Joseph Brown and
His Civil War Ironclads

ALSO BY MYRON J. SMITH, JR., AND FROM MCFARLAND

*Civil War Biographies from the Western Waters:
956 Confederate and Union Naval
and Military Personnel, Contractors, Politicians,
Officials, Steamboat Pilots and Others* (2015)

*The Fight for the Yazoo, August 1862–July 1864: Swamps,
Forts and Fleets on Vicksburg's Northern Flank* (2012)

The CSS Arkansas*:
A Confederate Ironclad on Western Waters* (2011)

*Tinclads in the Civil War: Union Light-Draught Gunboat
Operations on Western Waters, 1862–1865* (2010)

The USS Carondelet*:
A Civil War Ironclad on Western Waters* (2010)

The Timberclads in the Civil War: The Lexington, Conestoga
and Tyler *on the Western Waters* (2008; paperback 2013)

*Le Roy Fitch: The Civil War Career of a Union River
Gunboat Commander* (2007; paperback 2014)

Joseph Brown and His Civil War Ironclads

The USS *Chillicothe*, *Indianola* and *Tuscumbia*

Myron J. Smith, Jr.

McFarland & Company, Inc., Publishers
Jefferson, North Carolina

LIBRARY OF CONGRESS CATALOGUING-IN-PUBLICATION DATA

Names: Smith, Myron J., author.
Title: Joseph Brown and his Civil War ironclads :
the USS Chillicothe, Indianola and Tuscumbia / Myron J. Smith, Jr.
Description: Jefferson, North Carolina : McFarland & Company, Inc.,
Publishers, 2017. | Includes bibliographical references and index.
Identifiers: LCCN 2017012244 | ISBN 9780786495764
(softcover : acid free paper) ∞
Subjects: LCSH: Brown, Joseph, 1823–1899. | United States—History—
Civil War, 1861–1865—Naval operations. | United States—History—Civil War,
1861–1865—Riverine operations. | United States—History—Civil War,
1861–1865—Campaigns. | Armored vessels—United States—History—
19th century. | Armored vessels—United States—Design and construction. |
Chillicothe (Ironclad) | Indianola (Ironclad) | Tuscumbia (Ironclad)
Classification: LCC E591 .S653 2017 | DDC 973.7/5—dc23
LC record available at https://lccn.loc.gov/2017012244

BRITISH LIBRARY CATALOGUING DATA ARE AVAILABLE

**ISBN (print) 978-0-7864-9576-4
ISBN (ebook) 978-1-4766-2680-2**

© 2017 Myron J. Smith, Jr. All rights reserved

*No part of this book may be reproduced or transmitted in any form
or by any means, electronic or mechanical, including photocopying
or recording, or by any information storage and retrieval system,
without permission in writing from the publisher.*

Front cover: Joseph Brown (Emerson W. Gould,
50 Years on the Mississippi, 1889); USS *Tuscumbia*,
showing damage suffered against the Confederate batteries
(Naval History and Heritage Command)

Printed in the United States of America

*McFarland & Company, Inc., Publishers
Box 611, Jefferson, North Carolina 28640
www.mcfarlandpub.com*

In Memory of Karen Herbert Lime

Table of Contents

ACKNOWLEDGMENTS ix

INTRODUCTION 1

1—Joseph Brown: The Honorable Steamboat Captain 5

2—War and Gunboats 42

3—Building Capt. Brown's Ironclads 55

4—The *Chillicothe* Goes to War: Yazoo Pass and Red River 107

5—*Indianola*: The Shortest Cruise 177

6—*Tuscumbia*: The "Broad Giant" vs. Vicksburg 229

7—Joseph Brown, Enterpreneur and Mayor Again: Life After Gunboats 279

CHAPTER NOTES 329

BIBLIOGRAPHY 355

INDEX 373

Acknowledgments

Personnel at a number of libraries and archives helpfully provided insight and access to resources during the research and writing stages of this book. Among them were the kind folks manning the libraries and collections of the U.S. Navy Department; Library of Congress; National Archives; Emory University; University of Tennessee; Mississippi Department of Archives and History; University of Southern Mississippi; Missouri Historical Society; Rosenberg Library, Galveston; University of Arkansas; University of North Carolina at Chapel Hill; Duke University; East Tennessee State University; Kentucky Historical Society; U.S. Army Historical Center; Vicksburg National Military Park; Louisiana State University; Tennessee State Library and Archives; Illinois State Library; Indiana Historical Society; Chicago Historical Society; Ohio Historical Society; Ohio State University; and St. Louis Public Library.

For their insights, I would also like to thank those who have offered comments or other suggestions regarding Vicksburg and subjects related to it on the *Civil War Navies Message Board*. These include Alan Doyle, Tom Ezell, Henry E. Whittle, Ed Cotham, Mark Morss, George Wright, Mark Jenkins, Shawn Clark, David Adams, Gary Matthews, and Terry G. Scriber.

Terrence J. Winschel kindly provided assistance and answers to several questions. His work *Vicksburg Is the Key: The Struggle for the Mississippi,* coauthored with William L. Shea, also supplies useful detail.

A special tip of the hat goes to several colleagues who have been especially helpful. Their interest and assistance has aided this project tremendously. Warren Steel of the University of Mississippi cleared up several points regarding the relationships between several of Capt. Brown's subcontractors, and noted postcard collector Don Prout pointed out details regarding the Cincinnati Marine Railway, as shown on his Web site, cincinnativiews.net. Brian Combs from the Alton Museum of History and Art offered his thoughts on Joseph Brown's father, while Mike Meiners, director of News Administration at the *St. Louis Post-Dispatch,* helped with photos and encouragement.

David Meagher, historian and blueprint artist, has significantly advanced our understanding of the size and layout of the three Brown ironclads. In a series of thought-provoking communications, this colleague gave both solid data and the challenge to dig deeper. His generosity in allowing the use of his plans is very much appreciated.

Most especially, appreciation goes to Alton historian Catherine E. Bagby. "Chatty

Kathy," as her e-mail handle goes, was tireless in tracking down little tidbits regarding the Brown family and a number of articles from the local Alton newspapers that I had missed or could not locate. Her assistance and support was in many ways a key to unlocking the story of Joseph Brown and his family.

Special thanks is extended to Charles Tunstall, reference and interlibrary loan librarian, at the Thomas J. Garland Library, Tusculum College, for his diligent pursuit of titles not locally available.

Introduction

The Civil War was approaching the first anniversary of its beginning when the following advertisement ran in newspapers throughout the United States:

Proposals Wanted for the Immediate Construction of Ten New Gunboats
  WASHINGTON, March 11. The Secretary of War desires proposals for the immediate construction of ten gunboats of the same description as those now in use at Cairo and on the Cumberland. Proposals may be sent by telegraph and must specify the price and time when they will be ready for use.
  E.M. STANTON, Secretary of War[1]

On April 30, contracts were awarded for the first three of these units, all to Joseph Brown of St. Louis, Missouri.[2] They would become the *Chillicothe*, the *Indianola*, and the *Tuscumbia*, so squat and ungraceful in appearance they could be labeled the "Three Ugly Sisters."

Civil War gunboat construction on the Western Waters, with which I have dealt in other volumes, is most often associated with the gifted engineer James Buchanan Eads, also of St. Louis, who built the seven "City Series" partial ironclads that saw their first action at Fort Henry on the Tennessee River in early February 1862. Indeed, Eads received two of the seven remaining contracts for the vessels noted above. All ten were follow-ons to his seven originals, purchased to augment a growing riverine force in a war that was not over in the six months many had initially expected.

But who was Joseph Brown, how did he seemingly come out of nowhere to obtain his contracts, and what happened to him later on? His name always pops up in any discussion of the *Indianola* or *Chillicothe* or *Tuscumbia* and he was responsible for modifying dozens of small steamboats into light-draught gunboats known as "tinclads." But no Civil War histories actually profile him and those that do mention him in connection with his construction largely dismiss him as a Cincinnati boatbuilder. The principal purpose of this work is to review the story of Brown's ironclads, with heavy emphasis on their construction, along with brief operational histories and their ultimate fates. At the same time, we want to accomplish two other goals. First, because he was one of the most successful if least known Civil War contractors, we attempt to give readers an uncritical account of the life story of Joseph Brown, a man who left no personal papers except scraps of autobiography and who was never profiled in print beyond a few entries in several biographical directories. While his ironclad trio were not considered successful warships almost from the time they were laid down, he was a man who had many talents, interests, connections, and more than his share of pluck and good luck.

The youngest son in a Scottish immigrant family, Brown, along with his brother George T., was involved in politics and commerce from the 1830s onward, becoming acquainted with and influenced by many famous regional and several national names of his day including Webster, Lovejoy, Trumbull, Douglas, and, particularly, Abraham Lincoln. Both brothers served as mayor of Alton, Illinois—a decade apart. Born a Presbyterian, Joseph became a Spiritualist in the 1850s and practiced that religion for most of the remainder of his life. Unlike his brother, he remained an enthusiastic member of the Democratic Party until the day he died.

While George T. became a force in Illinois affairs, Joseph concentrated on the family business of milling, soon recognizing that in order to better get his grain to market he had better invest in and otherwise become involved with steamboating. The great river steamers were the principal method of bulk hauling in the Mississippi Valley of the mid-19th century and the successful Brown found himself with huge quantities of wheat and corn in need of delivery to ports as far south as New Orleans. Diving head first into river logistics, he became not only a shipper but also a captain and, subsequently, a builder as well. Further, he became a keen student of river commerce and the emerging technological advantages of railroads.

Unlike Captain Eads, Joseph Brown did not answer the War Department's initial 1861 call for river ironclads. He was still engaged in steamboating until, along with many others, it was seen that the rebellion would go on longer than first imagined. As the conflict deepened, Brown observed the Union river buildup and held himself ready to join the war effort, hoping for a way to eventually make use of his many talents, contacts, and skills, not only as a riverman but also as an entrepreneur and minor politician. And if he could earn a profit along the way, so much the better.

Whether or not Joseph Brown learned of the government's new proposal request for heavily armed river gunboats from the newspapers or from river acquaintances, many of his 19th century biographies indicate that he was definitely informed of them by his brother George T. Brown. The Senate sergeant at arms, knowing of his younger sibling's interest and river expertise, summoned him to Washington, D.C., to offer a proposal and make a bid. The invitation was similar to, if far less prominent, than that given James B. Eads by Attorney General Edward Bates the year before.

Joseph Brown was not a trained naval architect. He had worked with various Western boatmen in designing a number of steamboats during the antebellum period, including the famous *Mayflower*. What he did have was a great deal of knowledge concerning the Western rivers, steamboat construction, and Midwestern business and political accommodation. He also had an "in."

At some point after arriving in Washington, D.C., Brown and his brother George T. obtained an appointment and paid a visit to their old friend Abraham Lincoln in the White House. The old Illinois colleagues, perhaps following brief recollections of prairie politics and Alton friendships, got briefly down to business. As a result, on March 28 the president wrote the naval board then considering submitted blueprints and sketches asking that it "do me a personal favor, as well as the country at large, by giving the plans presented by him [Brown], that attention, which I have no doubt their merits entitle them to."[3] At the beginning of April, Brown was awarded a contract for three ironclads.

The former Alton mayor immediately set to work locating a shipyard and subcontracting various components and during the remainder of the year oversaw assembly of three huge scow-like gunboats designed to carry huge 11-inch Dahlgren cannon. The building process was not without challenges, but all of them were met to one degree of satisfaction or another. Along the way, Brown won the support, if not outright admiration, of the first commander of the USN Mississippi Squadron, RAdm. David Dixon Porter.

The admiral gave a benediction for the *Chillicothe, Indianola,* and *Tuscumbia* in a February 1864 report to Washington. "The builders never claimed that they should be considered more than temporary expedients with which to harass the enemy," wrote Porter. That said, he continued that the trio "certainly may be considered very good vessels, and have fairly repaid all the money spent on them, taking into consideration the work they have done."[4]

Despite the spotty combat records of his ironclads, Brown, who never mentioned any of them after the loss of the *Indianola,* devoted himself to the efficient, almost assembly-line modification of small sternwheel steamboats into light draught gunboats. When the war was over in 1865, he had the extreme satisfaction of knowing he had converted 55 of the 66 tinclads acquired by the U.S. Navy during the conflict, including a number that served with the West Gulf Blockading Squadron.[5]

Joseph Brown led a most interesting and diverse life in the years before he built the three ironclads and it remained interesting after the War of the Rebellion. He was a man who throughout his life won and lost fortunes regularly, in steamboating, real estate, railroads, and even gold mining. He was seldom without an idea or position, while sharing the sentiment of most Missourians regarding race and Western expansion. Brown was deeply devoted to his wife and adopted daughter, both of whom tragically died before he did.

Brown was not one of those Civil War participants who just faded away, but he instead took an active role in the commercial, civic, economic, and social life of his community, gathering even further laurels as a businessman, politician, and raconteur. A mayor of a small town before the great conflict, he served two terms as mayor of the country's fourth-largest city in the early 1870s.

His two-term administration was regarded as both colorful and successful. Brown supported education, including what became the St. Louis Public Library, and was a fanatical opera fan. During the Panic of 1873 he used his own fortune to personally guarantee scrip issued by the city ("Brownbacks") and organized a soup kitchen that fed 1,200 destitute people every day in cold weather. And yet, the only real way to follow his various activities, including his personal life, is through the newspaper. The man left no written record and, like his brother George T., no photograph of him exists.

In addition to profiling Brown and examining the construction of his ironclad naval vessels, we intend, through the story of the *Chillicothe, Indianola,* and *Tuscumbia,* to round out the remaining unchronicled operational portion of our Western waters saga begun seven volumes and a decade ago with a biography of famed tinclad captain Lt. Cmdr. Le Roy Fitch.

In *The Fight for the Yazoo, August 1862–July 1864: Swamps, Forts, and Fleets on Vicksburg's Northern Flank,*[6] I reviewed in great detail the many naval and amphibious activities above the Confederate citadel. The *Chillicothe* played a major role in one component of that tale and, as we note here, was the only one of the trio to survive the capture of Vicksburg in good enough shape to serve later, which it did in the Red River Campaign of 1864.[7]

While looking at the short careers of the *Indianola* and *Tuscumbia*, we return to the waters of the great river that ran between the eastern bank of the state of Mississippi and Louisiana's De Soto Peninsula and then continued down toward Port Hudson, Louisiana. That portion of this tale was begun in our *The CSS* Arkansas*: A Confederate Ironclad on Western Waters*, and it is now finished here with our accounts of four of the most important naval adventures of the Vicksburg operation. We begin with the February 1863 failed cruise of the *Indianola*. With her gone, we turn to the *Tuscumbia* and her April 1863 passage of the Vicksburg batteries with other elements of the U.S. Navy Mississippi Squadron. She is then profiled in the Battle at Grand Gulf later that month, and the bombardment of the Vicksburg water defenses in May and June.

In 1896 "Captain Joe," as he was later known, went home to Alton, Illinois, and delivered a lecture in support of a subscription monument to his mentor, Elijah P. Lovejoy. As his presentation closed, Brown confided a hope to his audience for himself. It was his wish that those who heard of him in the future "will condone my faults and remember me for the good I have done." We hope that this work will rescue the man from obscurity while throwing new attention upon his three wartime "ugly sisters": *Chillicothe, Indianola,* and *Tuscumbia.*[8]

1

Joseph Brown: The Honorable Steamboat Captain

An immigrant possessed of great business and political acumen, Joseph Brown was well known on the Western rivers when the Civil War began but is all but forgotten today. In order to more fully understand how and why he was able to build three ironclads for the Union navy, to say nothing of numerous tinclads, and enjoy a successful social, commercial, and political career, we must journey back to the antebellum period to reveal the man's personal enterprise.

Joseph Brown was born in Jedburgh, in southeastern Scotland about 50 miles from Edinburgh, in April 1823. His father, Thomas Sr., a man of good position in the community (and not to be confused with the local philosopher-poet of the same name) was a neighbor and acquaintance of the novelist Sir Walter Scott and knew from him firsthand the origins of many of the characters who appeared in that writer's works.

In 1832, Joseph and his family sailed from White Haven, England, and came ashore at Quebec following a voyage of eight weeks and three days. They went directly to Little York, as Toronto was then called, and made that place their home for fourteen months. In 1834 the family moved, via Cincinnati, to St. Louis, Missouri, being part of a great wave of settlers then enlarging the population of the Mississippi Valley. Not wishing to remain in a slave state, Thomas moved his brood 24 miles up the Mississippi River to Upper Alton, on the Illinois side of the Big Muddy. Thomas's family at that time included his wife, Margaret, four sons (two Josephs, Leo, Thomas Jr., and George T.) and two daughters, Flora M. and Helen, the latter nicknamed "Ellen."[1]

Founded in 1818 by lawyer and land speculator Rufus Easton (1774–1834), Alton is located at the end of a great string of bluffs on the Illinois shore of the Mississippi River, with the mouth of the Illinois River 16 miles to the north and that of the Missouri River seven miles south. Some of the limestone cliffs rose almost sheer from the waters below. Below the residential portion of the town the "Big Muddy" swings sharply south, leaving a broad space comprising many thousands of acres in a floodplain between the bluffs and the river.

The growing influx of settlers who arrived to inhabit this area, as well as other hills and valleys, swelled the community. Within three years of the arrival of the Brown family and within six of the commencement of mercantile business, Alton had a population of 2,500. According to James T. Hair there were "20 wholesale and 32 retail stores and groceries; eight attorneys; seven physicians; seven clergymen (in addition to circuit riders); four hotels; a large steam flour mill; four large pork slaughtering and packing houses; various and sundry mechanical shops; three print shops that issued three weekly newspapers; schools; four churches (Presbyterian, Baptist, Methodist Episcopal, and Methodist Protestant); two banks; one insurance office; lodges for the Odd Fellows and Masons; a lyceum; and a mechanics' association." Local Alton historian Judy Hoffman further reveals Alton's flavor: "Most of the residents of Lower Alton were Southerners from Kentucky and Virginia, while the majority of Upper Alton's inhabitants were Northerners from New England and New York. Alton was a city divided by the Upper Town and the Lower Town, by Northern Yankees and Southern sympathizers, by an upper business class and a lower laboring class, by temperate teetotalers and intemperate 'Mint Juleps,' by anti–Jackson Whigs and pro–Jackson Democrats."[2]

Around this same time, several Alton citizens, transplanted from elsewhere and who would impact the lives of the Brown brothers, were achieving local importance. Among these was Capt. Benjamin Godfrey (1794–1862), an Atlantic sailor from the age of nine. After service in U.S. gunboats during the War of 1812 the merchant captain made and lost fortunes in the West Indies trade and as a businessman in Mexico. He made a third fortune in New Orleans in the Mississippi River shipping and commerce trade and in 1832 came north and located in Alton. Meanwhile, Winthrop Sargeant Gilman (1808–1884), who had immigrated to St. Louis from the East in 1830 to open

Steamers at the Landing. Taken at Memphis, this photograph is typical of the prewar commercial activity at Alton and other river cities Joseph Brown frequented (Library of Congress).

A Mississippi River Packet. Near Memphis in 1906, this side-wheel packet was identical in many ways to earlier vessels that plied the Mississippi and with which Joseph Brown was most closely identified. Note her rudder arrangement aft and her staging planks forward (Library of Congress).

A Mississippi River Steamer. This stern-wheeler, photographed in 1906, was almost identical in profile to those of her type plying the Ohio and Monongahela rivers. Brown was intimately acquainted with the building of these vessels and would convert many of them into tinclads during the Civil War. Note the huge cloud of smoke escaping her tall chimneys (Library of Congress).

a wholesale grocery business, also arrived in town, joining with Godfrey to form the warehouse and commission concern Godfrey, Gilman & Company, a freight forwarder. Another resident, John Marshall Krum (1810–1883), was elected the first mayor of Alton in 1837, the same year in which future U.S. senator Lyman Trumbull (1813–1896), author of the 13th Amendment, arrived from Georgia to practice law.[3]

Brown and his siblings attended what was known as "day school," with boys and girls often together in the one room of the small frame schoolhouse on the corner of the Stanford block. In later life, he remembered his schoolyard fights and several youthful love affairs. Mostly, however, he recalled how his mind turned to the great Mississippi River, for which he developed a "passion." Having arrived with his family by boat in what was then called "the west," Brown was enamored of the many steamboats which visited at Alton. The region's coming community, according to some pundits, and not St. Louis, "was considered the head of navigation for St. Louis boats."

Douglas Meyer notes that the driving force behind Alton's economic success was "the impact of upstream steamboat commerce and evolving marketplace agriculture in its upland hinterland of Goshen." In addition to human industriousness, there also was a natural cause. Between St. Louis and Alton a rock ledge appeared during low water and "often hindered upstream steamboat travel," especially for vessels of sizeable draft. Even so, many steamers from the Ohio River and the upper Mississippi also "came to Alton and turned back from there."

Joseph was drawn daily to the river and spent as much of his free time as possible at the wharf watching the comings and goings of the many visiting steamboats. Alton was becoming a "bustling river port," as Hoffman puts it, "a melting pot of businessmen and frontiersmen, of missionaries, merchants, doctors, lawyers, dockhands, fishermen, and farmers." Undoubtedly, Brown was inspired by the September 22, 1835, inaugural arrival of the packet *Tiskilwa* from St. Louis, which had departed the Missouri town that morning and, having unloaded at the Alton riverbank, returned downstream that afternoon.

Brown was also impressed with the speedy Ohio River boats *Paul Jones* and *Champion*, the latter a low-pressure Lake Champlain steamer specifically taken west to beat the time of the *Jones*. Brown had a skiff from which he often waved to these and the other great vessels as they turned toward shore. "If I hadn't oars handy," the riverman wannabe recalled, he would hang his "legs over behind the skiff and work it like a stern-wheel boat." Yet for both him and other members of the family, the necessities of livelihood and family dominated most days.

Thomas Brown ran a successful retail business, eventually adding a gristmill, while his oldest son, George T., also worked in the family enterprise and studied law under newly arrived attorney Lyman Trumbull. Years later, an Alton pioneer remembered that the store, built of stone, was located at the corner of Second and Piasa streets. Afterwards, "the rear portion next to the levee was used as a flouring mill, as well as the store."

When he became a teenager, Joseph clerked at the shoe store of Royal Weller. Each morning before school he took down the shutters and swept out the establishment, earning $7 per month. Alton was in a boom period in 1835 and 1836; simultaneously the Illinois State Bank, located in town, was extremely generous in its support of local

Greeting a Steamer. From his first days in Alton, young Joseph Brown was fascinated by the steamers that visited his city. He had a skiff from which he often waved to the great vessels as they turned toward shore. If he didn't have oars, he recalled years later, the riverman wannabe would hang his "legs over behind the skiff and work it like a sternwheel boat." The scene was often repeated by others, as here when boaters greet the *Quincy* off Muscatine, IA, in 1900, a year after Brown's death (Library of Congress).

businesses like that of Thomas Brown, offering loans and other assistance. In the two years after the family arrived, real estate rose in value by over 1,000 percent. "By day, the city was filled with the noisy clamor and rank aromas of frontier progress," Judy Hoffman tells us, but at night, as was the situation in other border towns, the character changed. While the "pious and temperate" citizens (including Thomas Brown and his family) retired to their comparatively safe Upper Alton abodes at night, "the bustling river port became a brawling river town" where the "restless and unruly" gathered in numerous saloons and other bawdy locations.

All of this ended because of the national economic downturn known as the Panic of 1837. Noticeable difficulties occurred in March and the bottom fell out in April. The State Bank suspended specie payments in May and, in the weeks that followed, citizens and newspaper editors were hard pressed to accept

Lyman Trumbull. George T. Brown's teacher and long-time political patron, Trumbull (1813–1896) was Illinois secretary of state (1841–1843) and an Illinois Supreme Court justice (1858–1853) before he was appointed a U.S. Senator in 1854. An important figure in the new Republican Party, he insured George T.'s appointment as Senate sergeant-of-arms in 1861, cowrote the 13th Amendment to the Constitution, voted not to impeach President Andrew Johnson in 1868, and, having become a Populist, joined with Clarence Darrow in defending Socialist Eugene V. Debs before the U.S. Supreme Court in 1895 (Library of Congress).

that the bubble of prosperity had burst. The downturn paralyzed community trade, destroying local values, especially real estate. Brown later remembered that Alton town lots dropped from $1,000 to nothing and many were sold but could not even be redeemed for taxes.

Young Brown was exposed to stern religious requirements at an early age. His initial spiritual experiences were so strict that he actually developed "a positive dislike for Sundays." Fire and brimstone raged, as after Sunday school he was required to attend church services—offered by a traveling minister from St. Louis at the schoolhouse at 11:00 a.m., 2:00 p.m., and 7:30 p.m. At home at other times on the Sabbath, his mother, a strict Scottish Calvinist, insisted that Brown remain indoors until it was time to leave for church. All frivolity was curtailed, including laughing and even whistling.[4]

In "constant foreboding of the future life" after listening to his mother and the Sunday ministers, Brown the same year discovered an "oasis" in the "desert of Calvinism" by the name of Elijah Parish Lovejoy (1802–1837). A Maine native, the Princeton-trained Presbyterian minister and journalist was run out of St. Louis in July 1836 by mobs opposed to the semi-abolitionist views expressed in his newspaper, the *St. Louis Observer*. Invited to move to Alton by Winthrop Gilman and other newly settled eastern businessmen, Lovejoy published his views in a free state and soon found that many of his new Illini neighbors were no more sympathetic to his views than the mobs of St. Louis had been. Lovejoy and his supporters would see four printing presses (costing $284 each) destroyed over the next year by unruly crowds, one right after the other.

Brown, then 14, and his brother developed a close association with Lovejoy, who in turn briefly served as Joseph's teacher and the boys' mentor. Lovejoy also became a friend of Thomas Brown, who, the local newspaper would reveal years later, was also an abolitionist at heart and "an ardent sympathizer with Lovejoy." The reverend, remembered the future St. Louis mayor and ironclad builder, was strong of principle yet possessed of a "very loving nature, with fine expression of countenance and a voice as soft and tender as a woman's." He spoke not of hell and damnation but of "the love of God to man and the ways he had provided for his salvation." Was it "any wonder," Brown later confided, "that I should love and revere such a man and should desire to perpetuate his memory?"

The Brown brothers were also introduced to politics at this time when one of the greatest orators of the day paid a visit and then, at the end of July 1837, Alton was chartered by the state legislature. Among those who made investments in western lands (including those around Alton) earlier in the decade was a noted Massachusetts Whig, Sen. Daniel Webster (1782–1852), one of four losers from his party in the 1836 presidential election. Beginning the following May, Webster took his family on an inspection tour of his far land holdings, a trip which, according to biographer Claude Moore Fuess, he hoped would propel him into a dominant position among western Whigs, thus making him a "preferred presidential candidate." Among his many outbound stops, made primarily by steamboat, were the cities of Pittsburg (the Pennsylvania city did not employ an "h" in its name at that time), Wheeling, Louisville, and St. Louis. Returning East (where he would also stop at Springfield, Peru, and Chicago before heading home), Webster, his family, and a party of St. Louis citizens headed first to Alton.

As the steamer *H.L. Kinney* reached the wharf, a gigantic explosion erupted from a nearby river bluff. As was later reported in northern newspapers, the blast, caused by four barrels of gunpowder tamped into a big hole in the cliff, was meant to serve as a salute, as the town did not have a cannon. Sixty years later, the detonation was remembered as the "heaviest and biggest gun fired off" in Webster's honor during his whole tour.

A ceremony of welcome was then held in the expanding town and the great man was feted and talked politics with civic and Whig party leaders in the Alton House Hotel on Front Street. It was later remembered, in the 1912 Madison County history, that "champagne flowed freely and Webster afterwards made a rousing political speech from the porch where he was said to have maintained his equilibrium by holding on tightly to the railing." The Brown brothers Joseph and George T. were mesmerized by the power of the oratory in the famous man's speech. "More like a king than a senator," wrote historian McCampbell, he was "greeted with adulation and spoke before immense throngs in each city. " Joseph later opined that, like many of the speakers he saw early in his life—and later—Webster appeared to be one who "made his best speeches while partially intoxicated."

Before his return to the wharf and departure, Webster, within earshot of the Browns, was invited by Major Charles Hunter, an important real estate developer whose Hunterstown would be an important stop on the Underground Railroad, to see his nearby farm lands, particularly his grazing pastures.

Webster at Alton. The Brown brothers, Joseph and George T., were drawn to politics in late July 1837 when Massachusetts Whig, Sen. Daniel Webster (1782–1852) spoke at Alton. In the audience assembled outside a local hotel, the two young men were mesmerized by the power of the great man's oratory. Later, after becoming a well-known public speaker in his own right, Joseph opined that, like many of the speakers he saw early in his life, Webster appeared to be one who "made his best speeches while partially intoxicated" (Library of Congress).

"_____ your pastures," the senator reportedly replied. "Hunter was," Brown recalled, "religiously paralyzed," but the two soon rode out to see the grassy acreage. Although Webster's western swing was a success, the growing depression caused him significant financial difficulty.

Meanwhile, throughout the spring and summer of 1837, Lovejoy transformed his views on slavery and abolitionism. It was no longer enough to denounce the former as sin while also deploring the excesses of the abolitionist movement. As his views on the evils of forced servitude stiffened and his concern over the methods employed to eliminate it faded, his editorials became harsher and he became the subject of increased opposition, both in print and in person. Threats against the man and his newspaper intensified and violence followed, two presses being destroyed between August 21 and September 21.

From October into November, Alton's business, religious, and professional leaders organized public meetings to debate the fate of Lovejoy's newspaper. Some people urged him to depart the town; however, the minister pledged to remain, maintaining his press and expressing his views. On the night of November 6, a fourth printing press arrived from Cincinnati aboard the steamer *Mozelle*. With protection from 30 armed supporters, Lovejoy oversaw its placement on the third floor of the Godfrey, Gilman & Company riverfront warehouse, a "double building of stone" measuring some 100 feet in length by 50 in width. A large vacant lot lay next to it and at its southern end was a small lumber pile. The next day was given over to public meetings amidst "mutterings of threatened trouble." Lovejoy's opponents pledged that the press could be set up if he would avoid any discussion of slavery; the Princeton minister refused, citing freedom of speech and the press. Discussions ended without conclusion, but all knew the night would be long.[5]

Trouble was indeed imminent and Alton had no real police force with which to confront it. As ruffians and others muttered determination to destroy the press and grew their courage in Second Street saloons, 20 men, including Winthrop Gilman, Royal Weller, and George T. Brown, stepped forward to serve as warehouse guards through the hours of darkness. Other Lovejoy supporters agreed to reinforce them if necessary. As the storm gathered in late afternoon and into the evening, Weller requested that his young employee, Joseph Brown, who had made several trips to his father's store to bring back provisions, mold as many bullets as possible using an old led mold.

About 8:00 p.m. Brown returned with them to the warehouse via the river end of the building as a liquor-agitated crowd gathered at the other end. There he found his brother and the others in urgent conversation with Rev. Lovejoy as to what course should be followed in case of an attack. Lovejoy famously said he would not leave and would die if necessary to defend his press; the others, some wavering, were inspired and agreed to fight to the death if need be.

About this time, Judge John M. Krum arrived with a message from the mob demanding Lovejoy surrender his press. Krum, later the 11th mayor of St. Louis (1848–1849), was chosen the town's first mayor when it was chartered by the Illinois legislature back on July 31. Counseling compliance while doing what he could, in the words of Thomas Dimmock, to take "precautions against unlawful interference," Krum insisted he had tried—and failed—to reason with the pro-slavery band. Gilman replied that he and his group would fight to the death to avoid handing over the press. Krum left the warehouse to convey the determination of those inside to the men gathered outside. The angry pro-slavery demonstrators were asked to disperse and were warned that the mayor would instruct the few Alton police to shoot anyone attempting arson. According to Louis S. Gerteis, Krum was, in the end, "ignored by the mob and the police."

Led by a carpenter, Lyman Bishop, late of New York, the mob then attempted to storm the warehouse, using a long lumber 2" × 4" to batter down the front door. The assault briefly stopped after an unidentified second floor defender shot and killed Bishop. Then, amidst shouts of "Burn Them Out," a ladder was placed against the wall of the warehouse and a youth scampered up it with a torch. As he neared the top, Lovejoy and Royal Weller, hiding outside behind the nearby lumber pile, rushed around, pushed the ladder over, and retreated inside the building. When the ladder was replaced, the tactic was retried, but this time Lovejoy and Weller were seen by the mob. Shots rang out and both Lovejoy and Weller were hit, with the former mortally wounded by

Pro-Slavery Riot at Alton. On November 6, 1837, a new printing press arrived at the Godfrey-Gilman warehouse for abolitionist minister the Rev. Elijah Lovejoy. The next day agitators threatened to destroy it as Lovejoy and 20 defenders fortified themselves in the building. Fourteen-year-old Joseph Brown, a student of the minister, made several trips to his father's store to bring back provisions and to mold as many bullets as possible. About 8:00 p.m., Brown returned to the warehouse once more as a liquor-agitated crowd gathered outside. The Rev. Lovejoy famously told his followers he would not leave and would die to defend his press. The others inside, including George T. Brown, agreed to fight to the death if need be. When the mob attacked, Lovejoy was mortally wounded (Library of Congress, via Catherine E. Bagby, Alton, IL).

five bullets (though some say it was a shotgun blast). As the roof took fire, those inside the warehouse surrendered and determined members of the crowd swept inside to destroy Lovejoy's press, hurling it down onto the riverbank and its pieces into the Mississippi River. Lovejoy, widely remembered, was buried two days later on his 35th birthday. He was quickly hailed, according to Harold Holzer, as "a martyr to public liberty." The town in which he died was castigated by eastern newspapers as a "lawless community" and this poor public opinion added to Alton's economic woes.[6]

As a direct result of the Panic of 1837, Godfrey and Gilman within a short time suffered the loss of their businesses and most of their investments, with Gilman returning East. Indeed, the financial downturn led to higher taxes and the cancellation of many state improvement projects, while bankruptcies and foreclosures became commonplace. Land speculators went bust and lots were sold for taxes. As the port of St. Louis expanded, landings at Alton's wharf dried up. Many of the town's best citizens moved elsewhere and many of those remaining faced bleak prospects.

Even as hard times had an impact upon himself and Winthrop Gilman, Capt. Benjamin Godfrey, who was not directly involved in the Lovejoy tragedy but was heavily involved in local financial activities, including railroad development, continued to have a dream for the education of young women. The owner of some 10,000 acres in the area known as Scarritt's Prairie, north of Alton, spent some $53,000 to construct the Monticello Female Seminary (later Shurtleff College), employing both local and outside labor. On behalf of his father Joseph Brown, well known to Capt. Godfrey, often visited as the 5-story facility was finished and made ready for classes in April 1838.

Later, Brown, an 1838–1839 student, recalled that Godfrey was "a grand man" "devoted to all that was good and noble." He also remembered that Godfrey was very prompt with his daily evening prayers, which he said publicly in the Monticello lobby at 10:00 p.m. Anyone present was expected to participate. More than once, the younger man recalled, he arrived back at 10:00 with a "young lady in company." The arrivals were then compelled to "kneel down and listen to his time-honored prayer." Telling this tale before an audience in 1896, Brown, with tongue in cheek, suggested, "I fear I shall have to repent in dust and ashes for the sin of whispering to my young lady friends while at prayer."

Thomas Brown died on November 23, 1838, and his sons, Joseph and George T., were left to manage the family business as co-owners and to provide for their mother and younger siblings. George operated the concern for two years while Joseph attended college in St. Louis for two years. Joseph then returned to Alton at the age of 18 in 1841 for the purpose, according to Scharf, "of engaging in business, in which he was very successful."

With George T. now beginning his law practice, Joseph Brown, in the first of numerous non-family partnerships, joined with newly arrived Henry Lea (1803–1881)—an experienced businessman who knew of Alton from his brother-in-law Joshua G. Lamb and who had previously run concerns in Cincinnati, Bolivar, Tennessee, and New Orleans—to operate the store and flouring mill once owned by Brown Sr.[7]

Future U.S. president Abraham Lincoln (1809–1865) twice visited Alton in 1840 while Brown was in St. Louis. He returned again in 1842 under unusual circumstances, which initially grew out of a political difference. Lincoln (along with Mary Todd [1818–1882]. it turned out), was responsible for a series of inflammatory letters in a local Springfield newspaper that humiliated Illinois state auditor James Shields (1810–1879). Taking offense, Shields demanded that the two men face each other on the field of honor and it was agreed that they would duel. Lincoln admitting that he was responsible for the bad press, consented and Sunflower Island, in the middle of the Mississippi River near Alton, was chosen as the dueling ground. The island was Missouri property and such grievance redress was legal in that state.

The two men arrived at Alton on the appointed day, September 22, and were accompanied to the island by a number of local backers and citizens. There Lincoln, the challenged party, was given the right to choose the weapons and he selected large and long cavalry swords. The 6' 4" politician then demonstrated his advantage over his smaller opponent by cutting off a branch from a tree just above Shields' head. Anticipating the outcome of any actual fight, the seconds for the two men intervened and the duel was cancelled.

Another large group back at the Alton landing awaited news of the outcome. By and by a rowboat approached with what appeared to be a body, covered by Shields' cloak, with several men waving cooling branches over it. Gasps were heard as rumors began that Shields was dead. The gambit was a prank by Constable Jake Smith, who jumped up from the boat just before it landed and shouted to the crowd that there was no fight: "The one was afraid and the other darsen't!" When Shields and Lincoln landed,

1—Joseph Brown: The Honorable Steamboat Captain 15

James Shields. *Lincoln the Railsplitter*, 1909.

Shields-Lincoln Dispute. As the result of a purposeful humiliation of Illinois state auditor James Shields (1810–1879), future U.S. president Abraham Lincoln (1809–1865) was challenged to a duel. On September 22, 1842, the two met to fight it out with cavalry swords on Sunflower Island, in the middle of the Mississippi River near Alton. The 6'4" politician than demonstrated his advantage over his smaller opponent by cutting off a branch from a tree just above Shields' head. Anticipating the outcome of any actual fight, the seconds for the two men intervened and the duel was cancelled. When the contestants returned to Alton, Joseph Brown, in the crowd, watched as the two "lost no time" in jumping into their waiting carriages and making "their way up State Street out of town" (Library of Congress).

Brown, among the people fooled by Smith, watched as the two "lost no time" in jumping into their waiting carriages and making "their way up State Street out of town."[8]

Although Alton suffered some reversals due to the great Mississippi River flood of 1844, both Brown brothers seemed to weather that natural disaster and continued their pursuits as the decade advanced. As Joseph became more deeply engaged as a miller, his brother George T. practiced law and turned to politics and was elected Alton mayor, serving in 1846 and 1847. Following his term as mayor, George T. won election as the Third Ward alderman (1850–1851). In 1852 he almost became the Democratic Party's candidate for Illinois lieutenant governor and the same year established the *Alton Daily Morning Courier* newspaper, which he would edit until 1859.[9]

While George T. shifted his interest further away from commerce, Joseph intensified his, seeking ways of expanding his flour business and taking it beyond the Alton area to St. Louis and other locations. "Up to the year 1845," he later wrote for an encyclopedia, "steamboats were doing all the transportation business in the West and the trade had then reached its zenith." In 1846 the flour supply in New Orleans was reported to be very short and Brown, by judicious management, found himself with a surplus so large that it filled his entire mill and a rented storehouse.

To take advantage of this business opportunity, Brown travelled to St. Louis, rented the side-wheel steamer *North Alabama*, and took her back to Alton, where she was loaded with 18,000 barrels of flour. The vessel was then dispatched downstream under a contract captain to deliver the bounty to the Crescent City. As she descended, the flour supply in New Orleans improved and the price per barrel stabilized at $2.60 a barrel.

The *North Alabama* ran aground at President's Island below Memphis and lay stranded for twelve days. Brown, when he received word, "nearly went wild," as he had drawn bills of credit on the cargo and was fearful that the bills would become due without the money from the sale of the flour to pay them. Fortune then stepped in as war broke out between the U.S. and Mexico. The price of flour skyrocketed to $3.50 a barrel and the Alton entrepreneur cleared $30,000 on that one boatload simply because she was late in delivery. In recalling the episode, Brown later remarked in a phrase worthy of Yogi Berra, "I tell you there's nothing so successful as success."

Later the same year, Brown took a small interest in the *Little Eagle*, a steamer built and operated by Capt. William Pierre LaMothe (1817–1898). The Quebec, Canada, native had arrived in Alton nine years earlier and used a small inheritance to acquire his little vessel, built in the late 1830s for the ferry trade across the river and to St. Louis. Painted all black and with but a single engine, the vessel was 90 feet long with a 16-foot beam. Her cabin was located aft of her shaft and like other boats of that time had no upper cabins. Brown remembered that it required about seven hours for her to make the voyage between St. Louis and Alton and that she was extremely noisy. "You could hear her screaming," he recalled, "for an hour before she reached the landing."

In January 1844 LaMothe, in partnership with the St. Louis wholesale and retail grocery concern Starnes & Springer, built the 162-ton stern-wheeler packet *Luella* at Nashville and entered her into the Alton–St. Louis service just after the great flood. The craft was 10 feet longer than the *Little Eagle* and was powered by an engine from a much larger boat formerly on the New Orleans trade. Her increased power, which, according to Frederick Way, Jr., "made her speedy," allowed her to become, as Joseph Brown remembered, "the fastest boat of her day running above St. Louis." The following year the region's largest stage line, based in Chicago and owned by John Frink and Martin Walker, diverted their new Illinois River steamer *General Briggs*, under noted Capt. James E. Starr, into competition with the *Luella*. Frink "realized that steamboats were logical extensions of the company's transport of mail and passengers" and hoped his expansion would prove profitable.

After his 1846 success with the *North Alabama* flour sale, Joseph Brown took a sizeable stake in the *Luella*, leaving LaMothe in command to operate her against the stagecoach people. In 1847, Brown and LaMothe offered rapid service between Alton and St. Louis for $1 per head, giving their passengers supper on the way up. One might conjecture it was from this that Brown developed his love of steamer speed; his idea of fast boats, coupled with developing business skill, would stand him in good stead in the years ahead.

During the winter of 1848, the miller, hoping to expand his business yet again, travelled to Galena, IL, to buy wheat. There as yet being no railroads in his part of the West, Brown made the trip aboard a Frink & Walker stagecoach. The springs of the vehicles, he later remembered, were made of "great leather straps" and if, as was the case during his trip, there were only a few riders the passengers were "likely to have a pretty rough time of it."

Successful in his mission, Brown returned to Alton and promptly bought out Capt. LaMothe, wishing to devote most of the *Luella*'s capacity to hauling flour between Alton and St. Louis, where it could be sent south to New Orleans on other steamers. He then joined with Frink & Walker and agreed to pool their two boats under a single joint-stock company. The *Luella*, now under Capt. George E. Hawley, remained on the Alton–St. Louis run, while the *General Briggs* initially concentrated on the Illinois River.

By 1848, the steam mill and warehouse complex operated by Brown, situated on Piasa Street and extending from Front to Second, had been significantly upgraded and renamed Madison Mills. Henry Lea and J.G. Lamb were now his partners and their principal building, made of stone, was 113 feet long, 55 feet wide, and four stories high. Lea often handled day-to-day activities while Brown handled acquisitions and transportation. In an 1856 review of the local milling scene, George T. Brown pointed out that his brother's concern employed two steam engines, each with a 14-inch cylinder with a four-foot stroke, and three boilers, each 36 feet long and 42 inches in diameter. The plant ran five pairs of burrs and the 12 employees could produce between 275 and 300 barrels of flour every 24 hours. The daily payroll came to $100, and the mill complex used about $12,000 active capital and did a yearly business of $250,000.

At this point, brothers Sebastian and Peter Wise (dba S & P Wise) stepped into the picture. The two had arrived in Alton from the East in 1839 to operate a gristmill initially established in 1830 as the Alton Manufacturing Company. In 1842, they built a new steam-powered concern on the levee, near the state penitentiary, in a building initially operated as a store by Godfrey, Gilman & Company. The Wise operation, slightly smaller than Brown's, could produce 250 barrels of flour per day. Joined by Capt. Starr and several other investors, they elected to begin an opposition line to Brown's and, hoping to take some of the flour-hauling trade away from him, acquired the fast and large steamer *Tempest* for Starr to captain against the *Luella*.

Starr and Hawley now engaged in a spirited and warm fare war over the Alton–St. Louis route, with each hiring a band to play and entice or amuse passengers. Brown and Hawley cut their fares in stages down from one dollar (supper included), to 75 cents, to 50 cents, to 25 cents, and then to 10 cents. Finally, passengers were carried free with only a nominal charge for freight. The Wises and Starr followed suit. On top of these tactics, each vessel dueled for the fastest time between the Illinois and Missouri ports. At that time there were no laws restricting the amount steam vessels could carry, so the engineers of these two boats (like others aboard other steamers) freely mixed rosin and turpentine with the usual wood fuel. Speed—and risk—were thus increased.

The war between the two lines continued for nine months. On December 15, 1848, the naturalist S.W. Woodhouse departed St. Louis for Alton, later recording his thoughts in the only known account by a *Luella* passenger. The vessel had proceeded only 10 miles when, at 4:00 p.m., a thick river fog forced it to move into the bank and tie up

Competition. Initially moving into steamboating to transport his milled flour, Joseph Brown soon became involved in offering passenger services between Alton and St. Louis. When other men also came onto the route, the competition between them, based on price and speed, was intense. Leaving the operational posts of pilot and master to others, Brown wisely concentrated on investment and management in those early years (John C.J. Taylor, *The Pilot House*, in Charles D. Stewart, *Partners of Providence*, Putnam, 1906).

for the night. The voyage was continued at 7:30 a.m. and a half hour after its resumption "the wind came out of the north West and the fog soon disappeared." The *Luella* duly landed at the Alton wharf at 9:00 a.m., where her passengers disembarked and her cargo was unloaded.

The competition between Brown and the Wises could not economically be maintained. An amicable compromise was reached as, in the words of the W. R. Brink & Company county history, "The owners of the boats came to the conclusion that a better way could be devised for the management of their business." Frink & Walter sold their interest in the *Luella* company to Brown, who in turn bought out the Wises. The *Luella* ran in the trade during the spring of 1850 and the *Tempest* the balance of the year and the whole of the year 1851.[10]

Meanwhile, in January 1851, a new steamboat-building yard was established at Fort Pickering, Memphis, Tennessee, by Primus Emerson (?–1877), a shipwright later famous for his construction of the Confederate ironclad ram *Arkansas*. During his itinerant building career, Emerson made the acquaintance of Joseph Brown, who, perhaps remembering the long-ago glory of the *Tiskilwa*, was now casting about for a noted boat carpenter and mechanic to construct a large packet. Assuming half interest (and the mastership), he was able to convince Gaty, McCune & Co. of St. Louis and Peter Wise of his recent partners, S & P Wise, to each assume a quarter interest. Samuel Gaty (1811–1887), the foundry official who, according to Van Ravenswaay, "helped make St. Louis a shipbuilding center" and was the first major manufacturer of steamboat machinery in the West, was authorized to design the steamer with input from Brown and, initially, from Emerson. Brown let the contracts with Emerson and other subcontractors and also served as construction superintendent.[11]

The construction of a big steamboat at Memphis for a St. Louis concern was a novelty of the day, as the Missouri city was recognized as an important boat-building community and, as the Tennessee newspaper reported, the milestone was "gratifying to our citizens." The *Altona*, as she was named, was launched before the end of May 1851, but, as Emerson's yard was not adapted for her completion, the side-wheeler was towed on August 27 to St. Louis for completion. Many other boats were also taken there from inland yards for finishing, as that community boasted extensive woodworking and foundry facilities.

The *Altona*, according to Brown, was 232 feet long with a 32-foot beam and a seven-foot draft. During her initial construction, the majority owner elected to stress his growing interest in speed and so conferred with Gaty and probably Emerson, plus his engineers, mechanics, and foundry people, regarding the vessel's power plant. The foundry representatives advised that four boilers would make her "the fastest boat above St. Louis." Brown wanted to "make her the fastest boat on the river" and so ordered one more. Her engines were each 36½ inches in diameter with a 10-foot stroke. In a further effort to increase efficiency, Brown opted for a pair of unique paddle wheels, called by rivermen "oral wheels." Each was 32 feet in diameter (extreme) with 13-foot buckets and blades of different width. Brown later reported his vessel had a "36-foot water wheel and a 16-foot bucket."

While the *Altona* was being completed at St. Louis, Brown took the opportunity to marry. His wife was Virginia C. Keach (1831–1881) of Carrollton, IL, the daughter of prominent Greene County saddlery manufacturer and land dealer Hiram Keach (1802–1868), a native of Abingdon, VA. The bride and groom were united on October 1. Brown and his wife had met at Shurtleff College, Upper Alton, perhaps through her brother, John R. Keach (1830–1888). Keach completed his education at Shurtleff and thereafter became a steamboat captain on the Keokuk to Rock Island trade. Brown and his new wife purchased a home at the corner of Market and Third streets, where, according to a World War I era newspaper article, an establishment called the Illinois Hotel was later built.

On December 10, Capt. LaMothe, with Brown and his wife embarked, skippered the *Altona* on her trial run from St. Louis to Alton and back, with hundreds watching the departures from the shores of the two towns. By month's end, the $100,000 vessel was ready to enter licensed packet service between Alton and St. Louis. It was during the second quarter of 1852, as reported by the Alton *Daily Telegraph*, that the *Altona* gained Capt. Brown's desired reputation as the fastest vessel on the Mississippi: "On Saturday afternoon [May 19] the *Altona* made the run from St. Louis to this city, about 29 miles, against the strong current of the Mississippi in an hour and 37 minutes, or ¼ mile every four minutes. This is the quickest time ever made upstream by any boat between the two places. At this rate, the *Altona* could make the trip from New Orleans to Alton in three days and a few hours."

The following week the newspaper added a few details concerning the record-breaking run, one which was never bettered. "Several hats were bet," it reported, that "she would do it in one and a half hours." Travelling against a 5-mph current, the *Altona* "was so hot when she arrived at the levee that it was deemed advisable to run her upstream somewhat farther to allow the boilers to cool somewhat before a landing." Joseph Brown wrote an encyclopedia article in which he noted, "There was no United States law regulating the amount of pressure that might be carried in the boilers, and the result was that some reckless engineers, encouraged by their captains [and perhaps their owners], often carried a pressure of 180 to 200 pounds of steam to the square inch in boilers 40 inches in diameter, and with a shell not more than 3/16th of an inch in thickness."

Capt. Brown was extremely proud of his boat's transit times, to the point of boastfulness. On March 13, 1852, he sent out a challenge to other steamboat owners and masters via the newspapers of the various Mississippi River towns where she touched. His steamer had "proven herself the fastest craft on the Mississippi," and so he would "present a gilded eagle to the first steamer that beats the *Altona*'s time in a trial from St. Louis to Alton." Brown never had to cough up the prize.

On May 24, the big side-wheeler, with LeMothe in command, once again with Brown and his wife embarked, made two round-trips with mail and passengers between Alton and St. Louis, the first occupying the morning hours between 6:30 and 11:30. Brown ordered the *Altona* operated as deep into the winter as possible, even when the river was filled with ice and "the St. Louis ferry-boats were tied to the bank." With no vessels leaving St. Louis save the *Altona*, the Illinois miller quickly earned back his boat's building cost. In September, the Chicago and Sangamon Railroad purchased the *Altona*, paying Joseph Brown and his associates $100,000. The railway, completed to Springfield, would employ her to finish their route from Chicago to St. Louis. Before turning her over to the railway, the captain claimed the boat's bell as a personal souvenir.

Employing his share of the proceeds, Joseph Brown and Virginia travelled to New York in early fall. There the captain met the Fox sisters, Kate and Margaret, and was drawn into their world of spiritualism. He would be a fervent follower of mediums until almost the day he died.[12]

In 1848, the 937-ton side-wheeler *St. Louis* was built in her namesake city for the trade with New Orleans. Reported to have a length of 307 feet (though Capt. Brown later claimed 350), with a 45-foot beam and 10-foot hold, she was one of the largest steamboats of her day. It was initially hoped she might be able to churn the miles north or south between the two cities in three days, but because she was so heavy and "unable to rise on the water" as designed, she could never make the trip under seven. Her great weight also kept her from taking advantage of her extreme size and the potential for loading her to her guards, thereby cutting her freight profits even further.

The bursting of the larboard boiler of the *St. Louis*, on the 23rd of February 1851 resulted in the deaths of 20 of the 25 souls aboard. "Timbers, large masses of machinery, brick-work, and ashes were hurled aloft in every direction," recorded Scharf. It would be several years before the vessel could be rebuilt. In the meantime, the surviving chief engineer was indicted for manslaughter and underwent a lengthy trial that found him innocent. Rebuilt, the vessel "dragged along" in commercial service, with her captain "discouraged without making any money out of her."

In early 1853, following his disposal of the *Altona* and the repair of the *St. Louis*,

The *Altona*, Brown's revolutionary steamer, built with Primus Emerson, who would later construct the CSS *Arkansas*, quickly gained a reputation as the fastest vessel on the Mississippi. Unfortunately, as with most of the captain's craft, no *Altona* photograph exists. Some idea of her hard-charging service between Alton and St. Louis can be taken from Jacob Dallas's illustration *Up the Mississippi* (*Emerson's*, October 1857).

Capt. Brown, while maintaining his other Altona business interests, took a 50 percent interest in the latter from her builder and captain, George Taylor, hoping to earn a profit on the St. Louis–New Orleans trade for which she was originally planned. Not long after the transaction was completed, as she prepared for her initial departure downstream a yellow fever epidemic broke out in the Crescent City. It quickly became so virulent that most of the other Mississippi River boats engaging in trade to the town were laid up and refused to enter her port. The situation caused the profits from freight hauling to skyrocket and Brown, deeply in debt for his share of the *St. Louis*, decided to make the run.

Loading his vessel to her guards, Brown proceeded to New Orleans, where upon his arrival he learned that over 100 people per day were dying in the city and more than half of the population had evacuated to avoid the plague. As his craft was unloaded, her captain, later admitting to "morbid curiosity," elected to visit one of the local cemeteries, where he found 99 unburied caskets. It was raining, as it had for days, and "the ground was so full of water that as fast as they dug the hole it filled with water." As soon as possible, the *St. Louis* departed "for up the river" and away from the disease. "I cleared $10,000 on that trip," Brown later remembered, "and I think I earned it."[13]

While Joseph worked the river "getting fabulous prices for freight and taking great

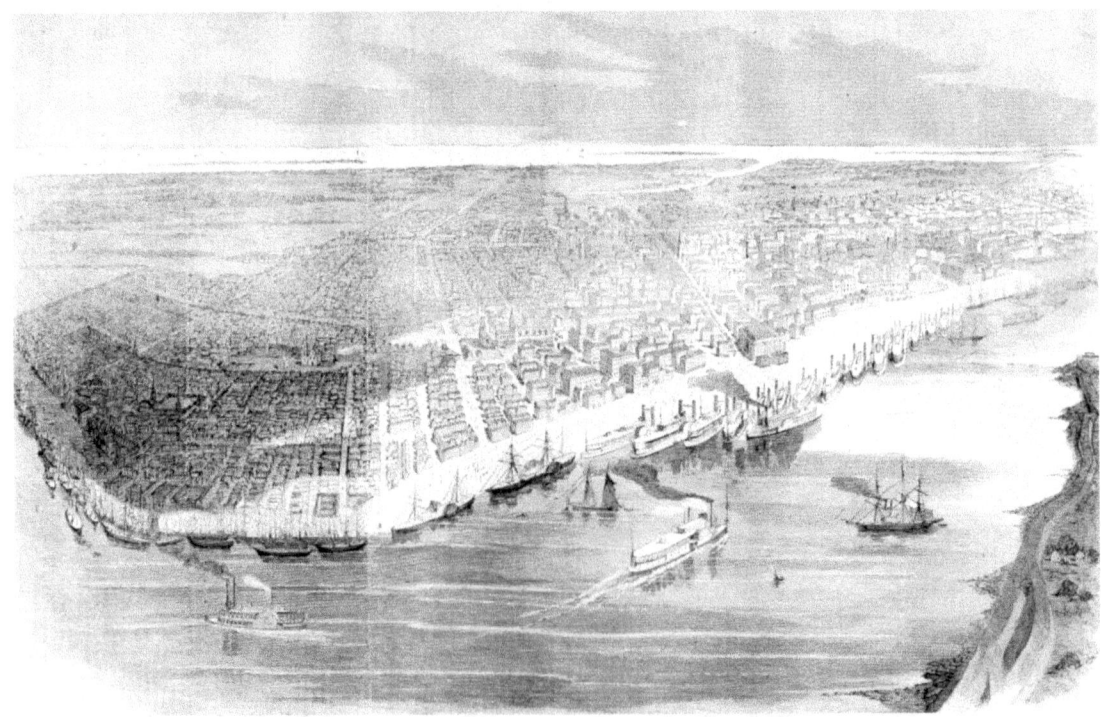

The St. Louis. Half owner and master, Brown took the steamer *St. Louis* to New Orleans in 1853, only to find that the city was in the grip of a virulent yellow fever epidemic. Most of the other Mississippi River boats engaged in the trade refused to enter that port and the situation caused profits from freight hauling to skyrocket. Despite the loss of 100 Louisianans a day to the disease, the big side-wheeler made the run. "I cleared $10,000 on that trip," Brown later remembered, "and I think I earned it" (*Harper's Weekly*, May 10, 1862).

risks," his older brother George T. became increasingly involved in state politics. Working from the offices of his *Alton Daily Courier*, the bachelor joined men of anti-slavery sympathy from various political parties in intense opposition to the Kansas–Nebraska Act of 1854. That federal legislation, authored by Illinois senator Stephen Douglas (1813–1861), would allow territorial citizens to determine by vote whether their locale was free or slave. A winning November candidate as an "Anti-Nebraska Democrat" for a seat in the state legislature, George Brown actively supported Abraham Lincoln's summer-fall statewide tour of anti-act speeches. He was on hand in Peoria on October 16 when Douglas and Lincoln presented their cases before a large gathering.

Early in 1855 it became obvious that the new state legislature, elected at the end of 1854, would have the opportunity to name a U.S. senator (this was years before the 17th Amendment). Lincoln sought the seat and, although he had the support of Free-Soiler Brown in the effort, he did not have the votes to win over other candidates on the first ballot. To assure the choice of an "anti–Nebraska" man, he then threw his support to Congressman Lyman Trumbull, Brown's former law teacher, who triumphed and launched an 18-year Senate career. A year later, Brown helped create the Illinois Republican Party, presiding over its Bloomington Convention. His obituary would later claim, "In truth, from 1855 to 1860, he was the acknowledged leader of the Republican Party in Southern Illinois."

George Brown, as a newspaperman, was in a unique position to further his beliefs. Lincoln scholar Harold Holzer recently observed that by this time in the American West "newspaper publishers were routinely and overtly participating in grassroots politics and vice versa." Earlier, Mark E. Neely noted that newspapers were almost a "branch of government." In a spirit of mutual support, the journalists provided print support to their favorites while the politicians bought subscriptions and paid for print advertising and such things as handbills.

The political friendship among Brown and Trumbull and Lincoln deepened as the antebellum period became more turbulent. Trumbull and Lincoln were not personally close, though they were politically allied. Joseph did not become a Republican but remained a Democrat and would enjoy electoral success under the old party banner.[14]

During this time of the anti–Nebraska political maneuvering, Capt. Brown, disappointed in the *St. Louis'* ability to generate memorable income, again dreamed of building the finest steamboat on the Western waters. Joining once more with Samuel Gaty and John S. McCune, as well as several lesser partners, he travelled to the boatbuilding centers on the Ohio and Monongahela rivers, where numerous construction sites had blossomed over the previous decade or so. Construction locations at towns and cities like Madison, IN, and Cincinnati, OH, were seen, as well as Pittsburg, PA. "Due to the rush of emigration at that time," they knew that this production expansion was due to the fact "boats could not be built fast enough." The men hoped to find builders who could provide a large hull that could be finished at St. Louis.

The captain later reported a meeting with Stephen Phillips (1780–1855), the well-known steamboatbuilder at Freedom, Pennsylvania, in Beaver County on the Monongahela River north of Pittsburg whose facility helped supply the demand. Phillips' concern kept on hand "a lot of the straight bodies of boats put up [built]." "When a man wanted a boat," Brown remembered, Phillips or his associates "took him down to the yard and asked him how long he wanted her." Once the dimensions were provided, they could "just put two ends onto a body and he had a boat." After this review ended, Brown and his associates continued their search, visiting other Pennsylvania boatbuilding towns downstream.[15]

At some point, the Midwesterners arrived at Elizabeth, PA, below Pittsburg, where Samuel Walker (1798–1876) was recognized as the dean of Monongahela boatbuilders. His father having constructed the vessels used on the Lewis and Clark Expedition, Samuel, who had been building steamboats with him since 1826, took over the family business and expanded it to three yards along the waterfront. Also heavily involved in mercantile pursuits, he would by 1857 have finished all or part of 312 steamers (occasionally completing hulls that were towed elsewhere for outfitting). After a detailed discussion in which Brown explained his requirements and his hopes for a new vessel: a "floating palace" that would draw passengers in a very crowded transport business. To meet his need, he wanted to construct a giant craft "with three decks so as to furnish better accommodations for deck passengers." Only one other three-decker had been built, the *John Simmonds*.

An arrangement was thereafter completed whereby Walker would build the hull and much of the superstructure for a 310-foot vessel with a 47-foot beam for $186,000. Her upper works were "fitted up in elegant style" with large staterooms for wealthy travelers, while the middle deck had cabins for 250 regular passengers. So elegant were the upper cabins there was an oil painting on each panel of each door and a large painting of the *Falls of the Colorado* that according to one writer "looked so natural that many thought it was real." There was also space for 400 steerage passengers and 2,500 tons of freight. Certain of her woodwork would be completed at her home port.

Walker completed the hull for Brown's three-decker just prior to the holidays in 1854, and on January 1, 1855, it arrived at the foot of Broadway, Cincinnati, under tow of the steamer *Buckeye State*. On January 20 the boat's owners took out a $5,000 insurance policy with the Phoenix Insurance Company to guard her "against fire and the perils of the river" for a period of one year. She was authorized to navigate "the usual waters" of the Mississippi, Ohio, Illinois, Tennessee, and Cumberland rivers carrying all manner of freight plus passengers. The only proviso was that she could not engage in the cotton trade unless her owners obtained the express written consent of the underwriter.

The incomplete vessel was towed by the side-wheeler *Natchez* from the Queen City to St. Louis where Brown's partners installed her boilers, machinery, and ironwork. She was given seven boilers and engines that were 34 inches in diameter with a 12-foot stroke. Her two paddle wheels were 40 feet each, with 17-foot buckets. When completed, the giant lady, christened *Mayflower*, displaced 890 tons. She was widely admired as having "more good points than any other steamboat of her day."[16]

The *Mayflower* entered service in the St. Louis–New Orleans trade in May 1855. Unfortunately, the passengers were not there as emigration West via the Crescent City had dramatically slowed. Unable to realize a profit transporting passengers alone, Brown and his partners elected in July to cut down the vessel by a deck, so fitting her as to serve as a regular packet offering round-trips between her new home port of Memphis, TN, and New Orleans. The work was completed in mid–September.

The Triple-Decked *Mayflower*. Joseph Brown's most famous commercial steamer, the only one for which any illustration exists, was the *Mayflower*, which entered St. Louis–New Orleans service in May 1855. Unprofitable carrying only passengers, she was cut down by one deck and home-ported at Memphis, and from there she offered packet service south while also hauling freight and cotton (Library of Congress).

On September 21 the *Memphis Daily Appeal* and *Cincinnati Daily Enquirer* carried these two advertisements, reprinted here in that order:

> MAYFLOWER—Joseph Brown, Master—Memphis and New Orleans regular Tuesday packet. This new and splendid steamer, built the past season at a cost of more than $100,000, has been placed permanently in the Memphis and New Orleans trade, and will remain the entire season, leaving Memphis on Tuesday, the 20th of September, at four o'clock P.M., and every alternate Tuesday thereafter. Shippers may rely on the *Mayflower* running permanently in and becoming identified with the trade, as hereafter she will be permanently owned in Memphis. The passenger accommodations are superior to any on the western waters, having larger rooms, with linen outfits, tables set restaurant style, etc. For freight or passage, apply on board, or to Duval, Algeo & Co.
>
> MEMPHIS AND NEW ORLEANS—Regular Tuesday Packet *Mayflower*—Joseph Brown, captain, Henry Filbrun, clerk. The middle deck of this magnificent steamer having been taken out for the purpose of making her suitable for the Memphis and New Orleans trade, she will commence her regular trips about September 25, and continue during the season. Shippers may rely on her remaining permanently in the trade. Duval, Algeo & Co., Lavalette & Morris, agents.

At this time, the principal "freight" exported from Memphis and points along the lower Mississippi River was cotton, which constituted the bulk of all cargo carried by steamers making regular runs between Memphis and the Crescent City. Even occasional and much smaller Ohio River boats sometimes participated in the trade. There were other cargos, such as machinery or farm produce, but given the economy of the region most large shipments were of cotton.

Captain Brown fully intended to engage in this lucrative business when he altered the *Mayflower*, but for whatever reason he and his partners failed to obtain permission from their insurance underwriters. Perhaps the matter was simply overlooked or perhaps the men anticipated a rejection of their application or, as he had with the *St. Louis*, Brown accepted the danger of uncovered loss as just a part of turning a profit. After all, the policy, if paid, would only cover 10–20 percent of the cost of his vessel.

Having completed her sixth voyage—a late November run to New Orleans transporting a number of passengers and some 3,700 bales of cotton—the *Mayflower* returned to Memphis about 11:00 a.m. on Saturday, December 1, and Captain Brown received from his agents a contract to carry some 12,000 to 15,000 sacks of corn south on future voyages. Approximately 4,800 of the total being loaded aboard at Bradley's Landing above the city later in the day, Brown's craft returned to Memphis near 11:00 p.m. and tied up to the wharf boat *Mary Hunt.* The next afternoon, Mrs. Brown, who wanted to visit Cuba, came aboard to take passage downriver. It was anticipated that 3,000 bales of cotton would be loaded on Monday before the steamer cast off on Tuesday.

Sometime between midnight and 1:00 a.m. on December 3 a fire broke out onboard the packet *George Collier*, which lay on the other side of the wharf boat. In less than five minutes, the conflagration was out of control and the steamer's captain gave the order to abandon ship. Some men jumped onto the lower deck of the *Mary Hunt* and others leaped into the river. Within seven minutes not only was the wharf boat engulfed but so too was the *Mayflower.* Captain Brown and his wife managed to escape to the levee in their nightclothes but Brown's assistant barkeeper, Arthur Dignan of Philadelphia, was killed. Between 12 and 15 of the 65 to 70 passengers aboard the *George Collier* also perished and the cargoes of both vessels were lost. Within 10 minutes, all three vessels burnt to the water's edge. "In 15 minutes," Brown later remembered of his boat, "what cost $220,000 was a smoldering wreck that sold for $1,500." In an autobiography published four years before his death, he remembered how he had made great fortunes but in this instance "lost $100,000 in a single night."[17]

After the loss of the *Mayflower*, Brown, Gaty, and McCune contested the refusal of the Phoenix Life Insurance Company to make good on its policy with them. After a loss in lower court, the case made it all the way to the Missouri Supreme Court, in 1861, where the ruling was affirmed (*Gaty et al., Plantiffs in Error, v. Phoenix Insurance Company*," 56–62).

Although the loss of the *Mayflower* was a financial blow, Capt. Brown quickly found other opportunities. Returning to Alton, he joined with the miller John James Mitchell (1813–1903), as well as Capt. LeMothe and McCune and Co. to form the Alton–St. Louis Packet Company. Miller and his brother had taken over the Brown milling concern in the 1840s, continuing its expansion. Acquiring two boats, the *Winchester* and the *Reindeer*, from failing interests, the parties contracted with the Chicago and Mississippi Railroad (begun as the Alton and Sangamon Railroad) to ferry freight and passengers from the Illinois community to St. Louis.

Brown might have captained a number of packet runs for the line but spent much of his time ashore in Alton regaining local prominence and rekindling good will among a few of his many local family friends and acquaintances that his time on the river had dimmed. Though, as his 1899 *St. Louis Post-Dispatch* obituary put it, he was a man "slight of stature and of medium height, not a strong man in point of muscle, but splen-

Loss of the *Mayflower*. While tied to the Memphis wharf boat on December 3, 1855, a fire aboard a similarly secured nearby steamer spread to the *Mayflower*. All three boats were lost, along with 65–70 people. "In 15 minutes," Brown later remembered of his boat, "what cost $220,000 was a smoldering wreck that sold for $1,500." In an autobiography published four years before his death, he remembered how he had made great fortunes but in this instance "lost $100,000 in a single night" (*Harper's Young People*, February 1893).

did vitality," Brown, considered to be of "unusually stalwart character," now put his energy into local politics. In April 1856 he was elected the town's eighteenth mayor. Years later, the *Alton Telegraph* would summarize his one year term in a single, lengthy sentence: "Mr. Brown was a progressive man; whatever he did he pushed with vigor, and the result was that during his term as Mayor he started improvements which ultimately resulted in great good for Alton."

Just as he would be later in St. Louis, Brown was keenly interested in beginning and pushing infrastructure improvements. His greatest mayoral contribution was the initiation of a paving program for city streets, during which "nearly every street between Piasa and Henry was more or less graded," including Piasa, Alby, Market, Third, Fourth, Fifth, and Sixth. Hundreds of men were employed by the town on the work. After reviewing plans and overseeing the appointment of a building supervisor, Capt. Brown next launched construction of a fine "City Building." Costing some $40,000, it was completed in 1859 and provided quarters for not only city hall (which occupied the entire top floor) but also rooms for city offices, a city council chamber, and space for the fire department.

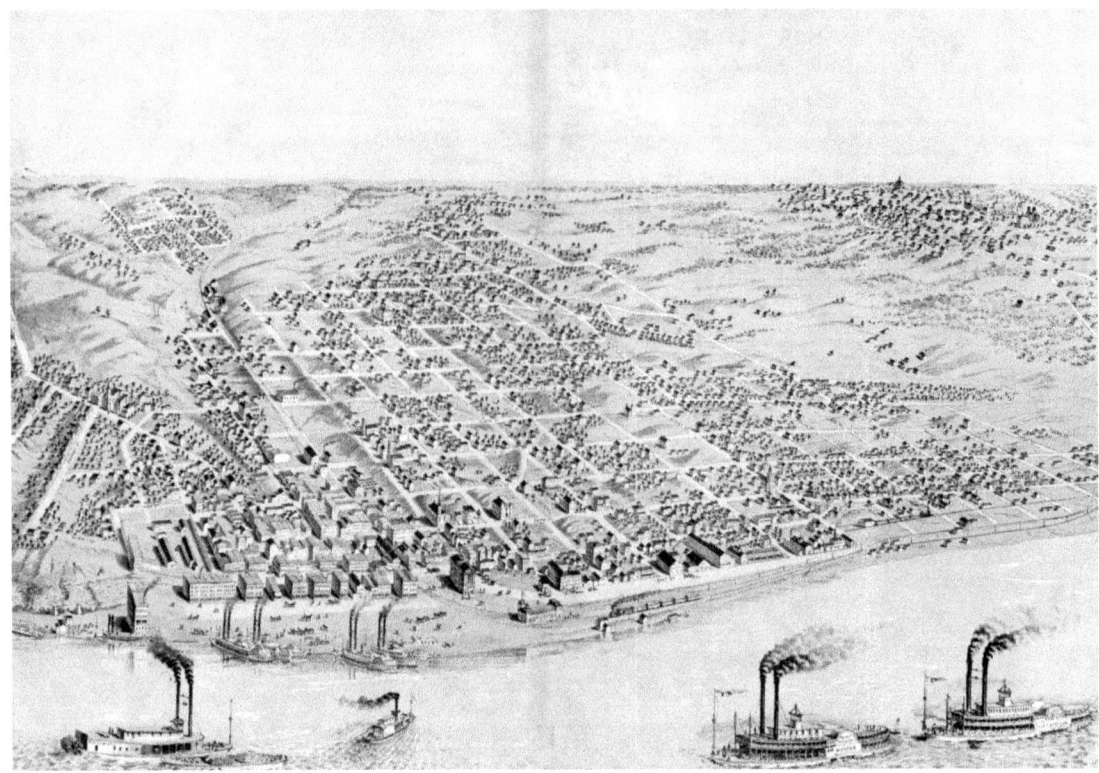

Alton City Hall. Joseph Brown was elected the 18th mayor of Alton, IL, in April 1856. During his single year in office, he pushed infrastructure improvements, which resulted in the paving of a number of city streets and beginning construction of a city hall building completed in 1859.

Brown continued his interest in the Alton–St. Louis Packet Company while in office and worked quite diligently to insure that the Chicago and Mississippi Railroad continued its affinity for the city. It was later recorded by several historians, including Reavis in St. Louis, that, because of his diligence, "the claims of commerce were finally admitted to be paramount to all others, and the railroad passed through instead of around the city."

Alton was the center of attraction in early fall 1856 when, after months of preparation by public entities and private citizens, it hosted the fourth state agricultural fair, the first outside Springfield. There every manner of exhibition normally associated with such an event (even today) could be seen, with entries judged from local communities and throughout the Midwest. Encouraged by the fair superintendent J.A. Miller, and supported by Mayor Brown as part of his civic improvement program, the new Alton Gas Company laid miles of pipe, and gaslights illuminated every street in town. The streets leading to and from the fairgrounds were also graded. Brown even got the city council to order the city marshal to begin enforcing a long-disregarded ordinance that made it a misdemeanor for one to "permit hogs to roam at large in the business portion of the city."

Transport to the September 29–October 2 exhibition was by rail and road from points in Illinois and, under contract with the Alton–St. Louis Packet Company and the

St. Louis and Keokuk Line, by steamboat twice daily from St. Louis. Three of the four steamers engaged were even employed at night, tied up at the levee to serve as floating hotels supplementing the city's establishments.

One boat, the *Winchester*, with 200 souls aboard, struck a log above Madison, IL. Broken, she landed on a sand bar, where her passengers were taken off without injury and sent on to Alton. Capt. James B. Eads (1820–1887) and his partner Capt. William Shaw Nelson (1817–1878), operators of a "wrecking" business in St. Louis (the Missouri Wrecking Company), accepted the contract to salvage the vessel. Although Brown later claimed to have met Eads when the Hoosier engineer and Nelson operated a St. Louis glass factory a decade earlier, it is quite possible that the two actually interacted at length at this time.

By this time, Lawrenceburg, IN, native James Eads (whose mother was a cousin of future president James Buchanan) was a highly regarded Missouri entrepreneur, a "rags-to-riches" businessman who got his financial start by selling apples on river packets. There being many wrecks along the river during those early steamboating days, Eads saw a chance to make money by salvaging some of them. Knowledgeable about the shipping business from being employed as a steamboat purser, he demonstrated an early mechanical aptitude when in 1842 he devised a successful diving bell that could be operated from a special "snag-boat" he built with Capt. Nelson called a "submarine." After entering into a partnership with Nelson in the Missouri Wrecking Company at St. Louis, the men became rich cleaning out river-bottom wrecks. To satisfy his new bride and alleviate health problems doubtless caused by his pioneering underwater salvage work, Eads quit the Mississippi. New energy and his fortune were poured into the establishment, at St. Louis, of the first glassworks west of the Ohio River, but it and he were financially ruined at age 37 by the Mexican War. Required by fate to replenish his empty bank accounts, Eads returned to the salvage business, improved his earlier innovations, and earned a second fortune. In 1855 poor health forced him to retire from active underwater participation in his business at the age of 55. Later (1867–1874), he would construct the steel Mississippi River arch bridge at St. Louis (a bridge still in use today). Here he would again encounter Joseph Brown, then mayor of that city. Eads would thereafter oversee river jetty improvement

James B. Eads, Another Future River Legend. When a steamer bringing passengers to attend the Illinois State Fair, held at Alton in the fall of 1856, went aground, Mayor Joseph Brown offered a contract to the St. Louis–based salvage firm headed by James B. Eads to get her off. Although Brown later claimed to have met Eads when the Hoosier-born engineer operated a St. Louis glass factory a decade earlier, it is quite possible that the two now actually interacted at length for the first time. Their paths would intersect several times during the next quarter century (Library of Congress).

projects at New Orleans. At the time of his death he was planning a ship-railway across Mexico's isthmus of Tehuantepec.

Draughtsman, construction engineer, and inventor William Nelson arrived at St. Louis from New York in 1840, remaining partnered with Eads in his river salvage firms. During the Civil War Nelson was superintendent of the City Series ironclads built by Eads at Carondelet, MO. He was the expert selected by the U.S. Navy in 1863 to examine the wreck of the Brown-built ironclad *Indianola*. Later he served as construction superintendent for both the Eads bridge at St. Louis and the famous New Orleans river jetties.[18] Whether or not he met Eads at this time, Mayor Brown probably enjoyed his responsibility of introducing many of the politicians who took the opportunity to offer oratory in his town during a state and presidential election year. Being originally scheduled to speak earlier, George T. Brown's friend Abraham Lincoln was not able to make it to town until the afternoon of October 2, when he was introduced by the mayor and spoke before a large gathering at the Presbyterian church in support of the Republican presidential candidate John C. Fremont. Senator Stephen A. Douglas could not make it to town before October 8. At the fairgrounds, he praised the Democratic candidate James Buchanan before a crowd of 500.

A then largely unnoticed event occurred on March 30, 1857, that would bring Lincoln and Brown together again a year later. About 2:00 that morning, according to the mayor's recollection, an Irish immigrant and Shakespearean actress named Mary Mcready arrived on the Keokuk packet to present a series of public lectures. As she was making her way to a local hotel, she stepped into an old, uncovered, and unseen cellar door in front of a grocery store, badly injuring her back, a leg, and an ankle. Attended by a local physician, Mcready was laid up at the Franklin House for some time before she removed to Peoria and Springfield for further treatment.[19]

Stephen A. Douglas (National Archives).

Abraham Lincoln (Library of Congress).

1—Joseph Brown: The Honorable Steamboat Captain

Following the end of his mayoral term, Joseph Brown maintained his home in Alton. About this time, the Chicago and Mississippi Railroad was reorganized, becoming the St. Louis, Alton, and Chicago Railroad. Although the cross-river Alton-to-St. Louis connection continued to be maintained by the Alton–St. Louis Packet Company, the captain took this opportunity to withdraw his interest in the line. Also in 1857, Brown agreed to travel to Madison, IN, on behalf of his friend and colleague John S. McCune to oversee final construction of the *City of Louisiana*, a new side-wheeler packet for the St. Louis and Keokuk Packet Company named in honor of the Missouri river town. Upon the completion of her hull, she was towed to St. Louis and, like the *Mayflower*, was finished by Brown's old partner, Samuel Gaty. With a length of 250 feet and a 40-foot beam, the steamer entered service to Keokuk and other points in the fall, with Brown a part owner, though not her initial master. "She was not a long carrier," the captain remembered in 1891, "but a good runner."

On March 13, 1858, Brown and his brother George T. were both asked to serve on a jury empanelled to hear evidence in the death of an Alton Penitentiary inmate who had taken a guard hostage three days earlier and held him until the perpetrator was mortally wounded by the prison warden. Of the 12 men and true asked to review the situation, three were past Alton mayors and the fourth was the current mayor, Samuel Wade. The warden's action was quickly justified.

Meanwhile, Mary Mcready convalesced at Peoria and Springfield, where she was treated by physicians and incurred medical bills in excess of $500. Being unable to work during her rehabilitation—or pay her bills—she retained the services of Lincoln and Herndon in the spring and they filed suit in June at the Federal District Court at Springfield against the City of Alton. The suit charged the town with negligence in failing to maintain its sidewalks. Mcready sought $20,000 in personal injury compensation. Alton denied any responsibility for the lady's injuries. It being determined that the case could expeditiously proceed, the U.S. marshal ordered former Mayor Brown, several Alton city officials and two city council members to appear in court. The town would be represented by St. Louis, Alton, and Chicago Railroad attorney Levi Davis (1808–1897) and lawyer and former Alton mayor (1851–1852) Henry W. Billings (1814–1870). The jury was empanelled on June 29, with U.S. District Court judge Samuel Treat presiding.

According to his recollections, Brown and Levi entered the courtroom before the proceedings commenced and saw Abraham Lincoln and Mary Mcready seated inside the bar waiting for the court to open. Shortly after the two men from Alton took their seats at the defense table, Lincoln rose and came over, asking Brown if the two of them couldn't have a private word. Widely quoted but not independently verified, Brown recalled the exchange, with Lincoln beginning:

> Mr. Brown, I don't like to take this suit against your town; can't we compromise it in some way? I said: "I don't see how we can, as we don't think the city is liable for an injury done to the lady by a man having bad cellar doors." "Ah," he said, "but the city is liable for its sidewalks, and I feel sure we shall get the judgement." "Well," I said, "if you do, she can up and help herself to the Market House (which at that time was an old dilapidated concern)." "Well," he said, "I think it is best to compromise if we can. How much will you give the lady? She is lamed for life with a stiff ankle." I said: "I can't make any offer; we have no money." "Well," he said, "will you give her $3000?" "No," I said, "there isn't that much money in the town!" Finally he got down to $1,500, and I felt that it was best to compromise at that, so I said: "If we give the $1,500 are we to have the damaged

limb?" Lincoln said: "I will go over and ask," which he did, and after talking with her a little while he came back and said: "If you are an unmarried man, and as you are pretty good looking, you can have the entire woman!" So we compromised, but I did not accept the lady's offer.

Two physicians and a Peoria chamber maid testified on behalf of the Irish actress, recounting the circumstances of both her injury and her subsequent treatment. The trial was continued to June 30, on which morning testimony was taken from Brown, personnel from the Alton hotel where Mcready had stayed, and a Madison County deputy sheriff. The 12-man jury, after deliberation, returned their verdict, finding the City of Alton guilty and awarding Mary Mcready $300, the real cost of her medical expenses. Both sides were ordered to cover their own legal costs.[20]

Needing employment, Brown now accepted the position of master aboard the *City of Louisiana*, landing at various Mississippi River towns between St. Louis and Keokuk, Iowa. Among the destinations in Illinois were Alton and Quincy; in Missouri, Louisiana and Hannibal; and in Iowa, Keokuk, Fort Madison, and Burlington. Earlier in the year, the town of Hardin, IL, opened its first public school and among its students was the captain's nephew, George Child. Learning that the facility needed a bell, Brown donated the bell of the *Altona*, much to the pleasure of his sister Ellen and his brother-in-law Benjamin F. Child, which was, according to a Kansas newspaper years later, "dedicated with much pomp and ceremony."

During this time, Abraham Lincoln became a candidate for his state's U.S. Senate seat, then occupied by Stephen A. Douglas, who was up for election. In August the two men agreed to formal debates in seven of the nine Illinois congressional districts—the seven where Douglas had not already spoken. The process would begin at Ottawa on August 21 and conclude at Alton on October 15. Lincoln and Douglas held their sixth debate at Quincy on October 13. The next day the pair, accompanied by numbers of their handlers as well as newspaper reporters, repaired aboard the *City of Louisiana* for a leisurely overnight voyage 100 miles downstream. Always solicitous of his passengers, Capt. Brown doubtless spent time visiting with his notable guests at table or otherwise. The vessel landed her passengers at dawn on Friday, October 15; both candidates were met by local delegations (including some dignitaries who had arrived from elsewhere) and were escorted to Democratic headquarters at the Alton House for breakfast. Samuel Pitts, Jr. (1833–1912), son of the establishment's owner, remembered the table conversation between the two great men as being "very friendly." After the meal ended, Lincoln was led by his supporters, including newspaperman George T. Brown, to the Franklin House, which was serving as Republican headquarters (this was the same establishment where actress Mary Mccready had been laid up just over a year earlier). Here Lincoln caucused with his supporters, including U.S. senator Lyman Trumbull and George T. Brown.

After lunch the politicians and their people made their way to a speaking stand at the corner of the new, almost finished city building. The sixteen-foot-long stand, sparsely decorated, held a number of supporting dignitaries, including George T. Brown. Crowds now gathered in front of it and on nearby sloping hills. Among them was Capt. Brown, who always enjoyed hearing expert orators. The debate ran three hours.

"I heard Lincoln and Douglas speak at Alton when they ran for Congress," Brown recalled, "when Lincoln sprung the question of the 'irrepressible conflict.'" The steamboat master summed up the feelings of many: "Douglas was the greater orator, but

Lincoln was the most profound and prophetic." In the end, Lincoln lost the senatorial contest. Two years later, he would be elected the 16th U.S. president.[21]

Capt. Brown continued as master of the *City of Louisiana* off and on in the months ahead. In 1859 he purchased a home in St. Louis and became the chief St. Louis representative of the newly finished Carondelet Marine Railway and Dock Company, where Roger C. McAlister was president and employed his old *Altona* acquaintance Primus Emerson. During this time, the *Mayflower* insurance case was settled by the courts in favor of the Phoenix Insurance Company. Attorneys for Gatty, McCune then appealed it to the Missouri Supreme Court.

Early in 1860 Capt. Brown traveled to Madison, IN, where he contracted for the hull for a new steamer, the *Jeannie Deans*, which would replace the St. Louis and Keokuk Packet Company vessel of the same name destroyed by fire at St. Louis in 1856. The body of the 503-ton side-wheeler was 244.7 feet long, with a beam of 39.8 feet and a six-foot draft. Having overseen its construction, Brown accompanied the hull when it was towed to St. Louis, where Gaty, McCune installed the engines and ironwork, including four boilers, each 46" × 24' with five flues. Ready by fall, the *Jeannie Deans* entered the St. Louis to Keokuk packet trade with which her owner was so familiar.

Commemorative Stamp (U.S. Postal Service).

Lincoln-Douglas Debate Site (courtesy Catherine E. Bagby, Alton, Illinois).

Lincoln-Douglas Debate, October 1858. Now captain of the steamboat *City of Louisiana*, former Alton mayor Joseph Brown delivered both U.S. Senate candidates Lincoln and Douglas to Alton, IL, on October 15, where he joined both men, his brother George T., and city officials at an Alton House breakfast. Both Browns, with 5,000 others, heard the subsequent three hour seventh debate between the notables. Joseph later recalled, "Douglas was the greater orator, but Lincoln was the most profound and prophetic." The event was commemorated by a special postage stamp in 1958 and is forever recalled by two statues created by Jerry McKenna and dedicated in Alton's Lincoln-Douglas Square in October 1995.

Able to carry only some 750 tons of cargo, she specialized in passenger and mail service.

As Capt. Brown later told Capt. Gould, he came up with the idea of employing the *Jeannie Deans* on the Lower Mississippi during the fall and winter months when the Upper Mississippi was unprofitable. Realizing that it took vessels with greater hauling capacity longer to make the turn-around-trip between St. Louis and New Orleans, Brown decided to "whip" his vessel through in a series of rapid round-trips. To accomplish this goal, he would push his side-wheeler at top speed and enter and exit each port along the way on "the same day, making 2,480 miles in eleven days." Twelve trips into this winter cycle, disaster nearly occurred, as Brown told Gould: "I was commanding the *Jeannie Deans* in the New Orleans trade when we carried 180 pounds of steam to the square inch, and had it at the time when she picked up a snag that came up through the lower guard, straddled the copper steam pipe and bent it through the boiler deck, until it hemmed in a man in his berth, so that when the boat was stopped, he had to climb over the bent pipe to get out of his berth, and yet the pipe did not burst and we ran to St. Louis (800 miles) with the bent pipe, but not with 180 pounds of steam as may be supposed." The steamer was diverted to Carondelet for repairs and Brown returned to command of the *City of Louisiana* while she was on the ways.[22]

Snag. While pushing upriver from New Orleans in the winter of 1860 Capt. Brown's steamer *Jeannie Deans* hit a snag, which entered the hull, bent a pipe, and pinned a passenger into his bed. The customer escaped uninjured and the damaged vessel steamed 800 miles to undergo repairs at Carondelet, MO (Mark Twain, *Life on the Mississippi*, 1883 first edition).

To say that the political situation was tense in the wake of the election to the White House of Illinois native Abraham Lincoln on November 6 would be a huge understatement. On December 3 the second session of the 36th U.S. Congress assembled in the nation's capital and in the days that followed, newspapers from cities large and small intensified their reporting of uncertainty-filled public discourse. Many sectional leaders from the South threatened secession while significant blocks of northern citizens sought compromise to avert the union's dissolution or demanded that the government stand fast and impose its laws in the South.

On December 18 Senator John J. Crittenden (1787–1863) offered a compromise, rejected by Lincoln and his followers, that would recognize even further the "rights" of the slaveholders. Allies of the president in Congress were strongly committed to compromise, both on political grounds and because of the perceived impact the crisis was having upon the national economy.

Despite the spreading web of the railroad, among the possibilities most feared by those at the northern end of the river system as the secession movement unfolded in 1860–1861 was the creation of a hostile, southern, indeed foreign, power that could choke off trade. As the soon-to-be-called Confederates became increasingly aggressive and civil war threatened, opinion and concern in the upper Midwest crystallized behind the slogan "Free Navigation of the Mississippi." Many northerners began to consider the extreme measures that might be necessary to protect their vital water arteries to the south and to the world in the event compromise failed. While it was true that commerce with the eastern seaboard had grown, citizens of the upper Midwest also recognized that much of their prosperity was still tied to the cotton South.

Midwestern legislators participated in the ferocious legislative debates that surrounded the Crittenden Compromise and several other proposals designed to find some middle ground between the crisis's extremists. As trade with the South began to dwindle during this time of uncertain political conditions, merchants, shippers, farmers, and others, especially in Ohio, Indiana, and Illinois, supported work by state legislatures and Congress to find national compromise. Though it was not recognized as such that day, the work of the peace advocates was, in fact, really doomed on December 20 when South Carolina enacted an ordinance of secession.

In rapid succession between January 9 and February 1, 1861, Mississippi, Florida, Alabama, Georgia, Louisiana, and Texas seceded from the United States. On February 8, the seceded states met in convention at Montgomery, AL, and established the provisional government of the Confederate States of America. Even as various efforts were undertaken to achieve compromise and avert war, the new entity began to discuss or exercise the various prerogatives of national government, including those affecting mid-continent river commerce.

In his March 4, 1861, inaugural address, Abraham Lincoln, the tall, former Illinois lawyer-politician, rejected compromise with the South. The reaction from southern newspapers was acerbic. The *Charleston Mercury* screamed that "the Ourang-Outang at the White House" had sounded "the tocsin of battle," while the *Richmond Dispatch* in still-loyal Virginia concluded that the speech "inaugurates civil war."[23] While the politicians and newspapermen debated the national future and Midwesterners of all occupations worried for their livelihoods, commerce continued up and down the Mississippi River and its tributaries. This flow was occasionally subjected to excited patriotic fervor, particularly on the waters below Memphis, TN.

On January 9, as reported in the *Cincinnati Daily Enquirer* six days later, Mississippi governor John J. Pettis (1813–1867), reacting to intelligence received from Louisiana, ordered action taken to stop two steamers, the *Marengo* and the *Silver Wave*, that were believed to be bringing ordnance downriver to reinforce federal installations.

Walking down to the state arsenal in Jackson, the Democrat executive ordered the Quitman battery to move over to positions on the landing at Vicksburg and in the Walnut Hills, there to "prevent any hostile expedition from the Northern States descending the river." All vessels ascending the river were to stop and submit to inspection by specially appointed officers. If a hailed vessel did not stop, the gunners were to fire a blank first and employ live ammunition thereafter.

By the time the Jackson cannoneers joined with other units already at Vicksburg, rumors about the *Silver Wave* expedition had mushroomed. Not only was the steamer, which was expected on the evening of the 12th, carrying cannon; it also was transporting 500 hooligans—"Wideawakes"—who would come ashore and pillage the town. The *Silver Wave* did not materialize as expected, but the volunteer defenders were not to be disappointed. The following evening as the men stood ready and waiting at their 6-pounders., another steamboat rounded De Soto point in the dark and headed toward the town landing. Betrayed by sparks from her chimneys and the chugging sound made by her engines, the regularly scheduled Cincinnati–New Orleans packet *A.O. Tyler* was targeted for the first blank round. Captain John Collier, part-owner of the craft, did not know what to make of the firing and so continued on.

Another shot, this one live, was fired across the bow of the *A.O. Tyler* and splashed into the muddy Mississippi water beyond. As the artillerymen prepared to shoot again, the *City of Louisiana*, en route to New Orleans and whose identity was known, steamed between the defenders and Collier's boat, bringing a lull in the action before continuing down.

Collier was now hailed by the Mississippians and ordered to bring his craft in. At the dock, he was advised of the "Wideawake" scare and ordered to take his boat upstream to a point below Fort Hill where it could be inspected—even though both he and the *Tyler* were well known. By-and-by, as the *City of Louisiana* continued down the river, the *Silver Wave* appeared. She too was searched and when neither contraband of war nor ruffians were found, both steamers were permitted to depart.

U.S. Navy commander John Rodgers (1812–1882) would later purchase the *A.O. Tyler* at Cincinnati and have her converted into the gunboat USS *Tyler*. Seven months to the day later, on August 13, the *Tyler* would, according to several writers, fire the first hostile naval shots heard on the Western waters. Seventy-one years later, historian Charles Henry Ambler would refer to the January incident as "possibly the first shot of the Civil War."[24]

On Brown's next trip, just after the *City of Louisiana* shoved off from the St. Louis wharf, the captain was somewhat surprised to find that approximately 100 of his passengers were young men returning, by parental request, to their Crescent City homes from college in the north. All the way down, he noticed that the fellows would gather in small knots and, putting "their heads together, would hold animated conversations."

1—Joseph Brown: The Honorable Steamboat Captain 37

Bound Down the River. As Capt. Brown's *City of Louisiana* approached Vicksburg on January 10, 1861, she was witness unwittingly to what some historians now say were the first shots of the Civil War, rather than those fired on Fort Sumter. Local militia had fired on a steamer, the *A.O. Tyler*, which was suspected of harboring Yankee saboteurs. As the artillery prepared to fire again, the *City of Louisiana*, en route to New Orleans and whose identity was well known ashore, steamed between the defenders and the *A.O. Tyler*, bringing a lull in the action. This 1870 photograph depicts two steamboats approaching a Mississippi town from the north, just as Brown's vessel and the *A.O. Tyler* had (Library of Congress).

At other times, Brown remembered in 1891, they could be heard "singing snatches of red-hot patriotic songs applicable to the South."

Like others across the land, Joseph Brown had watched the sectional storm as it continued to gather, discussing its import with fellow steamboatmen and river people. All the way down the river "there was a strong undercurrent of thought, an uneasiness that was constantly coming to the surface." Wherever his vessel landed, whether village or larger town, crowds seemed to be in motion. Some were depressed and thoughtful, he remembered for a St. Louis newspaper, while many were "excited and boastful."

When the *City of Louisiana* reached the Crescent City levee on the morning of January 26, it was crowded with excited people making inquiry of the few incoming boats concerning conditions in states farther upstream. Most of the northern-owned vessels had withdrawn back to upper river ports and those coming in found that all local business was suspended. Capt. Brown went aboard the *Natchez No. 5*, the Vicksburg packet tied up next to his craft, to discuss developments with his good friend, pro–Southern Captain Thomas P. Leathers (1816–1896). Leathers would gain lasting

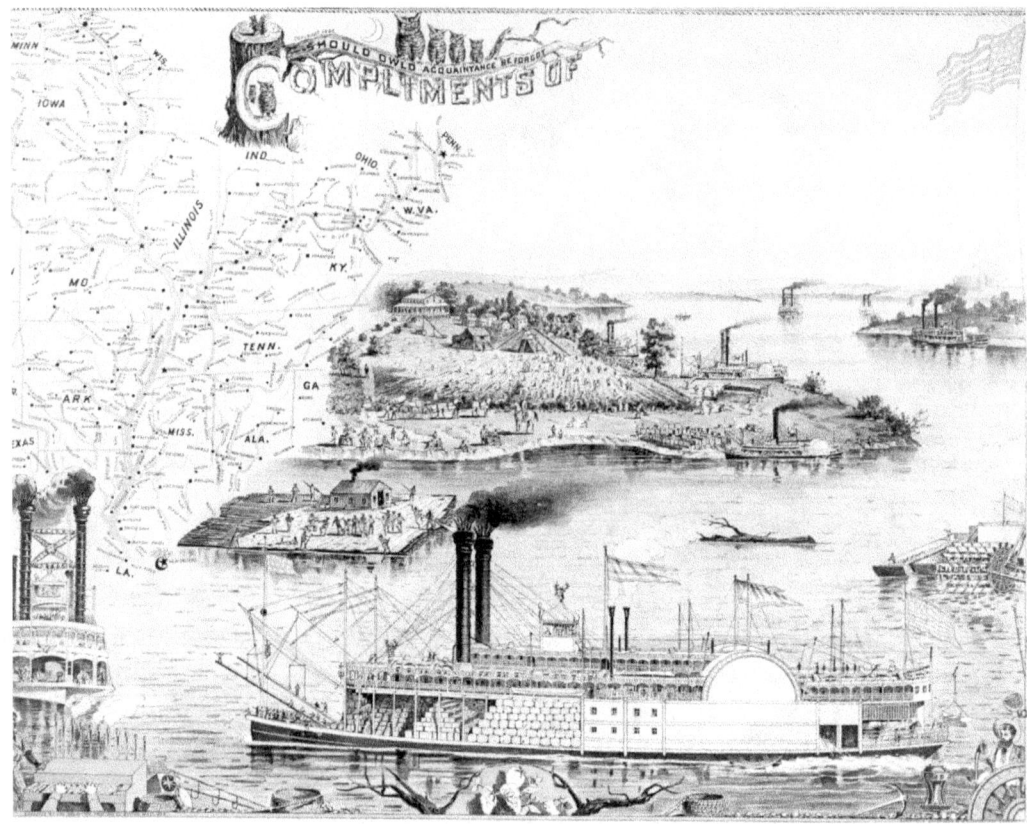

War Enthusiasm. En route to New Orleans in mid–January 1861, the *City of Louisiana* made frequent logistical stops at towns along the Mississippi, with ever more ominous news given to Capt. Brown and his men at each point. These landings are depicted in William Alyward's painting *Steamboating Through Dixie*. Not all aboard were displeased, as approximately 100 of his passengers were young men returning, by parental request, to their Crescent City homes from college in the north. All the way down, it was noticed that the fellows would gather in small knots and, "holding their heads together, would hold animated conversations." At other times, Brown remembered in 1891, they could be heard "singing snatches of red-hot patriotic songs applicable to the South" (*Harper's Monthly*, September 1915).

fame as master of the vessel that lost to the *Robert E. Lee* in the great steamboat race of June 1870. At 11:00 a.m. as the two men conversed, the U.S. flag was lowered over the customs building signaling to all that Louisiana had seceded from the union. The two now engaged in what the Illini master remembered as "quite an animated discussion on the subject of secession." Both men espoused the virtues of their beliefs and the prowess of men from their geographical divisions, North and South. Brown worried that Louisiana authorities might attempt to confiscate his boat, while Leathers did not believe war would come because the North would recognize the Confederacy.

Alton's former mayor was not prepared to take any chances and was determined to depart right away, even if it meant returning to St. Louis without freight. Recollecting the trip down, Brown estimated that if he did not make it past the pro–Southern hotbeds at Napoleon, AR, and Greeneville, MS, his boat would probably be stopped and confiscated. Returning to his vessel, the master immediately engaged his crew and every available nearby worker he could hire (over 100 men) to offload his present cargo. They then loaded her "with pine knots and resin, enough to carry the boat to Cairo without stopping," or, as he remembered in 1891, two-hundred sixty cords of pine knots, 800 boxes of Pittsburg coal, 100 barrels of resin, 20 barrels of turpentine (in which to dip the wood), and 30 barrels of tar (which could be spread on green wood if they were forced to refuel with same while en route).

While the laborers handled their tasks, Capt. Brown spoke several times with his chief engineer, George Lewis, an old Alton acquaintance, impressing upon him the need to make all speed back to their Missouri home port. Obtaining assurances from the engineer, he turned to the carpenter, who warned that one of the paddle wheels was damaged and in need of repair. After some discussion, it was agreed that it could be mended by 4:00 p.m. if all the men necessary to complete the task could be hired. With the paddle wheel repaired and such passengers aboard "only as were anxious to get away while they could," Brown made ready to cast off in late afternoon.

Just before the *City of Louisiana* cast off, an officer in a new uniform came aboard and served a writ on Capt. Brown that demanded he acquire papers from the new Confederate custom house before he could leave. The vessel blew off steam from her safety and other valves while the master went ashore to pay a fee for new documents headed "Confederate States of America." Returning aboard, Brown ordered his pilot to get underway and at dusk the steamboat "was off up the river like a shot out of a cannon." About 53 minutes later, she passed Richmond, 12 miles upriver, her speed being estimated at 22 mph rather than her normal 12 mph against the current.

The passage began without incident. However, "trouble was expected in getting past Napoleon." To provide as innocent a profile as possible, Mrs. Brown, along for the trip with several St. Louis lady acquaintances, came up with a novel idea. To celebrate the vessel's Louisiana name, painted on the paddle wheel houses, it was decided that a white flag with a black pelican, the state emblem, would be made and flown from the steamer's jack staff. Employing their undergarments and a cutting from the lining of Capt. Brown's coat, a state flag (entirely unofficial) was quickly created and hoisted in place of U.S. colors.

On his way down, the master had spied a pair of cannon planted on the riverbank at Napoleon, which lay above Vicksburg (just south of the mouth of the Arkansas River) approximately 390 miles south of Cairo. On the second day out of New Orleans, the *City of Louisiana* approached the Arkansas town just before dark. Peering through his telescope, Brown saw that the cannon were still there and ordered his pilot to get by, if possible, without landing. Just as Brown had feared, when the *City of Louisiana* came abreast of Napoleon the Southern gunners sent a warning shot across her bow, forcing her to heave to. They then hailed her master, ordering him to land his vessel at the bank. "As soon as she touched the shore," Brown later related, "at least 400 thirsty men jumped on board. In less than 20 minutes, the bar was empty and the barkeeper received nothing."

Having consumed the vessel's libations, the visitors began to debate whether or not they should confiscate the boat and turn her over to the Southern cause. More men than not shouted in favor of the idea and it appeared that the vessel would be taken over, with Brown, his crew and passengers stranded ashore. While the discussion went on, Brown made use of his political and oratorical skills, boldly jumping up on a cabin table to proclaim, "Gentlemen, this boat belongs to St. Louis and I am part owner, with slaves on board, and if you want Missouri to go out of the Union, with the other Southern States, I would advise you not to confiscate her citizens' property." The men argued and discussed the ex-mayor's words and decided to release the craft, though pledging to abduct any other Northern steamers passing their town.

Although the possibility of trouble also existed at Greenville, MS, that town was passed at night. The longest halt of the entire voyage was made at Memphis. There a number of prominent passengers boarded, including James B. Eads, the salvage expert and future gunboat and bridge constructor, with whom Brown had been acquainted for some time, and his partner Capt. William Shaw Nelson. Two other possible danger points, Hickman and Columbus, KY, were also passed without difficulty. Reaching Cairo, IL, everyone aboard breathed a sigh of relief and the *City of Louisiana* thereafter proceeded to St. Louis at normal speed. Brown had completed this round-trip to New Orleans in the record time of nine days and 18 hours.

Brown completed only a few more runs before civil war broke out on April 12. When it did, the steamboatman, a staunch unionist, returned home to Alton, where he unfurled a large (9' × 14') U.S. flag over his residence. With the coming of actual conflict, traffic on the inland rivers largely dried up. A newspaperman visiting the St. Louis levee

A Great Escape. After arriving in New Orleans in late January 1861, Capt. Brown watched as the U.S. flag was lowered over the customs house, signaling Louisiana's secession from the Union. Loading the *City of Louisiana* with as much fuel as she could hold and all willing hands and passengers, he sped north to avoid his boat's being confiscated. Employing a ruse flag and bold talk, the ex-mayor of Alton avoided difficulties, reaching St. Louis in a record nine days and 18 hours (*Harper's Weekly*, February 16, 1861).

at the beginning of June found it to be as quiet as a graveyard. Brig. Gen. Joseph Totten (1788–1864), in the Mississippi Valley on a transportation fact-finding mission for the U.S. War Department, noted that 150 steamboats were idle at St. Louis alone. Rivermen based in that town feared a total suspension of freight and passenger services and several prophesied that grass would soon be growing on the wharf itself. Except for local packets, the Mississippi River below Cairo, IL, was closed to commercial navigation for the first time in 60 years. The same suspension also occurred on the Ohio and its tributaries. The blockade had a devastating impact on river trade as business dried up and insurance companies refused to assume risks. Some daring rivermen tried to operate flying two flags as needed in a *ruse de guerre*, but this didn't last long. Most just tied up their boats "and settled down to watch the outcome" of the growing struggle. As Louis Hunter has noted, the great streams were "plunged into a depression from which there was little relief until the second year of the war."

Brown was one of those who was able to participate in the local packet trade, his vessel plying the waters between St. Louis, Alton, and points north. As the conflict deepened, he observed the Union's river buildup and held himself ready to join the war effort, hoping for a way to eventually make use of his many talents, contacts, and skills not only as a riverman but also as an entrepreneur and minor politician. And if he could earn a profit along the way, so much the better.[25]

While Joseph Brown was engaged in the increasingly dangerous if slowing steamboat trade, his brother George T. Brown found new opportunities in Washington, D.C. The printer and former proprietor/owner of the *Alton Weekly Courier* (which he sold on January 1, 1860), by now moderately wealthy, had followed other business pursuits and participated in the 1860 election in support of his political associates Lincoln and Trumbull.

The 36th U.S. Congress adjourned on March 4, 1861, the day Lincoln was inaugurated as president of the United States. The same day, with numerous southern states seceded or seceding and withdrawing their representatives, the Republican pluralities elected in 1860 to the U.S. Senate and House became the governing majorities of the 37th national legislature. Fort Sumter at Charleston, SC, was attacked by Confederate forces on April 12 and thus the long-dreaded civil war began.[26]

2

War and Gunboats

As tensions continued to escalate in the Mississippi Valley, the steamboat trade between northern and southern ports on the great river steadily declined, having something of a ripple effect on steamboating in the waters north of Memphis. Although Joseph Brown continued to operate his *City of Louisiana* on sporadic trips, he now also spent more time observing developments and reviewing real estate opportunities in St. Louis from his new residence at 226 Olive Street, a home he would own into the 1870s.

When news of Fort Sumter's fall on April 13 and President Abraham Lincoln's subsequent call-up were received in St. Louis, MO, Brown's river colleague engineer James B. Eads, a passenger on the *City of Louisiana* during the last leg of Capt. Joe's perilous January run up from Memphis, wrote to his Missouri friend U.S. attorney general Edward Bates (1793–1869). Eads, famous for his Mississippi River salvage operations, called for aggressive action to defeat the Rebels and suggested he had a plan that might prove helpful in wresting the lower Mississippi away from the South. In the attorney general's April 17 acknowledgment, Bates advised Eads that the riverman's presence would soon be required in the nation's capital, as "it will be necessary to have the aid of the most thorough knowledge of our Western rivers and the use of steam on them."

Eads arrived in Washington and on April 29 was taken by Bates before President Lincoln and the cabinet to explain his ideas for creating a river navy to aid in a joint U.S. Army-Navy campaign to recover the river valley. The proposed campaign would be based on a navy operating from the low-lying town of Cairo, Illinois, where the Ohio River flowed into the Mississippi and where those two streams physically separated pro–Union Illinois from the border states of Kentucky and Missouri. Eads later delivered his ideas in writing to an appreciative Navy Secretary Gideon Welles (1802–1878). In the confusion, excitement, and inter-service rivalries that marked the Federal buildup, Eads' plan was amalgamated into one sponsored, financed, and controlled by the War Department, which in peacetime exercised jurisdiction over inland waterways.[1]

On May 1, 1861, the Union army chief, Gen. Winfield Scott (1786–1866), a hero of the Mexican War, wrote to Lincoln describing a strategy for crushing the rebellion. At the heart of this "Anaconda" victory plan lay the idea of strangling the South along the Mississippi and its tributaries, using inland river highways to mount and support amphibious assaults to crush the strong points of the divided parts, eventually reopening the mighty stream to United States commerce. Scott based his strategy on a powerful U.S. Navy coastal blockade and called for a decisive "movement down the Mississippi to the ocean, with a cordon of posts at proper points ... the object being to clear out

Unfinished Capitol Dome. When the Civil War came in the spring of 1861 the U.S. Capitol Dome, shown here during President Lincoln's March 4 inauguration, was incomplete. While work on it proceeded, James B. Eads arrived from St. Louis to present his plans for a river-based strategy to the new administration (Library of Congress).

and keep open this great line of communication." Although this game plan, similar to that of Eads, had its critics, it was, with modifications, successfully followed. The Confederacy, for its part, devised no real countermeasures to the Union strategy and such preparations as could be made to resist the scheme would, in the end, prove useless.[2]

The first problem faced in implementing the Eads-Scott strategy was one of matériel: there were no Union gunboats on the rivers. On May 16, 1861, Cmdr. John Rodgers, USN, was ordered to report to Brig. Gen. George B. McClellan (1826–1885) at Cincinnati "in regard to the expediency of establishing a naval armament on the Mississippi and Ohio Rivers." McClellan earlier in the month had recommended to Scott that three gunboats be constructed to protect the occupation of Cairo, Illinois, and Secretary Welles quickly cut the orders that sent the sailor west to serve as nautical advisor to the soldiers. Although Rodgers fell under army orders and funding, he was allowed to make requisitions upon the Navy Department for ordnance—and to make all the recommendations the generals would hear. In addition to establishing at Cairo what would become the inland navy's administrative seat and one of its most important bases, Rodgers, with the help of two subordinates and naval constructor Samuel M. Pook (1804–1878), purchased and oversaw the conversion at Cincinnati of three river steamers: *Lexington*, *Conestoga*, and *A.O. Tyler* (shortened to *Tyler*). The *Tyler*, it will be recalled, was fired upon off Vicksburg in early January. Laboring in the face of a

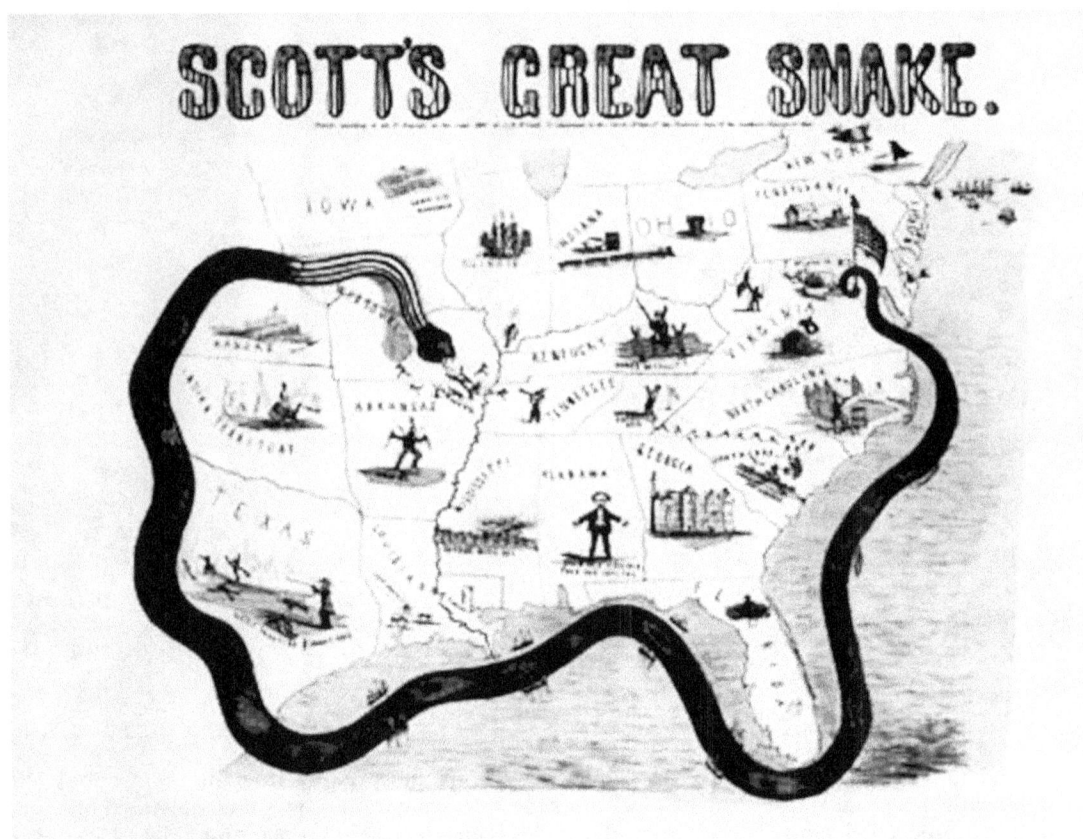

Anaconda. Another idea for overall Union strategy to quash the new Confederacy came from Union army chief Gen. Winfield Scott (1786–1866). Envisioning riverine elements similar to those offered by James B. Eads, it came to be known as the Anaconda Plan. Although it had its critics, this scheme was, with modifications, successfully followed to victory (Library of Congress).

civilian-military logistical nightmare, the navymen were able to get these three steamers outfitted, armed, crewed, and, following a low-water delay, down to Cairo by August 12. With the "timberclads" (so called because of their wooden armor) in hand, the U.S. Army could begin implementing the Scott-Eads plan and the naval war on inland waters could proceed.[3]

When Brig. Gen. Joseph Totten, chief engineer of the U.S. Army, completed his spring fact-finding survey regarding transportation assets on the Western waters, he returned to Washington on June 1. The purpose of his mission had been to determine, among other things, which additional types of purpose-built gunboats beyond the timberclads might assist in implementation of the Anaconda Plan. To that end, he sought the insights of John Lenthal (1807–1882), the chief of the navy's Bureau of Construction, Equipment and Repair. Lenthal provided a set of gunboat plans that were eventually forwarded to Cmdr. Rodgers and Naval Constructor Pook for modification.

In the meantime, on July 4, President Lincoln called Congress into extraordinary session to approve war measures. By this time, Senator Lyman Trumbull was the ranking member of the Senate Judiciary Committee and he, like many of his colleagues, continued, as they had since March, to seek and dispense patronage appointments. On Independence Day he thus arranged for George T. Brown to be elected U.S. Senate sergeant-at-arms and doorkeeper the following morning, the first Republican to hold that post. As such, he served, with a decent budget, as the legislative body's protocol and chief law enforcement officer and was the principal administrative manager for most of its support services. He was not universally beloved, but as we shall see this appointment would prove crucial to our story.[4]

The U.S. Congress, on July 17, appropriated a million dollars to the War Department for "gunboats on the western rivers." Responsibility for their construction fell upon the quartermaster general, who was also to account for all project expenditures. Within a few days, with the Pook modifications of the Lenthal hull and superstructure plans in hand, QM Brig. Gen. Montgomery C. Meigs (1816–1892) placed the first in a series of construction ads. The one that appeared in the *Chicago Daily Tribune* on July 23 appears below:

Cmdr. John Rodgers and the Inland Navy. Working under U.S. Army orders, U.S. Navy commander John Rodgers (1812–1882) established an inland flotilla during the spring and summer of 1861 that employed converted riverboats known as timberclads. One of these was the former *A.O. Tyler* (shortened to *Tyler* in service), which was shot at by Vicksburg militia back in January (Library of Congress).

GUN-BOATS

The Quarter Master General of the United States Army is actively engaged in preliminaries for constructing gunboats for the Western waters. Plans and specifications for their hulls are at his office and also at the quartermasters' offices at Pittsburg, Cincinnati, St. Louis, and Alton. These boats are to be delivered at Cairo. The bids should be sent to the Quarter Master General's office by the 1st of August.

Another notice appeared in the *St. Louis Daily Missouri Democrat* on July 29:

Gunboats for the Western Rivers
Quartermaster General's Office
Washington, July 18, 1861

Proposals are invited for Constructing Gunboats Upon the Western Rivers. Specifications will be immediately prepared and may be examined at the Quartermaster's office at Cincinnati, Pittsburg, and this office. Proposals from boatbuilders alone will be considered. Plans submitted by builders will be taken into consideration.
M.C. Meigs
QMG U.S.

Once the final plans for gunboat engines were adopted, QM Gen. Meigs signed off on the entire project and specification revisions were made available. The *Daily Missouri Democrat*, on August 1, was paid (as were other river city newspapers) to adjust its advertisement:

> Western Gunboats
> Proposals for Building Western Gunboats will be received by General Meigs, QM General, Washington City, D.C., until August Fifth when the bids will be opened by him and contracts awarded.
> Drawings for inspection and specifications for distribution at the office of The Collector of Customs, St. Louis.
> The bids to be endorsed, "Proposals for Western Gunboats."

As the adjusted ads passed to the western newspapers, three noted residents of St. Louis, including Postmaster General Montgomery Blair's (1813–1883) brother, Francis P. Blair, Jr. (1821–1875), wrote the quartermaster general that they had learned from a high government source that the War Department was planning to actually build river gunboats. This eminent lobby reminded Meigs of Missouri's many facilities for steamboat building and suggested that the best locations for gunboat construction were the towns of Cape Girardeau and St. Louis. The latter, besides being a center of machine manufacture, had dry docks and a great number of able workers. In a letter sent along a few days before the bids were due to be inspected, the postmaster general also wrote Meigs to support any claims that might be submitted by St. Louis builders.

Even though he had never seen a real gunboat before (although he might have read of their use in the Crimean War), James Eads was convinced that, because of his knowledge of river steamers, he could build one. After formulating his proposal for what he no doubt considered bargain-basement craft, he posted it to Meigs in Washington on August 1. So confident was he of his abilities Eads even included unique phrasing that would permit the government to penalize him X-amount of dollars for every day he was late. On Tuesday, August 5, seven gunboat bids were opened in the office of the quartermaster general. When all the letter openers were down, it was discovered that Missourian Eads had, indeed, sent in the lowest proposal. Blair's friend stated that he could build from four to sixteen ironclads at $89,000 each and deliver them to Cairo, IL, on or before October 5, 1861.

Eads, who had come to the capital city, was notified of his success on August 7. He had never built a boat, ship, or any other kind of nautical craft, but he was extremely confident when he exited the contract signing that he could construct the vessels designed to provide the heavy punch necessary to achieve the riverine goals of the Anaconda plan.

Six other Ohio River boatbuilders had also submitted bids, ranging from a high of $110,000 per unit quoted by Madison, IN, constructor Capt. A.F. Temple, down to the $75,000 from New Albany's William Jones Company. Temple, superintendent of the Madison Marine Railway Company, was so upset he lost the bid that he wrote to his U.S. Senator, Henry S. Lane (1811–1881), complaining that Eads was not a legitimate builder but merely a wartime speculator. His appeal fell on deaf ears, largely because none of the other bidders had offered to build so many boats at so low a figure and none volunteered a penalty clause.

Before he could start, Eads was faced with the task of finding four men who would post a bond of $30,000 to insure that he would faithfully perform his part of the contract. With a copy of the agreement in his pocket, the engineer set to work locating his backers (one of whom was his partner, William S. Nelson) and then building his gunboats from nothing but a rough set of plans in only 64 days. As one student has summed it up, " The program had all the characteristics of a problem contract; subject to political pressures, time constraints, interservice rivalry arising from a navy design procured by the army and administered by local naval superintendents of shipbuilding, and not least the difficulties of the new technology of ironclads.⁵

Almost identical when completed, seven were built around a casemate pierced for 13 guns and constructed with many subcontracted components at yards in Mound City, Illinois, and Carondelet, Missouri (the St. Louis suburb). The latter, known as the Carondelet Marine Railway and Drydock Company, had previously been operated by Primus Emerson, who with several partners purchased Carondelet riverfront property and incorporated this yard in 1855, growing it over the next four years to a point where it was a $150,000-per-year operation, based on Emerson's patented marine railway. In 1859 and 1860 it also employed Capt. Joseph Brown as its St. Louis sales associate.

Ironclads Sought. With plans and specifications in hand, the U.S. Quartermaster General, Brig. Gen. Montgomery C. Meigs (1816–1892), bid out the construction of the first U.S. armored warships. James B. Eads won the contract with the lowest bid, offering to build from four to sixteen ironclads at $89,000 each and deliver them to the river navy's forward base at Cairo, IL, on or before October 5, 1861 (National Archives).

When war came and the steamboat business initially dried up, Emerson, who had Southern political leanings, accepted a steamboat repair contract at Memphis. Ironically, through his association with John T. Shirley (1823–1873) of that city he became the prime builder of the Confederate armor-clad *Arkansas*, which would later deal harshly with Eads' boat *Carondelet*. While Emerson remained decamped in the South, the Carondelet company passed into the hands of company president Roger McAlister, a longtime Eads acquaintance who gladly leased the operation to the Hoosier-born entrepreneur. Eads enhanced the size and scope of McAlister's yards, which he renamed the Union Iron Works, and appointed William S. Nelson as his project's chief draughtsman and construction superintendent.

Having occasionally employed its services for his own earlier activities, Eads was doubtless familiar with the boatyard nicknamed "Emerson's Ways" that was established during the 1850s and was now the largest in the West, rivaled only by facilities in Madison, IN. What drew the attention of Eads and Nelson to this particular facility, of course, was the special railway system in its title that Emerson had invented: "the largest and most complete to be found in the West, 'in fact in the United States.'" Coming onto the company grounds, the visitor immediately saw tracks laid out into the river. Over them, a powerful 50-horsepower steam engine could haul a steamboat out of the water by car or cradle in about 30 minutes. Once out of the stream, it was sent directly into a shiphouse (a very large shed) for repair or, conversely, a new or repaired one could be taken to the water and launched.

By 1861, Emerson's treeless boatyard, in addition to the shiphouses, included a dozen ways, a variety of hoists and cranes, and the marine railway. By now, other boatyards on the Ohio—at New Albany, Mound City, and Cincinnati—were also modeled after Emerson's concept, but none were as close to St. Louis. So it was that Eads chose to lease this facility for the construction of his gunboats and over the next few years, as he accepted other government work, to improve it.[6]

Eads, as prime contractor, not only had to find facilities in which to assemble his hulls and casemates, but he had also to subcontract for all of the major components, from wood and spikes to engines and armor. For example, iron plate was ordered that was being rolled by Gaylord, Son & Company's mills at Newport, KY, and Portsmouth, OH. The gunboat engines would be assembled by Hartupee and Company of Pittsburg. This acquisition process was common in 1860s shipbuilding, whether for river craft or ocean steamers.

Holdups in construction, usually because of financing, caused the craft to be delayed well beyond their initial delivery dates. Upon delivery, they were named for prominent river cities: *Carondelet, St. Louis, Louisville, Cairo, Cincinnati, Mound City,* and *Pittsburg.* In addition to these purpose-built ironclads, two larger conversions were made using existing steamers. Thus the snagboat *Submarine No. 7* was reborn as the *Benton* and the ferryboat *New Era* became the *Essex.* Various tugs, auxiliary steamers, and a number of barges converted into heavy mortar platforms were also ordered or purchased. As the construction of the vessels for the War Department's Western Flotilla progressed toward completion in January 1862, non-matériel problems were also addressed, including the succession of Cmdr. Rodgers by Capt. Andrew Hull Foote (1806–1863).[7]

Between September 1861 and January 1862 Capt. (later Flag Officer) Foote literally struggled with the U.S. Army, as well as the builders and contractors, to complete his flotilla. The seven City Series ironclads were finally accepted by the government on January 15, 1862.[8]

The Scott-Eads plan for the Union's reduction of Confederate positions in the West and an associated great move south along the Mississippi River was not a secret. Indeed, when Tennessee became the last southern state to secede, on June 8, 1861, the outline of the Yankee scheme was widely accepted as strategy on both sides of the Mason-Dixon Line and a guide to the way the Western conflict would be fought. Union supporters and a number of Yankee generals soon believed that a strike into the heart of

Building the Federal "City Series" class ironclads. The Union ironclad building program at Carondelet, MO, site of a shipyard previously operated by Primus Emerson, the constructor of the *Arkansas*, became a model of supply and efficiency. The yard's activities would be similar to those of others along the great western rivers engaged in the construction of river gunboats. Notice the vessels on their stocks and the timber scattered about.

the western Confederacy via the Tennessee and Cumberland rivers would pay huge dividends. As famed Civil War authority Allan Nevins would write in 1960, "A mere glance at the map would seem to reveal that the Tennessee-Cumberland river system offered the North a heaven-sent opportunity to thrust a harpoon into the very bowels of the Confederacy."

Maj. Gen. Henry Halleck (1815–1872), "Old Brains" as he was known, reviewed the strategic situation in the West in the weeks following his November 1861 posting to Cairo, IL, as one of two senior Union military commanders in the West. U.S. Army organization in the region was, by presidential order, just then being reconfigured into what would prove to be two rival departments. One was Halleck's Department of the Missouri, which covered several states west of the Cumberland River. The other, under Maj. Gen. Don Carlos Buell (1818–1898), was the Department of the Ohio, which came with specific access to the Ohio and Cumberland rivers. It did not take Halleck, for

Later, after launch, the incomplete craft completed outfitting at Cairo, IL.

one, long to determine that thrusting Nevins's harpoon into the area of Middle Tennessee between the rivers could be "the turning point of the war." Still, due largely to the fact that the Eads' ironclads were not yet finished, neither he nor Buell authorized any move against the two Tennessee fortifications.[9]

At the end of January 1862 Maj. Gen. Halleck received intelligence that the defenders of the Tennessee river forts might be reinforced by fresh troops from Virginia. On January 29 he authorized Maj. Gen. Ulysses S. Grant (1822–1885) to take Fort Henry on the Tennessee River. Heavy rains slowed the arrival of the bluecoats, but the navy had no problem with the rising water in the stream. When the federal gunboat and transport fleet arrived at Bailey's Ferry near Fort Henry, they were spied by Rebel lookouts. The defenders witnessed a most

Flag Officer (later RAdm.) Andrew Hull Foote (1806–1863) succeeded Cmdr. John Rodgers in command of the Western Flotilla in September 1861. Foote guided the construction of the Pook turtles and made recommendations for the ironclads that followed, including three built by ex-Alton mayor Joseph Brown. He led the Western Gunboat Flotilla during the February 1862 Battles of Forts Henry and Donelson and in the campaigns against Island No. 10, Fort Pillow, and Memphis, but he was forced to depart when wounds received at Donelson made it impossible for him to continue (Library of Congress).

Maj. Gen. Henry Halleck (1815–1872) was Western Theater commander until July 1862. "Old Brains" was responsible for the direction of military demonstrations in the months leading up to the Battles of Fort Henry and Fort Donelson. In later years, Halleck served in Washington, D.C., as army chief of staff—working for Lieut. Gen. Grant (Johnson and Buel, *Battles and Leaders of the Civil War*).

Ulysses S. Grant (1822–1885) was deeply involved in the Western theater from the fall of 1861 through the fall of 1863 before departing east to command all Federal forces. The general from Ohio worked particularly well with his U.S. Navy colleagues, whose vessels unceasingly fought to support his campaigns, from Fort Henry, TN, through the capture of Vicksburg, MS (Library of Congress).

novel sight. "Steamboats," wrote Cumberland River historian Douglas, "had been used for many various purposes, but never before in an amphibious military operation to transport an entire army."

On February 6, following a spirited hour-and-a-half morning exchange between Rebel gunners and those aboard the *Essex*, *Cincinnati*, *Carondelet*, and *St. Louis*, Fort Henry, nearly awash due to its low-lying position, was surrendered to Flag Officer Foote. Yankee soldiers did not arrive on the scene until the afternoon, by which time the soggy citadel's main Confederate garrison had escaped to Fort Donelson, on the left bank of the Cumberland River 12 miles southeast of Fort Henry north of the little town of Dover.

Fort Donelson's guns were not at water level; indeed, its formal cannon were mounted on a bluff some one hundred feet high overlooking a straight stretch in the river below. It would later be praised as "the strongest military work in the entire theater of war." On February 14–15, the ironclads *Carondelet*, *St. Louis*, *Louisville*, and *Pittsburg*, supported to the rear by two timberclads, steamed to within 600 yards of the Rebel batteries and engaged them in furious close-range exchanges of fire. This time the gunboats did not prevail, as plunging fire took a terrible toll on the ships and their sailors,

Fort Henry. The February 6, 1862, bombardment of the Federal gunboats was particularly difficult for the Confederates to defend because the Tennessee River was at full flood stage and the bastion's guns were not elevated sufficiently to achieve any kind of plunging fire into the lightly armored top decks of the Yankee ironclads. After a spirited fight of an hour and a half, the fort was surrendered to Flag Officer Foote (*Harper's Weekly*, March 1, 1862).

Fort Donelson's guns were not at water level; indeed, its formal cannon were mounted on a bluff some one hundred feet high overlooking a straight stretch in the river below. In action against them on February 14, the Union gunboats did not prevail as plunging fire took a terrible toll on the ships and their sailors. Still, the navymen contributed materially to the victory achieved when the bastion surrendered to Grant on February 16 (*Harper's Weekly*, March 15, 1862).

including a wound to the fleet commander that would eventually lead to his death. "Actually, the Western Flotilla at Fort Donelson was," as historian Douglas later noted, "thoroughly whipped by the land batteries." Still, the navymen contributed materially to the victory achieved when the bastion surrendered to Grant on February 16.[10]

The Confederate defense line in the West was shattered by the twin Union triumphs

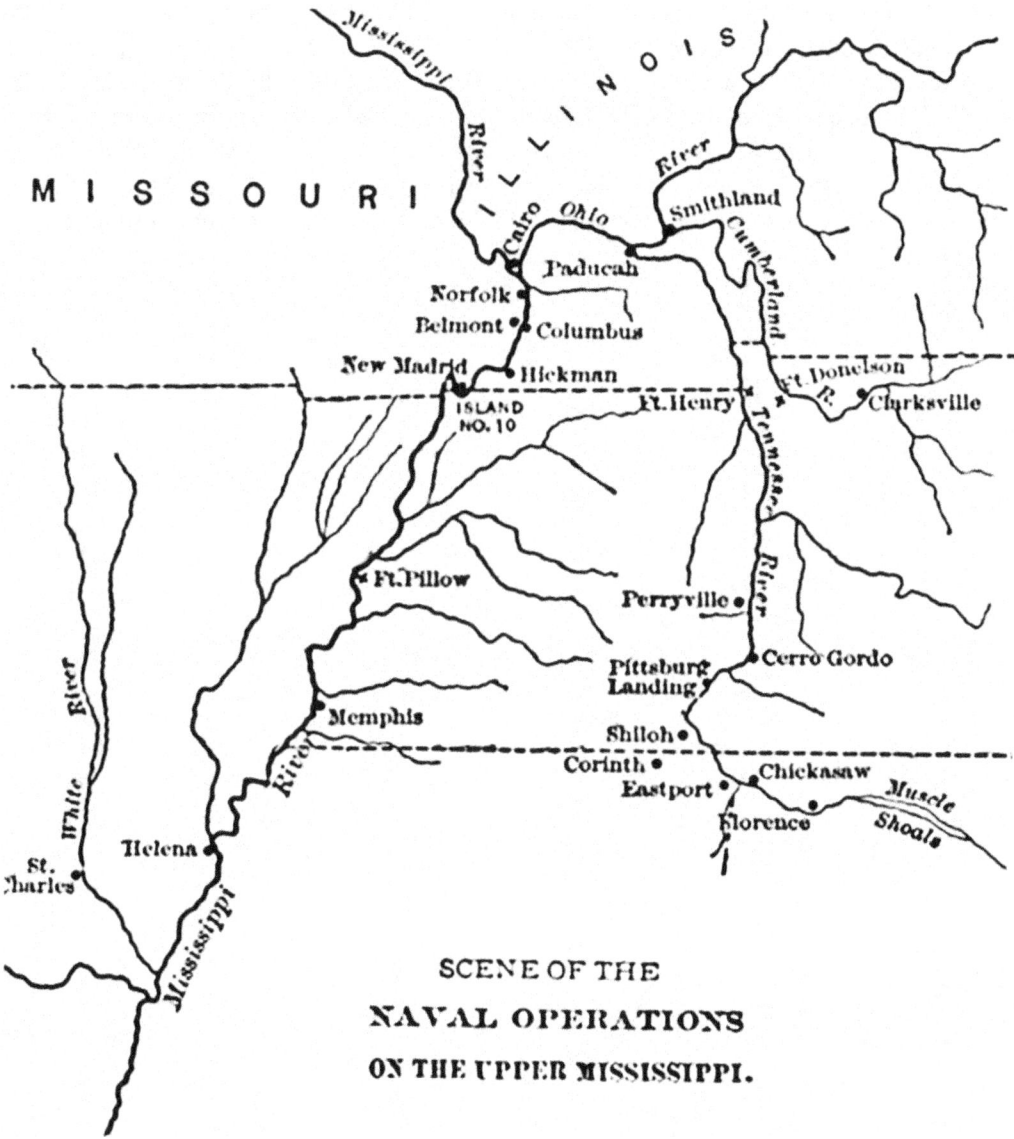

Map of the Upper Mississippi. Shown are the most prominent towns and cities visited by the U.S. Western Flotilla during the first six to eight months of the Civil War (Maclay, *A History of the Navy*).

on Tennessee's waterways, two of "the most significant battles of the Civil War." Confederate commander Gen. Albert S. Johnston (1803–1862) was forced to advance the timetable for his evacuation; troops departed Bowling Green, Kentucky, on February 17 and over the next week soldiers marched out of Nashville, while stores and equipment were sent to Chattanooga. The Union occupied Clarksville on February 19 and Tennessee's capital on February 24–25. "The loss of Nashville had a paralytic effect upon the Confederacy, politically, psychologically, and from a military standpoint."

In addition to Nashville's loss, Columbus was about to be abandoned and control of the Mississippi River was yielded as far south as Island No. 10. Gen. Pierre G.T. Beauregard (1818–1893), of Fort Sumter fame, who was then in the West, summed up the Confederate position in a March 3 memorandum cited in the official record. The main Southern forces, he reported, now occupied a line from Island No. 10 down across West Tennessee to Corinth, Mississippi, and in between those extremes lay a number of small defensive outposts: Fort Pillow, Union City, Paris, and Jackson. Washington's control, however tenuous, had been largely established over Kentucky and a portion of Middle Tennessee.[11]

3

Building Capt. Brown's Ironclads

Earlier, in mid–February 1862, in the wake of several successful naval events, including the work of the Western Flotilla on the Cumberland and Tennessee rivers, Congress appropriated an additional $15 million for the construction of ironclad gunboats. Charles Baldwin Sedgwick (1815–1883) of New York, chairman of the House Naval Affairs Committee, in moving the funds, noted that the gunboats already built had proved "a perfect success." Charles A. Wickliffe (1788–1869) of Kentucky added that "more such boats would be needed before the war was over." On February 21, the *New York Tribune* reported that, in light of the funding, the Navy Department would issue, the next day, proposals for the building of a number of steam men-of-war and that the "construction of gunboats will be urgently pushed." On March 25, Secretary Welles would inform the Senate Naval Affairs Committee that his department "proposes to construct a few vessels of light draught, great speed, and heavy armament for the Western waters."

The actions of the gunboats under Flag Officer Foote, the dramatic impact of the Confederate ironclad *Virginia* (the subject of much speculation before she fought the USS *Monitor* on March 8), and growing concern over British/French intentions toward the Union—as well as spy reports on possibly more Southern armor clads being built—had a definite impact upon the Federal Navy Department. Secretary Welles, together with his assistant secretary Gustavus Fox (1821–1883) and various officers, realized a pressing need for more Federal ironclads. This view was shared by the War Department's Secretary Edwin Stanton (1814–1869), whose organization oversaw the gunboats on Western waters. He now authorized Quartermaster General Montgomery C. Meigs to accept proposals for new vessels.

The U.S. Navy had formed an Ironclad Board in 1861, which, to its credit, recommended construction of the *Monitor*. The board's term having ended, Welles now appointed a new board to consider the many proposals certain to come in for new vessels from all quarters. He also promised Stanton that its members would first review and make recommendations concerning Western requirements before moving on to ocean and harbor craft. Turning to his available experts in naval architecture and engineering, the secretary appointed Com. Joseph Smith (1826–1862), chief of the U.S. Navy Bureau of Yards and Docks, a leading ironclad critic and carry-over from the earlier panel, as group chairman of a new board of construction, with John Lenthall, naval engineer Benjamin Isherwood (1822–1915), assistant naval constructor Edward Hartt (1825–1883), and former naval engineer Daniel Martin as the other members. The

Gideon Welles. Realizing a pressing need for more ironclad vessels in light of the duel between the *Monitor* and *Merrimac* and the battles with the Tennessee River forts, the U.S. secretary of the navy announced in March 1862 that his department would "construct a few vessels of light draught, great speed, and heavy armament for the Western waters." This decision was shared by the War Department, which organization oversaw the Western gunboats. Quartermaster General Montgomery C. Meigs was authorized to accept proposals for new vessels (U.S. Army Military History Institute).

John Lenthall. The long-time chief of the USN Bureau of Construction and Repair was one of three members assigned by Welles to comprise the new Ironclad Board to discover and recommend the best design for armored vessels. Lenthall had participated in discussions concerning Western gunboats since before the time of the timberclads in 1861 and, with the new board functioning out of his office he would offer important observations on what was required in any new craft (Naval History and Heritage Command).

board's composition would be made known to the public in the newspapers on March 28.

On March 7, Assistant Navy Secretary Fox wrote to Flag Officer Foote advising his Western commander that, under the new law, the Navy Department intended to construct some of the authorized vessels in the Mississippi Valley. It was strongly suggested that, having had actual ironclad gunboat experience in battle, his opinions concerning what would be needed in the new boats would be very helpful if communicated "either directly to the Department or to some of those persons West who propose to meet the advertisements of the Department."

In Hampton Roads, VA, next day, the Confederate ironclad *Virginia* rammed and sank the U.S. frigate *Cumberland* and destroyed with hot shot the frigate *Congress*. On March 9, she was engaged in an inconclusive duel by the Federal ironclad *Monitor*. The actions on both days would have a lasting impact on naval history, including the design of vessels employed on Western waters.

While the navy awaited suggestions and an assessment of the Pook turtles from its Western flag officer and digested the sea fighting events of March 8–9, Secretary Stanton went ahead on March 12 and placed small advertisements in a number of regional newspapers, including a few in East Coast journals such as the *Boston Herald*, seeking plans for new river ironclads "of the same description as those now in use at Cairo and on the Cumberland." "Proposals may be sent by telegraph," the communication read, "and must specify the price and the time when they will be ready for use."

In order to provide as much assistance to the department as possible, Foote wired the Bureau of Ordnance directly on March 13 listing his concerns with the ironclads under his command. These, he was compelled to state, were defects that could not be changed, as the vessels were modeled and partly built before he took over the flotilla. First, the commander emphasized, was the inability of the boats to hold position when anchored in a swift current. This defect arose from the positioning of rods between the fantails forming their sterns, which caused the craft to yaw their unarmored sterns about and face the opposite direction. So positioned, the vessels, displaying unarmored sterns, and shipping but two aft-mounted 32-pounders, could not effectively fight downstream.. The defect, painfully obvious in the Mississippi River above Island No. 10, forced the ironclads to anchor to shore and offer bombardment from less than ideal locations.

A second major defect in the "turtles," as noted by Foote, was the center-wheel propulsion unit. Contractor Eads was familiar with this system common to many Western ferryboats. He used it to propel the catamaran snagboat *Submarine No. 7*, which was converted from his salvage operation into the fleet flagboat *Benton*. He also chose to purpose-install the system into the Pook ironclads chiefly because it could be at least

Stern of Eads-built Ironclad. Tied up to a riverbank, the famous City Series gunboat *Carondelet* clearly shows her unarmored stern and rear cannon. Despite this planning defect, the vessel went on to become the most famous of all the Civil War river warriors (Naval History and Heritage Command).

partially protected by their armored casemates. Driftwood, the bane of all steamboats, was particularly hard on center-wheels. These often huge logs and other flotsam could "take" (i.e., break) the wheels even if they were pushed by a powerful engine. Com. William D. Porter (1813–1864), when assessing "propelling apparatus" for a May 6 report, issued an objection to the center wheel known to most rivermen—"want of speed." On March 16, the U.S. Western Flotilla, from locations on the bank of the Mississippi River, opened the bombardment of Confederate positions on Island No. 10, which would be captured on April 7.

It is known that Foote was well acquainted with James B. Eads, the contractor who had provided most of his inland fleet. Indeed, days after the Island No. 10 bombardment began, Eads visited Foote on the flagship *Benton* after having come down from Cairo on the fleet mail tug. "We withdrew to his cabin," the entrepreneur later remembered, to consider plans he had drawn for new gunboats. After a 15–20 minute discussion of Eads' gunboat ideas, the two men "returned to the deck" to observe the fall of shot, Union and Confederate.

We today are not aware if Foote was as familiar with Joseph Brown or any of the other Midwest steamboat captains, foundry operators, or boatbuilders who would shortly submit proposals as he was with Eads. Foote met many civilians while in St. Louis during the fall of 1861, but it is not likely that he made many, if any, close acquaintances among them. It is even more doubtful that he would have communicated his gunboat concerns to any real or potential contractors (save perhaps Eads, who had already been required to remedy certain Pook turtle structural defects prior to their January acceptance). Beyond observations of the man as a self-starting entrepreneur demonstrated in our first chapter, we do not know for certain how or why Brown became interested in building gunboats. He, like Eads, was a War Democrat, quite patriotic and supportive of Union political and military aims. It is quite probable that he visited the Carondelet boatyard during or after the time Foote's gunboats were constructed. After all, he had represented the interests of that yard in St. Louis in 1859–1860.

Brown might have been present at the launching of one or more of the Pook turtles, beginning on October 12, 1861. Louis S. Gerteis reminds us "the launching of gunboats at Carondelet became occasions for popular celebration." He might also have discussed the craft with Eads there or at St. Louis, where he perhaps also was introduced to Flag Officer Foote. What is known is that by early 1862 Brown was at least mentally designing gunboats he believed would be superior to the Pook turtles. He had long made it his business to know sundry St. Louis business leaders, including those in transport, railroads, and iron and machinery. Among his acquaintances was Charles W. McCord (1842–1872), proprietor of McCord & Co. (dba Franklin Foundry), which was founded in 1853 when McCord left the engine-building works of Samuel Gaty. It is not unlikely that, in discussion, McCord opined that he could construct more efficient propulsion units than those that propelled Eads' ironclads and dreamed of perhaps building gunboats himself.

McCord actually caught Brown's gunboat-building fever and after joining the former Alton mayor in his ironclad building enterprise contracted in early 1863 to build one light draught monitor (*Etlah*) and subcontract the entire construction of another (*Shiloh*). Changes required by the navy delayed completion of both vessels beyond the

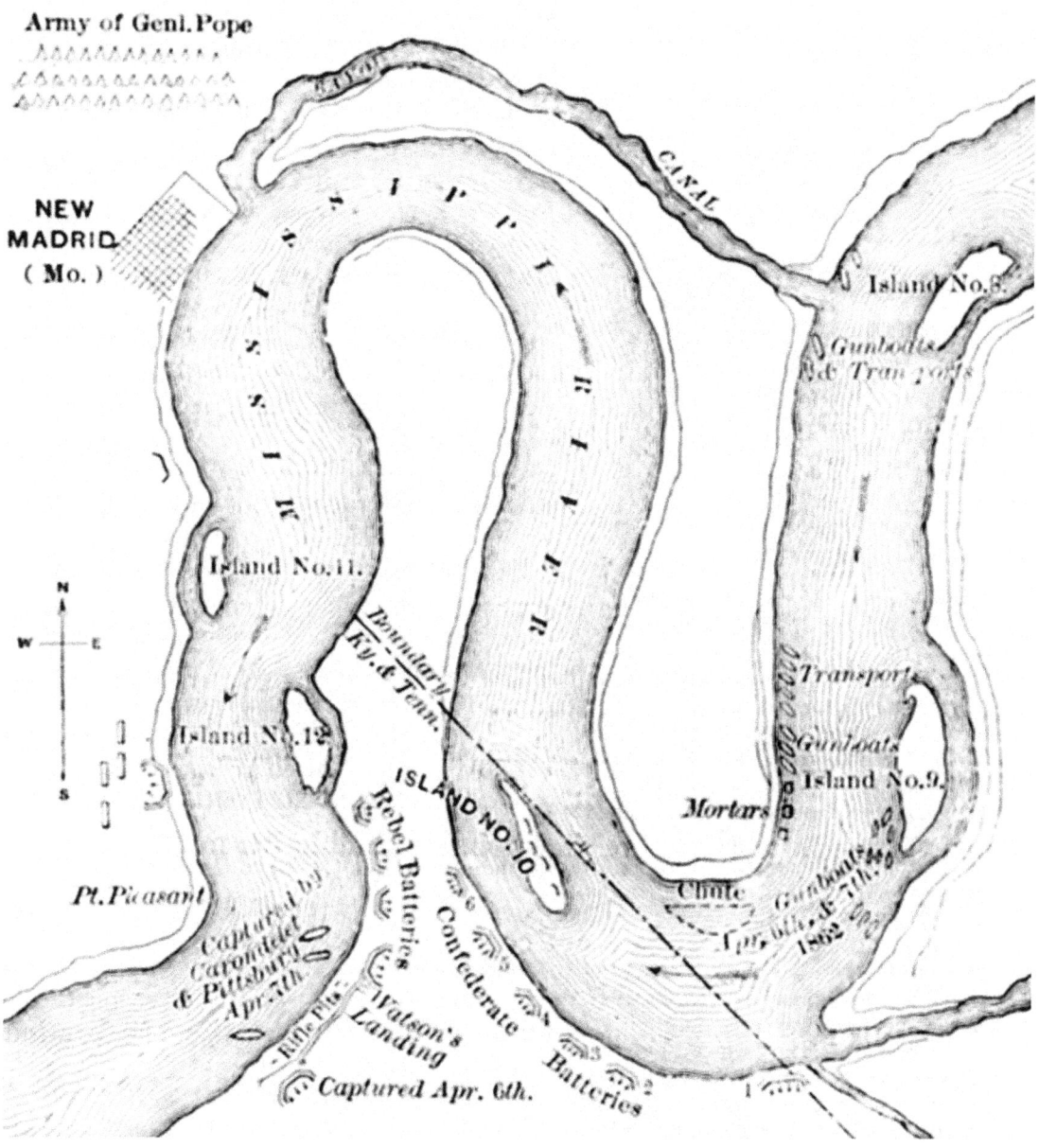

Island No. 10. The attack by the U.S. Western Gunboat Flotilla on the Mississippi River island citadel known as Island No. 10 began on April 16. The operation, successfully concluded on April 7, exposed a number of weaknesses in the City Series ironclads constructed by James B. Eads. As Flag Officer Foote informed the Ironclad Board, the boats were unable to hold position when anchored in the swift current. This defect arose from the positioning of rods between the fantails forming their sterns, which caused the craft to yaw their unarmored sterns about and face the opposite direction. So positioned, the vessels, displaying unarmored sterns and shipping but two aft-mounted 32-pounders, could not effectively fight downstream.. The defect, painfully obvious in the waters above Island No. 10, forced the ironclads to anchor to shore and offer bombardment from less than ideal locations (Hoppin, *Life of Foote*, 1874).

end of the war and neither ever saw service. The resulting cost overruns bankrupted McCord and fiscally damaged one of his most active creditors, James Harrison (1803–1867) of Chouteau, Harrison & Valle.

It is possible that Harrison, of Bremen, North St.Louis, then managing partner of the iron rolling mill and nailing manufacturer Chouteau, Harrison & Valle, might have joined Brown and McCord in any vessel discussions between the two, voicing his opinion of the iron requirements needed to make gunboats truly armor clad and remarking upon the fact that Eads' seven sisters were not completely protected all-around. Harrison undoubtedly agreed to join in any ironclad building project for which Brown could win a contract.

A native of Bourbon County, KY, James Harrison, prior to the 1857 depression, oversaw the largest St. Louis manufacturing concern and in August 1862 would answer a navy advertisement for the construction of iron river and harbor defense vessels, placing bids for two at $675,000 a copy. When his proposals were not chosen, he joined McCord's effort to build two light-draught monitors, providing their armor, but he then died suddenly on August 2, 1870.

Whether or not Joseph Brown learned of the government's proposals for fast, light-draught, heavily armed river gunboats from the newspapers or from other river acquaintenances or from Foote, many of his biographies indicate that he was definitely informed of them by his brother, Senate sergeant at arms George T. Brown, who, knowing of his interest and river expertise, invited him to Washington, D.C., to make a bid. Evidence that he knew, though it is not overly strong, can be taken from the fact that on March 12, 1862, documents were signed leasing the *City of Louisiana*, which Brown had

Joseph Brown. Beyond observations of the man as a self-starting entrepreneur, we do not know for certain how or why 39-year-old Capt. Joseph Brown, of whom no photograph exists, became interested in building gunboats. He, like James B. Eads, was a War Democrat, quite patriotic and supportive of Union political and military aims. Not a trained naval architect, Brown had worked with various Western boatmen in designing a number of steamboats, including the famous *Mayflower*, during the antebellum period. What he did have was a great deal of knowledge concerning the Western rivers, steamboat construction, and Midwestern business and political accommodation. The former Alton, IL, mayor also had an "in." His brother, Senate sergeant-at-arms George T. Brown, tipped him off to the military's decision to sponsor additional gunboat construction, leading him to design plans and travel to Washington in hopes of securing a contract (Emerson W. Gould, *50 Years on the Mississippi*, 1889).

continued to command and in which he held an interest following Fort Sumter, to the Western Sanitary Commission. The steamer was immediately outfitted as a hospital boat and dispatched, under a new captain, down the Mississippi from Cairo to join the Western Flotilla at Island No. 10.[1]

Stanton's earlier call for construction ideas was amplified on March 24 in a brief article which appeared in the *Daily Cleveland Herald.* The Ohio newspaper had learned that the secretary of the navy was issuing a call by telegraph for proposals for gunboat construction on the Western waters. These were, as noted by Stanton two weeks earlier, to be "built mainly on the model of those now in service on the Mississippi." It was further revealed that the Navy Department would be employing the recommendations, based on experience, of Com. Foote and his gunboat commanders. "One suggestion," already in hand was "that heavy guns should be mounted in the stern as well as the bow." In a similar vein, the *Cincinnati Daily Commercial* stressed the requirement that any new river warships be "ironed and made ball proof all over."

A number of Midwestern boatbuilders and interested persons had already answered the call for the Federal government and provided proposals and drawings. Among these was Brown, whose plans, including engine specifications from McCord, as now presented were less than detailed. Many other schemes of greater or lesser substance were from individuals who, unlike Brown, were not familiar with the peculiar requirements of Western river navigation. Also on March 24, the *New York Tribune* ran the following lament: "The propositions for building gunboats for the Western waters which have thus far been submitted to the War Department are all of them formed to require too great a draught of water to meet the contingencies of the service. The Secretary of War invites plans and estimates for gunboats of as shallow a draught as the mechanical ingenuity of the West can devise. Quartermaster General Meigs has special charge of the subject and may be corresponded with accordingly." The next day, the *New York Times* reported that fewer bids were put in for the Western gunboats by the proposal deadline than was expected and that contract awards would not be made for several days. It was, however, noted that the plan of the Eads' boats "is highly approved by scientific men."

Also on March 25, Secretary Stanton convened a morning meeting at the War Department to discuss a new worry, intelligence from St. Louis that the Confederates farther south were building armor-clad gunboats potentially powerful enough to "destroy Commodore Foote's flotilla and burn the steamboats in the Western waters." Present for the discussion on "the best mode of meeting the rebel boat" were a number of Western boatbuilders." It is quite probable that Capt. Brown, not yet sufficiently noteworthy on the national scene as to have his name in the newspapers or Official Records in conjunction with the war effort, was present.[2]

Joseph Brown was not a trained naval architect. He had worked with various Western boatmen in designing a number of steamboats during the antebellum period, including the famous *Mayflower.* As discussed in the introduction, what he did have was a great deal of knowledge concerning the Western rivers, steamboat construction, and Midwestern business and political accommodation. He also had an advantage.

At some point after arriving in Washington, D.C., Brown and his brother, George T., obtained an appointment and paid a visit to their old friend Abraham Lincoln in the White House. The old Illinois colleagues, perhaps following brief recollections of prairie politics and Alton friendships, got to the business which resulted in the following March 28 message from the Executive Mansion to Com. Smith and his naval board colleagues, whom the President addressed as "Commissioners to Examine Plans and Award Contracts for Building Western Gun-Boats":

Gentlemen: Capt. Joseph Brown is well known to me, as one of the most successful boatbuilders on the Western Waters having built some of the finest, as well as the fastest Boats on the Mississippi River & he is also a man of great energy.

The commission will do me a personal favor, as well as the country at large by giving the plans presented by him, that attention, which I have no doubt their merits entitle them to.

ABRAHAM LINCOLN

Lincoln's message was handed to Smith's working group when it assembled in Lenthall's office later in the day to begin its reviews of the proposals received.[3]

Capt. Brown's original gunboat proposal might have benefited from the advice given by Com. Foote at mid-month. The Alton native could have heard comments on ironclad performance in person from Foote, Eads, or Western Flotilla officers or have been made privy to the March 13 Foote telegram. His concepts might have been based upon actual examinations (up close or from the deck of the *City of Louisiana*) of the Pook turtles abuilding or in service, or perhaps he had conversations with those who helped in their construction or outfitting. The ideas offered may also have simply profited from the steamboatman's knowledge of Western river boat construction as well as of the Western gunboats that were seen in person or drawn in the press. Brown may also had some inspiration from reports on the ironclads *Monitor* and *Merrimac/Virginia*, which had recently dueled at Hampton Roads, VA.

Lincoln Recommends Brown. At some point after arriving in Washington, D.C., Capt. Joseph Brown and his brother, George T., obtained an appointment and paid a visit to their old friend Abraham Lincoln in the White House. The old Illinois colleagues, perhaps following brief recollections of prairie politics and Alton friendships, got to business, which resulted in a March 28, 1862, message from the Executive Mansion to the USN Ironclad Board vouching for the riverman as a qualified builder and concluding, "The commission will do me a personal favor, as well as the country at large by giving the plans presented by him, that attention, which I have no doubt their merits entitle them to." Brown signed contracts for a trio of casemate ironclads with the Bureau of Construction and Equipment on April 30 (Library of Congress).

What the Smith board received from Brown was a proposal for three ironclads, one that was 170 feet long by 70 feet wide and two that were 170' × 50'. In actuality, the sizes of the actual craft would range small, medium, and large. Each would have a wide, shallow, riverboat hull (sometimes referred to as a "scow"), with funnels and paddle-wheel boxes showing above deck. Additionally, a slant-sided armored casemate was to be built athwartship. It was designed to permit heavy cannon mounted on pivots inside to fire forward or from each side (the casemate "ends"). Western newspapers later reported that the trio were "of the *Monitor* order, that is, their armaments are carried in turrets, impregnably encased in iron." The definition of turret was clarified so that readers would understand it was not the rotating unit of the Ericsson vessel but a "shot-proof tower."

The powerplant for Brown's ironclads, as recommended by Charles McCord, would consist of two side paddle wheels and twin screws on the medium and large vessels and paddle wheels only on the smallest. Canney suggests that the motive arrangement, particularly the screws, was introduced "to provide additional steering power, above and beyond the rudders." A newspaper article (republished in the April 1, 1863, issue of the *San Francisco Daily Evening Bulletin*) regarding the medium-sized ironclad was specific: "In order, however, that the boat might be turned with rapidity and in a narrow stream, she was provided with a wheel on each quarter stern and two propellers between the wheels." Various and significant differences in the three vessels would prevent these light-draught ironclads from being referred to as a "class" of warships like, for example, the *Cairo*-class, another name for the Pook turtles.

As the naval review group examined Brown's suggestions and those from other builders, the Western Flotilla continued to slog away in the waters above Island No. 10. The delay in capturing the Confederate bastion brought considerable protest in certain quarters and in part of the Northern press. Because of their success at Forts Henry and Donelson, the gunboats were held in high esteem by the public, some of whom understood and overlooked the inability of the Pook turtles to fight downstream. Now, even though they were as good as they ever were, revealed the *Boston Daily Advertiser*, "every sort of abuse is lavished upon these boats" some now held up as "expensive failures." The boats were only partially armored, and newsmen advised that Eads' craft should never have been presented as "ironclads." The press not being privy to the deliberations of Smith's committee, it was announced that the "government now needs badly some really ironclad boats for the Mississippi service."

In order to quickly satisfy the needs of Secretary Stanton, Com. Smith's group initially reviewed plans for Western river gunboats before turning to plans for harbor and coast defense ironclads. Member John Lenthall, who had initially provided plans from which the Pook turtles were modified, voiced the opinion that henceforth only hulls of iron would be of value. In a May 11 letter to Flag Officer Samuel Francis Du Pont (1803–1865), commander of the South Atlantic Blockading Squadron, Lenthall noted his position that "wooden vessels covered with iron, when wanted, will be found to be rotten and unless for temporary immediate use ought not to be." Several of the new Western vessels were seen by the committee as being for that "immediate use" and so plans for them were approved.

The results and recommendations of the naval board were forwarded to navy secretary Welles on April 9 and, after passing them to the White House and U.S. Senate for comment, they were announced in the press on April 14, which was probably several days after the winning contractors were notified and allowed to start assembling their building combinations. As James M. Merrill later put it, "With the *Monitor-Virginia* contest still fresh in their minds and with little knowledge of Western rivers," the government signed contracts for the building of "untested vessels."

Eight craft would be built at river communities on the Western waters, including two paddle-wheel river monitors by James B. Eads at Carondelet, the monitor *Ozark* by Hambleton and Collier of Peoria, IL (to be built at Mound City, IL), the iron-hulled *Marietta* and *Sandusky* by Tomlinson and Hartupee at Pittsburg, and three wooden vessels by Joseph Brown (two at Cincinnati and one at New Albany, IN). Because the demands of river service subjected all else to the goddess of shallow draft, William H. Roberts has identified what all eight physically had in common": relatively light construction and broad, scowlike hulls." The aggregate cost for the package was to be $1,229,500.[4]

Joseph Brown signed contracts for his trio of casemate ironclads with the navy's Bureau of Construction and Equipment on April 30, 1862, simultaneously turning over to that body more detailed plans and specifications. These refined documents detailed the interior bulkhead and compartmentalization arrangements, power plants, and protection. The smaller of the three, *Chillicothe* (named for the capital of Ohio from 1803 to 1810) would be 158 feet long and powered only by paddle wheels. The two larger 170-footers, *Indianola* and *Tuscumbia*, would also employ propellers.

The aggregate cost of the three ironclads was to be $450,000, with another $70,000 to the Franklin Foundry for engines and machinery. Brown, like the other ironclad builders before and after him, was subjected to fiscal requirements that were nearly identical to those Eads had labored under with the Pook turtles. His fixed price contract promised him a series of progress payments as work was completed (though no incentive contracts for speedy construction), but also threatened financial penalties if the vessels were late in delivery or completed in a manner inconsistent with the contract, e.g., too great a depth of hold. Indeed, so rigid was the depth requirement that the government could reject the vessel if it was exceeded. Left vague was any mechanism for compensation for government required alterations or intervention that delayed construction. "Organizing a network of subcontractors and suppliers was," William Roberts reminds us, "a key element in the shipbuilders' preparations." Construction of the original Pook turtles had required the coordination, often in a mad and scrambled fashion, of the raw materials, manpower, machinery and armor plate needed for the boats built by Eads in the Carondelet yards. Suppliers who delivered the goods and equipment and members of the skilled workforce gathered to install or assemble had to be individually recruited.

Louis Hunter tells us that just as Eads, Brown, and the others were commencing their gunboat projects, "boom times" returned to the river. Federal victories on the Cumberland, the Tennessee, and especially the Mississippi, accompanied by a general business revival fueled by war demands, brought new requirements. Shipyards which were idle began "to operate at full capacity in the effort to supply the soaring demand for tonnage and to repair and refit old boats." Prime contractor James B. Eads now faced the component ordeal again, one which would be intensified when he agreed to produce the four additional monitors. "June found Eads in St. Louis," said Lawrence M. Pockras in his October 1959 talk before the Cincinnati Civil War Roundtable, "begging Eastern mills for armor plate and engine parts, trying to build his shallow draft monitors. He wrote everywhere for men, skilled or unskilled."

Eads was not, however, alone in his setup and recruiting difficulties. Securing components and laborers to see their naval projects finished was a challenge for all Civil War ironclad builders, north and south. For example, though the process of obtaining workers, armor, and machinery to assemble the CSS *Arkansas* at Memphis was certainly more frustrating, Primus Emerson, Capt. Brown's old friend, went about acquisition in much the same manner as Eads or John Ericsson (1803–1889), builder of the USS *Monitor*. Capt. Brown, who knew the intricacies of civilian boatbuilding first-hand, had begun in mid–April to assemble his own military supply and subcontracting teams, beginning with Charles McCord, who would build the propulsion units.[5]

The most pressing need Brown faced was location of modern shipbuilding facilities that were both suitable and available. Yards with marine railways and not already pledged to other contractors were required. Eads continued to undertake his projects at Carondelet. William Hambleton (1825–1883), his brother Samuel T., and their partner Collier, who had constructed several of the Pook turtles at Mound City, had charge of the yards at that Illinois facility. East from the St. Louis and Mound City areas along the Ohio River were numerous other boatbuilding centers, including those in and around New Albany and Jeffersonville, IN (which handled most of the boatbuilding contracts out of Louisville, KY), Cincinnati, OH, and Pittsburg, PA. All had access to needed raw materials and also featured supply, foundry, and component centers that could create, fashion and build necessary fixtures.

In the late 1940s, Hunter described the steamboat-building system of the 1860s. While meant to describe the birth of commercial boats, the process also applied, at least partially, to the construction of the gunboats of Eads and Brown and others: "The building of the hull and the framework of the superstructure remained in the hands of the boat yards, with their complements of shipwrights; other firms directed the carpenters, joiners, and decorators in building the cabin and giving the boat its over-all finish. Furniture, utensils,and equipment of various kinds came generally to be supplied and installed by firms specializing in these articles." The scholar went on to note a key business arrangement Brown would employ in his relationship with whichever boatyard(s) he employed. "Sometimes," the historian noted, "owners made a single contract with a builder, who assumed responsibility for the entire vessel, but again, contracts were made with each of the various firms contributing to the completed vessel." In addition to considerations involved in his choice of a builder or builders, the experienced ex-Alton mayor knew that geography and river stage made several of the smaller Ohio River yards less than desirable.

A point 369 miles from the mouth of the Ohio and 150 miles west of Cincinnati was the only major natural navigational barrier on the river that concerns us, the Falls of the Ohio. These falls, located at Louisville, are a series of rapids where the river flows over hard, fossil-rich limestone beds. The first Ohio River locks were built here before the Civil War to circumnavigate them; the Louisville and Portland Canal was 2.5 miles long and 50 feet wide, and its lock could pass a boat through that had dimensions up to 180 feet long and 49.7 feet wide. In 1860 a total of 1,520 steamboats and 1,299 other craft transited the canal. This limitation led to the steamboat construction custom, summarized Victor Bogle in 1953, of building "the larger boats for the lower river trade at points below the Falls." New Albany thus became "the most important boatbuilding center below the Falls."

In addition to the Falls of the Ohio, the changing depth of the river itself offered problems, as Cmdr. John Rodgers had learned the previous year when he sought to get his converted timberclads downstream from Cincinnati to Cairo, IL. Generally, the hotter summer months saw a drop in the river stages, particularly in the upper half of the Mississippi Valley; water levels could fall so far as to greatly restrict navigation or prohibit it entirely. Skilled rivermen aboard both naval and civilian steamers could tell a river's stage, rising or falling, by using a lead or even watching driftwood. When Brig Gen. Joseph Totten stopped at Madison, IN, during his spring of 1861 Midwestern river inspection tour, he was given specific information regarding drafts of water in the Ohio: "Four feet draft with some certainty after middle of October; five feet draft 1st of November; six feet draft with great certainty after 15th of November. This, in ordinary seasons, a very dry summer and dry early autumn, will give less water in October, but the middle of November will very surely give from five to six feet draft."

Capt. Brown, however, had more concerns than just the physical when considering boatbuilding site possibilities on the upper Ohio. Politics and previous experience with large or unusual steamer construction would also play roles in the decision he made regarding his subcontractors. William Roberts reminds us that during the Civil War "there was a political need to spread the wealth of government contracting." Many Washington officials worried about issues of loyalty in the supposedly Southern-oriented regions along the northern bank of the Ohio. Increased manufacturing and government contracts should, it was thought, boost the prosperity of that sector and "yield increased loyalty."

Pittsburg was the first upper Ohio city considered. Brown knew the Pittsburg area well from his steamboating activities, particularly his 1854 tour of boatbuilding centers on the Ohio and Monongahela rivers he made prior to the construction of the *Mayflower*. He also knew how Cmdr. John Rodgers had, in the spring of 1861, overseen the purchase by army advisor and Three-Rivers steamboat captain William J. Kountz

Cincinnati. Capt. Joseph Brown, who knew the intricacies of civilian boatbuilding first-hand, began in mid-April to assemble his military supply and subcontracting teams. The most pressing need he faced was location of modern shipbuilding facilities that were both suitable and available. Yards with marine railways and not already pledged to other contractors were required. After a thorough search that took into consideration the challenges of Ohio River steamboat construction, facilities were chosen at Fulton, a suburb of Cincinnati, OH, and New Albany, IN (*Harper's Weekly*, September 27, 1862).

(1817–1904) of three Pennsylvania-built steamers for conversion into gunboats for a military flotilla. "Pittsburgh," Theodore Parker proudly hailed almost a century later, "was the first place where this force began to function."

Rodgers was initially undecided about a location to have the steamers modified into warcraft. It was initially thought that one of the yards near Pittsburg would be chosen. Then the naval officer learned that the low waters of the Ohio during the summer would prevent the vessels, if they were finished there, from steaming out to the Cairo, IL, war zone. Thus he decided to have them remodeled at Fulton, Ohio, then a suburb and now part of Cincinnati.

A year later, when Brown sought a building site, the steamboat captain was forced to consider the same water stage challenge as well as the fact that, due to new construction activity, many of the area's most desirable boatbuilding locations, including those at Brownsville and Elizabeth, were pledged to other entrepreneurs or already under contract. Indeed, by October more steamers would have been constructed at the Western Pennsylvania yards in this 1862 spring-fall building period than in any year during the previous decade.[6]

With Pittsburg never really in contention for his project, Capt. Brown turned his attention to Fulton and New Albany. Both were noted boatbuilding and repair centers, though the actual construction business in the former location was in decline by 1859, according to Charles Cist, being concentrated instead on remodeling and repair work. Interestingly, Fulton, which covered a two-mile stretch of the north bank of the Ohio River in line with low hills that ran parallel, was annexed by Cincinnati in 1854 but continued to be known as Fulton. It has been claimed that between 1816 and 1880 some 900 steamboats were built there on the strip of land adjacent to the river between Kemper Lane and Torrence Road. Both Fulton and New Albany experienced the same wartime shipbuilding boom as Pittsburg, becoming quite busy with new construction early in 1862. One of the city's three largest yards, Cincinnati Marine Railway, already had some military experience, having been paid to convert one of the steamers acquired at Pittsburg a year earlier by Cmdr. Rodgers and Capt. Kountz.

A local son, Capt. Daniel H. Morton, was a prominent Cincinnati steamboat operator who also built and converted vessels at his boatyard, Dan Morton & Co. He was a partner in the Cincinnati Marine Ways, which he had opened with John Johnson in 1849. One of the three vessels purchased by Rodgers and Kountz was his, the *Conestoga*. Morton remained the vessel's temporary captain and was given a $41,000 U.S. Quartermaster contract to convert *Conestoga* and one of the others, *Lexington*, into wooden timberclad gunboats. A third, *A.O. Tyler*, was also taken in hand and finished as a timberclad at the Marine Ways, a huge site which occupied a six-block area a short distance down the riverbank from Morton's yard. Much of the work performed at both locations was overseen by Naval Constructor Samuel M. Pook; however, completion was delayed and, then, because of low water, the vessels did not actually arrive at the Union military's Cairo, IL, advance base until August.

Brown also considered the shipyards of New Albany, IN, which offered the possibility of constructing gunboats that could steam to Cairo without having to first navigate through or around the Falls of the Ohio. Of these, the most appealing was that of Peter Tellon & Son, which occupied a section of the riverfront extending from West Fourth

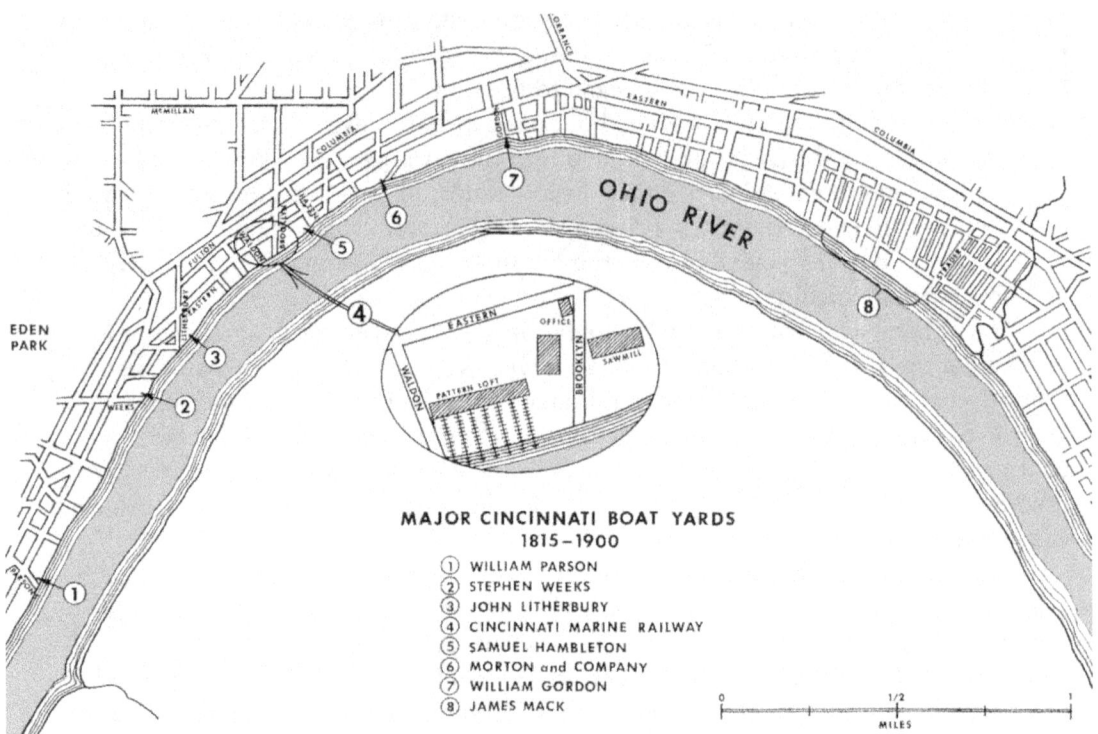

Cincinnati boatyards. With Pittsburg out of contention for his project, Capt. Joseph Brown turned his attention to Fulton, OH, where a number of boatyards were engaged in the construction and repair of commercial steamboats. Several of these would be chosen by other operators as sites to build other of the new Union ironclads that the Navy Department was letting contracts for in the spring and summer of 1862. The *Chillicothe* and *Indianola* were built here, then taken to New Albany for completion and hence delivery to the military (Map courtesy Don Prout, cincinnativiews.net).

Street to West Sixth Street. The facility included Tellon's well-known American Foundry, plus shops for machinery, boilers, and sheet iron. Tellon (1795–1862), quite senior in years, was probably known by Brown.

Both the Cincinnati Marine Ways and Peter Tellon & Son indicated a willingness to accept Capt. Brown's gunboat project, and thus arrangements were made with each. The hulls for two of the vessels, *Chillicothe* and *Indianola*, would be built at Cincinnati, while that for the *Tuscumbia*, a much larger craft, would be constructed at New Albany. The application of side armor and mounting of ordnance would be handled at points below the Falls, while McCord addressed engine and machinery installation at both locations. Brown probably did not recognize it at the time, but his decision to spread out the work on his ironclads geographically would have consequences. Two years later, the Mississippi Squadron commander, RAdm. David Dixon Porter, summarized: "He had three vessels building at different places, which is a bad idea. A builder cannot do justice to the government in that way, especially as some of his work is let out by contracts, and he has to depend upon superintendents."[7]

Brown, quite probably in the company of his wife, Virginia, took up residence at

Burnet House. Capt. Joseph Brown, quite probably in the company of his wife, Virginia, took up residence at Cincinnati's leading hotel, the Burnet House, in May or June 1862 and eagerly undertook his construction task. The decade-old world-class hostelry was well known after having hosted President-elect Lincoln in February 1861. The hotel would serve as Brown's base of operations throughout the war, even during the time part of it served as headquarters for Lt. Gen. Ulysses S. Grant (March 1864) (Library of Congress).

Cincinnati's leading hotel, the Burnet House, in May or June 1862 and eagerly undertook his task. He was particularly anxious to work with Capt. Hercules Carrel (?–1890), president of the Marine Ways, and his chief superintendent, Oliver P. Tharp. Although Brown had most likely visited the facility earlier, he was eager to become more familiar with their concern, which not only included the marine railways but a large mill room and pattern loft building, located at the head of the inclined railway, plus various ship houses, a foundry and machine shops. Cabins, interior spaces, and other steamer superstructure would be fashioned by several groups of subcontractors, including cabinetmakers.

Capt. Carrel's marine railway was not greatly different from that operated by James Eads (and Primus Emerson before him) at Carondelet, MO, or, for that matter, Peter Tellon's shipyard at New Albany. Firmly anchored in position, pairs of heavy timbers (called ways) ran from below low-water level to the top of the high riverbank in groups of eight. Atop each pair of ways was a substantial cradle, the bottom of which rested on the ways while the top remained horizontal to keep held craft level. The cradle was attached to big winding drums at the top of the bank by heavy chains. The drums, in turn, were on a lengthy continuous line shaft powered by a steam engine equipped with

Harper's Weekly, July 13, 1861

(Postcard courtesy Don Prout, cincinnativiews.net).

Cincinnati Marine Ways. Opened in 1849 as a partnership between John Johnson and Capt. Daniel H. Morton, a prominent Cincinnati steamboat operator, this shipyard had modified the steamers *A.O. Tyler* and *Conestoga* into timberclads the previous spring. Brown was particularly interested in working with Capt. Hercules Carrel, president of the Marine Ways, and his chief superintendent, Oliver P. Tharp. The three men would conduct business together through the end of the conflict. Our first illustration noted the construction of the timberclads while the second is a postcard reproduction of a much later scene that nevertheless gives an excellent portrait of the manner in which vessels at the yard were positioned.

clutches that could operate through nine gear sets. This combination allowed vessels set for repair to be floated onto the cradles sideways, hauled up the riverbank to a chosen location, and blocked in place. The cradle could then bring another vessel so that, in practice, more than one boat could be on the ways at a time. The process was reversed when vessels were returned to the river. New boats, built on the ways, could be lowered sideways into the Ohio in the same fashion.

As soon as Brown and Carrel were on the scene, construction of the two smaller gunboats began at the top of the ways, adjacent to the mill room and pattern loft building. The process would be the same as if the vessels were civilian steamboats. First, the hull lines for the craft were drawn full size on the loft floor according to Brown's plans and clearly showed elevation and section views. Next, the head carpenter traced the dimensions for each piece of frame or planking. Using wood supplied by yards in western Virginia (now West Virginia) or Pennsylvania, carpenters, as John White informs us, then "sawed, machine shaped, and dressed" the needed timbers. Once that was finished, construction of the boats would begin over the inclined ways, "parallel to the river with the bow upstream and on top of the stocks and blocking."

With the hulls begun, Brown next turned his attention to his major subcontractors, McCord and Harrison. Orders placed with both gentlemen for the construction of

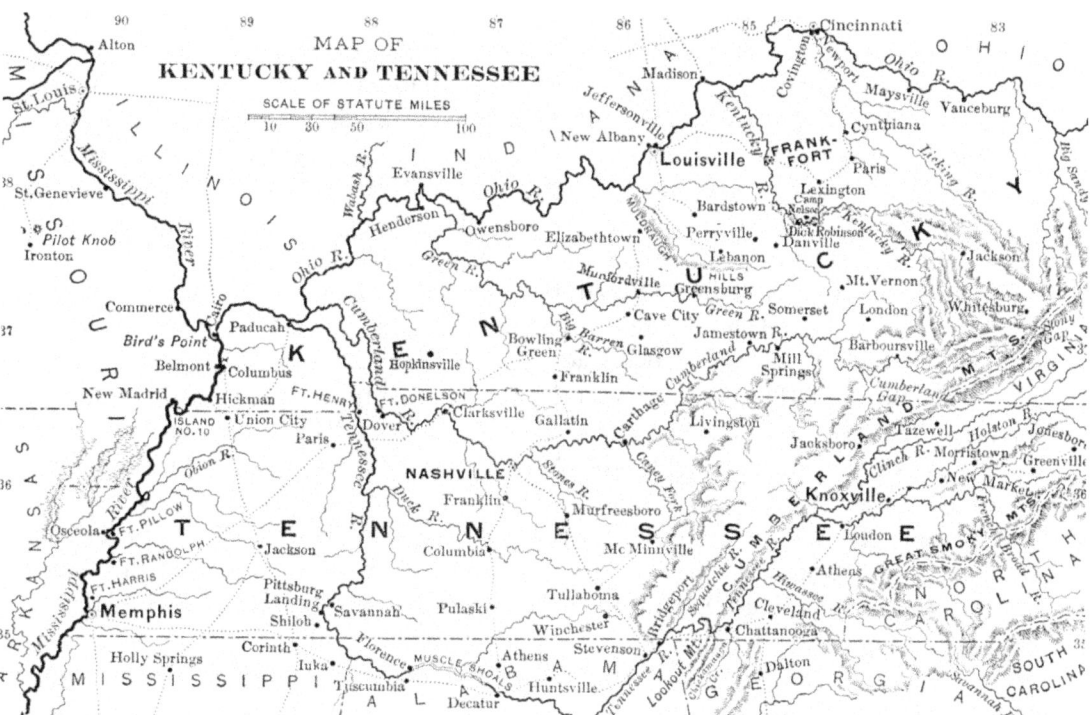

Map of Kentucky and Tennessee. In addition to displaying the locations of principal Western Theater operations in 1862, this map shows the location of the major Ohio River boatbuilding communities noted in our story: Cincinnati, Jeffersonville, New Albany, Louisville, and St. Louis. Also cited is Cairo, IL, home base for the Western Gunboat Flotilla (Johnson and Buel, *Battles and Leaders of the Civil War*).

engines and the rolling of armor plate at their facilities in St. Louis shortly after the boatyards were signed up were confirmed. Arrangements were made that when finished the product would be shipped to the building yards at Cincinnati and New Albany.

Reprinting an article from the *St. Louis Daily Republican* of a few days earlier, the *Louisville Daily Journal* on May 21 gave its readers their first information on the Brown gunboat enterprise, including names of the principals and some fiscal data, though they proved to be incorrect as to the construction site, Cincinnati, OH not Cairo, IL:

> Messrs. Brown, McCord, and Sanger of St. Louis, have contracted with the government for the building of three iron clad gunboats, at an aggregate cost of $450,000. These will be constructed on the plan submitted by them and approved by the Board of Construction [U.S. Navy Bureau of Construction and Equipment]. The iron mail of these boats will cost $100,000. Their machinery, which is now in a very forward state, is being constructed by Messrs. McCord & Co, of the Franklin Foundry, and will cost some $70,000. The *Republican* says two of the hulls are on the stocks at Cairo and are nearly completed.

On May 27, the *Cleveland Daily Herald* reported "the Marine Railway and Dock Company at Cincinnati are constructing two new gunboats, of oval deck and iron clad." The short article continued: "The Government says it is intended to make them invulnerable, all sorts of military projectiles glancing from the sides without producing any impression." This was the first public print indication that Capt. Carrel had taken on Brown's project.[8]

Leaving Carrel, Morton, and Tharp to attend to matters in Cincinnati, Brown next traveled to New Albany, IN, to consult with Peter Tellon. Born in France, Capt. Tellon had settled in New Albany four decades earlier, engaging in both foundry and boatbuilding occupations. By the opening of the Civil War, the aging entrepreneur's business was operated on a day-to-day basis with his sons, William and Martin. Like Carrel in Cincinnati, the Tellons, Brown learned, were well equipped to construct the largest of his three ironclads. Work on her hull was also pushed ahead and over the next several months, Brown traveled back and forth between the Ohio and Indiana communities overseeing component deliveries and checking on progress. Local superintendents, presumably Tharp and the Tellons, oversaw daily construction details.[9]

While Brown and his associates were busily getting their gunboat projects going, the Navy Department, as was the case when any major warships were built, appointed officers to oversee construction. In mid–May, Secretary Welles reached for the retired list to bring Capt. Joseph B. Hull (1802–1890) back into service, ordering him to St. Louis as overall superintendent of gunboat construction. The fourth cousin of Flag Officer Foote had joined the U.S. Navy in 1813 and risen to command the Brazil Squadron and the Paraguay Expedition (1856–1859), participating in the 1861 Atlantic Blockade. Although he would not arrive in Missouri until July, at which time he was promoted to the rank of commodore on the reserved list, Hull would have an active assistant.

Edward Hartt, the naval constructor who had served as part of the Smith Review Board, which had given a final boost to Brown's proposals, was appointed by Welles on May 19 to serve as Hull's operational lieutenant. Also based at St. Louis, he was to supervise the actual work performed by the builders "in all matters pertaining to the hull, cladding, equipment, and accommodations" of the warships (but not their steam

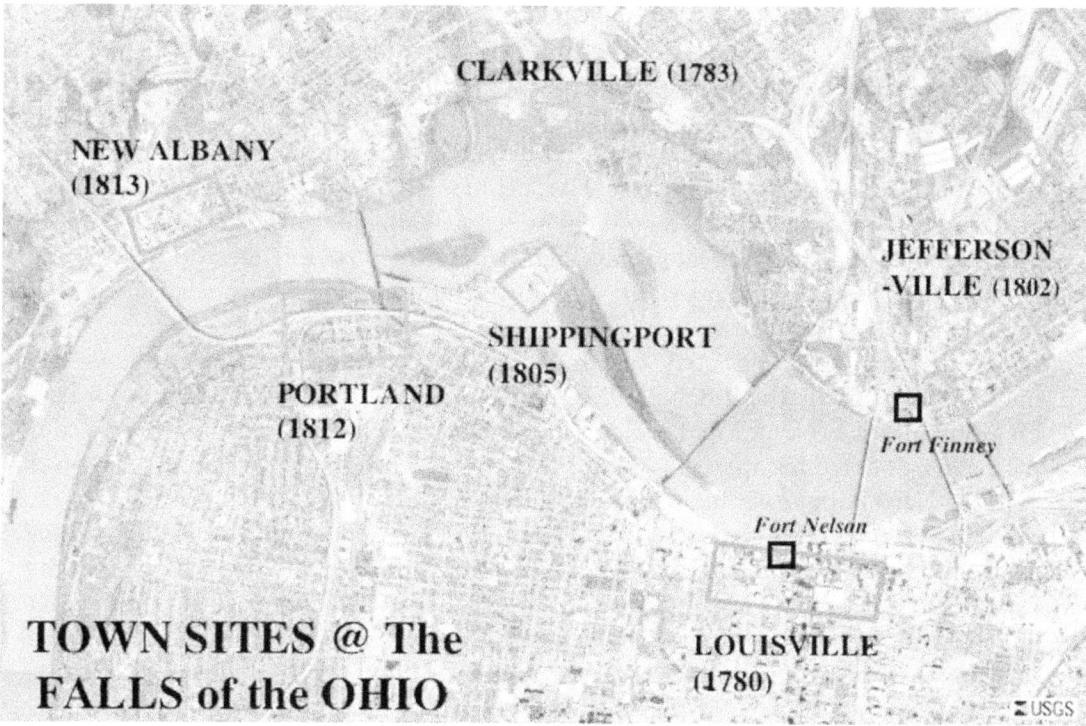

Towns at the Falls of the Ohio. Seen in a modern aerial map, these towns and the long-famous natural obstruction near them play an important part in the story of the three Brown ironclads. Low water at the Falls of the Ohio prevented larger craft from making an easy passage down the Ohio River to Cairo, IL, where the Western navy was based. Understanding this difficulty, the captain chose to build his largest vessel, the *Tuscumbia*, at the New Albany, IN, yards of Peter Tellon & Sons. The application of side armor and mounting of ordnance aboard the trio were handled at points below the Falls (US Geological Survey).

machinery), making certain all work was properly completed and inspected and certifying all payments. He would become intimately familiar with the gunboats built by both Eads and Brown, later working closely with the former when he was contracted to convert several light draught steamers into "tinclads."

Years afterwards, several historians suggested that one or more of Brown's three ironclads was actually designed by Hartt. The respected warship historian Paul H. Silverstone states frankly that Hartt designed the *Chillicothe*. Angus Konstam argues that the plans for Brown's vessels were "based on a series of designs produced by the naval constructor Edward Hartt." If the boats were found wanting, "neither man," according to Konstam, "was capable of coping with the design challenges they were faced with." On the other hand, the *St. Louis Daily Republican* of August 4, 1862, frankly notes, "The plans for the three vessels were submitted by Capt. Brown." Donald L. Canney attributes the original "general concept" of the ironclads to Brown, who "rightly feared the consequences" when RAdm. David Dixon Porter ordered structural alterations to the two larger units in late September.

We know that Brown conferred with Hartt on several occasions regarding improvements or specialized installation requirements to his three ironclads. It is possible that Hartt conferred on the former Alton mayor's original proposal when they were in Washington in March and April, even though Hartt had his hands full working on proposals for Com. Smith's ironclad review board. The visits between the two appear to have become less amiable after RAdm. Porter ordered very specific changes to Brown's trio at the beginning of October. In fact, Hartt conferred, per the responsibilities of his position, with all of the Western gunboat builders, taking his duties as superintendent quite seriously. James Eads later paid high tribute to Hartt for his work in revising certain difficult details and providing assistance on the Carondelet ironclads, "working for days at a time in my drawing room."

Still, Hartt was not directed West until mid–May, at which time Brown was already in Ohio working with the Cincinnati Marine Railway and Eads was in St. Louis focused on his monitors. Both men had projects underway and, while appreciating Hartt's contributions, doubted his appreciation of Western steamboat construction. Neither ever credited Hartt with designing their gunboats for them.

It was Hartt's close superintendancy of the building process and his ability to troubleshoot design flaws that gave Brown the impression that he and the craftsmen of the Cincinnati Marine Railway had lost some of the construction authority they had earlier enjoyed. The following March when his boats were finished, Brown complained, "I had none of my own way [during the construction of the *Chillicothe*], the second [*Indianola*] a little more [and] the third and last [*Tuscumbia*] a little more." This observation doubtless caused Silverstone, Konstam, and others to attribute the actual design of the Brown gunboats, especially the *Chillicothe*, to the naval constructor.

In the months after Porter arrived, Brown came to consider Hartt a nit-picker and difficult to work with. On the other hand, Brown and Porter did in fact, and frequently, arrange modifications, especially to the *Tuscumbia* and *Indianola*, and failed to inform Hartt. This lack of communication occasionally resulted in Hartt's threatening to withhold contract payments if the contractor failed to notify him of every modification. While Brown remained a Porter favorite, Hartt not only lost the admiral's confidence but was castigated by him when opportunities arose. In a May 1, 1863 letter to the assistant secretary of the navy, Gustavus Vasa Fox, following the Battle of Grand Gulf, Porter was blunt: "The Brown gunboats are entire failures, which I attribute to that man Hartt (who disobeyed my instructions in relation to these boats in every respect)—who ought to be hung for neglecting matters when the lives of the men, and the honor of the nation is at stake. I have said as much as this officially, I believe. I don't know if it will remove an incompetent and dishonest man." Hartt's future was pretty much linked to that of Com. Hull. Late in 1864, Hull and Hart were both transferred to the Philadelphia navy yard, where Hartt was promoted to the rank of naval constructor on July 25, 1866.[10]

Shortly after his arrival at St. Louis, Com. Hull learned that the smallest of Brown's vessels was now at the riverbank. This development encouraged him to undertake an inspection trip to Cincinnati and New Albany to examine the work being performed on Brown's three ironclads—the floating *Chillicothe*, as well as the *Indianola*, and *Tuscumbia*, both of which were still on the ways. Arriving first at Cincinnati, he found the hulls of the two there ready to receive their power plants. As can be seen in two contemporary photographs of the *Indianola*, construction was off to a fine start.

Many of the men hired to build the Cincinnati and New Albany gunboats were Irish, French, and German and came from yards all along the Ohio River, including those at those two towns, as well as at Jeffersonville, Louisville, and upriver toward Pittsburg. Particularly sought for the work were ship carpenters and skilled mechanics. As more laborers joined the effort, the adjacent town area near New Albany and Cincinnati's Fulton suburb swelled in terms of people and structures. In addition to the various buildings and machinery of the boatyards, new houses were constructed, along with several stores, saloons, boardinghouses and restaurants. Insofar as the workforce was concerned, the government idea of spreading the work around seemed to take hold.

By mid–July, progress on the Cincinnati boats was substantial, while work on the hull of the *Tuscumbia* was advancing at New Albany. Observers, including Hull, could envision how the finished vessels would appear. As with the Pook turtles, there were similarities between Brown's creations; conversely, there were also major differences. As Eads found when building the City Series gunboats a year earlier, changes would have to be made during assembly. Each unit was originally designed with a very shallow flat-bottomed and rather short hull and small-diameter paddle wheels. In Brown's original sketch, they would each appear from the river like a big square-bowed steamer, with a single flat main weather deck with a wide breadth, a triangle-shaped casemate structure atop the deck athwartships forward (with two funnels or "chimneys" right behind), and further back, covered paddle wheels, one on each side. The crown, or camber, of the main deck (its athwartship roundup or highest point from the boat's bottom), which allowed rainwater to run down to the side of the hull and hence overboard and also demonstrated hold depth, was to be only six inches.

The hull of each vessel, built on eight-to-ten-inch floor timbers, rose from a central 15" × 30" keel and two side keelsons. The nine-inch thick sides, with frames set 15 inches apart, were built of oak and some pine. Stretching around the hull and extending below the waterline was what Capt. Brown called a beveled "fascia," an architectural term meaning, according to Henry Saylor, "a horizontal band of vertical face." Brown's beveled outer ribbon was a foot thick and two feet deep. Despite also having two side and two knuckle keelsons, rigidity problems were anticipated immediately for the gunboats given their designed short length-to-breadth ratio and their shallow hulls.

The solution to this challenge, Brown thought, was to install three full-length bulkheads aboard each boat. That in the center would be waterproof and 2½ inches thick fore-to-aft. The ones on either side athwartships were of an arched lattice design, four to six inches thick. This series of diagonal cross braces ran 10 feet apart from bow to stern. There was at least one giant 32-inch timber arch located directly beneath the casemate. If the specifications proved to be correct, this unique system of heavy arches, together with the central bulkhead, would distribute design weight and provide the desired hull rigidity. In the end, however, fore and aft hog chains, common on many Western steamers but increasingly augmented with braces, would need to be employed in a continuing effort to redress strains, both athwartships and longitudinal.

The main decks of Brown's ironclads were not constructed in a conventional fashion. None had either the normal lateral deck beams or fore-and-aft planking. Instead, the contractor chose to lay eight-by-eight–inch pine timbers side-by-side athwartships, These were in turn secured edgewise to each other and through the arch lattice bulkheads with one-inch–thick iron bolts. The main decks also received no conventional support over the boiler area; instead, it was supported from above by a bridge tree and chains. This main deck assembly, as Budd remarks, "provided no longitudinal support" for the hulls. A rectangular casemate, constructed of solid nine-inch–thick white pine and sloping on a 26½-degree incline, was placed forward, atop the main deck of each gunboat and was initially referred to as a "turret" or "tower." It was not, reported a *St. Louis Daily Republican* journalist on August 4, "as in the *Monitor*, revolving, but stationary, with sloping sides and a ball-proof grating overhead." The casemate was pierced for gunports that permitted both side and forward fields of fire from two big cannon mounted on Marsilly carriages. All of the gunports were enclosed by shutters three inches thick, which were slid back and forth via tracks on each side. As for dimensions, the turrets aboard the *Chillicothe* and *Indianola* measured 22 × 42 feet at their base and rose to a height of seven feet. They were framed with 12-inch–square pine that received nine-inch–pine overlays. The casemate aboard the *Tuscumbia* at deck level was 62 feet by 22 feet and the pine covering was a foot thick. Initially, Brown made the same design error as Eads had with the Pook turtles in not providing for a proper armored pilothouse. The former Alton mayor placed his steering wheel in the casemate right between the two forward gunports. Without 360 degree visability, the boats' pilots would be handicapped in their ability to see anywhere other than straight ahead.

While work on the hulls and superstructures moved ahead, Charles McCord completed, with the help of local subcontractors, the propulsion plants for the three warships. The *Chillicothe*, the smallest of the three, would be powered only by paddle wheels, while her "yard sister," *Indianola*, would also, like the *Tuscumbia*, be outfitted with propellers. All of the ships' machinery would be located belowdecks, filling up almost all of the hold space.

The powerplant of the *Chillicothe* featured two high-pressure engines with inclined cylinders (one per side paddle wheel) measuring 23 inches in diameter by four feet, with an eight-foot stroke. Steam was generated in three amidships, five-flued boilers, each 28 feet long and 40 inches wide. Alongside the boilers on this ship and the other two were the coal bunkers, nearly seven inches thick. Also in the hold, forward of the coal bunkers (and under the forward casemate), were the magazine and shell room. The former contained space for 100 eleven-inch shells and 10 barrels of powder. It would take just three hours of fighting to expend all of these.

Two independently operable fifteen-foot paddle wheels in unprotected houses, or paddle boxes, were provided, though moved forward 18 feet from their original recess location as first specified. Exhaust exited via two 20-foot–high hinged chimneys. Steam also powered a pair of capstans and a donkey engine, it being anticipated that the power of the former would be sufficient to pull the vessel, in shoal water, over a bar in two feet of water.

By late July, the *Chillicothe* was approaching completion, with her hull, most of her superstructure, power plant, and wheels ready. At some point during this time, a short trial trip was made upstream during which she was able to attain a 9-mph speed, far in excess of her contract requirement of 4 mph against a 2-mph current.

The two paddle wheels located on the sides of the *Indianola*, approximately three-fourths of the length back from her bow, were powered by a pair of high-pressure inclined cylinders, each measuring 24 inches by six feet, with a six-foot, six-inch stroke. Recessed below the waterline at the stern of the hull were a pair of four-bladed propellers, each six feet in diameter. Each of these was handled by a beveled-gear engine 18 inches in diameter by two feet, four inches, with a 20-inch stroke. Steam came from five amidships, five-flued boilers, each 28 feet long and 40 inches wide. The capstans, donkey engine, and chimneys were identical to those aboard the *Chillicothe*.

The extremely-wide *Tuscumbia* required additional power and so was outfitted with six 40" × 28' five-flued boilers to move her two propellers and two side wheels. The two high-pressure engines mated to the former measured 30 inches in diameter by six feet, with a seven-foot stroke. The beveled gear engines for the latter were 20 inches by 20 inches, with a 20-inch stroke. Again, the donkey engine, steam capstans and exhaust chimneys were identical to those aboard the *Chillicothe*.

As Brown and McCord personally labored on the three boats, handling on-site details and conferring with the builders, back in St. Louis James Harrison, of Chouteau, Harrison & Valle, sought to provide the needed iron armor. Some of the iron employed would come from Kentucky furnaces. Unlike on the Eads projects centered in Carondelet, he would have not only to manufacture the plate but also ship it to the banks of the Ohio. The latter was viewed as an iffy proposition in July.

Starting on July 4, John Hunt Morgan (1825–1864), leading 900 cavalrymen, made his celebrated "First Kentucky Raid" deep into the rear of the Federal army. In three weeks, he captured over a thousand Northern soldiers, hundreds of horses, and a large

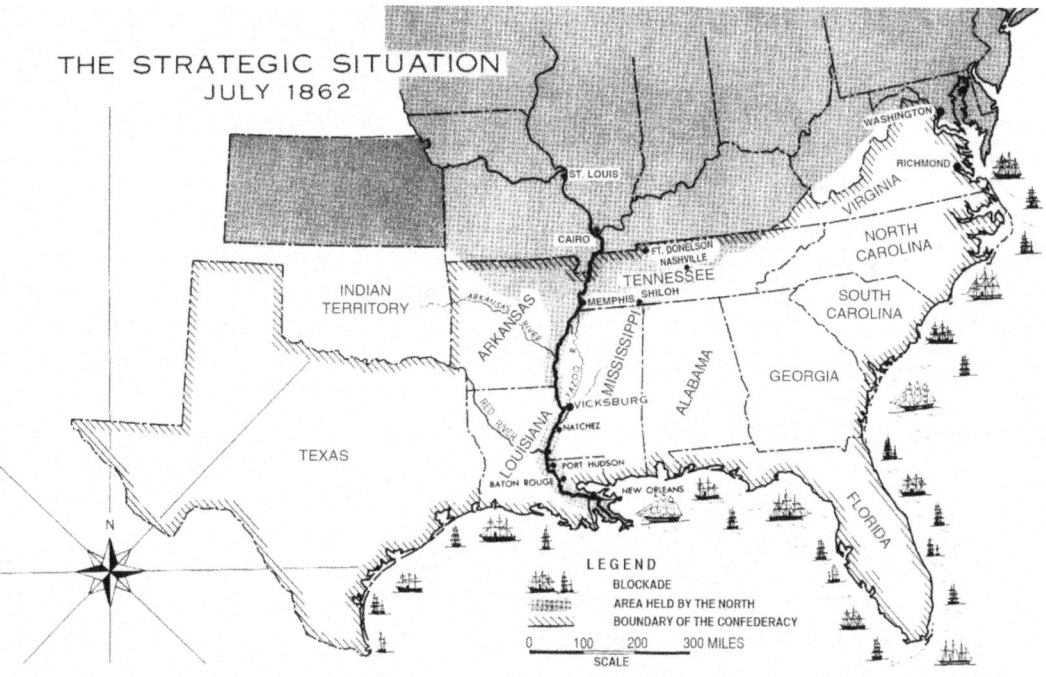

The Strategic Situation. When Joseph Brown began construction of the *Chillicothe* and *Indianola* at Cincinnati in July 1862, the South controlled vast swathes of territory. However, implementation of the Federal Anaconda Plan had begun (National Park Service).

quantity of supplies. What was more important, he unnerved Kentucky's Union military government, causing rumors to fly around the Bluegrass State and beyond for several more weeks concerning all manner of Yankee military and logistical dangers. To his own superior, as recorded by Woodworth, Maj. Gen. Edmund Kirby Smith (1824–1893), commander of the Department of East Tennessee, the "Thunderbolt of the Confederacy," as he would be known, opined, "The whole country can be secured, and 25,000 or 30,000 men will join you at once."

At St. Louis, Harrison not only had to worry over production and military concerns, he also had to participate in an ongoing debate as to how much iron production was actually required. This discussion, along with his other considerations, slowed down manufacture and shipment. In August, Joseph Brown explained his ironing concern in a letter to the editor of the *Louisville Journal*:

> In the present march of improvement in firearms, it would be difficult to say what would constitute a perfectly ball-proof boat. The question resolves itself into this shape, with regard to these three boats: is the iron thick enough and not are they iron-clad. I will here state it has been a question in my mind whether there was iron enough on certain portions of the boat; and, with a view to increasing it, I wrote to the Bureau of Construction at Washington, asking permission to increase the thickness of iron on the sides to three inches, and on the casemates, or towers, to six inches. From the nature of their reply, referring the matter to Commodore Hull, at St. Louis, I presume it will be done.

There was, of course, a tradeoff if more armor were added, something Brown undoubtedly discussed with his associates: Tharp, the Tellons, Harrison, and perhaps also Com. Hull, the latter during his July inspection. Brown would even bring the matter up with the new fleet commander, RAdm. David Dixon Porter, following the sailor's October appointment: "Now, let us see. The contract depth of the *Indianola* was for six feet and she draws six feet, so that she would have been six inches under water." Brown further pressed his case to the Louisville newsman. "There is," he noted, "this drawback to adding more weight, viz: the draft of water." By contract, he could not increase the hold depth of the trio because "I am bound down to draft of water, the penalty for over running which would make the hair stand on your head!" In the end, an undocumented compromise was made with the government. The armor thickness of the three gunboats was not increased. However, the main deck crown was permitted to rise from six to eight feet. Despite this change, the *Chillicothe*, smallest of the Brown three, would be, according to Canney, "the lightest-draft armored vessel built for the river fleet." Just as her depth of hold was increased, so too was *Chillicothe*'s length, from 158 to 164 feet. The middle craft, *Indianola*, measured 175 × 52 × 5 feet and the huge *Tuscumbia* was 178 × 75 × 7. By way of comparison, the City Series Pook turtle *Carondelet* measured 175 × 51 × 6 feet and the *Benton* was 202 × 72 × 9 feet.

Skipping ahead slightly, let us take this opportunity to review where the iron was placed aboard these craft and in what thickness. Also discussing these details with the Louisville editor, who in turn printed the remarks for all the world to read, Brown revealed that, as of August, his three gunboats were being protected as follows: "Thickness of iron on the entire deck, one inch; on the sides, two inches; on the bow two and a half inches; and on the towers [casemates] three inches; which as you will perceive, includes the entire boat except the wheels, which are left un-protected, as to cover them would very considerably increase the draft of water, and was deemed unnecessary, as two of the boats are provided with propellers under water as well as wheels."

Knowing that main deck protection might raise questions in certain circles, the contractor noted that some might think "the iron on the deck, being only one inch, is not thick enough." But, he argued, "from the actual test on the *Monitor*, it is found to be ample, as that is the thickness of her deck-iron." In addition, both the side and bow armor extended a foot below the waterline. To help guard against plunging fire, the builders fastened heavy gratings to prevent shell penetration. He noted later that every scuttle and hatch "was equally well covered." Later critics would decry Capt. Brown's brushing aside of wheelhouse armor, regarding that as his vessels' greatest weakness. Still, as his trio took shape on the Ohio that summer, the industrious riverman apparently familiar with reports on the protection given both Ericsson's ironclad and the Pook turtles believed his gunboats were better covered than those of Eads.[11]

On July 26, the *New York Times* published a lengthy review of new warships under construction for the Union navy, on both the East Coast and the Western waters. Upon receipt of the eastern paper, *St. Louis Daily Republican* publisher and chief editor Nathaniel Paschall (1804–1866) planned to run the statement in his journal on July 31. Familiar with river affairs, he was aware that it "omits to mention three of the most powerful and impressionable iron-clad gunboats contracted for by the War Department." He further knew that they were being constructed "under a contract with Capt. Joseph Brown, a St. Louisian so well known here and in Alton, Illinois, that he will be recognized at once." A reporter whose name we do not have was called in and immediately sent to Cincinnati to interview Brown and write an article about his project. Paschal's man arrived at Cincinnati early on July 31 and immediately paid a visit to the Cincinnati Marine Railway, where he found the *Chillicothe* afloat, the *Indianola* on the stocks, and Capt. Brown and numerous yard workers and superintenandants busy about the yard. Always eager that his various enterprises receive the best press, the one-time mayor took the scribe in hand and toured him all around, including a stop aboard the *Chillicothe*, describing his vessels and the progress of their creation in great detail.

The *Chillicothe* was found to be "nearly finished." Brown was pleased to point out that "she had all of her machinery in, her deck-plating completed, her turret more than half plated, and much of her bow and stern plating on." The vessel's beam was so wide that the side plating could not be affixed until after she had passed downstream through the canal around Louisville's Falls of the Ohio. After confirming the thickness of the iron plating, the journalist learned she would be armed with a pair of Dahlgren 168-calibre guns (11-inch smoothbore cannon). Then, while touring the spaces below the main deck, it was pointed out that *Chillicothe*'s "officers' rooms and machinery," located in the hold, were "perfectly protected from shot." Finally, the *Daily Republican* writer was shown the boat's paddle wheels and told that she had "made a trial trip and easily makes five miles per hour up stream." While stepping ashore to continue their conversation, the contractor intimated to the writer that the *Chillicothe* "was so nearly done" that he "expected to take her down during the present week."

The "powerfully and heavily built" *Indianola*, a somewhat larger gunboat, was visited next. Her machinery was in and because her five boilers and powerful engines would connect both with paddle wheels and with screws it was expected she could

***Indianola* Under Construction**. The first of two remarkable pre-launch building shots of the *Indianola*. These are the only ones extant showing any of the Brown ironclads other than the *Tuscumbia*. Workmen here are shown undertaking various tasks near and aboard the hull (bow to the right of the photograph), along with uninstalled engine gears on the deck. The photo is controversial, it long being believed this was a salvage rather than a building portrait. The Naval History and Heritage Command labels the photo as a building image while students debate that idea in a series of posts of "Another Misidentified *Indianola*" on *Civil War Talk* (Naval History and Heritage Command).

move "without trouble ten miles per hour up stream." In fact, while in service she made just barely seven mph (6.9 knots). Designed for ease and speed in handling, she, too, would have a pair of 11-inch Dahlgrens. Both men agreed she would be "a war vessel of formidable strength and Brown expected to have the *Indianola* ready for service in six weeks.

The St. Louis reporter was not able to see the *Tuscumbia*, which was "being built at New Albany, her size being such that she could not be carried through the canal." Though larger, she was, he learned from Capt. Brown, the same "in every way" as the *Indianola*: general layout, side wheels and propellers, immense engines, thickness of iroin armor, 11-inch guns. She, too, was to be completed within six weeks and would be "far in advance of anything now on the Western waters."

Throughout his visit, the reporter jotted down Brown stories and vignettes concerning both the boats and their contractor. Noting that their initial plans were accepted by Washington with but "slight modification," the newsman observed, "Since the contract was awarded to him, he [Brown] has pushed the building to completion with that resolute, driving energy which is known as a characteristic of 'Capt. Jo,' as he is called in everything he undertakes. The admirable manner in which the vessels have been built, under his immediate and constant supervision and direction, furnishes the highest evidence of his fidelity, as well as his excellent judgement and skill."

Com. Hull made his Ohio River inspection tour within a few days of the *St. Louis Daily Republican* writer's Cincinnati visit, but he was not able to file his report with the Navy Department until August 12. He, too, found the *Chillicothe* "nearly ready to be removed to New Albany for purpose of putting on the side plate." In other respects, she was nearly ready to receive her big guns and other "equipment for service." Hull, like the newspaperman ahead of him, believed the *Chillicothe* to be "a fine vessel," the work on her being "well done throughout."

The building of the *Indianola*, also at Cincinnati, was likewise discovered to be far advanced. "The deck is laid and the casemate formed," Hull observed, "the engines and boilers in place, and the work is progressing very well and is well done." In accordance with an earlier arrangement between the chief supervisor and contractor Brown, the latter "deepened her hold two feet three inches," a decision that would allow her to "stand out of the water."

Immediately following Hull's departure from Cincinnati, Capt. Brown and a makeshift crew provided by the Cincinnati Marine Railway took the *Chillicothe* downstream, most likely at the beginning of the first week of August. When she left Cincinnati, it was reported that the gunboat transported her hull side armor as deck cargo. It could not be "put on until she had passed through the canal at Louisville, her width being such that she can barely go through without the plates." The downriver trip was

Stern Construction View of the *Indianola*. Another building photo of the *Indianola* that emphasizes her stern configuration and scow-like hull lines prior to the placement of the paddle wheels and their houses in the recesses shown. Note the screw propellers already installed (*Miller's Photographic History of the Civil War*, vol. 6).

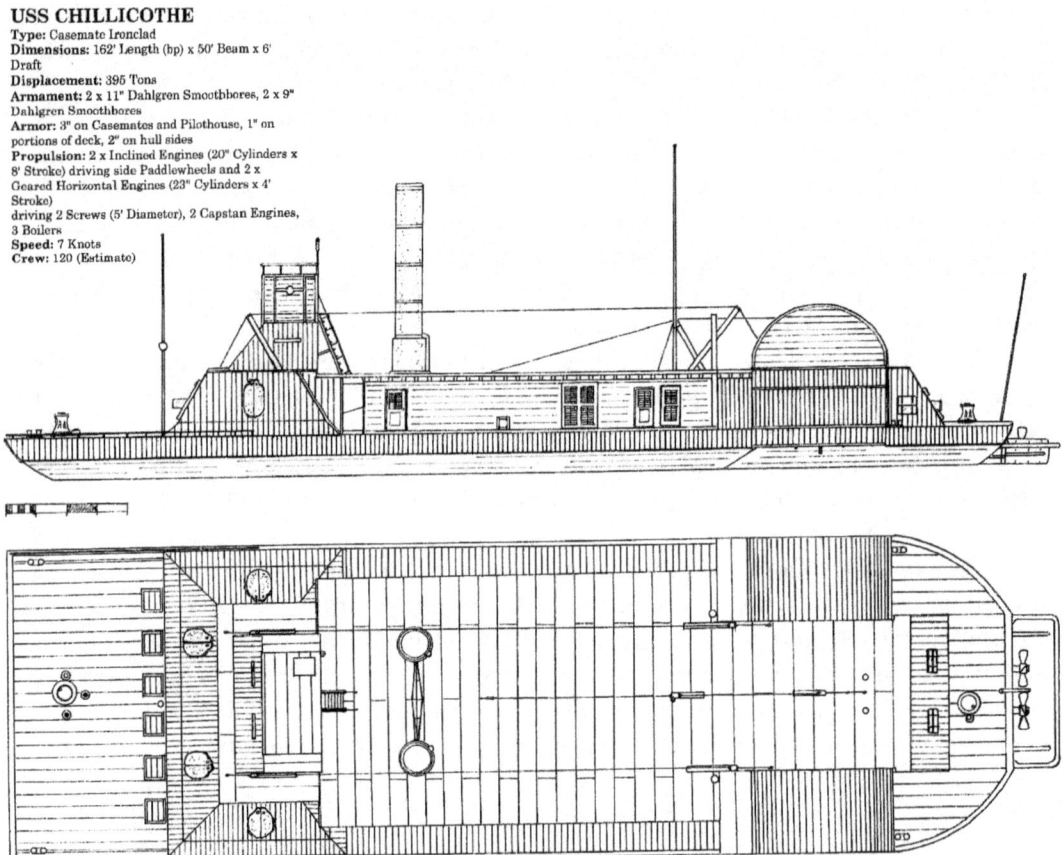

USS CHILLICOTHE
Type: Casemate Ironclad
Dimensions: 162' Length (hp) x 50' Beam x 6' Draft
Displacement: 395 Tons
Armament: 2 x 11" Dahlgren Smoothbores, 2 x 9" Dahlgren Smoothbores
Armor: 3" on Casemates and Pilothouse, 1" on portions of deck, 2" on hull sides
Propulsion: 2 x Inclined Engines (20" Cylinders x 8' Stroke) driving side Paddlewheels and 2 x Geared Horizontal Engines (23" Cylinders x 4' Stroke) driving 2 Screws (5' Diameter), 2 Capstan Engines, 3 Boilers
Speed: 7 Knots
Crew: 120 (Estimate)

Copyright © 2006 - David J. Meagher

***Chillicothe* Finished First.** The smallest of the three Brown ironclads, the *Chillicothe*, was the first completed and was dispatched, minus guns and armor, to New Albany, IN, at the end of August 1862. Low water there would keep her from proceeding to Cairo, IL, until January 1863. Still, she was a major force after two 11-inch Dahlgren smoothbore cannon were mounted aboard on September 17–19 (c2006, David J. Meagher; used with permission).

uneventful, except that *Chillicothe*'s main deck actually leaked a bit while underway, as did her bow. This seepage did not bother Brown, who proudly proclaimed that his gunboat was so watertight "even the bilge water smelled." It is not known, but not altogether unlikely, that the ironclad was given her nickname during this inaugural movement: "Chilly Coffee."

Unhappily, the water was so low and the canal so narrow that the *Chillicothe* could not pass below the Falls of the Ohio and so was docked at Jeffersonville, IN, to await a rise. It was most likely at this time that Acting Master Edward Shaw (1813–1887) came upon the scene from Cairo, IL. Shaw, first master of the U.S. timberclad *Tyler*, was being seconded to the Brown project while his vessel, badly damaged in her July 15 engagement with the CSS *Arkansas*, was under repair.[12]

The success of Morgan's First Kentucky Raid in July, meanwhile, had convinced Confederate major general Smith that it would be possible to mount a large incursion, wreaking even more damage on the Union hold on Kentucky and Tennesse; protecting Vicksburg, MS, the South's last Mississippi River bastion after the fall of New Orleans and Memphis; convincing additional men to join the Southern army; and acquiring vast quantities of supplies. Smith successfully lobbied his superior, Gen. Braxton Bragg (1817–1876), commander of the Army of the Mississippi, regarding these possibilities, and after meeting at Chattanooga on July 31—the same day Capt. Brown showed off his boats to the St. Louis reporter—the two Rebel leaders devised an ambitious plan. If it were successful, much of what Smith proposed would be accomplished and the northern border of the Confederacy would rest on the southern bank of the Ohio River.

Moving on to New Albany as August began, Com. Hull met with the Tellons and observed that the "hull of the *Tuscumbia* is nearly done." The boilers were being placed and workmen were "putting up inside bulkheads and partitions for the different apartments and preparing to lay the deck." Construction of this craft was also "being done well."

While at Cincinnati the previous week, Hull and Brown had discussed the possibility that, once she had her side armor installed, the *Chillicothe* would proceed down the Ohio to Cairo, IL, where she would receive her guns, crews, and other outfits at the main Western Flotilla operational base. Now, the master superintendent, who did not know the *Chillicothe* was at Jeffersonville, like other officers at regional Union headquarters, both military and naval, began to hear significant rumors regarding Confederate movements in, and designs upon, Kentucky.

On Friday, August 8, Com. Hull sent a message to Capt. Brown advising him to proceed no further than New Albany. The naval officer would return to St. Louis, where he could have more direct contact with authorities and soon advise the former Alton mayor as to when the boat's detention might end. Although reports and stories regarding Southern incursions continued to circulate, the Confederate "Heartland Offensive" did not officially begin until August 13 when Maj. Gen. Smith departed from Knoxville, TN, riding north with 11,000 men.[13]

The same day Smith quit Knoxville for the Blue Grass State, Hull in Missouri informed Capt. Brown in Indiana, ordering him to keep the *Chillicothe* where she was until further orders were received. He also advised the contractor that an invoice was received for guns and other articles which were en route to New Albany and Cincinnati for *Chillicothe* and *Indianola*. Upon their arrival, it would be Brown's responsibility to find a safe depot for them until they could be installed. Ordnance and outfits for the *Chillicothe* were to be put aboard as soon as possible and if any advice was required from constructor Hartt, then also at St. Louis, on their fitting, the contractor was to ask him "soon." Brown quickly arranged for Hartt to come out to Jeffersonville and supervise the installation.

Returning to Cincinnati, contractor Brown found the hull of the *Indianola* nearly ready for launch. Noting that she was very "strong in the bow," he perceived that it might be possible to strengthen her even further, turning her into an ironclad ram, perhaps on the model of the famed Confederate *Arkansas*. On August 14, he proposed this idea to Com. Hull, who rejected any bow alterations out of hand a few days later. Disappointed, the former mayor remembered the following March that he nevertheless "did all I could, consistently, to make her extra strong in that locality."

Gen. Bragg eventually departed Chattanooga for the Blue Grass State on August 27, forcing Maj. Gen. John Carlos Buell, commander of the Army of the Ohio, to eventually move from Nashville on September 7 to position himself between Bragg and the cities of Louisville and Cincinnati. Earlier, on August 30, Smith had defeated the Federals at Richmond, KY, and two days later occupied Lexington. These Southern triumphs caused a panic throughout Kentucky and southern Indiana and Ohio. There appeared to be little to prevent a successful Confederate march north via Frankfurt toward the vital Union logistical hubs at Cincinnati and Louisville.

On September 1, the worried Department of the Ohio commander, Maj. Gen. Horatio Wright (1820–1899), began formulating plans for his defense of the Ohio River country, not knowing for certain what Maj. Gen. Smith had in mind beyond his next obvious goal: Frankfurt. Moving to Louisville that afternoon, Wright ordered Maj. Gen. Lew Wallace (1827–1905), future author of the novel *Ben-Hur*, to assume command at Cincinnati. Both communities would be placed under martial law, commerce would cease, and the populations rallied and given roles to play. Across the river from Cincinnati at Covington and Newport, the likely eastern and western river approaches for any Confederate attack, only 15 unmounted guns, without either ammunition or crews, were available for protection.

The Hoosier-born general arrived at the Queen City the next day and established his headquarters at the Burnet House (where Brown and his wife were also residing). At the same time, the *Cincinnati Daily Enquirer* assured the world that the town's citizens were "manifest to give General Wallace all the assistance in their power." Wallace, in turn, issued a proclamation of expectations under the slogan "Citizens for Labor, Soldiers for the Battle." Earnest activities to strengthen the defenses of Cincinnati, Covington, and Newport commenced.

Also, in the morning of September 2, Indiana governor Oliver P. Morton (1823–1877) wired Capt. Brown, via Peter Tellon and Son at New Albany, regarding his perception of the necessity, as part of river defense, to quickly commission the *Chillicothe*. The contractor immediately wired the message on to Com. Hull at St. Louis, reporting that the *Chillicothe*'s iron work was just about finished save for the gunport shutters. Temporary ones could

Maj. Gen. Lew Wallace. On August 27, 1862, elements of Gen. Braxton Bragg's Army of the Mississippi began a large incursion into Kentucky designed to protect Vicksburg, threaten the Union hold on Tennessee and Kentucky, and capture supplies. Within days, Maj. Gen. Lew Wallace (future author of the novel *Ben-Hur*) assumed military command at Cincinnati to undertake its defense if Rebel forces approached (U.S. Army Military History Institute).

be fitted, Brown indicated, though it would be necessary to ship cannon from Cincinnati or Pittsburgh, as none were aboard. Ascertaining that Western Flotilla fleet captain Alexander M. Pennock (1814–1876), then also in St. Louis, could send a crew to Jeffersonville on short notice, Hull referred the matter to navy secretary Gideon Welles in Washington.

While Maj. Gen. Smith paused at Lexington, KY, to organize a provisional Confederate state government, units of his cavalry occupied Frankfurt on September 3, finding the roads to Cincinnati and Louisville largely undefended. Brig. Gen. Henry ("Harry") Heath (1825–1899) now approached Smith asking if he might attempt by quick march to capture either Cincinnati or Louisville. Heath waited all day for a reply. Finally, just before midnight, Smith came to his quarters and granted permission for him to "make a demonstration on Cincinnati." With four brigades of infantry and one of cavalry, he would set off for the Ohio River after sunrise.

In addition to rallying the citizenry of Cincinnati, Maj. Gen. Wallace on September 3 also started to bring in militia units from elsewhere in Ohio. Wallace also established a maritime patrol force, placing it under command of riverboat pilot John A. Duble (?–1901), former first master of the U.S. gunboat *Conestoga*. Wallace had met Duble late in 1861 when the general accompanied the timberclad on an early reconnaissance of the Tennessee River to the vicinity of Fort Henry. From the steamer *Emma Duncan* the former gunboatman assumed overall command of 16 steamers, armed with field pieces as ersatz warships.

At St. Louis that morning, Com. Hull received permission from Secretary Welles to commission the *Chillicothe* as Gov. Morton had requested. Additionally, Hull was permitted to "make any arrangement the emergency requires." At almost the same instant, a wire arrived from Cincinnati. General Wallace had taken charge of the *Indianola* and ordered her launched the next day. News of this development was wired on by Hull to Secretary Welles.

A new telegraph was next composed by the commodore to Cmdr. John M. Berrien (1804–1883), the assistant inspector of ordnance at the Fort Pitt Ordnance Works at Pittsburgh. Berrien would command the monitor *Monaonock* in 1864 and retire a commodore, but he was then the navy's man at the facility where its large cannon were cast. "Shells, cartridges, fuses, and other articles necessary to use two XI-inch guns" were required immediately for the *Chillicothe* at Jeffersonville, IN.

After his plea was off to Berrien, Hull next wrote to fleet captain Pennock, formally noting that the *Chillicothe* was under threat and asking him to send "with all possible haste" a force of 50 sailors and an officer "to take command of her temporarily." Assuming his request would be honored, he wired Capt. Brown saying that the men would be arriving as soon as possible and meanwhile Brown was to "go on with the preparations for the guns as fast as you can."

Also during the first week of September, Lt. Cmdr. Oscar C. Badger (1823–1899) arrived at Cincinnati from the East to serve as assistance ordnance inspector for the Western Flotilla. From his room in the Queen City's Broadway Hotel, he wrote to Com. Hull advising him of his arrival. After a briefing on the developing military situation, he visited the Marine Railway and interviewed President Carrell regarding progress with the *Indianola* and *Chillicothe*. Noting later that two XI-inch guns were aboard,

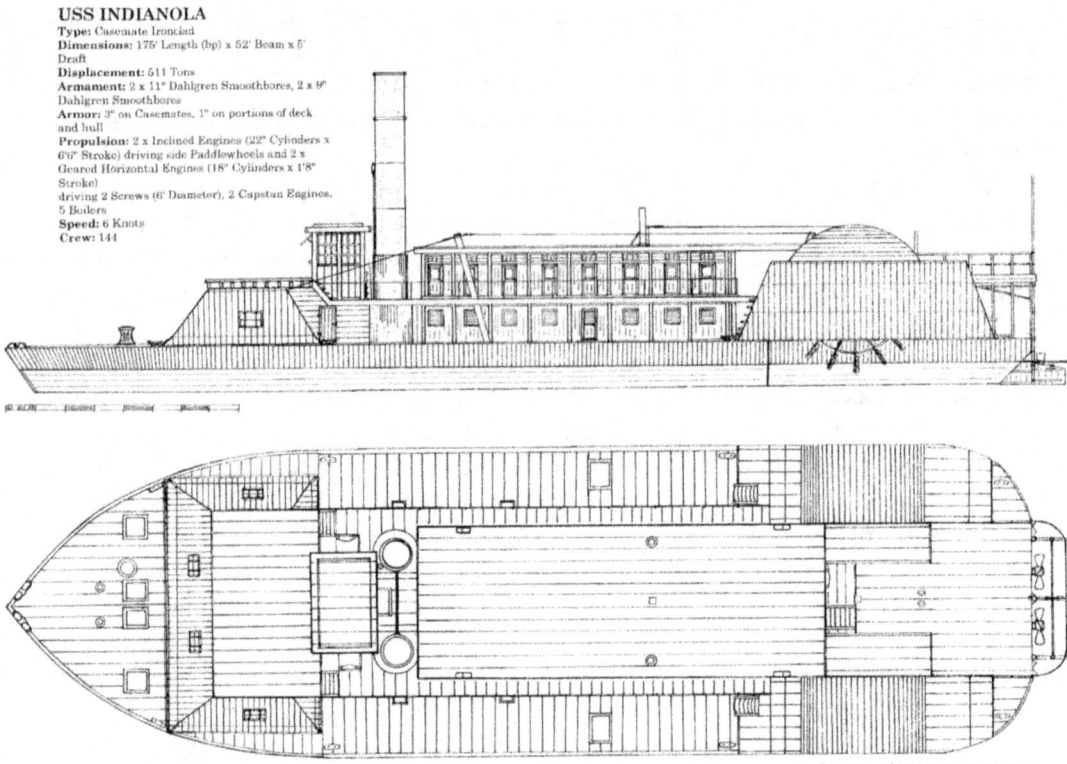

Indianola Impressed into Service. Taking charge of the incomplete *Indianola*, Maj. Gen. Lew Wallace had her launched on September 4 and readied to help in the defense of Cincinnati against Confederate forces believed approaching in strength. A pick-up crew was assembled under Lt. Cmdr. Oscar Badger and efforts were made to obtain armaments. Fearing that he could be bankrupted if the vessel were severely damaged or destroyed while in army hands, Capt. Brown protested to the government, which failed to support his claim (©2006, David J. Meagher; used with permission).

Badger was present at the launching of the *Indianola* on September 4 and began to handle her outfitting. With no ammunition available for the guns, he quickly took steps to procure a limited amount.. The ordnance man also inquired how he was to cover the considerable outlays being rung up for transportation, labor, etc., asking for the appropriate forms upon which to forward the expenses.

Badger also took it upon himself, working with Capt. Duble, to assemble a pick-up crew for the *Indianola* led by three Western Flotilla acting masters. The acting captain was the still available Edward Shaw, while the executive officer was John A. Yates (1815–1881), currently on medical leave, a Seminole War veteran and acting master wounded aboard the ironclad *Essex* during the February 1862 Battle of Fort Henry. It was at this time that the vessel's chief pilot, William J. ("W.J.") Anschutz (1811–1883) was appointed, while power-plant expert Thomas Doughty (1828–1896) transferred aboard from other Western Flotilla duties. Both longtime veteran steamboat officers, after being captured aboard the ironclad in February 1863 and then paroled, would return to the Federal river navy. Anschutz filled the same billet for the rest of the war aboard the *Forest Rose* (Tinclad No. 9), while Doughty ran the engine room aboard the monitor *Osage*.

About this same time, Com. Hull wrote to naval constructor Hartt at Jeffersonville indicating that two XI-inch cannon were en route. Hartt was ordered to contact Badger and determine when ammunition would be arriving. He was also to reinforce to Badger the commodore's desire to "do all he can to equip the boat."

As the gunboat outfitting at Jeffersonville and Cincinnati continued apace, Capt. Pennock, at the Cairo naval station, using authority previously received from the Western Flotilla commander, answered Com. Hull's appeal of September 3 and dispatched Lt. Cmdr. Joseph P. Sanford and a contingent of 50 sailors to take temporary charge of the *Chillicothe*. The contingent arrived within a day or two.[14]

Not yet having received communication from Lt. Cmdr. Badger regarding the acquisition of ordnance supplies and ammunition, Com. Hull, early on September 5, took it upon himself to seek them from the St. Louis military arsenal. Col. (later Brev. Brig. Gen.) Franklin D. Callender, Department of the Missouri chief of ordnance, was requested to expedite a hundred XI-inch shells and 10 barrels of cannon powder each to Jeffersonville and Cincinnati "for use of the United States gunboats." Badger did not mention that this was the total amount the vessel magazines could hold.

Hardly had he contacted the St. Louis Arsenal than Badger's Queen City dispatch arrived at Hull's office. Tearing it open, the commodore read of developments at Cincinnati and immediately answered his subordinate's queries with a single sentence: "You will remain on the Ohio River as long as the present necessity requires your presence and use all efforts to equip the boats at Cincinnati and Jeffersonville." After saying that the local arsenal would be sending shells and powder (but no fuses or primers), Badger was asked to also run a survey of the quantity of ordnance equipments, guns, etc., at various locations on the Ohio that might be diverted to the use of the flotilla.

The rush to outfit Brown's two ironclads continued without letup on September 5–6, as did the efforts of Maj. Gen. Wallace to bring reinforcements to the field and, largely using civilian fatigue parties, strengthen Cincinnati's lines of defense. On the latter day, Confederate advance parties rode into Walton, 20 miles to the south of the Queen City. When he arrived, Heath went into camp and sent scouts and other riders fanning out over the approaches to Cincinnati, seeking intelligence on Federal defensive preparations.

Fuming over the military takeover of the *Indianola*, Capt. Brown was worried that he and his partner could be bankrupted if the vessel was severely damaged or destroyed while in army hands. Laying the groundwork for any possible claim, Brown and McCord formerly protested Wallace's action. In a strongly worded message to Com. Hull, the St. Louisianans reemphasized that the vessel was no longer in their possession or under their control and management. Gen. Wallace had deprived them, they complained, of "completing said gunboat in accordance with the letter and spirit of our contract with the U.S. government."

When Hull received the Brown/McCord complaint the next morning, he forwarded it on to Secretary Welles. Never quite coming down on the side of the contractors nor finding truth in their assertions, the sailor noted that it "appears" that Wallace, reacting to the Cincinnati emergency, had taken over the *Indianola*, prepared her with "a military organization," and now had her "in his possession." As it "was desirable" that the ironclad be under the direction of the navy, Hull asked his superior to order a permanent commanding officer and crew to her, allowing the badly needed Badger to step away and get on with his full-time ordnance duties. While he was at it, Hull also requested that Cmdr. Sanford be relieved from and replaced aboard the *Chillicothe* because "his services are important at Cairo."

More ominously, a plot was uncovered against the *Chillicothe* on September 8. Union military authorities, according to a newspaper report, discovered a Confederate "special forces" stratagem to cross the Ohio River at some point near Louisville. Graycoat soldiers would then proceed down the Indiana shore to Jeffersonville and attack the gunboat, which was still largely defenseless even after the arrival of Sanford and his men. Fortunately for the boat, when Brig. Gen. Gordon Granger (1821–1876), whose men were stationed near New Albany, received information on the enemy intentions, he "adopted measures which efficiently circumvented the vandals in their meditated raid."[15]

While moving the *Chillicothe* on the day of the reported Rebel gambit, Capt. Brown was horrified when a half-inch seam opened over her engines, which occurrence was blamed entirely upon "the weakness inherent in her beamless deck." Observing the event, Lt. Cmdr. Sanford believed the boilers would fall right through the boat's bottom, which dropped some 10 inches. He was blunt when he wired Com. Hull, saying the gunboat was now "unsafe for guns or as a gunboat." In a similar vein to the same recipient, Sanford said of the *Chillicothe*, "I have never met with a more complete failure."

In his first order of business on September 10, Com. Hull wrote to Edwad Hartt, who had returned to St. Louis a few days earlier to work on the designs of the Eads ironclads. The naval constructor was to immediately return to Jeffersonville and inspect the *Chillicothe*, determining whether or not she was safe to carry cannon. As soon as he knew what repairs might be in order, he was to consult with Capt. Brown and give him such directions as would allow Brown to "repair the defect." On the other hand, if the two XI-inch guns could not be safely mounted, Hartt was to remove them to a safe location ashore and then return to St. Louis while Hull and the Navy Department determined what action should next be taken. The seam defect was pronounced fixed after iron straps were bolted over the problem area. In one of his regular reports to Secretary Welles on the condition of various vessels under construction, Com. Hull noted that the *Chillicothe* remained at Jeffersonville with her temporary 50-man crew from Cairo. The *Indianola* was taken over by the military at Cincinnati and was being prepared by it for service. Meanwhile, at New Albany, the *Tuscumbia* was receiving her machinery.

Also on September 10, Brig. Gen. Heath's outriders returned to his camp, bringing information regarding Union defenses at Cincinnati and the nearby area. Although Florence, KY, was protected, several of the roads leading to Covington were now in Confederate hands. There would be two days of skirmishing in the Florence area, none decisive.

During this stressful week, Lt. Sanford continued to despair over the *Chillicothe*'s belowdecks situation. The engine room was so hot and poorly ventilated that her "black gang" could not remain at their posts for over 20 minutes at a time. A visitor from the U.S. Army, when shown below, immediately bolted back up the ladder shouting that he

Ohio River Defense. As the Confederate threat to Cincinnati faded in September 1862, defenders from the city were released to reinforce other threatened Ohio River communities, including Louisville. Many went by steamboat, escorted by a number of ersatz Union gunboats under army command. It was shortly thereafter that Maj. Gen. Lew Wallace returned control of the *Indianola* to the Western Flotilla, which would become the U.S. Mississippi Squadron on October 1. In the waters off Louisville, meanwhile, the *Chillicothe*, a force in being, prepared to play a defensive role, which was, in the end, not required as Southern forces withdrew from the area (*Harper's Weekly*, September 20, 1862).

was suffocating and recommending in a voice large enough for all aboard to hear that the ironclad "be abandoned and all work stopped."

A message arrived at the camp of Brig. Gen. Heath on September 12 ordering him to withdraw to Lexington, where he, together with Maj. Gen. Smith, would await the arrival of Gen. Bragg. Limited contact continued in the Florence area for the next five days. On September 14, the *Cincinnati Daily Gazette* proclaimed, "Thanks to the promptitude of Generals Wright and Wallace, and the patriotism, courage and valor of the people, the Rebel movement toward Cincinnati has been frustrated and rolled back." David Smith, in his insightful Civil War Roundtable talk, concludes: "The scene shifted towards the western part of the state, as the cat and mouse games of Buell and Bragg began to unfold."

Over the next week or so, Gen. Bragg's force continued north toward Louisville, where, as Maj. Gen. Buell moved toward the same town, its defenders, under Maj. Gen. William "Bull" Nelson, prepared defenses. The Confederates now hoped to destroy the giant Federal depot town and, on top of that, smash the Louisville and Portland Canal

As Heath's men continued to depart the Covington area and Bragg bore down on Munfordville, KY, Gen. Wright, by the 19th, concluded that it was safe to send Union reinforcements to Louisville from the Queen City. That day, he ordered Capt. Duble, employing six of his ersatz gunboats, to guard a relief convoy of 15 steamers and a ferryboat downriver, transporting 13 infantry regiments. By late the next day, upwards of 40,000 Union soldiers had arrived at Kentucky's major riverfront city.

While the Union military now concerned itself with the protection of Louisville, U.S. Navy commanders continued to fret over Brown's ironclads. On September 13

Com. Hull learned that two Dahlgrens would be mounted on their Marsilly carriages aboard the *Chillicothe* within the week. Lt. Sanford, meanwhile, had continued to warn Hull regarding the gunboat's deficiencies. The heat in his cabin made it impossible to work belowdecks and he desperately required a transfer. The sympathetic commodore again wrote to the Navy Department requesting a replacement for *Chillicothe*'s acting commanding officer. Under the direction of naval constructor Hartt and acting captain Sanford, Capt. Brown's workmen mounted the two XI-inch Dahlgrens onboard the *Chillicothe* during September 17–19. A few days later, on September 21, Theodore E. Underwood (1836–1877), a civilian riverboat pilot, enlisted and was sent aboard to be the vessel's chief pilot.

Writing from Washington on September 15, Secretary Welles, in reaction to Hull's request, ordered that the commodore turn over the *Indianola* to RAdm. Charles H. Davis (1807–1877). The Western Flotilla commander would, in turn, provide her with officers and a crew.

Back in Cincinnati on September 18, Acting Master Shaw received a letter from Lt. Cmdr. Badger belatedly ordering him in writing to assume temporary command of the *Indianola*. Shaw, in turn, wrote to Com. Hull noting this development and the fact that, in his opinion, "work on the vessel is progressing finely under the supervision of the various contractors." He also held himself ready to "promptly and faithfully attend" any orders from Hull.

Though Shaw temporarily held day-to-day command on the scene, the military still controlled the *Indianola*. Believing that naval officers were quickly required for the *Indianola* to replace those temporarily placed in charge of her by authority of Maj. Gen. Wallace and Capt. Duble, Com. Hull sent a list of acting captain Shaw's complement to Western Flotilla commander Davis, then off Helena, AR, on September 19. It was attached to an order from the Navy Department requiring Hull to turn over the ironclad to Davis's jurisdiction and hence to any officer whom the admiral might designate as her captain.

Knowing the list would be read by Captain Pennock at Cairo, Hull asked for his review of the Shaw crew's qualifications—save the engineers who had received their commissions from the Navy Department—and his input in arranging a more permanent officer group. The vessel superintendent also revealed that the ironclad, while launched, was not yet ready for action. "The engines have not been tested as required by the contract," Hull emphatically stated, "and the screw engines require some changes in the values, which will be done soon." Noting that work on the *Chillicothe* and *Indianola* was interrupted by "their being kept in a state of readiness for service," Hull also informed Secretary Welles in a different communication that work continued on the *Tuscumbia*, though he had received no reports on exactly what progress had been made.

As Hull anticipated, Pennock as fleet captain read his report on the *Indianola* officer corps and rendered his opinion in a message sent to Davis on September 20. He recalled Shaw from the *Tyler*, but Yates he did not know, though "he is well spoken of." Acting master George L. Johnson had once served aboard the *General Bragg* but had been dismissed from the service earlier that summer. Pennock assured his superior that he could find enough sailors to man the Cincinnati vessel, but finding a qualified captain might be problematic. If necessary, he would personally travel to the Queen City for a few days "to organize this vessel without delay."

Given the end of direct Confederate interest in Cincinnati, such a step wouldn't be required. A few days afterward, RAdm. Davis had an interview with Lt. Cmdr. Oscar Badger, his assistant ordnance inspector then acting as de facto commissioned captain of the *Indianola*. The flotilla chief was opposed to the retention of Acting Master Shaw in command, as well as the officers appointed by Capt. Duble and others in the gunboat's crew, save engineering personnel, all of whom received their subsistence from the military's Cincinnati commissary. Davis agreed to send replacements.

Although there was no longer any danger to Cincinnati, the Union defenders of Louisville expected the Confederate invasion force under Gen. Bragg to reach their city by midnight on September 23. As preparations to meet an assault were pushed, the Southerners actually remained at Bardstown resting. Next day, Federal vigilance continued at a fever pitch. So as not to unnecessarily alarm the local citizenry, the *Louisville Daily Journal* cautioned its readers not to panic if large explosions were heard coming from the direction of the Ohio River. The *Chillicothe*, it warned, would be test firing its newly installed cannon.

Despite the completion of arrangements to do so, Lt. Sanford's new ironclad did not test fire her guns on September 24. "The reasons we did not learn," reported the newspapermen who were earlier alerted. Although it is very possible that the *Chillicothe*'s ordnance was not ready for live fire, it is also likely that the event was postponed when it was learned that Maj. Gen. Thomas L. Crittenden's 12,000 men, the first of 60,000 from Maj. Gen. Buell's army, had begun entering Louisville that afternoon, causing the town's defenders to breathe a sigh of relief: "Louisville is now safe."

Generals Bragg and Buell would continue to eye one another until they engaged in the October 8 Battle of Perryville, which ended the Confederate invasion of the Blue Grass State. Meanwhile, as September waned, work on the three Brown ironclads proceeded apace. On the 27th, Com. Hull briefly noted to Secretary Welles, "*Chillicothe* is at anchor in the river near Louisville, ready for service; the *Indianola* in commission at Cincinnati, working on the armor; the *Tuscumbia* is nearly ready to launch."[16]

It is not likely that Gideon Welles did more than glance at Hull's report upon its receipt. Bigger developments were about to occur with his Western operation. Back on July 16, Congress, having been made aware of the deficiencies inherent in the army operation of a large river gunboat fleet under naval direction, passed a law transferring the Western Flotilla to the U.S. Navy, effective October 1. During the planning interim, the Navy Department was required to make ready numerous adjustments in the operation of the inland fleet, which would be known as the Mississippi Squadron. The law also required organizational changes with other previously established squadrons and the process of changeover was time consuming.

Among the most important decisions Secretary Welles had to make with regard to the establishment of his new fighting force was who to appoint as its leader. Charles Henry Davis, in charge since June 17, was believed to lack initiative. Whether that view was accurate or not, the river sailor, one of the navy's greatest scientists, was seen as the best candidate to become chief of the Bureau of Navigation. After much consideration and consultation with others, up to and including President Lincoln, the decision was taken to bypass a number of more senior officers and give the post to 49-year-old Cmdr. David Dixon Porter (1813–1891), former commander of the West Gulf Blockading Squadron's Mortar Flotilla. Neither Welles nor his War Department opposite, Edwin Stanton, were fans of Porter, but both acknowledged that the energetic, ambitious, and sometimes unscrupulous sea dog was a fighter. Besides, his appointment would be as an *acting* rear admiral, a rank that could be withdrawn quite easily if the need arose. Welles, who actually met with Porter beforehand to discuss his advancement, officially informed his newest rear admiral of his appointment on October 1. Simultaneously, the Western Gunboat Flotilla, brought into being by Cmdr. John Rodgers and Flag Officer Andrew Hull Foote, under jurisdiction of the War Department, finished a little over 13 months of service.

Porter was directed to take up his duties at Cairo, IL, as soon as possible. However, on his way west, he was directed to make stops to inspect the various gunboats under construction at Pittsburg, Cincinnati, Mound City, and St. Louis. He left Washington, D.C., on October 9, planning to reach the headquarters of his new command about a week later. After reading through reports on the progress of the various new Western ironclads and visiting those abuilding at Pittsburg, Porter arrived in Cincinnati on October 12 to discuss the *Indianola* (and by implication the *Chillicothe* and *Tuscumbia*) with Joseph Brown. His initial impression of the gunboat, as conveyed to the navy's assistant secretary, Gustavus Vasa Fox, later that day, was not positive. "I was quite wild, I assure you," he began. There were too few cannon, the armor was too thin, and the crew spaces were abysmal. A variety of changes were required and ordered.

Some of the shortcomings, especially those relating to officer and crew accommodation, had long since been recognized by Brown and his associates, the contractor having tried to win approval from Washington for changes. "His ideas are all good," Porter believed, "and he seems an energetic fellow." Still, the Western boatmen were found to be too new to naval construction procedures, while the naval constructors and building superintendents did not understand steamboat creation. "Mr. Brown and myself would make up the internal plans in one hour, whereas he has to wait three weeks before he can get answers to his letters [of inquiry]."

Porter, who would continue to "have a good deal of confidence in Mr. Brown ... having found him very zealous, and doing the work for the government well and cheaply," admitted that he would not permit the contractor "to carry out his plans" for some of the ironclads' arrangements. Porter agreed with Brown's recommendations to deepen the vessels as well as his original August 14 plan to strengthen the bow of the *Indianola* "to perform the part of a ram." Brown agreed to make all of the other alterations Porter wanted, though not without objection to the addition of more iron and ordnance on the two larger gunboats.

Continuing on for a meeting with James B. Eads in St. Louis next day, RAdm. Porter, together with Com. Hull, naval constructor Hartt, and others, received a tour of the contractor's facilities, laid on by Eads in an effort to impress the sailors not only with the building of his ironclads but also the modifications that were changing purchased civilian steamers into small gunboats. The idea for these "light draughts" came from RAdm. Davis, who required a way of processing operations on streams too shallow for the ironclads. Showing off the *Signal* (Tinclad No. 8), the smallest warship present at Carondelet that day, her former owners, Thomas C. and Andrew J. Sweeney, told the admiral that the new gunboat, when finished, "would float on a heavy dew."

Porter came away from this inspection impressed and with the belief that "tinclads" were "admirably adapted for ascending shallow rivers." That night he wrote to Secretary Welles asking that the number available be boosted by ten, all to be armed with 24-pounder howitzers. While publicly endorsing the light-draught idea, Porter remained cautious regarding their birth in the St. Louis yards where heavy units were abuilding. Wanting as many of these little vessels in service as quickly as possible, he made a mental note to order the next several from Joseph Brown at Cincinnati.

Brown, mostly using his own plans, had demonstrated some skill to Porter in his construction of his ironclads, completion of which was momentarily expected. It should be possible for him at that point to work with the owners of his leased Queen City facility on a tinclad building program. Indeed, the admiral believed Brown could easily handle the rapid and simultaneous modification of several light draughts. Centering the work in Ohio would not only be of economic, hence political, benefit in the Cincinnati area, but it would also permit Porter's own newly appointed superintendent, Lt. Cmdr. Watson Smith (1825–1864), based on the local rendezvous, to oversee and assist in the work rather than Com. Hull and Constructor Hartt, whose primary emphasis would remain the large—and delayed—St. Louis ironclads *Choctaw* and *Lafayette* plus a growing number of river monitors.

Having arrived at Cairo on October 15, Porter immediately assumed command from RAdm. Davis, who returned to Washington, D.C., to take over the Bureau of Navigation. Jumping immediately to business, the new squadron chief launched into an organizational overhaul of his new command, reviewing the disposition and calibre of both men and equipment.[17]

Two days after assuming his new duties, RAdm. Porter received a letter from Lt.Cmdr. Badger at Cincinnati, covering a clothing requisition made by Acting Master Edward Shaw for the small crew of the *Indianola*. Badger, the squadron's assistant ordnance inspector, took this opportunity to review his past involvement with the still-incomplete ironclad, pointing out the need of her men for "clothing, hammocks, etc." Since RAdm. Davis had not acted, Badger politely but bluntly asked Porter to "appoint some one to command the vessel and retire me from further responsibility in the matter."

In fact, the new Mississippi Squadron commander had captain vacancies for two ironclads, as the billet aboard the *Chillicothe* was not yet occupied. In response to Badger's missive, Porter, on October 20, ordered Lt. Cmdr. George Brown (1835–1913) to command of the *Indianola* and sent Lt. Cmdr. John G. Walker (1835–1907) to Jeffersonville, IN, to take over the *Chillicothe*. Once in charge, both men would also open naval rendezvous facilities (recruiting stations) ashore to ship fleet crewmen, arranging to use the two ironclads as receiving ships.

The work of Acting Master Shaw was not overlooked. He was ordered to St. Louis to outfit the new light-draught *Juliet* (Tinclad No. 4). Promoted to the rank of acting volunteer lieutenant on November 7, Shaw became her first captain on December 14. Acting Master Yates was confirmed as the *Indianola*'s executive officer.

A native of Indiana, Brown was appointed a navy midshipman in 1849, advancing to the rank of lieutenant in 1856. He was aboard the steam sloop *Powhatan*, under Lt. David Dixon Porter, when she sailed to the relief of Fort Pickens, FL, in 1861. Later that year Brown was posted aboard the six-gun, 829-ton *Octarora*, which was attached during the fall to Porter's Mortar Flotilla, a division of RAdm. David G. Farragut's (1801– 1870) West Gulf Blockading Squadron. The Hoosier sailor participated in the capture of New Orleans in April 1862 and the squadron's sojourn up the Mississippi River to Vicksburg in May, June and July.

When RAdm. Porter took over the Mississippi Squadron in October, Brown was one of the men ordered to his growing new command. Remaining in the navy for decades thereafter, he was promoted to the rank of rear admiral in 1893. His relationship with the *Indianola*'s creator, as the former Alton mayor remembered, was cold, as the two men were "in no way connected with [one another], or related." Indeed, they did not even develop "any particular friendship for each other."

Brown's opposite number aboard the *Chillicothe* was a birth-year contemporary from New Hampshire, who was appointed a navy midshipman from Iowa in 1850. A Naval Academy graduate, John G. Walker was advanced to the rank of lieutenant in 1859. From the steamer *Connecticut* cruising the Atlantic Coast early in the Civil War, he was posted to command of the West Gulf Blockading Squadron gunboat *Winona* in the fall of 1861. Like Brown, Walker had participated in the capture of New Orleans in April 1862 and Farragut's passage upriver to Vicksburg in May, June and July before being detached and ordered to Cairo, IL, in mid–October. He too would remain in the navy after the war; he became a rear admiral a year after Brown.[18]

Walker was the first regular naval officer to assume command of a Brown-built ironclad, taking charge of the *Chillicothe* from Lt. Cmdr. Joseph Sanford on the morning of October 22. Having seen her from the riverbank upon his arrival, Walker thought she looked like a square-bowed scow, an observation confirmed even as he stepped aboard. After taking over her leadership, the New Englander made a hasty inspection with Sanford, who was anxious to return to his regular duties. The gunboat was weak, Walker noticed, and her hull lacked "knees or anything to strengthen her." This weakness, together with poorly attached armor, had caused the main deck leak already described (and others) during her transfer downstream from Cincinnati. In addition, heated cement was ordered run under iron plating to seal other openings.

Contractor Brown had ordered that she be braced with iron rods ("straps") running fore and aft under the deck and bolted through it. These would help to draw the boat's bow and stern together. Workmen, the two officers observed, were also putting up a light hurricane deck, running from abaft the wheelhouses forward to the top of the casemate. Additional strengthening would come through the use of a system of chains and rods called hog chains that paralleled the hurricane deck. The forward hog brace ran through the casemate diagonally and the aft hog brace met the chain before the wheelhouses. Moving belowdecks, Capt. Walker was appalled when shown the tiny spaces set aside for the officers and crew. These quarters were "small, badly ventilated, and extremely uncomfortable." Given that the *Chillicothe* had but one substantial main deck and a very light draft, historian Canney, from a future vantage point, was able to observe that "living conditions were comparable to the monitors," though without "forced-air ventilation." Walker immediately recommended that several small, inexpensive deckhouses be constructed on the *Chillicothe*'s main deck, for the "health and comfort of the officers." That idea was not implemented, though a small cabin for pantry and stores was built, and on occasion in warm weather was employed by sailors to hang their hammocks.

Continuing his introduction, the captain visited the ironclad's casemate, forward on the main deck. Here he found other laborers addressing gunports cut 5 inches in the wrong size. Wood and iron patches already applied were deemed deficient in strength. This would be remedied, to a measure, when the heavy gunport covers, or shutters, were affixed. The *Chillicothe*'s steering wheel, Walker learned, was in her gun tower, right between her two forward gunports. This was a major design flaw, inconvenient for helmsmen and gunners alike. The pilots, meanwhile, were so situated as to be able to only see straight ahead. This was, "in the river, I take it ... a grave objection." The blue-water veteran, innocent of either river gunboat or monitor experience, suggested the construction of "a pilot house abaft and joining the gun tower high enough to look over the top of the tower, with lookout holes in all directions." This recommendation was implemented.

Bidding Sanford farewell, Walker began to organize his small ship's company and the mechanics of his order to establish a rendezvous at Louisville. On October 25, he reported his observations to RAdm. Porter, noting his expectation that Capt. Brown would have the *Chillicothe* finished in about two weeks. Then, if the river level in the Ohio would just rise some six feet, his pilots could manage the vessel over the Falls of the Ohio and on to Cairo.[19]

A hundred miles to the northeast at Cincinnati on October 23, Lt. Cmdr. George Brown began preparations to open a naval rendezvous as RAdm. Porter was directed. It was hoped by the squadron commander that the Queen City, along with Louisville and St. Louis, could provide a thousand bluejackets for his growing fleet. However, before large numbers of recruits could be enticed to serve, bedding, clothing, and even the forms necessary for them to sign had also to be secured. A location ashore would soon be had for a suitable rendezvous facility and the shipping of men could begin immediately thereafter.

So far, Brown informed his chief two days later, twenty seamen were aboard the *Indianola*. Brought aboard irregularly during the Cincinnati emergency in September, all were rated seamen. There was also confusion in the appointment of firemen and coalheavers, who were all drawing $39 a month regardless of any naval rating. Brown expected to be able to straighten out the paperwork puzzle before future men were acquired and thereafter properly make all reports. Fortunately, Ensign Benjamin Sebastian had reported to the rendezvous and could take over much of the recruiting workload.

Capt. Brown's primary responsibility, along with Acting Master Yates, was to ready the *Indianola* for service, making certain that her construction was appropriately completed. Some of the building grew out of the letter contractor Brown had received from RAdm. Porter confirming arrangements made during the squadron commander's inspection earlier in the month. In light of reports received at the shipyard regarding the difficulties of the *Chillicothe* during her voyage to Jeffersonville, workmen were taking off her bow plates and rebending them to make certain that, upon reinstallation, they fit snugly. The rough edges and projections were also chipped away while more work was performed on the hold. A number of details were carried out on the strength of Porter's requirements and not necessarily those of naval constructor Hartt, who was not consulted any more than absolutely necessary.

Iron plate was bolted onto the vessel's sides and casemate and, in addition to putting up a pilot house not unlike that suggested by Lt. Cmdr. Walker for the *Chillicothe*, laborers built a light upper deck, complete with" light rooms" on the main deck. This description is somewhat misleading because the "light rooms" were actually a two-story deck cabin that stretched from the paddle-wheel housing forward to the pilothouse and forward casemate. In appearance, the structure was not unlike that found aboard most larger side-wheel commercial steamboats.

By order of RAdm. Porter, contractor Brown was also required to add a second 17-foot armored casemate at the stern of this vessel (as well as the *Tuscumbia*) between the paddle wheels, wherein would be mounted a pair of IX-inch Dahlgren smoothbores. Unprotected on the forward side, the sides of the oak casemate were covered with inch-thick plate and the after end with two inches. Gunports would allow the cannon to be trained four points or 45 degrees on each quarter. This new weight added several hundred more tons of displacement, thereby seriously increasing "both longitudinal and athwartship strains." A series of fore-and-aft hog chains, similar to those aboard the *Chillicothe* and the *Tuscumbia*, were put into place aboard the *Indianola* in an effort to remedy the difficulties.

When the three ironclads were finished, their displacement would be progressively greater on an alphabetical basis. *Chillicothe* came in around 395 tons, while *Indianola* was 511 and *Tuscumbia* 915. By way of comparison, the City Series Pook turtle *Carondelet* was 512 tons and the mighty *Benton* was 633 tons.

With structural work nearly completed on the *Chillicothe* by this time, Capt. Walker was ordered to proceed downstream a short distance below Jeffersonville on a 72-hour shakedown cruise. Everything aboard the new ironclad would be tested, with special emphasis on her big guns and the power plant. Having "got down the river" that first week of November, the new warship was ordered to test fire her cannon at targets identified on uninhabited spots along the riverbank. Giant shells were lobbed at random ranges from 1,000 yards down to 100 yards. When these initial shoots were concluded, Walker and his gunners were pleased to note that there was, in the words of an accompanying newsman, "no recoil, no shaking of decks, no bursting of turrets, or giving away of gun gear." In short, the ordnance tests were successful "in every sense."

Upon her return to Jeffersonville, the *Chillicothe* was run at full speed. She turned in a handsome top performance of eight miles an hour against the Ohio River current, two miles per hour more than her contract required. Tying up to the building dock on the 26th, Walker wired a report to Com. Hull, while the contractor's men returned aboard to finish off her construction and the reporter filed his story. The first of the "Ohio River Iron-clads" would soon be "actively employed."

On October 27, Com. Hull dispatched his weekly report to the Navy Department concerning progress made toward the completion of the Western gunboats. Regarding contractor Brown's work, the naval officer noted that a soon-to-be finished light hurricane deck was being installed aboard the *Chillicothe*. Laborers were at work installing plating on the sides and casemates aboard the *Indianola*. They were also putting up the pilot house, "light rooms on deck," and a light upper deck. Onboard the *Tuscumbia*, men in the employ of the Tellons were working "on the bevel timbers on the sides, the inside flooring, etc." The hold was already deepened three feet, 10 inches. Lt. Cmdr. Badger, meanwhile, had also been dispatched to New Albany in order to place within her casemates "the pivot centers, circles, etc."

Inspection of the construction process at this time was later pointed out to be spotty at best. It was suggested that the superintendent of the vessel neglected his duty and actually "injured her efficiency in the most important point." That point, and others, was identified in the U.S. Navy armored vessel report of 1864:

> The *Tuscumbia* looks as if she could stand anything. The material used in her construction is of the best kind. The only difficulty is the manner in which the iron is put on, and the want of sufficient backing of wood under the iron.... The arrangement of the magazine is due to the ordnance officer [Badger] who had charge. It would have been much better on deck, exposed, than the way it is now. The vessel depends too much on hog chains, the cutting of one of which brings all the weight on her ends.[20]

The *St. Louis Daily Republican*, following up its report on the shakedown of the *Chillicothe*, published an update on the construction progress of the *Indianola*. Details concerning her ordnance, armor, and machinery were glowing and exceptionally detailed. For example, it was revealed that her two 11-inch Dahlgrens were "exceedingly smooth and beautiful," each weighing 1,570 pounds and capable of throwing a 182-pound cannonball two miles. The "plating or slabs of iron" was secured to her hull "by long iron bolts." Waxing even more eloquently, though inaccurately, it was alleged that "officers and crew have comfortable berths in their quarters below, which resemble the Liverpool steamers." *Indianola* was expected to be ready for service within a fortnight.

Com. Hull was greatly incensed when the news reports of the *Chillicothe*'s trial and the *Indianola*'s building appeared in the St. Louis press on November 8. He was particularly unhappy that the correspondents had provided technical details regarding the vessels, down to the thickness of her armor plate in various locations onboard and the functioning of their machinery. Such descriptions, he reasoned, gave intelligence to the Confederacy. That morning Hull wrote to Lt. Cmdr. Brown in Cincinnati, as well as to Lt. Cmdr. Walker and presumably contractor Brown, reminding them of Navy Department regulations prohibiting the presence of correspondents during warship trials or other unauthorized or unofficial communications with the press, in order to prevent intelligence reaching the Confederacy. As his vessel was the latest to surrender her secrets to the newspapers, Lt. Cmdr. Brown was enjoined to take special security precautions and, if he could determine the source of the story regarding his gunboat, to forward the name of the offender(s). There is no evidence that the *Indianola*'s commander ever fingered a source of the story concerning his vessel. Given the glowing terms in which she—and also the *Chillicothe*—were depicted, it is not unreasonable to believe that the descriptions might have been given by Joseph Brown himself and that the reporter involved may have been the same one who interviewed the former Alton mayor back in late July.[21]

By the middle of November, Maj. Gen. Ulysses S. Grant and William T. Sherman (1820–1891), in collaboration with RAdm. Porter, had initiated plans for a second

Federal effort to overwhelm Vicksburg and "liberate" the last 250 miles of the Mississippi held by the Confederacy. While Grant came in from the East, Sherman and Porter would undertake an amphibious operation up the Yazoo River. If the strategy worked, the Southern citadel would be squeezed between the Federal forces and the wide river.

Such an expedition had been the talk of the river—and of newspapermen reporting from its local towns—for some time. On November 11, Junius Henri Browne of the *New York Tribune* told his readers that there was considerable doubt in his mind—and Porter's, he presumed—that a water-borne campaign could get "fairly under way before a rise occurs in the river." Still, Porter was beginning to intensify naval preparations, pre-positioning as many warships and supply vessels as possible down the Mississippi. Naturally, he was quite anxious that the powerful new Brown ironclads join his squadron at the advance base at Helena, AR, as soon as possible.

As part of his fleet reorganization, RAdm. Porter, on Monday, November 10, ordered Lt. Cmdr. Walker of the *Chillicothe* to transfer into the same billet aboard the Pook turtle *Baron de Kalb*, formerly the *St. Louis*, then at Cairo. One of the seven original Eads ironclads and renamed earlier in the fall, she would be active throughout the campaigns to conquer Vicksburg and Walker would remain aboard her until the following August.

Walker's successor aboard the *Chillicothe* was a Hoosier, Lt. Cmdr. James P. Foster (1827–1869), recently come West from the North Atlantic Blockading Squadron. Arriving in Indiana from Cairo on Friday, November 14, he learned that the contractor's work was all but finished and that his new command was "ready to leave at any moment." Having found that Lt. Cmdr. Walker's rendezvous was not yet up and running, he rented a room ashore in Louisville for the work and began shipping men the following Monday.

It was hoped that within a week or so it would be possible for the *Chillicothe* to steam downstream to Cairo. As the gunboat was entirely too large to go through the local canal, her further movement was entirely dependent upon the Ohio rising enough to permit her to float over the rocks on the falls. The stream was also rising at Cincinnati, where workers were completing the *Indianola*. With the summer dry spell ending, this deepening water level was soon anticipated. On October 22, a Louisville correspondent arriving home by boat from Cincinnati observed that the river would, within a day or so, "doubtless feel the water here, which is pouring into it from all the upper tributaries, and then these powerful adjuncts to the Mississippi flotilla, released from the long drought blockade, will soon be in active service." The next day, Lt. Cmdr. Brown at Cincinnati confirmed to RAdm. Porter that the level of the Ohio River was, indeed, rising, and that he expected to depart the Queen City within a week. The captain informed his superior that he had a few requisitions to make in the meantime and hoped to learn where they would be filled. "Mr. Brown furnishes very few articles, but, as there will be a scarcity of room," the lieutenant commander said, "requisitions will necessarily be small."

Still, on a positive note, the contractor had assured him that the remaining construction work could "be done twice as fast at Louisville as at this place." Besides, with the ironclad gone, Brown could concentrate on converting more steamers into tinclads. Some of those finished were ready to sail, abeit with lean crews. RAdm. Porter, though, as he had done earlier, could not resist requiring certain improvements. For example, in December he ordered gun ports cut a foot higher than originally planned.

The water level did not actually rise as fast as anticipated and would not permit the departure of either of the ironclads as quickly as their commanders had anticipated. On November 24 a frustrated RAdm. Porter ordered the *Chillicothe*'s pilot, Theodore Underwood, to conduct a survey of the river stage between Louisville and Cairo, looking to see whether it would soon be possible to move the heavy gunboat downstream. Several days were required to make the examination and the findings were negative. As the ship awaited a favorable water stage, she was formally commissioned on December 3.

The water level at Cincinnati grew enticingly, but still too slowly to permit the *Indianola* to make an early departure. On November 26, RAdm. Porter, after giving Lt. Cmdr. Brown instructions on how to turn over the Queen City rendezvous to subordinate officers, directed him to steam to Louisville as soon as possible, bringing every man shipped. There he would cross the Falls of the Ohio at the first opportunity and he was cautioned not to lose his first chance "to get down." Not quite as ready to cast off as his commander might like, Brown delayed further, bothering Porter at Cairo again on December 2 with additional questions concerning the Cincinnati naval rendezvous and certain requisitions. Somewhat exasperated, the squadron commander wrote him back two days later: "Don't wait for anything, but get here, if you have nothing onboard but a handspike!"

Even as preparations continued for the joint army-navy expedition up the Yazoo River he was supporting with Maj. Gen. William T. Sherman, Porter was unable to get his newest ironclads downstream. On December 12 he sent a mixed report to Secretary Welles. Although his officers were able to recruit a bare minimum of men to man the *Chillicothe* and *Indianola*, the two giants could not join the Yazoo operation "for want of sufficient water to enable them to come down."

On December 19, the *Indianola* conducted a 72-hour shakedown cruise in the Ohio River downstream from Cincinnati. Although a speed check was not conducted, ordnance and machinery drills were. As Com. Hull informed Captain Pennock on January 12, these were "reported satisfactory." By Christmas, Lt. Cmdr. Brown was able to relax slightly in the knowledge that he had a complete complement of officers, even if his enlisted crew spaces still had openings. In addition to Acting Master Yates, the ship was home for two acting ensigns, William S. Pease (1832–1915) and Thomas McElwill; acting assistant paymaster Thomas Carstairl; chief engineer Thomas Doughty; first assistant engineer Wallace B. Hovey; second assistant engineer, David Hawksworth; four third assistant engineers, Thomas E. Scholes, George Wardell, George A. Boice, and Josephus Blake; four acting master's mates, William Shaw Ward (1843–1917), Gardner Fitch, P.H. Hipps, and Lewis Kenny; one acting gunner, Joseph E. Keys; and pilots William Anschutz and Daniel V. Stewart. The veterans Anschutz and Doughty had been with the vessel since September, while Ensign Pease had joined in October (following his release from a Confederate POW camp the following summer he would join engineer Doughty aboard the monitor *Osage*). Acting assistant surgeon Henry Mixer would arrive by transfer from the *Chillicothe* a few days later.

As the year wore down, there was good news from the yards of the Cincinnati

Marine Railway. By December 20, Fleet Captain Pennock had learned that sufficient funds ($56,000) had been received from the Navy Department to cover the cost of converting six Queen City tinclads at $8,000 a copy. All of the money that could be spared from the coffers of the fleet paymaster were sent to Joseph Brown to help defray his expenses.

On December 28, the *Detroit Free Press*, along with other Midwestern newspapers, announced, "The gunboat *Indianola* has been examined in Cincinnati and accepted by the government." She would leave for down the river "on the present rise of water in the Ohio River." In fact, the official paperwork would take a couple of weeks longer, as Com. Hull still needed an official release from the Bureau of Construction in Washington. On New Year's Day 1863, Lt. Cmdr. Foster passed orders for the 385-ton *Chillicothe* to raise steam and depart Jeffersonville for Cairo. Joseph Brown's two vessels built in the Queen City were now finished and those interested in the completion of his contract could now focus full-time upon the wide giant at New Albany.[22]

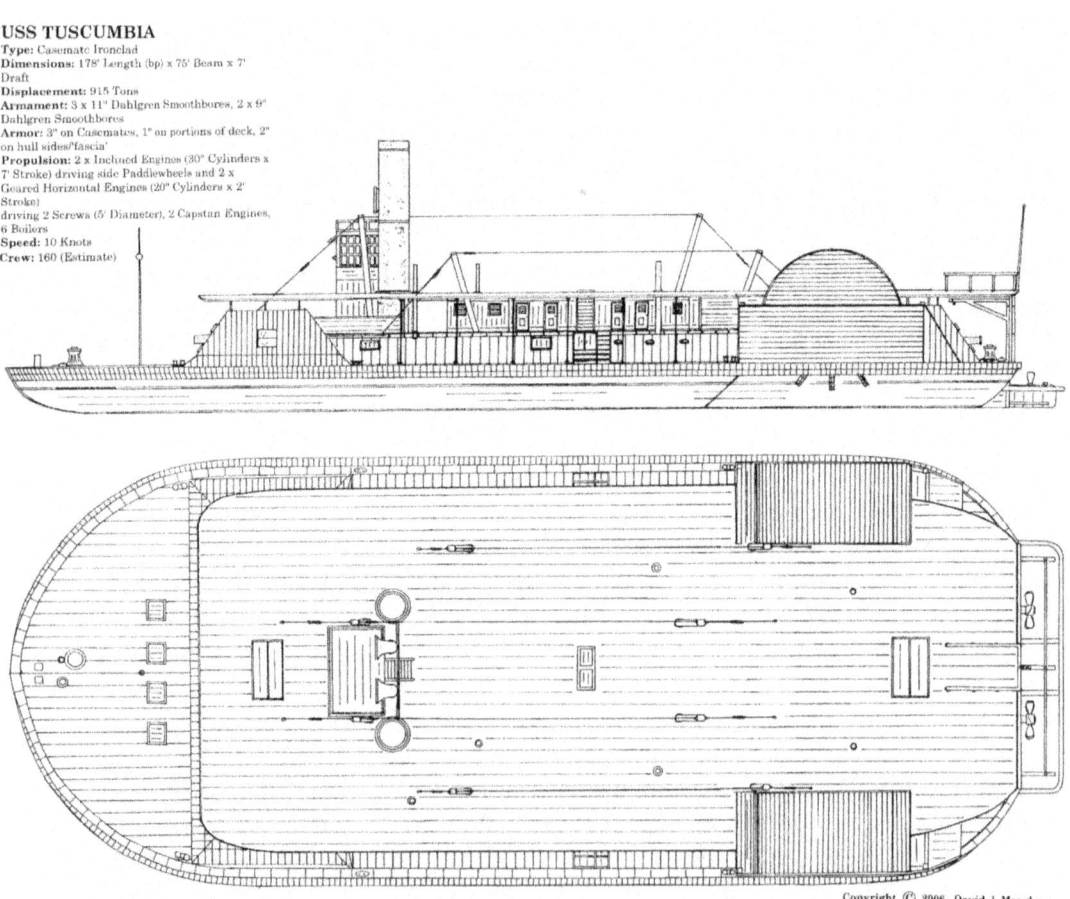

***Tuscumbia* Is Last.** The widest U.S. Navy vessel built prior to the 20th century, the *Tuscumbia* was the last of Capt. Joseph Brown's three ironclads constructed, not being launched until December 12, 1862. Her beam was so extreme in order to allow the shipping of a third 11-inch Dahlgren smoothbore cannon. Otherwise, her outfit was similar to that of *Indianola* (©2006, David J. Meagher; used with permission).

While RAdm. Porter and his lieutenant commanders, Brown and Foster, pushed to get the *Chillicothe* and *Indianola* to the war zone, at New Albany the *Tuscumbia*, the largest of the three new ironclads, was under construction. On November 29 readers of the *New York Times* learned that her 11-inch guns had just arrived and would "soon be placed in position." The gunboat was quietly launched on December 12 and, according to Donald Canney, "had the dubious distinction of being the widest U.S. Navy vessel built" prior to the 20th century. Referred to as "the broad giant," *Tuscumbia* "was probably the maximum width possible in a flat-bottomed boat." There was little newspaper coverage of her entry into the Ohio, perhaps because at this time journalistic concern was focused on the local activities of the North's real and imagined internal war opponents, the Copperheads and the Knights of the Golden Circle (KGC). Dissatisfaction with the politics, economics, and war aims of the Lincoln administration had resulted in the formation of an opposition movement, largely centered on radical elements within the Democratic Party, of unknown size. Nowhere was this potential insurgency considered to be stronger threat to the Union than in southern Indiana. By the last quarter of 1862, rumors of impending Copperhead and KGC actions around the Hoosier state were rife. The latter, in particular, was, according to Jennifer Weber, "supposedly plotting to depose the governor, seize the state arsenal and its 15,000 arms stored there, and establish a new confederacy of the Western states.

At New Albany, speculation regarding war opponents in the local, regional and national press worried many manufacturers in industries supporting the Federal cause. William and Martin Tellon grew so concerned for the safety of the unfinished *Tuscumbia* that they appealed for protection to Com. Hull on December 30. That officer turned once more to his ordnance expert, Lt. Cmdr. Badger, ordering him to the vessel's Indiana construction site to ascertain the cause of the subcontractor's concerns and, if necessary, make arrangements to either protect her in place or remove her down the river to Mound City or Cairo. Simultaneously, Hull requested that Fleet Captain Pennock dispatch a 20-man squad of U.S. Marines, plus an officer and sailors, from Cairo, to the *Tuscumbia* for temporary guard duty. Pennock responded from Cairo on New Year's Eve that unhappily there were neither sailors nor marines to spare. So desperate was the squadron for manpower that three newly arrived tinclads could not be crewed. If he felt guards were really necessary, Hull was advised to approach the military at New Albany for a protective force.

When Badger arrived at New Albany, he found that the Tellon brothers had, in fact, panicked. There was no immediate pressing requirement for active duty boat guards and the U.S. Army command in the area had already assigned convalescent soldiers to provide protection. "Even in her present condition," he found, "with her guns in position and ammunition on board, she is a most formidable vessel." Formidable, indeed, with three 11-inch Dahlgrens in her forward casemate and two 9-inch in her rear casemate.

Still, the ordnance man reported, enhanced precautions should be taken in order to prevent the enemy from acting on any temptation "to get possession of, or to destroy her." The vicinity around the town "swarms with secessionists and the guard of convalescent soldiers is not so reliable as could be wished." He would feel much better if the *Tuscumbia* could be "furnished with a crew of at least two officers and 30 men" equipped with small arms, along with an engineer and two firemen.[23]

Copperhead Threat. Dissatisfaction with the politics, economics, and war aims of the Lincoln administration led to the formation of an opposition movement of unknown size, largely centered on radical elements within the Democratic Party. Nowhere was this potential insurgency considered to be a stronger threat to the Union than in southern Indiana. William and Martin Tellon grew so concerned for the safety of the unfinished *Tuscumbia* that on December 30, 1862, they appealed for protection to U.S. Navy leaders at Cairo, IL, who did not have the manpower to help. Lt. Cmdr. Badger, dispatched to check the claim, found that the Tellon brothers had, in fact, panicked. There was no immediate pressing requirement for active duty boat guards and the U.S. Army command in the area had assigned convalescent soldiers to guard the nearly finished "broad giant" (*Harper's Weekly*, February 27, 1863).

While workers from the Tellon shipyard continued to fashion the *Tuscumbia*, Capt. George Brown at Cincinnati received direct movement orders from RAdm. Porter on January 3, 1863. Having heard that the Ohio River was higher than, in fact, it was, the squadron commander, aware that the gunboat had passed her trials and been accepted, wanted Brown to steam the *Indianola* down to Louisville and make ready to pass the Falls of the Ohio even though his crew was still quite short. On January 7, the same day the *Chillicothe* arrived at the Cairo fleet base, the *Indianola* halted at Jeffersonville. Announcing the news in a message to Porter, then off the mouth of the Yazoo River, Captain Alexander Pennock promised to have the former quickly coaled and provisioned and expressed his hopes that the water up the Ohio would rise quickly enough that the *Indianola* might soon get over the falls.

Although the boat was designed for a crew of 144, that of the *Chillicothe* was both short and mixed, featuring a few veterans and many recruits. Included among officers were a large number of men with previous riverboat experience. A few weeks later, a reporter from the *Chicago Daily Tribune* would reveal their names in yet another vessel profile. Thus we learn that, in addition to Capt. Foster, his clerk Alfred Ryan, and chief pilot Theodore Underwood, the *Chillicothe* hosted two acting ensigns, William T. Powers and Walter Muir; two master's mates, Henry Baker and Horace J. Hamond; acting assistant surgeon Henry Mixer (soon replaced by William C. Foster, Jr.); acting assistant paymaster James H. Hathaway (1825–1924); chief engineer H.W. Hardy; first assistant engineer J.D. Rice; second assistant engineer, Charles W. Reynolds; four third assistant engineers, John J. Briggs, Watson B. Fleming, Daniel Lantz, and Charles Trotter, who would replace Rice within the month; and the second pilot, David. M. Doyden. Ensign Muir was tapped to serve as executive officer.

The "Chilly Coffee," as her crew had come to know her, departed the tip of Illinois within a few hours en route to join RAdm. Porter's flotilla. En route south, her men, under Acting Ensigns Powers and Muir, conducted numerous gun and other drills and amazed passing vessels with her unusual architecture. Below Memphis on March 10 she encountered the famous old Pook turtle *Carondelet* paddling north from the war zone under her intrepid commander, Henry Walke (1808–1896). A naval officer since 1827 and a renowned Romantic painter, the taciturn captain would become the last commander of the Mound City naval station and then retire as a rear admiral. During the hour-long rendezvous, two of *Carondelet*'s crewmen who were keeping diaries penned their impressions. Coxswain John G. Morrison observed, "In the forenoon, we met the new style gunboat *Chillicothe* on her way down to join the fleet. She is the queerest-looking specimen for a warship that ever I seen. She may be a useful boat, but I vow she is not a handsome one." Captain's Steward Terry P. Waters revealed that at "9:30 the U.S.G. Boat *Chillicothe* hove in sight. She rounded to and Capt. Walke went on board. All eyes were turned to this new novelty of naval architecture, which appeared to be nothing but a scow, with a steam-engine on board, and a pilot-house with 2 Eleven inch guns mounted inside."

Pennock at Cairo and Brown at Jeffersonville were officially notified on January 12 that contractor Brown had completed his work and that the Bureau of Construction and Repair had officially approved acceptance of the *Indianola*. She was, therefore, released that day to her captain and the leadership of the Mississippi Squadron. Two days later, the ironclad was formally commissioned in a low-key ceremony. Although the *Indianola* remained above the Falls of the Ohio continuing her wait for a river rise, the *Chillicothe* by January 16 had arrived at Fort Hindman, in the Arkansas River, where she joined the squadron flagboat *Black Hawk*, the Pook turtle *Louisville*, and three tinclads. Porter had still not departed the scene of victory following the January 9–11 Battle of Arkansas Post.[24]

About the time the *Chillicothe* arrived in the Arkansas River, the *Indianola* was finally able to depart Jeffersonville, getting over the Falls of the Ohio on January 19 and speeding downstream toward Cairo, IL. Joseph Brown later remarked, "Her log to Cairo showed that, with half her complement of firemen, she made 11½ miles per hour, and could make seven miles per hour upstream." The ironclad, unlike the Pook turtles, handled easier, so much so that Brown bragged "her pilots said she was the easiest handled vessel they ever steered." The *Indianola* arrived at the Mississippi Squadron upriver base during early morning on January 23. There the resident scribe from the *New York*

Times caught sight of her as she put into the anchorage and in a brief notice to his readers proclaimed her "a great addition to the active gunboat fleet on the Mississippi."

Promising to have the large new gunboat victualled and coaled, Fleet Captain Pennock messaged RAdm. Porter the next day that the *Indianola* would depart for "down the river" on the 26th, carrying several personal items for the squadron commander that had arrived from the East. While she was en route three days later, Porter, at the mouth of the Yazoo River, drew up a new order of battle for his anchored vessels, including two ironclad divisions. Captain Henry Walke was placed in command of the 1st Division, which included the *Chillicothe*, while the *Indianola* was assigned to the 2nd Division under Lt. Cmdr. S. Ledyard Phelps (1824–1885). A participant in the laying of the Atlantic cable, the brother-in-law of Cmdr. John Rodgers joined the Western Flotilla in early 1861 and remained with it (and the Mississippi Squadron) until the end of the 1864 Red River campaign, after which he resigned to join the merchant marine.

Contractor Brown's two ironclads were both available to the Western naval command by the beginning of February. A week into that month, RAdm. Porter sent Secretary Welles a lengthy report on the activities of his ships, as well as observations on the new pair, which had "not been tried under fire." Based on reports received from different quarters concerning their construction, there was doubt over their ability to "bear battery" when both were tried a short time hence. He continued: "The details of these vessels are not credible to the superintendents of the work, and many things have been slighted which a naval constructor should not have overlooked. Though the vessels are better than I expected, they show a great want of attention on the part of those overlooking the work. With the exception of their batteries (XI-inch guns), they are not as serviceable as the old Pook vessels." Porter had yet to see the finished *Tuscumbia*, which "drags along slowly, though promised three weeks ago." On January 13 the admiral directed the veteran captain of the timberclad gunboat *Lexington*, Lt. Cmdr. James W. Shirk (1832–1873), to take over the giant at New Albany. As soon as he had "read himself" into command, Shirk was to proceed up to Erie, PA, and spend a week recruiting her crew.

An Erie County native, Shirk had joined the navy in 1849, serving as a midshipman during the 1850s' "Opening of Japan." Aboard the *Lexington* since early 1862, he participated in the April Battle of Shiloh, the June White River Expedition, and the Chickasaw Bayou campaign in December. Late in 1863 he would take over the squadron's Seventh District, serving on the Tennessee River and becoming the longest-serving officer in unit history. He would die of pneumonia while on Washington, D.C., duty.

While waiting for construction and recruiting to progress, perhaps the reader will enjoy a visit to *Tuscumbia*'s New Albany construction site.[25]

The 915-ton *Tuscumbia* was nearly finished by the end of January and it was fully expected she would leave for Cairo by mid–February. Her shakedown cruise was undertaken January 26–27 with no major problems encountered with either her machinery or her ordnance. Her hog chains appeared to steady her hull as hoped. Along for the ride, contractor Brown did later remind RAdm. Porter of the importance of having deepend her hold: "I deepend the hold of the *Tuscumbia* three feet 10 inches and yet, when she is running upstream full speed, the water is ready to wash her decks; and what would have been the case if I had not deepened her? Why, just as you [had earlier] stated ... a perfect failure of both—yes, all three vessels."

On January 28 the *New Albany Daily Ledger* published a glowing report on the new ironclad. Despite the news blackout imposed by the Navy Department and Com. Hull earlier, the unnamed writer had obviously interviewed William and Martin Tellon, as well as Joseph Brown, in the process of preparing his story. "This monster ironclad vessel," the piece began, "is rapidly approaching completion and two weeks hence with all her armament aboard will be ready to sail to any point indicated by Com. Porter." One of the "largest vessels in the Western fleet," the *Tuscumbia* "in strength of timbers, imperviousness of her coat of iron mail, staunchness of build, and completeness of outfit ... will rank among the very best of the iron-clads yet built." After reviewing the vessel's dimension, power plant, and armored protection, the newsman went on to praise the builders claiming, "The carpenter work of the boat is one of the most substantial jobs ever done upon a vessel and reflects the highest credit upon the contractor, the late Capt. Peter Tellon, as well as upon every man engaged upon it. Since the death of Captain T., his sons, William and Martin Tellon, have superintended the woodwork, and had it finished up in the most satisfactory manner. We cannot, indeed, say too much in praise of the staunchness and superiority of the workmanship in every department of the boat." The story continued, adding other details not readily available in modern vessel histories: "The *Tuscumbia*'s engines and machinery were made by the well-known firm of McCord & Co., St. Louis, and is one of the best and most perfect jobs ever set up on a boat. The setting up of the machinery, the iron plating, and all the iron work of the boat has been personally superintended by Mr. C.W. McCord and gives evidence of his superior skill as a mechanic." A few other points need to be quoted from the *Daily Ledger* account, which was later reprinted in the *Scientific American*: "A bulwark of iron, loop-holed for musketry, is placed around her guards. Her speed will be about 12 miles an hour against the current. She will be manned by 150 marines [i.e., naval officers and sailors]." With a crowd of 10,000 cheering people watching from the shore, the *Tuscumbia* departed New Albany for Cairo, IL, at 5:00 p.m. on February 28.

And so ends our tour.

The next morning, Joseph Brown wrote to RAdm. Porter confirming that the vessel was on her way downstream. "This winds up the contract for the three vessels," the one-time steamboat captain indicated. Having already turned his attention full time to the mass modification of light draughts, the contractor nevertheless took time to reflect in his letter upon certain supervisory and fiscal concerns. While refraining from directly criticizing Porter, a patron for future alteration business, Brown made known his intense displeasure with what he perceived to be the high-handedness of naval constructor Edward Hartt. The latter had recently, and again, refused, over Brown's lack of notification on a given point, to recommend a progress payment to the contractor for work Porter required on the ironclads. "I will never again work under such men as were sent to superintend me," Brown lamented, meaning both Com. Hull and constructor Hartt. About this time, Hull and Hartt were ordered to concentrate their efforts on speeding construction centered in St. Louis; other superintendents would be assigned to Cincinnati with the support of a sympathetic Porter.

Revealing that the "government have only paid me about half on the *Tuscumbia*" and had yet to provide "a single cent" on three tinclads he had on the ways, Brown highlighted a second worry. He informed the admiral, "If you do not help me through this [financial] difficulty, I shall be a ruined man." Feeling much the way Eads must have when he built the Pook turtles on his own credit, Brown cried, "I am largely in debt. It makes me feel like going back into the woods and living on corn bread, rather than be harassed to death." Brown's financial concerns were eventually alleviated when he was paid in full for all three of his ironclads. The total was $503,022.25 ($92,690.00 for the *Chillicothe*; $182,662.52 for the *Indianola*; $227,669.73 for the *Tuscumbia*). Adding required modifications had raised the finished price by $54,000 over the original contract sum.

During the months that immediately followed, Capt. Brown may have inwardly wished his protests over the lack of freedom in construction practices granted by Hull and Hartt had been less intense. When men other than naval constructor Hartt came to voice concern over the viability under fire of his three ugly sisters, the one-time Alton mayor found it necessary to publicly defend his creations.

The Mississippi Squadron commander continued to regard contractor Brown with pleasure, taking his side in the dispute over the qualities of constructor Hartt and encouraging the one-time steamboat captain as he moved steadily ahead with his Cincinnati and New Albany partners to develop an efficient process for rapid warship conversion. As 1863 progressed, the time for tinclad alteration from purchase to commissioning accelerated to a period as short as five weeks. This success, coupled with the delivery of other ironclad and monitor units to the squadron by various contractors, allowed criticism of his ironclad boats to be muted, filed away for future use or conveniently forgotten. RAdm. Porter gave a benediction for the *Chillicothe*, *Indianola*, and *Tuscumbia* in a February 1864 report to Washington. "The builders never claimed that they should be considered more than temporary expedients with which to harass the enemy," wrote the admiral. That said, the trio "certainly may be considered very good vessels, and have fairly repaid all the money spent on them, taking into consideration the work they have done."

The physical limitations of the *Chillicothe*, *Indianola*, and *Tuscumbia* revealed in combat must be included as we now chronicle "the work they have done." Their individual wartime service and eventual fates fill the next three chapters.[26]

4

The Chillicothe *Goes to War: Yazoo Pass and Red River*

As 1863 began, the military forces of the United States had recaptured much of the lower Mississippi River from the Confederacy, including Memphis and New Orleans. The sticking point to complete supremacy lay in a stretch of the stream anchored by the fortress cities of Vicksburg and Port Hudson, LA. The former had already been subjected to two unsuccessful Federal campaigns (June–July and December 1862), the most recent ending as the new year started.

To prevent harassment of their supply lines, Union forces steamed up the Mississippi and in a short January 9–11 operation captured the Southern bastion of Fort Hindman at Arkansas Post on the Arkansas River. However, while the bulk of the Mississippi Squadron's gunboats were attending to this matter, regional Confederate leaders took the opportunity to gather supplies for their fortress garrisons.

Across the "Big Muddy" about midway between the two eastern shore river towns lay the entrance to the Red River, which wound its way up to Alexandria and Shreveport, LA, and beyond. This trans-Mississippi sally port was a key, along with the Yazoo River country about Vicksburg and the Big Black River lands below, to the Confederate logistical chain that supplied Vicksburg and Port Hudson even in the face of blockading U.S. gunboats.

The *Chillicothe* arrived off Fort Hindman on Sunday, January 16, too late to participate in the fighting. There she joined the Mississippi Squadron flagboat *Black Hawk*, the Pook turtle *Louisville*, and three tinclads. RAdm. David Dixon Porter had not yet departed the scene of victory, remaining to provide support as U.S. Army forces destroyed the bastion's remaining defenses and sent away the prisoners of war. Joined by Capt. James P. Foster's new gunboat in a line ahead formation, Porter quit the Arkansas headed south on a stormy Monday afternoon. The fleet passed Island No. 93 early on the afternoon of the 20th, picking up an escort from among several of the naval vessels left behind earlier off the mouth of the Yazoo River above Vicksburg.

Imbedded with the transports, *New York Herald* scribe Findley Anderson told his readers that there "were rumors of a rebel ram having come out of the Yazoo." So, when two supply steamers passed down beyond the escorting gunboats and did not immediately return, there was real fear that they were taken. A speedy transport was sent to catch up and turn them back. "There were several hours of suspense," Anderson noted.

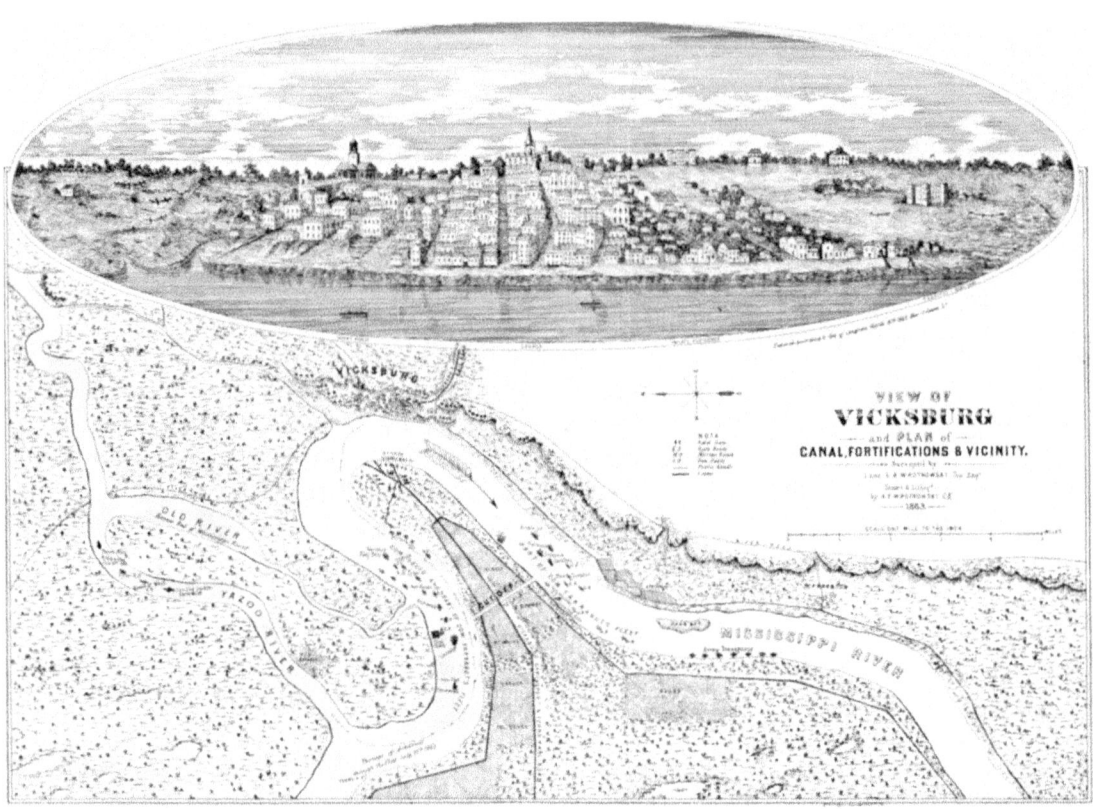

Vicksburg and Environs. This contemporary map, upon which is superimposed an illustration of the Terraced City, shows the Mississippi and Yazoo rivers, plus many geographical features and the positions of Union naval elements. After a brief halt at Arkansas Post, the *Chillicothe* arrived off the Confederate citadel in late January 1863 (Library of Congress).

However, early on the morning of January 21, "the appearance of the missing boats assured us all that the lost were found."

The weather having cleared, the fleet touched at Milliken's Bend and then at Young's Point on the Louisiana side of the Mississippi. As the soldiers disembarked, both they and the sailors on the vessels offshore were able to view a portion of the vastness known as the Yazoo Delta. Criss-crossed with various lakes, small rivers, and bayous, the Yazoo Delta lies on the eastern side of the Mississippi River between Vicksburg and Memphis. Much of the land is rich, black farming soil, but due to faulty drainage in Civil War times, most of it was either swamp or flooded land. As Maj. Gen. William T. Sherman and RAdm. Porter had discovered the previous December during their adventure to Chickasaw Bayou, it would be a difficult, if not impossible, task to take the route up the Yazoo River to the high ground northeast of Vicksburg. Across the Mississippi, the

Opposite: *Chillicothe* **Configuration.** Most of the men of the USN Mississippi Squadron assembled off Vicksburg had never seen a vessel like the *Chillicothe*, with her enormous turret, huge wheel houses, and low profile. The noted naval vessel plan expert David Meagher here shows us in detail the vessel's layout (©2006 David J. Meagher; used with permission).

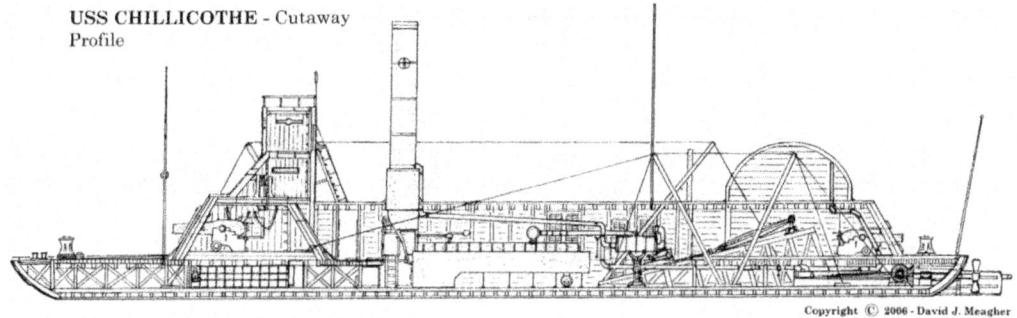

Cutaway Profile.

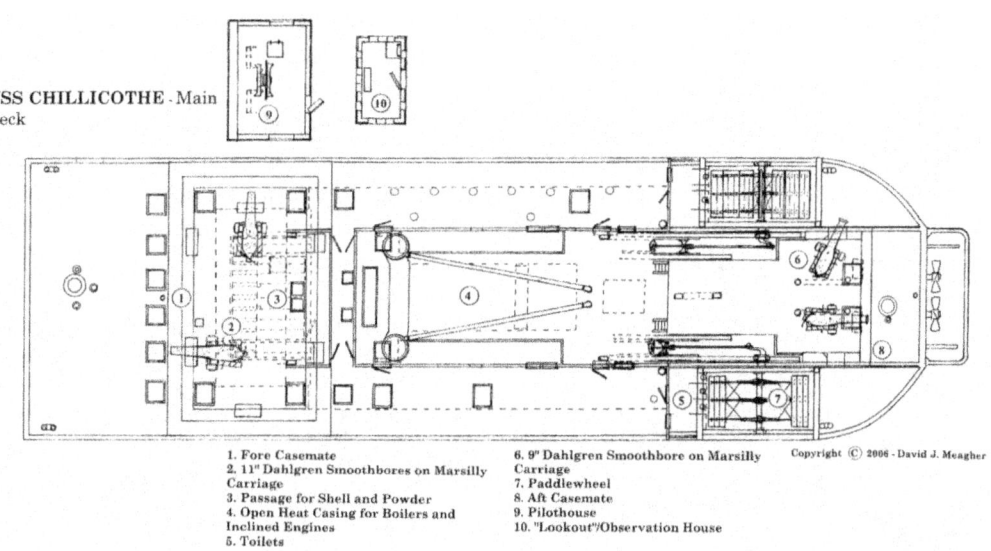

1. Fore Casemate
2. 11" Dahlgren Smoothbores on Marsilly Carriage
3. Passage for Shell and Powder
4. Open Heat Casing for Boilers and Inclined Engines
5. Toilets
6. 9" Dahlgren Smoothbore on Marsilly Carriage
7. Paddlewheel
8. Aft Casemate
9. Pilothouse
10. "Lookout"/Observation House

Main Deck.

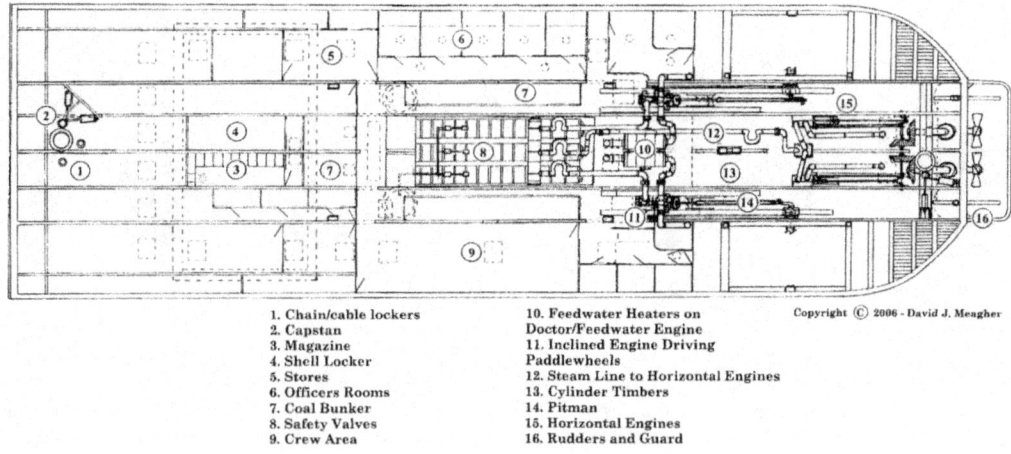

1. Chain/cable lockers
2. Capstan
3. Magazine
4. Shell Locker
5. Stores
6. Officers Rooms
7. Coal Bunker
8. Safety Valves
9. Crew Area
10. Feedwater Heaters on Doctor/Feedwater Engine
11. Inclined Engine Driving Paddlewheels
12. Steam Line to Horizontal Engines
13. Cylinder Timbers
14. Pitman
15. Horizontal Engines
16. Rudders and Guard

Hold/Hull Areas.

situation for an invader was no better. The land there was also low and overly wet. It would be suicidal for any Union army to try to cross the river and attack the high batteries defending the city and eastern banks. Perhaps the geography of the area is best summed up by that old observer Thomas Bangs Thrope: "The country through which [the Mississippi] flows is almost entirely alluvial."

The vessels of the Mississippi Squadron, including Capt. Foster's, anchored in an advanced position at the mouth of the Yazoo River. According to a Chicago newsman, it was located seven miles from Vicksburg by water and about three by land. In addition to normal fleet business, including logistical and protective, there were several fights with the gunners of the enemy's fortress city. On January 26 the *Chillicothe*, believed to be a "formidable ironclad," shelled Vicksburg's lower batteries. The *Chicago Daily Tribune* reporter "Omega," who witnessed the one-sided duel, later told his readers that her shoot did not provoke any Southern return fire. "It was thought," he added, "she was trying to learn the range of the enemy's guns." A Pennsylvania sailor who served aboard gave his hometown newspaper a brief description of his gunboat's appearance: "Only about two feet of her is above water and five feet below, and is covered with three inches iron all over her decks and sides. Her boilers and machinery are below the waterline, leaving nothing but the turret and wheels for them to shoot at."

Vicksburg Bombardment. Just a few days after her arrival, the *Chillicothe* was ordered to test her giant 11-inch Dahlgren cannon against the Southern river fortress. The *Chicago Daily Tribune* reporter "Omega," who witnessed the one-sided duel, told his readers that her shoot did not provoke any Southern return fire. "It was thought," he added, "[that] she was trying to learn the range of the enemy's guns" (*Harper's Weekly*, January 9, 1864).

The next day, DeBenneville Raldoph Keim (1841–1914) of the *New York Herald* wrote of that day's bombardment. When several of the ironclads moved more closely to Vicksburg's upper defenses, Confederate gunners took them under fire. There ensued "for an hour and a quarter quite a brisk cannonade" maintained by both sides. "Our boats," Keim, noted, "[held] their positions and came out of the action uninjured."

As additional Union naval forces congregated off the mouth of the Yazoo over the next week and more troops were off-loaded from transports, Maj. Gen. Ulysses S. Grant arrived on the scene to restart the dormant Yankee advance upon Vicksburg. There would be no more direct attack upon water defenses like those at Haynes Bluff or Chickasaw Bayou. He believed that with the aid of Porter's vessels it was time to find a way of getting behind the town's defenses. Schemes to that end would begin to unfold within days.[1] Nearly until spring, the Federals would occupy themselves with several "momentary contingencies," or "half-baked schemes," as Grant biographer Smith called them, "to get around the city via man-made Louisiana canals that reached the Mississippi below the town or murky alternative eastern shore bayou routes that promised to enter the Yazoo above the Snyder's salient.

For purposes of this book, the Louisiana canals do not directly concern us. On the other hand, two truly amphibious adventures were initiated on the eastern side of the Big Muddy. The first attempted to move via the Yazoo Pass, and when it faltered a second steamed into Steele's Bayou. Both were, it has long been thought, designed to turn the right flank of Vicksburg. If successful and the high ground were gained, the city could be attacked by Union columns from the northern Yazoo approaches above Snyder's Bluff. It is the first of these, in which the *Chillicothe* participated, that will occupy us.[2]

On January 29, Porter re-formed the heavy units of his squadron into two divisions. The *Chillicothe* was assigned to the First Division with the *Louisville*, *Cincinnati*, *Baron de Kalb*, *Carondelet*, *Lexington*, and *Conestoga*. The unit would be commanded by Capt. Henry Walke when he arrived with another new gunboat, the

Captain of the *Chillicothe*. Hoosier Lt. Cmdr. James P. Foster (1827–1869) was appointed the *Chillicothe*'s first captain in November 1862 and guided her through the Yazoo Pass Expedition. Forced to succeed the expedition's ill naval commander, it was he who withdrew it from danger in early April 1863. Transferred to the giant ironclad *Lafayette* in September, he would command her through the remainder of the war. He died off the coast of South America while attached to the Brazil Squadron (Naval History and Heritage Command).

THE BAYOU EXPEDITIONS
FEBRUARY – APRIL 1863

Four unsuccessful attempts by Grant to strike Vicksburg from the rear by moving his army on transports through the rivers and bayous to the bluffs north or south of the city.

Yazoo Pass Expedition blocked by the guns of Fort Pemberton.

Lake Providence Route abandoned; unable to clear route for navigation.

Steele's Bayou Expedition cut off in Rolling Fork.

Duckport Canal Expedition abandoned because of low water in the bayous.

Bayou Schemes. Nearly until spring 1863, the Federals occupied themselves with several "momentary contingencies," or "half-baked schemes," as Grant biographer Gene Smith called them, "to get around the city via man-made Louisiana canals that reached the Mississippi below the town or murky alternative eastern shore bayou routes that promised to enter the Yazoo River above the fortress. The *Chillicothe* was a participant in the first of these, the Yazoo Pass Expedition (National Park Service).

4—*The* Chillicothe *Goes to War: Yazoo Pass and Red River* 113

Grant and Porter Cooperate. Working in cooperation with RAdm. David Porter, Maj. Gen. Ulysses S. Grant coordinated the effort against Vicksburg. Throughout the months ahead until the citadel surrendered the two merged their interests to insure a remarkably smooth tactical and logistical approach to the resolution of their strategic objective (Naval History and Heritage Command).

Lafayette. Later that evening, just hours after Maj. Gen. Grant arrived at Young's Point, the Union theater commander held a council with several of his subordinates and RAdm. Porter to consider efforts that might be undertaken to capture Vicksburg. Passage by the river past the citadel's big guns then seemed suicidal and no one wanted to repeat December's attack on the Snyder's Bluff salient. For the moment, the options seemed limited to a Louisiana canal or obtaining access to the upper Yazoo and hence the city via some route as yet unknown. The possibility of an entrance to the upper Yazoo via the old Yazoo Pass, an idea on the table, for a week floated to the top of the discussion list.

As a result, Lt. Col. James H. Wilson (1837–1925), an engineer on Grant's staff, was detailed to go examine its technical feasibility. A boy wonder of the conflict, Wilson became a Union major general just five years after graduating from West Point. After serving as a volunteer aide-de-camp for the Federal commander at the Battle of Antietam, the engineer was sent to Grant and served in the West for the remainder of the war save for a brief spring 1864 stint in the East. He retired from the army in 1870, but returned to duty during both the Spanish American War and the Boxer Rebellion.[3]

While Lt. Col. Wilson, supported by a navy tinclad, examined a levee established on the State of Mississippi riverbank below Helena, AR, that kept back the Mississippi from the Yazoo Pass, RAdm. Porter wrestled with a challenge that dated back to the beginning of his western tenure and beyond—manpower. Finding sufficient crewmen and marines for the Mississippi Squadron had been a problem ever since its predecessor organization, the Western Flotilla, was established in 1861. Without going into detail better provided elsewhere, it is sufficient to say that by the time Wilson was detailed to Helena, Porter was reduced to borrowing men from Maj. Gen. John A. McClernand just to complete outfitting the *Chillicothe*. During the day, the admiral wrote a formal request to Maj. Gen. Grant asking that enlisted soldiers, without commissioned officers, be transferred over to him by companies. If he were now forced into action without them, Porter emphasized, "I should be able to fight but very few of my guns." If the theater commander would honor his request, the navy, it was promised, would return them when the need ended and they would be "the best drilled and the best behaved men in the Army." Grant was quite sympathetic to the need of his nautical colleague. Within a few days, he had not only endorsed the navy request all the way to Washington but had also transferred almost 600 soldiers: the entire 58th Ohio Volunteer Infantry, two companies from the 29th Illinois, and four companies from the 101st Illinois.

These men, Grant later noted, would initially "go to act as Marines for the occasion." At this point, both the military commander and RAdm. Porter believed any incursion into the Yazoo Delta would be a naval operation devoid of a large-scale army contingent. By February 5, army and navy colleagues working together had blown an entrance through the Snagey Canal/Grant Pass levee that allowed the Mississippi to flood into Yazoo Pass and the Yazoo Delta beyond. When news of the success coupled with engineer Wilson's optimistic prognostication reached Young's Point, the project was given a green light to proceed.

That evening, while visiting with Maj. Gen. William T. Sherman, the major general commanding authorized final arrangements for the 58th Ohio to be transferred to the gunboat service. Grant also instructed that the entire contingent of 600 men being seconded to the Yazoo Pass expedition report aboard the transport steamer *Magnolia* the following morning for transport to Helena. RAdm. Porter, whom Grant may also have seen, was acquainted with Lt. Col. Wilson's report.[4] Orders and reports preparatory to undertaking the Yazoo Pass expedition flew about the Young's Point anchorage and adjacent levees through February 6. A report on expedition preliminaries, enclosing Wilson's information, was forwarded on to army headquarters in Washington, D.C. It concluded that prospects looked good for "a safe passage into the Yazoo River by way of Yazoo Pass."

The force of 600 soldiers supplied by Grant would, he told his Washington-based superiors, be put aboard a task force organized by RAdm. Porter. It would then "thoroughly explore" the pass route and, it was hoped, capture "all the transports in the Yazoo and tributaries, and destroy two gunboats said to be in course of construction." They would also attempt to ascend the Yalobusha to Grenada and destroy the railroad bridges at that town. If that task could be completed, the Confederates would be unable to employ the vital Mississippi Central Railroad. Next Grant sent a message to RAdm. Porter with "respectful" advice for the upcoming "voyage." This included such basic intelligence on the interior as he had at that moment. It was recommended that all of the navigable streams and bayous "be well reconnoitered before the expedition returns."

According to the army's commander, the town of Greenwood, near where the Yazoo was created from the confluence of the Tallahatchie and Yalobusha rivers, was not fortified nor did it have a battery commanding any of the waters. Interestingly enough, he did not mention that only a few miles above the town the Tallahatchie and the Yazoo flowed past one another on opposite sides of a neck of land that was only a few hundred yards wide. Nor did he note that the little populated place of Le Flore lay directly in the junction of the two streams.

The great prize of the campaign was Yazoo City. Here was, "in all probability," where the steamers known to be in the Delta would "be found and, if any Gunboats are

4—*The* Chillicothe *Goes to War: Yazoo Pass and Red River* 115

being constructed, it is likely at this place." As newsman Thomas M. "Tom" Cook said of the rams, "Whatever they have got up the Yazoo or its tributaries will be pretty much certain to be brought to light by this expedition." On the other hand, there was also information that many transports were up the Sunflower River. "They have a fleet of 40 of the finest river steamboats somewhere in this system of rivers," the Chicago newsman wrote. Capturing the transports would largely eliminate the flow of grain and livestock into Vicksburg from the countryside. Finally, in the event the naval vessels could reach Grenada on the Yalobusha, there were two key railroad bridges that required attention. "If these bridges can be destroyed, it would be a heavy blow to the enemy and of much service to us."

Having digested Grant's recommendations, the Mississippi Squadron boss called Lt. Cmdr. Watson Smith, commander of the fleet's First Division Light Draught Vessels, aboard the *Black Hawk*. Porter placed Smith in charge of the Yazoo Pass expedition and the two men spent some time discussing details based upon the Wilson reports and the information supplied by the army. Porter assured his subordinate that the success of the mission, if performed as outlined and expected, would "strike a terrible blow at the enemy, who do not anticipate an attack from such a quarter." Porter may also have spoken of another one of his ideas. Once he knew that Smith was above the Snyder's Bluff salient on the Yazoo north of Vicksburg, he would send other vessels up to join in a coordinated attack, either destroying the batteries or forcing their abandonment. Smith departed in early afternoon to organize his departure while his superior wrote out a full set of instructions and had them couriered over to the campaign flag boat, the light draught *Rattler* (Tinclad No. 1).

After a sailor delivered the instructions to his cabin, the Yazoo Pass commander tore open the envelope and read his chief's detailed orders. Smith, the instructions read, was to depart the waters off Young's Point as soon as possible and rendezvous with three other tinclads while en route to the mouth of the White River. Continuing to believe this to be a rapid, purely navy show, Porter wrote that the *Chillicothe* was being added to engage any heavy batteries encountered. Thinking in a postscript concerning logistics, the admiral cautioned his deputy that it would probably be best if all of his vessels first stopped at Helena and fueled. Not only were they to take aboard all the coal they could transport themselves, but at least two filled barges were also to be obtained from the naval supply kept at the town. These could then be towed with the vessels during the upcoming operation. Porter explained that some 600 to 800 soldiers were being detailed to serve as marines aboard his tinclads. Additionally, before starting, all of the pilots in residence at Helena who knew anything about steaming the waterways of the Delta were to be employed.

After Smith's vessels reached the entrance to Snagey Canal/Grant's Pass, where Wilson had blown an entrance into the Yazoo Pass, they were to refrain from entering until it was certain that the water rushing in had become quite slack. Even then, soldiers were to be transferred to a small army steamer that was to be sent ahead of the gunboats. The bluecoats aboard her would then clear the way by cutting down the overhanging trees and branches that might endanger the warship's chimneys. All activities were to be carried out at low speed and "only in the daytime."

Porter's orders further called upon Smith to execute the remainder of his mission with great speed, but at the same time, he was to exercise great care and "guard against surprise." Being relatively unfamiliar with the Delta, Porter did not detail what actions should be taken by Smith if he encountered either significant natural or Confederate opposition. Of course, protection of the Union warships was vital. If a major attack developed and the gunboat force was overwhelmed, all the steamers were to be run onto the bank and set afire. The bearded naval chief, assuming smooth steaming on the part of his task force, now laid out a program of objectives to be captured or destroyed. Once the vessels reached the Tallahatchie River, they were to quickly ascend it as far as the railroad crossing and quickly destroy the rail bridge at that point, as well as cut the telegraph wires. Smith's group was then to steam back down the river to the mouth of the Yalobusha. After the Federal gunboats reached the Yalobusha, they were to pause and coal ship. Leaving the barges under guard of the tail-end light draught, the remaining vessels, including the speedy *Chillicothe*, were to "dash on to Grenada." There they were to completely destroy the railroad bridge so fondly desired by Maj. Gen. Grant. With the exception of small boats encountered, nothing else at that location was to be eliminated.

Back at the Yalobusha, the vessels were to refuel once more before proceeding into the Yazoo River. The entire force was to then attempt to get into the Sunflower River, where Porter had been advised "all the large steamers are stowed away." If it was successful, the pace of the operation would not permit the time needed to capture any of the Confederate riverboats. Those encountered were to be destroyed and an account kept, as best as possible, of the value of the prizes liquidated. Lt. Cmdr. Smith was also to obtain all the information he could about the ironclads the Rebels were supposedly building on the Yazoo. If he came across the construction site for any of these, he was to eliminate the vessels "while they are on the stocks." Once all of the tasks entrusted to him were completed, Smith was to return back up the Yazoo Pass and, upon reaching the Snagey Canal/Grant's Pass entrance, speed a dispatch boat to the admiral with reports on the expedition. Not long after this message was sent, RAdm. Porter wrote out another, to Lt. Cmdr. James P. Foster. The commander of the *Chillicothe* was ordered to proceed up to Helena, coal, and find Lt. Cmdr. Smith at Delta or down at the levee cut. Smith had one further evening conversation with Porter, where several minor points were clarified.[5]

Lt. Col. Wilson reported to Helena army headquarters on the morning of February 9. There he learned that Maj. Gen. Grant had under consideration a far larger incursion into the Mississippi Delta than was originally intimated, one involving a much larger body of Union troops in addition to those slated to serve aboard the gunboats. The engineer was also apprised that the Confederates were fully aware of Federal movements and were completing "arrangements for our reception." The young man, who earlier had heard something similar from prisoners of war, did not believe this information was very reliable.

By the morning of February 10, several hundred Iowa soldiers from Helena had been detailed to clear such vegetation that clogged the mouth of Old Pass, getting inside it for about one mile. From there the real work and danger of removing the obstructions began. The bluecoats, stripped to their waists and their pant legs rolled up, encountered the obstacles placed by time, nature, and man. Low-hanging branches ripped the light work of the work steamers and grabbed at their chimneys. Wild grape vines and muscadine as strong as rope cable was interwoven into unbreakable mats and sawyers poked up from the current of the stream. Newsmen have left quite vivid descriptions. The first looks at movements from the Mississippi to the Old Pass, via Moon Lake, the second at Yazoo Pass itself.

The narrow Snagey Canal/Grant's Pass channel, about 100 yards in from the Mississippi, made a sharp 90-degree turn. It was noted that "long boats, without the most skillful management, could not make this turn." Continuing about a mile into Moon Lake, a crescent-shaped body of water, vessels were required to steam on about four or five miles more in a voyage much as that described by *Chicago Daily Times* reporter Tom Cook several weeks later: "The lake ... is a very picturesque and beautiful sheet of water, the entrance to and exit from which, both being so very narrow and through thick woods, can scarcely be seen a hundred yards away from their mouths. The shores are high and dry. On the eastern bank there are two or three fine plantations, but, with these exceptions, the surroundings are an unbroken forest. Its isolation, and consequent quiet, have made it a great resort for aquatic birds of all kinds.... The water being deep, cool and comparatively clear, abounds with fish of all kinds."

Lt. Col. James H. Wilson. A boy wonder of the conflict, Wilson (1837–1925) became a U.S. major general just five years after graduating from West Point. Assigned as an engineer to Maj. Gen. Grant, he served all but a few months of his war in the West. His memoirs have far less to say about the Yazoo Pass Expedition, his first significant assignment, than one might expect. Wilson retired from the army in 1870 but returned to duty during the Spanish American War and the Boxer Rebellion (Library of Congress).

Old Pass was found to be "a good wide channel, with four fathoms and upwards," but "neither so large or straight as it is nearer the river." The channel was 20 to 30 feet deep, but the current was very strong. Its average speed was found to be 3–4 mph. However, it could run as much as 5 mph or, where the stream widened, it could slow to just 2–3 mph. The newsman's pen expanded the picture: "The width of the Pass in no place exceeds 100 feet, excepting where the banks are overflowed and the water finds escape from its narrow bed by spreading out into the woods." Cook continued: "Sometimes it narrows down to 50 feet, when the current dashes along with almost fearful violence." As far as the eye could see, there was significant overhang from "wild, jagged and crooked" trees, plus vines and other brush. The entire route, as recorded by the Chicago pressman, lay "through an unbroken

Daunting Task. *Chicago Daily Times* reporter Tom Cook reported the difficulties facing the Federal Yazoo Pass Expedition as it was launched, noting that its route lay "through an unbroken wilderness of the largest growth of cypress, sycamore, and cottonwood trees, with an entanglement of cane and wild grape vines beneath and clinging to the larger wood, forming a most perfect jungle." Added to the natural maze were man-made obstructions hastily made by Confederate defenders (*Harper's Weekly*, May 9, 1863).

wilderness of the largest growth of cypress, sycamore, and cottonwood trees, with an entanglement of cane and wild grape vines beneath and clinging to the larger wood, forming a most perfect jungle."

Another newsman along later noted the following: "Through this jungle the Pass winds and twists in the most serpentine course imaginable, frequently doubling on itself after describing a wide circuit of several miles, and forming a narrow neck across which a stone can be easily thrown. The channel is nowhere perfectly straight. It would be hardly possible to find a place throughout its entire length where one can see in either direction 500 feet—its bends form very acute angles frequently, and all the way the course is but a succession of very small letter s's." All of the hardwoods, he went on to say, had "a greater gravity than water." The felled trees were mainly green sycamores and cottonwoods and some of those were four feet through at the butt and weighed 35 tons." When driftwood, stumps, trees growing in midstream, vines and other debris were mixed in, the Old Pass barricades proved to be "of no trifling nature." Indeed, so thick were the barricades that in some places soldiers could walk across them from one side to the other without getting their feet wet. "Long branches protrude entirely across the stream quite frequently," observed one reporter and, seemingly only yards ahead "some tall sycamore is to be found, leaning so far over the water as to completely block the passage." On other occasions, one would be encountered standing so tall as to "form a perfect arch over the little stream, but so high as to seldom interfere with the passage of boats beneath it." Unfortunately, the tree obstructions were more common than not.[6]

Maj. Gen. William Wing Loring (1818–1886), CSA, the commander at Grenada of the 2nd Military District, Department of Mississippi and East Louisiana, who was more or less in charge of defending the Delta area, was alerted to the incursion by scouts and citizens of the Moon Lake region by February 11. A hero of the Mexican War (during which he lost an arm), Loring was commissioned a Confederate brigadier general in 1861. Serving in Southwest Virginia, he was promoted in 1862 and posted to Vicksburg, where he would gain fame for turning back the upcoming Yazoo Pass expedition but would later be blamed for the Southern defeat at Champion's Hill. Second in command during the battles of Franklin and Nashville in 1864, he surrendered in North Carolina. Later, he served a picturesque tour of duty as a general under the Khedive of Egypt (1869–1879).

On the evening of the 12th, Lt. Cmdr. Watson Smith, aboard the *Rattler*, arrived at Helena with two other light draughts. There he found the *Forest Rose* (Tinclad No. 9) and the *Chillicothe*. He also found that the work of cutting through Old Pass was going to be a far greater chore than was initially expected and, most depressing, the mission was no longer a surprise to anyone. Smith was hardly ashore before a military officer told him that he had learned of the expedition while in Memphis. Both Union and Confederate forces realized that there was no way for the Federals to secure the lower end of Old Pass; their work could be done only from the upper end. As the Northern soldiers labored vigorously to remove the "Red River rafts" and other obstructions, natural and manmade, the Southerners gradually pushed back toward the Coldwater in an effort to fill the channel with wood and thus delay their enemy. "Things began to take on the appearance of an impasse," wrote Charles Dana Gibson, "as each side worked feverishly to undo the other's efforts." At least, as the historian observed, the fallen trees served as "a shielding barrier between the two groups of axmen."

Early on Friday, the 13th, Lt. Cmdr. Smith commandeered the steamer *Stephen Bayard*, which had three barges (containing 30,000–40,000 bushels of coal) under tow. There was little navy coal remaining in the town and the expedition naval commander was reluctant to obtain any from the army stock. Lt. Cmdr. Smith, at mid-morning, boarded the *Forest Rose* and was taken downstream to obtain a more detailed view of the Snagey Canal/Grant's Pass cut than was possible as his little task group had passed up the river a couple of days earlier. The soldier wished to check on the progress of his men, whom RAdm. Porter later praised as having "worked like heroes in clearing away the obstructions." Smith was impressed with his initial view. "This was a work of nature," he exclaimed. The saltwater sailor found, as the tinclad steamed through, that the current passing in the cut was now moderate, rising and falling with the Mississippi.

When he returned to Helena, Watson Smith found a message from RAdm. Porter restating his aims for the forthcoming expedition. In reply, the task force commander warned his superior that developments with the expedition had not been kept from the enemy. On top of that, he passed on a warning from Special Pilot John L. Morton (?–1865) that the Little Tallahatchie and the Yalobusha to Grenada could also be blocked by felled timber. Fortunately, the Tallahatchie proper could not.

Kentuckian Morton, who had served before the war on the Mississippi, Missouri, and Ohio rivers as a pilot, master, and vessel owner, was found by RAdm. Porter in January to be the only pilot in the whole Union squadron assembled above Vicksburg to have ever traveled the old Yazoo Pass route before the Magnolia State sealed it off as a flood control measure a decade earlier. In conversation, he had told the admiral "the passage could be made practicable." Consequently given an honorary title and detailed to accompany Lt. Col. Wilson, Morton would witness the upcoming operation from the pilothouse of the *Chillicothe*. Returning to the river after the war, he died at St. Paul, MN. His son, born in New Orleans, became a prominent member of the Missouri legislature.

Having found that it would take many more days for Old Pass to be cleared, Lt. Cmdr. Smith, who was not feeling well, waited, strengthening his force for the upcoming mission. According to Richard West, he was becoming "depressed over the prospects."[7]

As the channel clearing project continued, Brig. Gen. Benjamin M. Prentiss (1819–1901) became commander of its sponsoring department, the Federal District of Eastern Arkansas, on February 14. The Mexican War veteran and former Illinois congressman was named colonel of the 10th Illinois Infantry in early 1861 and a brigadier general in mid-year. A hero of the Battle of Shiloh in April 1862 and promoted to a major general in March 1863, Prentiss would remain at Helena after the upcoming operation, winning a decisive victory on July 4. Resigning due to poor health that fall, he was thereafter a lawyer active in Missouri politics.

The same day, Lt. Cmdr. Smith, working to strengthen his delayed expedition at Helena, petitioned RAdm. Porter for the addition of several Ellet rams. Continuously reviewing his charts aboard the *Rattler*, the task force boss now estimated that he would be required to steam 1,500 miles in order to complete his mission. Meanwhile, a sailor aboard the ironclad *Chillicothe* remarked on the pleasantries of the Southern spring, noting to his Pennsylvania correspondent that he supposed "you have sleighing and skating yet in Erie." Following divine services the next day, Lt. Cmdr. Smith notified the rear admiral that a few small Rebel steamers were reported on the Coldwater River and the Mississippi was falling. Still, from what he had seen and heard, the Yazoo Pass would not be cleared for another six or seven days, even with 2,000–3,000 men working on it. There were, as there had been for most of the past 10 days, almost 2,000 Union men laboring on the pass obstructions. The obstacles in front of them were becoming "more and more formidable." It would take another 10 days, it was predicted, to cut out "the drift from the cut-off." Even then, many of the divers had little confidence that boats as large as Smith's ironclads would be able to steam through.

Secrecy, the project commander noted, was "out of the question, as it was as fully known in Grenada what we are doing as it is here." As if to bear out this observation, "De Soto," the Cairo correspondent of the *New York Times*, who was most likely William George, sent a dispatch to his eastern editor that would be published four days later. In it, he confided, "Arrangements are completing for dispatching a small fleet of our tinclads, known as the 'Mosquito Fleet,' through Yazoo Pass so as to get in the rear of and out below the Rebel stronghold on the Mississippi."

Maj. Gen. Grant now wrote to Brig. Gen. Prentiss to say, "I send with this steamers to take on board Gen. Leonard F. Ross' [1823–1901] Division to be used on the Yazoo Pass expedition.... If this expedition should succeed in getting into the Coldwater, I want Gen. Ross to take with him all the force he starts from Helena with."

"Judge" Ross raised the 17th Illinois in 1861 and became its colonel. He served at Fort Donelson in February 1862, was promoted, and fought at Corinth in November. His posting to the command of the XIII Corps' 13th Division came only a few weeks before the start of the Yazoo Pass expedition. Ross resigned later in 1863 and was active thereafter in Republican politics.

The theater commander was anxious that there be no delay. "Time," he added, "is now growing important." The boats he was sending for what *New York Herald* reporter Keim would call "the sternwheel expedition" were all light, narrow-beamed transports with their single paddle wheels at the stern. In the press of business, Maj. Gen. Grant somehow failed to include RAdm. Porter in this decision and did not even tell him about it. While it may have been all well and good to enhance the invasion force, it would take more time for it to be assembled. The sailor complained to his chiefs in Washington on March 12: "At the last moment (and without my knowing it), 6,000 soldiers were ordered to join the expedition."

On February 16, Grant forwarded to Washington the latest reports from Lt. Col. Wilson. Additionally, he went on to tell his superiors that he was "sending an addi-

Brig. Gen. Leonard Ross. Photographs of most of the leading figures in the Yazoo Pass Expedition are, sadly, absent, including Lt. Cmdr. Watson Smith, overall naval commander. We do have a drawing of the U.S. Army commander, Ross (1823–1901), who had earlier served in the Fort Donelson and Corinth, MS, campaigns. His posting to the command of the XIII Corps' 13th Division came only a few weeks before the start of the Yazoo Pass Expedition. He resigned late in 1863 and was thereafter active in Republican Party politics (*Harper's Weekly*, April 4, 1863).

tional division of infantry, with a few pieces of artillery, without horses, to accompany the expedition." The task force would have as its first order of business the destruction of the railroad bridges at Grenada, a town which, according to intelligence, was not now heavily defended.[8]

One of the big navy coal barges at Helena grounded on February 17, requiring that the entire crews from the *Rattler* and *Chillicothe* be sent to remove its fuel into smaller barges. Even though it would take two days to complete the transfer, this may not have been an altogether bad development. Lt. Cmdr. Smith was aware that large barges could not be easily managed in Yazoo Pass and tha, after the coal was shifted the smaller barges could be "dropped ahead" of the steamers during transit. In practice, this would not prove to be much better and would limit the column to the speed of the current.

Reacting to a large number of incoming warnings, the Confederate department commander, Lt. Gen. John C. Pemberton (1814–1881), communicated with Brig. Gen. Loring in late afternoon. Born a Pennsylvanian, Pemberton, a Mexican War veteran, was appointed a major general at the beginning of 1862. After service in South Carolina he was advanced to lieutenant general and in October was sent to command the Department of Mississippi and East Louisiana. Exchanged several months following the loss of Vicksburg in July 1863, he never held another major command, and after farming in North Carolina (1866–1876), returned to Pennsylvania. Pemberton suggested that Loring immediately seek the best location on the Yazoo or Tallahatchie to make a stand against the Federal advance. There was very little time to determine whether to fortify some spot on those streams or on the Yalobusha.

Loring had earlier dispatched scouts out to a distance of 100 miles to seek locations from which to defend the Delta from the Federals. After considerable exploration and some argument, word was sent back that the ground at Clayton Bayou, a little above the town of Greenwood, might prove ideal. Located between the Tallahatchie and Yazoo, it was only 300 yards wide. It should be possible to erect impregnable fortifications near Point La Flore where the Yalobusha and Tallahatchie joined and further safeguard it by obstructing the Tallahatchie. Not knowing of this recommendation, Lt. Gen. Pemberton spent most of February 18 messaging his area subordinates in an attempt to coordinate a Delta defense. His communications were neither specific nor helpful, but all stressed the need for action. Additionally, heavy ordnance, including a rifled 32-pounder, was ordered up to Yazoo City from the northern Vicksburg defense line. On the Mississippi far to the northwest, the ironclad *Baron de Kalb* and another tinclad arrived at Helena and reported to Lt. Cmdr. Smith their readiness to participate in the Yazoo Pass expedition. The *De Kalb*, Seaman Frederic E. Davis told his parents in a letter home to Providence, RI, was headed to the Coldwater in "the heart of the Confederacy."

Lt. Cmdr. Smith, as he did almost daily, conferred with Brig. Gen. Prentiss. The latter now admitted that the channel the soldiers were clearing might not be wide enough to allow troop transports to get through. In the light of the possibility that military boats might be lost, Smith now spoke of his steaming plans. When the force departed up into Old Pass following its clearance, his warships, led by the *Chillicothe* and *Baron de Kalb*, and including the light draughts (with 100 soldiers shipped aboard each as marines), the towboats and their coal barges would all proceed with the army transports. That way, if any troop vessels were lost, the navy could carry on. That night, the barge from which the *Chillicothe*'s crewmen had been retrieving coal at Helena sank with the loss of 2,000 bushels of coal. Fortunately, those contents were all retrieved and set out to dry.

On February 19 Lt. Cmdr. Smith paid a visit to the Old Pass entrance that ran southeast out of Moon Lake. In a report to his superior, the seaman confirmed what many others were saying, namely that the Rebels had felled the heaviest trees possible across the waterway. The labor of clearing them out was extremely tedious for the army fatigue parties engaged in the removal. Trees cut by the Confederates were not the only obstacles. A number of trees could not be felled because to do so would result in their falling directly into the channel. These were left, but a warning was sent to the fleet that their overhanging branches would need to be severely trimmed. If the water level fell four or five feet, it should be possible, according to Lt. Col. Wilson, to avoid cutting and just pull the offenders inland with lines. The importance of this news, Smith went on to say from his desk in the cabin of the *Rattler*, was the impact it would have on his task force. The width of the channel cleared was, he admitted, "about wide enough to admit vessels of the length of this to pass around its turns." Noting that the water at the Moon Lake entrance into Yazoo Pass had fallen about six feet, Smith announced that his part of the expedition would steam to that location the next day.

Meanwhile, at about 5:00 p.m., the steamers *Edward J. Gay* and *Hope* arrived at a new camp named for Lt. Gen. Pemberton that was being established at the point earlier recommended below Greenwood. Once their landing stages were dropped on the bank, two battalions of Waul's Texas Legion went ashore and set up camp, taking the house of the local ferryman, named Beck, for their headquarters.[9] At Camp Pemberton on Friday morning, Col. Thomas N. Waul (1815–1903) met with the scouts who had suggested this spot. The South Carolinian was a local judge when the war broke out. Elected to the first Confederate congress, Waul resigned in February 1862 to raise the Texas Legion. He was active at Vicksburg through its surrender and later fought in the Trans-Mississippi Department, participating in the Red River campaign of 1864.

The three men agreed that their present location offered the best spot for the construction of suitable defenses against the looming Federal incursion. Beck's Ferry was four miles by water and 2.5 miles by land below Greenwood on a 500-yard-wide neck that separated the Tallahatchie and the Yazoo. The narrow land, surrounded by water on three sides, offered the advantage of rising eight feet above the streams and providing an ideal location for gun emplacements that could project a plunging fire. Work was immediately begun on "staking out the ground in a zig-zag way" and erecting fortifications and gun emplacements. "Slaves," wrote Frank E. Smith years later, "were conscripted to furnish a good part of the labor." The pokey Federal advance would permit the Confederates to largely finish a respectable choke point.

Maj. Gen. Loring arrived at Camp Pemberton on February 21. The Mexican War hero of Chapultepec was so pleased with the progress already launched by Waul and the others that he could not help but express his confidence that, when finished, the works would "do much toward preventing the passage down of the enemy." In order that a defensive position be created as quickly as possible, a large quantity of cotton for bulwarks was required. Two steamers were immediately ordered up the flooding Tallahatchie and Yalobusha to acquire cotton bales, with the first loads arriving by dark.

There was considerable preparatory action at Helena that Saturday morning. Having been advised that the work of clearing Old Pass was nearly finished, Lt. Cmdr. Smith's invasion squadron raised anchor and, with great clouds of black smoke rising from 14 chimneys, steamed down below Delta to the Snagey Canal/Grant's Pass entrance from the Mississippi into the Yazoo Pass. By afternoon, the *Chillicothe*, *Baron de Kalb*, *Rattler* (flag), and three other tinclads, together with the *Stephen Bayard* and three barges containing 27,000 bushels of coal, had entered Moon Lake and pushed through to anchor "all snug" at the entrance into Old Pass. There the U.S. Navy would await the completion of the army's obstruction-removal work and the arrival of Brig. Gen. Ross.

About this same time, General Prentiss wrote out campaign orders for the army contingent Brig. Gen. Ross would lead on the expedition. Over the weekend, the 13th Division (178 officers and 3,502 men) was to be embarked upon 13 steamers currently at the riverbank, with each man carrying 160 rounds of cartridges and rations for 15 days. In accordance with orders from Maj. Gen. Grant, the mission would be a fast one, so few tents were to be loaded. On Monday, Ross was to lead his boats through the levee cut, down the channel connecting the Mississippi with Moon Lake, and then down that waterway. They would rendezvous with the navy vessels waiting at the entrance into Old Pass. Thereafter, his force was to follow the gunboats into that forbidding stretch and steam toward the Coldwater, assisting in every way to clear any leftover or newly placed obstructions. To that end, the division was not to depart without "a large quantity of axes and spades."

Given the nature of the streams ahead, it was understood that the Federal formation would proceed only during daytime. Additionally, both Ross and Smith knew that their descent would be made in stages: Old Pass to Coldwater; Coldwater to the confluence of the Yalobusha and Tallahatchie; a sweep up the former to Grenada and continuance into the Yazoo Valley. Temporary bases or depots might be established at any of those points as necessary. That evening, Lt. Col. Wilson reported to Grant that the work of removing the obstructions found in Old Pass by the Helena-based soldiers "was accomplished." Plans were made to make an early reconnaissance out into the Coldwater.[10]

By February 22, the weather in the Greenwood area had improved significantly; the sun shone brightly and work on the little Confederate fort progressed rapidly. As procured, the big 400–500-pound cotton bales were stacked in their designated positions two tiers high and six deep. After being joined together with sheet iron, these breastworks were partially covered with dirt and sand. Constructed from cotton bales, logs, and mud, the parapets were covered with rawhide, said to cause cannonballs to bounce off. To keep the works from catching fire, the whole could be wetted down with river water during battle. The next day, as preparations continued apace and additional southern soldiers arrived, Maj. Gen. Loring was able to procure from Yazoo City two giant cannon originally promised to rebel defenders in the Trans-Mississippi department. The 6.4-inch piece would arrive before the day was finished.

As February 24 progressed, Union transports from Helena all entered the Snagey Canal/Grant's Pass leading into Moon Lake en route to their rendezvous with the task group of Lt. Cmdr. Smith. There were 13 vessels, all stern-wheelers and most of them previously engaged in the Ohio River trade. The Federal Yazoo Pass expedition got underway at daylight Wednesday morning, February 25, in an incessant rainstorm. Two ironclads, five light draughts, the chartered steamer *Key West No. 2*, with a surplus of soldiers too numerous to put aboard the tinclads, the *Stephen Bayard* and her three coal barges, plus 13 army transports ("said to bear 4,500 troops") began their quest into the Mississippi Delta.

Brig. Gen. Prentiss joined the procession as a guest on the leading *Chillicothe*, finding that Smith's boats "had no trouble up to the time I left." *Chicago Daily Times* reporter Tom Cook observed that a "blind man, working in the dark and trying to describe a very crooked stream, could scarcely exceed the reality of the Yazoo Pass." Cook's *New York Herald* colleague DeB. Randolph Keim, as he signed himself, lamented, "Should one propose to run a steamboat to the moon, he would be considered equally sane by those who had seen the Yazoo Pass." Lt. Allen Wood Miller of Co. C, 36th Iowa, wrote in the diary he always kept handy: "Steamers have gone through the Pass. We try tomorrow. Rain. Beautiful lake. Men characteristically American—rush to destruction as to a feast."

Of the three, it was Prentiss's opinion that was misleading. From the start, Lt. Cmdr. Smith, in the words of Bruce Catton, "found himself mixed up in a sailor's nightmare." First, the stream they would follow "wound and turned on itself interminably and was full of snags that could rip the bottom out of an incautiously piloted gunboat." On top of that, the powerful current "made it impossible to steer properly" and even the wind could push around the tall but lightly built tinclads and transports. Further, "artful Confederates swarmed all about," felling trees to clog the narrow waterway. The nightmare would continue for days.

It had been known for some time that the width of Old Pass would permit only line-ahead steaming and so, for maximum protection of the unarmed military steamers, the tinclads, positioned after the ironclads, were spaced between the troop boats, so that all could supposedly maintain 300-yard intervals: *Rattler*, *Volunteer*, *Marmora* (Tinclad No. 2), etc. The problem, quickly identified by newsman Keim but obvious to all of the participants, was that no place could be "found in the whole stream where they could see one-third of this distance ahead or behind them." The speed of this necessarily elongated formation was, from the start, "much less than had been hoped for." Indeed, by nightfall the lead ironclads had steamed only about two miles. Still, Prentiss and Ross, conferring together, were convinced, as the former wrote Grant, "that the Yazoo Pass is the route to Vicksburg." Writing to RAdm. Porter from Yazoo Pass the next day, Lt. Cmdr. Smith indicated that his daylight-only voyage, even if challenging, was, so far, progressing without serious difficulty. Traveling only by day was, as Richard West noted, "another time killer," but to do otherwise invited certain disaster. To give his superior some idea of what they faced, the task force commander indicated that the width of Old Pass was about sufficient for one of the squadron tugboats "if handled skillfully." The forward speed of the vessels was necessarily less than the current, "as backing is our only and constant resort against dangers and to pass the numerous turns." The boats backed frequently to escape snags or tree-covered banks, while lines were in constant use to help navigate the narrow turns and to avoid colliding with the shore or remaining bush.

Every vagrant floating log, it seemed, tried to foul the paddle wheels and many of them did so. As a result, delays were frequent. *New York Herald* reporter DeB. Randolph

Keim suggested as it moved on that the expedition be renamed "the back water expedition" or the "hold water expedition." This was because, he suggested, the only way it could advance was "by holding back." The exhaust pipes, the railings, and all of the "gingerbread fixings" were swept away. These damages, if inconsequential, were frequently suffered. The *Baron de Kalb* and *Chillicothe* were able to cruise through with more ease and facility than the light draughts and troop boats. "If we get through this with our casemates up and our wheels serviceable," Smith concluded, "it will be as much as can reasonably be expected."

The fleet could only make a few miles a day "and often at night the starting point of the morning was in sight." Observing as a guest in the pilothouse of the *Volunteer*, correspondent Keim later wrote, "Once, indeed, we did catch a glimpse of the *Rattler*, flagship. She was just abreast of us, and about 100 yards away, going in an opposite direction to us." Thinking the boat was close to Smith's, the *Volunteer*'s master ordered her tied up for the night as darkness fell.

An indication of Smith's forward movement was received aboard the *Black Hawk*, anchored above Vicksburg, on the morning of February 27. Personally unfamiliar with the distances involved, RAdm. Porter expected, due to a misunderstanding with his subordinate, that Smith's group could appear in the waters above Haynes' Bluff by midnight. Having earlier ordered that his subordinate fire a predetermined number of guns upon his arrival, the admiral now sent the ironclad *Carondelet* into the mouth of the Yazoo to keep a bright lookout. If the agreed-upon signal was heard, she would immediately send word to the flag boat. Having duly gotten underway at first light, the *Volunteer* paddled on, believing herself closely following the unseen expedition flag boat, *Rattler*. Then, just as the sun was at its meridian, the transport "passed the spot where we had seen our file leader 18 hours earlier." The lead vessels of the Federal task force snaked their way to a point in Old Pass a mile or two from its entrance into the Coldwater River by 1:00 p.m. There they halted for the night. *New York Herald* scribe Keim took the opportunity to observe the vessels around him. The *Chillicothe* and *Baron de Kalb*, like icebreakers, had enjoyed fairly smooth steaming through Old Pass, crushing what did not bounce off.

Keim was optimistic regarding the ability of the following lighter craft to make their way through Old Pass. After all, as he looked astern, it was clear, in his opinion, that the lead vessels had worked the hardest to clear a path. "The others," he suggested, "have only to avail themselves of our improvements, like an avaricious tax title claimant to lands." Actually, on the other hand, the narrow and tortuous channel impeded all of the following vessels, damaging or crippling most of them, with many forced to halt to make repairs to their engines, wheels, or superstructures. Branches had wrecked cabins and light upper works, "tearing away stanchions and braces, and sometimes even the light bulkheads around the upper works." In fact, Keim opined when he saw them next day, "all the vessels look as though they had been in a hard fought battle and had been badly worsted." Because the expedition was inching along in single column, all vessels behind a halted boat had to stop as well. Even when all of the paddle wheels were biting water and the column moved ahead its average forward speed, Commodore Smith was forced to concede, was only a mile and a half per hour.

Whether under steam or halted, the warships and transports were frequently visited

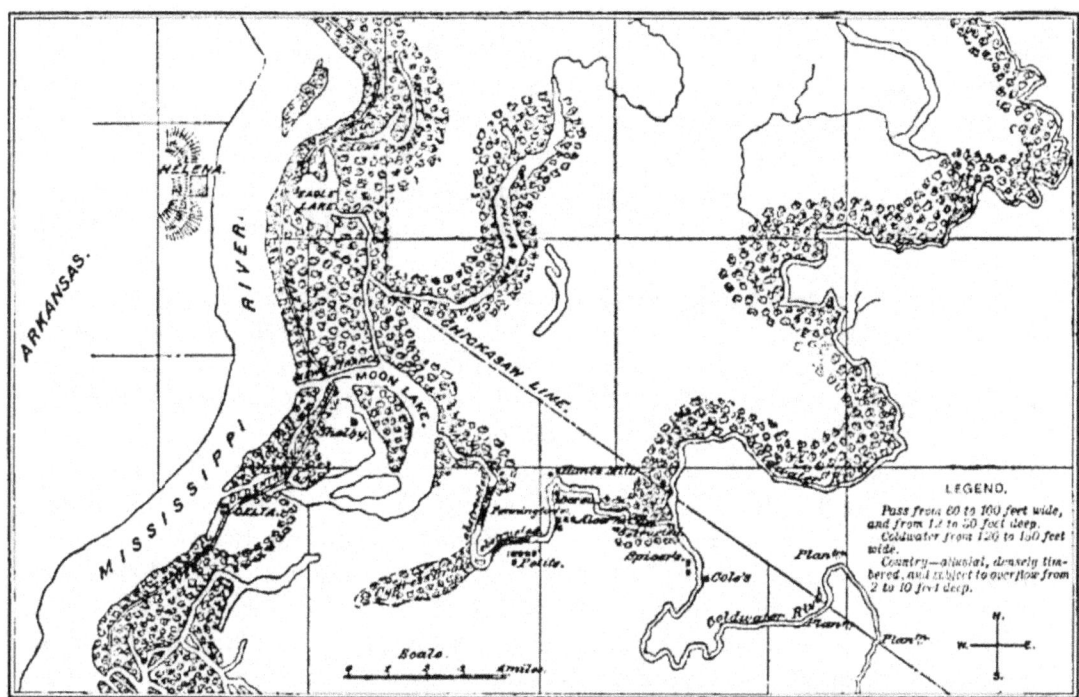

Route of the Yazoo Pass Expedition from the Mississippi into the Coldwater. Lt. Col. Wilson's detailed map, in which one foot equals four miles, shows the torturous path through which the Federal vessels, led by the *Chillicothe*, steamed in February-March 1863. The entire stretch, from the Mississippi through Moon Lake and then beyond into the Coldwater, was, because of the possibility of its ultimate destination, known as the Yazoo Pass (*Official Records of the Union and Confederate Armies*, vol. 24).v

by all manner of uninvited nonhuman residents, harmful and innocent alike. Whenever an overhanging branch swayed, it was likely to drop one or more squirrels, opossums, raccoons, rats, mice, lizards, snakes, spiders, big beetles, or other vermin. Alligators and turtles were often encountered, as were panthers and even bears. Many species were received in good humor, others with fear or loathing.

The Union ironclads *Chillicothe* and *Baron de Kalb*, followed by the *Rattler* and *Volunteer*, reached the confluence of Old Pass and the Coldwater River about noon on February 28. There they lay to as the other vessels of the expedition, strung out behind them, made their way through the twisty channel and closed up. It would take some of the vessels much longer than others. Still, the idle was not without its pleasure, as spring appeared to be opening in this latitude. The sun shown bright and warm in a clear sky. "Birds of every hue are twittering about in all directions," recorded one correspondent, "and already vegetation begins to show itself in its most beautiful greens."

The expedition was at something of a crossroads, as Richard West pointed out 50 years ago. "Since surprise was out of the question," he wrote in his pioneering essay, "everything now depended either upon getting across the Yazoo Delta before the Confederates could block the way or upon the power of his ironclads to eliminate any defenses which the Confederates might improvise." Though pressed by Ross and the ironclad captains, Smith, an ordinarily cautious man, pointed out Porter's orders to "proceed carefully ... [and] guard against surprise." It was important, he believed, that the fleet be kept together; sending ahead the ironclads would leave the transports or the ironclads themselves vulnerable to attack by whatever naval forces or rams the enemy might have available. Interestingly enough, just two days later out on the Mississippi 30 miles below Vicksburg, the *Chillicothe*'s near-sister ship, *Indianola*, was sunk by Confederate rams from Red River including the captured Federal vessel *Queen of the West*.

Throughout the expedition, Lt. Col. Wilson continuously excoriated the task force commodore in his reports to his superiors. Smith was, he bluntly said, "entirely responsible" for the ... failure of the expedition, and responsible for no other reason than his timid and slow movements." His refusal to allow the ironclads to speed ahead and thereby supposedly prevent the erection of Fort Pemberton was seen by Wilson and Foster, his successor as task force commander, as incompetence at best and cowardice at worst. Because the little armada halted frequently, Brig. Gen. Ross would later join Wilson and Foster in criticizing Lt. Cmdr. Smith for not pushing his two most powerful vessels on downstream. They could probably, he asserted, have made it to Greenwood within two days and thus have prevented the enemy from erecting the fortifications that would prove the undoing of the expedition. While Smith waited for the rest of his fleet to catch up on March 1 he ordered that the smallest coal barge be emptied and its contents crammed into the bunkers of the several warships.

Still, the expedition slowly continued. "Persons well acquainted with the country bordering on Yazoo Pass and Coldwater," the *Richmond Daily Dispatch* told its readers on February 28, "say if the enemy succeed in getting their gunboats in the Coldwater, they will never get out." The capital city newspaper went on to say that "an army of 1,000 men could hold at bay and destroy an invading force of 50,000 of the enemy."[11] During the time men aboard the lead elements of the Union expedition already through Yazoo Pass anticipated linkup with the trailing army transports and remaining naval vessels, numerous housekeeping activities were handled. Repairs were made to damaged smokestacks, and wheels and bales of cotton were collected for vessel bulwark protection.

Lt. Cmdr. Smith was clearly worried even early on. "I imagine that the character of this navigation is different from what was expected," he would observe the next day. "We will get through in fighting condition, but so much delayed that all the advantages of a surprise to the rebels will have been lost." As if to add emphasis to Smith's words, it was discovered, per Chicago newsman Cook, that "at a point about a mile below where we are lying, a huge tree has been felled directly across the channel and below that the stream has not been explored." Even more worrisome to the expedition leader was the plain truth, as the correspondent wrote: "We are, therefore, in utter ignorance of the obstacles we may meet with." The vessels still in Old Pass continued to halt frequently because of obstructions.

A significant number of steamers bearing the 13th Division, but definitely not all, and the tinclads interspersed among them finally arrived in the Coldwater in the hours after 11:00 a.m. on March 2. Lt. Allen Woods Miller of Co. C, 36th Iowa, embarked aboard the *Lavinia Logan*, dejectedly opined in his diary, "Little progress. O horrible how slowly the cause moves." Pvt. Newton Robert Scott, Company A, also of the 36th Iowa, wrote to his friend and future wife, Hannah Cone, back in Alba, IA: "We was 6 days coming 18 miles through the Yazoo Pass one of the Crookedest & narrest [sic] Channels that a Steam Boat Ever went Before. But we Have got through with about 25 Boats all together. We Have Some 6 or 8 gun Boats with us & we are now Penetrating into the verry Heart of Dixie." This accomplishment of Smith's task force in passing from Moon Lake to the Coldwater was, as RAdm. Porter wrote Washington a little over a week later, not performed without some damage to the engaged units. "The vessels had to work their way through a narrow creek for over a hundred miles," he enthusiastically wrote, "while two vessel can not pass each other." Continuing, the bluewater seaman added: "They had to remove trees that had grown up thick and intervened and sometimes they would not advance a mile per day. Vessels had their pipes knocked down, wheels carried away, and cabins swept off, but they all got through in fighting condition."

News coverage of the Yazoo operation was widespread North and South, even though Federal leaders urged correspondents to restrain their reporting. Colleagues from other Confederate theaters inquired of Lt. Gen. Pemberton whether the enemy could actually make a serious attempt on Vicksburg via the Yazoo Pass route. The newspapers, he was told, were all reporting that the enemy was working on such an outcome from that direction. New reports constantly reached them, directly or through their subordinates. For example, Capt. Edward E. Porter, commander of Porter's Rangers (Company B, 18th Mississippi Cavalry Battalion), sent word to Maj. Gen. Loring at Camp Pemberton: "The Federals left General Alcorn's farm this morning down the pass with 13 transports and five gunboats." This news was sent along to Jackson. Cmdr. Isaac Newton Brown (1817–1889), CSN, at Yazoo City also took an opportunity this day to acquaint Pemberton with developments from his vantage point. "Latest advices represent the enemy steadily passing their forces into Coldwater. Two first-class ironclads are said to be with them and the ram *Lancaster*." The Federal land force was estimated at 20,000 and the sailor was convinced that their "demonstration will be made in force."

Kentuckian Brown, a Mexican War veteran and contemporary of the Union's Capt. Henry Walke, was currently the de facto Rebel naval chief on the Western waters. Having served on the Mississippi since 1861, he won immortality with his command of the ironclad ram *Arkansas* during the first Vicksburg campaign in July 1862. He would return East after the fall of Vicksburg to command an ironclad at Charleston, SC. Residing postwar in Mississippi and Texas, he was not restored to full citizenship for almost 20 years after the end of the war. Declining to participate in civic or political affairs after 1875, he did, however, agree, to author a history of the *Arkansas* and of his role in the torpedo defense of the Yazoo River for *Century Illustrated* magazine in the 1880s.

The Union's Yazoo Pass expedition crawled farther down the Coldwater River on March 3–4. The light draughts and troop transports, underway at sunrise, were pestered by wind and current and surrendered pieces of themselves to their surroundings "as mementoes of the trip." Only the mighty ironclads continued to appear immune to the ravages of the grasping shoreline forest. Even so, the *Chillicothe* managed to locate a snag on the latter day that loosened a plank in her hull. The Federals watching from their boats as they passed farther down found the countryside devoid of clearings or patches with shacks "to relieve the monotony of the unbroken wilderness." Reporter

Keim noted that not a living soul was seen, so no one could be questioned as to what might lie ahead.

Writing to his editor from Young's Point that evening, William George, the correspondent from the *New York Times* who wrote under the pen name "De Soto," brought up a matter seldom mentioned in studies of the bayou campaigns. Given that warm weather was approaching, Union soldiers, "as well as the naval part of the Mississippi expedition," would soon need clothing adapted to the climate. They would not be able to continue providing "effective service in the heavy woolen garments which have been issued to them for use in colder climates."

The Coldwater proved less torturous on Thursday, March 5, allowing the speed of the Federal armada to be increased. In better spirits, Lt. Cmdr. Smith opined that his advance elements might reach the Tallahatchie that evening. "We are better off than the army," he observed cheerfully, because "we have a fair supply of coal." As the gunboats approached the confluence of the Coldwater and the Tallahatchie in late afternoon, scouts sent along the shore by Brig. Gen. Ross found a small Confederate battery stationed to block Union progress. The Southern soldiers chose not to stand and the threat was quickly eliminated by the Northern patrol.

Navigating the Coldwater and the Tallahatchie. The huge leading *Chillicothe* crashed through the Coldwater undergrowth with relatively little difficulty, though at one point on March 4 she managed to locate a snag and loosen a plank in her hull. The U.S. Army transports and the light-draught gunboats interspersed among them were able to join up with her some 15 miles below the mouth of the Coldwater on March 7, from which point the task force continued down the Tallahatchie. Three nights later, the Northern invasion fleet, in heavy rain, tied up to shore about 20 miles from a half-mile-wide neck of land that was believed to be just a few leagues above Greenwood, MS, by water (*Harper's New Monthly Magazine*, January 1865).

A survey was now taken to determine the extent of rations left to the navy vessels. No vessel had more than a month's supply; the *Chillicothe* was down to seven days. Joint army and navy parties foraged daily, retrieving beef for dinner and cotton for protection. In the process, the bluecoats learned that large numbers of impressed slaves were fortifying both Yazoo City and Greenwood. "I do not place the same credit in the reports concerning Greenwood," Smith told Ross and wrote Porter.

At Young's Point during the day, Maj. Gen. Grant elected to reinforce the Federal expedition. He wanted to be able to carry off a coordinated attack by all of his forces upon Vicksburg and believed that the incursion now being made from the north through the Mississippi Delta offered the best opportunity to obtain a position on the east bank of the Yazoo River. Besides, rumors had been heard that Vicksburg was sending forces, in the words of Steven Woodworth, "to counter the Union force coming through Yazoo Pass." To add further insurance to the current Union effort aimed at the Yazoo, he wrote to Maj. Gen. James B McPherson (1828–1864), commander of the XVII Army Corps then working on the Lake Providence Canal project upriver in Louisiana. Wanting a lodgment at Yazoo City or another good location, Grant ordered his subordinate to organize his corps so as to "get in there as rapidly as possible." Brig. Gen. Isaac F. Quinby's (1821–1891) Seventh would be the first of two divisions started.

A master of detail, Buckeye McPherson had become chief engineer of the Army of the Tennessee in 1862 and commander of the 2nd Division before his elevation to corps leadership. He led that field army after Grant was sent East but was killed in the Battle of Atlanta. A new Jersey native and a teacher before the war, Quinby had been a veteran of Grant's western campaigns since the spring of 1862, becoming intimately familiar with the Corinth sector. Though he was active during the remainder of the Vicksburg campaign, poor health forced his resignation in December 1863.[12]

Having passed out of the Coldwater early on the morning of March 6, the lead vessels of the U.S. Yazoo Pass expedition enjoyed relatively smooth steaming during the day. "The weather is very warm for this time of the year," observed one shipmate, "the Holly tree is robed in her beautyfull [sic] robe of green; the woods will all soon be in full leaf." Led by the *Chillicothe*, the naval portion of the task force passed down the Tallahatchie about 12 miles before dark. The "extreme upper part of this river and the lower part of the Coldwater were moderately good rivers," newsman Keim later testified, and would permit the column to make upwards of 20–30 miles per day. During this portion of the trip, numerous stops were made along the bank to obtain cotton bales, which willing hands stuffed into every available opening aboard the light draught gunboats and some of the transports. Some bales were also employed aboard the *Chillicothe* and *Baron de Kalb*.

Although March 7 was a Saturday, it was no less a busy day for the soldiers and sailors aboard the slowly moving Federal invasion fleet than any of the others before it. The U.S. Army transports and the light draught gunboats interspersed among them were able to join up with the *Chillicothe*, *Baron de Kalb*, and *Rattler* some 15 miles below the mouth of the Coldwater. The vessels toward the end of the column finally entered the Tallahatchie between noon and about 2:00 p.m. Brig. Gen. Ross and Lt. Cmdr. Smith then conferred on what steps to take next.

The matter of ironclad coaling now became a point of angst between Ross and

Smith, with the former believing it wasted precious time. The contract army boats could employ foraged wood in their boilers; the navy, especially for the ironclads, needed to use the anthracite bedded in the two unwieldy barges tended by the *Stephen Bayard*. It was decided between the two leaders that after the naval craft were coaled that night a depot would be established when they came to the confluence of the Yalobusha and Tallahatchie. Once this supply point was set up, it would be protected by a tinclad. That evening, as bluejackets aboard the *Chillicothe* and *Baron de Kalb* labored to refuel, Smith and Ross, a long way yet from the Yazoo, wrote out reports for their superiors. The U.S. naval commander dwelt upon the added protection captured cotton gave his units, including the two ironclads. Writing to Brig. Gen. Prentiss, Ross set out the timetable he hoped the task group would execute: mouth of Yalobusha Monday evening (March 9) and on to Greenwood the next day, having possession of that community by noon. Just after midnight, the Union gunboats stationed at the mouth of the Yazoo River heard what was thought to be signal guns from Smith's expedition as it descended that stream. It was speculated at Cairo two days later, when the dispatch boat *General Lyon* arrived with the down river news, that if the signal really was "from the *Chillicothe*, as conjectured, Yazoo City has already fallen into Federal hands." Hindsight shows such was not the case.

The coaling of the *Chillicothe* and *Baron de Kalb* took longer than was anticipated, meaning a late departure for the task force on March 8. Brig. Gen. Ross was quite upset by the schedule maintained by the commodore. "The work should have been done by 2 o'clock this morning and we on our way by 5:30," he steamed, "but it was 7:30 this morning before we started." Although the general was "a little, yes, considerably disgusted with these necessary delays," he still expected the joint Union army-navy expedition to steam some 40–50 miles. Ross would later report himself most indignant over the fact that "on several occasions the gunboat immediately in my advance stopped and lay to an hour for dinner." The vessels causing his unhappiness were the two ironclads and the *Rattler*.

The banks of the Tallahatchie for its first 20 miles were found to be high, with "well-cultivated plantations in abundance." The owners, remembered the *New York Herald* correspondent aboard the steamer *Volunteer*, "were, as a general thing, at home attending to their ordinary avocations as though there existed no war in the land." Thereafter, however, the banks became low and were overflowed by the high river stage. For the next 40 to 50 miles, there were no plantations seen nor any wilderness break experienced because "the course of the stream became exceedingly tortuous, the bends sharp and abrupt, the timber scraggy and hanging far over the water, and the whole appearance wild and forbidding." The crooked waterway would delay progress more than was anticipated when the fleet broke out of the Coldwater into the upper reaches.

Preparations continued at best speed on March 8 to fortify the neck of land at Fort Pemberton. "Cotton bales and dirt" enhanced the natural strength of the position, the eastern end of which, according to one soldier from Co. G, 22nd Mississippi, was literally anchored "in the Yazoo." According to Ron Field, with Federal forces approaching Loring also "cut the levees and flooded the surrounding area, ensuring that the only approach to the fort was by water."

Laborers prepared a defensive log raft to protect its river flank and several cannon

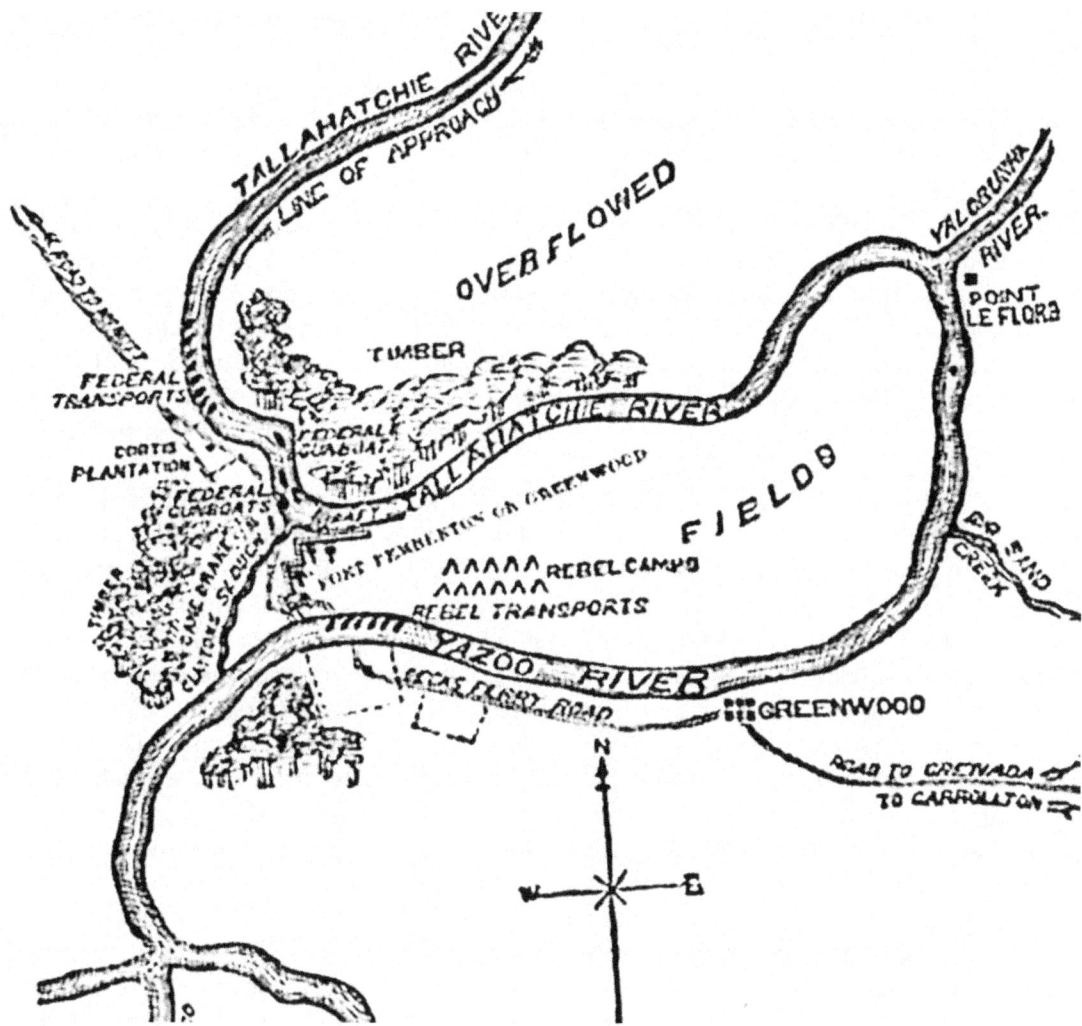

Fort Greenwood or Fort Pemberton. The Southern cotton-bale bastion just above Greenwood, MS, as was common during the Civil War, wore a different name depending upon one's affiliation, North or South. The name Fort Greenwood was taken from the nearby community, while Fort Pemberton honored Vicksburg's commander. The author's rendering shows the reader not only the main points of battle but also the geography of the river confluence and the direction, and is based on maps appearing in the *New York Herald*, March 25, 1863, and the *Official Records of the Union and Confederate Armies*, v. 24.

were emplaced including the rifled and banded 32-pounder, sometimes known as a 6.4-inch rifle. Captured perhaps at Norfolk, VA, there were hundreds of smoothbore 32-pounders available to the Confederacy at the beginning of the war. Some of these long-barrel pieces had their inner bores rifled and so could no longer fire cannonballs but instead shot elongated rifled 68-pound projectiles. Several replicas are today on display, including those at Fort Macon. Often these guns were mistakenly identified as 6.4-inch Brooke rifles.

It also began to rain incessantly. Noted both at Confederate camps and aboard the

Union invasion fleet, the downpour showed no signs of cessation. The rivers ran over their banks at every low spot and the countryside in many locations became even more inundated. Despite the heavy and oft times violent downpour that soaked the Yazoo Valley for the next two days, newsman Keim noted the rain was good for the Yankees, "as it prevents the operations of guerillas or other forces of the enemy against us along the river."

On March 9 Maj. Gen. Loring received a message from Lt. Gen. Pemberton stating that, despite several requests, there were no more heavy guns to send nor spare troops. In his return wire Loring stated simply, "From every information I can get, enemy's gunboats will be down tomorrow. They were 75 miles from here today." Scouts and citizens, openly or hidden in canebreaks, watched as the vessels, great clouds of black smoke belching from their chimneys, paddled past. Throughout the time of the expedition, the Federal boats were anything but quiet, great puff-puff propulsion sounds or whistles being regularly audible.

Just before 4:00 p.m. the ironclad *Chillicothe* hove in sight of a flaming and nearly incinerated steamboat. A cutter was sent to inspect the scene and its occupants learned that she was the *35th Parallel* and had been hauling cotton for the defenses of Greenwood. The Federals continued on and the wreck, "in flames [and] almost consumed," per Lt. Cmdr. Smith, sank as the *Rattler* passed. Aboard the flag boat, Lt. Cmdr. Smith was displeased and worried. His allowance of coal had been calculated upon "prompt movements" and did "not include delays." The problem was, of course, that delays were constant. Although every effort was being made to push ahead as rapidly as possible "speed was far below" expectations. With "strict attention" to "using coal economically," Smith believed his ironclads might have sufficient for the mission. Even so, his towboat, the *Stephen Bayard*, was now "a worn-out vessel." Her owners, the commander asserted, would probably "be pleased" if she was just "left down here."

At approximately 1:15 p.m. on March 10, the black-hulled *Chillicothe* took possession of a flatboat loaded with furniture. The contents were set ashore—except for confiscated contraband—and the craft burned. On shore, her tars also fired a sawmill. At Camp Pemberton, Cmdr. Brown got off a brief message to Lt. Gen. Pemberton: "The enemy in great force are very near our works."

Throughout the day as his craft approached Greenwood, Lt. Cmdr. Smith took every opportunity to gather intelligence from local people, mostly African Americans, along the riverbank. The stories collectively provided a picture of what supposedly lay just ahead. According to this information, there was a single line of cotton-and-sand breastworks facing westward not far above the town. These, together with their parapet, were circled by a deep slough, or ditch, extending across the narrow neck of land. The slough was quite close to the Confederate works at the upper end but gradually receded from them until, at the lower end, it was removed by several hundred feet. Beyond this slough was an extensive canebrake, and a deep woods reached even farther back into the country. The right flank of this cotton-bale bastion contained three guns, one a rifled piece, plus field pieces and, some believed, upwards of 7,000 soldiers. Lt. Cmdr. James P. Foster, captain of the *Chillicothe*, would later report that there were five cannon. Four of them could launch both shot and shell and were believed to be 12- to 30-pounder rifles. The fifth, mounted *en barbette*, was a monstrous 6.4-inch gun ("an old 32-

pounder, altered") that employed conical steel-pointed shells. Directly to the right of the Rebel works was a log raft ready to be swung into position along with a block ship prepared for sinking in the river passage. Smith understood that he, Ross, and the rest of their contingent would not see the fort until they were about 400 yards distant.

In fact, the Confederate breastworks, made from cotton bales covered with earth, contained seven cannon mounted en barbette, meaning they could be elevated, according to Warren E. Grabau, to fire "over the top of a smooth parapet, rather than through embrasures." The pieces included one banded 32-pounder (6.4-inch) rifle; one 12-pounder rifle; one 18-pounder (3-inch) Whitworth; and two 12-pounder rifles on siege carriages. There was one 6-pounder and one 3-inch rifle emplaced on the left flank and a 6-pounder Napoleon in the center. Several ersatz "Quaker" guns were also in place, painted black and looking real. Ammunition, including some shells that received final assembly on the spot, was stored in three cotton bale and earth magazines.

Col. Waul continued his overall command of the troops at the post under the supervision of Maj. Gen. Loring, who now assigned his inspector general, Capt. John D. Myrick, to take charge of the batteries. As the Yankees appeared, they "found us but poorly prepared to receive him," the commander of the cotton bale bastion later recalled. That night, the Northern invasion fleet, in heavy rain, tied up to shore about 20 miles from a half-mile-wide neck of land that was believed to be just a few leagues above Greenwood by water. At sunrise on a rainy March 11, the men at Fort Pemberton were sent to their stations on the breastworks. The Smith-Ross Union task force, meanwhile, steered for Dr. Curtiss's plantation, a point in the Tallahatchie about five miles from Greenwood on a direct line, but 12 by that stream or the Yazoo.

Seeing the great clouds of black smoke approaching closer from up the river, Maj. Gen. Loring ordered the patrolling 2nd Missouri Cavalry to fall back to the south bank of the Yalobusha. With the commander of the still-incomplete little bulwark looking on, his gunners aimed the available cannon down the Tallahatchie as other soldiers rushed to handle two other last-minute defensive details. The defensive raft was swung into place across the river, as was a block ship. Now if the Federals managed to get by the outer defense of the fort it would remain for the famous old wreck and the raft to stop them.

Forward Union progress was blocked, in the words of Brig. Gen. Ross, by "a strong fortification," extending from the Tallahatchie to the Yazoo, across a neck of land some 2.5 miles below. For all practical purposes, the Federals found, upon easing into the bank about 9:00 a.m., a "low, horizontal silhouette" downstream of them, the Rebel strongpoint "entirely surrounded by water." Lt. Cmdr. Foster aboard the *Chillicothe* later remembered it was about three miles "distant from the Yazoo." The first order of Union business now was a reconnaissance. To that end, Brig. Gen. Ross, Lt. Cmdr. Smith, and Lt. Col. Wilson all boarded the *Chillicothe* promptly at 9:00 a.m. Moving slowly ahead, the ironclad turned through a long bend. About 70 minutes later she came in sight of the Confederate batteries 800–900 yards upstream, at which point she was taken under fire. Out of 25–30 shells thrown at her from what Foster believed were five enemy cannon, four struck his boat, causing some damage and obstructing visibility with huge clouds of smoke.

The initial Confederate shell from Fort Pemberton to strike home was a shell that sliced into the port bow of the gunboat about 18 inches above the waterline. It did not penetrate the armor but all but buried itself in the iron plating. The second missile hit the starboard side of the *Chillicothe*'s forward casemate, her stationary turret, approximately four feet from the forward starboard gun port and six feet above the deck. Identified as a "conical rifle shot," the projectile indented and fractured both turret plates and smashed in the 9-inch pine framing (or backing) abaft of where it hit, splintering it. It also broke off or started several bolts; one of the former flying around inside the turret gave a crewman a shoulder contusion. A third round also hulled the vessel, "making as great an indentation as possible without breaking through," as one more glanced off the deck. We do not know exactly what sort of projectiles hit the ironclad. One can be fairly certain that Loring's assertion is correct that at least one was a 6.4-inch round, while another came from the 18-pounder Whitworth gun.

In reply to the Confederate fire, the *Chillicothe* sent three 11-inch Dahlgren shells landward, though to what effect was unseen because of the smoke trapped under the tree branches along the riverbank. At 11:00 a.m., after being in action about 20 minutes, the ironclad hauled off and backed up around the point, halting when all but her black bow and the forward face of her turret were concealed by trees within ¾ mile of the fortifications. Smith and Ross departed to discuss their next moves and her crew were immediately put to work placing well-pressed cotton bales against the turret. As he had seen done on Lt. Cmdr. Walker's boat at Arkansas Post back in January, Foster now ordered his tower "slushed." Refuse cooking fat and grease were then believed capable of helping to turn cannonballs and shrapnel. Once the cannon fire stopped, Maj. Gen. Loring composed a set of messages that couriers immediately took away. He recapped the action for Lt. Gen. Pemberton and asked that ammunition be sent to him and if additional troops were available at Vicksburg they be dispatched to Yazoo City.

Following a reconnaissance by two Federal regiments, their colonels reported to Brig. Gen. Ross that the geography of the area was quite unfavorable for land operations. To get at the fort it would be necessary to cross some 600 yards of cleared ground and a bayou containing water four feet deep. They could not sneak up through the woods that bordered the fields because they were well within the range of enemy cannon. The contest ahead would be purely a ship-shore slugfest, much in the manner of Fort Henry up on the Tennessee River just over a year earlier. Unlike that at Fort Henry, the waterway here was so constricted the gunboats would be unable to obtain a good angle of fire. On top of that, as Steven Woodworth reemphasizes in his study of the Army of the Tennessee, "dry land—limited as it was to the curving strips of the natural levee—was so scarce that Ross' division could not deploy and use its strength against the much weaker Confederate garrison."

About 3:00 p.m. lookouts aboard the U.S. ironclads saw what appeared to be the removal of cattle and other goods from the battery they had engaged in the morning. It was thought in some circles that "they were preparing to leave." Events would prove that had been a bad interpretation of a Southern precautionary move as the Federals returned to the attack in late afternoon. Loring's biographer, James Raab, calls the livestock withdrawal a trick, designed by "an old frontier fighter" to lure his enemy into making another attack.

Lt. Gen. Pemberton, at Jackson, now received a delayed report on the enemy opposition from Maj. Gen. Loring. According to a spy who had escaped his Federal captors, the armada approaching down the Tallahatchie comprised two ironclads, seven gunboats, a mortar boat, and upwards of 27 troop transports. Believing the enemy was fully apprised of Confederate strength at Yazoo City, the agent indicated that the avowed Union intention was to bypass that town "with a view to operate in rear of Vicksburg."

At 4:10 p.m. the *Chillicothe*, followed by the *Baron de Kalb*, steamed down to within 800 yards of Fort Pemberton, having strengthened themselves with additional pressed cotton bales before advancing. "The short distance and the stream being narrow," Lt. Cmdr. Smith later wrote, "prevents the easy use of two vessels upon the fort." Given that only one gunboat at a time could attack, the former opened the ball when at 4:15 p.m. she commenced firing upon a steamboat lying just beyond the Rebel bastion. Seven big 5-second, 11-inch shells were launched. Two appeared to burst well over the fort and two others were seen to apparently strike the steamer *John Walsh*. A Federal soldier on land later remembered the noise of the ironclad shoot as "a perfect roar, louder than any thunder." Capt. Thomas N. Stevens of the 28th Wisconsin admitted that the *Chillicothe*'s shoot was the "first sight" and "first sounds of real war" many in the regiment had ever experienced. Every gun at Fort Pemberton now opened on the strange-looking Union ironclad, as well as the troops along the riverbank. Simultaneously, Lt. Cmdr. Smith hailed orders for the ram *Lioness* to be kept ready as he prepared to bring up the *Rattler* and transfer from her back aboard the *Chillicothe*. Once the ironclads silenced the fort's guns, the ram would surge ahead and push the hulk of the block ship out of the way for the army transports. Smith wouldn't get the chance to board his boat or use Master O'Reilly's boat against the sunken steamer.

One of the necessities of in the *Chillicothe*'s unusual design was that her forward 3-inch-thick gunport slide covers needed to be kept sufficiently ajar while the cannon were being loaded to permit the rammer handles to pass out. The men of the forward port were loading a shell with the slide covers ajar, but as the charger was cutting the shell fuse they had not yet tapped it home. At that precise moment, a Confederate 6.4-inch steel pointed rifle shell sailed through the crack and hit the tulip of the 11-inch Dahlgren, resulting in a disaster. The bursting 6.4-inch Confederate shell ignited the 11-inch shell of the *Chillicothe*. The explosion carried away the two slide covers (weighing about 3,200 pounds between them) in front of the piece, which, although slightly fractured on the interior rim of its muzzle, was amazingly not disabled. Years later, a Confederate soldier paid tribute to that piece of Federal ordnance when he said its manufacturer "'builded well,'" so well, in fact, the piece "did good work in subsequent actions." One of the blown-out slide covers was lost overboard. The blast also carried away a part of the turret backing, ripped the bolts out of large swaths of armor, and set ablaze the packed cotton bales earlier placed forward of the turret. The No. 2, or forward port, gun crew was "rendered perfectly useless." Three men were killed outright, 11 others were badly wounded (one mortally), and three others were temporarily blinded by powder in their eyes. Special Pilot Morton was among the wounded, though he would recover.

Lt. Cmdr. Foster, a reporter from the *New York Herald* later wrote, "exhibited the utmost coolness and courage when the severe accident befell him, ordering his men to remain quiet, and giving the necessary directions to bring his starboard gun into range."

***Chillicothe* vs. Fort Pemberton.** This depiction of the Federal casemate ironclad, dated February 22, 1864, was published by Bufford's Print House, Boston, Massachusetts. With no photographs of the craft known to exist, this is the only artistic print we have of her other than the Meagher plans shown on other pages. Other illustrations depict her yard mate, the *Indianola*, and there are photographs of her big sister, *Tuscumbia*. *Chillicothe* was damaged in her engagements with Fort Pemberton, with several men lost and defects exposed. Repaired at Mound City, IL, she returned to active duty with the Mississippi Squadron on September 6, 1863 (Navy History and Heritage Command).

This was his last shot of the day. Historian Donald Canney later suggested the freak shell-melting on the *Chillicothe* "did much to tarnish her fighting reputation." The Confederates truly had the range of the *Chillicothe* and hit her three more times. One round smacked into the bow deck, another carried away the jackstaff, and the last impacted aft. Several dumbstruck crewmen watched as the latter approached, passed over the port quarter and aft of the turret and between the paddle-wheel houses. Later, a chunk of the boat blown off into the water and still carrying a shell fragment washed down with the current and floated against the raft opposite the fort.

During the seven-minute action, Fort Pemberton was believed to have fired 20 rounds at the *Chillicothe* while she got off four 5-second shells before backing down the river out of range. The *Baron de Kalb*, her bow at times touching the *Chillicothe*, participated in the shoot, but details of her success or any damages are lacking. Smith, "on going aboard the *Chillicothe* found her already much injured by the shot of the enemy." Fragments from several Rebel shells that struck the Federal boat were later recovered. From these, the task force commander knew that he was facing a 6.4 and most likely a 24-pounder and a 3- or 4.5-inch rifle. As he later intimated to Smith, Lt. Cmdr. Foster was now convinced his craft was "a failure" due to "the ease with which the enemy's shell ... penetrates the armor." She would remain so, in his opinion, until "alterations are made in the backing of the turret" or, left unsaid, she was sunk.

The two ironclads were now withdrawn as orders were passed for additional cotton armoring to be installed. Not long afterwards, a Rebel called over warning the Federals that they had a vessel of their own, ready presumably to attack and board the *Chillicothe*. If such were possible, Lt. Cmdr. Smith was ready. The ironclad's crew would go below while other Union vessels closed and swept her with gunfire, presumably dislodging any successful boarders.

During the day's actions, most of the ammunition for the Confederate 6.4-inch rifle was expended, but the fort's defenders took no casualties. Loring, in reporting the second confrontation with the *Chillicothe*, remarked, "Our 32-pounder shot nearly exhausted; they are our main reliance." At 7:15 p.m. the post commander sent one last message by courier to Pemberton: "From all the information we can gather, the enemy's strength is five gunboats and about 5,000 men, indicating the advance of a huge force." Late that night Smith retired to his cabin aboard the *Rattler* to write out his daily report for RAdm. Porter. The *Baron de Kalb* was very awkward in maneuvering; however, the *Chillicothe* "worked well." The turret armor of the *Chillicothe*, on the other hand, was poorly backed. Indeed, neither she nor the *Baron de Kalb* would be able to "stand the rifle shot." The soldiers "serve[d] the guns well," but there was insufficient manpower overall to do more than partially man most other vessel departments. The fear of Rebel activities required that steam now be kept up at night as well as during the day, thereby further exhausting the coal supply.

While the military people wrote out their reports, correspondents attached to the fleet penned their own observations, beginning not with columns but with a series of short dispatches that would be sent out on returning supply steamers for fast passage up the Mississippi to Memphis and hence to newspapers all over the North. The reporters, like the sailors, were stunned by the pounding taken by Foster's ironclad and they reported accordingly. Messages published in the *Philadelphia Press* and the *New York Times* on March 20 revealed "the *Chillicothe* was struck sixty-four times and damaged seriously." She was also out of ammunition. The *Cincinnati Daily Commercial* piled on, telling its readers that "during the engagement, one of the *Chillicothe*'s guns exploded, killing three or four of the seamen and injuring seriously a dozen others, mostly soldiers belonging to Ohio regiments." On the other hand, the named correspondents Cook and Keim and several others embedded in the expedition began to polish relatively objective pieces that would be sent off to their journals in the next few days. Keim, unlike several others on the scene, was impressed with the resilience of Capt. Foster's ironclad, reporting that *Chillicothe* had been under fire "a little over an hour and a half" that day: "She was not withdrawn till long after the enemy had ceased firing and then only because her store of ammunition was about exhausted and requiring a replenishment of her magazine. The Rebels singled her out as their principal target, and they peppered her well.... Her massive iron plating was indented all over her front where balls had struck her. Yet she withstood the terrible ordeal, and is tonight as good for a fight as she was this morning."[13]

There was no action at Fort Pemberton on March 12. The entire day was spent by the Federals repairing the damages to the *Chillicothe*, increasing the protection of both that boat and the *Baron de Kalb*, and loading shells. In what would prove to be his final letter home, Seaman Frederic E. Davis aboard the latter told his parents that his boat had been "feeling" the enemy's strength and he expected a decisive battle within the next 24 hours. He would be glad when the campaign was over as the *De Kalb* had been away from the fleet for almost a month and was much damaged by trees, etc., in the narrow rivers.

News of the previous day's engagement had spread throughout the Delta by late afternoon. At Rokeby Plantation on the Yazoo River, some five miles below Yazoo City, its owner, James Oliver Hazard Perry Sessions, wrote in his diary: "Yesterday the Yankees attacked our batteries at Greenwood on the Yazoo. Great consternation in the country—a good many running away. If they succeed in passing there, the whole valley is gone." Campaign information of a more fictitious kind was published in the *New York Tribune*, based on stories already floating about Memphis. "The Yazoo Pass expedition," it read, "is a complete success. The gunboats have arrived above Haynes' Bluff, which is poorly fortified against attack from above." Additional wishful thinking revealed that the Union fleet had "captured 26 transports up the Yazoo, eight of which were burned." The story would be repeated in numerous Northern newspapers, including the *Cincinnati Daily Gazette* and the *Brooklyn Daily Eagle* on March 16 and the *New York Times* a day later. Even the most famous western reporter for the *Times*, Franc B. ("Galway") Wilkie, accepted it as fact and went on to analyze it in his column published on March 19.

Just before midnight, Maj. Gen. Loring wired Jackson to report that Greenwood was quiet and there was no further action taken against his position during the day. Following 24 hours of preparation, Lt. Cmdr. Smith was nearly ready to reopen the attack upon Fort Pemberton early on Friday, the 13th of March. Only a few last-minute details needed tending. The weather was great and, according to the *New York Herald* man on the scene, "like a June morning in the Northern states."

After completion of the customary warship breakfast hour that so infuriated the army leadership, the naval commander made certain that conditions were ready for a coordinated attack. In the two hours after 9:00 a.m. men newly detailed to the *Chillicothe* from two tinclads to serve as the ironclad's fresh No. 2 gun crew were rigorously drilled by Lt. Cmdr. Foster and his officers. The *Chillicothe* let go her lines and at 10:30 a.m. started downstream. Unhappily, there now occurred some difficulty in getting the expedition's lone mortar boat into position and this prevented the *Baron de Kalb* from moving. For 15 minutes, the *Chillicothe* waited until it was possible for her Eads-built consort to make steam. At 10:45 a.m. the two Union ironclads advanced down the Tallahatchie, the *Chillicothe* steaming some 50 yards ahead of the *Baron de Kalb*, toward their assigned positions about 800 yards from the Rebel works. To make certain that the vessels would be kept in the best bombardment position in the stiff current, a technique used many times earlier (most recently during the *Benton*'s duel with Snyder's Bluff in December 1862) was again employed—the gunboats were tethered to the shore. A line was run from the stern of the *Chillicothe* to keep her steady, along with a breast line from the starboard side forward. The *De Kalb* was similarly secured. Small boats were also put into the water to help guide the larger craft and to provide emergency towing. Now, if necessary, both gunboats could be kept from turning or could be drawn back out of view if disabled. It was, of course, unsaid that the lines were also designed to make certain that a disabled boat did not drift with the current down the intervening distance into the hands of the enemy.

While the Union ironclads were being secured, the "ball was opened" by one of the Union land cannon put ashore two days earlier. Lt. Cmdr. Foster believed the guns of Fort Pemberton were in action against "Battery Wilson" for at least three minutes before the *Chillicothe* answered with her forward port and starboard Dahlgrens at 11:25 a.m. The gunboat remained in action until 12.58 p.m., during which hour and 38-minutes she expended 54 five-second shell and shrapnel and all of her five-second fuses. As near as could be ascertained, the big Northern target floating on the Tallahatchie was hit 38 times. The Confederate fire was extremely punishing. Huge clouds of smoke hung over the area between the *Chillicothe* and Fort Pemberton. Atop the cotton bale and mud ramparts of the latter Maj. Gen. Loring rushed back and forth urging on his gunners: "Give 'em blizzards, boys. Give 'em Blizzards!" The phrase would give the one-armed Mexican War hero the sobriquet "Old Blizzards," which would stick to him for the rest of his life.

During the attack, projectiles from Fort Pemberton struck the ironclad ten times within a 10-foot space on the port side of her turret forward. Some shots bounced off (believed to be 20-pounders), but the 6.4-inch conical rounds did "mischief." Seven missiles went through the wheelhouses (with pieces striking the paddle wheels) of the *Chillicothe* and the remainder hit in and about her bow, on the starboard side of the turret forward, and on her port quarter and hurricane deck, including several that riddled her weather roof. Additionally, her launch was "stove to pieces," while her pennant was shot away and her American flag was shot through four times.

Watching with his spyglass from shore, Lt. Cmdr. Smith himself "saw three hit in one place, under the edge of the hurricane deck, port side forward." Those so bent down the grating as to confine the steering wheel. Additionally, the forward port gun port lid was struck three times before bouncing out, and the other was disabled. All of the cotton bales placed against the turret, while undoubtedly helping to prevent further damage, were thrown out of place. Three times they caught fire, but on each occasion African American firemen hosed down the flame, extinguishing it. Out of ammunition and on fire, Foster received his superior's permission to retire to fill more shell and cut fuses. Six men were wounded aboard the *Chillicothe*, but today there were no deaths. Her commander was particularly proud of the new No. 2 gun crew. "Although never drilled until the morning of the action" and "never under fire before," it "behaved remarkably well."

After the *Chillicothe* withdrew back up the river "around the bend, 800 yards distance, showing only one gun," Maj. Gen. Loring got off a message to Jackson announcing the fight. Noting the enemy withdrawal, he sadly revealed his own losses. "Thank God, our losses small so far," he wrote. "Enemy's must be very great." A newsman from Jackson noted a while later in the day: "Two empty boxes floated down and lodged against our raft, marked Com. J.B. Hull, U.S.N., steamer *Chillicothe*, 11-inch shell."

While the *Chillicothe* engaged Fort Pemberton and was peppered in return, the *Baron de Kalb* also fought the Confederates bows-on. Capt. Walker later remembered that the fighting was particularly severe until her consort withdrew. Thereafter the old

Eads-built ironclad retained her position, firing at the Confederates at 10–15-minute intervals. After dark, at Smith's order, the gunboat backed up to her previous anchorage.

The inability of the Federals to spot their fire kept them from knowing that several 11-inch shells from the *Chillicothe* had been effective. Pvt. Edwin E. Rice of Waul's Texas Legion recorded in his diary, "Several times they came very near dismounting our two largest guns."

A Dahlgren projectile from the *Chillicothe* smashed through 16 feet of cotton and earth protecting the magazine of the Confederate Whitworth gun, manned by Company B of the Pointe Coupee Artillery. Although the shell failed to explode, it "ignited a tub of cartridges in the magazine" that caused a fire so serious it claimed the lives of the lieutenant commanding the piece and 15 Louisianans from his gun crew. Another naval shell burst over a different battery, killing another soldier and wounding four others.

After inspecting the damages aboard the two ironclads, Lt. Cmdr. Smith made an assessment of his major instruments: "Those two vessels do not resist shot well." In a report to RAdm. Porter, he elaborated: "With much opposition, the *Chillicothe*'s turret would be demolished. The *De Kalb* is pretty strong directly in front. If this expedition meets with this kind of opposition, other and better vessels will be required. The *Chillicothe*'s thin white pine backing will not stand."

Remaining extremely anxious for the success of the expedition, Maj. Gen. Grant, at Young's Point, had not yet heard of the encounters between the gunboats and Fort Pemberton. Still, wild rumors were circulating that because the Federal fleet was about to pass into the Yazoo the heavy guns at Vicksburg were being dismounted and preparations taken to evacuate the town. Hungry for concrete information and unable to see any reduction in the town's water battery, he wrote to Brig. Gen. Prentiss: "Give me all the news you receive of the Yazoo expedition promptly and direct, without sending through the army corps commander." At 7:50 p.m. Maj. Gen. Loring, now unofficially known as "Old Blizzards," got off a dispatch to Jackson. In it he acknowledged that the Federals had opened up on him again and kept "it up with great spirit until after sunset." His men would be working through the night to effect repairs to the parapet. Perhaps just as important as Loring's recap, or more so, was his confirmation that reinforcement steamers were approaching from Yazoo City. "Ammunition for heavy guns arrived just now," he cheered. It would supplement the cartridges for the 6.4-incher that were being prepared as he wrote.

About 11:00 p.m. a very discouraged Lt. Col. Wilson, writing by lantern light aboard the steamer *Volunteer*, poured out his disappointment in a letter to a colleague, a disappointment born of disgust mingled with lack of sleep. Unable to "perceive any advantage gained," the engineer was extremely frustrated that the heavy naval units present were stopped by a single 6.4-inch rifle. Admitting they had not stood up well to the big conical shells, Wilson believed that the ironclads should have moved to a closer range, where a chance shot could have put the Rebel piece out of commission. The exhausted Wilson asserted that Lt. Cmdr. Smith, whom he mocked as the "able and efficient rear admiral, commodore, captain, lieutenant commander," was overly timid in not placing his vessels closer to the enemy. Rather than 1,100 yards, Wilson cried, "They ought to go up to 200 yards and 'make a spoon or spoil a horn.'" If they got in close, "one chance shot will do the work." Of course, it was likely that one such shot might not have been made in a thousand.

The arrival of a brigade on three transports with cannon and ammunition, both from Yazoo City, "relieved us a great deal," remembered Texas Legion private Edwin Rice. As the troops disembarked with their equipment, they were quickly shown to their new posts. The remainder of Loring's garrison worked through the night repairing the breastworks and unloading the 8-inch naval gun, a 6-inch cannon, and a 20-pounder rifle, plus an ample supply of ammunition. The 8-inch piece was speedily mounted and a new magazine was prepared for her ammunition. The work was completed just as the sun began to rise.[14] Having worked through the night mounting new guns and further enhancing the defenses of Fort Pemberton, its defenders were somewhat surprised when, by 8:00 a.m. on Saturday, the Union invaders had not reopened their bombardment. March 14, like March 12, was, however, a day of recovery and preparation for the Federal expeditionary force below the South's cotton-bale bastion. Bluecoat wounded were attended to while repairs were made aboard both the ironclads. Lt. Gen. Pemberton also took the opportunity, in a situation report, to advise his superiors about operations on the Tallahatchie. He was pleased to announce the repulse of the attack upon Camp Pemberton made on March 11 as well as a second attack yesterday. The defenses were located "on a narrow neck six miles above Greenwood. A raft and steamboats sunk obstruct the river opposite the fort." The department commander was fully confident that Col. Waul, in tactical command, "can hold the place."

Pemberton's confidence was reflected in an article by the Chicago newsman Tom Cook, who gave all the credit for stopping the Federal enterprise to the lone Confederate 6.4-inch rifle. "Under ordinary circumstances," he raged, "it would be disgraceful that such as expedition as this should be held in check for a week by such an insignificant gun as this." In a column to be sent off by messenger that day, he continued:

> We have vastly heavier metal in abundance; we can cover them all over with 8, 9, 10, 11, and 13-inch shot and shell; but as yet, we have been unable to silence this one 64-pounder. That we have faithfully and bravely attempted it, let the scarred bows of the gunboats *Chillicothe* and *Baron de Kalb* tell. We have assailed it as never a battery was assailed before without demolition and it still stands to fight us. The acknowledged best 11-inch gunner in the United States Navy—the man who has had more experience than any other in working those enormous Dahlgren shell-pieces—Lt. Cmdr. Foster, has, on three occasions, attempted to silence this piece; but it still stands to hurl defiance at us.

One wonders what Cook would have written had he known that the piece in question was largely manned by Confederate navy gunners, several of whom had given the U.S. Navy "what fer" from aboard the mighty ram CSS *Arkansas* the previous July.

Toward sunset, Lt. Cmdr. Foster was able to report that the best possible repairs had been completed aboard the *Chillicothe*. A warning was, however, added in his message to task force leader Smith: "She is ... badly battered and shattered, and does not withstand the enemy's shot and shell near as well as expected."

The reports passed to the Confederate War Department in Richmond from Maj. Gen. Loring regarding his battles with the ironclads were now published in leading Southern newspapers. They appeared throughout the day in such journals as the *Jackson*

Appeal, the *Richmond Daily Dispatch,* and the *Mobile Advertiser and Register.* The *Appeal* added a few details of its own, later sharing them with the *Advertiser and Register* and the *Daily Dispatch.* A man who had witnessed the Union fleet buildup on the Coldwater traveled to Grenada, where he informed the newspaper's editors that morning that the enemy squadron included the "formidable ship-gunboats *Chillicothe* and *De Kalb,* along with two rams with cotton defenses, three gunboats (not deemed formidable), three batteries, 300 cavalry, and 10,000 men." The *Appeal* went on to say that it was informed by "a gentleman who witnessed the fight at Fort Pemberton" that "our troops waded to their waists to get a chance at the enemy." Also from the realm of the press, it should be noted that the *Brooklyn Daily Eagle* published a "special" from Memphis. Originally a telegram, this "seconded" story informed the paper's readers that RAdm. Porter was "momentarily expecting intelligence from Haynes' Bluff announcing the arrival of our forces there, which would be the signal for a combined attack upon that fortification." The same tale would be told in the *New York Times* two days later.

The ironclads did not resume their attack on March 15 "out of respect for the Sabbath," but throughout the daylight hours the Federal land battery maintained a light, short-time harassment of Fort Pemberton. In late afternoon plans were confirmed for another attack by the ironclads upon the fort, a coordinated affair with an amphibious component. Lt. Col. Wilson, in conversations with Lt. Cmdr. Walker and Foster, encouraged the two to take their vessels in closer to Fort Pemberton. "I tried to give them backbone," he later confided, "but they were not confident." Believing those officers would advance into a "close and desperate engagement" if ordered, the engineer found Lt. Cmdr. Smith, the expedition commander, as not "the equal of Lord Nelson" and without the disposition to make an all-or-nothing push. Wilson, in the words of his recent biographer Longacre, "singled out Smith for particular abuse laced with sarcasm … but his criticisms of Smith were hardly fair." Despite a deliberate style, the naval commander was "intelligent and conscientious and as willing to work hard for success." The engineer "grew impatient with anyone who seemed unable to give him the precise amount of cooperation and support he desired." Smith, Longacre reminds us, "would not be the last colleague whom he would abruptly condemn on such grounds." Despite his disappointment in the elan of Smith and his subordinates, Wilson fairly admitted that the *Chillicothe* in particular was "an inglorious failure." Looking ahead, he lamented, "if she is hit half as many times tomorrow at close range as she has been at long, she'll be in a sad condition." The *De Kalb,* as long as she could be fought bows on, "stands it well, though her sides do not fare well if hit."

Last-minute preparations were made aboard the *Chillicothe* and *Baron de Kalb* during the morning of March 16. Finally, a little before 1:00 p.m., they cast off their lines and steamed in the order named once more to the designated bombardment position, this one some 200 yards farther up than that of March 13. After they came to a stern line was rowed ashore from each and made fast to large trees on the right bank of the Tallahatchie. Although the ironclad was positioned at what Smith and Foster considered to be a relatively close-in position, Maj. Gen. Loring remembered the boat actually "got into position, bow on, at 1,200 yards range." The *Chillicothe* "opened the ball." Brig. Gen. Ross reported that the enemy "responded with spirit."

Fighting bows-on over the next 15 minutes, the *Chillicothe* discharged seven 5-

second shells into Fort Pemberton. *Chicago Daily Times* newsman Tom Cook counted fourteen Confederate counter-battery shots. At some early point, with her forward gun ports all closed, the unhappy Cincinnati-built gunboat was pounded by four Southern bolts. Two struck simultaneously on her forward gun ports, on her starboard slide ports forward and the other on her port slide port forward. So heavy were the enemy missiles (most likely 6.4-inch) that all the forward slide ports of both of the *Chillicothe*'s forward ports were either penetrated or so smashed in (or the bolts knocked out) that it was no longer possible to open them. The forward gun crews made every effort to overcome the problem and run out their guns but could not. Meanwhile, other Rebel projectiles smashed into her hull.

Lt. Cmdr. Foster initially believed that it was possible to open the forward starboard ports and to continue the action with that Dahlgren alone. He was quickly apprised of his error; the ports were held fast in their closed position by the armor bolts being so started out as to keep the ports from sliding. Having satisfied himself that it was not possible to shoot forward and in accordance with standing orders, Foster ordered his boat to slip her lines and back out of range to make repairs. The undamaged *De Kalb* was also ordered back. Watching from the parapets of Fort Pemberton, a *Jackson Appeal* correspondent wrote almost sympathetically: "They dare not turn round when they want to withdraw, as that would expose their tender parts. You may know that backing a clumsy gunboat upstream is no easy business." Before withdrawing, *Chillicothe* was struck by four smaller projectiles on her upper and lower decks. Now a smoking wreck, the *Chillicothe* did not return to action. Her total losses for the three days of combat to that point (11th, 13th, and 16th) were 22 killed, wounded, and drowned.

The ironclad's engagements had shown up several building deficiencies. To begin with, the use of pine alone (rather than in combination with oak as aboard the Pook turtles) as backing for armor plates was shown to be ineffective. When projectiles hit the *Chillicothe* and did not penetrate, most nevertheless stove in the iron and also "deformed the backing of adjacent armor plates." Another difficulty arose from the fact that there appeared to be some indifference on the part of Joseph Brown's builders with regard to the manner in which their workmen secured the highly vaunted armor and a failure on the part of superintendents and inspectors to order correction. Upon examination, it was found by naval officers that in some cases "four-inch drift (lag) bolts" were used to secure three-inch-thick iron plates to soft pine backing. Under fire, the heavy Confederate shells simply sheared off the tops of the bolts, sending them screaming as shrapnel into the casemate and elsewhere. As if this were not bad enough, it was discovered that many of the mounting bolts used to secure the casemate armor were not bolts at all but simply big-headed spikes.

Coming only days after the loss of his *Indianola*, the *Chillicothe*'s designer, Joseph Brown, could have been badly scandalized. His integrity and reputation as a prime contractor was opened to the question of whether he was able to properly oversee the work of his subcontractors. In turn, Brown, for his part, could have publicly railed against those who, to great acclaim from the New Albany newspapers, personally oversaw the installation of the protective plates. With his eye, to borrow a phrase, on the greater prize and always the politician, Brown chose not to complain about any shoddiness on the part of his St. Louis colleague. After all, the design failures aboard the *Chillicothe* were not actually known to the public at large. Those details that were shared about her, such as the profile "Sketch of the Iron-Clad *Chillicothe*," which appeared in the *New York Herald* on March 20, gave no hint of anything but strength, with her exploits portrayed as "brilliant." He preferred to let all believe that, as the paper put it, "her superior build and powers of resistance gave her the place of 'head boat' in the expedition in which she now performs so gallant and bold a part."

Perhaps the strongest newspaper criticism of the *Chillicothe* appeared in the *Philadelphia Press* on April 28 when a reporter noted that the boat "would have been one of the very best of the ironclads but that the contractors slighted her turret and her machinery." Indeed, in the same *Chicago Daily Times* article in which he had praised the Confederate 6.4-inch rifle, embedded reporter Tom Cook actually praised the vessel's success: "She was struck thirty-eight times and remained unhurt—a record that scarcely a naval vessel afloat can show."

Brown, as he had and would to the end, continued to claim that his ironclads, defects and all, were but stopgap projects designed to fulfill an urgent need for additional river ironclads. He never accepted any blame for specific defects or came forward to expose any, nor did he pillory his subcontractors, relying upon reporters like Cook and those interviewed during the building process to tell a positive tale. Consequently, the former mayor was not disciplined by word or coin, retained the favor of RAdm. Porter, and continued to receive government contracts to modify most of the civil steamers turned into tinclads. Still, when he grasped the magnitude of this astonishing defect, Lt. Cmdr. Foster was amazed "that the weight of the armor has not heretofore forced them out," with the obvious consequence that sections of it would have fallen overboard. Shaking his head, the sailor summed up his boat's situation: "The backing of the turret is shattered all to pieces and the iron plating on the turret is penetrated, knocked loose, stove in, and almost unfit for service."

Lt. Cmdr. Smith, in his report of the day's action, told RAdm. Porter that Foster would be writing directly to him concerning the weaknesses of his boat's turret. Until then, the task force commander hoped that the side slides could be taken off and, with the aid of blacksmiths from the other boats and the army, affixed in place of the destroyed slides. Pressed cotton bales would be used on the sides.

Although both the Union ironclads were out of action down at Greenwood, the Federal cotton bale battery in the woods continued to fire a few shells at Fort Pemberton off and on until dark. The Confederates were not hurt; indeed, the enemy "covered his heavy guns with cotton and replied to us with light field pieces." Brig. Gen. Ross was now convinced that the only way to take the fort was to have better gunboats and stronger artillery dispatched to his location, along with "plenty of ammunition."

Early on March 17, Lt. Cmdr. Foster was summoned aboard the Federal flag boat *Rattler*. There Lt. Cmdr. Smith, who had not been well or acted well for some time, admitted that he had, in fact, been quite ill since January. After assuming command, he had hoped that the surgeons with the task force could help keep him fit for duty, but the long hours of pressure endured had by now conspired to prevent that and forced him to his sickbed. He was going to have himself examined by the surgeons with the expedition the following morning but anticipated he might have to retire. Lt. Cmdr. Smith's examination (called a "medical survey") was completed on March 18. Many over the years have been unkind to the naval commander. The captains of his ironclads and the army officers accompanying the expedition regarded him as either mad or a coward and historians since have largely signed off on those diagnoses. RAdm. Porter later wrote that the man "showed symptoms of aberration of the mind," undoubtedly meaning a nervous breakdown, that caused him to often hamper Foster and Walker by issuing "contradictory orders which they felt bound to obey." Given the naval discipline of the day, they had "great difficulty getting him to pursue proper measures."

The story got started, and is repeated in a recent book on the Vicksburg campaign, that Smith "seemed to come apart when Rebel shells began to fall." Indeed, it has been alleged that, even though the man was not aboard at the time, when the two shells collided within the gun port of the *Chillicothe* on the afternoon of March 11, Smith fainted. Upon "being revived," he then supposedly "started issuing orders 'in the most complete gibberish,' the gist of which was an immediate withdrawal." Richard West, in his groundbreaking study of the campaign, was rather more sympathetic. "He seems to have been a victim of excessive strain and just plain nerves." Porter's comments regarding his supposed "aberration of mind," the historian suggested was actually more "a reflection of the admiral's disappointment than a medical diagnosis."

Not only at the time but also for years afterwards and even in his 1912 memoirs, Wilson blamed Smith for being too timid and unwilling to push his ironclads against the fort for fear that they might "be injured, become unmanageable, and prove a total loss. The expedition was therefore abandoned." Again, Longacre reminds us, Wilson was being unfair to one of his associates who worked just as hard as he for success. "In times of stress and ill fortune," the biographer notes, Wilson himself could seem to come unwound and his "determination to succeed often carried him far beyond the limits of fair play." Although Lt. Col. Wilson was openly hostile to Smith, Brig. Gen. Ross was most gracious. Acknowledging that his naval colleague might have been more assertive early on, he recognized that the man was "in very feeble health, after arriving in front of the fort." Still, he was "indefatigable in his labors, and exhibited during the engagement the utmost coolness and gallantry."

Recently, the logistical historian Charles Dana Gibson put his finger on the underlying cause of Smith's difficulties. The expedition commander had a "debilitating illness (chronic dysentery)." Chronic dysentery, a nasty intestinal disease that was often fatal, according to Glenna R. Schroeder-Lein, could "last for weeks, or even years, severely weakening the patient." The lingering afflicted suffered "weight loss, weakness, and emaciation." This sort of dysentery was "a symptom of other diseases" and although it could be caused by microbes "much of it was associated with malnutrition" or possibly intestinal damage lingering after a short-time bout with acute dysentery. There were also insect-delivered diseases rampant in the pestilential swamps of the Delta and the lower Mississippi, led, of course, by malaria and dengue fever. The latter was then known as broken bone (break bone, bone crusher) fever from the great pain it caused joints, or the Drugue. It is, like malaria, an infectious mosquito-borne sickness. It is possible that Smith also had contracted it.

After writing out a brief summary for enclosure in a dispatch to RAdm. Porter, Smith now turned over control of the task force to Foster and returned, with the squadron commander's belated permission, to Cincinnati, via Helena and Cairo, aboard the *Rattler*. He would convalesce at home in Trenton, New Jersey. Before his departure "for a more salubrious climate," according to Lt. Col. Wilson, Smith advised Ross and Foster that "the present force of ironclads could not take the two Rebel guns in our front."

The captain of the *Chillicothe*, now the new task force commander, spent the remainder of Wednesday conferring with his military colleagues and Lt. Cmdr. Walker on the steps to be taken next. Everyone from Brig. Gen. Ross on down agreed with the departed Smith and admitted that it was impossible for the damaged ironclads to capture Fort Pemberton alone and that it was equally impossible, due to terrain, for the soldiers to participate in a combined attack. The *Chillicothe* was badly damaged and she, as the *De Kalb*, was nearly out of ammunition. There were also persistent reports that Confederate forces were coming down from the Coldwater to outflank the Federal expedition and effect its capture.

During the morning, as Lt. Cmdr. Foster engaged his colleagues in discussion, Maj. Gen. Loring continued to receive reports on the Quinby force now working its way through the tree-lined channel east of Moon Lake. It was believed to be "a most formidable one." Convinced that it would link up with Ross, Fort Pemberton's commander wrote Lt. Gen. Pemberton prophesying "a series of hard fought battles throughout the whole length of the Yazoo." Because he did not have the cipher, Loring was sending his messages in plain English. Writing without code, he made it clear that he needed more heavy guns "and plenty of ammunition." Additionally, he wanted some artillerists from the Vicksburg defenses to be seconded up as well. "We need them badly, and have none at all." This latter remark would, if known, have come as something of an insult to the Confederate naval personnel who made up much of the crew manning the 6.4-inch piece.

Given the various negative considerations facing the Union force tied up above Fort Pemberton, Lt. Cmdr. Foster, as the task force commander, elected to retreat. A message to that effect was prepared for delivery by messenger to RAdm. Porter. About 7:00 p.m. the Union troops onshore were ordered to "strike tents" and reembark aboard their transports, taking with them all of their gear and equipment. Battery Wilson was also rapidly dismantled and its pieces returned to the gunboats that provided them. With everyone and everything reloaded aboard the warships and transports, the Federal invasion flotilla departed the waters off Fort Pemberton at 5:00 a.m. on the morning of March 19, en route back up the Tallahatchie and headed for Helena. Having made its way "bag and baggage" up the river "as fast as Steamboats can go," Foster's retreating Federal armada managed to put a locally estimated 80–100 miles between itself and Fort Pemberton by nightfall. All during the trip, the men wondered about "the object of So precipitate a retreat."[15]

A retreat by Ross and the USN was the last thing Loring expected that night. In fact, according to Pvt. Rice of Waul's Texas Legion, both of the defending battalions at Fort Pemberton "slept in the breastworks as an attack was anticipated—but they were not disturbed." Rumors began to circulate around the Confederate cotton bale fort on the morning of March 20 that the Federals were evacuating their camps in the timber. Just before noon, Maj. Gen. Loring dispatched 200 men from Waul's Texas Legion, under Lt. Col. Barnard Timmons, to reconnoiter. Timmons and his men found the Federal camps and cotton-covered gun emplacement had been abandoned by Brig. Gen. Ross and that all of the steamers once tied to the trees upstream were gone. The cotton gun parapet was immediately burned. The Texans also found 15 Federal graves, including those of the *Chillicothe*'s Quarter Gunner Thomas Greenslade and Seaman Frederic E. Davis from the *Baron de Kalb*. At 11:00 a.m. the commander of Fort Pemberton, with great relief, got off a message to his superior at Jackson announcing, "In consequence of the crippled condition of their gunboats, the injury done to their land batteries, and from all we can learn, their great loss of life, the enemy have commenced a precipitate retreat up the Tallahatchie."

About noon next day, the *Chillicothe* and *Baron de Kalb*, leading the transports of Brig. Gen. Ross, turned a bend and encountered Quinby's vessels. The two groups halted while Ross and Lt. Cmdr. Foster retired aboard the newcomer's flag boat, *Prima Donna*, to confer with the ranking officer. Ross and Foster described to Quinby in detail all of the events that had occurred since March 10, including the seeming impregnability of Fort Pemberton and the grounds, made impassable by flooding, that surrounded it. Quinby, who did not know that Maj. Gen. Grant had decided Yazoo Pass was a bust and was now determined not to bolster the expedition further, believed it best if the now-enhanced force return and try again to take the place. "Falling back, after forcing our way our way thus far," would, he believed, "have a depressing effect upon our army and the country, and raise the hopes and the determination of the Rebels."

Quinby, supported by Ross and Lt. Col. Wilson, implored Lt. Cmdr. Foster, who was not in their military chain of command and therefore had a veto, to agree to return with him for the good of the country. After much conversation, the naval officer agreed, later admitting his realization that at least two additional heavy gunboats were required to make any assault a sure thing. News of the Quinby-Foster decision trickled down to every transport and gunboat present. Now joined under Quinby's command, the enlarged Federal invasion fleet rounded to and headed back down the Tallahatchie on the morning of March 22. Although the task group commander had hoped to make a landing above Fort Pemberton before dark, progress was slower than anticipated.

Maj. Gen. Grant, having changed his mind on Quinby's mission, sent a message to that effect to Maj. Gen. McPherson at Lake Providence. Although he would let the expedition "try Greenwood a short time longer," the theater commander could not see anything positive coming from sending in additional reinforcements. "I see nothing for it now," he told his subordinate, "but to have that force return the way they went in." Quinby's task group arrived at Clark's Plantation, about two miles above Fort Pemberton, just after noon on March 23. All morning the Confederate leadership at Fort Pemberton had received an increasing number of reports that a reinforced Federal force was on its way to attack again. Now they were here.

As the by now thoroughly discredited *Chillicothe* and her consort steamed down around the bend in a heavy rainstorm and made themselves fast to the shoreline around 2:00 p.m. Quinby and Ross traveled up the right-side riverbank to a viewing location about 700 yards from the Rebel works. From their position the two generals "could distinctly see the guns, but the gunners kept under cover, evidently reserving their fire for a nearer approach of the gunboats." There was no nearer approach and the pair of high-ranking scouts retired.

The *Chillicothe* fired three rounds toward the supply steamer *Edward J. Gay*, which was tied up near the Southern cotton-covered fort some 900 yards off, but she received no reply. The *De Kalb* did not fire. Both gunboats now withdrew, the former out of ammunition. As they were backing out, a tremendous explosion split the water. "We, along with those on shore," Lt. Cmdr. Foster later wrote, "were under the impression that the enemy blew up a torpedo just forward of the *Chillicothe*'s bow." Both tied up to the trees approximately three-quarters of a mile above Fort Pemberton. War Department assistant secretary and special Western envoy Charles A. Dana would write to Secretary Edwin Stanton a few days later, saying that the army officers attached to the expedition held Foster responsible for its failure "for not taking sufficient ammunition with him at the outset." The former newspaper man went on to say that if on this occasion the gunboat commander could "have fought his vessel a little longer, the fort might easily have been taken."

At Young's Point, Maj. Gen. Grant wrote to RAdm. Porter: "The expedition by way of the Yazoo Pass seems to have come to a dead lock at Greenwood." More troops were en route, but the Union theater commander did not believe they would be "of any service." Lt. Col. Wilson, "in whose judgement I place great reliance," believed, Grant continued, that there had been too much delay in reaching Greenwood and now land forces could not act until the batteries there were silenced. He noted that Quinby could determine whether or not to attack, but if he determined an assault was impracticable he was to return immediately.

Inclement weather prevented activities on the Greenwood front all day on March 24. The rain having stopped on the following morning, the remainder of the Federal soldiers disembarked from their transports and set up camps along the riverbank. During the day, Quinby had a disappointing meeting with Lt. Cmdr. Foster. After informing the navy man that more reinforcements were requested, the general was shocked when the captain of the *Chillicothe* revealed that, unless he received orders from RAdm. Porter to the contrary, he would be departing these immediate waters for Helena, via Moon Lake, with the gunboats on or before April 1. The dumbstruck Quinby immediately realized that the departure of the gunboats would leave his entire force "in a very precarious position, with nearly 200 miles of unguarded water communication" separating it from the Mississippi. Later, after composing his thoughts, the general determined to approach Foster and attempt to "change his determination" or, at the very least, induce him to leave his light draughts behind to protect the army transports.

Over at Eagle Bend on the Mississippi, Albert H. "Bod" Bodman, the noted correspondent of the *Chicago Daily Tribune*, made it clear to his Northern readers that no one knew for certain what was going on with the expedition. The previous day, he was told, the whole expedition was abandoned. Then, per contra, the next day it was learned that the rumors were false and the campaign was still on; in fact, it was said that now "the troops were landed, attacked the fort in the rear, and after an heroic struggle, captured and destroyed it." Of course, Bodman, with a war reporter's experience going back to 1861, was careful to hedge. "At this distance," he concluded, "we are unable to say which, if either, is true—'You pays your money and you takes your choice!'"

Very little action occurred near Fort Pemberton in the next days. Lt. Col. Wilson took the opportunity to return to Young's Point and report to Maj. Gen. Grant. After

Wilson gave a less-than-glowing assessment of the Greenwood situation on March 28, the Union theater commander informed the engineer that he was to return to the waters above that town with orders to Quinby that he discontinue his efforts and extract his force. Also on Saturday, Grant wrote to Brig. Gen. Prentiss at Helena: "The troops that have gone down the Yazoo Pass are now ordered back." Meanwhile, a young seaman who had joined the crew of the *Chillicothe* just two weeks earlier took the opportunity to send a few observations to his hometown newspaper, the *Erie Observer*. The unidentified lad's letter confided that the "Great Yazoo Pass Expedition" was "still occupying its old position near Fort Pemberton," probably waiting for reinforcement. He then provided the journal with a unique description of the view both Federal and Confederate had when seeing his boat in action: "Only about two feet of her is above water and five feet below, and is covered with three inch iron all over her decks and sides. Her boilers and machinery are below the water line, leaving nothing but the turret and wheels for them to shoot at. Taking her altogether, she is about as good a boat as one can desire to be on."

Grant's orders reached the waters above Greenwood on April 4. Ashore for the past several days, Union and Confederate forces engaged in artillery and other skirmishing but no operations of consequence. Brig. Gen. Quinby, after reading his orders, directed his men to break camp and reload and reembark aboard the transports. Loading the teams and equipment back aboard the many Federal transports took all of the remaining daylight hours and most of those on April 5. In late morning of that day, the Federal convoy, larger than it was when it first arrived almost a month earlier, started up the Tallahatchie led by the *Baron de Kalb*, the *Chillicothe* bringing up the rear. The return passage out of the Tallahatchie and up toward the Coldwater was made largely without incident, although there was some Confederate resistance from shore. The first returning boats actually soon encountered the last of those coming down with Quinby's reinforcements. These latecomers duly rounded to and started back upstream.

At Fort Pemberton, Maj. Gen. Loring wrote out a message for his superiors next day indicating that the enemy was progressing up the Tallahatchie, presumably toward the Mississippi. "We are certain," he added, "that our shells and shot did great execution in their crowded camps before leaving." Lt. Gen. Pemberton wired Richmond: "Enemy certainly leaving Tallahatchie." Pemberton's communication went on to say that a "negro captured from them says all the fleet is going to Helena."

The leading elements of the Federal convoy entered the Old Pass on the morning of April 8, a Wednesday. All aboard were pleased to see that the water had fallen almost 10 feet. The *Chillicothe* reached the river off Yazoo Pass late that evening and remained tied there until she entered the pass and made fast about 7:00 a.m. on April 9. Two hours later, she cast off and stood upstream, working very badly due to her damaged paddle wheel. About 11:15 a.m. Joseph Brown's smallest ironclad, which had hit a sawyer on the way in on March 4, ran onto an unknown underwater obstruction that stove in her starboard bow. Half an hour was required to extract the *Chillicothe*, which action caused her to leak so badly that hands had to be called to man the pumps and bail water with buckets. While the men pushed out the water, two hours were required by damage control personnel to plug the leaks and get the vessel ready to proceed. Her bow shoving on, the ironclad crawled slowly on up the river until about 6:00 p.m., when she swung against an overhanging tree. This accident demolished a large part of her port wheelhouse. While damage control sailors worked anew, the vessel made fast to the shore for the night.

Having made considerably greater speed on the way back than on the way down, the first of the steamers reached Moon Lake on April 10. Here the troops were able to disembark and make camp and here the Yazoo Pass expedition ended. The vessels of the Mississippi Squadron steamed to other duties, though many had first to offload a portion of the intact cotton bale armor with which they had returned. As the *Chillicothe* continued on toward the Mississippi, Lt. Cmdr. Foster took the opportunity to travel to Helena by tinclad to deliver his reports and to oversee, with Brig. Gen. Prentiss, the appropriate accounting of the cotton coming out of the pass on chartered steamers. Aboard the stricken vessel, Acting Ensign Walter Muir, the executive officer, effected such repairs as possible even as his crew daily sent more men to the sick bay.

On April 11 RAdm. Porter wired Washington: "The Yazoo Pass Expedition has returned safely." He also acknowledged that the campaign did some "harm to the enemy, though not as successful as I intended it to be." Three or four vessels were sunk by the Confederates to avoid capture and even Fort Pemberton was successfully neutralized for a day, though because the army leadership did not believe itself strong enough to attack they "waited for reinforcements and lost their chance." The squadron commander would send a follow-on message within 24 hours happily noting that the expedition fleet captured 558 bales of cotton. Discounting 125 that were handed over to the army for defenses, 433 bales were sent to the prize court at Cairo, IL. Years later, Porter dismissed the whole enterprise as "just one of the episodes of the war (my consolation when I met with failure) and I never wanted to hear of the Yazoo Pass again."[16]

The *Chillicothe* arrived at Helena around noon April 14. Many of her men were now quite sick, with some sent ashore. Next day late in the afternoon, available crew were drilled in small arms. Lt. Cmdr. Foster returned aboard from a dispatch steamer about 7:30 p.m. and immediately hands were detailed to transfer to her the 79 full bales of cotton remaining from that taken in earlier, some of which was used as armor. Early on April 16, Foster, having received orders north from RAdm. Porter, ordered his vessel to raise anchor and make steam up the Mississippi. She landed alongside the U.S. Navy coal barges at Memphis at 7:30 the next night and immediately commenced coaling.

It would take almost two weeks for the *Chillicothe* to return to Cairo and begin the repair process. The *Philadelphia Press* reporter "F," possibly J.F. McDevitt, told his readers on May 2 that upon the boat's docking at the Illinois naval base many of the sailors aboard were found to be ill and were sent back down to the new medical facility at Memphis. "The crew of the *Chillicothe* have mostly all been sent to the general hospital," he revealed, "in consequence of drogue or break-bone fever, contracted on the Coldwater and Tallahatchie rivers in the Yazoo Pass expedition."

Employing sailors from the facility as well as healthy members of the gunboat's complement, the damaged wheelhouses and casemate of the *Chillicothe* were now taken down. On May 2, Fleet Captain Pennock advised RAdm. Porter that *Chillicothe* would soon steam to Mound City, where she would go on the ways for hull work. It was initially anticipated that the vessel could be readied for combat shortly. (During 1863, the government, on behalf of the Mississippi Squadron, leased the Hambleton, Collier & Company's shipyard for $40,000 per year and began turning it into its principal construction and repair facility. It would later base most of its other activities there, where a large new hospital was also completed.) The ironclad was on the Mound City ways by May 17 and what the workers found was not encouraging. "She was in worse condition than was first supposed," Pennock confessed. She would have to undergo extensive repairs, which were already dragging behind due to the facility's heavy workload and a shortage of laborers. It was now impossible to say exactly when she could return to duty.[17]

Her hull and underwater structural questions addressed, the *Chillicothe* returned to Cairo in late June. There her casemate, superstructure, fixtures, and so forth were put right over the next two months by dedicated yard workers employed around the clock. Even as the Vicksburg campaign drew to a successful close in early July the work was overseen by Lt. Cmdr. Foster and his officers under the wary eyes of Fleet Captain Pennock, who frequently reported progress to RAdm. Porter. Other than repairs and strengthening with new bolts and fixtures, the casemate of the gunboat changed little and her heavy ordnance not at all. She was, however, given a wheeled 12-pounder boat howitzer for close-in or shore work. Meanwhile, on May 20, Porter, "with characteristic energy," had issued General Order No. 20, the inaugural official decree outlining a divisional administrative plan for the Mississippi Squadron.

This blueprint created six geographical sections, each, as the admiral later wrote, "extending between specified points." The admiral's divisions were "filled up with light-draft vessels, to cruise up and down the river and carry dispatches." The light draughts in this chain were intended to be "strung along the river between ironclads." Lookouts aboard were "to watch the shore very close and capture every strolling party they may come across." Boats and skiffs encountered along the banks were to be taken and "every available method" employed to break up and disperse guerrillas. The new geographical units, initially called "sections," were led by divisional officers, all trusted regular navy officers who commanded a certain number of named vessels. For example, Division Six, under Lt. Cmdr. Le Roy Fitch, comprised the Cumberland and Ohio rivers from Cairo to the mouth of the Kanawha River. The Third District, from Natchez to the Red River, was overseen by Lt. Cmdr. Frank Ramsey. These leaders were also charged with the maintenance of "strict discipline," for cooperation with various U.S. Army officers, and were to employ all of their spare time directly or by mandate to their subordinates, "exercising the men with the great guns and small arms."

The light draught vessels in Porter's new districts were responsible for patrol, convoy, and other work within the assigned boundaries, with the ironclads available as backup in emergencies. It was understood that boats within a district could not leave station without the authority of the district leader, who would also approve all acquisitions (except money) and forward on all communications from his subordinates to Cairo. This decentralized district plan worked well, though from time to time over the next year as the squadron grew in size it had to be amplified by later general orders, all of which are printed in the navy *Official Records*.

At the end of August, as repairs on the Brown-built ironclad neared completion, Lt. Cmdr. Foster was transferred aboard the *Lafayette*, succeeding Capt. Henry Walke, who was sent to the Atlantic. Foster would remain aboard the giant ironclad until 1865 (he served in the U.S. Navy after the war and died of disease while attached to the Brazil Squadron). Succeeding Foster in charge of the *Chillicothe* was Acting Volunteer Lieutenant Henry St. Clair Eytinge, a former New York City theater stage manager and merchant sailor about whom we know little. Before coming West he had wrecked his previous vessel, the South Atlantic Blockading Squadron four-gun, ship-rigged sailing vessel *Shepherd Knapp*, on a West Indian coral reef (May 23). As Foster departed, the newcomer received orders from RAdm. Porter to take his gunboat, as soon as she was ready, down to the Third District, where she would operate under the auspices of Lt. Cmdr. Francis M. "Frank" Ramsay (1835–1914).

Washington, D.C., native Ramsay had spent the first two years of the war on the African Station before receiving command of the giant Mississippi Squadron ironclad *Choctaw* in March 1863. Following the capture of Vicksburg that July, he took over the Third Division. He would transfer to the Atlantic coast in September 1864 and remain in the U.S. Navy after the conflict, rising to the rank of rear admiral in 1894.

Rebuilt but still possessed, in the opinion of her new captain, of a very heavy turret atop a very light frame, the *Chillicothe* departed Cairo for Memphis late in the first week of September. Unfortunately, low water and faulty piloting caused her to ground twice on the way down. Unable to float in less than six feet, three inches of water, the ironclad twice got into shoals, the second time becoming stuck at Plum Point Bend in only five feet, nine inches of water. After her hawsers were parted twice, the *Chillicothe* was successfully pulled into deeper water by the transport steamer *War Eagle*. At this point, Eytinge found "the stem seam on her deck from the gunwale starting away over an inch and the vessel taking a stream of water over the bow." Unable to make needed repairs, the captain ran his vessel at half speed down to the Memphis navy yard, where workers took her in hand on September 14. While the work was completed, the crew, "the greenest ... ever," was kept at work on daily chores and in practice with the great Dahlgrens. It was hoped that the ironclad could be underway again within a day or two.

By September 21 the *Chillicothe* reached her assigned position off Ellis Cliffs and Red River. There, on October 27, Eytinge was ordered by Lt. Cmdr. Ramsay to turn his craft over to her executive officer, Acting Ensign Muir, and to return north. Two months later Muir was succeeded as captain by Acting Volunteer Lieutenant Joseph Pitty Couthouy (1808–1864), an active officer whose zeal greatly impressed his commander. As famous a scientist as he was a naval officer, Couthouy was a master mariner and amateur explorer, an expert in conchology and invertebrate paleontology. A successful Atlantic coast blockader during 1862, he had also lost a ship, the steamer *Columbia*, when she was caught in a January gale off the North Carolina coast. Posted to the Mississippi Squadron base at Cairo, IL, in June, Couthouy became the first captain of the new river monitor *Osage*, constructed by James B. Eads. During July she was dispatched to the Ohio River to reinforce the light draught tinclads of Lt. Cmdr. Le Roy Fitch, then undertaking combinations to prevent the recrossing of the stream by Brig. Gen. John Hunt Morgan, who was then raiding in Indiana and Ohio. In August, *Osage* participated in the Federal armed reconnaissance of the Red River and thereafter patrolled in the Mississippi River off Adams County, MS. During that time, Couthouy and Ramsay became close personal friends, spending many pleasant hours together, often speaking of family, including the daughters treasured by the *Chillicothe*'s captain.[18]

4—The Chillicothe Goes to War: Yazoo Pass and Red River

Estimating the situation west of the Mississippi on January 4 Lt. Gen. E. Kirby Smith, CSA, wrote to a subordinate: "I still think the Red and Washita [Ouachita] Rivers, especially the former, are the true lines of operation for an invading column, and that we may expect an attempt to be made by the enemy in force before the rivers fall." Little did he know at that time that within eight weeks RAdm. Porter would be leading just such a joint expedition.

For some months Federal forces from Washington to the West had been involved in planning an incursion into the Confederate theater west of the Mississippi. Such would be part of an overall multi-pronged assault on the Confederacy via Virginia and Georgia. By the beginning of 1864, generals as diverse as Maj. Gen. Grant, Sherman, and Nathaniel Banks, the eventual leader, were on board with a plan to move up the Red River through Louisiana toward Texas.

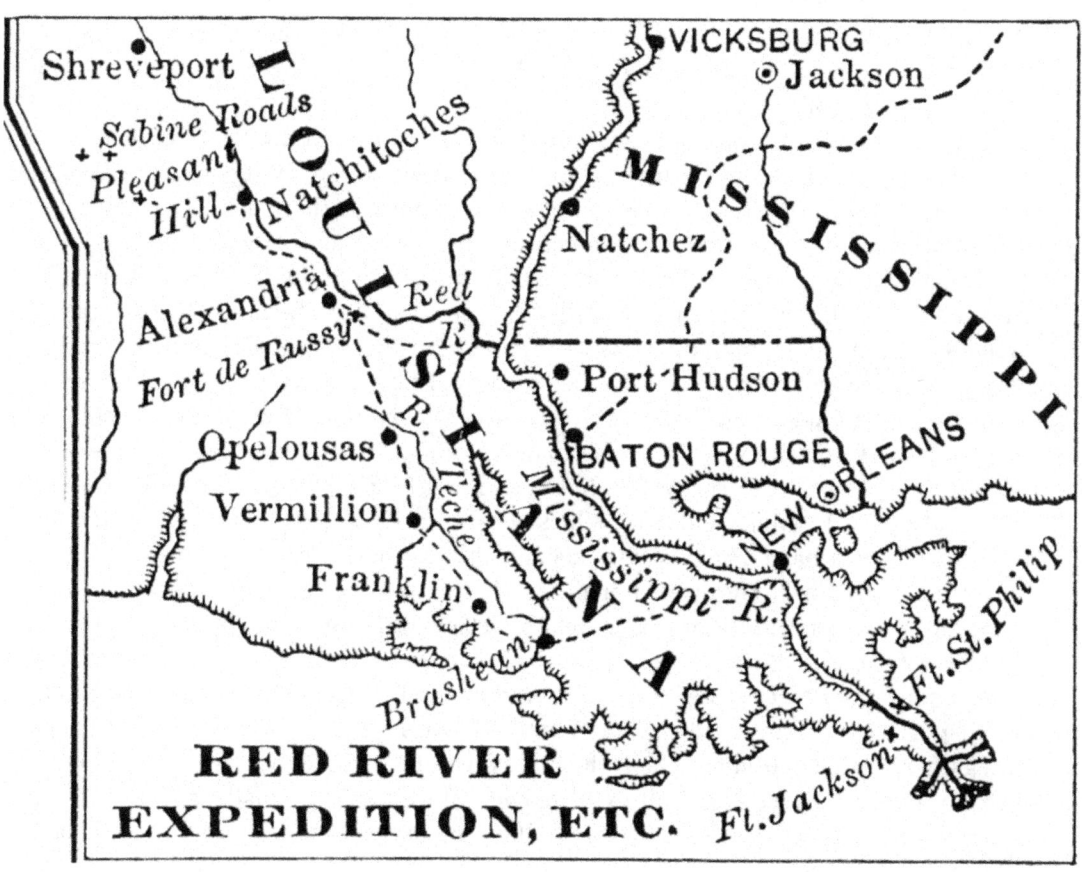

Map of the Red River Area. For some months prior to the beginning of 1864, Federal forces from Washington to the West were involved in planning an incursion into the Confederate theater west of the Mississippi, moving up the Red River through Louisiana toward Texas. In addition to purely military gains, this offensive could have disrupted Confederate commerce, allowing acquisition of vast amounts of cotton for New England manufacturers, and help to dissuade a northward advance by French forces then trying to subdue Mexico. Naturally, the Mississippi Squadron was invited along to provide support and guard the many necessary U.S. Army transports (Johnson and Buel, *Battles and Leaders*).

The forthcoming operation would, in actuality, be a "rather grand undertaking," in the words of historian William Riley Brookshire. Although championed on military grounds by, among others, President Lincoln and Maj. Gen. Halleck, the undertaking held other potential benefits for the North. In addition to purely military gains, a big Red River offensive could disrupt Confederate commerce while allowing acquisition of vast amounts of cotton for New England manufacturers. On top of this, the venture offered hope for dissuading a northward advance by French forces then trying to subdue Mexico. Although, in the end, it would really consist of a "loosely connected joint land and naval exercise," it did have as its ultimate military objective "completion of the subjugation of Louisiana and Arkansas." If this thrust was successful it "would effectively remove the Confederate Trans-Mississippi Department from an active role in the conflict." Naturally, the Mississippi Squadron was invited along to provide support and guard the many necessary transports. The *Chillicothe* was stationed off Fort Adams, MS, as the new year began, employed largely to interdict Southern river commerce. Between February 4 and 6, she prized nine bales of cotton directly across the Mississippi in the vicinity of Point Breeze, LA.

On February 21 Lt. Cmdr. Ramsay, commander of the Third District, reported that the water level of the Red River was falling. Three Confederate gunboats reportedly at Shreveport at the end of January could not get over the falls there due to the low river stage. While the ironclads and troop transports were assembled for the upcoming Trans-Mississippi campaign, RAdm. Porter arrived off the mouth of the Red River during the last week of February.[19] By the beginning of March, Maj. Gen. Richard ("Dick") Taylor (1826–1879), a transplanted Louisianan and son of President Zachery Taylor, knew that a large Federal force would soon be headed his way. To meet it, he had just 25,000 men. Maj. Gen. Banks and RAdm. Porter enjoyed a force superiority of 42,000 men, including 10,000 on loan from Maj. Gen. W.T. Sherman and 15,000 more from Maj. Gen. Frederic Steele, although his VII Corps would, in the end, not fully participate, leaving the land force total at 32,500. Maj. Gen. A.J. "Whiskey" Smith (1815–1897), a career soldier and later St. Louis postmaster, arrived with his men at the mouth of the Red River on March 11 aboard 21 transports. They were borrowed; Sherman wanted his men back by April 15. These soldiers, their munitions and their supplies, would be guarded by the Mississippi Squadron of the U.S. Navy.

In addition to the civil steamers chartered by the U.S. Quartermaster Department to transport Union army soldiers and supplies, RAdm. Porter, over the previous few days, gathered what was later called "the most formidable force that had ever been collected in the western waters." It drew from every flotilla in the squadron. The admiral was "determined there should be no want of floating batteries for the troops to fall back on in case of disaster." The task force comprised 13 ironclads, including the *Chillicothe*, the last of the Brown-built ironclads to see action. In reviewing this naval strength, the embedded *Philadelphia Inquirer* reporter was moved to observe that "a more formidable fleet was never under single command than that now on the Western rivers under Admiral Porter." On the other hand, "it might be said, also, never to less purpose. At the time of departure, the strength of the Rebellion in the inland waters had been crushed."

Just before Smith's arrival, Porter received the news that heavy rains were delaying

Assembling the Fleet at Red River. A large fleet of Federal transports and gunboats, including the *Chillicothe*, assembled off the mouth of the Red River in late February and early March 1864. The Federal commander, Maj. Gen. Nathaniel Banks, was unable to join the task force at the appointed time and so, on March 12, RAdm. David D. Porter began this expedition, hoping to make progress before the army man arrived by capturing the Confederate citadel of Fort De Russy (Johnson and Buel, *Battles and Leaders*).

Maj. Gen. Banks. He could not possibly reach Alexandria, one of the principal targets, before March 21. Additionally, the sailor found that work on the completion of Fort De Russy, 30 miles northwest of Simmesport and about 25 miles below Alexandria, was being pushed hard by the Rebels. While the naval and military men bobbed on their vessels observing the overgrown marshlands ashore, RAdm.Porter and Maj. Gen. Smith held a meeting to decide what to do next in light of Banks' delay. The two men decided to capture Alexandria, LA, taking Fort De Russy while en route. Porter's invasion armada started up the Red River at 8:30 the morning of March 12. Several of the larger ironclads had difficulty making it over the big sandbar that guarded the entrance, the *Chillicothe* among them.[20] At the junction of the Old Red River and the Atchafalaya River, a naval task group was ordered to push ahead up the former to remove a series of obstructions in the river eight miles below Fort De Russy. Porter took the remainder of his fleet, including the troop transports, into the Atchafalaya to cover the army landing at Simmesport.

On the morning of March 13 the soldiers disembarked and pursued the Confederates falling back on Fort De Russy. Meanwhile, the task group sent up the Old Red River reached the obstructions that the Southerners had spent five months building. It would take hours to remove them. At 4:15 that afternoon the *Chillicothe* and other vessels lying off Simmesport stood upriver, leaving the flag boat *Black Hawk* and a large tinclad in the rear with troop transports. The fleet entered Old River about 5:20 p.m. and tied up for the night just over two hours later.

Before sundown on March 14, the Federal military force under Maj. Gen. Smith had converged upon Fort De Russy and compelled its surrender. Upon their taking possession, it was learned that most of the defenders had already withdrawn, leaving only a gallant 300 to offer what turned out to be token resistance.

The *Chillicothe*, together with other fleet elements, steamed up the Red River toward Alexandria on March 14–15, the *Osage* actually receiving its surrender on the former day without firing a shot. Some units, particularly the timberclads and several larger tinclads, were able to move much more quickly than the slower casemate ironclads and thus reached the town toward dusk. Maj. Gen. Taylor, who had decided not to contest the Federal occupation, sent his steamers upriver to Grand Ecore, the port city of Natchitouches, ordering other units to make rendezvous at or near that point also.

Nine Union vessels arrived at Alexandria by the morning of March 16 and landing parties entered the enemy town. Overall command of the sailors ashore fell to Acting Volunteer Lt. Couthouy, with Acting Ensign H.A. Hanson in charge of the *Chillicothe*'s

To Alexandria. Following the capture of Fort de Russy, the *Chillicothe*, together with other fleet elements, steamed up the Red River toward Alexandria on March 14–15, with the *Osage* actually receiving its surrender on the former day without firing a shot. Some units, particularly the timberclads and several larger tinclads, were able to move much more quickly than the slower casemate ironclads and thus reached the town toward dusk.

20-man contingent. Happily for the gunboatmen, the troop transports arrived at 1:30 p.m. and Maj. Gen. Smith's men more fully occupied Alexandria. RAdm. Porter was not at all pleased that Maj. Gen. Banks, plagued as he was by heavy rains, remained absent. The campaign seemed to be at a stand-still. Shreveport, the principal objective, was still 350 miles up the Red.

Banks' troops began entering Alexandria on March 19. When, eight days late, the last of them trekked into the city on March 26, the Federals finally were able to assemble what Ludwell Johnson called "an impressive display of military might—the greatest in the history of the Southwest." But could it be effectively employed?

Meanwhile, sailors from the Mississippi Squadron continued to assist in the occupation of the town, concentrating on its waterfront and the provision of river pickets. Additional landing parties under Capt. Couthouy and his ensigns went ashore on March 21, while a six-man boarding crew under Acting Ensign C.A. Calvert transferred aboard the tug *Dahlia* to perform picket duty over the next two days. On the 23rd, half a dozen unidentified horsemen were seen at a house on the left riverbank. Acting Ensign Calvert and 16 men were sent off in the *Chillicothe*'s cutter to determine their identity. A number of prisoners were returned to the ironclad for interrogation; found unsuspicious, all were released and returned ashore. The house was then destroyed. On March 26 Maj. Gen. Smith's corps undertook a march to Bayou Rapides, 21 miles above Alexandria. Units from the Mississippi Squadron were needed to provide support.[21]

By direct order of the Confederate War Department, an obstruction had been ordered constructed the previous year, between Tones Bayou and Bayou Coushatta on the Red River near the village of Coushatta. Accordingly, Southern engineer Capt. Thomas P. Hotchkiss built a raft-like dam located near the southern bend of Scopini Island near the river cutoff bearing its name. Sometime between March 18 and April 5, as the Union invasion started, the dam was blown, draining most of the water (about 75 percent) from the Red River above Grand Ecore "like pulling the plug out of a bathtub." As soon as the Confederate black powder barrels exploded, mountains of water flowed into an old channel known as Bayou Pierre, located about 30 miles south of Shreveport. As it cascaded in, a 19-mile wide flood plain was created as 75 percent of the stream's water was diverted. As the water level fell over several days, as observed by the Union navy, a small amount of water exited Bayou Pierre into the Red, giving the false appearance of a rise. Most of the water remained trapped for some days before backing up into the Red River as planned, a few miles above Grand Ecore. This Confederate river manipulation, and not an accident of nature, was the reason the Union navy later in the campaign found the water level so low. The little freshet occasioned by the backup gave Porter the encouragement needed to advance from Alexandria toward Grand Ecore. In the end, it nearly cost him his fleet.

Electing to keep below a number of vessels obviously too deeply laden, the Mississippi Squadron leader sent others ahead into the danger zone. The river stage looked passable for some vessels, though questionable for others. Almost as soon as this effort began, Lt. Cmdr. Seth Ledyard Phelps' giant ironclad, *Eastport*, taken along due to a continuing fear of possible Shreveport-based Rebel gunboats, grounded. She would, in the end, have to be scuttled.

On March 29, Porter sent a letter to navy secretary Welles announcing that he was

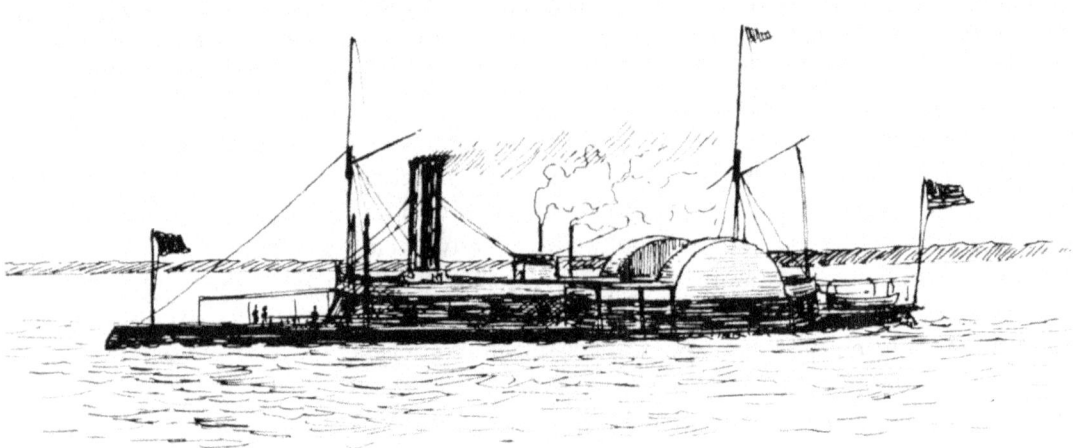

Stopped Above Grand Ecore Having learned of Banks' defeat at the Battle of Mansfield on April 8, RAdm. Porter two days later ordered a Shreveport-bound task group, which included the *Chillicothe*, to round to and return to Grand Ecore as quickly as possible and hence back to Alexandria. A difficult journey ensued during which a number of vessels were damaged and the mighty ironclad *Eastport* was lost before safety was reached on April 27 (courtesy Andrei nacu, via English Wikipedia).

about to depart for Shreveport "or as high up the river as I can get." The low level of the Red River continued to hinder efforts to get his gunboats above the rapids at Alexandria for the mission. The admiral added, "I shall only be able to take up part of the force I brought with me, and leave the river guarded all the way through." When all were available, the waterborne Porter-Smith expedition resumed its trek up the Red River on April 2. As the line moved ahead, the *Chillicothe* took station astern of the *Carondelet* and *Lexington*. By mid-afternoon, the armada was a long gray line that strung out nearly 30 miles from its first units back to the location of Mayor Brown's ironclad. Maj. Gen. Banks and his men, meanwhile, marched overland.

By noon next day, the task force reached Grand Ecore, the little west bank town four miles north of Natchitoches. Here the bluffs were 120 feet high and contained fortifications dating back to the Mexican War. Upon arrival, "Whiskey" Smith's soldiers disembarked, save for the XVII Corps Provisional Division, which was detailed to remain with the transports. Banks joined Porter and Smith at the little river community later in the day.

Just before 5:00 p.m. the *Lexington* led a small task unit up the river to search for Rebel torpedoes that may have been laid in the Red. The river narrowed above Grand Encore as the speed of its current grew more swift. The banks were elevated at a number of points from the surrounding countryside but not so high as host major Rebel fortifications. The vessels were also to look into reports that Confederates were burning large quantities of cotton near the riverbank. The rumors were true and when the timberclad, followed by the *Fort Hindman* (Tinclad No. 13), *Chillicothe*, *Neosho*, and *Osage*, arrived on the scene about five miles above Grand Ecore, Rebel horsemen were seen "lurking about." The *Lexington* fired two howitzer rounds at the butternut riders, who returned fire immediately. Indeed, the men on the bank opened fire at all four vessels as they passed the blazing cotton, the *Chillicothe* now at the end of the line. As the ironclad's commander, Capt. Couthony, stepped up to the pilothouse to see what the shooting was about, a minie ball passed through the starboard chimney and entered his body at the waist. The wound was mortal.

As the gunboats above Grand Ecore fought the Rebel horsemen, the Union army and navy commanders congregated at the town. There the generals agreed to a new plan for the rapid capture of Shreveport. The National Expeditionary Corps, comprising Banks' corps and most of A.J. Smith's, both of which thus far had moved mainly along the Red River, would strike inland away from water along the Shreveport road on April 6, headed toward Mansfield, and Porter would move upstream on April 7 taking a military force, headed by Brig. Gen. Thomas Kilby Smith (1820–1887), on transports. (Smith, a Buckeye and a former member of Maj. Gen. Grant's staff, served as a U.S. counsel after the war.)

Meanwhile, up the Red, the *Fort Hindman* ran onto a sandbar. As she was backing off, the wind blew her stern into the bank, unshipping her starboard rudder and breaking her tiller. Putting the damages right consumed most of the night, the other undamaged gunboats anchored or tied up nearby. During this episode, the surgeon from the monitor *Neosho* arrived aboard the *Chillicothe* to examine her stricken captain. There was nothing he could do as Couthouy suffered through the night, conscious most of the time.

The naval portion of Banks' grand scheme did not unfold immediately. As preparations for departure continued, the *Lexington* and her consorts, especially the repaired *Fort Hindman*, undertook a torpedo sweep on April 4. Aboard the *Chillicothe*, which was tied to the left bank, Lt. Cmdr. Couthouy expired around 8:00 a.m.

Armed cutters from all four vessels, called away near Madame De Roe's plantation, not far from Campti, now dragged the river for the nefarious mines. During the process, they sounded the channel's depth. The bluejackets had dragged for just over an hour when Union cavalry from the Army of the Gulf attempted to make a reconnaissance into the town. Riding in, they were met by a hail of gunfire from approximately 125 Confederate defenders hidden in houses. At the beginning of this skirmish, the sweeping boat crews returned to their respective vessels, while those jacks remaining aboard were beat to quarters. The gunboats got underway and headed upstream toward the sound of the guns. Meanwhile, the 3rd Rhode Island Cavalry was ordered to push into Campti from the flank and fire the defenders' houses. Out on the river the first gunboat on the scene was the *Fort Hindman*, which fired five rounds toward suspected Confederate positions in the town. The *Lexington* passed her a few minutes later and also threw in a number of shells, as did the howitzer onboard the *Chillicothe*. The navy shoot made it impossible for the Rhode Islanders to get to the homes, which were spared—for now.

As the cavalry pressed in from the front, Liddell's men retreated through some woods and over a bridge across a bayou, which structure they burned behind them. Toward 9:00 a.m. soldiers from the 5th Minnesota Infantry arrived and joined the troopers, charging on the butternut positions. Continuous musketry could be heard from all four gunboats, which continued firing on targets of opportunity for an hour. Once the dust settled ashore and the Confederates were driven off, the Union force burned Campti. When the bluecoats withdrew back to Grand Ecore, Liddel simply moved back into the void, planning to harass the Northern fleet whenever possible.

The Federal gunboats, meanwhile, had tied up to the riverbank. Signal flags ran up the *Lexington*'s halyards, sending the anti-torpedomen back to work. The river was dragged and sounded until just after 11:00 a.m. Once the hands had returned aboard and consumed lunch, the craft got underway and stood upstream. Meeting no further obstacles, the four gunboats tied up to the right bank at 6:40 p.m. and threw out pickets. Just before 9:00 the morning of April 5 the *Chillicothe* got underway and ran alongside the *Fort Hindman*. The remains of Capt. Couthouy were put aboard the *Fort Hindman* in an air-tight lead coffin for shipment north. Within the hour, the Brown-built ironclad proceeded up the river at the rear of the task group, steaming slowly.

Just after midnight on April 7, lookouts aboard the *Chillicothe* spotted a number of suspicious persons moving abreast of them along the riverbank about 100 yards south of town. One of these fired a rifle shot at the ironclad, doing no damage. Acting Ensign Muir immediately had the crew beat to quarters and ordered one 5-second shrapnel shell fired at the strangers from the ship's howitzer. The day's highlight aboard the Brown-built ironclad occurred around 6:00 that morning. Recovered somewhat from his experience up Yazoo Pass a year earlier, Lt. Cmdr. Watson Smith, just returned to the Mississippi Squadron from medical leave, came aboard and assumed command. With the coming of full daylight, Smith was ready to join the nautical force in shoving off from Grand Ecore. Even so, he took the time to reassure his officers that the body of Lt. Cmdr. Couthouy was even then headed east to his friends in Boston.

As the water-borne portion of the Shreveport expedition was governed largely by the depth of water in the Red River, RAdm. Porter was forced to leave his heaviest units behind. So it was that the chosen task group was the same that had operated near Campti, with the addition of the sternwheel light draught *Cricket* (Tinclad No. 6), from which Porter flew his blue flag. If the water level would only began to rise the remaining gunboats could be brought up. Those warships with the admiral were deemed sufficient, for the moment, to protect the U.S. Army convoy. As the task group prepared to depart the Grand Ecore hills, no one aboard knew that the water, now visibly falling, was going down because Rebel engineers had blown the Bayou Tones dam up ahead.

The parade departed Grand Ecore at 1:00 p.m. on the four-hour trip to Campti. Steaming behind the monitors, the *Lexington* led five troop transports and seven supply steamers. The *Fort Hindman* and *Chillicothe* paddled toward the rear, the latter specifically instructed to guard the steamer *Clara Bell*. The naval contingent was supported by the tug *Dahlia* and the towboats *Benefit* and *William H. Brown*. Not immediately known to the admiral, Maj. Gen. Banks' quartermasters had inserted an additional 10 supply transports into the convoy even after squadron leadership had expressly stipulated that they not be added.

Finding the Banks transports waiting at Campti, Porter immediately ordered them to the rear of the fleet. Included among the new arrivals was the ammunition-ordnance steamer *Rob Roy*. The monitor *Osage* was tasked to follow them. In addition to the extra supply vessels, the headquarters boat of the XIX Corps, the *Black Hawk*, was also present. She was not the same boat as the navy flag tinclad now at the mouth of the river.

Even though the ironclads with the deepest drafts were left behind, those with Porter, including the *Chillicothe* along with some of the larger transports, began to experience very rough navigation. The muddy water often made it almost impossible to spot obstructions such as stumps or snags under the surface. Many bottoms scraped or struck hidden bars and rocks. Damage to paddle wheels and unshipped or broken rudders was common. Steaming around the numerous sharp bends against the current was laborious, to put it gently, and the maximum speed of the entire fleet was just one or two miles per hour.

In addition to navigational problems, Porter's gunboats continued to suffer fuel shortages. The fleet supply of coal having long since been exhausted, the vessels depended upon wood for their motive power. The problem was that there were not many suitable trees available and, even with those being mostly cottonwood, the work of cutting and trimming them would take much time. So it was that fence rails, basically small trees already shaped by farmers and ranchers, became a happy substitute.

From the start of the expedition, with some exceptions, Porter's gunboats and the quartermaster steamers tied up every night two hours before sunset for the express purpose of hunting rails. Whole crews, including those from the *Chillicothe* as well as soldiers from the transports, scoured the countryside. Every man was expected to return with at least two rails. After they were handed over, the poles were then sawed up by the "black gangs" of engine-room personnel into the lengths necessary to fit into the various furnaces. While bluejackets from the *Chillicothe* were ashore hunting poles on April 9 they also managed to prize 11 bales of cotton. Lt. Cmdr. Smith later wrote that these were found at a deserted and uninhabited place on the left bank of the Red River. They were obviously free for the taking, as "no persons, black or white," were in view and "the houses were somewhat damaged."

Porter's gunboats and the army transports slowly steamed up the so-called Narrows towards Shreveport for three days. Rebel riflemen treated them to regular lead greetings. A favorite tactic was to lie in wait for the craft as it entered the upriver side of a bend below a high bluff. Having volleyed, the butternuts would disappear before the return shells could explode and race across the hill to the downriver side and fire down on the continuing vessels as they passed below. Very few men on either side were actually badly hurt during the trip, but many Northern nerves were undoubtedly frayed. By and by the boats arrived as scheduled, about 2:00 p.m. on April 10, at what was believed to be the mouth of Loggy Bayou. Perhaps stroking his beard, the admiral wondered why the stream was not the same one marked on his map.

Gary Joiner has looked into the question of just where Porter halted. The admiral's own writings are contradictory and it is possible that he just did not know. Springfield Landing, where he thought he might be, was four miles west of the Red River and 30 miles below Shreveport. On the other hand, he might have been at the mouth of Loggy Bayou or even the nonexistent Shreveport River. "It is possible," Joiner wrote in 2006, that the task group "was as close as two miles south from Tones Bayou or as much as four to five miles below the bayou."

Here, nearly 100 miles in the rear of Banks' army, they were stopped cold by Confederate ingenuity. In conjunction with their blowing the dam, the large scuttled steamer *New Falls City*, her hull filled with mud, was stretched end to beached end, directly across the river. An invitation writ large to a Shreveport ball, Porter later told Maj. Gen. Sherman, "was kindly left stuck up by the rebels, which invitation we were never able to accept." Before the bluejackets could manhandle the broken packet out of the way of the fleet, units of which stretched at various intervals back downstream, a courier from Maj. Gen. Banks streaked to a halt on the riverbank with terrible news. The courier revealed the Federal defeat at the Battle of Sabine Cross-Roads near Grand Ecore and indicated that the Army of the Gulf and the attached corps from the Army of the Tennessee were retreating toward Pleasant Mill. Though the fact was not fully realized by all at that moment, the Union's Red River campaign had reached its zenith.

RAdm. Porter later told Maj. Gen. Smith that his disappointment was great upon learning "that all our perseverance and energy had been thrown away." As that thought took hold with others, Banks' rider relayed a verbal command for Brig. Gen. Smith from Maj. Gen. Banks: the amphibious XVII Corps Provisional Division, just disembarked, was to return aboard its steamers and find Banks' main force near Grand Ecore as fast as possible. Porter and his military colleague elected to quickly retreat south in order to avoid entrapment. "The confusion which immediately followed" the revelation of Banks' defeat "was frightful," remembered Nicholas Smith, an officer aboard the steamer *John Warner*. Interviewed by the *Columbus (WI) Democrat* in 1895, Smith recalled that the quartermaster transport "captains became frantic and disorder seemed to control every movement."

The commanders of the gunboats were signaled to meet aboard the *Cricket*, where RAdm. Porter informed them of the army's defeat and retreat. He also revealed his decision that the boats would be returning to Grand Ecore. A plan was quickly worked out in conjunction with the also-present Brig. Gen. Smith to provide a maximum of defense against the Confederate troops, regular and irregular, that were anticipated on the southern exodus. During the trip downstream the gunboats were to be distributed among the transports, with the *Osage* remaining at the rear. Soldiers from the various regiments aboard ship would construct and defend rude breastworks of hay and cracker boxes on the hurricane decks of their steamboats.

Guerrillas and others were not the only obstacles to cause concern. The river's going back down would be just as hazardous or worse than it was coming up. Although the speed of the convoy might be a fraction faster because it was not paddling against the current, a significant negative was the fact that the larger craft, particularly the *Chillicothe* and the monitors, would be almost unmanageable. "The river was exceedingly narrow and torturous," remembered Brig. Gen. Smith, "the bottom covered with logs and snags and the banks full of drift, rendering the navigation most difficult and dangerous." On top of that, the banks in some stretches were even taller than the pilothouses of the boats, a situation that greatly favored the Rebel defenders.

Within a couple of hours of encountering the *New Falls City*, the Federal convoy was ready to return. Smith and Porter knew that they did not have the width of river required for the boats to round to, so orders were given that "the fleet back down the river in the order the boats then lay." Once the procession began, the rearmost boat, the monitor *Osage*, took the lead downsteam. The parade had barely begun, however, before the *Chillicothe* struck an invisible snag and became stuck. All afternoon the gunboat's tars worked without success to get her off the hidden stump. After 4:00 p.m. the

4—The Chillicothe Goes to War: Yazoo Pass and Red River

transport *Black Hawk* came down, maneuvering to take her largest hawser, with which she pulled off the ironclad.

Though it would take the whole night, the elements of the Union convoy would turn as the bayous and pockets of the stream afforded facility. Steamers of the day were not built for such backward motion over an extended distance and it was known that the physical strain on propulsion and steerage functions would be significant. The number of miles the vessels had to travel in reverse was directly related to their size, with the smaller ones able to turn sooner. By 6:00 the morning of April 11 all had rounded to or otherwise come about, with the *Osage* once more at the rear. From this point on, Porter, his gunboats and the military transports faced a desperate battle against falling water and Confederate riflemen to avoid entrapment above the Alexandria rapids.[22]

Maj. Gen. Banks' corps reached Grand Ecore on April 11 and went into camp behind rapidly constructed entrenchments. It would remain at this location for the next 10 days. During the day the Porter-Smith armada worked its way down the frustrating Red River. The men aboard did not know that at dawn Maj. Gen. Taylor had dispatched a brigade of cavalry and a battery to cut off the boats at the docks of Bayou Pierre. Luckily for the Federals, they passed Grand Bayou Landing several hours before the Rebel horsemen arrived.

On several occasions, Confederate riflemen atop the riverbank bluffs peppered the vessels with musketry just as they had on the way up. Such bee strings continued to elicit massive cannon fire in response. For example, about 4:30 p.m. Confederate riders opened musket fire on the transports *Black Hawk* and *Benefit*. All of the nearby Union warships immediately replied, including the tugboat *Dahlia*. Then, at 6:30 p.m., the *Chillicothe* was asked to shell the woods on the left bank where a concentration of enemy was believed to be assembling. Four 5-second shells were dropped on the shoreline by the starboard Dahlgren.

"In the first years of the war," Richard Taylor wrote later, it "was popularly believed that the destructive power of these monsters ... could 'not be resisted.'" Many of the Confederate soldiers pursuing Porter's task group still believed this, though a few did not.

April 12 did not begin well for the men of the return convoy. Underway at 6:00 a.m., the vessels encountered what Brig. Gen. Smith called "exceedingly difficult" navigation. In an effort to avoid collisions while turning the narrow bends the fleet was ordered to separate as much as possible.

At 6:30 a.m. Confederate troops in buildings along the shore had opened small arms fire on the *Chillicothe*, to which she replied with five 5-second howitzer shells. An hour later, Acting Ensigns Muir and Hannon, with two master's mates, went ashore with an armed party to engage the bushwhackers. The sailors soon engaged in a brisk firefight that lasted 20 minutes before the Southerners were driven back. Once the Confederates were gone, Muir ordered the structures fired and the men then returned aboard their ironclad, which continued downstream about 7:15 a.m.

As the army steamer *Black Hawk* and the monitor *Osage* passed up shortly thereafter, they, too, were fired into by Confederate troops along the shore. As this assault on Union river traffic continued, Porter, from the *Cricket*, sent dispatches to his gunboat captains ordering that they shoot into the woods and brush back of the banks in an effort to keep the Southerners at bay. His order to Capt. Watson Smith arrived around 8:00 a.m. and the *Chillicothe* was "beat to quarters" and undertook a brief bombardment, expending one each XI-inch and 12-pounder shrapnel shell. The huge billowing clouds of wood smoke puffed out by the Northern vessels was visible for miles. Thus, the progress of the Yankee craft was easily and continuously monitored by Southern troops. Most of the wooden transports, guarded by the tinclads and the *Chillicothe*, were up ahead and passed Blair's Landing before noon. Those few army transports at the rear were covered by the *Lexington* and *Osage*.

Not long after the sun reached meridian, Mayor Brown's smallest ironclad rounded to and came to anchor below Blair's Landing. There, over the next four hours, she shelled the right banks at intervals, sometimes aiming at actual targets and other times at suspected rebel locations. When the shoot ended in late afternoon, gunners examining the magazine found that four XI-inch and five 12-pounder shells had been expended. Further upstream, other steamers, including the monitor *Osage*, had engaged attacking Texas cavalry, killing their commanding general. The death of Brig. Gen. Thomas Green (1814–1864), a prominent prewar military and political leader and a dashing horseman, slowed the Confederate onslaught. Brig Gen. Smith was uncertain whether or not the Southerners would resume their attack that evening. Taking no chances, either with his crews or the men and supplies aboard the transports, Porter, just before 8:00 p.m., ordered the fleet to make the best speed away from Blair's Landing as river conditions permitted. Actually, the progress of the Union task group was not very fast considering the many sandbars encountered. In pitch dark, the boats had only torches by which to navigate the risky stream. Several struck rocks and grounding was only a sandbar or low riverbank away.

While proceeding downstream about 8:40 p.m. the *Chillicothe* ran aground in a river bend, near the right bank. After she had made several attempts to free herself, Lt. Cmdr. Watson Smith hailed the transports *Southwester* and *Sioux City* for help, but, being too long, they were unable to assist. While an ensign was sent to alert RAdm. Porter of the *Chillicothe*'s immobility, Confederate infantry in the bluffs off the starboard bow raked the two passing transports with musket fire. The gunboat's crew was immediately beat to quarters and shelled the elevations. About 11:30 p.m. the *Fort Hindman* also came down and shelled the cliffs while passing.

After pounding the woods for two hours, the side-wheel tinclad came back to assist the *Chillicothe* early on April 13. The ironclad's heaviest hawser was passed over and, after several attempts, the Brown-built craft was finally pulled free into deeper water. The withdrawal to Grand Ecore resumed about 6:00 a.m., when it was light enough to check for obstructions ahead. As the ironclad steamed downstream, Lt. Cmdr. Smith had his gun crews blast the same wooded area hit by the *Fort Hindman* hours earlier. Half a dozen XI-inch shells departed her casemate, including a stand of grapeshot. About 7:30 a.m. the flag boat *Cricket* arrived towing a barge and also fired into the brush along the shore. As the hour advanced, the craft headed down the river, the *Chillicothe* leading the tinclad.

Not much further into the morning, the quartermaster steamer *John Warner*, while moving through a dense patch of fog, hit a snag and grounded so firmly she could not be immediately worked off. Finding himself in a situation not unlike that faced the day before, Brig. Gen. Smith immediately sent a courier to Grand Ecore and hoped that his superior, Maj. Gen. Smith, would come up soon. Word of the running ship-shore battle had actually reached Grand Ecore hours earlier. "Whiskey" Smith immediately set about organizing a relief force. When it was ready that morning, he set out toward Campti leading two brigades, two batteries of field artillery, and cavalry.

Confederate forces who continued to follow the fleet along the river were now determined to take advantage of the *Warner* situation to harass the Federals again. The two sections of field artillery available to them (two 6-pounders and two 12-pounder howitzers) were unlimbered atop the hill overlooking Bouledeau's Point, where the grounded steamboat lay. Between noon and 4:00 that afternoon Rebel gunners attempted to hit her or any of the vessels strung out across the river under a bluff, realizing that a lucky shot might blow up an ammunition steamer or penetrate a boiler. Their efforts were supported by riflemen whose balls were dangerous from that distance to Union crewmen but not, if they came no closer, to their vessels.

Because the *Warner* blocked the river the *Chillicothe* was unable to steam to her assistance. While attempting to renew the effort about 2:00 p.m. the ironclad dragged her stern anchor and grounded on logs. Unsuccessful in working her way free, Lt. Cmdr. Smith ordered the big 11-inch hawser taken aboard the nearby steamer *William H. Brown*. Puffing mightily, the dispatch boat pulled off the warship, but in the process it carried away Smith's cathead and port bitts, swinging his vessel into the transport *Universe*, which action carried away the port gangway and a boat davit. Once this episode was sorted out, the *Chillicothe* was able to get underway again, shortly thereafter encountering the transport *Black Hawk*, which was towing the monitor *Osage*.

Armed only with howitzers, the *William H. Brown*, in continuing downstream, opened fire upon Confederate gunners concealed behind a bluff. The grayclad cannoneers immediately replied and struck the transport in her steam drum, completely disabling the stern-wheeler. Simultaneously, the *Chillicothe*, right behind, went to general quarters and opened fire on the enemy's position and the surrounding woods. About 4:00 p.m., as her Dahlgrens continued to speak, Smith's command reached the *Brown*, which was brought alongside. Her crew was taken aboard and the vessel itself was taken in tow behind the ironclad. As the pair continued, the transport *Sioux City* was encountered about 4:45 p.m., she having broken her rudder. She hailed the *Chillicothe* for assistance and, after some maneuvering, took the *Brown* off Lt. Cmdr. Smith's hands, using her rudders to steer by as she moved on with the dispatch boat in tow.

Along about 5:30 p.m. Rebel cavalry appeared on the hill overlooking the gunboat's location but stayed out of range of her guns. Once the *Sioux City* and the other transports and warships were past Bouledeau Point the *Lexington* followed, bringing up the rear. Most of the convoy reached its destination by late afternoon. The *Chillicothe* came to anchor around 6:30 p.m. As the quartermaster steamers reached Campti, a number of them grounded. Despite coming to difficulties, most of the soldiers and sailors aboard the fleet were excited when Maj. Gen. Smith and his men arrived at the village about 4:00 p.m. The man nicknamed "Whiskey" was overjoyed that Kilby Smith's craft had arrived. He had "by energy, good judgment, and rare good fortune, succeeded in running the batteries and land forces of the enemy without the loss of a boat." Though to be accurate, it had to be admitted that "some were completely riddled with shot."

The exodus downstream continued on April 14. As the spring sun shone high above, the gunboats and steamers continued en route to Grand Ecore. Any building not completely destroyed earlier in the month was set ablaze when the soldiers withdrew from Campti, The *Chillicothe* and other fleet elements anchored at Grand Ecore by early evening as Porter traveled to Alexandria to confer with Maj. Gen. Banks. Although many of the vessels that had so far escaped bore the marks of Rebel sharpshooters, the transports and gunboats reassembling at Grand Ecore were, in fact, little the worse for their ordeal. Still, the *St. Louis Daily Missouri Democrat* newsman embedded with the army transports called the fleet's escape to Grand Ecore "one of the most daring, as well as one of the most successful ... feats of the whole war."

With their admiral away, the Mississippi Squadron vessels made repairs and awaited developments. Around noon on April 18 lookouts aboard the *Chillicothe* recorded that the *Louisville* was hard aground off Harper's Plantation, with a steamer working hard to get her afloat. Later in mid-afternoon, just after the steamer *White Cloud* was passing a short distance ahead, she was taken under fire by Confederate riflemen. This action brought the "Chilly Coffee" men to general quarters and within minutes, six XI-shells (shrapnel) from the Dahlgrens flew into the woods along the bank, together with two howitzer rounds. The Confederates faded away.[23]

April 19 was barely an hour old when RAdm. Porter, having returned, ordered his fleet to evacuate Grand Ecore and steam down to Alexandria. For a number of Federal naval craft, the new voyage would be as trying as that just past. Starting out, the *Chillicothe* followed the *Ozark* and *Louisville*, with the *Pittsburg*, *Carondelet*, and *Mound City* behind. Around 4:00 a.m. the *Ozark* grounded, halting the entire procession and forcing these ironclads to briefly tie up to the bank while she was freed. While these vessels made their way downstream, the next several days were taken up with a desperate struggle to save the mighty *Eastport*, which had grounded due to a torpedo strike at a point about six miles below Grand Ecore.

The *Chillicothe* was not directly involved in the unsuccessful effort to save the *Eastport* (scuttled on April 26) nor in the heated exchange that day between the *Lexington* and *Osage* versus Confederate troops at Deloges Bluff. Reaching Alexandria on April 27, she, like the other ironclads of her fleet, faced the challenge of getting past the Alexandria rapids. Indeed, Porter later confided that he not only had the rapids to deal with but also the rocks below them, which were "for a mile quite bare, with the exception of a channel 20 feet wide and 3 feet deep."[24]

On April 28, RAdm. Porter advised Navy Secretary Gideon Welles of his precarious position, due to the falling water level of the Red River as well as Banks' withdrawal. "I find myself blockaded," he wrote, "by a fall of 3 feet of water, 3 feet 4 inches being the amount now on the falls; 7 feet being required to get over." Facing the distinct possibility that he would need to destroy twelve gunboats (worth $3 million), as he had the *Eastport*, to keep them out of Confederate hands, he lamented to his superior, "[Y]ou may judge of my feelings at having to perform so painful a duty." On April 29, Porter had some initial success in getting at least a portion of the transports and his flotilla through the available little 20-foot-wide channel. Still, the heaviest vessels, including the *Chillicothe*, remained above behind the falls. That night, Lt. Cmdr. Smith, ranking officer and one-time expedition commander, established the nightly picket routine, assigning

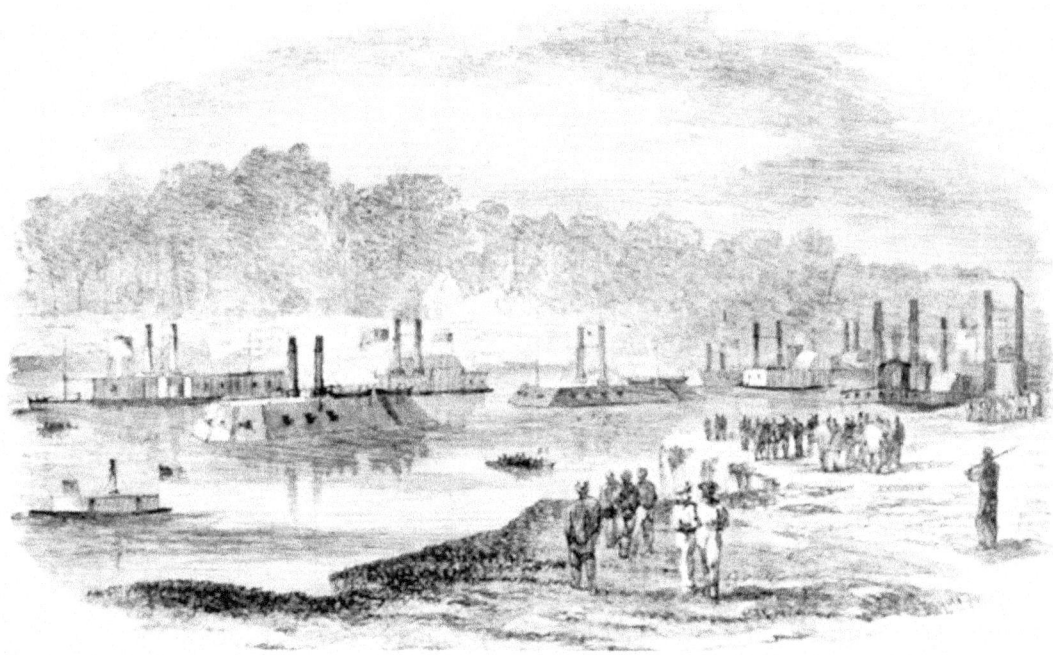

Above Alexandria. The Mississippi Squadron units that escaped Grand Ecore were trapped by low water above the Alexandria falls. Many were, in actuality, tied to the riverbank and not spread out as depicted. Nevertheless, the drawing conveys the sense of urgency that faced every Union sailor present in the days before a dam, built by XIX Corps staff engineer Lt. Col. Joseph Bailey (1825–1867), was completed (*Harper's Weekly*, April 30, 1864).

two officers and three men from ten gunboats to alternate going ashore and keeping posted.

Working with Maj. Gen. Banks and his officers, the Mississippi Squadron chief fortunately came up with the correct solution and the right man to carry it out, XIX Corps staff engineer Lt. Col. Joseph Bailey (1825–1867), whom Nicholas Smith decades later called "the Moses of Porter's fleet." For years, the story of Bailey's dam was the most celebrated single event of the entire Federal Red River fiasco. The presence of the one-time 4th Wisconsin Cavalry officer with the Banks expedition was, wrote Smith and Castille in 1986, "one of those coincidences of history that sometimes result in turning the course of events." So it was that, on April 29, Bailey was tasked by Banks and Porter with constructing a dam that would raise the water sufficiently to allow the fleet to escape. Straightaway the next day, Maj. Gen. Banks set over 3,000 men to work chopping down trees or dismantling whole buildings, finding stone and rock, and hauling the materials to the sites on either bank where the dam would be constructed. Interestingly, Black troops worked the Alexandria side, while soldiers from Wisconsin, Maine, and New York labored on the Pineville shore.

Around the clock for eight days the men strained without cessation, beginning the initial dam not far above the lower, downstream rapids where the river was about 758 feet wide. It was hoped that when the project was finished the water behind the structure would have risen enough to float the gunboats over the upper rapids. Then when the

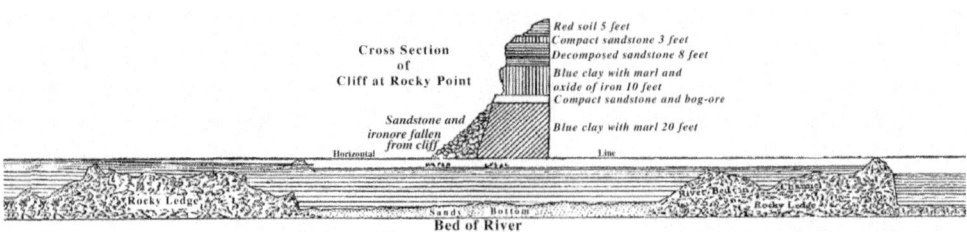

MAP AND SECTIONS OF THE RED RIVER DAMS ABOVE ALEXANDRIA.

Red River Dams Above Alexandria, LA, May 1864. On April 30, over 3,000 men began work chopping down trees or dismantling whole buildings, finding stone and rock, and hauling the materials to the sites on either bank where the dam would be constructed. Interestingly, Black troops worked the Alexandria side, while soldiers from Wisconsin, Maine, and New York labored on the Pineville shore. The top drawing shows the construction of the dams while that on the bottom depicts their placement (Johnson and Buel, *Battles and Leaders*).

time was just right, the dam could be broken and the gunboats could rush free over the lower rapids, carried by the force of the released water. On May 5 RAdm. Porter made inquiry of Lt. Cmdr. Smith about what kind of preparations had been made aboard the *Chillicothe* to keep her dry during a run up the river. Smith replied that, within minutes of casting off, each hatch (including the fire room hatch) would have its heavy grating secured, with a heavy tarpaulin battened over it and the combings, and a strong wooden cover spiked down all around. Additionally, the chimneys would be closely boarded, with 10 inches of space to a height of 4.5 feet from the deck.

Despite a 9-mph current, the work continued and gradually the water level began to rise. According to soundings ordered by RAdm. Porter, the water level for the *Chillicothe* anchorage at the upper falls on May 6 was three feet with a rough and bumpy bottom. Downstream at the lower falls the depth was nine feet. On May 8, the stage on the upper falls was up sufficiently to allow the lighter gunboats and monitors to move down and make ready to pass the main dam the instant it was ready. Early the next morning, great crashing sounds were heard in the vicinity of the dam. The tremendous water pressure against the dam forced two of the barges employed in its construction to burst loose, and they were swinging in below the dam on one side. The *Lexington*, the only one of the gunboats with steam up fully ready to go, immediately passed the upper falls, ran down over the rocky stretch before the level fell, and exited to safety through the dam. Anchoring below the town, her crew observed the monitors *Osage* and *Neosho* and the big tinclad *Fort Hindman* come down a short time later. The successful passage of these boats proved Lt. Col. Bailey's dam would work and he resumed his work on it with spirit. Still, as it was being mended, strengthened, and completed, the *Chillicothe* and her consorts remained stranded, "locked in by a reef of rocks across the river just below."

About 11:00 a.m. RAdm. Porter sent orders to the remaining boats to remove their cannon, much of their ordnance and other stores, and their side armor. Capt. Smith pushed his crew to lighten ship. Tons of shot and shell, powder and stores were sent ashore. As darkness fell, a line was gotten up to the gunboat from the dam and plans were made to utilize it in pulling her agonizingly ahead. After 9:00 p.m. a council of war was held aboard the *Cricket* as the captains were informed of the fleet's next moves. By late evening the *Chillicothe*, which still lay in the channel at the head of the falls just ahead of the *Carondelet* and *Mound City*, had about four inches more water under her keel than when she first grounded. Tons of iron plating were loosened from her casemate turret by midnight and readied for disposal. At 5:15 a.m. on May 11 Watson Smith's craft, with her hatches all battened down, weighed anchor and dropped downstream stern first. In passing over the upper falls, the ironclad grounded on the rocks. Utilizing heavy lines, the crew of the Brown-built ironclad, working with hundreds of soldiers ashore, were able to get the vessel over those falls at noon, permitting her to anchor above the dam a half hour later.

The fleet withdrawal continued on May 12, and at 10 a.m. on May 13 RAdm. Porter sent orders aboard the *Chillicothe* that she go over the dam at the lower falls. As Lt. Cmdr. Smith readied his vessel for the dash, the *Louisville* went over several minutes later. Not long after she cleared, Smith's vessel and the *Ozark*, for reasons unrecorded,

Escaping Over Bailey's Dam. The heavier units of the stranded Mississippi Squadron were lined up and escaped over the Red River falls at Alexandria, LA, via Lt. Col. Bailey's dam. Prior to her run on the morning of May 11, 1864, the *Chillicothe* (shown second from left) was lightened by the removal of significant stores and armor plating. With her hatches all battened down, she weighed anchor and dropped downstream stern first, but in passing over the upper falls she grounded on the rocks. Utilizing heavy lines, the ironclad's crew, working with hundreds of soldiers ashore, was able to get her over those falls at noon. She anchored above the dam a half hour later (*Frank Leslie*'s *Scenes and Portraits*, 1894).

were each directed to send one big shell over a nearby point. As the morning fled, the *Chillicothe* was cut loose and steamed up river past the *Ozark*, taking a position behind that vessel and tying up to the bank. After she had done so, the *Ozark*, accompanied by a tugboat, cast loose and steamed over the dam. Around 11:40 a.m. Lt. Cmdr. Smith ordered the *Chillicothe* to drop down and she, too, passed safely over the dam, tying up to the right bank. During the remainder of the day and next morning, the ironclad and her consorts reloaded their provisions and ammunition, coaled, and departed downstream guarding a convoy of transports. Union forces, including the *Chillicothe* and the other gunboats, exited Alexandria on the afternoon of May 14, leaving the city in flames. About 2:00 p.m. a volley of musketry was fired into Smith's vessel from the left bank. No casualties were taken and within 10 minutes his crew beat to quarters and shelled the nearby woods with the boat howitzer.

The *Chillicothe* was tied up with other fleet elements at Simmesport, LA, late in the afternoon of May 16 when two officers from the staff of Maj. Gen. Banks arrived from Army of the Gulf headquarters some 10 miles inland on the right bank of the Red. Smith was informed that the Federal force would begin arriving at Smith's location by the next day, ready to embark for the Mississippi. Next day, Lt. Cmdr. Smith received a message from RAdm. Porter. The light draught *Forest Rose* (Tinclad No. 9) was then towing two empty coal barges to a nearby location. Upon delivery, they would be placed in the river to serve as a "pontoon" (bridge) across.

Late on May 18, Maj. Gen. A.J. Smith came aboard to confer with Lt. Cmdr. Smith, and to report to his naval colleague on the status of the Army of the Gulf's withdrawal. The soldier explained that the day's fighting had been heavy and his pleas to Maj. Gen. Banks for reinforcements had gone unfulfilled. Smith had taken it upon himself to form his steamers into a continuous ferry ("a bridge") across the river, thus allowing his troops to move to the left bank. He asked the naval commander to keep his vessel and others under his direction available to provide gunfire support if needed. On the morning of May 19, as bluecoat troops continued to move across the river, Maj. Gen. Banks sent a message to Smith asking that 100 tons coal from the navy's stock be diverted to supply the steamers carrying his troops to the left bank. Smith refused to do so unless he had direct orders from RAdm. Porter. Banks' exodus continued through the day. Toward evening, one of the *Chillicothe*'s pilots, John Dean, reported to Smith that rumors ashore indicated Confederate soldiers had already crossed the river below and were taking up positions to further engage the retreating Federals.

RAdm. Porter returned to the mouth of the Red River on May 30, where he wrote out vessel assignments for his squadron's various districts. "And thus ended the 69-day Red River expedition," Lt. Cmdr. Thomas Selfridge wrote in his *Battles and Leaders* contribution, "one of the most humiliating and disastrous that had been recorded during the war."[25]

Once the Army of the Gulf was across, Lt. Cmdr. Smith approached RAdm. Porter and asked for a 45-day leave of absence. He made no complaint of illness, remaining anxious to return and perform whatever duties the admiral wished upon his return. The squadron commander, however, was quite concerned for his subordinate's health, thinking that he was now demonstrating "symptoms of breaking down in mind and body." The "longer leave than usual," was explained in his endorsement to Navy Secretary

***Chillicothe*'s Fifth Captain, Lt. Cmdr. Francis Munroe "Frank" Ramsay.** This D.C. native spent the first two years of the war on the African Station before receiving command of the giant Mississippi Squadron ironclad *Choctaw* in March 1863. Following the capture of Vicksburg that July, he took over the Third Division, becoming the ironclad's fifth captain on June 8, 1864. He would transfer to the Atlantic coast in September 1864 and remain in the U.S. Navy after the conflict, rising to the rank of rear admiral in 1894 (Library of Congress).

Welles: "This officer joined me out here after having gone through a severe illness, and after having sustained a domestic clamity which seriously affected and partly impaired his mental faculties. This he partially recovered from, though from the close attention to the duties I assigned him he recovered slowly. I thought the life of a valuable and brave officer of too much consequence not to be looked after by his commander." Smith traveled back to his Trenton, NJ, home, where he died on December 19.[26]

Following Smith's departure east, Third District commander Lt. Cmdr. Frank Ramsay assumed command of the *Chillicothe* bright and early (5:30) on June 8 as the ironclad was coaling. The former captain of the *Choctaw* had received information that Confederate activity was being renewed in the Simmesport, area, including artillery possibly from Boone's Louisiana Battery and the Crescent Artillery, also known as Hutton's Company, Louisiana Artillery, in newly dug breastworks. Members of these units, Ramsay might have known, had served aboard the steamer *Dr. Beatty* (also spelled Batey, Battie and Beaty) and ram *Webb*, respectively, when, in a tale we relate below, they helped ruin the Brown-built ironclad *Indianola* below Vicksburg in February of the previous year.

Formed by Capt. Richard M. Boone in March 1862 as a part of the 2nd Louisiana Volunteer Battery but later often operating independently, this unit spent most of its time prior to July 1863 in the defenses at Port Hudson, LA. After its surrender and the parole of its members, the unit was re-formed at Alexandria, LA, in December 1863 under Lt. Maunsel Bennett. In March it was given two pieces of siege artillery at Shreveport. When the Porter-Banks expedition began to withdraw in early May, it took over a pair of 30-pounder Parrott rifles captured from the sunken navy light draught *Covington* (Tinclad No. 25) and participated in the fighting at Mansura on May 16.

Like Boone's Battery, the Crescent Artillery was formed in March 1862, though specifically to serve aboard the Confederate ironclad *Louisiana*. After the fall of New Orleans a month later, Capt. Thomas H. Hutton's unit saw service on the Red River. During the fall of 1863 and spring of 1864 the cannoneers manned artillery positions at Shreveport, Grand Ecore, and Fort De Russy. Although most of the men were captured when the latter fell to the Union on March 14, others served at Alexandria. Six were present with Lt. Bennet at Simmesport this day.

Determined to ascertain the accuracy of his intelligence, Ramsay got up a small task group, which included his new command, the monitor *Neosho*, and the light draught *Fort Hindman* (Tinclad No. 13), and proceeded up the Red River in that order. At 8:00 a.m. the crews were beat to quarters and minutes later the trio entered the Atchafalaya River. Steaming upstream for an hour, the Federal gunboats came upon a body of Confederate troops encamped behind thin breastworks on the shoreline about a mile and a half from Simmesport. It was 9:15 in the morning when Lt. Bennett opened on the vessels, which, according to Ramsay, "stood on until in good range, then opened." With the tinclad remaining behind about two miles, the two ironclads advanced steadily to a range of 600 yards, firing shell and shrapnel at the Southerners.

When the fight began, the Confederate infantry, stationed behind the levee to support Bennett's people with musketry, withdrew about 300 yards in a dry bayou behind a point of woods. Shortly thereafter, one of the Boone's Battery gunners was killed by the explosion of a shell that landed in front of his piece. The other Parrott suffered a burst breech at its third discharge, wounding one of the men serving it. The artillerymen from the disabled gun were moved to an area near the mouth of Bayou de Glaise while the other continued an impossible duel with the *Chillicothe* and *Neosho*. "I fired principally solid shot," remembered Lt. Bennett, and "those that struck hitting obliquely and glancing off." As the engagement continued, Bennett ordered his surviving cannon wheeled across the river road where it could be better hidden in a ditch to the rear of the levee. He also repeatedly sent messages to the commander of the supporting infantry seeking support to help prevent the Lincolnites from landing. It did not come.

After about 90 minutes of cannonading, the three Union vessels closed the right bank intent upon landing. Sailors from both ironclads were detailed to man armed boats and go ashore; however, because a few men still surrounded the Parrott in the ditch, this initial deployment was aborted. While Bennett was in urgent personal conversation seeking help at an infantry outpost 200 yards away, the gun's protectors disappeared and a party from the *Neosho*, which drew abreast, went ashore with a hawser.

Even though they were targeted by riflemen and Seaman Charles Sower was mortally wounded, the bluejackets were able to make their line fast and after signaling, the monitor's steam winch dragged the gun over the breastworks and down to the beach.

Even as the *Chillicothe* and *Neosho* continued to blanket the area with large shells, the latter cast off and stood up the river. This retreat made way for the *Fort Hindman* to land and for her men to take aboard the serviceable Parrott, as well as thirty-six 30-pounder cartridges, six muskets, and a captured Confederate soldier from the Crescent Artillery (the cannon was subsequently shipped to the main squadron base at Cairo). Lt. Cmdr. Ramsay ordered his vessels to cease firing about noon, any sign of Confederate activity having ceased almost an hour before. While returning downstream to spend the evening replenishing ordnance and ammunition, the *Chillicothe*'s gunner took stock of his magazine. During the shoot, his vessel alone had fired 69 XI-inch shells, more than during any other engagement of her wartime career, including the battles with Fort Pemberton.

This sojourn up the Atchafalaya River put paid to the action accounts of the *Chillicothe*. The ugly little ironclad had now seen more combat operations than either of her larger sisters, actually becoming the only one of the three to see service after 1863. Upon the vessel's return to the waters off Fort Adams, Lt. Cmdr. Ramsay returned to the *Choctaw* and was succeeded as captain by Acting Volunteer Lieutenant George P. Lord (1842–1866), who would remain aboard until the ironclad was laid up in May 1865. A native of Delaware, Lord joined the U.S. Navy in 1861 and was immediately transferred to the U.S. Western Flotilla as a master's mate. Promoted to the rank of acting volunteer lieutenant in October 1862, he became executive officer of the giant

Left Below Cairo. The *Chillicothe* was sold at a giant public auction on November 29, 1865, to Cutting & Ellis for $3,000. Having no real use for her beyond the iron spikes and other fittings of her hull, her engines and tackle, her owners left her on the riverbank below Cairo until 1872, when her remains were burnt during preparation of a railroad right-of-way (*Miller's Photographic History of the Civil War*).

Benton and then, in spring 1863, was given command of the light draught *Covington* (Tinclad No. 25). About 25 miles below Alexandria, LA, on April 27, 1864, while protecting the steamer *John Warner*, the vessel and a consort were attacked by Confederate infantry in force. After five hours of bitter fighting, the transport was captured and the two escorts were so badly damaged that they had to be abandoned. After *Covington* was set on fire by her crew, Lord and 32 of *Covington*'s crew escaped to Alexandria. Exonerated for the loss, Lord then became captain of the ironclad *Chillicothe.* Honorably discharged on February 22, 1866, Lord and his brother-in-law, Peter Eltinge, operated a Memphis, TN, grocery business until the former naval officer died in August.

The *Chillicothe* survived six months longer than her last commander. She was sold at a giant public auction with the *Indianola* and *Tuscumbia* on November 29 to Cutting & Ellis for $3,000. The buyers having no real use for her beyond the iron spikes and other fittings of her hull, her engines and her tackle, she was left on the riverbank below Cairo until 1872, when her remains were burnt during preparation of a railroad right-of-way.[27]

5

Indianola: *The Shortest Cruise*

While the *Chillicothe* enjoyed the longest service career of the three Brown-built ironclads, the *Indianola* suffered the shortest. She wouldn't survive a month in the combat zone.

Having departed Cairo, IL, for "down the river" on January 24, 1863, the new Brown-built ironclad *Indianola* reached Memphis, TN, the midway point of her journey, five days later. There she coaled and continued downstream. All the way downstream from Tennessee, as before, her crew drilled at the great guns in the forward and stern turrets and conducted various other drills designed to enhance their efficiency. Both the men and their acting ensigns were quite green and in need of rigorous education.

Acting Master's Mate William Shaw Ward later remembered the ironclad's arrival in the Vicksburg arena on January 31:

> The air was filled with sunbeams, and the sky above with broken, fleecy clouds on that memorable afternoon ... when the United States gunboat *Indianola* rounded into the mouth of the Yazoo River. The decks of Admiral Porter's fleet were crowded with eager gazers, awaiting with anxious interest the approach of this, their new and formidable ally. So much had been told of the coming ironclad, and so much was expected of it, that there were probably many doubters among the old salts and seamen who stood with those expectant watchers. The first view proved that the *Indianola* was far from graceful in its lines, and somewhat commonplace in model; but it was an ironclad, and to those who knew the number and power of the Vicksburg batteries by a desperate experience, the question of armor was more vital than that of armament.

A newsman, seeing her for the first time, observed for his New York readers that the strange-looking vessel was "nondescript in architecture, embodying some ideas borrowed from the famous *Monitor*, and others entirely original to her." She sat "very low in the water," he continued, "showing forward and amidships but about two feet of hull." A colleague from the *Daily National Intelligencer* told his audience in Washington, D.C., that "in her architecture" the *Indianola* "combines the monitor and the ram, setting very low in the water...."

During the ironclad's downriver voyage, RAdm. David Dixon Porter, the fleet commander, remained concerned not only with direct action plans to capture Vicksburg, MS, but also with that fortress city's ability to obtain sustenance from the surrounding countryside. A particular thorn in his side was the Red River, which emptied into the western side of the Mississippi between Vicksburg and Port Hudson, LA. Vast quantities of foodstuffs arrived from such upstream communities as Alexandria and Shreveport, LA, and were taken by steamer across the "Big Muddy" to waiting troops at both the

Following 4 photographs: *Indianola* **Configuration.** Having departed Cairo, IL, a week before, the *Indianola* anchored above Vicksburg on January 31, 1863. Yard mate of the recently arrived *Chillicothe*, she, too, was conspicuous among fleet units with her enormous turret, huge wheel houses, and low profile. The noted naval vessel plan expert David Meagher here shows us in detail the vessel's layout.

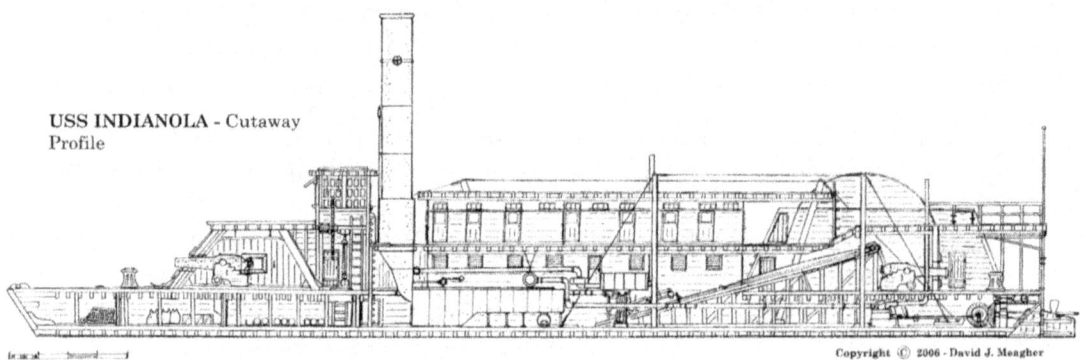

Cutaway Profile (©2006 David J. Meagher; used with permission).

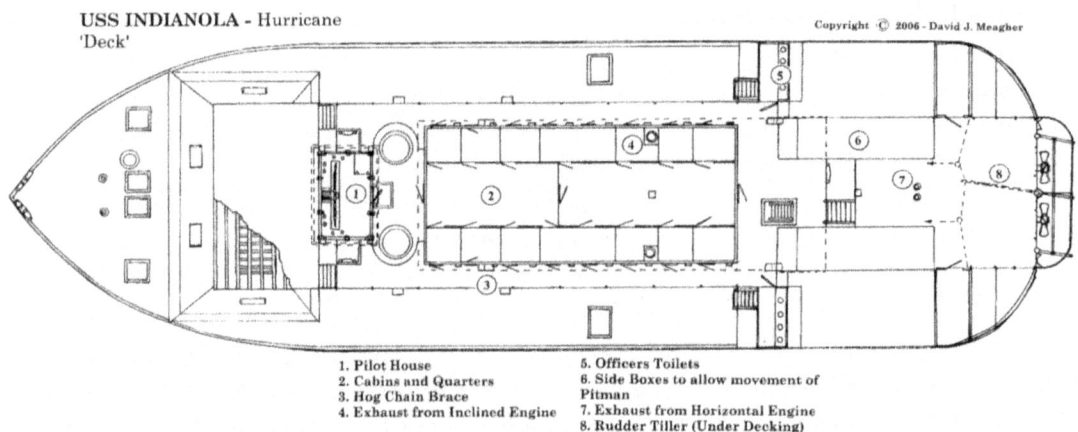

Hurricane (Top) Deck (©2006 David J. Meagher; used with permission).

eastern-bank Mississippi and Louisiana citadels. Since the previous fall, the big guns at Vicksburg and Port Hudson had closed off to Union vessels that portion of the Mississippi River that lay between them, while safeguarding Southern craft operating out of the Red and Big Black rivers. Now, as January closed, word wafted upriver that the Confederates planned to create additional defenses by converting the steamer *City of Vicksburg* into an ironclad. After some thought, Porter, as he walked the deck of his flag boat, *Black Hawk*, anchored above the mouth of the Yazoo River, decided upon a plan to destroy the unarmed Dixie steamer then docked at Vicksburg and being readied for conversion. He might also be able to disrupt the larger annoying Confederate supply effort on those waters below him. Porter would send swift raiding vessels down on the fast current past the upper fortress. The vessel(s) would not only be fleet but also pow-

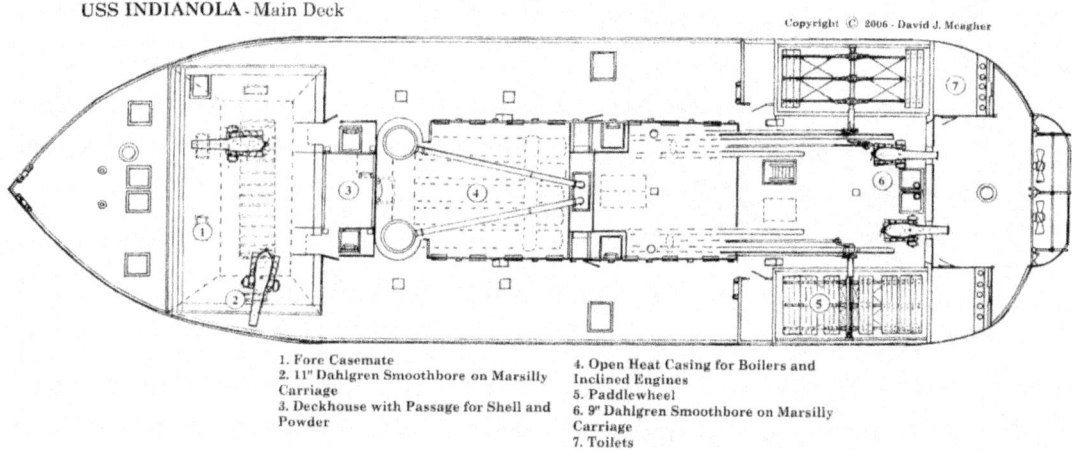

1. Fore Casemate
2. 11" Dahlgren Smoothbore on Marsilly Carriage
3. Deckhouse with Passage for Shell and Powder
4. Open Heat Casing for Boilers and Inclined Engines
5. Paddlewheel
6. 9" Dahlgren Smoothbore on Marsilly Carriage
7. Toilets

Main Deck (©2006 David J. Meagher; used with permission).

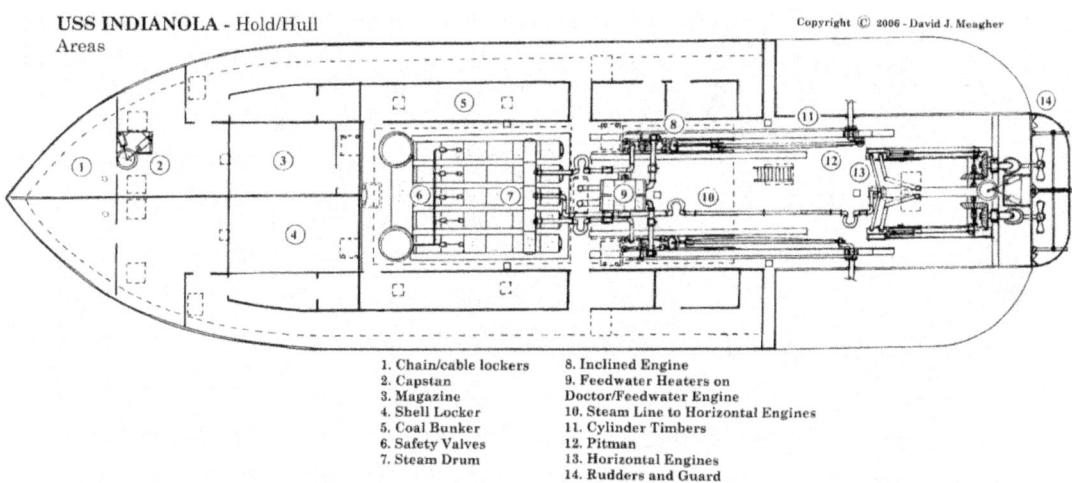

1. Chain/cable lockers
2. Capstan
3. Magazine
4. Shell Locker
5. Coal Bunker
6. Safety Valves
7. Steam Drum
8. Inclined Engine
9. Feedwater Heaters on Doctor/Feedwater Engine
10. Steam Line to Horizontal Engines
11. Cylinder Timbers
12. Pitman
13. Horizontal Engines
14. Rudders and Guard

Hold/Hull Areas (©2006 David J. Meagher; used with permission).

erful enough that when the mission was finished it could steam back up to that area of the west bank territory controlled by the Union.

On February 1 the admiral ordered Lt. Col. Charles Rivers Ellet (1843–1863), commander of the U.S. Ram Fleet, to take his flag boat *Queen of the West* past the Vicksburg batteries and sink the *City of Vicksburg*. A decade-old commercial side-wheeler constructed at Cincinnati, the 406-ton *Queen*, as she was sometimes called, was 181 feet long, with a beam of 36 feet and a six-foot draft. Acquired by the U.S. Quartermaster Department in May 1862, she had been turned over to Charles Ellet, the lieutenant colonel's father, to form part of the War Department's Mississippi Ram Fleet. The senior Ellet had her strengthened for use as a ram, specifically by the addition of solid, heavy timbers in her bow. Additional protection was provided for her wheelhouses and other deck spaces both with light wooden construction and a double row of cotton bales that

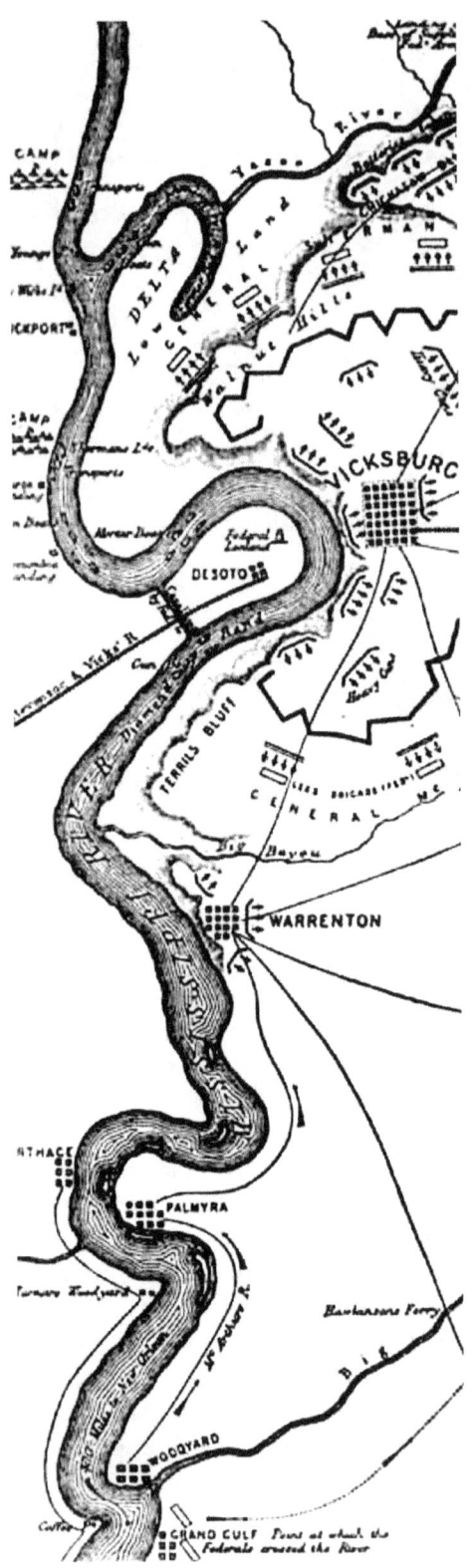

extended from just ahead of the port wheelhouse forward, around the front of the boat, and back down the other side.

The next day, the Union ram seriously damaged her quarry but was also damaged herself before moving on down the river. Although the plan did not go exactly as initially imagined, Ellet, after making quick repairs, was freed to become the only Union warship cruising between Vicksburg and Port Hudson and to "find, sink or burn" all Southern vessels in that Confederate stretch. Just after his departure on February 10, Porter promised Secretary Welles that he would reinforce Ellet's wooden ram at the "first favorable opportunity."

After taking three prizes and surveying the area for fortifications, Col. Ellet returned to Union positions above Warrenton, MS, seven miles below Vicksburg, on February 4. There he communicated with his superiors, navy and army, acquired a pair of military cannon for the *Queen of the West*, and received orders from the admiral to return downstream. Porter, impressed by the possibilities offered for rich prizes and destruction of enemy property, advised the soldier in his communication not to be surprised if he saw the *Indianola* below. "Don't mistake her for a rebel," he warned. "She looks something like the *Chillicothe*."[1]

RAdm. Porter had decided to send a more powerful vessel down to protect the *Queen of the West*, while maybe also joining in her war on Rebel logistics. After the fleet commander apparently spoke with Lt.

Vicksburg Area Down to Below Grand Gulf, MS. This contemporary map gives the reader a good idea of the principal location where the ironclad *Indianola* operated during her brief lifespan. Although she was able to get as far south as Natchez during her initial foray, her fatal combat with the Confederate rams occurred in the area just north of Grand Gulf, MS (*Harper's Weekly*, May 10, 1862).

Left: **Lt. Cmdr. George Brown, *Indianola*'s Captain**. Appointed the ironclad's captain by RAdm. David Dixon Porter on October 20, 1862, this Hoosier was appointed a U.S. Navy midshipman in 1849, advancing upward to the rank of lieutenant in 1856. He was aboard the steam sloop *Powhatan*, under Lt. Porter, when she sailed to the relief of Fort Pickens, FL, in 1861. Later that year, Brown was posted aboard the six-gun, 829-ton *Octarora*, which was attached during the fall to Porter's Mortar Flotilla, a division of the West Gulf Blockading Squadron. Brown participated in the capture of New Orleans in April 1862 and the sojourn of the WGBS to Vicksburg in May–July. After time in Libby Prison, he returned to duty and participated in the Battle of Mobile Bay in 1864. Brown remained in the navy after the war, rising to the rank of rear admiral in 1893 (Library of Congress). **Below: *Queen of the West* Attacks the *City of Vicksburg*.** On February 1 RAdm. Porter ordered Lt Col. Charles Rivers Ellet (1843–1863), commander of the U.S. Ram Fleet, to take his flagboat *Queen of the West* past the Vicksburg batteries and sink the *City of Vicksburg*, then fitting out as a ram. Although the assault was unsuccessful, Ellet, after briefly returning to base, remained below Vicksburg to "find, sink or burn" all Southern vessels in the Confederate-held stretch of river extending down to Port Hudson, LA (*Harper's Weekly*, February 28, 1863).

Queen of the West. RAdm. Porter, having decided to reinforce Lt. Col. Ellet, directed that the ironclad *Indianola* rush below Vicksburg on the night of February 12, a plan scrubbed in bad weather. Meanwhile, the *Queen of the West* began up the Red River of Louisiana seeking targets of opportunity (Naval History and Heritage Command).

Cmdr. George Brown, captain of the *Indianola*, regarding the idea and informed him of his upcoming mission, Acting Master's Mate Ward tells us that several days were spent by those aboard "in busy preparation" getting ready for departure. A pair of coal barges were located, filled "with about 7,000 bushels each," and tied alongside to provide fuel for the expedition and extra hull protection. In addition to normal preparations, sailors thoroughly covered the gunboat's sides and casemates with tallow and slush.

On February 11 the crew, still scanty in number, was, remembered Ward, "partially reinforced by detachments from other vessels of the fleet." The whole number remained thin and there were still insufficient bluejackets to fully man the cannon in both the forward and after turrets. An exact ship's roster is impossible to reconstruct. A reporter for the *Memphis Daily Appeal* in Vicksburg the day after the *Indianola* was captured reported that 112 prisoners were taken to Port Gibson after the fight, along with four African Americans claiming to be freedmen and two recaptured slaves. One U.S. jack was killed, two wounded, and seven were missing, with three or four people known to have escaped. By this count, Brown's crew comprised 139 or 140 men.

After breakfast on Thursday February 12, two days after the *Queen* cast off to resume her career as a raider, RAdm. Porter cut orders for the *Indianola* to follow Ellet's ram down. The directive was quite specific. Later that night, Brown was to slip his lines and run past the Vicksburg batteries. Once below, he was to find Col. Ellet, confer with him on a plan of action, and then execute it, perhaps even ascending the Red River in pursuit of Southern river commerce. Brown was reminded that Porter had ordered the

Indianola's bow strengthened "to perform the part of a ram." Therefore, the captain should not "hesitate to run anything down." If possible, he was to capture both steamboats and cotton, while making certain not to use up all his fuel. He was to retain his coal barges, destroying them if there was any chance they might fall into enemy hands. Though it was not contained in his written orders, Brown was apparently told, according to William F.J. Shanks of the *New York Herald*, that if circumstances required him to depart the Red, the *Indianola* was to steam to the Big Black River. There he was to turn into the stream, which empties into the Mississippi at Grand Gulf, and attempt to ascend it 15 miles to the site of the Vicksburg-Jackson Railroad Bridge and destroy the span. If that could be accomplished, the connection between Vicksburg and points east would be destroyed. Whatever he and Ellet undertook, they were to "try and have no failure." Indeed, Porter demanded, they were to bear in mind the adage that it might be better to pass on risky strikes as "a failure is equal to defeat."

As Porter's orders were being delivered to Brown, Lt. Col. Ellet's *Queen of the West*, together with a coal barge and the support steamer *De Soto*, arrived off the mouth of the Red River, having destroyed a number of skiffs and flatboats while moving downstream. Entering the confluence, the pair proceeded up to a branch with the Atchafalaya Bayou, where the auxiliary was anchored, allowing Ellet to continue up the Atchafalaya destroying Confederate property. During the Atchafalaya sweep and attack on Simmesport, James D. Thompson, first master aboard the *Queen of the West*, was wounded, at which point Ellet elected to return to the *De Soto*'s anchorage so that the two vessels might return together to the mouth of the Red River.

On the morning of February 13, Lt. Col. Ellet returned to the location of Thompson's wounding, extracted retribution on three plantations, and continued on up toward the mouth of the Black River. En route, he learned that a number of steamers were active on the upper Red. What was more important, one had just exited the Black and was headed up the Red toward Alexandria transporting a 32-pounder for the Confederate ram *William H. Webb*, known to be there and the only enemy vessel about which Porter had specifically warned the young light colonel.

Originally constructed in New York City in 1856, the 655-ton side-wheel ocean liner, later a tugboat, *William H. Webb* (called *Webb* in Confederate service) was sold into Confederate service at New Orleans in May 1861, being outfitted as a ram with a reinforced bow which Adm. Mahan tells us "was filled in solid for more than eight feet." The *New York Herald* later revealed that the vessel was "noted as being a very powerful and quick boat" because she was equipped with "two separate engines, working independently of each other." Transferred to Shreveport upon the fall of New Orleans in April 1862 and armed with four 12-pounder field guns and a volunteer crew, the highly maneuverable vessel was feared by Union sailors. It was said she could "easily make 20 miles-per-hour up the Mississippi or 30 miles when moving with the current." Many U.S. Navy officers concluded that there was "no other boat on the river that could hope to cope with her in point of speed." The *Webb* would indeed figure in the upcoming story just as Porter advised, though it would be mid-month before she was actually ready for combat. Few at the time realized that she was actually larger than the *Indianola*, which she would fight.[2]

Not yet having been tapped to join the Yazoo Pass Expedition, *New York Herald* reporter DeB. Randolph Keim was present at Young's Point when the *Indianola*'s mission began, his colleague Findlay Anderson having been embedded earlier with two other reporters on the *Queen of the West*. With Acting Master's Mate Ward, Keim detailed the story of the ironclad's departure from actual observation. Mayor Brown's ironclad was unable to get off as originally planned on the night of the 12th, the weather being unpropitious because a thick fog hung over the river making navigation impossible. The next night was not much better, being likewise described as "one of the most gloomy imaginable." The moon was absent and the faint glimmer of stars was hidden by thick black clouds. "The atmosphere was filled with a smoky haze, rendering the darkness so profound that nothing could be seen upon the river." Looking toward shore, pilots guiding the boats on the Mississippi found "it was barely possible to distinguish the woody banks in time to avoid running upon them." Refusing to wait longer, Lt. Cmdr. Brown, possibly the only officer aboard who knew the boat's destination, decided to cast off.

The *Indianola* departed the mouth of the Yazoo River about 10:00 at night on Friday the 13th. As she steamed downstream through the assembled warships, transports, and units in the fleet train, the "unusual and considerable noise" coming from her escape pipes and propulsion units "attracted general attention to her and gave sufficient notice to all her friends of what was up." Keim's description continued: "Nothing could be seen of her, but the noise was sufficient to disclose her whereabouts, the direction she was running, and the high rate of speed at which she was moving." When the Federal craft reached the top of the canal being built by Grant's soldiers along the Louisiana shore, Lt. Cmdr. Brown had his crew beat to quarters. Acting Master's Mate Ward remembered that at the call he took "his place between the eleven-inch Dahlgrens in the forward turret." To his right and left were the guns' crews and behind each giant piece was an officer, either Acting Ensigns Pease or McElwill.

Brown next ordered her steam engines idled way down to allow the vessel to drift with the current, then about 4 mph, with her great wheels moving, according to Ward, "with only enough speed to insure the proper steerage-way." As the boat passed the mouth of the Williams Canal (named for the U.S. Army general who had begun it back in July) and the mortar-boat fleet anchored nearby, the only sound Ward or the others in the forward turret were able to hear was "the whispered call of the pilot, stationed outside the port, and passed along to his assistant at the [steering] wheel." The "rattle of the rudder chains indicated an approach to the sharp bend above the town," Ward recalled. Silently the *Indianola* rounded the point and drove on directly below Vicksburg's high cliff batteries, headed toward the city's levee.

As she drifted, a flash occurred, followed by "a dull, low rumble." The men aboard looked at one another thinking their vessel discovered. Such was not, however, the case. "It was a flash of lightning and its succeeding thunder from the protecting clouds above us," wrote her acting master's mate in 1885. The bolt extinguished, darkness returned and the only indication of Vicksburg was its own flickering. "Lights were everywhere numerous along the levee" newsman Keim revealed, "and the voices of soldiers and citizens sounded as if they were close alongside."

The heavy black mass of the gunboat continued to float lazily along, every man aboard no longer exclusively wondering about when they would be discovered but entertaining the mental possibility that they might get by the citadel without being sighted at all. *Indianola* was very close to the eastern river bank. "Now the very houses of the city became plainly distinguishable, and even the forms of men upon the river bank could be readily made out in the glimmering light thrown from the windows and occasional lanterns carried by pedestrians."

About an hour after it began, the *Indianola*'s furtive cruise was undone, or so it was afterwards reported, by a fortunate Confederate accident. Both Keim and Ward agreed on the particulars, though Capt. Brown was silent. On the riverbank in the ironclad's path lay a Southern campfire, which could be dimly seen from the ship as she approached. As she came abreast of this bivouac, a bored soldier, just for something to do, picked up a burning brand from the fire and "threw it, carelessly, into the sluggish brown current that was lapping the shore at his feet." As the lit stick arched from his hand toward the water, its flash revealed to him, as Ward put it, "our vessel stealthily stealing by, like some dread intruder from the jungles upon the camp of the unsuspecting hunter." Startled, the soldier supposedly shouted, "Boat ahoy!" and discharged his musket toward the *Indianola*. The shot was enough to set off an initial alert. Thereafter, pandemonium reigned along the dark bank. Although the initial firebrand had provided some illumination, there was insufficient light thereafter for anyone to see the boat out on the water.

"Platoons of soldiers," the newspapers later reported, "drew up in line on the bank and discharged their muskets at random into the river, aiming at nothing and hitting nothing." At the same time, some Southern artillerists pointed their pieces upstream and others downstream with a full five minutes elapsing between the time the first cannon fired and a second followed. His boat's journey apparently discovered, Capt. Brown ordered a "change of tactics," to make headway under steam, gaining steerage and hence safety. The *Indianola*'s machinery was started up and steam began snorting out of the escape pipes as her paddle wheels briefly splashed the water. This loud noise drew additional musket volleys and was halted immediately.

Although the gunboat now drifted largely without sound or propulsion other than the current, the Confederates, having seen her once and heard her the second time, now fired off signal flares from points above and below her position and blasted the Mississippi a third time. At this point, Brown decided it best to make haste and ordered the steam again let on. "The great engines, that had been held under control so long, were now turned loose to run a race for life through this gauntlet of fire and iron hail. The great smoke stacks belched forth black smoke and crimson flame, and the paddles now thundered and beat the sluggish current as in angry protest against the resistless restraint of the preceding hours." The *Indianola* sprang forward downstream, her captain unworried about any noise she might now be making.

Soon Rebel cannon from the shore and heights joined the fray. The "deafening reverberations were so mighty," the *Chicago Daily Tribune* reported, that their shock quivered "steamboats stem to stern five miles distant." Though Capt. Brown later admitted the cannonballs, all coming from abaft, were "good line shots," none scored a hit because the Northern vessel hugged the left shore and the guns on the bluff could not be sufficiently lowered. Thus, according to reporter Keim, the Southerners used their cannonballs but charily. "As every shot was fired wild," he wrote later, "the gunners con-

***Indianola* Runs Past Vicksburg.** The *Indianola* departed her Yazoo River anchorage in the dark of Friday, February 13, and drifted on the river current as far down past Vicksburg's batteries as she could before she was discovered. When the Confederates saw her, she started her machinery and steamed out of danger. There were three distinct intervals of two, three, and five minutes between the firing of Confederate guns targeting the ironclad and only 18 shots were discharged in total (*Harper's Weekly*, March 7, 1863).

tented themselves with a single discharge each." There were three distinct intervals of two, three, and five minutes between the firing of Confederate guns and only 18 shots were discharged in total. Having sped by the citadel's defenses by11:41 p.m., the time of the final discharge and only 19 minutes after the first, "her loud whistle sent back the tidings that she had passed beyond the reach of the batteries to safety."

Showing two prearranged red signal lights on her starboard side to U.S. Army troops working on the Williams Canal, the *Indianola* put into the Louisiana shore near Bigg's Landing four miles below Warrenton. There Capt. Brown was able to get off a message to RAdm. Porter describing his successful passage. As soon as possible the next morning, the squadron commander telegraphed the Navy Department, crowing, "This gives us entire control of the Mississippi, except at Vicksburg and Port Hudson, and cuts off all the supplies and troops from Texas." When given the news, the Federal press regarded the *Indianola*'s passage as a complete success. It was attributed "to the coolness and wisdom displayed by Lt. Cmdr. Brown in the management of the boat—a cooler or braver officer could not well be found." "We had triumphed this time," remembered Acting Master's Mate Ward, "and whatever of disappointment and defeat awaited us, was postponed awhile."[3]

Brown cast off at 5:20 on the morning of February 14 and headed down the Mississippi, expecting to rendezvous at the mouth of the Red River with the *Queen of the West*. As she passed the plantation of a Mr. Sims, a few miles above Natchez, the *Indianola* halted to destroy a number of small boats pulled up at the landing and to capture or kill some beef cattle, in the process "liberating" two African American slaves waving from shore. The stop was triggered, according to a reporter for the *St. Joseph* (LA) *Gazette*, by Archy Pope, superintendent and overseer of a gang of slaves working on the Vicksburg fortifications who was caught crossing the Mississippi in a rowboat with two companions. As a gig from the *Indianola* swept down upon the trio, Pope destroyed several important papers he had on his person by tearing them up and swallowing them. The Southerner eluded capture by diving overboard, and, as the correspondent crowed, "they couldn't catch him."

About the same time as the Pope episode, the Ellet ram began up the Red, along with the *De Soto*, and soon captured her first prize, the steamer *Era No. 5*, which had aboard two Confederate officers. (None of the army officers aboard from either side could know that before the day was over both the *Queen* and the *De Soto* would be captured.) Learning from his "guests" that three big steamboats lay, with steam down, about 30 miles above (75 miles from the mouth of the Red) at Gordon's Landing, Ellet decided to attempt their capture. Sending a prize crew aboard the *Era No. 5*, which was then anchored with the coal barge, the colonel got his other two vessels underway. He did not anticipate that news of his earlier activities had reached Southern defenders, who had taking strong measures to halt his advance with emplacements near the landing's Fort Taylor.

When the leading *Queen of the West* spied the steamers lying under a bluff near Gordon's Landing, she charged toward them—only to be met by a barrage of cannon fire from four Confederate 32-pounders. Ellet immediately ordered the ram to back down, but in the process she ran aground on the right bank of the river within point blank range of the Rebel guns. The *Queen* was hit several times and one ball cut her steam pipe, stopping her engines. Deterred from setting the vessel alight to save the life of Master Thompson, Ellet ordered "abandon ship." A short time later, the Southerners put a prize crew aboard and she was taken to Gordon's Landing (also called Norman's Landing) for repair.

Most of the Union soldier-sailors reached the *De Soto*, which now began her own panicky escape. The craft almost immediately ran onto the riverbank, where she lost her rudder and became unmanageable. Unable to guide her flight, Ellet ordered her to drift downstream on the current. As she descended, alternately using her side wheels for primitive control, Ellet picked up other survivors floating on logs or cotton bales before reaching, in thick fog, the anchored *Era No. 5* about 10:00 p.m. Two Yankee vessels were now gone, leaving Joseph Brown's big ironclad out on the Mississippi as the only northern vessel between Vicksburg and Natchez. With her two coal barges in tow, the *Indianola* made good progress down the Mississippi during the 14th and also that night riding the current without interception while Lt. Col. Ellet adventured up and then down the Red River.

Early in the post-midnight darkness of February 15, the *Era No. 5* rapidly descended downstream toward the mouth of the Red, desperately seeking to escape a swarming force of Confederates ready to begin pursuit. Later, at 3:00 p.m., according to local

Loss of the *Queen of the West*. Surprised by Confederate defenders at Gordon's Landing on the Red River, the *Queen of the West* was captured. Lt. Col. Ellet and many of his crew escaped; however, the U.S. ram was repaired and put right back into Southern service (*Harper's Weekly*, March 21, 1863).

Confederate government agent George W. Koontz, the *Indianola* passed Natchez. At this point, the weather turned. Newsmen Albert H. "Bod" Bodman with Ellet recalled that "the night was a terrible one—thunder, lightning, and fog." The pyrotechnics and touchable dampness caused Lt Cmdr. Brown to halt his voyage and bring the *Indianola* to anchor four miles below Natchez.[4]

The *Era No. 5* broke into the Mississippi just after dawn on February 15, being yet buffeted by heavy rain and dense fog. The elements stirred the river, and driftwood smashed paddles off her wheels, thereby decreasing her speed. As the crew were nearly out of fuel, wet wood was obtained at Union Point. It proved to be so damp that when fed into the boilers it could provide steam sufficient for only two miles per hour against the heavy current. Opposite Ellis Cliffs, the steamer's pilot ran the vessel aground, requiring hours of delay while she was worked free. Once her crew shoved her off, the *Era No. 5* rushed on in the fog, though her starboard paddle wheel, damaged by drift, now began "dropping to pieces." With luck, perhaps they could make it up to Biggs Landing.

Far upriver that morning, the Confederate ram *Webb* arrived off Fort Taylor. She had been under repair at Alexandria for several days, but her new captain, Lt. Col. William S. Lovell (1829–1900), had her ready in time to steam downstream shortly after sunrise. His vessel was accompanied by two others, Capt. J.M. White's *Grand Duke*, which helped to man Lovell's boat with a draft of 100 Southern soldiers, and the *Louis d'Or*, another unaltered Cincinnati-built side-wheeler. William Lovell, the fifth son of U.S Army surgeon general Joseph Lovell and the brother of Maj. Gen Mansfield Lovell, was born in Washington, D.C. He was appointed a U.S. Navy midshipman on November 8, 1847, graduating from the U.S. Naval Academy at Annapolis, MD, on June 10, 1853. Posted to the Home Squadron, he participated in Atlantic and South American cruises, including the Kane relief expedition. Promoted to the rank of lieutenant on September 16, 1855, Lovell married a lady from Natchez, MS, in June 1858 and on May 3, 1859, resigned his commission to move to Adams County, MS, to become a cotton planter and plantation owner.

Lovell enlisted in the Confederate States of America military on April 11, 1861, as an artillery captain, transferring in October to New Orleans, where his brother, Mansfield, was in command. Promoted to the rank of lieutenant colonel, William moved with his brother to Vicksburg, MS, in late spring 1862 following the loss of the Crescent City to the Union fleet under RAdm. David Glasgow Farragut. William Lovell served as an assistant inspector general under Lt. Gen. John Pemberton, who on February 4 ordered him, because of his naval experience, to report to the commander of the Department of Western Louisiana, Maj. Gen. Richard Taylor, who put him in command of the *Webb*, then refitting at Alexandria. Lovell would return to Vicksburg shortly thereafter. He resumed his career as a cotton farmer after the war.

Lovell found the *Queen of the West* being repaired by Southern laborers and also received news that Ellet had burned the *De Soto* and was now fleeing downstream aboard the captured *Era No. 5*. Pushing on "with all speed" into the fog, the *Webb*, *Grand Duke*, and *Louis d'Or* sped along as carefully as possible toward the river's mouth. En route to the Mississippi, *Webb* stopped to pick up nine U.S. Army sailors making their way in one of the small boats once davited on the *Queen of the West*. They immediately told their captor that Ellet might soon be rescued by an ironclad expected down several nights before. The three Confederate vessels were forced by very thick fog to heave to upon reaching the confluence and tie up for the night.

While Ellet's men were engaged in shoving off their craft and continuing their getaway with Lt. Col. Lovell in hot pursuit, the *Indianola* weighed and continued downstream below Natchez looking for the *Queen of the West*. As she passed Natchez, she was glimpsed through thick fog by various citizens ashore, including the editor of the *Natchez Weekly Courier*. He did not think her very formidable and assured his readers that she was simply a "Cincinnati tub."

Crewmen aboard Capt. Brown's warship would have been amused had they been able to read the account of their progress reported by the Young's Point *Chicago Daily Tribune* reporter for dispatch to his paper (via Memphis), which printed it three days after they were captured. "The turret ironclad *Indianola*," he penned, "is understood to be above Port Hudson, and to have destroyed a steamer that was laying under the guns of that place."

Having cruised four miles beyond her night anchorage, the ironclad was alerted by her lookouts on the morning of February 16 that a strange steamer approached. The *Indianola* was simultaneously identified by Ellet through a break in the fog. The *Era No. 5* began blowing her whistle and carefully approached the large warship, which had, meanwhile, stood across the river. Newsman Bodman later remembered the rejoicing aboard the prize steamer when she came abreast of the *Indianola*, completing her "miraculous escape." Capt. Brown hailed the newcomer and soon both vessels were adjacently anchored. The jacks aboard the ironclad could not but notice that some of the men on *Era No. 5* wore rags without caps or shoes; all were hungry. "The good people of the *Indianola* acted the part of good Samaritans; they clothed and fed us and made us comfortable." At the same time, Lt. Col. Ellet was invited to Capt. Brown's cabin, where he informed the navy man of the loss of the *Queen of the West* and of his hasty retreat out of harm's reach.

Surprised at the ram captain's reversal of fortune, Capt. Brown conferred now with the lieutenant colonel regarding their combined next step. Ellet, ever aggressive, recommended that they proceed back up the Red River. There they could destroy the batteries at Fort Taylor and capture or sink the *Queen of the West*, now undoubtedly being repaired by the Confederates. If Brown would be so good as to wait until *Era No. 5*'s paddle wheels were repaired, Ellet would gladly lead the way. With luck, they might even come up with and destroy the *Webb*. Although they suspected she was on the loose, neither Union man knew that as they spoke that afternoon the Confederate vessel was at Ellis Cliffs, where she learned that the *Indianola* had come down and where Lt. Col. Lovell decided to slow down and proceed with caution, leaving his companions at the mouth of the Red and cruising on alone.

Around 4:30 in the afternoon, the two U.S. gunboats weighed anchor and proceeded downstream, the *Era No. 5* in advance. At 5:10 p.m. lookouts aboard Ellet's craft spied a steamer approaching from abreast Ellis Cliffs below, identifying her through the fog as the Confederate *Webb*. Simultaneously, Lt. Col. Lovell's lookouts also saw "two chimneys sticking up through the fog," recognizing them as belonging to the *Era No. 5*. The Southern vessel opened her throttles to give chase and shortly thereafter her captain saw another pair of chimneys. This second steamer appeared "very low in the water in the fog," a circumstance that convinced Lovell and his officers that they faced an ironclad. In his later report, Capt. Brown also indicated that he, too, recognized the vessel "as being the rebel gunboat *Webb*" and steered toward her "at full speed." Perhaps hoping to bag the young Federal raider before her heavy companion arrived, Lovell's command dashed into the miasma at flank speed while, about two miles or so away, the *Era No. 5* turned back, sounding her alarm. Capt. Brown's gunners, who were cleared for action when Ellet's whistle was heard, prepared to shoot, elevating their big forward Dahlgrens as far as "the ports would admit of."

Quickly thereafter, two giant 11-inch shells were sent in greeting to the oncoming *Webb*. The pair were reportedly "good line shots; one struck within at least 50 yards of her." Because their target was slightly out of range, the *Indianola*'s first offensive rounds of the war were ineffective, though the geysers they sent up from the river were quite spectacular. By the time the *Indianola*'s shells fell, the fast *Webb* had slammed her wheels into reverse, backed around, and disappeared into the fog "with all dispatch," disappearing fully from sight around a bend in the river. Prior to her retreat, according to her captain, the vessel had attempted to return the ironclad's fire, but her friction primers failed. Shortly thereafter, she entered the Red River and headed back up from whence she had come, turning back two Mississippi-bound steamers encountered on the way. The *Indianola* pursued her enemy around the bend, but with the fog now thickening it became impossible even to see the *Webb*'s smoke. The speedy Southern warship returned to the Red, where she, together with her two consorts, headed back toward Alexandria.

Not knowing for certain where the Rebel ram was and believing it possible that she might have anchored close to shore in the thick pea-soup mist, Capt. Brown now elected temporarily to give up her pursuit and halted for the night under Glasscock Island. After all, it would not do to drift past Lovell's boat in the dark, letting her escape in his rear. When the *Indianola* and *Era No. 5* were securely anchored, Lt. Col. Ellet returned aboard the ironclad, where he was informed that they would weigh again in the morning after Brown was certain that he could "run with safety and be certain of seeing everything on either side of the bank" as they passed. The two men now resumed earlier conversations on what course to follow next.

By early afternoon on Tuesday, February 17, the fog had sufficiently lifted to permit the *Indianola* to weigh anchor and head downstream in company with the *Era No. 5*. During the transit, a deserter was taken aboard from the *Webb*. The two Union craft anchored off the mouth of the Red River about 5:00 p.m., where Brown sent across the Mississippi for Col. Joseph A.S. Acklen (1816–1863). A wealthy Southern landowner and veteran of the Texas Revolution but rather ambivalent toward slavery, the Tennessean had moved farther south from Nashville when it was occupied in early 1862. Reaching the plantation house from Acken's Landing, the patriarch was informed by the sailors that the captain of the powerful and just-arrived Federal gunboat wished information regarding the situation ashore and up the Red. Acklen, for his part, was curious about the iron monster anchored over at the mouth of the Red and wanted to visit her.

When Acklen arrived aboard, he was greeted both by the ironclad's captain and Lt. Col. Ellet and immediately escorted to the commander's quarters for debriefing. Here it was learned that the *Era No. 5* had been pursued not only by the *Webb* but also by three other steamers. On top of that, Ellet, perhaps not to his surprise but to Brown's, was told that the *Queen of the West* was under repair at Gordon's Landing and that this refit would be quickly accomplished, as only her steam and escape pipes were damaged in the original encounter. The military officers learned further that Lt. Col. Lovell, who was in charge of the Confederate vessels, expected the Federals to ascend the Red, where they would be met by the *Webb*, *Queen of the West*, and Fort Taylor's defenses when they reached Gordon's Landing. Two additional Confederate cottonclads were being outfitted at Port Hudson, the men learned, though for what purpose their contacts could not say. Both were supposedly armed with small cannon and, more important, carried boarding parties. Capt. Brown fully expected that his mighty warship could take on and defeat both the Confederate rams, as well as the Port Hudson boats. The *Webb*'s deserter had informed him that the principal enemy vessel had no iron reinforcing her bow, though her machinery was protected by many bales of cotton, that is to say, all except the walking beams of her engine, which were not guarded and thus quite vulnerable to Dahlgren fire.

The Union vessel commanders now resumed their discussion of tactics and it was decided, in keeping with RAdm. Porter's original orders, that the *Indianola* would not move up the Red after the *Webb* and Ellet's old command. Confident of his strength, Brown decided to guard the river mouth and interdict any Southern steamers that approached out of it, thereby stopping Southern river communication. Col. Ellet for his part would return to Biggs Landing. There, in addition to his own reports and commentary, he would make certain that RAdm. Porter received a summary that Brown now wrote out for delivery. He would also turn over several prisoners taken during his sojourn.

Following his recapitulation of events over the past week, Brown in his message assured Porter that although he could remain alone where he was for some time it would be quite helpful to have another serviceable vessel with him, presumably another of the Ram Fleet craft. The river was expected to rise, cutting off the land approaches to Port Hudson and thereby increasing Confederate need for river-borne logistics. The commander of the *Indianola* then expressed his greatest concern—coal. Although he kept the bunkers of the ironclad filled at all times as earlier instructed, he needed to also maintain a quantity sufficient for any vessel the admiral might send down. Looking after and towing his two coal barges was a problem. They could be hauled upstream only at a very slow rate and he dared not take the risk of losing them, either through an accidental separation or by placing them in a temporary guarded anchorage.

On February 18, the *Indianola*, despite being unable to find any Red River pilots, commenced her blockade, steaming upriver and down off the mouth of the Red with her two coal barges in tow. On the same day, the *Webb* and her two auxiliaries returned to Alexandria, where Lovell received orders from Maj. Gen. Taylor to take command of Fort Taylor. In his absence, Maj. Joseph L. Brent (1826–1905), chief of artillery and the senior artillery officer in the CSA Army of Western Louisiana, had arrived. He was a confidant of the general, but without naval experience, asked to oversee repair of the *Queen of the West*. In Special Orders No. 49 of February 19 Taylor made him commodore of a small task group that included the two rams and any auxiliaries, while also ordering him to assume charge of, prepare, and shove off as quickly as possible on an expedition to destroy the *Indianola*.

A transplanted Californian and the son of a Maryland lawyer, Joseph Brent, with several other Southern sympathizers, was captured at Panama City while returning east at the beginning of the war. Released by order of President Abraham Lincoln in order to avoid a diplomatic incident with Columbia, Brent and his companions eventually, in February 1862, reached Virginia, where he was given the rank of captain, later major, and participated in the Peninsular Campaign. Transferred west to the District of Western Louisiana, he was now embarked upon what would prove to be his most noteworthy posting. On April 17, 1864, Taylor's artillery was reorganized and Brent was promoted to the rank of colonel. When the District's new 1st Louisiana Cavalry Brigade required a chief, he accepted a promotion to the rank of brigadier general and agreed to switch arms from artillery to cavalry in order to lead it. Brent thus became the only California citizen to become a Confederate general.

While workmen were completing repairs to the *Queen of the West* it did not take long for word to spread across the Alexandria waterfront that Maj. Brent would be momentarily departing "for down the river" to seek and find the Federal ironclad. Numerous volunteers, many with military experience, quickly signed on. On February 21 the *Queen* steamed down to Fort Taylor, where she and the *Webb* were coaled and victualed and received ammunition. Maj. Brent arranged for Capt. James McCloskey, the Confederate quartermaster at Alexandria who was then in temporary command of the *Webb*, to take over the *Queen*, while the *Webb* was given to Capt. Charles J. Pierce. Capt. Thomas H. Handy of the Crescent Artillery had command of the troops aboard the latter.

Another auxiliary, the *Grand Era*, was secured to replace the *Grand Duke*, aboard which smallpox had erupted. A side-wheeler like the *Grand Duke*, the *Grand Era* was a 323-ton Louisville packet constructed in 1853. After this sortie, she would remain at Alexandria, where she would be broken up in 1864 and her machinery used aboard the CSS *Missouri*. She had previously been operated on the New Orleans–Vicksburg route by the brothers John H. and George L. Kouns, who took her up the Red following the Union capture of the Crescent City in April 1862. One or the other was in command of her on this expedition, but which one is not known.

Having learned that a Confederate "fleet" was preparing to attack his lone vessel, Brown ordered her back upstream the same morning. If he had the chance, he would look into ascending the Big Black River. Also at dusk that Saturday, Ellet, who had departed the Red River area at noon on February 18, arrived at Biggs Landing, and from there he set off to brief RAdm. Porter.[5]

The U.S. Navy Mississippi Squadron commander read the Ellet and Brown reports on the morning of February 22 and, as he wrote Secretary Welles later in the day, was forced to admit that "the best calculations are liable to be upset and mine have been disarranged." The plan to starve the Port Hudson garrison by cutting out the flow of Confederate relief available via the Red River had failed, thanks to Ellet's failure to patiently await the arrival of the *Indianola* prior to his taking any offensive action up that stream. Porter reflected further on his new ironclad, which was now "there by herself." He could not communicate with Capt. Brown, upon whom he depended "for carrying out my cherished plan of cutting supplies." Powerful but with faults, the vessel was not as strong against the Mississippi River current as her builder had promised, being capable of only two knots per hour going upriver. "Whether the commander will have the good sense not to be surprised," the unit boss worried, "remains to be seen." No mention was made of actually sending another vessel to support the *Indianola*. There were no regular navy vessels available that could handle the stream and Ellet's remaining rams were, in Porter's opinion, "fit for nothing but towboats."

While the admiral awaited further word on the mission below (and also hoped for the best from the *Chillicothe* and company in the simultaneous Yazoo Pass Expedition), Capt. Brown continued up the Mississippi. That Sunday, following divine services, he halted at Alcorn's Landing and acquired a sufficient number of cotton bales to create bulwarks aboard his craft as further safeguards against boarders. According to *Chicago Daily Tribune* reporter Bodman, who had departed the area with Lt. Col. Ellet, Alcorn was anxious to sell the Federals all or part of the 1,200 bales of cotton he had ready for

***Indianola*, by Oscar Parkes**. After conferring with Lt. Col. Ellet, who returned to base, Lt. Cmdr. Brown maintained a blockade of the mouth of the Red River with his ironclad from February 18 until February 21, when he learned that a pick-up flotilla of Southern rams had been dispatched to hunt him down. Believing the enemy far behind, the *Indianola* began going slowly back up the Mississippi, her officers and men expecting reinforcements would be sent to their support from above (*Official Records of the Union and Confederate Navies in the War of the Rebellion*).

market. These compressed barricades rose from the main deck of the *Indianola* almost to the level of her hurricane deck and filled the gangways between her wheelhouses and the casemates. Capt. Brown thought that this added protection would help make his command "better able to repel the boarding parties." Those of her crew not engaged in such work assisted in the tasks of otherwise readying the ship, including topping off her coal bunkers.

Steven Mayeux, the most recent historian to review the story of the *Indianola* but not a fan of her captain, has cast doubt upon the need for these enhancements, claiming that the warship certainly "did not need any additional armor." Rather he points out, "Brown makes no mention of how valuable those bales would be when he returned with them to Union-held territory, nor does he mention what his share of the prize money for those bales would have been, but one would have to be very naïve to think that he was not aware of those things."

It is true and a well-established fact that RAdm. Porter had a thirst for prize money (as has every sailor in every navy since the time of Drake) and had instructed Brown to acquire cotton, the commodity most easily adjudicated a prize. It is probable that the ultimate end of the cotton acquisition could be profits into the bluejackets' pockets. However, Brown was originally expected not only to disrupt Red River traffic, but also to take (as well as sink or burn) any decent Confederate steamers he could. These, if they successfully made it into Union shipyards, could be transformed into tinclads or fleet auxiliaries. Prize vessels would need protection in order to run back upstream past Vicksburg's batteries and the squadron commander first of all wanted the cotton bales to barricade captured steamers. Also, it should be remembered that there was a rigid discipline structure in the U.S. Navy at this time and gunboat captains exerted every measure to fulfill the wishes of commanding admirals rather than face their wrath. Operational initiative contrary to Porter's orders was seldom approved unless previously granted. Brown's contemporaries, such as Lt. Cmdr. Le Roy Fitch and Seth Ledyard Phelps, both outstanding officers given much responsibility, had constantly to watch over their shoulders for Porter's disapproval. The *Indianola*'s commander may have been as concerned with this fleet structure as he was regarding any reward he might earn.

Mayeux's observations regarding Brown's motives may or may not be correct, but losing a vessel then, as now, could get a boat captain beached. Given some of the then-known difficulties with Mayor Brown's ironclads, if adding some cotton bales might help in the *Indianola*'s defense, her captain should be applauded for their acquisition. It might have been one of the few events on this short cruise that was accomplished without setback.

Her armor augmented, the *Indianola* continued upstream. Having yet to receive reinforcement, Brown still thought he might receive succor from above, but until it arrived he elected to continue up the Mississippi to his squadron's base, thereby allaying any concerns Porter might have for the safety of the ironclad. On the outside chance that he might meet another Federal warship, he elected to retain his coal barges, suspecting that any newcomer might be low on fuel after running past the Vicksburg batteries. Rather than the prize money some suggest he dreamed of, Brown might have been more interested in getting back up safely and returning the actionable responsibility for commerce raiding below Vicksburg to his superior.

Meanwhile early that Sunday morning, Maj. Brent's three vessels cast off from the riverbank below Fort Taylor and began their adventure. As the trio made their way down the Red River, the gun crews, many of whose members were innocent of artillery practice, were continuously instructed and exercised. Signalmen practiced a code of lanterns and whistles devised for the hunt while soldiers serving as sharpshooters were assigned positions.

When approximately 20 miles downstream, Brent's task group encountered the Confederate steamboat *Dr. Beatty*, cutting her way up from Port Hudson, under the command of Lt. Col. Frederick B. Brand, a former Confederate navy lieutenant. The 281-ton side-wheeler, built at Louisville in 1850, previously on the trade out of New Orleans, had been taken to Shreveport by her commander, Capt. John Hiern, at the beginning of the Civil War. There she was sold into Confederate service and operated in the Trans-Mississippi supply of Vicksburg and Port Hudson. While at Port Hudson, the *Dr. Beatty*, held in port to keep her away from Ellet's *Queen of the West*, was assigned to Lt. Col. Brand, deputy to Col. William R. Miles, commander of the 32nd Louisiana Infantry (Miles Legion). Brand was ordered by the city's commander to take her in search of the *Indianola*. Sending aboard two small field cannon from a Louisiana battery, several officers, including 2nd Lieutenant Charles H. Frith and 250 volunteer riflemen from the regiment, the vessel, protected with stacked cotton bales stem to stern, had put out into the Mississippi the previous day. During the brief mid-river meeting between the commanders of the two endeavors, Lt. Col. Brand, who outranked Maj. Brent, graciously acknowledged Maj. Gen. Taylor's order placing his chief of artillery in command of the chase. Brent willingly accepted the former navyman's craft, assuming there might be a use at some point for the large body of Louisianans in any multi-vessel boarding assault.

The fleet, now swelled to a quartet, reached the mouth of the Mississippi after dark. Finding neither the *Indianola* nor any other vessel, Brent needed to know whether he should guide his men left or right on the Mississippi. To that end, he put into Acklen's Landing and made his way to the home of the former Nashvillian to see if there was any news. Brent found Acklen to be "an intelligence and observant man" who had seen all of the Federal boats that had operated on the Mississippi adjacent to his farm over the past year, including the *Essex*, which had passed the Vicksburg batteries in July. The *Indianola*, he guessed, was "the most formidable of all." Maj. Brent told Acklen of his plans to tackle the Union ship. Horrified that the soldier would take on the big gunboat with his weak little fleet of basically civilian craft, the plantation owner advised that the enterprise be abandoned, "declaring it simply an act of folly." Pursuit of this mad scheme "would simply result in the loss of my boats and men," Brent later remembered his saying, "without any possibility of success." Thanking Acklen, Brent returned to his armada and ordered the four boats to shove off and head upstream. When he arrived at Natchez on Monday morning, February 23, he found that the *Indianola* had passed the city at 3:00 a.m. that morning. The task group commander was elated. He had understood from Col. Acklen that the gunboat was two days ahead of him, but now he learned from local observers that she was only 24–30 hours ahead.

Also that Monday, Lt. Ellet met with RAdm. Porter, amplifying his report and commenting on the situation at Red River. At the same time, the Southerners, with ample supplies of wood and coal for their boilers, were steaming furiously after the Federal ironclad, some boats pushing ahead of others. The race horse *Webb* scouted ahead, followed by the slower *Queen of the West*. The *Dr. Beatty* was so slow that the relatively fast *Grand Era* had cut her own speed to provide her with a tow. While the *Indianola* crawled ahead, reduced by her barges to a speed of 2 mph, the *Webb* and the others gained upon her steadily, their captains using all available time to feed boilers and drill their crews. Up ahead, the leading *Webb* chose not to lag behind with the slower vessels but sped ahead to halt at every landing, checking with anyone around to learn when the Union warship had gone by and calculating gain. From these reports, Maj. Brent, whose vessel was cruising at 5 mph, knew he was catching up to his quarry.

Aboard the *Indianola*, lookouts checking astern were able to see smoke rising from vessels far back down the river, exhaust fumes that never seemed to dissipate as the big vessel continued upriver. One-half of the watch aboard was now ordered to alternate watch on deck with the other. The gunboat pushed on upstream. Although the smoke seen by his observers presumably came from pursuing Confederates, Lt. Cmdr. Brown gave thought to the Big Black River objective, while simultaneously hoping that another Union vessel craft would appear around the next bend ahead. Fuel would undoubtedly be required by any consort so he refused to cut away his coal barges, ordering his engineers and pilots to make their best steam north all through the night.

Farther behind, Maj. Brent charged on, his four vessels strung out on the river, *Webb*, *Queen of the West*, and *Grand Era* far back towing *Dr. Beatty*. By noon on February 24 lookouts aboard the *Webb*, still first in line, clearly sighted the smoke belching from the chimneys of their enemy. Aboard the *Indianola*, Brown and his people looking aft could clearly see vessels gaining upon them. The entire complement hourly expected to be caught and attacked, but as the cool late winter afternoon of that Tuesday passed no attack was made. Not wishing to give the Federal gunners a chance to fire upon his craft in daylight, Brent had long since decided to attack her at night, and, as things were developing, that night would be this one. Stopping at Rodney, the major left a letter with rendezvous instructions for the trio following and then continued on to Berry's Landing, eight miles above, where he hove to and marked time for the next several hours.

Up ahead, the *Indianola* arrived off the mouth of the Big Black River at Grand Gulf. There, three guns in a Confederate battery on the bluff above fired a round at the ironclad and missed. The greeting was returned by Brown's two 11-inch Dahlgrens, a shell from one of which set a house ablaze. Knowing that Confederate vessels were in pursuit, the Union captain elected not to ascend the Big Black but to continue his return north. The Confederate task group re-formed at Berry's Landing in mid-afternoon and completed preparations for a night attack. Darkened, the *Queen of the West*, to which Brent now transferred, would attack first, followed by the *Webb*. The *Grand Era* and *Dr. Beatty* would keep their lights on and attempt to distract the Union gunners from the attacks being mounted by the rams. When the Confederate fleet reached the Grand Gulf it paused while Maj. Brent took a boat ashore. There he was informed that his opponent had steamed by no more than four hours earlier and could not be more than 10 miles ahead of him.

The *Indianola* continued to plod upriver, nearing the head of Palmyra Island (also called Davis Island because it was owned by Joseph Davis, the Confederate president's brother) and Island No. 370. According to Adm. Mahan, the island lay a little above New Carthage, LA, where the river was quite wide. There was a channel above the atoll that embraced the eastern shore but crossed to the western a little above the island. Although both sides of the island could be navigated, vessels normally took the chute closest to the town. As darkness fell, nature, within about 30 minutes, cleared the river of fog and presented moonlight, though it was somewhat faint due to clouds.

At 9:30 p.m.. with the *Indianola* about a half-mile above New Carthage, the lookout stationed on the starboard wheelhouse spotted lights from two of Brent's four vessels rounding the bend below them at the head of upper Palmyra Island about two to four miles off. These were the *Grand Era* and *Dr. Beatty*, the two rams blacked out and moving quickly. Responding to his sailor's hail, Lt. Cmdr. Brown ordered his men to clear for action. Even though he was only about 25 miles from Biggs Landing, he now had to give up any hope of help from above. The gunboat continued on for a short distance as crewmen raced to their stations. Orders were then given to come about and steam downriver to meet the Confederates.

With too small a crew to man the guns in both casemates, Brown directed that the principal attention be paid to the guns mounted forward. He was also aware, from RAdm. Porter and also conversations with contractor Brown, that his bow had been reinforced and might be employed to ram if the opportunity presented itself. In the meantime, the coal barges, which had so slowed the *Indianola*'s progress, might now provide additional protection against the enemy rams. These were lashed to each side of the big gunboat, their forward ends extending beyond her bows and the after halves reaching back as far as the wheelhouses. The giant warship headed toward the interlopers, presenting them with her port bow

Simultaneously, spotters on the *Webb* and *Queen of the West* saw a large, dark mass in the distance steaming at them "with her head quartering across and down river." If sketched out ahead of time on paper, it would have seemed a forlorn hope that the Southern vessels could triumph against the iron monster. After all, Maj. Brent had only one game plan, which he later revealed in his 1926 memoir: "My plan of battle was simple: to ram the enemy, and to continue ramming him as long as our boats held together and floated. I did not have enough men to think of boarding, as we knew he carried a numerous crew, and hence our only resource was to undergo his fire and ram, and ram, until the contest was decided." And so, in the dark, the ball was opened.[6]

Having switched fuel from wood to coal to increase steam pressure, the *Queen of the West* now became the first ram to ever assault two ironclads, her first having been the CSS *Arkansas* back at Vicksburg in July 1862 when she was flying the Stars and Stripes. With the moon allowing light to filter down through stringy clouds, the wooden warship, with her men ordered to hold fire until the last moment, began to charge across the two miles that separated the two combatants.

The *Webb* was following and awaiting her turn a half mile astern and the other two units in the group, lashed together, were off to the side farther back still, their lights providing some distraction. The *Queen*'s advance was not met by any immediate response from the *Indianola*'s forward Dahlgrens, even as she herself moved slowly toward Capt. McCloskey's craft. When only 150 yards out, all three cannon and every musket aboard the Southern boat opened fire and, in the smoke of discharge, the *Indianola* was rammed. Aboard the *Dr. Beatty*, an embedded *Memphis Daily Appeal* correspondent, writing under the pseudonym "American Rifles," took careful notes for the account he would soon pen.

Just as the *Queen* approached, the Federal ironclad halted her forward progress and instead churned rapidly astern. This action caused Maj. Brent's command to miss hitting the target, the *Indianola*'s unprotected hull abaft the port wheel. Instead, it sliced into and through the intervening coal barge and its cargo, which was set adrift and sank. Still, the shot was so powerful that the ram was able to not only break or break off numerous iron plates, but also, more important, damage the machinery that drove the boat's side wheels. Henceforth, the *Indianola* was forced to depend upon her propellers for all thrust and maneuver.

Although the *Queen* had managed to hurt her opponent, she too was initially caught. Her thrust into the side of the *Indianola* had resulted in her being initially hung up into the side of the ironclad and unable to back out. Even as her cannon and muskets continued to fire into the sides of the larger boat (without effect, as these projectiles simply bounced off), her captain and commodore pondered the possibilities if her reversed engines could not free her. At this point, the lines holding the surviving part of the smashed coal barge were cut by Union sailors and it slid off into the current,

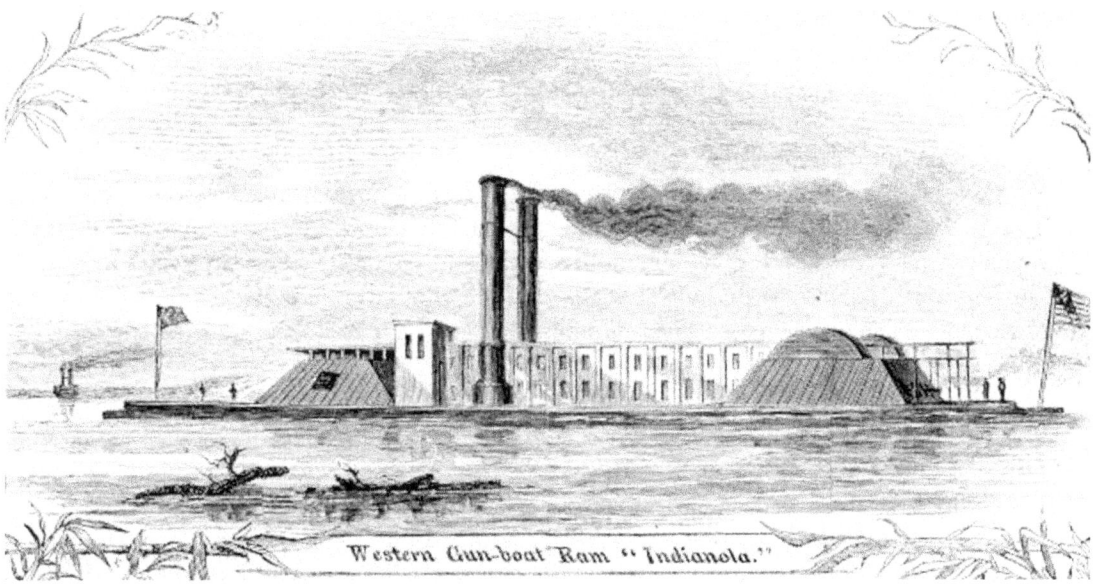

***Indianola* Meets the Enemy.** Though perhaps only a daylight depiction, this illustration might also, if deeply shaded, be taken to represent the moment on the evening of February 24 when lookouts aboard the *Indianola* sighted the pursuing Confederate rams and the ship was "beat to quarters." With no reinforcements having arrived from the Mississippi Squadron, the slow but powerful ironclad would have to face the enemy unaided (*Harper's Weekly*, February 7, 1863).

allowing the *Queen* to slip away. Even as the *Queen* backed away, Capt. Pierce's *Webb* passed her by, "running," as Maj. Brent had it, "like a railway express" right at the same spot hit by McCloskey's boat. When she was a hundred yards off, her lone big gun, a banded 32-pounder mounted forward (sometimes known as a 6.4-inch rifle) of the same variety as used aboard CSS *Arkansas* and also at Fort Pemberton, fired an 80-pound round into the side of the *Indianola.* The bolt made "a slight superficial scaling and an indentation of less than ⅛ inch."

Given that the *Indianola* was still backing, the *Webb*, like the *Queen*, missed the spot on her hull that was initially targeted. Instead, the Southern ram passed broadside to the ironclad, slightly striking her bow. Though the hit on the vessel was inconsequential, the angle at which the *Webb* struck was such that the coal barge tied to her starboard side was violently pushed back, snapping its lines and allowing it to drift away. Before the *Webb* could clear, however, the two XI-guns in the forward casemate of the *Indianola* blasted out at her, enveloping her in smoke and managing to hit her bow railing. It is unknown whether Brown was following his original orders from Porter: "If you are attacked by vessels protected with cotton bales, fire shrapnel, which are good incendiary shell."

As the *Webb* withdrew and headed upriver to circle and thrust with the aid of the downriver current, the *Queen of the West* returned for another round. As she approached, the *Indianola*'s forward guns spoke again, with both big pieces missing their target—again. As Maj. Brent had hoped, the dark of the night, to say nothing of the ironclad's lightly trained gunners, saved him from suffering as much damage as Capt. Brown may have liked. The *Queen* glanced off the port bow of the *Indianola*, running alongside. For a brief point in time, like their army cousins in formations ashore, riflemen on both vessels exchanged fire at one another (through protective loop holes), sometimes even employing revolvers. One of the Confederate shots killed a Union sailor, "greatly demoralizing the gun detachments."

Brown later commented on another physical problem that hindered his defense. "The peepholes in the pilot house were so small that it would have been a difficult matter to have worked the vessel from that place in daylight," he would write in May. Consequently, "during the whole engagement, the pilots were unable to aid me by their knowledge of the river, as they were unable to see anything." Those steering the *Indianola* were reduced to obeying orders from the vessel's captain "as they received them from me in regard to working the engines and helm."

The first of the crew released from Confederate custody (in April), Acting Assistant Surgeon Henry M. Mixer (1828–1909) was not impressed with the assistance given Brown by his subordinates, particularly in "working the guns." The brother-in-law of noted Western gunboat captain Lt. Cmdr. S. Ledyard Phelps, Mixer had signed aboard the *Chillicothe* the previous fall but transferred to the *Indianola* in January. He would serve aboard the timberclad *Lexington* for the rest of the war once he returned to duty during the summer. After the war, he practiced medicine in Neosho, MO. Back at the time of the battle, he observed that "it was perhaps too much to expect that young officers, in their first battle, in the horror and confusion of a night attack, and with such a multiplicity of assailants, should be cool and collected." According to Mixer, Lt. Cmdr. Brown, faced with structural problems caused by the vessel's construction and an ill-trained crew, was pretty much left to his own devices to save his ship: "To accomplish this, he exposed himself everywhere. He stood upon the hurricane deck, swept by volleys of musketry, grape, and canister shot, looking out for the rams, giving orders to his pilots, and, with his revolver, firing upon the pilots of the enemy. He stood on his knees on the grating on the main deck to see to it that the engineer correctly understood the orders from the pilots. He went to the casemate repeatedly and ordered the fire to be reserved until the rams were close upon us and then fire low. He aimed and discharged one of the guns himself."

Despite the observations of Capt. Brown and Surgeon Mixer, many would later question the competence of the ironclad's commander to fight his ship during the engagement. The descriptions by the two officers, comments Steven Mayeaux, gives the impression that "Brown was the only even remotely competent naval man aboard the vessel." That historian also agrees with most that the *Indianola* was manned "by a particularly inexperienced crew."

Meanwhile, the Confederates got ready for another round. "American Rifles," the *Memphis Daily Appeal* correspondent aboard the *Dr. Beatty*, was deafened by the incessant play of the riflemen shooting at the *Indianola*, mixed with the constant yelling of the ram crews. Dropping back, the *Queen* turned and rushed back for her third try. As she approached, the *Indianola*'s gunners fired again and missed again. Their continued poor shooting now allowed a major Confederate success as the ram ploughed squarely into Capt. Brown's warship, hitting her midway between the starboard wheelhouse and the stern. Every officer and man aboard both vessels was thrown to the deck. The butt was so hard that it smashed a hole in *Indianola*'s hull and crushed the starboard paddle wheel, starting a number of leaks abaft the shaft while also tearing off the starboard rudder.

Having seen the enemy approaching from starboard, Capt. Brown, before the crash, sent a number of gunners to the stern casemate and began to turn the *Indianola* away from the course she was on. This swing brought the *Queen*, as she backed away after striking, directly under the aft Dahlgrens. These now fired at such close range that their blast and smoke enveloped the Confederates. More important, one of the two 9-inch shells smashed into the port side of the *Queen* causing much damage, destroying guns, killing two men and wounding four, knocking out cotton bale armor, and destabilizing the boat, before exiting the starboard side. Far up the Mississippi at the mouth of the Yazoo River, RAdm. Porter and the bluejackets around him believed they heard heavy gunfire from down the river. They "supposed it was the *Indianola* firing at the batteries at New Carthage on her way up. The firing was very slow and not like that of an action."

Seeing the *Queen* limping off, the *Indianola* now increased power to her propellers and attempted to escape. She was barely underway when the *Webb*, moving in under a full head of steam and with help from the current, rocketed into the same spot aft on the *Indianola* that the *Queen* had just vacated, striking her "fair in the stern" and crushing her rudder box. Surgeon Mixer was later told that the blow not only put a huge hole in the hull but also carried away the outboard bearing of the shaft. As a result, "the wheel dropped down" and the vessel was no longer manageable. Watching from the *Queen*, Maj. Brent noted that "the sharp bow of the *Webb* penetrated as if it were going to pass entirely through the ship." Like a World War II destroyer running over a U-boat, the *Webb* came up out of the water, while the Mississippi River ran into *Indianola*'s smashed hull. Capt. Brown's gunners made no response to the *Webb*'s approach and could not now make one as she withdrew.

The captain of the Union vessel now knew that his ship was finished. He immediately threw his codes and signal books overboard and ordered the vessel to use her screws to run over to the Louisiana shore, where she could sink and her crew could escape to nearby Union lines. Due to the current, that maneuver was impossible, though four men were able to reach the western shore with a line, including an African American fireman called Isaac. The large warship was sucked back into the river and drifted downstream, helpless and a target for another strike by the *Webb*.

Having withdrawn from the stern of the *Indianola*, Capt. Pierce prepared for a third attack. No one aboard his craft knew that her previous plunge into the *Indianola* had punched a hole 18-inches long and a third that wide in the ram's hull approximately a foot above the waterline. Fortunately for the Southern crew, the third attack was not made, as it would have surely sunk them. At the same time, the river was rising through the holds of the *Indianola* and was now almost to the level of her grate-bars; she continued going down despite the frantic efforts of her crew to operate her pumps and to bail water.

As *Webb* approached at 11:07 p.m. a hail came from the *Indianola* announcing the warship's surrender and asking for a tow to keep her from sinking. Quickly taking possession of the immense prize, men from the Confederate vessel secured a hawser and began the requested tow. Unhappily, the line quickly parted as the ironclad, with two and a half feet of water in her hold, was too heavy for the former tug to handle alone. About this time, the *Dr. Beatty*, freed from the *Grand Era* and alerted by Maj. Brent that the *Indianola* was going down fast, moved alongside the ironclad pumping volleys of musketry and light artillery fire into her as she moved in. Col. Brand alerted his boarding parties to swing across, but before they could do so Lt. Cmdr. Brown yelled that he was sinking. Brand then demanded that he surrender (not knowing that he had already given in to Maj. Brent) and the U.S. officer gave up a second time. Brand and numerous soldiers than crossed aboard, where Brown handed his sword to the Port Hudson officer.

After an hour and 27 minutes of combat, the battle was over and the Dixie Lilliputians had won their impossible victory. Casualties aboard the *Indianola* were one dead, two wounded (one badly), and seven missing.[7]

The *Dr. Beatty*, along with the *Webb*, now secured to the *Indianola*, attempting to halt her drift downriver and her sinking in deep water where many would die and she would be lost as a prize. Shortly after they lashed on, the *Queen of the West* also made fast and Maj. Brent went aboard. His arrival was delayed by first having fallen into the river and being rescued by an African American stationed on the afterdeck of the *Webb*. Soggy and badly bruised, he was shocked to find the boat in chaos, the soldiers from the *Dr. Beatty* making no effort to secure the vessel or her crew, instead choosing to plunder both.

While his men looted the *Indianola*, Lt. Col. Brand was engaged in conversation with Lt. Cmdr. Brown, who was undoubtedly relaying the situation aboard while protesting the actions of the Southern soldiers. When Brent attempted to join the conversation, dripping wet and in a uniform not recognized, he was ignored by the naval officer. Angered, Brent ordered his superior to inform Capt. Brown "by what right I speak to him." Brand performed the introductions. "This is Major Brent, who commands the rams that captured you," he told Brown, who gulped and made apologies, smoothing

An Unrealized Dream. Having succeeded in taking the *Indianola* and her crew, it was widely anticipated by the local Confederate command and commanders, as well as RAdm. Porter, that the ironclad would be refitted and begin duty as a unit of the Confederate navy. One artist went so far as to depict what the vessel might look like in the service of Dixie (J. Thomas Scharf, *History of the Confederate Navy*, 1887).

over and improving a relationship with the Confederate leader that existed throughout the remainder of his time aboard.

Maj. Brent now appointed Lt Thomas Handy from the *Webb* to be the prize master and had Capt. McCloskey send over an armed guard under the Crescent Artillery officer to create order. As soon as Handy, 2nd Lt. Frith, and their men arrived, Lt. Col. Brand and his men were sent back to the *Dr. Beatty*, after which the crew of the *Indianola* was mustered on deck and then allowed to secure those personal belongings not stolen by the soldiers. Damage control parties and members of the recently named prize crew were sent around the *Indianola* to check on her situation and soon reported back to Maj. Brent that she was a wreck: the hull aft was breached, her engines and machinery were out of order, her paddle wheels were smashed or otherwise unserviceable, and although her armor protection and great guns were serviceable, water continued to quickly rise in the holds.

As the Federal prisoners were being transferred to the *Grand Era*, Maj. Brent determined to take the *Indianola* across the Palmyra Island channel to the eastern shore of the Mississippi, where she would, even if she sank, be on the Vicksburg side of the river. Additional cordage was located and the *Queen* and *Grand Era* were maneuvered into position, one on each side of the ironclad, and lashed alongside. Then, with the *Webb* towing and the other two providing support and propulsion, the captured vessel was slowly moved down and east across the current. As the procession progressed the *Indianola* continued to fill with water, and as she approached the eastern shore it appeared that she might actually sink, taking one or more of the Southern rescue boats down with her. At a point about 70 yards from the riverbank, Maj. Brent ordered the *Grand Era* and the *Queen* to cut their lashings and move away. The *Webb* reverted to her earlier role as a tugboat and pushed the ironclad, with her lower decks completely submerged, hard against a sandbar that jutted out from the bank a short distance above Hurricane Island, opposite the head of lower Palmyra Island, in 10 feet of water. Her final resting spot right out in front of Joseph Davis's farm, on an even keel with water up to a point two inches below her main deck, was, as Adm. Mahan noted, "near the plantation of the president of the Confederacy."

Following the burial of a wounded Union sailor who had died during the night, three of the vessels of Maj. Brent's Confederate task group set off downstream for Port Gibson early on February 25. Brent himself went aboard the *Queen of the West* to Warrenton to report and also obtain pumps and other equipment to use in raising the ironclad. Lt Handy and his prize crew were left behind to begin salvage work on the South's latest ironclad. "There appears to have been," an officer later wrote, "an utter want of authority, system, or plan." Joined by about 100 soldiers from shore, the men initially attempted to recover badly needed items thought to remain in the *Indianola*'s holds or storerooms. In the end, nothing was saved, "with the exception of the wine and liquor stores."

As Wednesday continued and the workers fished around inside the *Indianola* hull, the Union captives were moved to Vicksburg under an escort provided by Col. William Wirt Adams (1819–1888), commander of the 1st Mississippi Cavalry. A veteran of the Texas Republic's army and a successful local planter and businessman, Adams had formed his unit in late 1861, transferring it to the Delta area of Mississippi a year later.

He would remain defender of that area for most of the remainder of the war. President Grover Cleveland appointed him postmaster of Jackson, MS, in 1885. He died there in a street gunfight with his most bitter enemy, a local newspaper editor, three years later.

After the *Queen of the West* put in at Warrenton, Maj. Brent made his way to the headquarters of Vicksburg's commander, Maj. Gen. Carter L. Stevenson, seeking pumps and other equipment for salvage use. These were provided and the ram was directed to return to the wreck site off Hurricane Island with the items, there to serve as picket. Made aware of the major's exploit in a telegram from Lt. Col. Brand, Lt. Gen. Pemberton wired Richmond from his Jackson base giving brief details and noting that the *Indianola* was sunk in the Mississippi River and "shows bow and upper works out near Mr. Joe Davis' plantation." Plans were afoot, he added, to salvage her.

Meanwhile, the 112 crewmembers from the sunken *Indianola* reached Vicksburg, where crowds turned out to see them. According to the local reporter from the *Memphis Daily Appeal*, they had "acquired a great deal of notoriety by pillaging hen houses and negro cabins on the Mississippi." The officers and enlisted men were all accommodated in the Warren County Courthouse, "the best building in the town," and were occasionally given provisions by local citizens, in addition to military rations. Most of the men, it was believed, were from Illinois, Ohio, and Maine. It was anticipated that the men would depart shortly for the state capital at Jackson and hence to a POW camp.

About this time, telegraphic word of the ironclad's capture was sent from Vicksburg and reached other nearby Confederate communities, despite horrific weather that delayed reception in several locations. "Three cheers for our little navy," penned the editor of the *Natchez Weekly Courier* on February 26, "and blessings on the men of daring who accompanied this expedition." Unable to resist, he opined, "We think Federal rear admiral Porter will be a little more careful how he ventures his vessels in the lower country."

Farther north at the Union anchorage above Vicksburg, the fate of the *Indianola* was still unknown, though RAdm.

David Dixon Porter. One of the most colorful leaders of the Civil War, the 49-year-old Porter (1813–1891) was entirely mortified by the capture of the *Indianola*. Although it caused considerable consternation at the time, the episode did not damage his working relationship with Maj. Gen. Grant nor blunt his future opportunities, which included command of Federal naval forces at Fort Fisher in 1865 and great influence in the postwar navy. The loss of the vessel was attributed to incompetence by the *Indianola*'s builder, Joseph Brown, who nevertheless retained Porter's confidence and, thus, many tinclad alteration contracts (National Park Service).

Porter had heard what he thought was heavy cannon fire from down the river the night before. A correspondent from the *New York Times* reported that such fear of an attack by the *Queen of the West* or the *Webb* had spread through the Union transport fleet that the boats were kept "in a state of readiness to scatter like a flock of sheep at the first warning of their approach."

Union soldiers tasked with watching activities across the river at Vicksburg and Warrenton sent word that the *Queen of the West* was at the latter town flying a Confederate banner. Maj. Gen. Grant wired the War Department: "Distant firing was heard, lasting from 4 p.m. yesterday until 1 this morning. It was supposed to be the *Queen* and *Indianola*. Apprehension is felt for the safety of the *Indianola*."

During the day, Maj. Thomas H. Hayes (1837–1908) of the Kentucky Orphan Brigade was ordered to take the steamer *Frolic* across the Mississippi under a flag of truce in an effort to exchange 300 soldiers and win permission to land supplies at Vicksburg rather than Warrenton. He told those meeting him that the *Indianola* had been sunk, but many on the Union side "seemed to doubt the statement, thinking it only a ruse, and that the *Indianola* and *Queen* may yet be used against us."[8]

Locating the exact positions of Confederate gun emplacements in the Vicksburg defenses and of Union gun positions on the Louisiana shore was a task that busied observers in both armies. This probing occurred not only in the spring of 1863, but, in fact, was also a process that stretched back to the time to when the Federal navy first visited the city the previous summer. Telescopes and artillery exchanges were the usual ways of determining cannon sites. The Union army and navy at this time employed various methods for finding out where the Southern guns were situated. Shortly after the return of the Mississippi Squadron for the current campaign, RAdm. Porter ordered that at least one mortar boat be employed on a regular basis to bombard the Confederate fortress. On the appointed days, a tugboat towed down one of these scows, equipped with a 13-inch siege mortar, to a location directly across from where the suspected enemy batteries were located. From within "easy range," shells were lofted onto Vicksburg in an effort to draw fire. Sometimes the Confederates returned the Union compliments; mostly their few shells splashed into the water doing no damage to the little Federal craft.

Earlier on January 30, "Omega," one of the fleet-imbedded *Chicago Daily Tribune* correspondents, reported that engineers from both the army and the navy had begun making trips to within range of the Vicksburg cannon to look for Confederate artillery locations. The investigations, it was opined, added to the military's "knowledge and strength" of Southern positions. Having actually seen a number of these locations in action when the *Queen of the West* and *Indianola* passed down some days earlier and noticed that rapid firing, it was believed, caused several of the defenders' guns to burst, it was decided that another effort to draw fire might be profitable. The next effort would entail the creation of a mock gunboat, which could be sent past Vicksburg on the current, inducing the Confederates, it was hoped, to shoot at it and thus reveal battery locations (while also wasting ammunition).

During the day on Wednesday, Union soldiers and sailors, having acquired an old coal barge for the purpose, rigged her up to represent a gunboat. The *Jackson Mississippian* in reporting the incident called her "a flatboat with sundry fixtures to create deception." First Lt. Sebaldus Hassler of Co. E of the 37th Ohio Volunteer Infantry, in his report of her activities, revealed that she "had a square turret forward, with a mock cannon projecting toward the bow from within. Smokestacks made of four barrels, wheelhouse, etc. covered all over with a thick coat of tar." Later in the day as the homemade boat was being finished, one of the white crewmen, Seaman Benjamin Elliot, who had escaped from the *Indianola* along with several others and made it back to Union lines even as his messmates were being recaptured, was presented to RAdm. Porter. The unit commander debriefed the man, learning for the first time that the ironclad had been off the mouth of the Red River for three days before attempting to return to the fleet. Capt. Brown, he learned, had retained his two coal barges alongside, "giving the enemy all that advantage," and was thus caught by the Confederates. The sailor making this report told Porter that he had escaped in the confusion by jumping out one of the sinking *Indianola*'s ports and swimming ashore. He made his way through the Louisiana brush to the soldiers working on the Williams Canal, who forwarded him to Young's Point aboard a steamer. No one knew that the African American fireman Isaac was still in hiding and would shortly provide additional details. "His [Brown's] vessel must have been unmanageable," Porter reflected in a report of the interview. After the sailor, who could not actually confirm the vessel's loss, departed, the admiral confided his observations to paper, concluding that this was, for him at least, "the most humiliating affair that has occurred during this rebellion."

With his three other embedded *New York Herald* colleagues unavailable (Anderson was in Confederate hands, Keim was on the Yazoo Pass Expedition, and Frank Knox was under arrest), reporting the substance of the survivor's comments and preparing a summary of what was then known of the *Indianola*'s cruise fell to William F.G. Shanks (1837–1905), a *Louisville Courier* journalist before the war who later covered the Franco-Prussian War for the *New York Tribune*. His account, which was sent upstream by steamer before the ersatz target was launched, appeared on March 8 and has been cited above. His report fills in several operational details not previously published.

Just before midnight, the strange, remodeled Federal coal barge was towed to De Soto Point, where it was cast adrift to float past Vicksburg in the wee hours of Thursday morning, February 26, about 30 hours or so after the *Indianola*'s surrender. Events that followed would not only put paid to Southern hopes of raising their prize but also began a nautical tale of such prodigious size and duration as to make Davey Jones roll about in mirth on his underwater deck.

The tale of the first fake appeared in the pages of the *Memphis Daily Appeal* on March 11, 1863. Confederate 2nd Lt. Frith, several days after events, remembered when talking to a reporter from the pro–Dixie newspaper, that in the darkness a giant gunboat, which he was "pretty well assured was the *Tuscumbia*," made her appearance at a point several miles above the *Indianola* wreck site. She was still there on Friday. Penned by an unknown scribe, the New York news story, written on the morning of February 27 and which never once mentions either Porter or the U.S. Navy, appeared in the *New York Times* on March 12:

> The night was dark, and it was feared that the enemy would save their powder by not discovering it. It had scarcely drifted around the point in range of the batteries, before the "boom" of a huge gun showed the watchfulness of the enemy. Presently another and another, battery after battery,

opened upon it, until the long range of hills belched fire like a volcano, and through the humid atmosphere the bellowing of the artillery sounded like continuous thunder. It was "great cry and little wool," however, the innocent Quaker gunboat drifted safely through, and skiffs were sent out by our troops from below the point, and the craft was towed to shore, where it now lies, without the mark of a single shot in its formidable looking bulk.

The same day, the *New York Herald* ran a piece attributing the success of the disguised flatboat, which was called a "paddy-boat" or "dummy monitor," directly to Porter, though acknowledging that the initial purpose was to "run the Vicksburg batteries in order to ascertain their exact location." The vessel, said the news release, "frightened the rebels," causing them to "skedaddle on the double quick," blowing up the *Indianola* as they departed.

In his memoirs written in 1885, RAdm. Porter claimed, falsely, that it was he who had ordered construction of this "cheap expedient, which worked very well." Though he does not mention such a ruse in any of his contemporary reports regarding the loss of the ironclad below, he detailed in his recollections the manner in which the mock craft was ordered and assembled down to the use of smudge pots to simulate chimney smoke. He then asserted that it was this creation expeditiously dispatched that caused the Confederates to destroy the *Indianola*. Some have come to believe that Porter deliberately fabricated this story; though unlikely, it is possible that he was confused as to what scheme he had underway at which time. Acting Ensign E. Cort Williams, who saw the entire mock gunboat episode firsthand, acknowledged in his own recollection that the admiral was not aware of the *Indianola*'s fate when the first dummy vessel was dispatched, being concerned primarily with artillery site location. That view was confirmed by Adm, Mahan in his history of the river war.

On Friday, February 27, RAdm. Porter wired the Navy Department, via Memphis, to inform Secretary Gideon Welles that the *Indianola* had "fallen into enemy hands." "I do not know the particulars," he told his superior but guessed the tragedy had been caused by "a noncompliance with my instructions." The Mississippi Squadron chief advised Washington to warn the West Gulf Blockading Squadron headquarters at New Orleans. When Welles received Porter's telegraphic communication on March 2 he immediately wired back in cipher, noting that there was no way to warn the fleet at the Crescent City. Porter was told quite bluntly that the *Indianola* "must be destroyed."

Two days later, the squadron commander penned another message to Secretary Welles, saying that all of the information he had on the *Indianola* so far was basically "hearsay." The sources all agreed that the boat was captured after repeated ramming by the *Webb* and *Queen of the West* and that she was afterwards blown up. The ironclad, he was told, had not initially manned her after guns nor did she, at any time during the fight, "use her ram power." Porter, anxious to find fault with a subordinate who appeared to have let him down by losing his ship, concluded that the *Indianola* was "indifferently fought." Although her side wheels were damaged, the ironclad's sides did not "appear to be crushed." Without the facts regarding the strikes against her stern, those giving the admiral opinions believed "that she gave in too soon." Porter wrote back to Welles again by surface dispatch on March 7, explaining that he did not have a sufficient force to send past Vicksburg to rescue the *Indianola* at the time she was attacked. If she were still fit for service, he advised, she would "without doubt" have come upstream and

(Naval History and Heritage Command).

(*Harper's Weekly*, March 28, 1863).

made an attempt "to shell out our troops opposite Vicksburg." Later that day Porter wired Washington indicating that it was "pretty positively" known that the ironclad was far too damaged for early offensive use by the Confederates. Although she was a weak vessel, it remained unclear whether or not she existed. "If she exists," Porter added, "I hope to have her before a month is over."

Reports had since come in that she had been sunk in the action or run on a sandbar. The admiral went on to assure the chief navy official that those few members of the *Indianola* crew who had escaped her were concealed about a mile from her when she was destroyed. The handful who reached Union lines were all certain that she had exploded and they all agreed that the blast "shook severely everything in the neighborhood." Scouts meanwhile were dispatched and it was expected that they would soon report the facts of the episode more fully. Still, as late as March 7, "De Soto" (*New York Times* correspondent William George) wrote to his paper that "as there is a great variety of rumors afloat, however, it is difficult to believe anything except upon irrefutable testimony."

Although the story of the first sham gunboat had appeared in newspapers on March 11 and 12 respectively, the communication claiming credit for the initial mock-ironclad deception and its success was given to the *New York Herald* (before RAdm. Porter left on the 14th to participate in the Steele's Bayou Expedition) and was widely circulated, with an illustration, in *Harper's Weekly* on March 28. Only a few observers noticed that, three days before, a letter from Porter had appeared in the *New York Times* that specifically confessed that on the night the barge was sent downstream he did not know that Capt. Brown's vessel was actually captured. Porter did occasion an ersatz ironclad to be sent downstream, but that second and somewhat more elaborate creation was not launched until over a week after the first. As Porter wrote a fellow officer, enclosing the sketch of Theodore R. Davis that appeared in *Harper's Weekly* on April 11, a second "terrific monster" was created as a way of determining Confederate artillery locations. She was a "perfect imitation of the *Lafayette*, "which new ironclad had joined the squadron on March 3 and went downstream to bombard Vicksburg batteries on the afternoon of March 9."

This was the so-called Black Terror, the craft historians have come to say was the one that caused the Confederates to blow up the wreck of the *Indianola*. About 300 feet long with large wheelhouses and a wooden forward casemate from which extended logs ("Quaker Guns") representing cannon, she had old lifeboats hanging from davits and was able to produce smoke out of fake hogshead chimneys from burning oakum pots at their base. Covered with tar, the wooden wonder carried a skull and crossbones flag forward and a U.S. ensign aft. Across the sides of each wheelhouse was lettered the slogan "Deluded Rebels, Cave In." She reportedly cost all of $8.63!

About 11:00 that evening, the fake *Lafayette* was shoved off and made her way past

Opposite: Destruction of the *Indianola*. In response to reports of an approaching Federal ironclad, Confederate soldiers working to salvage the wreck of the *Indianola* blew up the vessel (or tried to) on the morning of February 26. Many thought it strange that the approaching giant intruder seemed to wallow in the shoal water above and not move down. The first sketch, of the USS *Wooden Dummy*, was made by RAdm. Porter, whose signature crosses the bottom, while the second appeared in *Harper's Weekly*.

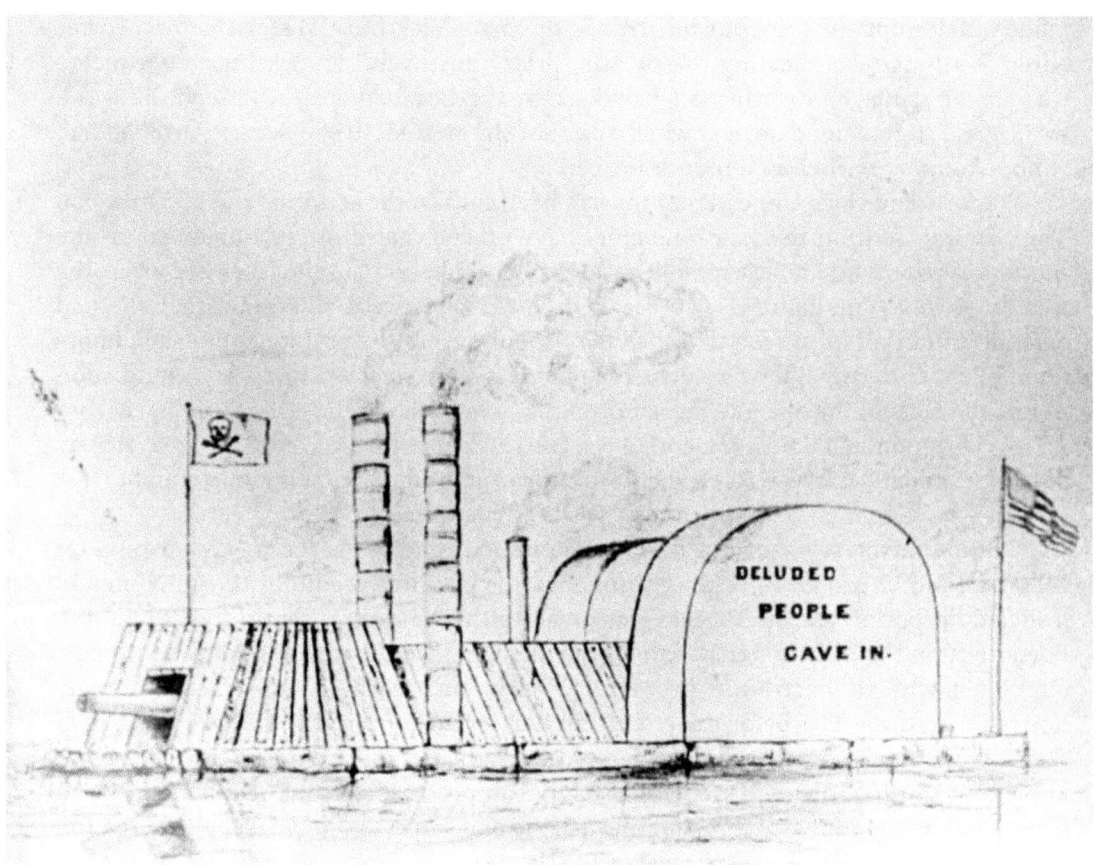

The *Black Terror*. This Theodore R. Davis sketch depicts the so-called *Black Terror*, the second of two sham gunboats sent down the Mississippi in the direction of the *Indianola* wreck. Long believed to be the creation that caused Southerners to blow up the ironclad, it reportedly cost all of $8.63! It was, in fact, the second of two dummy craft designed to reveal the locations of Southern artillery emplacements (*Harper's Weekly*, April 11, 1863).

the batteries at Vicksburg, Warrenton, and New Carthage, all of which shot at her with every gun available. "This little artillery sport," Porter told his correspondent, "must have cost the Rebels a thousand charges of powder and the bursting and dismounting of five or six guns." Steven Mayeux, who recently blew the whistle on this two-craft Porter error, tells us that the squadron commander's "version of the dummy gunboat story has taken on a life of its own and to this day refuses to die." The fact that there were two deceptions dispatched for two different reasons has been combined into the view that only one was sent and that one at Porter's instruction specifically to "stampede" the South into destroying Capt. Brown's ironclad.

A report on the second sham gunboat first appeared in the *Chicago Daily Tribune* for March 24, 1863; it was part of a larger dispatch sent from the Vicksburg area on March 10 and appears under the sub-headline "Another Mock Gunboat."

> Last night the enemy were victimized again by another "Quaker" gunboat, on which they must have expended three or four thousand dollars' worth of ammunition. The sham craft which ran

the gauntlet of their batteries at Vicksburg has been in course of construction for several days by the crews of our fleet, which lies at the mouth of the Yazoo. A small raft of logs represented the hull of a ram and gunboat sunk low in the water, with the supposed great weight of her metal; upon this a slight superstructure was built to represent the casemates; her smoke-stacks were represented by two logs set on end, and the whole painted black. The counterfeit was so accurate that even in daylight it was difficult to detect it at a distance of three hundred yards.

About midnight she was towed down to the point by one of the tugs and cast adrift to begin her engagement with the rebel batteries. A very small fire had been kindled inside the sham casemates to deceive the enemy into the belief that they caught glimpses of treacherous gleams of battle lanterns. She had scarcely turned the point before the watchful enemy opened a terrific cannonade upon her with their huge siege guns, which lasted nearly an hour.

Because the De Soto peninsula area was so flooded, observers could not immediately ascertain the fate of the sham vessel. Given the earlier visit to Vicksburg by the *Lafayette*, the Chicago reporter opined that the Confederates were doubtless "certain that it was she running the blockade to take the place of the *Indianola*. No one has left a better contemporary description of the second dummy ironclad than *New York Times* correspondent William George, writing as "De Soto." More detailed and complete than that of his Chicago colleague, it was penned two days afterward. Just before noon on March 9, he begins, "a mysterious craft was observed lying near the gunboat Louisville on the opposite side of the Mississippi River, just in the mouth of the Yazoo." The correspondent went on to describe her as "'long, low and black'—though not exactly a schooner." The entity had a "long casemated hull, close down to the water; two extensive wheelhouses and two high smoke-pipes were the prominent objects which attracted attention." Some army officers told the inquisitive scribe that the craft, then being pumped out, was a newly captured Confederate gunboat, "one of those rumored to be up the Yazoo, which had just been taken and partially sunk during a ferocious fight."

Correspondent George, "prompted by Yankee curiosity," crossed the Mississippi to get a better look at the curiosity, which upon close inspection he found to be "a very tolerable Quaker copy of the *Lafayette*." Constructed "at a total expense of ten dollars" by an "ingenious and rollicking engineer" assisted by numerous gunboatmen, her purpose was to run "past the Vicksburg batteries to feel their fire." About 150 feet long with a 40-foot beam, the dummy was built by wood "taken from vacant secesh houses on the Louisiana side of the river." Her sides were angled upward to resemble Federal ironclads with large side wheelhouses. Two pyramids of pork and flour barrels were stacked to make "an excellent substitute for a pair of very tall chimneys." At the right moment, smoldering fires could be lighted to make steam that resembled escaping smoke. Even in daylight, De Soto observed, it required close inspection to tell them from genuine smokestacks. A "barrel of coal tar furnished a pithy black coating everywhere expect the spaces on the wheelhouses, where, on the outside side of one was painted in large letters "CONFEDERATE MAIL PACKET NO. 1" and on the other "SECESH SOLD." A white cotton flag hung from the forward flagstaff. It was decorated with a skull and crossbones, "with the figure-head of a Yankee smelling the end of his thumb and twirling his fingers in the air."

Toward midnight the moon rose sufficiently, casting a light that was from time to time enhanced by lightning flashes. Given such an auspicious time for blockade running, the sham ironclad was taken in tow by a tug and, at the appropriate point, "pitchy black smoke" boiled out of her fake chimneys. Cast off, she went "a fluking down the rapid current of the swollen river." Before long, the northern creation, floating downstream, was taken under fire by Vicksburg's batteries. Each in turn "gave her a salute until every gun along the whole of the works as far as Warrenton had paid their respects." Turning to the accompanying newsman George, one of the tugboat crewmembers exclaimed, "I thought I should have died a laughing to hear them pegging away at the old raft." Another wag said he wouldn't have missed the fun of the shooting "for ten dollars." It was later reported that Confederate cannon had expended 94 rounds attempting to destroy the trickster.

When news of the ploy(s) reached eastern newspapers, there was relief. The *Brooklyn Daily Eagle*, one of those journals led to believe that only one fake was employed, opined, "The ruse was entirely successful on our part, and a formidable vessel, which should never have been out of our possession, was rendered useless for operations against us." That belief would be shattered over the next weeks as reports of the vessel's survival persisted.

To return to our story of the ironclad's destruction, we note that the initial Federal dummy ironclad passed downstream on February 26, being taken under fire by Vicksburg's batteries (which thus revealed themselves to Union observers). The mock ironclad was also seen from across the river by Capt. McCloskey, who ordered his crew to cast off and took the *Queen of the West* rapidly back toward Hurricane Island to warn the men aboard the wreck of the *Indianola*. While en route that Thursday, McCloskey encountered both the *Webb* and the *Grand Era* and "spoke" with their captains, reporting that another Federal ironclad was on its way. Lt. Col. Brand, on the latter vessel, was also apprised. With both rams damaged from their encounter with the Yankee ironclad, consensus now formed that drastic action regarding the *Indianola* was required. Indeed, the anticipated Union gunboat was causing what Brand later labeled "a stampede." Indeed, even as the *Queen* gathered way to leave her three-way meeting, she accidentally rammed the port side of the *Grand Era*, forcing her to reduce speed and slowly make her way to the wreck site, where she was to deliver 70 bales of cotton to assist in the salvage project.

The *Queen* and the *Webb* both stopped briefly at the *Indianola* location, where they took off about half of the workforce. The remainder volunteered to stay and work to salvage the vessel, refloating her as soon as possible. The two rams were barely out of sight before a new directive arrived from Vicksburg. The Confederate theater commander, Lt. Gen. Pemberton, from his Jackson headquarters, had wired commanders at Vicksburg early the morning of February 26 ordering that the ironclad be blown up. While the Southerners scrambled to get out of the way of the oncoming Federal monster, believed by 2nd Lt. Frith and others to be the *Tuscumbia*, it suddenly grounded near the end of the canal Union soldiers were building in Louisiana. A number of soldiers who were present watching its progress and reporting on Confederate cannon sites, after noting that it had a hole at the bow just above the waterline, helpfully pushed the mock monitor back into the four-knot current. She was then carried down the Mississippi, eventually grounding on a mud flat about three miles above the wreck of the *Indianola*.

When a cavalryman arrived with Stephenson's orders to blow the wreck, Lt. Handy and Frith, seeing the enemy vessel upstream, began making preparations to do just that. Efforts were made to destroy the Dahlgren cannon (Frith says three were actually thrown overboard) and then a fuse was laid to the magazine and lit. The lieutenants and crew scrambled ashore just before the great prize exploded with a tremendous roar. The burst succeeded in destroying the forward casemate and causing the hull to burn out above the water. During this time, the escaped U.S. Navy fireman Isaac was secreted in a barn near the riverbank; his safety was in the hands of local slaves, who took him food and information. There he heard the tremendous explosion out on the river. Within a short time thereafter, a Confederate cavalry patrol came to the farm and while speaking with an overseer near the barn one trooper reported that it was necessary to destroy the captured ironclad.

Before dawn, Isaac crept out of the barn and carefully made his way the riverbank in the darkness, the night's moon having gone down. There he saw the Federal gunboat drifting in the channel between the island and the main shore, eventually grounding on the former. At daylight, he found an abandoned canoe and immediately set off for her, thinking he could be reunited with a unit of the Mississippi Squadron. Upon reaching her, as it was later reported by the *New York Times*, the fireman "discovered her to be an innocent Quaker gunboat ... on which there was not a living thing except a few rats." Isaac returned to shore and watched as a few hours later the sham vessel was carried off "like the terrible body of the dead 'Cid,' to win yet other victories."

Isaac was able to make it back to Union lines by March 2. There he was first debriefed by Lt. Col. William Burnham Woods (1824–1887) of the 76th Ohio Volunteer Infantry Regiment. The engine room man freely admitted that he did not see much of the battle but believed (erroneously) that the *Queen of the West* was first to strike the *Indianola*, which, meanwhile, had fired into the *Webb* causing her to sink. He also relayed his story of the sham gunboat and the powerful impact it had on those Confederates working the wreck site.

A few days later, after having ascertained the particulars, the *Vicksburg Whig* on March 5 advised its readers of events regarding the gunboat's loss. The Yankees, its editors revealed, had dispatched a craft downstream the previous week that was reported to military headquarters as being an ironclad gunboat. Believing the *Indianola* in imminent danger of recapture, the garrison commander ordered her destroyed and orders were accordingly sent to the wreck site. "A few hours afterwards another order was sent down countermanding the first, it being ascertained that the monstrous craft was only a coal boat." However, before the new directive could reach Lt. Handy, the ironclad "was blown to atoms." When the article reached the Confederate capital, the editors of the *Richmond Examiner* caused it to be reprinted on March 12. The editors could not, however, avoid chiding all concerned by suggesting that if RAdm. Porter could just construct a few more log monitors the Union navy wouldn't need any ironclads because it could win the war with dummies.

The next day, according to newsman "Bod" Bodman, soldiers of the U.S. 8th Missouri Regiment, as was their custom, visited a point that jutted out into the Mississippi that was only 500–600 feet across from the Vicksburg landing. Here they were able to converse in shouts with town citizens and Confederate soldiers. One northerner was heard yelling over: "Where's the *Indianola*?" He was advised she was "gone to hell, where you'll go if you don't leave this latitude."⁹ The *Indianola* was not totally destroyed by the great blast. Three of the four cannon were, in fact, saved, as Maj. Gen. Stevenson on March 4 happily informed Lt. Gen. Pemberton, who also admitted that the infamous Federal ironclad was "a coal barge." Plans were underway for her salvage. However, as Pemberton lamented to his superiors on March 9, the "water [is] too high to raise the *Indianola* now."

The loss of *Indianola* was deeply distressing to the Union, as she was, as RAdm. Porter pointed out, the first ironclad in any theater to fall into the hands of the enemy. Northern newspapers offered various reports, official and otherwise, regarding the disaster. Published rumors suggested (incorrectly) that imminent action was expected to reclaim the vessel. "It is rumored at the [Chicago] naval depot that the whole of Porter's fleet has run by the Vicksburg batteries," reported the *Chicago Daily Times* on March 3. The same day, it was reported from Cincinnati that "it is believed that Porter has sent or will send a fleet of gunboats below to rescue the *Indianola* and *Queen of the West*." While neither of the events reported by the Chicago paper occurred, the loss of the *Indianola* ended RAdm. Porter's efforts to blockade the Red River by detached vessels while keeping the body of his fleet above Vicksburg. The crew of the ironclad was singled out for particular disdain. The *Indianola*'s builder, ex-Alton mayor Joseph Brown, was particularly critical of the ship's captain. After proclaiming the handling abilities of the *Indianola*, Brown, in a letter to the editor of the *St. Louis Daily Missouri Democrat* written from the Burnett House in Cincinnati on March 11, suggested that the reason for the disaster lay with the boat's crew, particularly her captain. Allowing, as all politicians do, that the public would come to form its own opinion of the cause, he bluntly stated, "Mine is that either cowardice, imbecility, or treason surrendered the vessel."

In addition to various newspaper editors, some members of President Lincoln's cabinet suspected Lt. Cmdr. Brown of Southern sympathies. Navy Assistant Secretary Gustavus Vasa Fox (1821–1883) wrote Porter that "the impression seems to be from those who are acquainted with his failure that he has acted treacherously." A former naval officer, a Mexican war veteran, and a New England manufacturer, Fox, as Gideon Welles' principal assistant, "remained uncertain" about Brown, but Porter gave him a half-hearted defense. "I think him loyal," the admiral told his superior, "but he acted like a fool—he never had a prettier chance to capture two vessels." William George, the *New York Times* reporter who wrote as "De Soto," summed up the thinking of most people: "The failure to avail himself of the information brought to him of the approach of the rebel rams and to get his vessel in trim for action was probably the fatal mistake." Over time, Brown's perceived inadequacies were forgiven and he retired as an admiral.

RAdm. Porter was not the only naval officer mortified by Maj. Brent's success, as indeed his half brother down the Mississippi was also distressed. There RAdm. David Glasgow Farragut commanded the "Big Muddy" from the Gulf to Port Hudson with his West Gulf Blockading Squadron. Foster brother of the naval Porters (David G. and William), Farragut had been in the U.S. Navy since he was nine years old. A year earlier, less two months, he had captured New Orleans and in May and July had visited Baton Rouge and Vicksburg, engaging CSS *Arkansas* in the process. He was presently making preparations to support a Federal military force tasked with investing Port Hudson. When he learned about the same time as Porter that the *Indianola* was captured, he too knew that Union control of the stretch of river between Port Hudson and Vicksburg was ended. Shortly thereafter, he wrote to Assistant Secretary Fox of his grief that the Mississippi Squadron had allowed the loss. "I confess," he added, "that the capture of the *Indianola* by two common river boats with no one killed has astonished me. I never thought much of Iron Clads, but my opinion of them is declining daily." Knowing that his relative had no fleet elements he could send below Vicksburg, Farragut wrote Secretary Welles on March 2 to say that "the time has come ... [and] there can be no more delay." Only he could move above the Port Hudson batteries to destroy the captured Union ironclad. By March 11, he had a good portion of his squadron back up the river at Baton Rouge.

The same day, the *Jackson Mississippian* offered news regarding the status of the *Indianola* wreck site. Its safety was assured and no more concerns needed to be feared regarding the craft. Hands were engaged in making repairs and it was anticipated that she might be raised and put back into service, this time for the South. Regarding that "awful coal boat about which so much nonsense has been circulated," the editor revealed it had been secured, together with a small quantity of coal found on board.

On the night of March 14, most of Farragut's vessels attempted to pass the guns of Port Hudson, with all but the *Hartford* and a smaller consort driven back and one, the historic paddle-wheel frigate *Mississippi*, destroyed. Continuing on toward Warrenton, Farragut learned that his costly passage was not really needed insofar as the *Indianola* was concerned.

Within a fortnight, it was decided that the *Hartford* should return downstream to the area of Port Hudson. Moving past Hurricane Island on March 31, tars aboard searched for the ironclad's wreck site but nothing was located. The admiral concluded that Lt. Cmdr. Brown's craft had sunk in deep water. Returning on south, the big flagship's mission to find the *Indianola* was a failure, though she would remain in the Port Hudson area for several weeks.

RAdm. David Glasgow Farragut (1801–1870). The foster brother of RAdm. Porter was below Port Hudson, LA, with elements of his West Gulf Blockading Squadron when news reached him of the *Indianola*'s capture. Believing her intact and that he would be able to destroy her, he made a costly and unsuccessful dash above that city on the night of March 14, eventually returning when it was realized that he also could not interdict the mouth of the Red River with only the two ships that made it past the citadel's guns (Library of Congress).

On March 27, the editor of the *Brooklyn Daily Eagle* commented on common confusion that would not be fully resolved for another month:

> The reports from the Mississippi have been so contradictory that it is almost impossible to tell what has actually occurred. We know that the *Queen of the West* and the *Indianola* were captured by the rebels, but further than that the information is very indefinite. The *Indianola* was reported to have been blown to fragments out of fear of a dummy ironclad which had been sent down the river, and of course was no more to be feared. Farragut is reported to have passed the batteries at Port Hudson with his flagship, the *Hartford*, and now we are told that he found the *Indianola*, ready for a fight—and took possession without opposition. The *Indianola*, like the old *Merrimac*, is a deceiving institution.

As if to confirm the New York opinion, the *Chicago Daily Tribune* reported two different tales next day: "The steamer *Indianola*, reported captured, is said to have been found half submerged, forty miles below Warrenton, where the engagement took place, in which she was taken. This is one story, while another is that the *Indianola* was blown up by the rebels and is a total wreck." These sorts of news updates and editorial comments continued in the Northern press. The *Brooklyn Daily Eagle* editor was totally exasperated by April 4 when he exclaimed in a column entitled "The Mysterious Ram" that "the mysterious ubiquity of the fabled craft of the *Flying Dutchman* has found more than a match in the *Indianola*." "We had just settled down to the conviction," he wrote, "that the *Indianola*, like the Army of the Rappahannock, was firmly stuck in the mud, when this morning we receive intelligence which would be startling if we were not used to it:

> The *Indianola* is up the Red River in fighting trim. We have had a good many mysterious affairs during the progress of the war, but nothing approaching the *Indianola* affair. We shall be surprised at no accounts we may hereafter receive of the movements of this incomprehensible ram. She may turn up in the Bay of Biscay in company with the *Alabama* chasing merchantmen, and may be simultaneously signaled off the coast of Newfoundland striking terror into the cod fisheries. The mystery of the iron mask was not a circumstance to this incomprehensible iron clad.[10]

On the night of April 16, in a move described in detail in the next chapter, eight heavy gunboats of the Mississippi Squadron, like the *Indianola* earlier, passed the Vicksburg batteries. Their intent was to cover and assist a cross-river U.S. Army invasion from Louisiana to that strip of Mississippi between the citadel and Port Hudson. For the next month, RAdm. Porter's vessels would provide both material and gunfire support. When in the early hours of April 17, the leading ironclad, the flagboat *Benton*, arrived off New Carthage, LA, she was immediately boarded by U.S. XIII Corps commander Maj. Gen. John A. McClernand (1812–1900). Greeted warmly by RAdm. Porter, the army officer reviewed local developments. He also took the opportunity to point out the nearby hulk of the *Indianola* and, as he reported to Maj. Gen. Grant later in the day, "suggested to him the importance of an examination, to ascertain whether she could not be raised and made seaworthy."

Porter, who remained anxious to know the situation with the *Indianola*, immediately agreed with McClernand's idea. Before noon, the Pook turtle *Pittsburg* anchored off the wreck site at the head of Palmyra Island. There her commander, Acting Volunteer Lt. William R. Hoel (1825–1879), according to orders received around sunrise, undertook a brief, preliminary survey of the sunken ironclad. A noted prewar steamboat pilot, Hoel had joined the Western Flotilla in October 1861 as pilot of the timberclad

Lexington. A year later, after several noteworthy adventures, he became captain of the *Pittsburg*, keeping that command for most of the war's remainder. Promoted to the highest rank for navy volunteers (acting volunteer lieutenant commander) in 1865, he resumed his civilian career after the conflict.

Hoel's initial examination gave his superior the most detailed description yet regarding the hulk of Mayor Brown's creation. She lay in nine feet of water in a straight position opposite Joseph Davis's plantation. The *Indianola*'s hull appeared sound, though all of the woodwork (superstructure) above the waterline was burned off. An experiment determined that no explosion had occurred in her magazine, though her forward turret, or casemate, appeared to have been blown apart, with its four sections "entirely disconnected and lying in different parts of the vessel's deck." Very little of the iron armor from the turret had been removed, though two of the 9-inch guns were missing. One of the 11-inchers had apparently burst, while the other had been lost overboard by the Confederates during their aborted salvage efforts. The engines were safe and undisturbed in the hold. The veteran pilot revealed that the hulk lay on a sandbar that for six months of the year was usually above water and dry. He anticipated that within two months the river depth would fall to a point where it was "entirely exposed." Hoel concluded his review with the optimistic opinion that "with proper facilities" the wreck "could be raised with but little difficulty." Following the inspection, the *Pittsburg* weighed for the new advanced Mississippi Squadron anchorage off New Carthage, LA, and reported his findings to RAdm. Porter. The fleet commander sent a message off to Secretary Welles before dark announcing both that his ironclads had passed Vicksburg and that the *Indianola* was "shattered."

On April 20 Porter detailed a visit to the wreck site by the *Pittsburg*'s sister boat *Mound City*. There her captain, Lt. Byron Wilson (1837–1893), was to amplify Hoel's first report and to remove what he could of the *Indianola*'s armor plate. A regular officer, Wilson had been given his present river command the previous June and would hold it for the remainder of the conflict. At the time of his death, he was the second ranking U.S. Navy captain.

The work began just after 11:00 a.m., but unbeknownst to Lt. Wilson his work was covertly observed from a nearby location by Confederate captain and future Virginia congressman George D. Wise (1831–1908), whose scout was later reported by his superior to Lt. Gen. Pemberton. Sent to reconnoiter Porter's newly arrived fleet, Wise found a skiff and ascended the Mississippi to within a few miles of the Joseph Davis plantation. There "he learned a large gunboat" was anchored near the *Indianola* and saw a part of her crew engaged "endeavoring to remove the iron." The squadron commander wanted the plate to strengthen the *Benton* and other ironclads that had just passed Vicksburg. The *Mound City*'s task was completed in time to allow the admiral to write an evening report and recommendation to the Navy Department. In it, Porter noted that Hoel's earlier observations on the physical condition of the lost vessel were correct. Wilson had sent down a diver to examine the riverbed next to the hull, where one of the 11-inch cannon was observed by Hoel. The man also found a number of shells lying about the bottom.

Porter acknowledged that it "would be a great comfort" to have the *Indianola* refloated and back in service and so, unrealistically, concluded that "with proper pumps and apparatus" she could be "raised in two hours." Knowing that his squadron did not have the wherewithal to do the job itself, he advised that as quickly as possible "a professional hulk raiser" should be hired and given "liberal compensation" for speed. Washington quickly responded to Porter's request. On May 1 John Lenthal, the chief of the navy's Bureau of Construction, Equipment and Repair ordered Com. Joseph Hull at St. Louis to contract with "competent parties" who could "ascertain if it can be done." If so, he was authorized to "make the most advantageous arrangements to the interest of the service."

The Mississippi Squadron was engaged in heavy action during the three weeks following RAdm. Porter's Washington report on the *Indianola*. At least two major bom-

(Both photographs: Naval History and Heritage Command).

Salvage of the *Indianola*. After elements of the U.S. Mississippi Squadron passed the Vicksburg batteries on April 16, RAdm. Porter immediately dispatched Acting Volunteer Lieutenant William R. Hoel (1825–1879) to the *Indianola* wreck site to conduct a survey. The captain of the ironclad *Pittsburg*, a prewar riverboat pilot and contemporary of Capt. Joseph Brown, the ironclad's builder, concluded his review with the optimistic opinion that "with proper facilities" the wreck "could be raised with but little difficulty." A number of officers were detailed to work on the project, including the captain of the ironclad *Carondelet*, Acting Volunteer Lieutenant John McLeod Murphy (1827–1871), an engineer who was also a naval officer before the war and one-time colonel of New York volunteers. Unfortunately, the vessel would not be refloated until January 5, 1865, at which time she was towed to the Mound City naval yard for disposal.

bardments were carried out in support of Union soldiers (22nd and 27th), with other shelling being intermittent. Still, every major gunboat passing the *Indianola* wreck site during this time was ordered to briefly halt and check its condition as well as the depth of the river around her. On May10 Lt. Cmdr. Elias K. Owen (1834–1877), captain of the *Louisville*, in a postscript to a general report, indicated that the hulk "is nearly high and dry. Her engines are in good condition, save the rust." Regular naval officer Owen retained command of that Pook turtle until the end of the war. Afterwards, he spent two years on special duty at the Mound City Naval Station overseeing the salvage of sunken vessels. He retired in 1876.[11]

Having participated in the bombardments of Vicksburg on May 22, one of the more famous of the Federal river ironclads, the *Carondelet*, was given as her principal duty the salvage of the *Indianola*. The captain of the veteran Pook turtle, Acting Volunteer Lt. John McLeod Murphy (1827–1871), a former navy midshipman, New York City surveyor, and first colonel of the 15th Regiment, New York Volunteer Engineers, had returned to sea service at the beginning of the year. When the *Carondelet* dropped anchor off the *Indianaola's* Hurricane Island wreck site on May 23, it was found that the hulk of Mayor Brown's broken vessel sat up straight in three fathoms of water about 20 yards from shore. The ironclad sent to the rescue was, however, very nearly sinking herself. Twice hit during the previous day's encounter with Vicksburg's water batteries, she required extensive pumping just to keep her afloat. In addition, the gunboat's boilers had not been cleaned for 41 days and it was unsafe to employ them any longer. When an order was received from Porter that night for the ironclad to join her sisters in the continuing bombardment of Vicksburg, Capt. Murphy sent word of his command's precarious condition. Ardently desiring to participate in the city's capture, the one-time army colonel had an even greater wish "not to suffer the well-earned reputation of the *Carondelet* to be diminished while in my hands." With other gunboats available and wishing no harm to come to the historic boat, Porter unofficially withdrew her from further bombardment duties. Stationed as she was at the salvage site off the head of Diamond Island, at New Carthage, the *Carondelet* was able to obtain pumps and make some of her own repairs while refreshing her power plant.

Work on the *Indianola*, meanwhile, was expedited as the fleet's construction chief, Com. Hull at St. Louis, began discussion with the Missouri Wrecking Company (the old salvage firm of James B. Eads) to raise her. A proposal was passed to the company's board by Hull, on behalf of Construction Bureau chief Lenthal, offering the concern $20,000 to raise the hulk and deliver her to St. Louis. Murphy, together with executive officer and acting ensign Oliver Donaldson (?–1866), who had come aboard at commissioning as the *Carondelet*'s carpenter, now began an organized review of the task before them. It was quickly found that there were no leaks in the *Indianola* except for those caused when the pipes in her bottom were severed. In addition, over 1,000 bushels of coal were found in the wreck's bunkers, most of which was usable. Within a few days, the captain had also arranged for the employment of approximately 40 African American contrabands, former slaves who sought Union protection.

On May 25, far away on the East Coast of the Confederacy, Lt. Cmdr. George Brown was paroled. A few days later, on May 31, he wrote to RAdm. Porter detailing his experiences, both with regard to the loss of the *Indianola* and his subsequent stays in eleven different Rebel prisons. He remembered his sojourn in Vicksburg at a time of great heat over the admiral's plans to execute Southern partisans attacking Union shipping. Telling of an interview with Lt. Gen. Pemberton, Brown relayed: "General Pemberton was quite anxious for you to hang someone so he could retaliate on me."

As Maj. Gen. Ulysses S. Grant's ground-pounding advance shoved around the Confederate fortress via the Big Black River, the supply, garrison and staging locations on the northwest side of the Mississippi River above Vicksburg were largely transformed into training and assembly points. A number of depots and hospitals were located close to the Louisiana shoreline. Southern leaders did not realize just how dramatically Grant's line of logistical support was shifting. They continued to believe that his supply route remained down the west bank of the river across from Vicksburg and that it was vulnerable to attack. As a result of this misperception, Richmond passed orders for Lt. Gen. Edmund Kirby Smith, commander of the Confederate Trans-Mississippi Department, to break up what was now a nonexistent supply line. Smith, in turn, ordered Maj. Gen. Richard "Dick" Taylor to mount this attack, to provide succor to Vicksburg, and to cooperate in every way with Lt. Gen. John C. Pemberton. To help carry off the assignment, Maj. Gen. John George Walker's (1821–1893) Texas Division ("Walker's Greyhounds") was assigned to Taylor's command. A career army officer before the war, Walker fled to Mexico after the conflict but was later appointed U.S. consul to Bogota, Columbia, by President Grover Cleveland. As Taylor and Walker approached the Mississippi from the Tensas River they learned that the Yankee supply line from Milliken's Bend was largely history. Still, it was reasoned, if a portion of the Louisiana shore could be captured and held, it might somehow be possible to herd cattle and send other supplies across to Vicksburg's beleaguered garrison.

Shortly before 11:00 p.m. on May 30, War Department special envoy Charles A. Dana (1819–1897), one of the North's leading prewar newspapermen, armed with orders from RAdm. Porter, came aboard the *Carondelet* seeking transport to a meeting with Maj. Gen Nathaniel Banks (Dana would later become editor and part owner of the *New York Sun*). As the request was endorsed by Porter, Murphy readily agreed to provide lift. Executive officer and acting ensign Oliver Donaldson was left in charge of the *Indianola* wreck site. Together with a small party he would begin checking over the hulk's damages. After making a mid-river rendezvous with the steamer taking Dana south, the *Carondelet* continued down to Perkin's Landing, MS, about five miles below James's plantation at New Carthage. Just after she dropped anchor, about 3:00 a.m. on May 31, Col. Richard Owen (1810–1890), commanding the position with a 300-man detachment, was granted permission to come aboard. While shaking hands with Capt. Murphy, the former commander of Camp Morton at Indianapolis and a widely known geologist, breathlessly explained that an attack from a large Confederate force was anticipated and that his communications were cut off. Owen went on to say that he had destroyed as much of the local depot's stores as possible and built an improvised but very light defense behind cotton bales at the river's edge.

After providing cover through the night, Murphy was relieved to see an evacuation steamer, the *Forrest Queen*, arrive about 9:00 a.m. and embark Owen's men. Loading the Union troops was far from finished when, 15 minutes later, a Confederate 1,400-man brigade from Walker's Texas Division "took the field and approached rapidly." The butternuts did not expect to find an ironclad, which quickly opened upon them "with such guns as could be brought to bear." The *Carondelet* bombarded the Southerners for an hour until they retreated. After the Rebels withdrew, the *Forrest Queen*, with Col. Owens' soldiers now all aboard, convoyed by the *Carondelet* up to James's Plantation. That place was also found evacuated, with "most of the negro quarters and outbuildings burning." The ironclad then proceeded up the river, arriving at the Mississippi Squadron anchorage below Vicksburg about 10:00 p.m. After coaling ship, she returned downstream next day.[12]

After her June 1 return to Palmyra Island, the *Carondelet* took no further direct part in the Vicksburg operation. She continued to guard and prepare the *Indianola* wreck for the remainder of the month. On June 13 Com. Hull in St. Louis heard from William C. Buchanan, president of the Missouri Wrecking Company, who indicated that an on-site inspection of the wreck would have to be made before his company could agree to the navy's salvage proposal. Buchanan's top expert "and most competent man," Capt. William Shaw Nelson, Capt. Eads' former partner, would make the trip to the Vicksburg area as soon as possible.

Acting Volunteer Lt. Murphy obtained the services of a group of 37 African American laborers from Turner's plantation at Point Pleasant, as well as the James place. These were fed with rations from the gunboat. They, with his bluejackets, were all to one degree or another busily engaged in the salvage work. With Acting Ensign Donaldson the daily on-scene superintendent, the sailors and day laborers were able to remove the mud from the *Indianola*'s interior, clean existing machinery, exhume a 9-inch cannon, making it ready for transport, and collect great piles of refuse. A considerable amount of coal was identified for reclaimation from the ironclad's bunkers, as well as a coal barge sunk opposite James's plantation.

On June 18 Murphy reported to RAdm. Porter that a clear trench was under construction around the hull of the *Indianola* and the African Americans were removing all portable weight. The New Yorker believed it possible to wait for the river to rise as it normally did toward fall and then to refloat her. Toward the end of the month, Capt. Nelson of the Missouri Wrecking Company visited Porter's flagboat, the *Black Hawk*. There he learned that the *Carondelet* workmen had caulked the *Indianola* hulk and had her ready to float into the river as soon as it rose. Expecting that he might, in fact, be able to get her up without contract assistance, the admiral nevertheless asked the expert to travel to the wreck site, conduct an on-scene inspection, and then report his findings back aboard the *Black Hawk*. Unhappily, and because of the necessities arising from the ongoing siege of Vicksburg, neither Porter nor Nelson was able to find transport to get the St. Louisian down to the *Indianola*, and he was forced to return north without gaining a firsthand impression either of the sunken ironclad or the work being conducted on her hulk by Acting Volunteer Lt. Murphy. When he returned to St. Louis, Nelson, via his company president, informed Com. Hull that, in his professional opinion, the *Indianola* could not be saved by waiting for her to float off. Indeed, if she did get up, "unless proper assistance" was at hand (meaning a Missouri Wrecking Company salvage vessel), she could easily "go into deep water and by some contingency be ultimately lost."

The death throes of Vicksburg continued through what remained of June and into the first days of July. On the fittingly symbolic date of July 4, after a 45-day siege, the fortress city was surrendered. The event, coming with the equally vital retreat of Gen. Robert E. Lee from Gettysburg in Pennsylvania, marked for all to see a reversal of the political tide that was the Confederacy. Like other vessels in the squadron up and down the rivers, the *Carondelet* command fired a 21-gun national salute at high noon.[13]

Just before and immediately after the fall of Vicksburg, Confederate mounted raiders stepped up attacks upon Mississippi River shipping in the area below the former Confederate citadel. Particular efforts were made to interfere with transports bearing supplies for Union posts or troops headed south. Still, the summer proceeded quietly at the *Indianola* wreck site. The heat remained ferocious and the water level declined. It was extremely hot, although the *Carondelet* sailors and the African American workers were able to obtain fresh fruit and poultry from markets and peddlers ashore. Bugs were everywhere. In a letter home, Acting Ensign Jordan confided that flies and mosquitoes were a problem but not nearly as bad as the one created by roaches.

By early August, the gunboat's sick list was down to nine. One of those was Capt. Murphy, who was so ill on Sunday, August 2, that divine services, over which he always presided, had to be cancelled. Fortunately, his bout was passing.

On August 11 an unidentified party of riders believed to be "guerrillas" approached the shore. As it was anticipated that they would attack the camp of the African American workers at the Davis plantation (referred to aboard the *Carondelet* as their "colony"), Capt. Murphy ordered his guns to fire on the men. Simultaneously, a 20-man landing party was sent ashore to see if it could capture any of the graycoats. Two men were taken and subsequently sent up the river.[14]

Late in August, Acting Volunteer Lt. Murphy became ill again. Evacuated to Memphis, he was treated aboard the *Benton* by that vessel's medical staff. There was great concern for Murphy's life and on September 1 he was comforted by the Roman Catholic bishop of Natchez, William Henry Elder, who was visiting in the Tennessee city. The *Carondelet*'s captain received the Eucharist under the special administration of Communion to the dying (Viatcum). The Last Rites were not administered; however, Elder promised to return if that necessity arose. Whatever his illness, Murphy soon appeared stronger. On September 6 he returned to the *Carondelet* onboard the *Forest Rose* (Tinclad No. 9). Unhappily, his improvement did not last and within two weeks he was forced to go on medical leave, this time returning home to recover. RAdm. Porter retained Murphy as commander of the *Carondelet* "on the books" through October. The gunboat's officers did not know the extent of his illness; most expected him back "pretty soon." Acting Ensign James C. Gipson took over the boat pending the skipper's return. Gipson, like Murphy, was popular with the *Carondelet*'s crew. Scott Jordan told his wife that his new captain was a very talented musician: "He can play or sing anything if he can hear it once—and he is always at one or the other unless when asleep." If he had a fault, Jordan confided later, it "is lack of education, which is quite a misfortune to anyone."

Temperatures off Hurricane Island moderated through the fall and the river slowly began to rise. Frost touched the wreck site on the night of October 25. Executive Officer Donaldson was also ill during much of this period, though he did not need to leave the ship. Ensign Jordan was his relief and conducted the gunnery divisions at practice every few days until early December while also overseeing the salvage task. Due to the increasing partisan threat, orders were received restricting the men to the *Carondelet* or the *Indianola* work site.

When in November it became clear that Capt. Murphy would not be back, Gipson was elevated. He would command the boat through January 1864. His popularity with his officers continually increased and he spent much time in the wardroom with them. Gipson often accepted the kind invitation of his subordinates to meals. He informed them that the pleasure of their company was a much happier arrangement than continuously eating alone in the captain's cabin as Murphy, and most gunboat commanders, did. On December 6 their repast included roast racoon, roast beef, Irish mashed potatoes with butter, boiled onions, canned peaches, bread, various sauces, and pumpkin pie.

Minor work on, and protection of, the *Indianola* continued without event under Gipson's eye. As Confederate cavalry and guerrilla attacks intensified along the Mississippi in the fall, RAdm. Porter cautioned that every protection should be taken to prevent a raid upon the sunken gunboat. Gipson, in a November 23, report, noted the removal of everything wooden from within a quarter of a mile of the wreck. Daily scouting parties went ashore to examine all possible approaches and "two negro scouts, mounted, rode backward and forward all the time between here [Hurricane Island] and the cut-off" above. Despite Gipson's precautions, 60 irregular horsemen approached the shore at the Davis plantation on December 11 intent upon destroying the wreck. The *Carondelet* opened fire, causing the Rebels to fade out of sight. To make certain they were gone, the gunboat captain led 30 men ashore toward the spot where the Confederates were seen. As the boat party approached, the riders, visible again, withdrew once more, this time for good. Thereafter, an African American armed guard was posted at the plantation.

On December 19 the *Carondelet* was transferred to the Fifth District (Vicksburg to White River), then under Lt. Cmdr. Robert K. Owen of the *Louisville*. Her work with the *Indianola* completed, the *Carondelet* steamed on December 29 to Skipwith's Landing, where, according to Owen, the locals "appear in constant dread of being attacked." When it was determined that no irregular assaults were about to materialize, the *Carondelet* was sent to Milliken's Bend, 70 miles farther south, on the last day of the year. Meanwhile, the historic ironclad was replaced at the wreck site by her sister, the *Mound City*.[15]

On January 25, 1864, Lt. Cmdr. Byron Wilson was transferred off the *Mound City* and succeeded by Acting Volunteer Lt. Amos R. Langthorne (1832–1877), a Canadian who had joined the U.S. Navy as an acting master in December 1861 and won acclaim for his handling of the light draught *Cricket* (Tinclad No. 6). A shipwright and deepwater mariner by trade, he would reside in Maine after the conflict. Reading himself aboard, the new captain let his crew know that their job was, according to his orders, to "keep a lookout on the *Indianola* and get her afloat when an opportunity occurs." Twelve days later, Langthorne was able to report that significant additional progress had been made in preparation of the sunken ironclad for refloating.

Although some of the work was actually accomplished under the tenures of Gipson and Wilson, the former *Cricket* captain indicated that the *Indianola* was now blocked up "on both sides, bow and stern." Trenches had been dug around her to force water to flow more readily below her and all the seams had been tried, being recaulked where necessary. All the seams in her bottom that could be inspected were found to be in good condition. Additionally, an empty U.S. Navy coal barge found nearby on the riverbank was brought alongside. Work was begun on removing into her all of the loose iron and other debris piled on deck and it was anticipated that this would "assist in floating her very much." The Mississippi was, Langthorne reported, rising at the rate of 14 inches a day and no difficulty was anticipated in floating her. If the river depth continued to deepen, it was expected that "the *Indianola* will be afloat in fifteen days." Following a period of short-time project supervisors, RAdm. Porter made another change on March 1, 1864, placing Acting Volunteer Lt. James Laning (1821–1891), captain of the *Rattler* (Tinclad No. 1), in charge. The experienced light-draught commander would finally see the *Indianola* raised and taken north for repairs.

The longest-serving chief of the ironclad's salvage effort was a Pennsylvania shipwright who signed aboard the ironclad *Essex* in September 1861 and was made stone deaf during the Battle of Fort Henry in February 1862. Remaining with his boat, he participated in the July Vicksburg campaign before he was posted ashore to superintend the construction of the giant ironclads *Lafayette* and *Choctaw*; he was later executive officer of the latter. Given command of the *Rattler* in summer 1863, Laning was ordered to Vicksburg in January 1864 and from there directed by RAdm. Porter to undertake a survey of the *Indianola* wreck site. His work was interrupted in February when his gunboat was required to participate in the repulse of a Confederate attack on Waterproof, LA.

When Laning received Porter's directive, he was off Natchez, MS, coaling. He proceeded up to Hurricane Island, where he relieved the *Mound City* on March 10 and began to exercise his instruction "to take care of the *Indianola* and have her kept in such order that when the river rises she will be floated and be in a condition requiring as little labor as possible to keep her so." It was expected that he would also complete the detailed review requested by his squadron commander in January. For assistance, Laning was authorized to call back for use of the tugboat *Hyacinth*. Reports on activities were to be sent in duplicate, with one set going to the bespectacled local Mississippi Squadron 5th District chief, Lt. Cmdr. James A Greer (1833–1904), who had joined Porter's fleet at the end of 1862, captained the *Benton* during the April-July Vicksburg campaign, and would rise to the rank of rear admiral two decades later.[16]

The Mississippi River began a steady rise around the time that Laning stepped aboard the hulk of the *Indianola* and by March 15 had risen over eight feet. Although a higher rise in the upper rivers (Tennessee, Cumberland, Ohio, etc.) was reported in the St. Louis press on March 9 (the last newspapers to which Laning had access), it was not as dramatic near the wreck site. At least another 13-foot depth would be required before the ironclad could be floated. Over the next month and a half, the water level around the hulk of Mayor Brown's ironclad slowly increased, even as newspapers arriving from the North aboard passing steamers indicated that the upper river conditions were in flood stage. A communication received on May 3 from Lt. Cmdr. Greer suggested that, from what Laning had previously reported, at least six more feet of water would be required to get the *Indianola* off the bottom.

The river level did not grow as steadily as anticipated, while numerous groups of

Confederate horse artillery became quite a scourge to civilian shipping. Needing another speedy light draught for the watery anti-guerrilla patrols being operated by vessels of his district, Lt. Cmdr. Greer, on May 22, ordered Laning temporarily relieved by Acting Volunteer Lt. Lanthorne and the *Mound City*. His *Rattler* would be assigned to the station between Waterproof and Bayou Pierre. For his part, Laning, who had by now completed his detailed review of the *Indianola* and submitted to paper his thoughts (with drawings) of what was required for her launching and reconstruction, requested leave on May 27. The next day, Lt. Cmdr. Greer ordered the *Rattler* to Natchez, leaving protection of the sunken ironclad to the light draught *Forrest Rose* (Tinclad No. 9).

After talking with Laning, Greer wrote to Porter on June 2 asking that the lieutenant's leave be granted and that he be given permission to visit Cairo, IL, to explain his plans to the admiral in person. It was hoped that ascent would be given to raise the ironclad as Laning recommended and that he be placed in charge of the enterprise. It was expected that Laning could complete his leave by the end of the summer, returning to locate facilities needed to make the articles he believed were needed to support the launch. "I cannot close this," Greer finished his report, "without paying tribute to the worth and sterling qualities Captain Laning possesses as an officer." RAdm. Porter readily agreed to Laning's recommendations on June 30 and placed him in charge of raising the *Indianola* and returning her safely to Cairo. On October 1, after Laning had completed his leave, Porter ordered that the *Mound City* return to the wreck site to become the permanent guard ship. Her crew was also expected to assist in launching her when "occasion requires." Laning's gunboat, the *Rattler*, would, of course, also be available to help provide protection and to assist in the launching, though she would on a daily basis be commanded by her executive officer.

Laning and his men worked diligently on readying the *Indianola* throughout the remainder of October. On October 28 Capt. Alexander M. Pennock, acting as temporary squadron commander while Porter was on leave, remarked in a message to his superior that "Mr. Laning is hard at work on the *Indianola*." He also noted that the river level was again beginning to fall.

On November 1 RAdm. Porter exchanged positions, becoming commander of the North Atlantic Blockading Squadron while its chief, Acting RAdm. Samuel Phillips Lee (1812–1897), took over at Cairo. A cousin of Gen. Robert E. Lee, the new fleet boss had extensive blue-water experience and had accompanied RAdm. Farragut to Vicksburg in July 1862.[17] The last commander of the Mississippi Squadron was also impressed with the work of Acting Volunteer Lt. Laning, particularly after reading the latest progress report forwarded by Lt. Cmdr. Greer on October 30. On November 9 Lee wrote directly to Laning informing him that he should consider himself officially detached from the *Rattler* as of October 1. He would henceforth devote his entire effort to launching the *Indianola* and taking her up the Mississippi to the naval yard at Mound City, IL. Laning was authorized to continue drawing rations for himself and his civilian mechanics and other work crews from the *Mound City*. After the sunken ironclad was launched, he was further authorized to apply to nearby district commanders for use of the rams *Avenger* and *Vindicator* as towboats. On the other hand, if he could work out "upon advantageous terms" for tow from private parties, that too would be permitted. Shortly thereafter, the *Avenger* was withdrawn from the offer.

To the great pleasure of everyone on the scene, the *Indianola* was raised and it was found that her hull was "very strong and in excellent condition, scarcely the least injury having been sustained either in the fight or by the long immersion it had undergone." Workers had it caulked by the end of the year. When the water rose sufficiently she was "launched," on January 5, 1865. Under tow of the *Vindicator*, now under the command of Lt. Cmdr. William R. Hoel, the resurrected warship reached the Mound City naval shipyard thirteen days later. When she arrived, Acting Volunteer Lt. Laning notified Acting RAdm. Lee that she drew but "3 feet 9 inches and is perfectly straight and tight."

News of the recovery of the ironclad was well received in naval circles, and was celebrated in the regional Union press. N.O. Delta, celebrating "An Old Warrior" in a Tennessee newspaper hoped that after she was rebuilt the ironclad would have "better luck in the next engagement it participates in." Far to the east off the Cape Fear River, RAdm. Porter, who had taken a special interest reclaiming her from the beginning, wrote a highly complimentary letter of congratulation to Capt. Laning on January 31. "There are triumphs of skill such as you have displayed," the lieutenant's former boss lauded, "as glorious as if the results were from combat." Nearly two years after the *Indianola* was taken by the Confederates, Acting RAdm. Lee also endorsed Laning's work in his own February 20 letter of commendation, written to Secretary Gideon Welles. A copy was sent to the lieutenant with Lee's thanks and a note of regret that the salvage manager had since resigned from the navy. Laning eventually served as president of an Illinois glass manufacturing concern.[18]

Although plans had been made to refurbish the Indianola, the end of the Civil War in April caused them to be shelved. Most of the vessels were ordered dismantled and readied for sale and naval bases were closed until only the one at Mound City was left.

After Acting RAdm. Lee hauled down his pennant and quit the west in early summer, caretakers continued to sell off the equipment, stores, and vessels of the ex-squadron. During this period, local contract Illinois workmen finished stripping the ironclads in ordinary. Armor plate and any items not required elsewhere, and which might show a profit if sold separately, were removed. There was little work to do on the *Indianola*, which remained basically a planked-over hull. Most of the tinclads and auxiliary boats were sold off in August and by the middle of November the remaining once-proud ironclads were little more than hulks.

The year would be truly profitable for one John Riley of St. Louis, a buyer and seller of steamboats and their equipment. A competent man by all accounts, he participated in the August gunboat sales and knew that the navy planned to sell the former ironclads. By November 21 he knew for sure, as their auction was advertised in most of the river papers. That morning, the *St. Louis Daily Missouri Democrat* and *St. Louis Daily Missouri Republican* both advised the public that some of the remaining vessels of the late fleet were going under the gavel. The selling would begin promptly at noon on Wednesday, November 29. All would be sold to the highest bidder, "together with their engines, tackle, and furniture."[19] We do not know for certain exactly how this particular ship sale progressed. It was one of many surplus auctions held around the country during 1865–1867 by the navy and the army Quartermaster Department. Although there are no accounts of it in known diaries or correspondence, and it was not widely

Mound City Naval Station. Although plans had been made to refurbish the *Indianola*, the end of the Civil War in April 1865 caused them to be shelved. On November 29 her hulk was sold to John Riley of St. Louis, MO, for $3,000. Within weeks, what remained of the *Indianola* was broken up for scrap (*Miller's Photographic History of the Civil War*).

covered by the public press, it undoubtedly unfolded much like the August sale, which was fully reported by several newspapers.

The future potential function of the *Indianola* may have been surmised by many of her prospective buyers, who saw the craft either during the war or at the time of the great August auction when they came to bid on other possibilities. Also, since the government was taking rather large losses to be rid of this surplus, the purchasers probably did not anticipate making large bids. One thing is certain, John Riley and his competitors had their financial arrangements completed. The advertisements specifically required that each bidder be able to place a 5 percent down payment on each vessel successfully won, the balance to be paid within a few months.

The morning of the appointed day dawned cold in Mound City; it was now less than a month until Christmas. At Cincinnati, ice was reported in the Ohio River as well as other tributaries. Although they may have had the opportunity over the prior week to inspect the boats and other surplus items, Riley and the other buyers undoubtedly arrived at the naval station fairly early and may even have attended the coal barge sale the day before.[20] The chief auctioneer, Solomon A. Silver, had presided over the August tinclad sale. The no-nonsense salesman, surrounded by naval station staff, gaveled the sale into session at noon. With 21 vessels, including the *Chillicothe* and *Tuscumbia*, and tons of equipment to be sold, a long afternoon was ahead.

It is quite probable that, as at the August sale, the one-time ironclads were unloaded alphabetically. When the name of the *Indianola*, raised with such determination from a Mississippi riverbank, was placed before the buyers, all assembled knew her story well, including the manner in which Joseph Brown had constructed her and her sudden and totally unexpected loss in February 1863. After a short period of back-and-forth, Riley pledged $3,000 and emerged the high bidder. Moving to the closing table, he paid cash and was awarded a bill of sale. Within weeks, what remained of the *Indianola* was broken up for scrap.[21]

6

Tuscumbia: The "Broad Giant" vs. Vicksburg

Nicknamed the "broad giant" from her extreme beam, the *Tuscumbia* was the last of former Alton, IL, mayor Joseph Brown's ironclads to join the war on western waters. By March 1, 1863, when the contractor informed the U.S. Navy the huge gunboat was finished, RAdm. Porter, commander of the Mississippi Squadron, was anxious that she steam down to his fleet anchorage above Vicksburg as soon as possible. It was hoped that she would rendezvous with the gunboat *General Price* at Memphis, TN, within the week and the two could continue downstream together. His desire, however, could not immediately be fulfilled.

Following her departure from her builder's yards at New Albany, IN, the *Tuscumbia*, guided by her pilots Joseph McCammant and Isaac N. Ashten, arrived at the Mississippi Squadron base at Cairo, IL, on March 3. The two river guides were probably not pleased with their working conditions. The vessel's pilothouse, located between the chimneys and above the magazine/shell room passages, was a small forward-mounted vertical structure only large enough to simultaneously hold one pilot and another officer. Protected to a height of four feet by two-inch thick oak planks, it left its occupants exposed.

Fleet Captain Alexander M. Pennock might not have been surprised to find upon greeting her captain, Lt. Cmdr. James W. Shirk, and touring her that *Tuscumbia* was "not prepared to go down." It is unknown whether the ironclad captain informed the base commander about her hull's biggest defect. Ever since he had taken charge, he later noted, it was seen that "she drew more water on the starboard bow and port quarter than she did on the port bow and starboard quarter, showing at once that there was a twist in her hull." In a telegram to navy secretary Gideon Welles, Pennock promised to have his ship outfitters "work day and night to get her off." The cabinet secretary received that same day a wire from Com. Joseph B. Hull, the Western gunboat construction superintendent, admitting that in response to requests from the military for additional escort vessels he had only the *Tuscumbia*, fitting out at Cairo, available for immediate service.

Since its capture in February 1862, Fort Heiman, on the Tennessee River, had been occupied by the U.S. 5th Iowa Cavalry, who held it as part of the Union strategy designed to protect shipping on the Tennessee River. The troops had many adventures (outside the scope of this story) during their tenure. Believing their mission completed, the Federal high command withdrew the horsemen on March 6, 1863. Four days later, at Cairo, IL, Fleet Capt. Alexander M. Pennock received various situational reports. The intelligence of proposed Confederate action along the Tennessee was extracted and was similar to that provided by special War Department commissioner Charles A. Dana to Secretary Edwin Stanton on March 20.

The Department of the Cumberland, Dana reported, had ordered Forts Henry and Heiman abandoned and leveled, as it was no longer believed manning them was essential. What troops had been stationed there could be transferred to, and better employed at, Fort Donelson, 12 miles away, which was being rebuilt to accommodate up to 3,000 men and 14 cannon. But before this could be accomplished, Confederate troops occu-

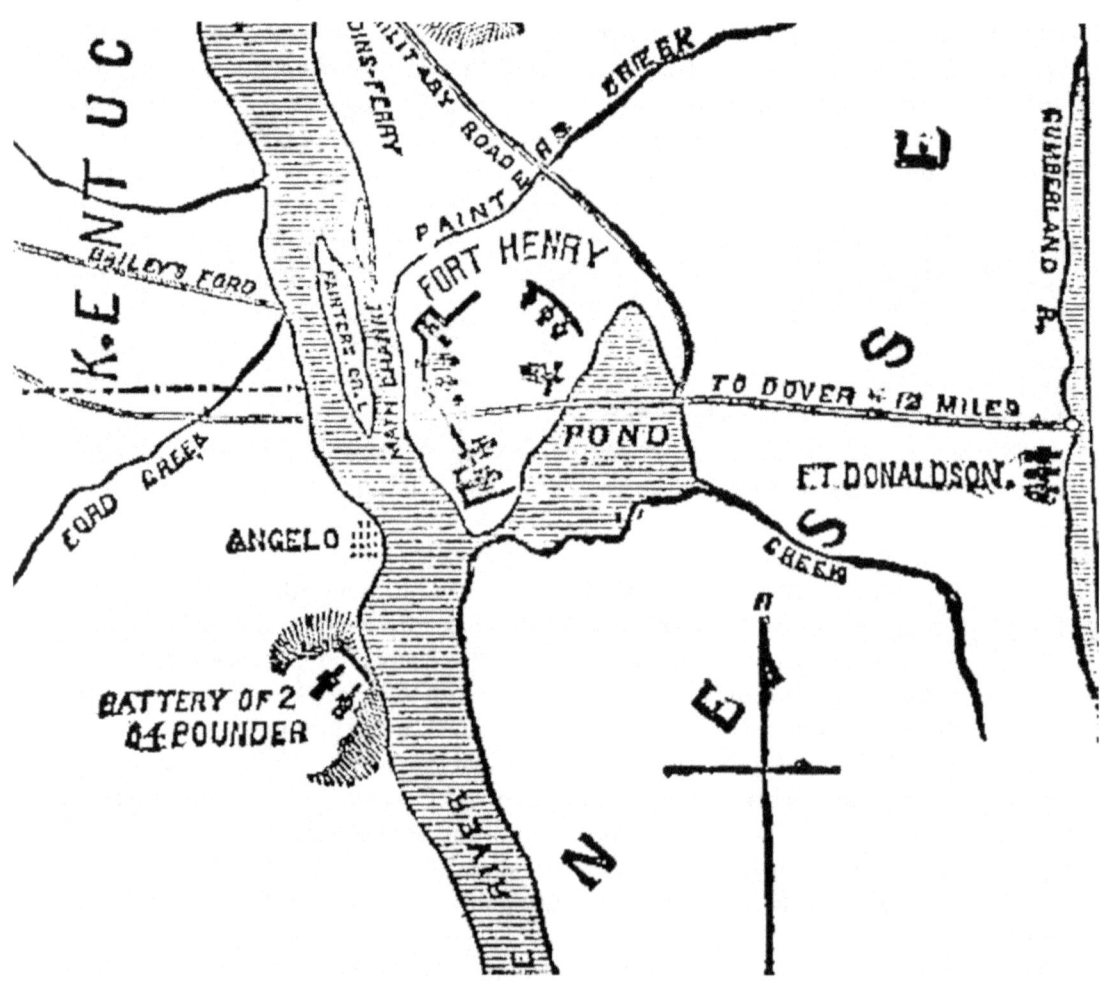

Fort Heiman. Commissioned on March 12, 1863, the last of the Brown-built ironclads, *Tuscumbia* (known as the "Broad Giant") was dispatched to protect the U.S. Army reoccupation of Fort Heiman on the Tennessee River. Directly across from Fort Henry, the outpost was abandoned by the Union and then reoccupied by Confederate forces in late winter. This Civil War map labels the site location as home to a two-gun battery. The *Tuscumbia*'s first mission completed, the huge ironclad returned to base on March 17 (*New York Herald*, February 8, 1862).

pied Fort Heiman. Out in Memphis, Sixth Corps commander Mjr. Gen. Stephen A. Hurlbut received information on the matter from Brig. Gen. Alexander Asboth (1811–1868), a one-time Hungarian freedom fighter who was now post commander at Columbus, KY. Both men, especially the latter, believed Heiman was a key to the protection of Columbus as well as Paducah. In anticipation of a consequential U.S. Army move back to Heiman, elements of the U.S. Navy were required in the Tennessee.

On March 12 Mjr. Gen. Hurlbut ordered Brig. Gen. Asboth to reoccupy Fort Heiman. As he stepped off, Asboth wired Capt. Pennock asking what the navy could do to help and wondering if the "gunboats from Smithland [are] already ascending the Tennessee?" Actually, the tinclads employed to regularly escort convoys had yet to depart, either as guard ships or as a relief force. In the meantime, in anticipation of possible trouble, the fleet captain decided to send the brand new *Tuscumbia*, under Lt. Cmdr. Shirk, up to Paducah, where she could enter the Tennessee to add her firepower if necessary. Notice was sent to Memphis that the newcomer would be delayed two or three days.

En route on her first wartime assignment, the *Tuscumbia* conducted gunnery and other drills under the watchful eye of her captain, her executive officer, Acting Master Augustus S. Tayon, and Shirk's aide, Acting Assistant Paymaster George A. Lyon (1837–1914). Young Acting Ensign Thomas M. Farrell seemed a quick study with the 11-inch Dahlgren mounted on the port side of the forward casemate; the other big guns, fore and aft, were overseen by Acting Ensigns Lewis Kenney, James Marshall, and A.H. Edson, with participation by Acting Master's Mate Ernest. M. Clark.

We know nothing of the life stories of Tayon, Kenney, Marshall, Edson, or Clark. Tayon was appointed to his rank on October 1, 1862, and would resign on June 16. Lyon, a Philadephia lawyer before the war, had transferred aboard from the timberclad *Lexington*. Sent to the North Atlantic Blockading Squadron in December, he would remain in the navy until 1899, retiring with the effective rank of rear admiral. Farrell joined the North Atlantic Blockading Squadron in April 1861 and transferred west at the beginning of 1863. He held command of the light draught *Linden* (Tinclad No. 10) from June until February 1864 and of the light draught *Peri* (Tinclad No. 57) from July 1864 until the spring of 1865. He lived in Harlem, NY, after the war.

Overseeing the engine room was Chief Engineer John W. Hartupee (1825–1886), together with his subordinates, Acting First Assistant Engineer Perry South, Acting Second Assistant Engineer William J. Milligan, and Acting Third Assistant Engineer Oliver Gough. Joining the boat later would be Acting First Assistant Engineer Joseph Hilliard. New Hampshire native Dr. Frederick E. Potter (1839–1902) was in charge of the *Tuscumbia*'s medical department. An 1859 University of Vermont medical school graduate, he was appointed an acting assistant surgeon upon the outbreak of the Civil War. After service with the South Atlantic Blockading Squadron, he transferred to the Mississippi Squadron, where he served until the war concluded. Potter remained in the sea service until 1876, after which he was a Portsmouth, NH, physician.

The giant craft was commissioned that very day before departing Cairo. Interestingly, at the same time, Com. Hull in St. Louis had received permission from USN Construction Bureau chief John Lenthal to transfer her to the Mississippi Squadron if she was finished "as represented." Leading a troop transport, the *Tuscumbia* departed the

Kentucky community early on March 13. The Tennessee River was very high at this time and, as had been the case in February 1862, Fort Henry was largely flooded. Fort Heiman, across the river on higher ground, was dry but actually unoccupied. Although the *Tuscumbia* had a design speed of 10 mph, she was slower going upstream than any of the Federal tinclads and so was quickly overtaken by a trio of smaller warships also ordered to join in the relief expedition. Within a short period, the five vessels were joined by two additional troop steamers carrying Gen. Asboth, his men, and artillery.

On the morning of March 14 a number of Rebels along the banks fired on the Yankee armada as it approached, "but the first shell from the gunboats made them run." Several local citizens later reported Confederates were lurking about "outback in the country." Asboth's soldiers reoccupied Fort Heiman without opposition under the guns of the fleet. Later in the day, the general wrote to Lt. Cmdr. Shirk thanking him for his assistance and promising to "follow the rebels up the bluffs behind Fort Heiman, where your shots forced them away." He closed with his personal appreciation and his hopes "to hear glorious news from the *Tuscumbia* before Vicksburg."

Upon completion of a tinclad sweep up the Tennessee on the morning of March 17, the *Tuscumbia* was able to depart the waters off Fort Heiman and return to Cairo, leaving protection of the earthworks to the light draughts and soldiers.[1] On March 27, as the *Tuscumbia* was making her way south from Memphis, RAdm. Porter and several of his Pook turtles returned from the unsuccessful Steele's Bayou Expedition, a Federal effort to outflank the northern defenses of Vicksburg. What some called the most romantically colored adventure of the campaign was over. With the nearly simultaneous failure of the Yazoo Pass Expedition, the North realized that advances

Lt. Cmdr. James Shirk. The veteran captain of the timberclad gunboat *Lexington,* Shirk (1832–1873) was given command of the *Tuscumbia* on January 13, 1863. An Erie County native, Shirk had led his timberclad in the April 1862 Battle of Shiloh, the June White River Expedition, and the Chickasaw Bayou campaign in December. Later in 1863 he would take over the Mississippi Squadron's Seventh District, serving on the Tennessee River and becoming the longest-serving officer in unit history. He died of pneumonia while on Washington, D.C., duty (Naval History and Heritage Command).

Opposite: *Tuscumbia* **Configuration.** Delayed by her sojourn to Fort Heiman, the newly finished "Broad Giant" was able to reach Vicksburg on March 26, 1863. Here sailors from the Mississippi Squadron, already having seen her sisters *Chillicothe* and *Indianola,* were amazed to see her extreme beam. Many officers had a chance to visit onboard, where they were shown her five giant cannon and reviewed her configuration. The noted naval vessel plan expert David Meagher here shows us in detail the *Tuscumbia*'s layout.

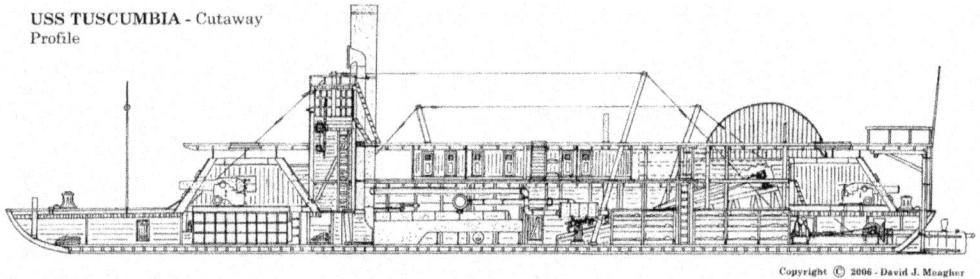

Cutaway Profile.

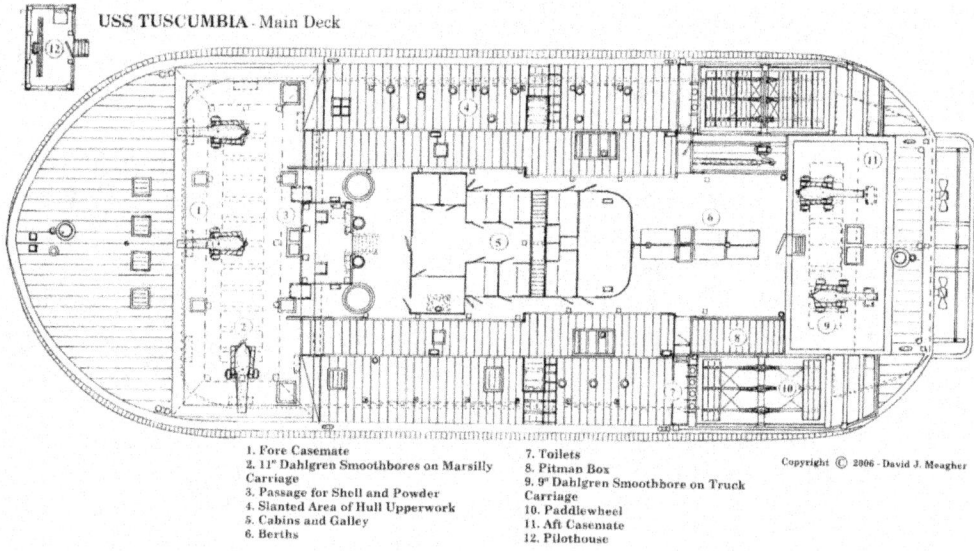

1. Fore Casemate
2. 11" Dahlgren Smoothbores on Marsilly Carriage
3. Passage for Shell and Powder
4. Slanted Area of Hull Upperwork
5. Cabins and Galley
6. Berths
7. Toilets
8. Pitman Box
9. 9" Dahlgren Smoothbore on Truck Carriage
10. Paddlewheel
11. Aft Casemate
12. Pilothouse

Main Deck.

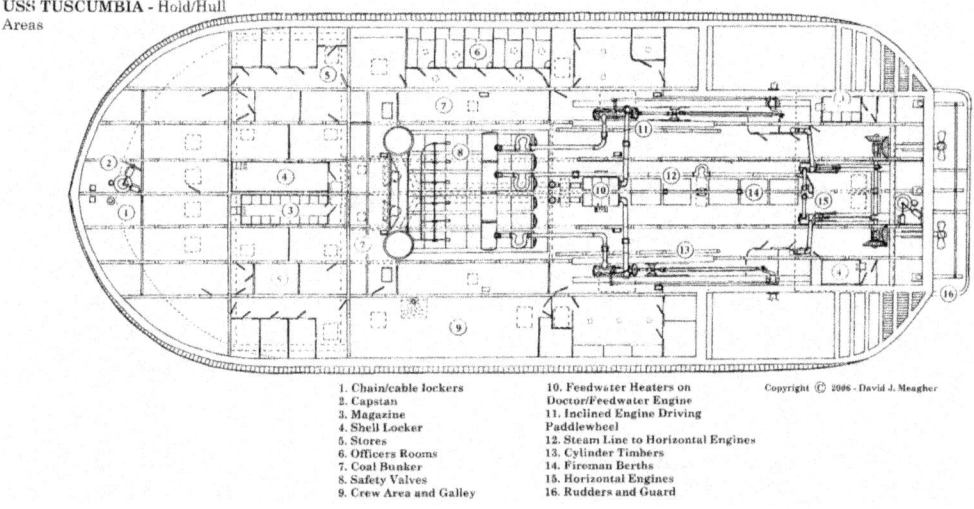

1. Chain/cable lockers
2. Capstan
3. Magazine
4. Shell Locker
5. Stores
6. Officers Rooms
7. Coal Bunker
8. Safety Valves
9. Crew Area and Galley
10. Feedwater Heaters on Doctor/Feedwater Engine
11. Inclined Engine Driving Paddlewheel
12. Steam Line to Horizontal Engines
13. Cylinder Timbers
14. Fireman Berths
15. Horizontal Engines
16. Rudders and Guard

Hold/Hull Areas (all photographs ©2006, David J. Meagher; used with permission).

upon the Confederate citadel via the Yazoo Delta were impossible. Their next question was how best the 60,000 bluecoats now in camps stretching 60 miles from Young's Point to Lake Providence, LA, could get into action against the Rebels across the Mississippi.

As sailors aboard the *Chillicothe* and *Baron de Kalb* made repairs after their ordeal in Yazoo Pass and those aboard Porter's Steele's Bayou ironclads did likewise, the *Tuscumbia* reached the Mississippi Squadron anchorage at the mouth of the Yazoo River on the afternoon of March 28. The downstream voyage had been glorious; azalea and dogwoods were in full bloom and the spring-like weather was warmer than many of the bluejackets aboard had experienced in months. After dropping anchor near the other assembled Union ironclads, Lt. Cmdr. Shirk was immediately summoned on board the fleet flagboat *Black Hawk*. There he was brought up to speed on the local situation and his vessel was assigned to the second division of ironclads RAdm. Porter had formed back in January.

Washington was aware of the change of season; the improvements seen in weather meant that the spring campaigning season could open. A message was duly dispatched from the War Department inquiring whether or not the Army of the Tennessee might somehow do something to aid the Department of the Gulf forces advancing on the fortress city of Port Hudson, LA, or, at the very least, destroy the growing Confederate chokepoint at Grand Gulf, MS, 30 miles below the guns at Warrenton. To accomplish this, it went almost without saying that some sort of combined operation would be required.

Warming to the possibilities of an approach other than the Yazoo Delta, Maj. Gen. Grant checked his maps for another way to pass Vicksburg and saw that it would be possible to march down the west bank of the Mississippi from Milliken's Bend to New Carthage, 15 miles below the Rebel batteries at Warrenton. Going another 15 miles down, they could come to a point opposite Grand Gulf, which was strategically located between Vicksburg and Port Hudson. Once the batteries atop the Grand Gulf bluffs were silenced, the military could be ferried across, take the fortifications, and march on Port Hudson or Vicksburg.

The developing Grant-Porter team was nothing if not innovative. Only two days after the ironclads returned to their anchorage from Steele's Bayou, the former was penning the latter proposing "one or two vessels be put below Vicksburg" in order to "insure a landing on the east bank for our forces." On his own, Grant dispatched soldiers overland down the Louisiana shore to scout out and begin opening a way to New Carthage, not far from the *Indianola* wreck site.

RAdm. Porter, meanwhile, was taking some heat from the Navy Department for the naval failures in the Yazoo Delta, as well as the earlier loss of the *Indianola* and several rams sent past the Vicksburg batteries. For a variety of reasons, he was extremely dubious of Grant's latest plan, as he later noted in a letter to navy assistant secretary

Opposite: **Vicksburg and the Mississippi River** The area of the Vicksburg campaign is shown in this contemporary map, with the "Big Muddy" extending from north of the mouth of the Yazoo River down past Grand Gulf. The *Tuscumbia*'s entire operational career from February to July 1863 would take place in this location (Library of Congress).

6—*Tuscumbia*: The "Broad Giant" vs. Vicksburg 235

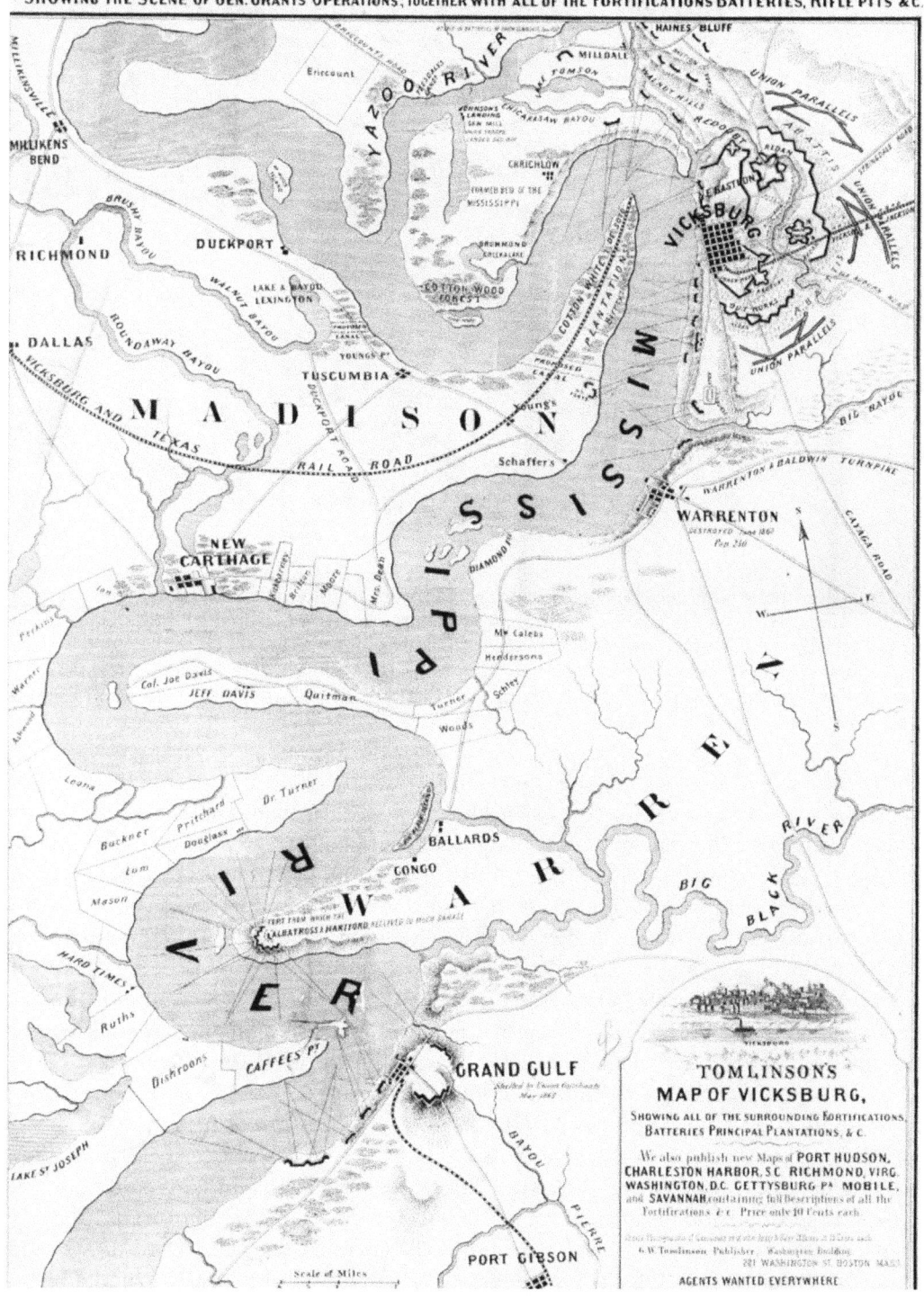

De Soto Peninsula This geographical feature was a three-mile-long peninsula formed by a twist in the Mississippi River before Vicksburg. Here Federal forces attempted to build a canal that would take them below the city's defenses across usually soggy ground that also provided basing. Some idea of the position can be seen in this contemporary illustration that looks across to De Soto Point and the peninsula beyond from the northern Mississippi shore above Vicksburg (*Harper's Weekly*, July 25, 1863).

Gustavus Vasa Fox. After all, the navy-army track record on combined operations around Vicksburg, albeit most of them had been in the Yazoo Delta, was not good. Indeed, Maj. Gen. Sherman and most of the corps commanders were opposed to Grant's thinking on operating below. Still, Porter was ready to support Grant's next plan. When the general wrote him on March 29 asking for ironclads to support half a dozen USQM support transports he planned to run by the city's guns, the reluctant squadron chief put away his doubts and promised to help, knowing full well that if he lost his fleet because of military miscalculation, the blame would, in the eyes of Washington, be his. Gideon Welles was bluntly in favor of going ahead—"The Department wishes you to occupy the river below Vicksburg"—and that was the way of the sea service.

Just to make certain that Grant, whom he had already assessed as an outstanding leader, understood the magnitude of what would or could happen, the fleet commander pointed out that his roll of the dice for a cross-river crossing would have to be total. Getting the ironclads past the Vicksburg batteries would not be too difficult, he imagined, but getting back upriver for any reason was a problem. None of Porter's heavy craft could make safe speed upstream against the current and if they tried they would be under Vicksburg's gun for a fatal length of time. On top of that, there would be no easy way for his task force to be resupplied, as Grant's quartermasters, via steamer, barge, or wagon, would have to supply every shell and lump of coal.[2]

To help firm up his decision to move down the Mississippi instead of up the Yazoo (and to make certain that he and Porter were not making an irrevocable decision in running big ironclads downstream), Maj. Gen. Grant arranged with his navy counterpart on April 30 to personally participate in an armed waterborne reconnaissance of the Confederate Yazoo River defenses the next day. At 8:00 a.m. on Tuesday, April 1, the *Tuscumbia* hove up anchor and headed up the Yazoo, in company with the light draught *Linden* (Tinclad No. 10).

As luck would have it, the Confederates at the river's main rebel defenses on Snyder's Bluff were also alert. A giant raft guarding the approaches had been damaged, forcing the men to become more vigilant. In addition to that concern, the soldiers, mostly from Louisiana, defending the post now received intelligence, confirmed by a signal gun, that the enemy warship activity had increased on the river below, with some believing them headed up their way. As Sgt. William H. Tunnard (1837–1916) of the 3rd Louisiana remembered years later, this alert occasioned a great deal of excitement and broke up "the usual monotony of camp life." As the men "eagerly" hastened to their posts, others, including officers, repaired to the brow of the hill to watch the Federal approach.

Grant Decides Warming to the possibilities of an approach other than those failing in the Yazoo Delta, Maj. Gen. Grant came to understand that it would be possible to march his soldiers down the west bank of the Mississippi from Milliken's Bend to New Carthage, 15 miles below the Rebel batteries at Warrenton. Going another 15 miles down, they could come to a point opposite Grand Gulf, which was strategically located between Vicksburg and Port Hudson. Once the batteries atop the Grand Gulf bluffs were silenced, the military could be ferried across, take the fortifications, and march on Port Hudson or Vicksburg. For his part, RAdm. Porter cautioned that once his ironclads were below the Confederate citadel, they would not be able to return north against the river current (Library of Congress).

A cloud of increasingly dense black smoke rolling above the treetops was visible to the people on Snyder's Bluff and marked the Union progress. Just after 10:00 a.m. the Mississippi Squadron flagboat *Black Hawk*, coming over from Young's Point and mistaken by the Southerners for a transport, landed at Johnson's Plantation, making rendezvous with the *Tuscumbia*, the *Linden*, and the *General Sterling Price* newly arrived off that location. Having made earlier arrangements, Maj. Gen. Grant, with Maj. Gen. Sherman and Maj. Gen. Richard "Uncle Dick" Oglesby (1824–1899), hosted by RAdm. Porter, went aboard a tugboat that transferred them to Lt. Cmdr. Shirk's huge ironclad a few minutes later. Oglesby, an Illinois Republican legislator before the war and a governor after the war, was acquainted with Grant from the earliest days of the war when both were in Cairo. Wounded at Corinth in October and just now returning to duty, Oglesby commanded the left wing of Grant's XVI Corps. Fred Grant had accompanied his father, the commanding general, up to Johnson's aboard the *Black Hawk*, but was not permitted join him on the big ironclad.

As soon as Porter and his guests were aboard, the *Tuscumbia*, escorted by the *General Sterling Price*, stood up the river. About noon, the two Union gunboats arrived in the waters below Drumgould's Bluff, a component of the Snyder's Bluff salient, which most of the Federals now referred to as Haynes' Bluff. In order to test the Rebel defenses, the ironclad moved slowly up and then, sheltered by a strip of woods on the adjacent bank, threw two shells at the Southern works from her starboard bow guns and two from her port side. The gunboat's shots were directed at those spots where masked batteries were suspected to be located. Sgt. Tunnard believed them to be badly aimed, as "they passed harmlessly over the men, exploding in the air, without injuring a single man." Disgusted at being unable to force a Rebel response, the Northern admiral later informed Secretary Gideon Welles "the enemy would not gratify our curiosity." Porter expected that the lack of Confederate response was designed to "get us among the torpedoes," this stretch of river being not too far above where the *Cairo* was sunk by a Rebel "infernal device" the previous December. As the minutes ticked away, Grant and his generals, with Porter and the ironclad's officers, aimed their spyglasses at the frowning fortifications ahead of them, debating among themselves the practicability of effecting a landing with a large amphibious force. Within 50 minutes, the soldiers had determined all they could regarding the hillsides and Porter ordered the boats to turn about down the river.

Aside from the uncooperative Confederates, the admiral was faced with another problem that perhaps his visitors had not noticed. In the course of coming downstream from Cairo and now this firing, the deck over the boilers of the *Tuscumbia* had dropped down about seven inches and her bottom rose ("hogging"), a not uncommon but serious structural defect. The deck in question now rested on the safety valves, while two of the fore-and-aft string pieces (girders) rested upon the steam drum. Similar to a structural problem experienced with the ironclad *Eastport*, it would be difficult to resolve with the means available to the squadron off the mouth of the Yazoo, though every effort would be made to strengthen her with what was on hand.

Porter was not pleased with his experience of being aboard Mayor Brown's creation the first time she sortied in the Vicksburg theater. She was, he apprised Secretary Welles, "to all appearances ... as strong as wood and iron can make her." But, he worried, "if

Reconnaissance. To check on the defenses of Snyder's Bluff, on the Yazoo River north of Vicksburg, Maj. Gen. Grant and RAdm. Porter, together with several other military leaders, went aboard the *Tuscumbia* on the morning of April 1, 1863. The mighty vessel, shown here underway, steamed up the Yazoo to a location, below the Southern defenses, from which she could open fire. Seeking a rebel response, the ironclad moved slowly up and then, sheltered by a strip of woods on the adjacent bank, threw two shells at the Southern works from her starboard bow guns and two from her port side. The gunboat's shots were directed at those spots where masked batteries were suspected. Disgusted at being unable to force the Southerners to shoot back at them, the Northern admiral later informed navy secretary Gideon Welles "the enemy would not gratify our curiosity..." (Naval History and Heritage Command).

she drops her deck owing to the firing of five guns, I do not know what she will do in action."

As the *General Sterling Price* exited, she, too, tossed several shells at the Southerners and these likewise went unanswered. The Southerners at Snyder's were left scratching their collective heads, unable to fathom a single clue "as to the purpose of this sudden visit."

It was 1:45 p.m. when the *Tuscumbia* and her consort returned to Johnson's Plantation, where the military leadership team went ashore to confer further. It was clear that Porter's agreement to help support any move below would be not only necessary, but, it was supposed, in passing Vicksburg's supposed formidable batteries, it would also be one of the great gambles of the war. Two hours later, the *Black Hawk* and *Tuscumbia*, accompanied by the *Linden*, returned to Young's Point, where they arrived not long after 5:00 p.m. The mission was apparently not widely discussed by the Yankee journalists of the "Bohemian Brigade." Franc (writing as "Galway") Wilkie of the *New York Times*, one of the most perceptive, did not even learn about it until the following Saturday. His next column thereafter mentions only that she tried the range of her guns and "met with no response," probably because the "rebels are evidently sparing of their ammunition."

Next day, Grant wrote to Porter admitting that he was now fully convinced "that an attack on Haynes' Bluff would be attended with immense sacrifice of life, if not defeat." He also revealed in writing to his sea service partner that he had ordered Maj. Gen. John A. McClernand, Lincoln friend, Grant enemy, and commander of the XIII Corps, to take and garrison New Carthage. Having determined to operate from that town over the river to either Warrenton or Grand Gulf, Grant emphasized the importance of keeping the Confederates from further fortifying either of those locations. He thought that once New Carthage was in hand a single corps "with the aid of two gunboats" could take and hold Grand Gulf until he could get the whole army there. To that end, Porter was once more asked to prepare to run past Vicksburg's guns as soon as possible. Grant would, meanwhile, organize or encourage a number of regional diversions to help focus Southern attention elsewhere and his quartermasters would undertake, upon the navy's success, to likewise send down unarmed supply steamers.

Getting Lt. Gen. Pemberton and his people to look elsewhere would not be a big problem. Already, the chief of the Confederate Department of Mississippi and East Tennessee had more than enough problems landing on his Jackson desk. Activities at Grand Gulf, Port Hudson, Grenada, Columbus and other Magnolia State and Pelican State points—as well as reports of Federal activities at Memphis and on the Mississippi, in addition to Vicksburg—fought for attention alongside logistical concerns. The commander of the Vicksburg garrison wrote to report on the previous day's Union gunboat reconnaissance to Snyder's Bluff. "After throwing a few shells," he summarized, "they retired." There were presently nine Federal gunboats off the mouth of the Yazoo, but they were there, the city's top military man believed, "to divert our attention from operations *above* [italics added] by making demonstrations against Vicksburg and Snyder's." Hopeful suspicion was mounting in Rebel headquarters that the Lincolnites would soon be moving north back to Memphis, from which Grant would send reinforcements to bolster the Federal army in Middle Tennessee. This idea was amplified by newspaper correspondents repeating them for readers across the South.

That night a member of Grant's staff arrived in Memphis and was immediately interviewed by Assistant Secretary of War Dana. The commander of the Army of the Tennessee, his subordinate reported, had absolutely no intention of either withdrawing the bulk of his army from Vicksburg or making a direct attack either on the city or Haynes' Bluff. Movement below the city was now contemplated and included not only the construction of a new canal from Duckport Landing but also the possibility of floating empty supply steamers past Vicksburg's batteries to a point below, from which point they could be employed to cross the Mississippi. News of the official abandonment of the Yazoo Pass Expedition was now also received and forwarded to Washington. His informant, like most army officers on the expedition, blamed the expedition commander, and especially the captain of the *Chillicothe*, for not taking sufficient ammunition at the outset.[3]

On April 2, Maj. Gen. Grant set in motion his new plan to capture Vicksburg from below. Requests were sent to St. Louis and Cairo for additional tugboats and transports, while engineers began widening a new road down the Louisiana shore leading to New Carthage. Some 20,000 XIII Corps men would soon begin marching over it. Grant and Porter met at Milliken's Bend, LA, on April 4 to further review the idea of moving down the great river and crossing it below. RAdm. Porter and the naval captains of the Mississippi Squadron all knew that it would be impossible to steam past Vicksburg and adequately cover Grant's army, let alone battle the Grand Gulf fortifications, with only the one or two gunboats requested. Rather, such a move would require them to take the heaviest ironclads available.

The bearded naval boss, who had been attempting to ascertain for months the exact number of cannon mounted along the 3.5-mile defenses stretched before Vicksburg, made it clear that the number was significant, requiring many more ironclads than just two make the trip down. Additionally, the fortifications at Grand Gulf were no less a tough nut to crack than those faced at Fort Donelson, TN, almost at the war's beginning. Although Porter did not have an exact cannon count for the Vicksburg River Batteries, historians quickly gained one, which was well refined in time for the centennial of the conflict. Mounted in the Upper, Middle, and Lower Batteries under the command of Col. Edward Higgins (1821–1875), the former artillery commander of Forts Jackson and St. Philip at New Orleans, were 37 big guns and 13 field pieces. These guns were located to take advantage of the De Soto Bend turbulence, which often impacted steamers passing through those waters, sometimes forcing them to circle off course. Although single vessels like the *Indianola* had managed to slip by them, Confederate defenders believed that wartime experience to date had adequately demonstrated that Union ironclads were vulnerable to the lethal damage of plunging fire. If a whole fleet appeared, they were confident it could be sunk.

The Upper Batteries, under Col. Andrew Jackson III's (1834–1906) 1st Tennessee Heavy Artillery Regiment, comprised six batteries, including two of the three most powerful along the entire line: the Water Battery and the Wyman's Hill Battery. Both were mounted about 30–40 feet above the water. The Middle Batteries of Maj. Frederick Ogden (1837–1886) contained just two batteries, while Lt. Col. Daniel Beltzhoover's (1826–1870) Lower Batteries, manned by the 1st Louisiana Heavy Artillery, comprised several batteries, including the powerful Marine Hospital Battery and the unusual banded and rifled 18-pounder "Whistling Dick," identified by the odd sound made by its shells as they flew though the air. Less than half a mile below the latter was perhaps the most interesting 5-gun iron defender, the Widow Blakely Battery, its principal piece being a 7.44-inch Blakely Rifle, the only one of its type in the theater. Five miles below Vicksburg at the town of Warrenton was a casemate cotton-bale battery. Extremely strong, it was, in the words of Warren Grabau, "covered with logs and sheathed with railroad iron, which in turn was covered with earth." Surprisingly, however, little is known of its armament. It certainly contained no heavy cannon, its cannon being mainly four Parrott rifles.

The Water, Wyman's Hill, and Marine Hospital batteries enjoyed the advantage of being dug in lower in the Vicksburg cliffs, making it less likely that ships passing close inshore could avoid their wrath. The barrels of the guns mounted higher up atop the cliffs had often to be depressed to reach such targets. Gun barrels not perpendicular could suffer "starts" (projectiles sliding ahead of powder charges), thereby reducing range and accuracy. For his part, Maj. Gen. Grant explained how he would march the Army of the Tennessee below and, once across the Mississippi, "would endeavor to turn Vicksburg and get to Jackson by a very practicable route." The two agreed that Porter would "pass the batteries of Vicksburg with most of the fleet."

Grant originally wanted to have six USQD steamers run the gauntlet. Reason prevailed as the initial scheme was deemed too dangerous. After discussion, the number of transports was halved. Only supplies such as rations and forage would be carried aboard the trio, no fighting soldiers. A number of barges would also accompany the fleet. Those loaded with coal would be lashed to gunboats or towed by steamers, while one with ammunition would be started later and allowed to drift separately with the current. As the U.S. Army started its own preparations, the navy off the mouth of the Yazoo did the same for a dangerous river descent. The eventual task force assembled would comprise both naval gunboats and army transports. To assist the busy army command, Porter also assumed responsibility for preparing and supervising the trio of USQM steamers.

In order to make certain that matters above Vicksburg could be addressed, the vessels of the lower Mississippi Squadron were now divided into two task forces. It was decided to retain at the mouth of the Yazoo the flagboat *Black Hawk*, the powerful new ironclad *Choctaw*, two Pook turtles, and all of the available tinclads and other auxiliaries. While all of this was going on, outwardly the situation with the vessels of the Federal armada appeared unchanged. As far as anyone knew, the major warships were more concerned with a large Confederate ironclad reportedly being constructed at Yazoo City than with the situation with Grant's army. On April 8, Franc ("Galway") Wilkie of the *New York Times* informed his readers that the "gunboats 'over there' in the mouth of the Yazoo" had their bows pointed up that stream, "like so many eager terriers with their noses at a rat-hole waiting for the animal to come out."

Accompanying Porter in the second group would be his flagboat for this operation, the *Benton*, followed by, in order, Capt. Walke's new *Lafayette*, and the turtles *Louisville*, *Mound City*, *Pittsburg*, and *Carondelet*. The tug *Ivy* would be tied to the starboard beam of the *Benton*, while the ram *General Price* was added as a counterweight to the side of the *Lafayette* and coal barges lashed to the starboard sides of the other gunboats, all "so arranged that they can be easily cut adrift." The ironclad *Tuscumbia* with her barge would bring up the rear following the three army steamers. It was hoped that the certain engagement between the ironclads and Rebel batteries would produce enough smoke to let the transports slip by largely unseen and untargeted.

RAdm. Porter issued secret written orders concerning preparations on April 10. When Lt. Cmdr. Shirk received his aboard the *Tuscumbia*, he learned that a night passage would be made past the Vicksburg and Warrenton batteries as soon as bad weather abated and that his vessel would have an important role to play in its success.

As was his way, the squadron commander's general order was quite specific. Union bluejackets, and their counterparts on the contract military steamers, were directed to make their boats as safe as possible, particularly their vulnerable machinery spaces. Hundreds of cotton bales (some captured up Steele's Bayou), some compressed, and numerous heavy logs were placed around the engines and boilers and other dangerous spots. Hay bales (useful later as animal feed) were also stacked about thinly armored portions of the decks, and heavy chains were also draped over the casemates. Sandbags were also stuffed around magazines and into spaces too small for cotton or hay. The hatch leading to the shell room and magazine passages was of particular concern. It had been located directly behind the large gun port in the center of the forward turret, abaft the center Dahlgren and below the pilothouse and steering wheel. If an enemy shell made it through that opening into either of the special storage spaces, the boat could be blown to atoms.

Getting by the batteries undetected for as long as possible required a minimum noise level—something steamboats, with their high-pressure engines, were not noted for at the time. In discussing the gambit with his superior a few days earlier, Capt. Henry Walke had pointed out that during his run by Island No. 10 a year earlier he had successfully muffled the *Carondelet* by diverting the exhaust steam from her engines into her wheelhouse. Porter ordered all captains to adopt this measure and added to it by directing that all livestock be sent ashore, particularly noisy chickens and dogs.

Remembering the cruise past the Vicksburg batteries made by RAdm. Farragut's ships the previous June-July and having received continuous input from several of his captains, including the *Pittsburg*'s famous prewar civilian steamboat captain, Acting Volunteer William Hoel, Porter passed along specific sailing directions. After casting off, the task force's dark monsters were to move slowly, keeping station single file with at least 50 yards separating one boat from the next. To help avoid collisions, everyone would steer a course in the wide river just slightly aport of the boat ahead. After coming around the point of De Soto Peninsula, the task force was to hug the Louisiana shore, hoping to take advantage of its dark levee, trees, and shoreline shadows. The admiral went on to direct that, as they departed and moved down, the

Porter Begins Preparations. Following the Snyder's Bluff reconnaissance, Maj.Gen. Grant and RAdm. Porter confirmed the necessity of moving against Vicksburg from below the citadel. Following an April 4 meeting, the U.S. Navy fashioned its support plan. In order to make certain that matters above Vicksburg could be addressed, the vessels of the lower Mississippi Squadron were divided into two task forces. It was decided to retain at the mouth of the Yazoo the flag boat *Black Hawk*, the powerful new ironclad *Choctaw*, two Pook turtles, and all of the available tinclads and other auxiliaries. The remaining ironclads, a gunboat, and three transports would make the dash. To encourage the civilian trio, the *Tuscumbia* was assigned to bring up the rear (Library of Congress).

gun ports of the eight warships were to be closed so that any light could not be seen from shore. When abreast of the town where combat was expected to start none were to open fire until they could do so safely without endangering either their pilots or the other gunboats. None were to fire their bow guns while abreast of Vicksburg.

Prior to departure, the guns were to be set to fire out to a range of 900 yards, which was expected to be sufficient for shells, and sometimes grapeshot, to reach enemy rifle pits and field artillery. This move was taken because the boats would be darkened and their gun crews would have to "work the guns without light on the decks." Such a storm of untargeted fire should be sufficient to suppress light harassing fire such as snipers firing at gun ports. Once engaged, the fleet was to shape course across the river and steam as close to the Mississippi shoe as possible. No vessel was to open fire until fired upon, but once the Confederates "opened the ball," it was every boat for herself. The vessels were to cease firing after passing the Middle Batteries "because the lower batteries are not worth noticing." After passing Warrenton, the *Benton* would burn a Coston signal, after which the following vessels would each hoist a red light so that the admiral would "know who is missing."

Of particular interest to the individual vessel commanders and their crews were Porter's orders regarding misfortune. If any of the gunboats were so damaged as to be in danger of sinking they were to attempt to land them in shallow water below the mouth of the army's Williams Canal. If any vessel grounded under any of the Vicksburg batteries and could not get off, she was to be "set fire to, thoroughly, and completely destroyed."

While Shirk and his crew handled the preparations required aboard the *Tuscumbia*, the civilian captains readying their steamers were slow, to say the least. As noted, there were three of these vessels, named *Forest Queen*, *Henry Clay*, and *Silver Wave*. The 419-ton *Forest Queen* had been constructed for the Cincinnati to Madison, IN, trade, though as an independent she often accepted contracts for cargoes on the Mississippi. On September 26, 1862, the vessel was nearly captured by Confederate irregulars as she was putting into a scheduled stop while en route from Memphis to Cairo. Thanks to quick thinking by Capt. C. Dan Conway and Pilot John H. Meeker she was able to back out and escape. Early in 1863 the six-year-old side-wheeler and her entire crew, including her well-known clerk, William ("Billy") Blenker, entered USQM contract service and by the following March found themselves off the mouth of the Yazoo. She would be burnt out at St. Louis, MO, in October.

The McKeesport (PA)-built *Henry Clay* entered service for the Northern Line on the Upper Mississippi in 1858. The side-wheeler entered USQM service in late 1861 under Capt. C. B. Goll, but by 1863 her master had become a man named Rider. John Taylor was her pilot. Built at Jeffersonville, IN, in 1854, Capt. John S. McMillen's 245-ton *Silver Wave* was an independent Ohio River sternwheeler that usually traded on the Pittsburg-Cincinnati-Louisville route. Her dramatic arrival at Pittsburg in May 1862 with Confederate arms captured at Island No. 10 was widely noted and led to the vessel's being chartered by the USQM. She was then sent west, where she was engaged in the logistical service that took her downstream to Vicksburg in February 1863 to assist in the Yazoo Delta campaigns. She would eventually be purchased by the U.S. government for work on the upper Mississippi. The civilian crews of the *Henry Clay* and *Silver Wave* balked at making the hazardous passage. As a result, a call went out for volunteers to help man the vessels. It was eagerly answered by Union soldiers from the brigade of Brig. Gen. Hugh B. Ewing, part of Sherman's command. As soon as the new hands were aboard, orders were received to protect the three boats with bales of hay packed around their boilers.

On April 12 RAdm. Porter updated Secretary Welles regarding the proposed operations below Vicksburg. Maj. Gen. Grant, whom the naval leader pictured as "sanguine," was positioned to march his army to New Carthage, "seize Grand Gulf under fire of the gunboats," and make it the base of his operations. For its part, the squadron would "pass the batteries and engage them while the transports go by in the smoke, passing down, of course, at night." In a follow-up report the same day, it was revealed that Maj. Gen. Grant was helping Porter to make up manpower deficiencies. Some 800 soldiers were sent aboard the vessels at the mouth of the Yazoo, including the *Tuscumbia*. In addition, about 600 African-American contrabands were employed in place of men whose enlistment terms had expired, with some sent to the engine rooms and others trained to man the cannon.

Over the next couple of days, Federal preparations continued. It was generally understood, reported Albert H. "Bod" Bodman of the *Chicago Daily Tribune* days later, that an attempt would be made to run the blockade, but "the extent of the enterprise was kept a secret until a day or two before it was carried out." Engineers worked to divert exhaust steam while most of the men not attached to the engineering departments were required to help add protection. Everywhere lightly guarded areas were perceived, cotton and hay bales plus sandbags were stacked or stuff. As most of the Northern ironclads were originally designed to fight bows-on in narrow streams, the armor around their sterns was notoriously thin. To address this very real concern, the after decks were covered with lots of wet hay (loose and in bales) and, in several cases, heavy logs were tied around vessel sterns at the waterline. Wherever possible, large chains were strung down over the aft casemates. The thinly covered machinery spaces and ammunition magazines and lockers were also liberally covered with cotton or hay. Aboard the *Tuscumbia*, a cotton bale was slung on each outboard side of the pilothouse.

As these activities continued, several jacks on every boat were detailed to rid them of livestock. Union sailors, like their civilian and naval contemporaries everywhere, usually kept large numbers of animals aboard for food or companionship. Goats, a few sheep, chickens, dogs, and cats were rounded up and sent ashore. Unhappily, the rats and cockroaches remained, though they, at least, were silent.

While the Northern tars made ready, the commanders in Vicksburg, grown comfortable since the defeat of the Steele's Bayou enterprise, chose to concentrate their attention upon preparations for an upcoming grand ball. The weather was spotty, with much rain and some thunderstorms. Even after a spy warned them that the Federals were planning to run boats past the city's batteries, no enhanced Southern defensive action was taken. Earlier orders to torch a number of tar barrels and old buildings on the riverbank opposite in the event of a Northern night passage continued in effect.

Over in Louisiana, almost since the beginning of the month, path-finding Federal units had made their way through rough terrain and swampy water, via the town of Richmond, toward the largely submerged riverbank community of New Carthage, 20 miles below Vicksburg. On April 6 the 1,300-acre Ion plantation of die-hard Confederate Joshua James was occupied by the 69th Indiana Volunteer Infantry, the vanguard of Maj. Gen. McClernand's XIII Corps, which sought cross-river assault points. About 80 acres of the plantation was above the surrounded flooding waters and a dry levee ran down about four miles to the steamboat landing at Perkins' Plantation, owned by John Perkins, Jr. (1819–1929), a former U.S. congressman and current Confederate senator, who had burned the mansion, "Somerset," to keep it out of Federal hands shortly after the fall of New Orleans a year earlier. A sizeable Confederate force was headquartered there and, visible across the river about three miles below, was Davis Bend, site of the plantations of Jefferson Davis and his brother Joseph.

To bluff their enemy into believing it stronger than it was, the regiment's lieutenant colonel (later colonel), Oran D. Perry (1838–1929), remembered that soldiers from his unit had rowed over to the nearby wreck site of the *Indianola* and retrieved her steam pipe. This was taken back to camp and rigged up as a "Quaker" cannon. Twice over the next week the Confederate gunboat *Queen of the West* (taken from the Federals just before the *Indianola* was captured) appeared intent upon shelling the bluecoats (now including the reinforcing 49th Indiana) but withdrew upon sighting the mammoth piece.[4]

Upstream at the mouth of the Yazoo, U.S. Navy preparations for the passage were intensified by April 14, as RAdm. Porter hoped to make watery charge that night. Indeed, Maj. Gen. Grant alerted Maj. Gen. McClernand that morning: "The Gunboat fleet and transports will run the blockade to-night." Unfortunately, the three civilian steamers designated to accompany the naval vessels failed to report for the trip by 4:00 p.m., so the mission was temporarily scrubbed. Early the next morning, the admiral examined the situation with the designated civilian craft and found that "they have made but little progress since yesterday." He then wrote to the commanding general emphasizing his desire to avoid delay and "to get off as soon as possible." To speed the process, Grant was asked to personally order the transports to report by 4:00 o'clock that afternoon. Porter could then "let the captains see the orders on which they will go down the river" and the enterprise could get away that night "if it is possible."

About midday that April 15, Pvt. Charles E. Affeld, of Battery B of the Chicago Light Artillery, wrote in his diary: "The *Dickey* ... took up a barge of hay; several others having previously been taken to the upper landing for the purpose of protecting the boats that are to run the blockade, for the report is that the transports, *Forest Queen*, *Henry Clay* and six more gunboats are to run the blockade in several days, and that they are to protect themselves by hay and cotton bales." Most of the gunboats were ready by late in the day. Regarding the transports, Grant, in the meantime, informed McClernand that it was possible that "these vessels will not run the blockade to-night. If they do not, they will go to-morrow night certain."

Downstream, the Hoosier soldiers of the 49th and 69th Indiana, knowing they had located an initial anchorage for Porter's fleet when it arrived, established a defensive perimeter at James's plantation and blocked the road south. Despite unsuccessful attacks on several nearby Union outposts during the day, the Hoosier held fast. Along with them, their commander, a Dutchman named Brig. Gen. Peter Osterhaus, who commanded the 9th Division, was convinced the enemy had grossly underestimated Yankee resolve.

At 12:15 a.m. on April 16 orders were brought aboard from the fleet tug *Thistle* directing that the fleet be ready to assemble into cruising formation within half an hour. Lt. Cmdr. Shirk immediately called all hands and ordered that their hammocks and any remaining bags be stowed in the engine room. The crew was then sent to quarters. At 1:40 a.m. a revised directive was received indicating that the operation was on hold until the three transports could complete their preparations. The last of those to finish readying herself was the *Henry Clay*, which at 7:45 a.m. came into the mouth of the Yazoo towing a barge. With the arrival of Capt. Rider's side-wheeler, the mission clock was restarted. According to the general's son, Grant and Porter held a final consultation before noon. Afterwards, the admiral had his participating captains report aboard the *Benton* for final individual briefings.

Amplifying his April 10 general order, RAdm. Porter informed the captain of the *Tuscumbia* when it was his turn that the passage of the three civilian transports by Vicksburg's batteries was essential to the entire war plan that he and Grant had forged. Shirk's giant gunboat was, therefore, being intentionally stationed aft of the USQM steamers, officially to render help if they got into trouble and unofficially to prevent their retreating back upstream when the cannonballs began to fly. In short, the imposing *Tuscumbia* was to be "the whipper-in to the fleet."

Per earlier orders, the boiler fires aboard the designated gunboats were lit early in the afternoon in order that by evening the hot power plants would be producing very little black exhaust smoke. As the remainder of the day progressed, finishing touches were made to shipboard defenses and the last barges were secured. At 5:00 p.m. the *Thistle* came alongside and transferred aboard the *Tuscumbia* 1st Lt. Samuel Bagley (?–1863) and Co. D of the 29th Illinois Volunteer Infantry Regiment. These newcomers, sent from the timberclad *Tyler*, had been among the soldiers recently sent by Maj. Gen. Grant to amplify the gunboat crews. Around 6:30 p.m. the *Tuscumbia*'s crew, as well as those aboard her consorts, were again beat to quarters and final preparations for running the blockade were completed. Over the next couple of hours, the three civilian steamers took their positions immediately ahead of the ironclad and directly behind the *Carondelet*. As the hour for departure approached, Franc ("Galway") Wilkie of the *New York Times* noted that Capt. Conway of the *Forest Queen*, the lead transport, calmly "carried a chair close up to the forward railing of the upper deck, seated himself, and lighted a cigar." Conway, the scribe later recalled in his memoirs, would remain in that position "during the tremendous fire through which he passed."

As the sun set, a small flotilla of steamers and yawls moved down from Milliken's Bend to Lower Landing, located about four miles by direct line from Vicksburg. This was one of those spots where, in daylight, the Confederate citadel could be clearly seen by any Northern observer. According to eyewitnesses, more than 30 vessels assembled in rather close proximity, "each of which was black with human beings." Maj. Gen. Grant and McClernand, their wives, and other officers were among the most important folks present at Lower Landing that night. Aboard the army commander's steamer *Henry Von Phul*, all of those invited received excellent seats forward on the hurricane deck as though they were at the theater. Correspondent Wilkie, the only reporter present on the headquarters steamer, scribbled in his notebook that Mrs. Grant had much improved her dress since he first saw her back in Cairo, while daughter Nellie wore "a very brilliant pair of nankeen pantalets." The uniforms of the officers or of young Fred Grant were, of course, so regular as not to elicit observation.

Down at the James Plantation, as Ion Plantation was also known, officers in the know and common soldiers who were not enjoyed a certain relaxation. On the second-floor gallery of the main house, McClernand, Ostrhaus, and Mr. James, plus those of lesser rank, anticipated the planned move of the navy ironclads. The Ion mood was

Starting Down Two hours after sunset, at 9:15 p.m. on April 16, lines aboard the Federal gunboats were cast off and the vessels moved away from their anchorage above the city with engines muffled and all lights extinguished to conceal their movement. Each boat was separated from the next by 50 yards (more or less), and to help avoid collisions everyone steered a course in the wide river slightly aport of the boat ahead (Abbot, *Bluejackets of '61*).

upbeat; indeed, a number of young Union officers formed a glee club and serenaded those present with a new and very popular ditty, "Rally 'Round the Flag." Despite considerable repetition of that and other patriotic songs, the listeners—even James— seemed to enjoy the music. The old Southerner did, however, allow to Lt. Col. Perry that his bluecoats showed remarkably high spirits for men who would soon be defeated.

Fifteen minutes after the two-lamp departure signal was hoisted aboard the flag boat *Benton* at 9:00 p.m., the vessels of Porter's downriver task force cast off from shore. William L. Shea and Terrence J. Winschel called the forthcoming adventure "the most dramatic episode in the long struggle for Vicksburg, and one of the most spectacular episodes of the entire Civil War."

In the dark two hours after sunset, the slightly staggered Federal line was duly established, each boat separated from the next by 50 yards (give or take a few). The night was, according to Wilkie and other observers, "moonless, starlit, placid, and balmy." This, despite a steady westerly breeze, was "not at all favorable," opined Albert "Bod" Bodman of the *Chicago Daily Tribune.* Not long after weighing anchor and starting up the Mississippi, Lt. Cmdr. Shirk ordered all hands below, with the exception of the No. 3 XI-inch Dahlgren in the forward turret and the men in the pilothouse.

Acting Master's Mate Charles Heckman ("Heck") Gulick (1836–1868), captain of the tug *Ivy*, later reported that the gunboats steadily passed ahead, with their engines "worked slow." As they began to turn into and around De Soto Point, all lanterns on each vessel were extinguished (save a red one at the stern) and the gun ports were closed to keep light from escaping the interiors. Coming abreast of the upper mouth of Williams Canal, the way of the craft was greatly reduced to just a little more than that of the current drift or the minimum speed needed by helmsmen for control.

According to the captain's report, the *Tuscumbia*, due to the necessity of getting the three transports into position ahead, was the last warship of the task force to actually move out, not actually starting down until 10:30 p.m. Once the rear echelon was underway it would move very slowly under twinkling stars until it caught up with the leading vessels at the head of the canal. Thereafter, *Tuscumbia* too drifted downstream until reaching the head of the point.[5] In Vicksburg, the grand Rebel ball was in full, happy progress about the same hour. A reporter from the *Memphis Daily Appeal* would later claim that partying by the citadel's defenders undermined the effectiveness of the town's defenses.

The lights of Vicksburg were clearly in sight to men aboard the approaching gunboats. Aboard the *Benton*, RAdm. Porter looked astern and saw the silent line following, not a light showing anywhere, like "so many phantom vessels." Indeed, as he remarked to the ironclad's captain, "The Rebels seem to keep a very poor watch." Porter had deliberately arranged for his vessels to be kept as invisible as possible. To the Federal observers off Lower Landing, the first gunboat came unexpectedly upon them, looking like a floating shapeless black mass. Quickly, as the witnesses all hushed, it disappeared, to be replaced by another and then another in what the *New York Times* man on the *Henry Von Phul* called "a long procession of bulky shadows, noiseless, mysterious, and drifting as without life or volition." As the task force continued on, it seemed to disappear, leaving only "a long low bank of pitchy midnight." Three quarters of an hour passed with no sounds reaching the Lower Landing observation boats. Nothing could be seen, as Wilkie told his readers on April 23, "save a long, low bank of darkness which, like a black fog, walled the view below and joined the sky and river in the direction of Vicksburg."

Even though much of the Confederate high command was not particularly vigilant, a number of pickets assigned to the river defenses of Col. Higgins were alert. These men not only lined the shore above Vicksburg's Upper Batteries but a number of them also nightly rowed several small yawls up the river in the area near the tip of the De Soto peninsula, keeping the watch Porter doubted. Unfortunately for the South, none of these men were at this moment sufficiently upstream to see the darkened Federal warships as they rounded the point in the obscurity permitted by the night's blackness. Still, and in the same manner as revealed to Grant's guests, the forms of the gunboats were picked up by the watery guards, who put their backs into their oars and rowed as fast as possible to sound the alarm. One of the yawls raced across the Mississippi and upon landing hurried men off to warn Col. Higgins, who immediately ordered all prearranged defensive measures into action. A large number of tar barrels had been placed along the Pelican State riverbank and soldiers raced to set them ablaze. The other Rebel yawls had meanwhile put ashore near the little Louisiana village of De Soto and scurried about preparing to light even larger fires.

As the gunboats continued down, Federal troops above, from commanding general to thousands of rankers, all watched the year's best show. Maj. Gen. Grant, with his son and staff, watched from the hurricane deck of his headquarters transport. Also aboard was Assistant Secretary of War Charles A. Dana, who recalled in his memoirs the "mass of black things ... floating darkly and silently." In an 1887 newspaper article, Fred Grant remembered how "suddenly a rocket went up from the shore. Then a cannon burst forth from Warrenton ... [and] soon fires were burning all along the shore, in front of the city, and the water was illuminated as by day's brightest sun." Maj. Gen. Sherman, meanwhile, also had a good seat, aboard a yawl near the lower end of Williams Canal. He hoped to be among the first to greet his friend Porter when the gunboats arrived below the citadel.

All along the Mississippi shore, fires shot up from the prepositioned oil barrels. As they came into range about 10:45 p.m., the Northern vessels were taken under fire by the 14th Mississippi Light Artillery and pickets from the 46th Mississippi Infantry. Over on the Louisiana shore, across from the powerful Water Battery, a whole series of buildings were put to the torch, including the Vicksburg, Shreveport and Texas Railroad depot. A little lower down, across from Maj. Frederick Ogden's Middle Battery, the house of Vicksburg sextant and undertaker John Q Arnold (1818–1910) was, according to the next day's issue of the *Vicksburg Whig*, also torched. Aboard the *Benton*, Capt. James Greer turned to the admiral and shouted, "The town is on fire."

The huge blaze backlit Porter's approaching fleet, while signal rockets alerted Vicksburg's batteries to commence firing. The resultant excitement quickly ended the Confederate dance as participants ran to their stations—or for cover. As the long roll sounded, many hundreds of curious citizens found viewing seats atop Sky Harbor Hill and Court House Hill, as well as other hillside vantage points, exhibiting "great excitement." The Federal craft were seen by hundreds of people in light and shadow creeping downstream close to the Louisiana shoreline. Fred Grant continued: "There in front of us, steaming down the river, were six gunboats, which looked to me like great black turtles, followed closely by three fragile transports, moving directly toward the batteries of the doomed city." The ironclads and USQM steamers were targeted by Southern guns as they came to bear, six minutes after the lead vessels crept by the silent batteries opposite De Soto Point. Confederate Maj. James T. Hogane later remembered seeing "Yankee gun boats slowly steaming down the river; nearer they came with almost a death-like motion, slow, and in harmony with the black, lithe, sinuous gliding of the river."

Aboard the *Lafayette*, the Number 2 boat in line, Capt. Walke pictured the gun flashes as "a thunderstorm along the river as far as the eye could see." The noise of the cannon fire was so loud it could be heard 60 miles away. The noise of musket balls rattling off the casemates and superstructures was far more intimate. Added to the din was the sound of Federal cannon, firing toward the Confederate bastion from two new batteries on De Soto Point. With their casemate interiors dark, it had been arranged that Union gunners would pre-elevate their cannon for ranges of about 900 yards and return fire with grape and canister. Power to the gunboat engines was now increased and the gun ports were opened. All the while, musket balls could be heard plinking into and off the sides. As the Federals bore down in the river above Wyman's Battery and launched a return bombardment, their nice staggered steaming formation was jumbled.

Blinding light flashes and thick clouds of smoke from cannon and burning buildings confused the pilots and serious collisions were a constant danger.

Viewing the event from one of the Lower Landing steamers, *Chicago Evening Journal* reporter Benjamin Franklin Taylor (who would become a well-known poet) observed, "The heavy roar of Dahlgrens, the keen, eager ring of Parrots, the explosion of shell, intermingling with each other, made the earth and water tremble with the sublime music of war." Watching from a vantage point on Wyman's Hill, the editor of the *Vicksburg Whig* recorded the scene: "The firing of guns, whizzing of balls, bursting of shells, the devouring flames that rose from Arnold's house, and the huzzas from the crowds that congregated on the hills, in the streets, and wherever a view of the passing boats could be obtained, was a sight beggaring all description."

At the James Plantation, Osterhaus, McClernand, and all of the others on its grounds heard a large booming begin about 11:00 p.m.; it would continue until almost 3:00 a.m. A great light filled the sky to their north that could be seen upriver of Grant's observation armada. At Milliken's Bend the earth trembled. Indeed, the sound of the warring guns could be head over a crow's-flight distance of almost 60 miles, from Lake Providence in the north to New Carthage. Aboard the *Henry Von Phul*, Fred Grant stood next to his father on the hurricane deck. Glancing toward the commanding general, he noticed that he was quietly smoking, "but an intense light shone in his eyes."

***Benton* Leads the Charge.** Henry Walke, captain of the ironclad *Lafayette*, was a well-known Romantic painter who sketched this drawing of the Federal gunboats, led by the *Benton*, passing the Vicksburg batteries on the night of April 16 (Johnson and Buel, *Battles and Leaders*).

Newsman Albert Bodman, on another steamer, gained the impression that the Rebels were not firing "as rapidly nor with half the vigor" that they had in other ship-shore engagements, such as Fort Donelson a year earlier.

Even as they hugged the Louisiana shore the gunboats first in line took a number of hits before they crossed the river to get close under the Vicksburg batteries. Those boats farther back were not initially as exposed as, say, the *Lafayette* or the *Pittsburg*. Even so, Lt. Cmdr. Shirk and the men of the *Tuscumbia* found themselves with quite an adventure on their hands.

It was noted aboard the "broad giant" that the Confederate guns opened fire toward her at 11:10 p.m. Ten minutes later her presence was addressed by Col. Jackson's Water Battery. The flash of his cannon was immediately answered by an XI-shell from the *Tuscumbia*, "which was answered by five guns from the enemy." Following this exchange, Lt. Cmdr. Shirk ordered all hands under cover of the casemates. The XI-inch Dahlgren was run in and its gun port closed. This was later seen as a mistake. Bearss and Grabau believed the captain squandered his one advantage, those giant forward cannon. "If he had kept his guns in action," they wrote a century later, "he would undoubtedly have reduced the rate of fire (and probably the accuracy) of the Confederate guns, and thus contributed to the safety of both his own boat and the transports."

By now, as newsman Wilkie recorded, a great cloud of smoke had "rolled heavily over the gunboats, and in this, the three transports entered and made their 'best way' down the river." What happened next has been discussed for 125 years. Over that time, the events we next discuss were ascribed to the vessels either being caught in the treacherous current as Confederate defenders hoped or succumbing to fear of the fire directed at them from the Water Battery. After the passage, Franc Wilkie talked to survivors and offered these reasons for why the transports *Henry Clay* and *Forest Queen* rounded to and headed back upstream, leaving the *Silver Wave* to push ahead unfazed.

The *Forest Queen*, in the advance, took a Confederate ball in her hull and another through her steam pipe, the latter instantly disabling her. The *Henry Clay*, next in line, stopped to prevent running into the van leader. It was at this time, according to Wilkie, that a Southern shot from the Water Battery plowed into the *Henry Clay* below the waterline and, almost simultaneously, a shell exploded among the cotton bales protecting her stern. Seeing the two civilian transports retreating, Lt. Cmdr. Shirk ordered his vessel stopped under fire in midstream in order to block their reverse progress. A confrontation was avoided when the true situation was ascertained. Demoralized crewmen aboard the *Henry Clay* were terrified by the Rebel guns and rushed about the decks in a panic.

With his ship ablaze, Capt. Rider ordered her abandoned. Last seen on the *Henry Clay*'s hurricane deck, the captain, together with a watchman named Metz, seemed to disappear. Two people, the ship's carpenter and the second cook, panicked and ran into the hold closing the hatches behind them. They were never found. Most of the crew immediately climbed into the vessel's two yawls and made their way to De Soto village, where they hid behind a levee before crossing swamps back to the Federal camp. Four survivors, including a woman, were picked up by Confederate rowboats next day and returned to Vicksburg. The unidentified lady told the *Vicksburg Whig* that about five crewmen had perished, including the captain and pilot. She also explained that the rea-

6—*Tuscumbia*: The "Broad Giant" vs. Vicksburg 253

Transports in Trouble. For the most part, Confederate gunners overshot the Union vessels passing below them. Still, the transport *Henry Clay* decided to head back upstream but was hit by a shell, caught fire, and was lost. The *Tuscumbia*, meanwhile, ran aground, attracting Rebel fire. While she was trying to back out of the mud, she hit the supply steamer *Forrest Queen*. Somehow the pair managed to survive, drifting downstream and out range. This sketch was made by Confederate Col. S.H Locket and gives the reader a vivid sense of the scene as seen from shore (Johnson and Buel, *Battles and Leaders*).

son for the passage was "to get all the boats possible below and then cross Grant's army to the Mississippi side, below Warrenton."

Pilot John Taylor remained at his post. He valiantly attempted to steer the *Henry Clay* down the river out of danger, but it wasn't to be. There was no way to con his vessel and none of the black gang in the engine room answered his bells for power. Acting Master Gulick of the *Ivy* later claimed that he picked up the steamer's captain "and most of the crew with the tug." He never learned what happened to Taylor or the balance of the hands, though Rider told him none had been killed onboard by enemy cannon fire. Now well alight, the steamer became an attractive target for the guns of the Water Battery, which blazed away at her as the *Forest Queen* came about and moved down the river, closely followed by the *Tuscumbia*. The transport, disabled when her steam pipe was cut, was forced to drift with the current. In order that he not pass her or break out of his place in the fleet formation, Lt. Cmdr. Shirk ordered his vessel to drift as well.

Hospital steward James Worthington, aboard the barge being towed by the *Henry Clay*, was convinced that Capt. Rider must have been drunk, so erratic had the sidewheeler's course become through the hail of shot and shell. As revealed in an article by James Arnold, Worthington believed that he and his shipmates were "going down into the Lower Regions." He did not know that Rider and most of the crew had already left the vessel.

As her escaping men reached shore, the *Henry Clay* was repeatedly hit and hundreds of her protective cotton bales, many of which were now individually on fire or parts of them were, popped out of the superstructure and landed in the water, each becoming a point of flame. Realizing that he could not save the vessel, Pilot Taylor made his way to the main deck, found a sturdy plank, and went over the side. At this point, meanwhile, Worthington's barge was cut free and she floated to safety. This fiery spectacle drew the attention of Vicksburg's crowds and her note-taking newspaperman. Capt. Rider's transport steamer, which everyone believed was a gunboat, had floated past the burning houses, herself on fire. Flames spread rapidly in her superstructure and "in a few seconds, the fearful glare of pallid light was dispelling the wild darkness of night in awful grandeur." The *Whig*'s correspondent continued: "Then cheer after cheer was sent up by our citizens and the soldiers at the guns and in the rifle pits. Cotton was thrown from the burning vessel and a long boat was seen to leave her for the Louisiana bank.... The burning vessel floated on, and when just above Burney's, she commenced careening and both her chimneys dropped off into the river. The flames gradually diminished and when she got to the mouth of the canal, a small light was all that could be seen above the surface of the water." Had the *Henry Clay* "been manned by men of nerve," opined Franc Wilkie days later, "the fire would have been extinguished and the boat carried through safely; the fact of her floating so far shows that her hull was undamaged."

The *Forest Queen* and *Tuscumbia* drifted round the lower end of De Soto Point about 11:30 p.m. At that point, the ironclad, running too close to the Louisiana shore, ran onto the bank. No damage was done and the captain immediately ordered her engines reversed. In backing into the stream in order to get her bow headed downstream, however, *Tuscumbia* accidentally collided with the *Forest Queen*, leaving the two craft locked together. The two fouled vessels remained hung up for the next five to six minutes, drifting down together closer to the Mississippi side as one big target. All along the Vicksburg bluffs, Southern soldiers and civilians cheered as the great defensive cannon concentrated their fire on the vulnerable pair. The *Tuscumbia*'s commander later reported that the rejoicing was so loud that it sounded as if it were "right over our heads." Despite the barrage of shells sent their way, the two Federal vessels were extremely lucky. The rate of fire and accuracy of the Confederate guns was pitiful, even for those pieces that did not "start" when being depressed.

Before the *Forest Queen* and *Tuscumbia* could free themselves of their embrace, the numerous Rebel guns were able to score only three times. Two shots hit the transport. One powered its way through the hull, while the second smashed the steam drum, preventing further use of the engines. Conway's craft began taking on water. The Rebels put a shell into the bow of the *Tuscumbia* below the waterline. This hit started seven planks and caused a serious leak, which was eventually controlled by diligent use of the forward force and siphon pumps. A 6-inch shot struck the iron lug that supported the rail upon which the starboard port of the after casemate traveled, making an inch-deep dent. After the two Union craft cleared themselves, they continued drifting down the river in close proximity. About 11:40 p.m. the pair passed the wreck of the *Henry Clay*, burning brightly, and within 20 minutes were out of range of Southern guns.

Just below the mouth of the Williams Canal, the *Tuscumbia*, having resumed steaming, passed the *Forest Queen*. Capt. Conway's steamer had 14 inches of water in her hold by now and was in serious difficulty, though the intrepid master may have believed his boat still capable of completing her mission. Whether Shirk noticed this situation in the dark or whether he offered aid and Conway waved him off is not known.

By 12:29 a.m. on April 17 the *Benton* had reached Biggs Plantation, below the mouth of the U.S. Army canal. Here Maj. Gen. Sherman, who had organized a small rescue flotilla of yawls out from Biggs Landing to pick up sailors in case of disaster, went aboard and met RAdm. Porter, congratulating him on a successful run. Sherman's lifeboats saved a number of men from the *Henry Clay*, including Pilot Taylor, whom the general personally assisted into his craft after he had drifted downstream nine miles from the spot where his steamer was disabled.

A few minutes later, about 12:45 a.m., the *Tuscumbia* came abreast of and "spoke" the Pook turtle *Louisville*. As the latter came alongside, she accidentally hit the *Tuscumbia*'s coal barge, starting a leak. From her, word was received that the *Forest Queen* was, in fact, totally disabled and in desperate need of assistance. Lt. Cmdr. Shirk immediately ordered the "broad giant" to round to and go to the aid of the vital USQM side-wheeler. Under the expert handling of pilots Joseph McCammant and Isaac N. Ashton aboard the *Tuscumbia* and their counterpart, John H. Meeker, aboard the *Forest Queen*, seamen were able, with difficulty, to secure a line from the transport. There were some problems. Porter wrote to Assistant Navy Secretary Fox later in the

Sherman Assists Survivors. Maj. Gen. William T. Sherman had a good seat, aboard a yawl near the lower end of Williams Canal, from which to observe the navy passage of Vicksburg's batteries. He hoped to be among the first to greet his friend Porter when the gunboats arrived below the citadel. He had organized a small rescue flotilla of yawls out from Biggs Landing to pick up sailors in case of disaster. Sherman's lifeboats saved a number of men from the *Henry Clay*, including her pilot, whom the general personally assisted into his craft after the survivor had drifted downstream nine miles from the spot where his steamer was disabled (Library of Congress).

day asserting that the reason it had proven difficult to get a towline rigged was because "all hands on the transport were drunk." True or not, shortly thereafter Conway's craft was beached at Brown and Johnston's Plantation, on the Louisiana riverbank at the lower mouth of the Williams Canal just across and above the town of Warrenton.

While Shirk was upstream, Maj. Gen. Sherman disembarked from the *Benton* and returned ashore. A lull in the firing lasting about 15 minutes elapsed as Porter's fleet now passed out of range of Vicksburg's lower batteries. The flag boat and those ironclads following her headed past Warrenton, continuing to their predetermined anchorage above New Carthage, close to the wreck of the *Indianola*. Bearss and Grabau later attributed the relatively easy success of their passage to weaknesses in the Confederate river defenses not earlier realized, including too few heavy guns for such an extended front and a remarkably low rate of fire, as well as Union gunners who so rapidly served their Dahlgrens as to make the slow Rebel loading and gun-laying extremely hazardous.

Her rescue mission accomplished, the *Tuscumbia* resumed her downstream voyage, passing the casemated Warrenton battery sometime after 1:00 a.m. As she slowly cruised by, Acting Ensign Thomas M. Ferrell's portside 11-inch Dahlgren, by Shirk's command, spit two 5-second shrapnel shells at the Rebel emplacement. "Six discharges from not more than four light guns" were returned toward the "broad giant," the captain remembered, none hitting.

Once Porter's flotilla was past Vicksburg and the firing had died down, the Federal observation transports at the Lower Landing above dispersed. Indeed, Maj. Gen. Grant's headquarters vessel, the *Henry Von Phul*, was among the first to leave, heading back to Milliken's Bend.

On his way back to base, the War Department envoy and former newsman Dana told everyone that he had counted 525 discharges during the two-hour event. Neither Grant, Dana, Wilkie nor any of the others noted above could know, given the volume of cannon fire, just how successful Porter's gambit had been. During the entire passage, only the transport *Henry Clay* was sunk.

Arriving at Milliken's Bend, Maj. Gen. Grant immediately summoned a few guards to horse and rode with them about 40 miles over the pioneer route to New Carthage. Arriving early the next day, the commanding general finally learned just how successful the navy had been. At Confederate army headquarters in Jackson, MS, Maj. Gen. Pemberton wired President Jefferson Davis seeking additional support and adding, "I regard the navigation of the Mississippi River as shut out from us now."

Approaching Diamond Island about 3:00 a.m., Capt. Shirk's boat was met by the *Ivy* with orders that she anchor. While delivering Porter's directive, her commander, Acting Master's Mate Gulick, learned from mates aboard the ironclad how "her 11-inch guns rattled the grape and shell into the city with great pleasure to all aboard." *Tuscumbia*'s were the last guns fired during the passage. Ashore, most of the men at James Plantation were able to go to bed, the Federals among them, "strong in the hope of success." The sailors aboard the gunboats set watch and repaired damages. No one had been killed during this adventure, but a dozen hands were wounded. "We suffered most from the musketry fire," Porter remembered years later. Aboard the *Tuscumbia*, the rest of the predawn hours were spent by all hands in a desperate attempt to save the leaking coal barge. Despite the use of portable pumps and spirited manual bailing, she could not be saved. At 4:30 a.m. her lines were cut and she was disappeared into the dark river.

In the U.S. Army camps above Vicksburg, not everyone was caught up in the drama or heard the heavy gunfire. After helping to dig a sort of levee behind his camp to keep the water out, an exhausted Pvt. Charles Affeld and his battery mates from the Chicago Light Artillery were mostly asleep. In his diary the next morning, the young Chicagoan confessed, "I did not hear it; being asleep, it did not waken me." Many gave thanks that the terrific thunderstorm of the previous evening did not occur during their recent passage.[6]

Back down the river at New Carthage, Maj. Gen. McClernand and his men, at about 7:00 a.m., watched for the Union task force from the shore as what remained of the wrecked *Henry Clay*, along with many cotton bales, floated by on fire about an hour later. She appeared to be keeping company with three barges, two filled with coal and the other with camp equipment. The XIII Corps commander ordered every available rowboat into the water in an effort to save the trio. Remarkably, given the size of the freighters vs. the little yawls, one coal carrier and the equipment barge were rescued. Found on the latter was an new outsize U.S. flag that Lt. Col. Perry, much to the consternation of Mr. James, had hoisted from the Ion Plantation mansion's balcony.

About 10:15 a.m., as the awaiting soldiers at James's wondered where it was, the squadron got underway and continued down. The *Pittsburg* was the first to arrive, putting into the landing about noon. As waiting soldiers rendered her joyous greeting, McClernand, together with his aide, Lt. Col. Henry Clay Warmoth (1842–1931), went aboard Capt. Hoel's gunboat, seeking aid in dispersing Confederate troops at Perkins' Plantation, five miles below. Protocol on such a decision required Porter's approval, the naval officer reminded, thus the former Illinois politician returned to his headquarters tent to await the coming of the admiral. Within a short time, the *Benton* and the other vessels hove to off the Louisiana beachfront. The bluecoat soldiers broke into wild celebration; "something to be remembered the rest of our lives," opined Perry. From his balcony, Mr. James watched in shock for a few moments as the gunboats arrived. He then fell to his knees, "sobbing as if his heart would break."

As Capt. Hoel had recommended, Generals McClernand and Osterhaus, with Lt. Col. Warmoth, immediately called upon the fleet commander. After words of congratulation, McClernand again made his request, which was quickly granted. "Now," the grinning Dutchman was heard to say, "those dampt fellers, dey'll catch it; give dem gunboat soup!"

While the three men conversed about the nearby wreck of the *Indianola*, an aide was sent aboard the *Ivy* to bring Lt. Cmdr. Shirk on board. When the captain of the *Tuscumbia* appeared, he was introduced to Lt. Col. Warmoth. Lt. Cmdr. Greer then showed the two dents in the *Benton*'s armor, as Shirk spoke of the *Henry Clay* and *Forest Queen*. Summoned over by Porter, the *Tuscumbia*'s commander was introduced to the two generals. Lt. Cmdr. Shirk, having largely addressed his passage damages, was then tasked with supporting Osterhaus, whose two Hoosier regiments would move overland to attack the Confederate camp at Perkins' Plantation. Specifically, he was ordered to rapidly throw grape and canister into their earthworks, which lay about 800–900 yards from their anchorage on the bank of the river. When, as was expected, the enemy fled,

***Tuscumbia* Supports the Army.** Shortly after her arrival below the Vicksburg batteries on the morning of April 17 the "Broad Giant" was ordered to steam downstream a short distance to support U.S. Army troops attacking Confederate positions at Perkins' Plantation. About 3:25 p.m. several Rebel horsemen were seen on the right bank and were chased off with three XI-inch shells. Over the next half hour the *Tuscumbia* continued to shell the woods running down to the river, and a number of men were seen running from the little fort. She then rounded to and returned back upstream to her New Carthage anchorage (Johnson and Buel, *Battles and Leaders*).

Shirk was to secure the cannon reported there and bring them back to the army at James's.

About 2:30 p.m. Brig. Gen. Osterhaus was welcomed aboard the "broad giant," which then weighed anchor and made down the river. About 3:25 p.m. several Rebel horsemen were seen on the right bank and were chased off with three XI-inch shells. Over the next half-hour, the *Tuscumbia* continued to shell the woods angling down to the river and a number of men were seen running from the little fort. She then rounded to and returned back upstream to her New Carthage anchorage.

En route back to base at dusk, the *Tuscumbia* passed close to the head of Palmyra Island, where most of her hands were able to see the wreck of the *Indianola*. It was the only time in the war when one of Mayor Brown's ironclads came within sight of another, even if one of them was but a hulk. RAdm. Porter was somewhat surprised by the speed with which Shirk had been able to accomplish his task and not at all pleased that he had returned without any Confederate cannon. The *Tuscumbia*'s captain was immediately summoned aboard the *Benton*, where the fleet commander, ever the great storyteller, remembered taking his report, curious about a knapsack he brought with him: "'What is that, sir?' I inquired, a little severely, 'and where are those guns?' The guns, he said, were four logs mounted on cart-wheels, and the knapsack contained all of the enemy's commissary stores, which he dropped as he was running away. In the knapsack was an old shoe and an ear of corn. Heavens! What a commentary on the war was this." During the fire support mission, Lt. Cmdr. Shirk's big ironclad expended 10 explosive shells and one shrapnel shell moving down the Mississippi and five explosive shells on the way back. Unbeknownst to the naval officers, the shoot was a waste of important ammunition. The small group of Confederate defenders had abandoned their positions and fled inland to the west bank of Lake St. Joseph.

Meanwhile, Grant, Porter, and other figures, including correspondents, wrote out the first dispatches announcing the successful passage of the batteries. These were hastily sent upstream to Memphis, where they arrived on Saturday, April 19, aboard the fast steamer *Silver Moon*. The welcome news was relayed as quickly as possible and soon began appearing in Northern newspapers as distant from one another as the *St. Louis Daily Missouri Republican* and the *Boston Daily Advertiser*.

By April 18, as the four divisions of the XIII Corps continued their march on New Carthage, Maj. Gen. Grant had determined that this location was inadequate as a staging area for a cross-river amphibious assault. Even though Maj. Gen. Sherman had provided Capt. Conway with all the materials needed to repair the *Forest Queen*, which was expected at New Carthage within two days, that vessel and the *Silver Wave*, even with help from the gunboats assembled off the Ion Plantation, were not enough to get his men across the Mississippi. It would be another two days before additional transports were available (allowing time, of course, for any repairs). In the interim, and as units of the Army of the Tennessee slogged down Louisiana from Milliken's Bend via interior corduroy roads, attention turned to the next target downstream, the fortress town of Grand Gulf, seen by some as a "backdoor to Vicksburg."[7]

As elements of the Army of the Tennessee moved down to the shore—first to Perkins' "Somerset" (also unsuitable) and then to Hard Times opposite the mouth of the Big Black River and three miles north of Grand Gulf—RAdm. Porter decided that it was time to take a closer look at the Rebel defenses that next awaited. For any assault crossing to be effective, the guns of Grand Gulf, he knew, would have to be silenced, but as had been learned earlier, the prospect of facing heavy plunging fire required caution.

A "southern extremity of the Vicksburg forts," as Prof. Soley put it, the unfinished Confederate fortifications at Grand Gulf, MS, 30 miles south of Vicksburg by road and double that south of Milliken's Bend, would be next to feel the wrath of the *Tuscumbia* and her consorts. It was unknown before the assault, but these defenses would not be conquered by the fleet. With this fact unrealized at the beginning, units from RAdm. Porter's ironclad task force began a week of reconnaissance on April 20. About 12:30 that afternoon, the *General Price* overtook the *Tuscumbia* near her Ion Plantation landing and her captain spoke with Lt. Cmdr. Shirk as the two vessels steamed along slowly. The two were ordered to drop downstream and observe Confederate activities on the bluffs at Grand Gulf and, while cruising, destroy any enemy river vessels (skiffs, barges, flatboats, etc.) encountered. Before the "broad giant" returned to her anchorage just prior to 9:00 that night her officers, together with those aboard the *General Price*, had observed Confederate workers busily fortifying the Grand Gulf heights. The captains from the two were then rowed over to the *Benton*, where they made their report to the admiral, who sent a digest of the findings, along with his opinions, to Maj. Gen. Grant. What the sailors saw with their spyglasses was ominous, according to Porter. As was the case at Vicksburg (and Columbus, Fort Donelson, and Fort Pillow before), the defenses at Grand Gulf, under the command of Col. John S. Bowen (1830–1863), covered bluffs well above the water. Porter noted, "Grand Gulf is the strongest place on the Mississippi."

Dug into the side of Point of Rock, Fort Cobun was 40 feet above the river and protected by a parapet almost 40 feet thick. This upper battery, manned by Battery A, 1st Louisiana Heavy Artillery, was being readied to mount a pair of 32-pounders, one 30-pounder Parrott rifle, and an 8-inch Dahlgren smoothbore. The river formed a bend here with difficult eddies. Under a covered way, two parallel rifle pits, held by the 3rd Missouri Infantry Regiment (C.S.), stretched three-quarters of a mile from Point of Rock to Fort Wade, the latter named for artillery chief Col. William B. Wade. This lower fort, just behind the little town of Grand Gulf, was positioned on an abutment 20 feet above and a quarter mile back from the Mississippi. That outpost, manned by artillerists from Guibor's and Wade's Missouri Batteries, was also being armed with two 32-pounders plus an 8-inch Dahlgren, as well as a huge 100-pounder Blakely rifle. A number of field places were emplaced at key points along the ridgeline at the top of the bluffs and also on hills overlooking the Big Black River. These guns were also manned by Missouri cannoneers.

Wishing that Grant or Sherman was present in person to take command of developments instead of McClernand, for whom he had no use, Porter stressed the need to quickly strike at Grand Gulf before all of the guns noted above could be emplaced. "My opinion," he confided, "is that they will move heaven and earth to stop us if we don't go ahead." While the Confederates enhanced their positions, a number of Porter's vessels, including the *Tuscumbia*, moved down the river on the morning of April 22, arriving in the vicinity of Grand Gulf about 11:00 a.m. Upon a signal from the *Benton*, they all came about and stood upstream, landing at Brown's Plantation, on the Louisiana shore in Hard Times Bend about four miles above and across from Grand Gulf. As the hands were called to their midday meal, all of the gunboat commanders, including Lt. Cmdr. Shirk, were ordered to join the admiral aboard the *Lafayette*. The officers were also joined by an invited correspondent, Franc ("Galway") Wilkie of the *New York Times*.

About 1:30 p.m., the *Lafayette*, accompanied by the *General Price* and the tug *Ivy*, dropped down to the waters abreast the Grand Gulf fortifications, where, with Porter standing "on the spar deck directing the firing," Capt. Henry Walke's gunners tested the great guns of his new ironclad against the Confederate defenses. Twelve times the cannon spoke, the results being eagerly observed by all aboard. The Rebels replied "eight times, their shells being good line short, but mostly falling short and exploding in the water." Although the *Lafayette* could not reach the batteries cresting the bluff, a number of Col. Bowen's work details in the lower works within range were dispersed. Several shells splashed into the water near the big gunboat but did no damage. Leaving the two warships off the citadel, Porter and his captains returned to their vessels aboard the *Ivy* later in the afternoon believing the enemy's work was not yet finished.

6—*Tuscumbia*: The "Broad Giant" vs. Vicksburg

Early in the evening, the Mississippi Squadron commander had the *Ivy* deliver a message to Walke advising that should he see the squadron coming down as a unit next day this was the signal for an attack on the Rebel batteries tested that afternoon. Contacted, Maj. Gen. McClernand quickly ordered Brig. Gen. Osterhaus to load his 9th Division aboard the repaired transport *Forest Queen* and a big barge. They would follow the gunboats down and if the Southern cannon were silenced would "take and hold the place." That night, six Federal USQM transports ran the Vicksburg batteries, with one lost. The civilian crews having refused to participate, the boats were, as reported by the *New York Herald*, made up of volunteers from Illinois regiments. The response of the Vicksburg batteries was heard until 2:30 in the morning aboard the *Tuscumbia* and the other gunboats waiting to attack above Grand Gulf. It would require several days to repair those that were damaged during the transit.

Although Osterhaus was able to assemble eight regiments and two field batteries by the morning of April 23, no attack was forthcoming. As the steamers were making their run during the night, RAdm. Porter had received aboard his flag boat a clergyman—"half Union," he believed—from Grand Gulf who proceeded to deliver a highly inflated count of the number of grayclad soldiers and guns facing him. The Rebels, so went the claim, had been working diligently on four forts (not two) for six weeks and more reinforcements were arriving daily, swelling the total available to Bowen to 12,000 men. Just after breakfast, the admiral revealed his information to Maj. Gen. McClernand, asking that his whole corps be hurried down to join Osterhaus. The general doubted the veracity of the preacher's report and, to make certain, volunteered to personally inspect the Grand Gulf fortifications, an offer Porter accepted. After noon, the Illinois general rode the *General Price* down to the waters off Col. Bowen's citadel and inspected the Confederate location with a spyglass. Not seeing four forts but only two, noticing little activity that would indicate incoming reinforcements, and counting far fewer exposed guns or emplacements, McClernand returned. Porter was immediately advised of the results of the scout. In confirming his finding to the squadron boss, the XIII Corps commander suggested that they wait until Maj. Gen. Grant arrived to decide what steps to take next. Meanwhile, fleet units could mount small gunfire raids to keep the Confederates from further entrenching.

Grant was on the scene by late in the day and listened as Porter advised against a direct attack on Grand Gulf's defenses. It was suggested, instead, that the Army of the Tennessee march farther downstream and, with gunboat assistance, go across even farther below. Again, as he had back on April 1 prior to the fleet's passage of Vicksburg, the commanding general wanted to conduct his own reconnaissance. With Grant and Porter embarked, the *General Price* steamed down to the vicinity off Grand Gulf early on April 24. As the Federals looked at them through their spyglasses, the Confederate artillerymen held their fire, wanting to make their opponents guess the quality of their defense. Like McClernand, Grant did not see the Grand Gulf batteries as being formidable. The place could be taken within two days was his estimate. Returning ashore, Maj. Gen. Grant ordered additional troops down from Milliken's Bend to Hard Times, while those present were to be loaded on the available transports as soon as possible. This desire was emphasized to Maj. Gen. McClernand when he met with Grant and Porter aboard the *Benton* that afternoon.

While the army buildup was underway, chief engineer John W. Hartupee and several of his assistants were engaged in helping to repair the transports damaged during the passage of Vicksburg's guns on April 22/23. A member of the *Cairo*'s crew before she was sunk the previous December, he was reassigned to the *Tuscumbia* as she finished construction in his New Albany hometown. He would remain with the "broad giant" throughout her career, before returning to the river in 1865. Their ironclad's carpenter, John Cronin, and his mates also lent a hand. About 9:30 a.m. on April 26, Maj. Gen. Grant and members of his staff were welcomed aboard by Lt. Cmdr. Shirk. The commanding general wished transport to Perkins' Plantation, which was provided courtesy of the ironclad's gig. About 11 hours later they returned with Maj. Gen. James M. McPherson; shortly after their arrival, the ship's cutter was tasked with returning them ashore.

That night, an army tug, with two barges, ran the Vicksburg batteries. Heavy firing was heard upriver at Vicksburg and presumably Warrenton between 3:00 a.m. and 4:30 a.m.[8] Having survived her ordeal, the army tug, with her barges in tow, rounded the point above the *Tuscumbia* on the morning of April 27, blowing her whistle. Her alarm, caused by the gradual sinking of one of her hay barges, was promptly answered. At 8:45 a.m. the little military newcomer began frantically whistling again, indicating that she, too, was going down; crewmen waved a white flag from her deck. A damage control party was then told off from the ironclad and sent with pumps to her assistance.

Aboard his flag boat, the *Benton*, RAdm. Porter wrote out and then dispatched to his ironclad captains about 6:00 p.m. specific general orders for the forthcoming assault they would make upon the Grand Gulf forts. In essence, the seven available vessels would divide their attention between the two Rebel emplacements: *Benton*, *Tuscumbia*, and *Lafayette* vs. the upper batteries at Fort Cobun, and the four Pook turtles vs. the lower at Fort Wade. The rest of the arrangements were the same as those made to pass the Vicksburg batteries, though Porter offered additional suggestions. For example, he recommended that each gunboat "should be well packed with hammocks, bags, and awnings around the pitmans." To guard against deckhouse fires, "water buckets and tubs should be kept filled all about the spar deck." Following the example first shown aboard the *Carondelet* at Fort Donelson in February 1862, members of the gun crews were to be "cautioned about sticking themselves out of the ports when loading." Every captain was to explain Porter's plans to all officers, who would share the plans with their subordinates. At 7:00 p.m., after the orders were read and conveyed aboard the *Tuscumbia*, Lt. Shirk ordered all hands called to quarters for gunnery drill.

The next two days were spent in preparing the vessels for combat and getting the bluecoats and their equipment loaded aboard transports and properly positioned. Maj. Gen. Grant was convinced that his naval colleagues could destroy the opposing guns making it possible for his assault landing to proceed. Lt. Cmdr. Shirk, aware of his vessel's limitations, again made certain that cotton bales were stuffed in vulnerable locations, with one each slung on each outer side of the pilothouse.

On April 28 two XIII Corps divisions (10,000 men) embarked upon three transports and a number of barges, leaving Perkins' Plantation for Hard Times about 10:00 that morning. Shortly thereafter the *Tuscumbia* and the other ironclads also cast off. At noon *Tuscumbia* rounded in the wake of the flag boat *Benton* in Hard Times Bend and in an hour tied up alongside her at the riverbank. Five other ironclads followed suit. There being insufficient transports available to bring down all of the XIII Corps in one lift, the trio making the first trip were sent back to Perkins' later in the afternoon to bring down the remaining two divisions. At the same time, the ironclad captains all assembled aboard the *Benton* once more to hear the latest intelligence and to exchange opinions. In continuing deference to his skills as a pilot and his knowledge of local waters, Acting Volunteer Lt. Hoel, commander of the *Pittsburg*, was "cheerfully," as Capt. Walke put it later, chosen to lead the squadron into action

By early morning on April 29 the XIII Corps was in the Hard Times area. Three divisions were then paddled down aboard seven transports to a holding area behind the Coffee's Point peninsula, about 15 miles below Perkins' Plantation and directly opposite the mouth of the Big Black River, where they would await and, it was hoped, watch the subjugation of Grand Gulf's batteries by Porter's fleet. Once the "all clear" was signaled from the *Benton*, the soldiers would dash across the Mississippi. After the steamers had unloaded their charges, they would return for the others. Watching from crowded decks, the bluecoats, covered by the gunboat *General Price*, would have a ringside seat for the great bombardment show. Grant himself would see it from a tug, about 1,400 yards above the fray. Several journalists from the Bohemian Brigade would also be watching, including Franc ("Galway") Wilkie, of the *New York Times*, who had just arrived after a 60-mile, 24-hour horseback ride from Milliken's Bend.[9]

Having assembled in the waters off Grand Gulf between 6:00 a.m. and 7 a.m. on April 29, the seven available Federal ironclads, their colors flying bravely, advanced slowly in the six-knot current upon their opponent's batteries. Led by the *Pittsburg*, the *Louisville, Carondelet, Mound City, Tuscumbia, Benton*, and *Lafayette*, at 150-yard intervals, came within about 1,500 yards of Fort Cobun around 8:00 a.m. Each had her bow guns ready with a mix of grape, canister, and shrapnel (cut to ½ second) and percussion shells. At 7:50 a.m., the four Pook "turtles" came past Fort Cobun, with its bend and eddies, opening the bombardment anticipated by both sides. The Confederate batteries at Point of Rock replied 25 minutes later, at 8:15.

The last big, loud ship vs. shore engagement of the Western riverine war was underway; those to follow on the Red River and at Nashville the next year would be small potatoes in comparison. Maj. Gen. Grant and Assistant War Secretary Dana observed from the tug *Ivy*, wondering when the transports could be called across.

After saluting the upper batteries, the four Eads-built ironclads continued toward Fort Wade. As the four veteran gunboats headed toward their assigned target, the *Tuscumbia*, at 8:25 a.m., turned around and engaged Fort Cobun with her 11-inch Dahlgrens. The *Benton* also participated in the shoot, as did the *Lafayette*, standing above and firing with her stern guns from a distance of about 600 yards. Occasionally, as the opportunity arose, shells were also lobbed at Fort Wade. Off this location, RAdm. Porter later told Assistant Navy Secretary Fox, "the current was six knots and the eddy three knots, and the vessels were turning around like a teetotum, fighting bow, stern, and side guns at the same time."

Blasting away from positions above, below, and abreast of the upper Confederate works, occasionally from no more than 50 yards offshore, the *Tuscumbia*, frequently troubled by the eddies, was quickly hit by return fire. At 8:35 a.m. a rifled shell hit the outer edge of the midships forward gun port, thereby opening it and continuing into

Fury of Battle. The fury of the Union ironclads against Confederate defenses at Grand Gulf, MS, is shown in this scene drawn by Capt. Henry Walke. The *Tuscumbia* is shown in action to the far right of the depiction, apparently early on before she was put out of action (Walke, *Naval Scenes and Reminiscences*, 1877).

the turret to explode, killing four men and injuring eleven others. Ominously, the Rebel round also threw sparks into the magazine passages and shell room, fortunately without cataclysmic consequences. Another Rebel bullet then hit both shutters of the same port, jamming it so that it could not be used. In addition, fragments from the first shell wounded Pilot McCammant as he was standing at the wheel. It also destroyed all of the bell wires and starboard speaking trumpets, forcing all orders to be passed through the port speaking trumpet.

The battle between the ironclads and the forts continued all morning as the ironclads poured broadsides up and into the Confederate parapets 40–50 feet above the river while the Rebels dropped their bombs into the water, raising huge columns of water if not sometimes striking home. Porter later confessed to Fox, "Very few of our shells burst, which made them about equal to round shot." The contest was eagerly watched by the thousands of Union troops assembled on transports across the way, as well as Confederates ashore. One soldier, Pvt. Isaac Jackson of the 83rd Ohio Volunteer Infantry, later admitted that the ship-shore duel was "something I longed to see." Now that he had done so, his "curiosity was satisfied."

A veteran since Fort Henry of reporting on ship-shore duels, Franc Wilkie of the *New York Times* observed that from the time the fight began until it closed "the gunboats moved constantly, passing the batteries, pouring into each their fire as they passed. The roar of the guns was terrific, and so continuous that it sounded almost like an unbroken roll of thunder. For awhile, the eye as well as ear would take in the scene, but soon great clouds of smoke rose, met above, and shut out the scene."

While attacking Fort Cobun, the *Tuscumbia* occasionally fired upon Fort Wade, employing the starboard stern Dahlgren. Around 11:00 a.m. the pilothouse was the next location visited by enemy fire, with a shell foiled in its attempt to enter by one of the cotton bales mounted on its side. Nevertheless, the protective iron was torn off and the oak backing started. Another round, according to Chief Engineer Hartupee in a letter later published by RAdm. Walke, entered the port side, passed through the cylinder timbers and pitman on that side, exploded between the cylinder timbers, and caused a fire that was quickly extinguished. By way of definition, Adam Kane tells us that the steamboat engines were each mounted on a pair of heavy timber frames called cylinder timbers. The gunboats continued to maneuver offshore, endeavoring to throw off the aim of the Southern gunners. All manner of shrapnel and thousands of Minie balls hit them as they twisted about the stream. A soldier from the 6th Missouri C.S. remembered, in 1910, "Many projectiles were seen to hit the iron sides of the gunboats, then glance off and go shrieking across to the Louisiana shore."

Later in the morning, two more shells entered the port side of the *Tuscumbia*, exploding against the cylinder timbers and tearing the stateroom of First Assistant Engineer Perry Smith to shreds, although no one was hurt. Almost simultaneously, a Confederate round plowed through the port wheelhouse and entered the after turret, detonating. All eleven members of the gun crew servicing that Dahlgren were disabled and Lt. Samuel Bagley was killed. Lt. Cmdr. Shirk later noted that the 8-inch thick wooden backing of the turret was too thin, contributing to the tragedy. Next, a shell entered the ironclad through her starboard side and exploded between cylinder timbers. Confederate round-shot, grape, and shells relentlessly pounded *Tuscumbia* and one of them entered the starboard wheelhouse, carrying away all of the wheel-chains.

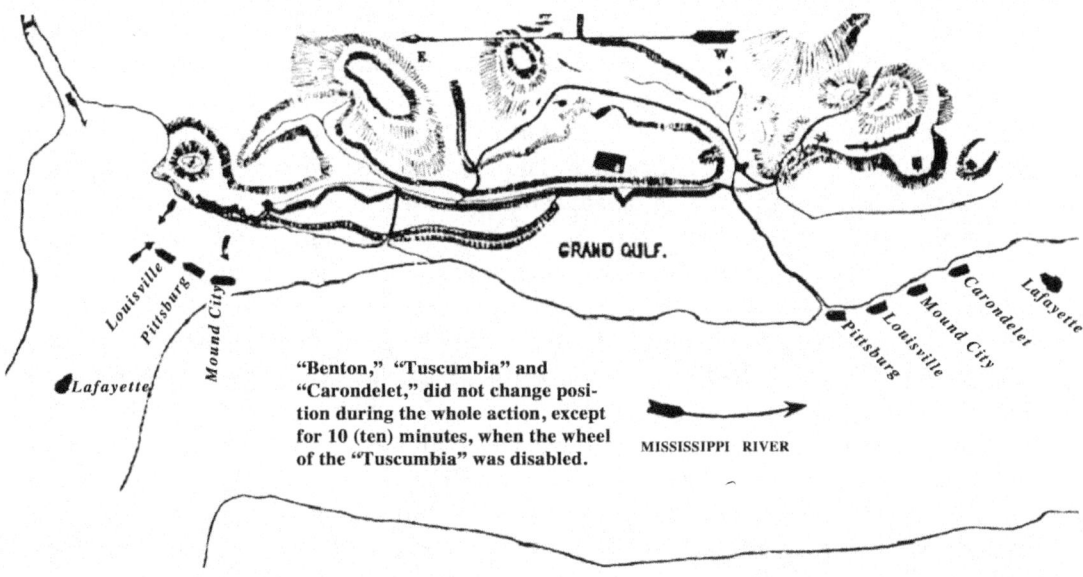

Capt. Walke's Grand Gulf Chart. A stickler for detail, Capt. Walke drew this chart of the fighting at Grand Gulf to prove a point in his memoirs. It is generally accurate (Walke, *Naval Scenes and Reminiscences*, 1877).

Material damage to the ironclad's forward turret was slight, though one armor plate was knocked off the starboard side of the forward turret and sailed over the side, while several others were started though not detached. Carpenter John Cronan, in his after-action report, commented on the "outrageously bad manner" in which the armor of the turrets was fastened to its pine backing with short drift [lag] bolts. As was earlier also seen aboard the *Chillicothe* during her fight with Fort Pemberton, the use of these spikes by the builders to mount the iron caused them to be started when hit by enemy cannonballs, while allowing damage to the light wood backing.

By now, all of the *Tuscumbia*'s hog chains and hog chain posts (20-foot-high stanchions) had been shot away but one. Two of the athwartship braces that supported the wheelhouse beams were gone, along with three deck chains attached to the bridgetree over the powerplant. The loss of support to one of the two bridgetrees supporting the deck caused it to sag down onto the boiler spaces, with the pressure causing a sprung bilge keelson. The vessel's ends now hogged about 7½ inches aft and 1½ inches forward and the bottom began to come up in the middle. The ironclad's light work and decking were riddled and her chimneys took on the appearance of colanders. The port piston was beginning to break as the stern of the vessel dropped, forcing the port paddle wheel to drop even and jam against the hull. The starboard engine continued functioning at full capacity, but, although not disabled, the port engine was now out of line. Several buckets were shot out of both paddle wheels.

About 12:35 p.m. a Rebel shell entered the side of the vessel and exploded between the port cylinder timbers. The blast disabled the port engine by breaking its full-stroke cam yoke. The boat had been designed to work with two fully functional wheels and now, with one down, the yaw of the remaining one caused loss of control and the vessel spun. Unable to employ his gunboat's paddle wheels, Lt. Cmdr. Shirk attempted to pass up and out of range using his propellers. These were unable to generate sufficient power to stem the current, requiring that the Brown-built ironclad simply drop out of the action below Grand Gulf. Passing downstream with the current, the captain quickly advised the flag boat of his plight and anchored until repairs could be made. Porter was sympathetic to the vessel's predicament, later telling Gustavus Fox: "The *Tuscumbia* supported us as long as she was manageable, but the great vessel, which I supposed would whip the whole [Mississippi] Squadron, was knocked into a cocked hat—she soon drifted out of action much to the mortification of her gallant commander."

Not immediately privy to the reasons for the *Tuscumbia*'s failure, *New York Times* reporter Wilkie nevertheless penned what he heard in his first description of the battle sent off overland to Milliken's Bend by messenger the next morning (it would not be published until May 11): "The *Tuscumbia*, a turreted iron-clad, was completely riddled in every portion not protected by plating. Her chimneys were perforated until they resembled huge graters, and her woodwork torn and splintered in every conceivable shape. Her turrets alone, in their thickest parts, were able to resist the projectiles hurled against her. She was finally disabled by a shot that cut one of her hog chains, by which, in river phrase, she was 'broken in two.'"

Chicago Daily Times correspondent Tom Cook, who had seen the damage inflicted on the *Chillicothe* during the Yazoo Pass Expedition, was explicit in his summary. She "must go on the stocks at once," he told his readers on May 11. The *Benton* was also roughly handled, with numerous casualties. For the only time during the war, Porter himself was wounded, though slightly. Meanwhile, the contest between the four Union ironclads—later backed by the *Lafayette*—and the Fort Wade cannon continued without a victor until the match was broken off. Two 32-lb. cannon in the lower Confederate citadel were disabled, the parapet was smashed, and Col. Wade was killed. At this point, the Pook turtles rounded to and moved up to support their heavier consorts off Fort Cobun. With the *Tuscumbia* fully out of action and the *Benton* temporarily sidelined, the *Lafayette* held her previous station while the *Pittsburg, Louisville, Carondelet,* and *Mound City* steamed in circles firing on Fort Coburn as their guns came to bear. A number of passes came as close to the enemy as 300 yards. Unhappily, owing to the "skillful and scientific arrangement of the embrasurers," the quartet scored few hits.

The fight with Cobun continued until Confederate resistance seemed to abate, somewhere around 1:00 p.m. The guns atop the bluff were not silenced but largely out of ammunition, despite the fact that nearly 2,500 Yankee shells had dropped into their works. When the guns were resupplied, they would be able to resume the contest almost as fresh as at its beginning.

Aware that the Rebel guns were still viable, but wanting to rest his men and confer with the military, RAdm. Porter ordered his ironclads to cease firing at about 1:15 p.m. The ironclads, less the *Tuscumbia*, withdrew to Hard Times and dropped anchor at 2:00 p.m.

As they left the scene, the Southerners at Fort Cobun gave the Yankee boats "a parting broadside," reported the *New York Herald.* Looking at his pocket watch, scribe Franc Wilkie noted that the fight had "lasted without intermission for five hours and forty minutes." The lengthy spate of noise from the Mississippi was heard all the way inland to the Mississippi state capital of Jackson, although it would be next day before the *Daily Mississippian* could confirm the cause for its readers.

Meeting ashore, Porter and Grant agreed that Grand Gulf was too tough a nut to crack by assault. An alternative idea was agreed to: after dark, the ironclads, again minus *Tuscumbia*, would make a demonstration off Grand Gulf while the XIII Corps transports slipped behind them. The soldiers, who had witnessed the ship-shore battery duel from the transports, were debarked and marched three miles across the base of Coffee's Point peninsula to De Sharoon's Plantation. The tug *Ivy* was sent to the *Lafayette* with orders to amuse the work parties at Fort Cobun, keeping them from completing some repairs. The little auxiliary then crossed to the *Tuscumbia*, relaying instructions for her to move down to De Sheroon's once her engine repairs were finished.

Lunch, meanwhile, was served aboard the *Tuscumbia*, Dr. Potter continued to attend the injured, and repair crews mended, as much as possible, battle damages received. Particular attention was, of course, paid by Chief Engineer Hartupee to the crippled engine. The men were able to change out the destroyed cam yoke and make other temporary engine room fixes, permitting Lt. Cmdr. Shirk's ironclad to get underway at 3:00in the afternoon and steam down to De Sharoon's, where she landed about an hour later. As Shirk's men worked to clear the wreck of their vessel, the other gunboats cast off after dark and steamed down upon Grand Gulf. Just after 9:00 p.m. the morning contest was resumed. It was "as fine a display of fireworks as I had ever witnessed," remembered one 6th Missouri soldier years later. This assault was, however, a ruse.

Blending into the shadows while hugging the Louisiana shore, five unarmed Northern troop transports passed down unscathed while the ironclads kept the Confederate gunners occupied. The gun smoke from the engagement completed the camouflage and within an hour the contract steamers were tied to the west bank at De Sharoon's, four miles below Grand Gulf. That bypass mission accomplished, the gunboats also withdrew, making their landing at a point a mile above the military's vessels.

Later in the evening, Maj. Gen. Grant completed plans for his next move as Capt. Shirk, with his colleagues, wrote out their after action reports. The *Tuscumbia* was hit 81 times during her engagement with Fort Cobun, suffered five dead and 24 wounded, and was effectively put out of action. Porter wrote to navy secretary Gideon Welles that evening to confess that the "broad giant" was "cut up a great deal and proved herself a poor ship in a hot engagement." Lt. Cmdr. Shirk was less generous, steaming, "Altogether, the *Tuscumbia* is a disgrace." Still, with most of the other vessels in fairly good shape, RAdm. Porter was able to close his own review of the day's fight to his superior with a hopeful forecast: "We land the army in the morning on the other side and march to Vicksburg." Contrary to the expectations of many, the bluecoats were unopposed when they stepped ashore at Bruinsburg, MS.[10]

Beginning at 4:30 a.m. on April 30, the officer of the watch recorded in the *Tuscumbia*'s log the embarkation of troops aboard the Federal gunboats and transports and their departure for "down the river" two hours later. Aboard the shattered gunboat, repair crews continued their efforts to put right the previous day's damages. At 1:55 p.m., the crew being assembled, Lt. Cmdr. Shirk read the Episcopal burial service and a few minutes later the bodies of Samuel Bagsley, Francis Adams, Henri Souquet, John Manly, and William Wright were taken ashore for interment.

Over the next several days the Army of the Tennessee, with aid from Porter's gunboats and the USQM transports, crossed the Mississippi and began its campaign against Vicksburg from the south. Early on May 3 the magazines of the Grand Gulf citadel were blown up as the post was abandoned by the Confederates. The place was occupied by the squadron before dark, at which point the wounded aboard the flag boat *Benton* were brought down and placed aboard the *Tuscumbia*. Mending of the latter continued around the clock. Progress was sufficient by sunrise on May 6 to allow the "broad giant" to stand up the river. Passing Hard Times Landing, she entered the Hurricane Island chute and landed at the Joseph Davis plantation about noon. The ironclad had no sooner come to a halt than a launch was dispatched up to the wreck of the *Indianola* with a shopping list of desired items. Following an afternoon successfully seeking hog chains, tools, and other items from the wreck of the Brown-built craft, Carpenter Cronan returned to the *Tuscumbia* at sunset. Having shifted to James's Plantation early on May 7, Lt. Cmdr. Shirk's crew resumed their labors. For several hours that afternoon, hands, under the direction of Dr. Frederick E. Potter, removed the sick and wounded from the *Tuscumbia* and took them ashore by boat to a makeshift naval hospital in the Negro quarters. While those men were attended to, the ironclad, though still partially disabled, remained on guard duty.

During the week, RAdm. Porter, with several of his vessels, steamed up the Red River on a mission to capture Fort DeRussy and to resolve logistical and strategic matters with the commanders of the West Gulf Blockading Squadron. While he was away, Lt.

Cmdr. Elias K. Owen of the *Louisville* was put in charge of the vessels left behind to support the Army of the Tennessee.

On May 9 a message was sent aboard the *Louisville* from the headquarters of Maj. Gen. Grant informing him that a new road had been opened from Young's Point to below the Warrenton batteries, one that would shorten the route over which the army had to transport its supplies. To help protect this artery and the depot at its upper end, the commanding general requested that the *Tuscumbia* be stationed off the latter point, with another boat at Grand Gulf.

After acknowledging Grant's requirement next morning he replied that Lt. Cmdr. Shirk's vessel, and several others would move accordingly. Simultaneously, he took advantage of an army tugboat headed south to inform RAdm. Porter of this development. At the same time, he revealed that the *Tuscumbia* had "her water-wheel beam up and her repairs generally nearly finished." With crewmen still patching her, the "broad giant" was ordered on May 13 to serve as something of a towboat/rescue craft. The

Confederate Batteries at Vicksburg. Just as had occurred in April, Union sailors gazing through their long spyglasses would have seen formidable defenses at Vicksburg in May when they were asked to bombard the city in cooperation with land operations by the U.S. Army. Three water batteries were situated for a distance of about three miles in front of the fortress town. The upper, located below Fort Hill, commanded the bend in the river above the city and were operated by the First Tennessee Heavy Artillery Regiment. The South Fork lower batteries, at the southern end of the citadel, were managed by the First Louisiana Heavy Artillery, while the center battery, those directly in front of Vicksburg, were fought by the Eighth Louisiana Artillery Battalion (*Miller's Photographic History of the Civil War*).

Carondelet had gone aground while moving up the chute at Hurricane Island. Arriving on the scene early next morning, the *Tuscumbia* took lines from the Pook "turtle" and within two hours had pulled her free. That afternoon, as she was proceeding back to the James place, Lt. Cmdr. Shirk's command was passed by the *General Price* carrying RAdm. Porter back from his Red River sojourn. After going ashore at Biggs Landing, the squadron commander walked back to Young's Point, where he boarded his normal flagboat, the *Black Hawk*.

Just after breakfast on May 15 the *Mound City*, under Lt. Cmdr. Byron Wilson, steamed upriver to reconnoiter the Confederate casemate battery at Warrenton. The *Tuscumbia* was ordered to join her. While standing offshore below the place with their hands at quarters, the Pook "turtle" sent a gig ashore to investigate and the landing party quickly made contact with the enemy. A signal was quickly sent to the *Mound City* that "rebels were about" and the sailors returned aboard.

The *Mound City* and *Tuscumbia* then opened Dahlgren fire upon the Southern battery, from which smoke soon arose. Other buildings were also on fire and within 15 minutes of the beginning of the shoot Wilson was able to send two gigs of armed men back ashore. The bluejackets found the battery abandoned and a number of storage facilities going up in smoke. Several additional houses were set afire by the tars before the boats returned. Going down in the *Black Hawk*, Porter personally examined the site the next morning "to be certain that the work was thoroughly destroyed." It was— and "a troublesome place," as he wrote Secretary Welles that night, that "merits its fate." The following morning while on an inspection of the area at and around James's Plantation, the squadron commander spent just over two hours aboard the *Tuscumbia*, speaking with Lt. Cmdr. Shirk and reviewing the hands and vessel readiness, and decided that the "broad giant" was once more battle ready.

Determined to play as big a support role in the end stage of the Vicksburg campaign as possible, Porter now took every opportunity to attack the riverside defenses of Vicksburg, with both mortar boats and gunboats. This process would not end until the fortress town surrendered.

About 4:00 p.m. on the afternoon of May 19, a letter headed from the "rear of Vicksburg" arrived aboard the *Black Hawk* from Maj. Gen. Grant. Tearing it open, the Mississippi Squadron boss learned directly that the Army of the Tennessee was investing the Confederate river fortress from above and on the left. Half of the enemy soldiers engaged in battle at Big Black River on May 17 and Champion's Hill the day before were unable to retreat back inside their fortifications. "If you could run down," he asked, "and throw shell in just back of the lower part of the city, it would aid us and demoralize an already badly beaten enemy." A message was rapidly sent to Lt. Cmdr. Greer of the *Benton*, who was temporarily in command of the gunboats on the Mississippi below the citadel while the admiral was up the Yazoo supporting the subjugation of the Haynes' Bluff salient. Greer was to take all of those vessels as unobtrusively as possible up toward the city to the opposite riverbank along the De Soto Peninsula. While not immediately opening fire, they were to remain prepared to place shells on enemy positions should Federal ground troops be seen on the attack.

However, if Greer actually observed the Confederates opening fire, he was to move up, together with the *Tuscumbia* and *Carondelet*, and open long-range fire upon the

6—*Tuscumbia*: The "Broad Giant" vs. Vicksburg 271

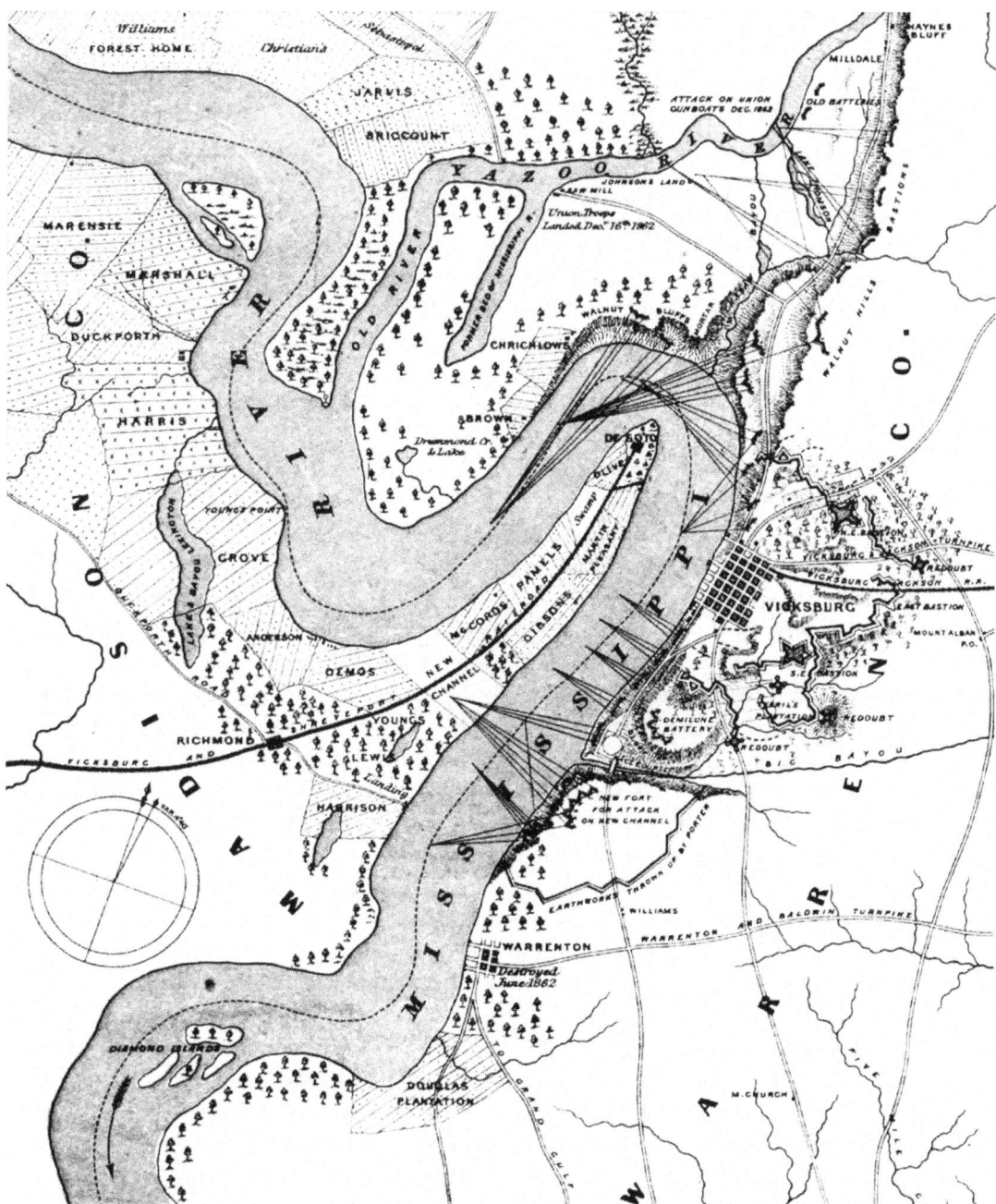

Map of Vicksburg's Defenses. This contemporary map gives the reader an idea of the river defenses of Fortress Vicksburg. In addition to the three principal batteries in front of the city, a smaller, casemated battery was manned at Warrenton. On May 15, the *Tuscumbia* and the Eads-built ironclad *Mound City* shelled the location, putting it out of action. It was "a troublesome place," RAdm. Porter wrote navy secretary Gideon Welles the evening after, and it "merit[ed] its fate." Determined to play as big a support role in the end stage of the Vicksburg campaign as possible, the Mississippi Squadron now took every opportunity to attack the riverside defenses of Vicksburg, both with mortar boats and gunboats (Library of Congress).

offending South Fort batteries on the hills above the bluecoat soldiers. The object would be to "disconcert the enemy," which is what Porter believed long-range fire could accomplish. No sooner had the admiral read Grant's missive and messaged Greer than another call arrived from Maj. Gen. William T. Sherman indicating that he was making an attack on the city's right flank. He too asked for gunboat support, particularly against one of the lower water batteries on the extremity of the Confederate positions, the one operating the famous 18-pounder "Whistling Dick."

Another order was quickly written out, this one handed to Porter's personal aide at 4:20 p.m. for delivery to Greer. The fleet commander wished the *Benton*'s captain to take his craft "up high enough" to lob shells into the forts and the city, keeping the vessels sufficiently separated so enemy gunners could not get their range. By "high enough" he meant initially the mouth of the uncompleted Williams Canal, but if the way were clear he was authorized to move farther up, always "looking out for your vessels."

Porter's directive failed to reach Greer. The veteran captain of the *Benton*, acting on his own hook, however, had steamed up to the foot of the canal that morning. There, at 12:30 p.m., "a large gun put up to control the canal" opened fire on his ironclad trio. None of its shots scored on the gunboats, which, in turn, "fired back, using heavy charges and long-range shell." These shells had fuses cut to 10 and 15 seconds, which gave them time to fly the estimated 2,100 yards over the river into the forts. The ironclads completed their shoot and then turned back to the riverbank on the De Soto Peninsula, where they tied up. At 4:30 p.m., the three Union gunboats cast off and got underway back toward the other side and "when in range, opened fire." Toward dark, the vessels retired to their makeshift Louisiana landing.

The assault by Sherman's soldiers was unsuccessful. "My troops reached the top of the parapet," he later remembered, "but could not get over." The Confederate soldiers in their strongly manned locations "fought hard and well. My losses were pretty heavy." Rebel 1st Lt. Calvin M. Smith of the 31st Tennessee, who kept a diary during the siege, summarized briefly: "3 gunboats moved up and exchanged a few shells and floated down. Flag came down but was run up again."

Later that night Porter, still in the Yazoo and unhappy that Greer had not received his order, was relieved to learn that his subordinate had nevertheless taken the initiative to engage Vicksburg's river defenses. Just before 10:00 p.m. another message was dispatched by aide to the *Benton* requiring that Greer's little task group shell the city from long range that night. If the *Tuscumbia*, which now had only 5-second fuses, was unavailable, she was to be sent back to Grand Gulf for more. By the time Greer received Porter's latest, it was already dark and the "broad giant" was returning downstream. Before his departure, Lt. Cmdr. Shirk wrote to RAdm. Porter telling of the afternoon's shoot, citing the reason for his withdrawal and indicating that he would be back next morning "ready to engage the enemy again."[11] The *Tuscumbia* returned a little later than expected and was unable to participate in the general bombardment of Vicksburg on May 20–21. About sunset on the latter day, RAdm. Porter received a communication from Maj. Gen. Grant announcing that three corps of the Army of the Tennessee would assault the city at 10:00 the next morning. The navy was asked to shell the town continuously for half an hour before the soldiers stepped off and 30 minutes thereafter.

Continued night harassment fire by gunboats and mortarboats beginning before midnight would also be appreciated.

Now available and wanting to make certain there was no communication difficulty, Porter decided that this time he would be in personal command, flying his flag from the tug *Ivy*. The Mississippi Squadron commander then wrote out and forwarded a set of instructions to his four participating ironclad commanders, acquainting them with the army's upcoming program and how their vessels were expected to participate beginning at 8:00 a.m. on May 22. The captain of the *Ivy* was routed out of his bunk at midnight and ordered to take one set of orders down to the *Tuscumbia*, then at Warrenton. Although the "broad giant" was still in "very bad condition" after the Grand Gulf fight, Lt. Cmdr. Shirk was informed that he just must get his vessel into action. "If she sinks," Porter confirmed, "the tug will pick up the swimmers."

Through the night, *Benton*, *Mound City*, and *Carondelet* ferried soldiers of the XVII Corps, 6th Division, across the river to Warrenton, where they could join with the left flank troops of Maj. Gen. McClernand's XIII Corps. Most of the harassing fire was left to the 13-inch mortars on their little scows anchored off the De Soto Peninsula. The *Mound City* was the first to start up the river, at 7:00 a.m., followed an hour later by the *Benton*, *Carondelet*, and *Tuscumbia*. As they reached the mouth of the Williams Canal, the quartet was observed approaching by the gunners of the 1st Louisiana Heavy Artillery. The little *Ivy* was readily seen flying a blue rear admiral's pennant and bobbing among the larger vessels.

As the ironclads passed on up, they prepared to fight bows on, keeping their vulnerable port sides shielded by the De Soto Peninsula. There followed, beginning at 8:55 a.m., a spirited slug fest with the South Fort "hill batteries," those guns originally sighted on the Williams Canal, in which the 18-pounder "Whistling Dick" was temporarily disabled. Once the enemy cannon were silenced, the northern vessels passed up, leaving the *Tuscumbia* behind to make certain that the inactive guns were not brought back to life to play upon the upstream ironclads.

The battle that followed between the forts near the Marine Hospital and the three ironclads was as vicious as the fight at Grand Gulf a month earlier as, Porter later claimed, the gunboats having to endure the "hottest fire the gunboats have ever been under." Still, the navy should have been at an advantage. Unlike Grand Gulf, the Confederate batteries fought from almost riverbank level instead of high above on cliffs. Porter's trio closed on the Marine Hospital batteries, fighting them from no more than 450 yards offshore. The Confederate guns were very accurate and both the *Benton* and *Mound City* were struck numerous times. The *Carondelet*, hit twice, took a shot that opened a huge gash just above her waterline that required quick damage control work. Ashore, 1st Lt. Smith observed that the three were dropping shells "thick and fast," but he was reassured because "we were ever secure in our ditches."

At this point, "a flame of fire and smoke leaped out of the earth, as it were," recalled *Ivy* captain Acting Master's Mate Charles Heckman ("Heck") Gulick. It was reasoned that three Confederate pieces were sighted specifically on them (or so it seemed). Porter directed the little boat to run alongside the *Tuscumbia* and, by speaking trumpet, Lt. Cmdr. Shirk was ordered to move up and join the contest. The two XI-inch Dahlgrens of the "broad giant," commanded by Acting Ensigns James Marshall and Thomas M.

Farrell (the only guns engaged), expended 55 shells. Once more, *Tuscumbia* was heavily damaged. Hits on her forward turret again loosened spikes holding on her armor while her pilothouse was badly dented, to put it mildly. Seaman Francis Reno, at the wheel, was wounded. On the *Ivy*, Mate Gulick observed that on one occasion a shot struck the ironclad's turret "and bounded over on her wheelhouse and from there on the forecastle of the tug." It did not, he opined, miss "the admiral's head six inches." In addition, the hog chains salvaged from the *Indianola* and newly installed on the *Tuscumbia* were shot through. For a second time, Lt. Cmdr. Shirk was forced to drop out of combat and once again, when given the opportunity to report on his damages, virtually shouted on paper: "I again most respectfully call your attention to the outrageous manner in which this ship has been put together." Fortunately, this time, unlike Grand Gulf, his ship suffered no casualties.

After two hours and 15 minutes, much longer than the army had requested, the *Ivy* came alongside the injured *Tuscumbia* and Porter ordered that she hoist signals to the squadron for discontinuance of the action. By the time the fight concluded, the Union ironclads, badly hurt, had begun to run out of ammunition. That night, the ironclads anchored abreast a crevasse. "The bank," according to eyewitness Gulick, "was a bluff and the hill was some 300 yards back with timber in the bottom."

In writing to Maj. Gen. Grant regarding the failure of his boats later that night, RAdm. Porter admitted that the Louisiana gun positions "were a tough nut to crack." Fortunately no one aboard any of the craft was killed and, in addition to "Whistling Dick" being put out of action, at least temporarily, the "Widow Blakeley" had burst at the muzzle. Grant was less successful still; his assault during the day was one of the largest single-day defeats of the Civil War, with some 3,000 casualties.

Porter's message to Grant passed one that evening from the commanding general to the admiral, admitting that in light of the military failures it would be necessary to put the city of Vicksburg under siege. To help him complete the ring around it, the navy boss was asked if it would be possible to steam even farther up the Mississippi and silence the Confederate Upper Batteries, enabling Sherman to control the Yazoo River area. This new request was not received until the morning of May 23. As much as he would have liked to push on up to help his army colleagues, RAdm. Porter had to write back saying that because of the strong river current his vessels could not buck it would be virtually impossible to attain the desired attack position "without sacrificing every vessel and man on board." The navy was doing all that it could and would continue to do its utmost with its "small means."

Ever hopeful and not personally acquainted with Porter's problems, Maj. Gen. Grant wrote back again on May 24 saying that his men could keep the upper water battery silenced by sharpshooting its gunners, and field guns could silence the guns. However, it remained essential for "one or two gunboats" to come and "enfilade the southern slope." Once more the admiral had to decline participation: "I have but one gunboat here [*General Price*]. She is unfit for the purpose. The *Carondelet* below is unfit to go into a fight. *Tuscumbia* disabled." He would, however, employ his mortars if that would assist. He did not add that not only was the "broad giant" disabled but she was also out of both coal and ammunition.

The *Tuscumbia* remained hors de combat for most of June and was anchored near

***Tuscumbia* Engaged.** To support a great May 22, 1863, Federal military assault on the defenses of Vicksburg, elements of the Mississippi Squadron engaged the citadel's batteries. Following a spirited shoot against the South Fork guns, the "Broad Giant" and three other ironclads took on the Confederate guns located near the Marine Hospital. The battle that followed was as vicious as the fight at Grand Gulf a month earlier was, Porter later claimed, and that the gunboats had to endure the "hottest fire the gunboats have ever been under." Once more, *Tuscumbia* was heavily damaged. Damage can be seen at the rear of her starboard paddle box in this partial photo. Moored inboard with her are the light-draught *Linden* (Tinclad No. 10) and two mortar boats, one with a 13-inch mortar mounted onboard (Naval History and Heritage Command).

where she had halted on May 22. She was unable to participate in the last bombardment attacks made by the Mississippi Squadron against Vicksburg before the siege concluded. In this timeframe, Acting Master Augustus S. Tayon went ashore and Acting Ensign James Marshall was appointed the boat's acting master. Fatigue parties struggled to put the *Tuscumbia* right during those weeks, while every effort was made to secure fuel for her boilers. Finally, on June 22, Lt. Cmdr. Shirk was able to inform RAdm. Porter that he had "got the last hog chain that had parted up again and a strain on it." He had also been able to secure about 150 bushels for coal from a barge sunk in a nearby crevasse. Within a couple of days, ammunition was secured and the ironclad was finally able to move from her temporary anchorage below Vicksburg to the Warrenton landing. On June 29 her captain informed his superior that an intercepted letter from a Confederate general had come into his possession indicating concern that the long-besieged citadel would fall on Saturday or Sunday, June 28 or 29. It fell on Saturday, July 4.[12]

Badly in need of a major refit, the Tuscumbia remained off Vicksburg until August, when she was ordered north to the U.S. naval station at Memphis. When Lt. Cmdr. Shirk was given command of the 7th District of the Mississippi Squadron in September he was succeeded as captain by Acting Master Marshall. Thinking it might be possible to rebuild the "broad giant," RAdm. Porter, on October 25, passed orders to the station commandant to have the *Tuscumbia* sent "to Cairo as soon as there was sufficient water to take her over the bars." She departed the same afternoon and arrived several days later.

Repairs at Cairo were distressingly slow, primarily because of a "want of hands." In May 1864, the "broad giant" was transferred to the Mound City naval station, but once again more pressing needs hijacked the workers who might have been employed in putting her right. In July, as he was leaving to take up duties as commander of the North Atlantic Blockading Squadron, RAdm. Porter confirmed what everyone involved already suspected: the *Tuscumbia*'s operational career was over and she would not be rebuilt. In a memorandum to his fleet captain, he ordered that men be found to get "the iron off her deck."

The decision to remove the giant ironclad from the fleet was questioned by Porter's successor, Acting RAdm. Samuel Phillips Lee, who took over the squadron on November 1. Five days later, he ordered the commandant of the Mound City naval station to have another survey taken on the ironclad, this one by naval constructor Charles F. Kendall. Unless the Cincinnati-born expert found some reason not to proceed, preparation of the *Tuscumbia* for service was to be "pushed."

Laborers at the Mound City yard duly turned their attention to the *Tuscumbia* in November and some minor, largely housekeeping, work was done on the flat-bottomed gunboat. By December, the decision was taken to dismantle her and by the end of February 1865 she was listed as being at the station "dismantled." When the Civil War ended in April, all of the squadron vessels, save just a few, were likewise withdrawn, demilitarized, and sold.[13]

We know that by August 2 twelve ironclads, including the *Tuscumbia*, the *Chillicothe*, and the hulk of the *Indianola*, were dismantled (or being dismantled), then inspected and moored in the towhead chutes above the naval station. All were "laid up in ordinary," the ancient term for an out-of-commission naval vessel being held in reserve for some future purpose. It was a state requiring only minimum maintenance and not dissimilar from the modern concept of "mothballing." Acting Volunteer Lt. George P. Lord, late skipper of the *Chillicothe*, a few other officers, and a handful of ratings were assigned to the skeleton upkeep crews. During the second week of August, Acting Rear Adm. Lee reported to Washington that all of the vessels to be liquidated were now in the hands of Com. John W. Livingston (1804–1886), the commander of the Mound City naval station. The Mississippi Squadron ceased to exist on August 14, when its commander hauled down his flag and returned East.

In the months after Lee quit the West, Com. Livingston continued to sell off the equipment, stores, and vessels of the ex-squadron. On November 21 the commodore advertised the auction of the remaining ironclads in most of the river papers. That

6—*Tuscumbia*: The "Broad Giant" vs. Vicksburg   277

Moored to the Riverbank. As the results of the damage suffered in combat against the Confederate batteries, the *Tuscumbia* remained hors de combat for most of June and was anchored near where she had halted on May 22. She was unable to participate in the last bombardment attacks made by the Mississippi Squadron against Vicksburg before the siege concluded. Fatigue parties struggled to put her right during those weeks, but the *Tuscumbia* remained off Vicksburg until August. Badly in need of a major refit, the "Broad Giant" was then ordered north to the U.S. naval station at Mound City. She did not return to the war but was sold out of service on November 29, 1865, to W.K. Adams for $3,300. Stripped of valuables, the hull languished a short distance from the mouth of the Cache River until October 1870, when the remaining woodwork was burned to get the hulk out of the way of river users (Naval History and Heritage Command).

morning, both the *St. Louis Daily Missouri Democrat* and *St. Louis Daily Missouri Republican* advised the public that some of the remaining vessels of the late fleet were going under the gavel. The sale would begin promptly at noon on Wednesday, November 29. All of them would be sold to the highest bidder, "together with their engines, tackle, and furniture." The newspapers also advertised the auction of 5,000 tons of the ex-fleet's coal and a number of coal barges for November 28 and the sale of 250–300 tons of "T" railroad iron—this being the armor of the dismantled City Series ironclads—on November 30. We do not know for certain exactly how this particular ship sale progressed. It was one of many surplus auctions held around the country between 1865 and 1867 by the navy and the army's Quartermaster Department. Although there are no accounts of it in known diaries or correspondence and it was not widely covered by the public press, it undoubtedly unfolded much like the August sale, which was fully reported by several newspapers.

At noon on a chilly November 29, auctioneer Solomon A. Silver gaveled the afternoon sale into session and began, probably alphabetically, to sell off the ironclads. It was rather late when he got to the *Tuscumbia*. With little competition from other bidders, W.K. Adams won the "broad giant" with a bid of $3,300. The ship broker immediately ordered his prize stripped of any iron and other valuables and had the hull towed downstream a short distance to the mouth of the Cache River, where it was beached. There it remained until October 1870, when the remaining woodwork was burned to get the hulk out of the way of river traffic.[14]

7

Joseph Brown, Enterpreneur and Mayor Again: Life After Gunboats

Joseph Brown led an interesting and diverse life in the years before construction of his three ironclads and did so again afterwards. He was not one of those Civil War participants who just faded away, but he instead took an active role in the commercial, civic, and social life of his community, gathering laurels as a politician and raconteur. Space does not permit a detailed biography after his three ironclads were built, but, in justice to his largely forgotten contributions, we do offer substantial overview.

When RAdm. David Dixon Porter took over the Mississippi Squadron in October 1862, one of the first major projects he pushed was a program for the construction of numerous light-draught gunboats suitable for use in the shallowest streams and waterways. Conceived by his predecessor RAdm. Charles Henry Davis, the "tinclad" type could be easily converted from civilian steamers, protected with thin iron armor, and armed with light cannon. Although the first of the vessels to be completed was actually launched in St. Louis, Porter saw merit in allowing the naval building yards of that city to concentrate on larger ironclads already under construction and to refer most of the tinclad construction to the Cincinnati Marine Ways, which Joseph Brown had leased and where the *Chillicothe* and *Indianola* were being finished.

Porter believed that the Cincinnati facility—where Brown as contractor worked closely with its president, Capt. Hercules Carrel, and his chief superintendent, Oliver P. Tharp—could easily handle the rapid modification of light draughts. Additionally, the work could be overseen by Porter's own newly appointed supervisors rather than Com. Joseph Hull and Constructor Edward Hartt, who were needed to complete the delayed *Choctaw* and *Lafayette*. En route to take up his duties at Cario, Porter enthusiastically wrote to the navy secretary, Gideon Welles, requesting permission to greatly expand the infant light-draught acquisition program. Appreciating that Porter had only a few weeks' tenure in his current post and would need more boats if he was to achieve this new directive, the secretary authorized the Cairo naval leadership to purchase and arm 12 to 15 more light draughts for use on the rivers emptying into the Gulf of Mexico. There was a caveat: someday they might all be transferred to the West Gulf Coast Blockading Squadron. As Welles put it, the boats would form a part of the Mississippi Squadron "until required in the Gulf." Above all, "that they are for any squadron but your own will be known only to yourself."

By the time Secretary Welles' communication was received in Cairo at the end of October, Porter had already contracted with Joseph Brown for the conversion of river steamers. It was quickly learned at the beginning of November that the overall demand for civilian steamboats, particularly from the U.S. Army, was driving up prices. Still, only new boats would be acquired, with their invoices forwarded to the Bureau of Construction. The admiral was able to obtain from Joseph Brown what he believed to be very competitive alteration rates of $8,500 per boat, including "outfit of every kind." Indeed, he was pleased that the modification cost was actually $2,000 per boat "cheaper than Mr. Hartt said he could do it for."

The arrangements worked out with Brown called for steamers—identified by naval officers asked to seek them out—would be paid for by the government and then delivered to Brown's leased yards for modification. Once in hand, the given craft would have her superstructure cut down to the boiler (main) deck, which was then strengthened to hold her cannon, and her boilers lowered into the holds. New bulwarks would be built, a pilothouse would be erected, and thin armor added to the pilothouse and superstructure. "These boats have been covered with iron all around and 11 feet high," Welles was informed by Porter. This made them "perfectly rifle proof and proof around the boilers against light cannon shot." The new tinclads had "every comfort and accommodation" and carried "eight 24-pounder howitzers in smooth water without any trouble." The boats were all "of good size" and could "carry comfortably 200 men for an expedition and accommodate a great many officers."

When the deck and casemate arrangements were complete, the boats altered by Brown at Cincinnati were then sent to the naval yards at Cairo or, later, Mound City, for their furniture, armament, and crews. When several vessels were purchased close together it was usual practice to send one of them awaiting her turn for alteration ahead to Cairo or Mound City loaded with furniture and other needs acquired in the Queen City. She would then return empty to Brown's yards for conversion. During late October and November, tinclad modification was launched full-bore at the Cincinnati Marine Ways. Seven tinclads were commissioned in December: *Forest Rose and Glide I* (December 3), *Romeo* (December 11), *Juliet* (December 14), *New Era* (December 1?), *Rattler* (December 19), and *Silver Lake* (December 24). These vessels and others besides were purchased and altered without much fanfare over the next two years. Additional physical changes were from time to time requested of contractor Brown by RAdm. Porter in the same manner as he requested alterations to the *Indianola* and *Tuscumbia*. For example, on December 15 the admiral sent orders to Lt. Cmdr. Smith: "If it can be done without delay in Cincinnati ... I wish the ports on these steamers cut up 1 foot higher; that the guns have no elevation."

It is true that, at least initially, there was some difficulty in adequately paying Joseph Brown's expense and reimbursement claims. On December 20 the squadron's Cairo-based fleet captain informed Porter that the Mississippi Squadron's chief bursar had previously sent the Cincinnatian "all the money he could spare" and had just received another $56,000 from Washington to complete payment. Porter, anxious for receipt of additional tinclads, attempted to make certain that his people stayed on top of payments. On January 14, 1863, he wrote Cairo from Arkansas Post inquiring whether sufficient funds were being regularly received to pay for the steamers "as they are bought." It was important, the commander continued, that as soon as Brown altered a steamer, he was to be paid for her at the rate of $8,500, plus extra charges for special modifications.

Earlier in January the squadron ordnance officer, Lt. Cmdr. Joseph P. Sanford, was dispatched to Cincinnati, along with Master Carpenter Charles F. Kendall, to assume responsibility for affairs at that city from Lt. Cmdr. Smith, including the supervision of tinclad alterations. Kendall at war's end would run a last survey on the Brown ironclad *Tuscumbia*. During his tenure at Cincinnati, Kendall, like Brown, would be criticized by certain naval officers regarding alleged defects in some of the delivered boats. One man opined, "Mr. Joseph Brown's work on these vessels is of the most worthless description.... Mr. Kendall seems not fit for his position."

Once the *Tuscumbia* was commissioned on March 12, 1863, Joseph Brown turned almost his entire attention to tinclad conversions. The aggressive Federal acquisition of suitable light-draught steamers and his conversion of them continued apace. (In early 1864 in the midst of all this Brown became the proud adoptive father of a little girl, whom he and his wife named Virginia, with the nickname of Jennie. Having lost two children a decade earlier, this seven-year-old would become the apple of their eye.) Late in 1864, a reporter from the *Chicago Daily Tribune* reviewed wartime industry in the Queen City. As he told his readers on December 1, 1864, twenty-one gunboats of all classes had been rebuilt and fitted out in the previous twelve months, including "a

Converted Wiggins Ferry Steamer *Queen City*. Two ferryboats belonging to the Wiggins Ferry Company of St. Louis, MO, were acquired by the U.S. Navy on February 13, 1863, and were transferred to Cincinnati, OH, where contractor Joseph Brown converted them into light-draught gunboats. The one shown, *Queen City* (Tinclad No. 26), was captured at Clarendon, Arkansas, on June 24, 1864, and subsequently destroyed (Naval History and Heritage Command).

number of sternwheel boats ... tinclads as the naval men call them." Aside from comments upon individual units joining the squadron, little more is heard about tinclad acquisition during the remainder of the war.

The last tinclad placed into service was Joseph Brown's own craft. During the war the *Tempest* (original name retained) was operated locally by the contractor, carrying supplies needed for the conversion effort. Brown sold the 161-ton stern-wheeler to the U.S. Navy on December 30, 1864, for $55,000; however, the finances of the transaction were not completed until February 10, 1865. She was then modified into Tinclad No. 1. Transferred West, she was taken in hand for her final outfit and commissioned at Cairo on April 26,1865, as the replacement for the command ship and flagboat *Black Hawk*, which was lost four days earlier.

When the war was over in 1865, Brown had the extreme satisfaction of knowing that he had converted 55 of the 66 tinclads acquired by the U.S. Navy during the conflict, including a number that served with the West Gulf Blockading Squadron. This record for steamer modification by the Cincinnati Marine Way far exceeded that of any other Civil War shipyard.[1]

List of Light Draught Gunboats
Modified by Joseph Brown, 1862–1865[2]

1862

Name & No.	Rig	Purchased/Captured	Alteration	Commissioned	Armament
Forest Rose 9	SW	11–15–62	Cincinnati	12–3–62	2 30pdr-r; 4 24pdr-SB
Glide I	SW	11–17–62	Cincinnati	12–3–62	6 24pdr-SB
Romeo 3	SW	10–31–62	Cincinnati	12–11–62	6 24pdr-SB
Juliet 4	SW	11–1–62	Cincinnati	12–14–62	6 24pdr-SB
New Era 7	SW	10–27–62	Cincinnati	12–1?–62	6 24pdr-SB
Rattler 1	S	11–11–62	Cincinnati/Cairo	12–19–62	2 30pdr-r; 4 24pdr-SB
Silver Lake 23	SW	11–15–62	Cincinnati	12–24–62	6 24pdr-SB

1863

Name & No.	Rig	Purchased/Captured	Alterations	Commissioned	Armament
Linden 10	S	11–20–62	Cincinnati	1–3–62	6 24-pdr-SB; 6 24-pdr-SB
Springfield 22	SW	11–20–62	Cincinnati	1–12–63	6 24pdr-SB
Cricket 6	SW	11–18–62	Cincinnati	1–19–63	6 24pdr-SB
Prairie Bird 10	S	12–19–62	Cincinnati	1–2?–63	8 24pdr-SB
Curlew 12	SW	12–17–62	Cincinnati	2–16–63	8 24pdr-SB
Covington 25	S	2–13–62	Cincinnati	3–?–63	2 30pdr-r; 2 50pdr-r
Argosy 27	SW	3–24–62	Cincinnati	3–29–63	6 24pdr-SB; 2 12-pdr-r
Hastings 15	S	3–24–63	Cincinnati	4–?–63	2 32pdr-SB; 3 24pdr-SB
Petrel 5	SW	12–22–62	Cincinnati	4–?–62	8 24pdr-SB
Fort Hindman 13	S	3–14–63	Cincinnati	4–?–63	6 8"-SB

Name & No.	Rig	Purchased/Captured	Alterations	Commissioned	Armament
Queen City 26	S	2–13–63	Cincinnati	4–1–63	2 32pdr-SB; 4 24pdr-SB
Naumkeag 37	SW	4–14–63	Cincinnati	4–16–63	2 30pdr-r; 4 24pdr-SB
Champion 24	S	3–14–63	Cincinnati	4–26–63	2 30pdr-r; 1 24pdr-SB; 1 12pdr-SB
Fawn 30	SW	5–13–63	Cincinnati	5–11–63	6 24pdr-SB
Kenwood 14	SW	4–3–63	Cincinnati	5–24–63	2 32-pdr-SB; 4 24pdr-SB
Exchange 38	SW	4–6–63	Cincinnati	6–?–63	2 32pdr-SB; 4 24pdr-SB; 1 12pdr-SB
Moose 34	SW	5–20–63	Cincinnati	6–15–63	6 24pdr-SB
Victory 33	S	7–14–63	Cincinnati	7–8–63	6 24pdr-SB
Reindeer 35	SW	6–13–63	Cincinnati	7–25–63	6 24pdr-SB
Wave 45	S	11–14–63	Cincinnati	WGCBS	6 24pdr-SB
Glide II 43	S	11–30–63	Cincinnati	WGCBS	4 24pdr-SB
Stockdale 42	SW	11–13–63	Cincinnati	WGCBS	4 24pdr-SB
Nyanza 41	S	11–4–63	Cincinnati	WGCBS	6 24pdr-SB

1864

Name & No.	Rig	Purchased/Captured	Alterations	Commissioned	Armament
Gazelle 50	S	11–21–63	Cincinnati	WGCBS	6 12pdr-r
Elfin 52	SW	2–23–64	Cincinnati	3–?–64	8 24pdr-SB
Fairy 51	SW	2–10–64	Cincinnati	3–10–64	8 24pdr-SB
Meteor 44	S	1–23–64	Cincinnati	WGCBS	2 32pdr-SB; 2 24pdr-SB
Undine 55	SW	3–7–64	Cincinnati	4–?–64	8 24pdr-SB
Tallahatchie 46	S	1–23–64	Cincinnati	WGCBS	4 24-pdr SB
Naiad 53	SW	3–3–64	Cincinnati	4–3–64	8 24pdr SB
Nymph 54	SW	3–8–64	Cincinnati	4–11–64	8 24pdr SB
Carrabasset 49	S	1–23–64	Cincinnati	WGCBS	2 32pdr-SB; 4 24pdr-SB
Elk 47	S	12–8–63	Cincinnati	WGCBS	2 32pdr-SB; 4 24pdr-SB
Rodolph 48	SW	12–31–63	Cincinnati	WGCBS	2 32pdr-SB; 2 24-pdr-SB
Huntress 58	SW	5–?–64	Cincinnati	6–10–64	2 30pdr-r; 4 24pdr-SB
Peri 57	SW	4–30–64	Cincinnati	6–20–64	1 30pdr-r; 6 24pdr-SB
Sibyl 59	S	4–27–64	Cincinnati	5–26–64	2 30pdr-r; 2 24pdr-SB
Siren 56	SW	3–11–64	Cincinnati	8–30–64	2 24pdr-SB

1865

Name & No.	Rig	Purchased/ Captured	Alterations	Commissioned	Armament
Grosbeak 8	S	2–3–65	Cincinnati	2–24–65	2 30pdr-r; 1 12pdr-SB
Colossus 25	SW	12–6–64	Cincinnati	2–24–65	2 30pdr-r; 4 24pdr-SB; 1 12pdr-SB
Mist 26	SW	12–23–64	Cincinnati	3–3–65	2 20pdr-r; 4 24pdr-SB; 1 12pdr-SB
Collier 29	SW	12–7–64	Cincinnati	3–18–65	2 20pdr-r; 6 24pdr-SB; 1 12pdr-SB
Oriole 52	SW	12–7–64	Cincinnati	3–22–65	2 30pdr-r; 6 24pdr-SB; 1 12pdr-SB
Gamage 60	S	12–22–64	Cincinnati	3–23–65	2 20pdr-r; 1 12pdr-SB
Kate 55	SW	12–23–64	Cincinnati	4–2–65	2 20pdr-r; 6 24pdr-SB; 2 12pdr-SB
Ibex 10	S	12–10–64	Cincinnati	4–4–65	2 30pdr-r; 4 24pdr-SB; 2 12pdr-SB
Abeona 32	SW	12–21–64	Cincinnati	4–10–65	2 30pdr-SB; 2 24pdr-SB; 2 12pdr-SB
Tempest 1	S	12–30–64	Cincinnati	4–26–65	2 30pdr-r; 2 24pdr-SB; 2 12pdr-SB

Long familiar with business activities in St. Louis, Joseph Brown planned, as the Civil War ended, to return to his Olive Street home in that city and resume his business career. To that end, he visited with Lewis Vital Bogy (1813–1877), president of the Wiggins Ferry Company, at the carrier's 207 Fourth St. headquarters and arranged to join that concern as its vice president and operational superintendent, as well as serving as a director. Founded in 1819 to provide a river crossing vehicle between St. Louis and Illinoistown, IL (later East St. Louis, IL), the Wiggins Ferry Company, named for the pioneer family of William C. Wiggins, who became company president upon its reforming in 1832. When the original Wiggins charter expired in 1853, the firm was reorganized. Wiggins remained chief executive; among the five board members was Lewis Bogy, who succeeded him in 1863.

By the time of the Great Rebellion, the firm had a monopoly over transfer of goods and passengers directly across the river. To accomplish that end, it operated three ferry boats, two tugboats, and several ferry landing barges. Capitalized at almost $1 million, the company held extensive business property, including warehouses, on both sides of the Mississippi, and employed around a hundred men, half of them dedicated to shore-based activities. Brown was acquainted with Bogy not only from his own prewar occupation as a steamboat captain and entrepreneur but also from his work during the conflict in converting vessels into light-draught gunboats for the U.S. Navy. In particular, two Wiggins ferry boats were acquired from the transfer concern, the *Covington* (Tinclad No. 25) and the *Queen City* (Tinclad No. 26), and taken to Cincinnati for alteration. Bogy, like Brown, was a Democrat.

During the summer of 1865 Brown was able to profitably settle his accounts with the government and the Cincinnati Marine Ways. He and his wife, Virginia, departed Cincinnati's Burnet House and returned to St. Louis, where as a result of his wartime contracting effort he was able to deposit a sum of between $600,000 and $800,000 in local banks. The historian Walter Barlow Stevens tells us he had come to St. Louis from Washington, D.C., "with a valise of $800,000 in currency."[3]

Vital if slight of stature and now sporting the distinguishing large mustache seen in all of his portraits, Brown reentered the St. Louis business and social circles with all of the flair exhibited in his prewar activities. Also, during his first year back in St. Louis, the First Spiritual Society of St. Louis was established by Andrew Jackson Davis (1826–1910) and was chartered by the state of Missouri. Weekly lectures, with Brown in attendance as often as possible, frequently from prominent spiritualism figures began in the Mercantile Library Hall, later shifting to Armory Hall.

Some of Brown's funds were invested in real estate, including properties along Second Street and Main Street, as he believed those thoroughfares would remain the principal commercial arteries of the city. He and others did not see the rapid outward urban growth just then beginning as a continuing trend and his acquisition choices would initially make money. About this same time, Brown also purchased the abandoned building of the St. Philomena School for Girls on Walnut Street and turned it into a modernized hostelry, the Paschall House. When it was opened the building had 100 rooms. It was placed in competition with the four most famous hotels of the town: the Southern at Fourth and Walnut streets, which had just opened in 1865; the Planter's House at Fourth and Chestnut; the Everett House on Fourth near Locust; and the Lindell at Sixth and Washington.

While dabbling in real estate, Brown also concentrated on the day-to-day activities of the Wiggins Ferry Company. He continued his lifelong interest in Mississippi steamboating, which was now, according to leading river historians, entering a sustained period of losing competition with the railroads, which had multiplied in size and scope during the recent conflict. It was at this time that the captain took a financial interest in the Pacific Railroad of Missouri. This carrier, established 15 years earlier, had reached Jefferson City in 1855. Thereafter, it established its own in-house steamboat line to connect passengers and freight between the state's capital town and Kansas City. Brown had probably seen, years earlier, the company advertisement that boldly stated "that at Jefferson City passengers could step from the train to the waiting steamboat and that by this route, the time from St. Louis to Kansas City had been cut to only 50 hours!" Even though the Pacific Railroad link between St. Louis and Kansas City would be completed that September, the fit between this company and its new investor seemed a natural and he soon began to play an important role in its direction. Eventually he would put more money into the line, advancing money to build surface tracks on Poplar Street and would serve as one of the railroad's directors.

A businessman through and through, Brown also remained an accomplished politician, a War Democrat deeply interested in the activities of government in St. Louis, both from a practical economic viewpoint with regards to the Wiggins firm and from deep social beliefs learned from Pastor Lovejoy so many years before. One of the most bitterly divided border states during the Civil War, Missouri emerged from the conflict governed by the Radical Unionists, a vehemently antislavery political party organized in 1863. It was this group that controlled the governor's mansion in 1865 and wrote a new state constitution that barred from public life all who in any way supported the Confederacy. Thousands of former officeholders and soldiers were thus effectively banned from civic participation. Brown, like others, believed this approach to be wrong and spoke on behalf of the disenfranchised.

Because the Federal government no longer needed as many steamer bottoms after the war, the coming of peace brought business depression to watermen and their interests throughout the Mississippi Valley. Many steamers were sold off and owners began to look at consolidating operations as a way of preventing further economic catastrophe. Late in 1865 discussions began in St. Louis between representatives from a number of steamboat lines concerning amalgamation possibilities. Early in 1866 "the most ambitious venture of its kind," as Louis Hunter called it, was incorporated at St. Louis under the name Atlantic and Mississippi Steamship Company. This combine of leading boatmen brought together a mass fleet of 24 big side-wheelers dedicated to providing reliable, regular passenger and freight service between the Missouri river port and New Orleans. The huge organization was capitalized at about $3.5 million, based on the value of the boats and funds from several stockholders, including Joseph Brown, who bought in for $70,000. As Brown later noted, the company started "under a load of heavy debt" because the owners of the line purchased into it their own vessels "at very high prices."

Capt. Brown's mother, Margaret, died at Alton, IL, on March 28. The lady was 88 years old and had resided in the Illinois city for over 30 years. We do not know her son's reaction nor what funeral arrangements were made. On a somewhat happier note, at least for the riverman, another well-known War Democrat visited St. Louis in 1866 and Brown helped shepherd his arrival—President Andrew Johnson. Between the end of August and the end of September, the successor of Abraham Lincoln decided to make a national speaking tour, hoping to gain popular support for his mild Reconstruction policies. Because it traveled from D.C. to New York and hence to Chicago and St. Louis before returning east through the Ohio Valley, it was labeled the "Swing Around the Circle." The campaign failed in its goal, but at some locations there were spectacular moments surrounding it.

When it became known in early August that the president would visit St. Louis, transferring from a train at Alton, IL, to steamers for the passage down the Mississippi, it was determined that two of St. Louis's most famous watermen would be on hand as city/state delegates and official greeters. James B. Eads would make the official welcome on behalf of the citizens of Missouri, while Joseph Brown would serve as commodore of the fleet of the 36 steamers (one representing each state) sent to provide lift for the chief executive and his entourage, which included Gen. Ulysses S. Grant, Gen. William T. Sherman, Adm. David G. Farragut, Secretary of State William H. Seward, Secretary of the Navy Gideon Welles, and many other civilian and military officials, aides, secretaries, etc.

The momentous day arrived on September 8, when Johnson's train came into the station at Alton from Springfield, IL. Following welcoming speeches by local dignitaries and the president's response, Johnson and his official party were escorted through large crowds to the river levee, where they were greeted by Capt. Eads. At the close of the famed engineer's official greeting and the president's rejoinder, bells on all of the steamboats at the levee and away from it sounded as a signal that the downriver portion of the tour was about to begin. The president and his party were escorted aboard the steamer *Andy Johnson*, which was lashed to the steamers *Ruth* and *Olive Branch*. Together, under Brown's direction, the trio turned their bows south with the current and were followed downstream by the others. The sun was bright and the weather was mild.

As soon as the fleet of gaily decorated steamers was well underway, the president and his party crossed over to the *Ruth*, passing up to their cabins escorted by a detachment of Knights Templar. At that point, Capt. Bart Able, a noted steamboat commander in his own right, suggested that, as the boats would soon pass the mouth of the mighty Missouri River, the party should, instead, be escorted to the upper deck to view the sight. The dignitaries were escorted to advantageous viewing locations on the hurricane deck of the *Ruth* and thereafter enjoyed their own company, as well as that of officials from Missouri. Grant, Farragut, Sherman, and the cabinet officers in particular were occupied with receiving and giving greetings. Passing majestically down the river, the armada was cheered by people on shore, and shouts came from other steamboats and vessels encountered or tied up at the bank.

President Andrew Johnson. At the close of the Civil War, Joseph Brown returned to St. Louis a wealthy man and took a position as vice president and operations superintendent of the Wiggins Ferry Company. When President Johnson, making a national speaking tour to gain support for his Reconstruction policies, reached Alton, IL, on September 8, 1866, he was welcomed by various officials, including St. Louis representative James B. Eads and Capt. Brown, commodore of a fleet of 36 steamers that would take him downstream to St. Louis. During the trip, a dinner was served on the flag steamer at which numerous invited guests, including Eads and Brown, were present and afterwards Johnson spoke with a number of selected individuals (Library of Congress).

"The steamer *Ruth*," wrote a columnist from the *New York Times*, "was overcrowded with passengers, crowds of whom gathered around the distinguished excursionists, either to gaze at or shake hands with them." Confusion and milling about were immense, he continued, but there was no attempt to restrain it. A dinner was served at which many of the guests, including Eads and Brown, were present and afterwards President Johnson spoke with selected individuals. The watery procession cruised to Carondelet to receive the salute of the military establishment of that place and then returned to the St. Louis wharf boat, where the official party disembarked at 4:30 p.m., proceeding into the city for additional activities to which both Brown and Eads were invited.[4] It is unknown whether or not Eads and Brown had any conversations during the Johnson visit or whether the two discussed the interest both held in the future of the St. Louis waterfront. Both knew that the contest for economic supremacy between riverboats and railroads was in full swing, with many in the latter group wishing independence from their forced reliance on steamboats to cross the Mississippi.

Brown, like many watermen, believed that overall river transport could be improved if the U.S. government would widen the many navigable streams. To that end, he now took on a role in the first of many multistate assemblies that would be held to lobby Congress for river improvements. When the second Mississippi River Improvement Convention was held at the Union Merchants' Exchange (ME) at St. Louis in February 1867, the Wiggins man found himself appointed a member of the executive committee

St. Louis Levee, 1871. After moving back to St. Louis, Capt. Joseph Brown took an interest in Democratic Party politics and also became a strong booster of inland river logistics, believing, like many watermen, that overall river transport could be improved if the U.S. government widened the many navigable streams. To that end, he became a leader in organizing and often chairing the several multistate assemblies held to lobby Congress for river improvements. He would continue this activity into the year of his death. Meanwhile, the 1874 completion of a bridge across the Mississippi at St. Louis brought unification of rail facilities on both sides of the river, thereby eliminating railroad dependence on ferries (*Harper's Weekly*, October 14, 1871).

7—Joseph Brown, Entrepreneur and Mayor Again: Life After Gunboats

charged with preparing a memorial for submission to Washington. The petition was duly sent off within a few weeks and Brown would remain an activist in the multistate improvement approach in the decades ahead.

After considerable jockeying between various other factions interested in ending reliance on river transport and relying more heavily upon the railroads, James Eads, the famous Carondelet gunboat builder who had interest in such an endeavor at the time of the presidential visit a year earlier, announced plans in the *St. Louis Daily Democrat* on July 21 to build a bridge across the river linking St. Louis and East St. Louis, IL. Costing an estimated $5 million, the steel, three-arch Illinois and St. Louis Bridge was expected to take approximately four years to finish once construction began the following year.[5]

At the start of 1868, Capt. Brown was a very busy man. Not only did he have a day job with the ferry company, which also now included supporting its interests against the location of the new Eads bridge, but he also had actively to follow his financial stake in the Pacific Railroad, the Atlantic and Mississippi Steamship Company, and in various St. Louis real estate holdings.

Brown's first significant diversification failure since his return from Cincinnati now occurred. Because of some reversals with his other properties, it became necessary for Brown to unload the Paschall House. The investment of the colorful, one-time Alton mayor would be sold off at a loss, but, interestingly, its disposal was handled in a most unusual manner—through a multistate lottery. In the era before lotteries were banned in Missouri, Brown's property had been joined with a large local farm and one in Memphis, TN, as prizes (valued at $315,000) in the Paschall House Lottery. The scheme, actively marketed by the Paschall House Lottery Association, attracted thousands of participants and was endorsed by local and state officials.

After the "Grand Drawing" was held at the St. Louis Fairgrounds on October 9, suit was brought claiming that those purchasing tickets were defrauded. The case received newspaper coverage as far away as London, England. When all was concluded on March 5, 1869, the chairman of the lottery association was found guilty and fined $1,000. The editor of the *American Agriculturalist* observed that "many fools lost their money and a few 'sharpies' made a 'pile.'" Noted St. Louis German historian Ernst D. Kargau confirmed "none profited by the transaction." Despite the public distaste engendered by the lottery, its conclusion had no adverse impact on the political or business fortunes of Joseph Brown.

In addition to these Missouri developments, the activities of George T. Brown, "Capt. Jo's" brother and still sergeant at arms of the U.S. Senate, were featured briefly on the national stage. His role during the Civil War had been played out largely behind the scenes, with only a moment or two of activity that caught the eye of reporters. As sergeant at arms, he served as chief protocol and law enforcement officer for the Senate, controlling access to the chamber and galleries, ensuring that Senate rules were followed, and handling special events or other assigned duties. In addition to overseeing security for the Capitol and distributing Republican campaign flyers to troops during the 1864 election cycle, Brown also signaled the crowds for silence prior to the second inaugural address given by Lincoln in 1865. He also was in charge of arrangements for Lincoln's funeral at the Capitol (including the specially constructed catafalque) and was sent to attend to the needs of dignitaries on the president's funeral train in April.

On March 7, 1868, Brown was sent by the Senate to the White House to present President Johnson with his summons to an impeachment trial. Taken directly into the office of the chief executive, Brown handed over the document. Johnson read it and gave it back, saying he would "attend to the matter." The exchange was drawn by artist T.R. Davis and appeared on the cover of *Harper's Weekly* a fortnight later. The days of George Brown's tenure with the Senate were numbered thereafter and, in March 1869, that body elected a former member of the House of Representatives as its new sergeant at arms.

Joseph Brown's older brother retired to Alton, Illinois, though he would, unhappily, be exposed to some unflattering newspaper commentary a few years later in connection with his long-time patron, Senator Lyman Trumbull. On July 6, 1872, the patronage arrangements of Senator Trumbull were castigated in the pages of the *New York Times*, which, in fact, labeled the former Alton mayor as the senator's "henchman." The famous newspaper, so politically opposed to Trumbull, further asserted that Brown had been given, and was maintained in, his post "by efforts often noticeable for their intensity and excess." The relationship between the two "present a case for outrunning all ordinary instances of getting a friend into office, or of being served by a friend in office." Two weeks later, while offering a fake bill of impeachment against Trumbull, the newspaper tore into the Illinois senator once more, partially because of Brown, "the late luxurious and pompous Sergeant at Arms of the Senate, who built the magnificent block on Capitol Hill where he and Trumbull so long lived, out of the spoils of office, and who lived in such regal style, was a protégé and pet of the Illinois puritan, and was brought here by him from his own state."[6]

The wealthy Joseph Brown also devoted considerable energy to one of his favorite charities, the St. Louis Bethel Association (also called the Bethel Mission), founded on October 30, 1868 as a revival of an organization initially established in 1841. Formed to support the work of the Western Seaman's Friends Society in St. Louis, it provided temporal and spiritual relief to needy rivermen and their families neglected by other church organizations. Brown was one of fifteen men who readily agreed to serve on the board of trustees. He would maintain his relationship with this group for the rest of his life.

Having retained an active interest in politics, Capt. Brown, now often known as "Capt. Joe," ran in the fall election as a War Democrat for the Missouri State Senate from the 31st District. Continuing to champion the disenfranchised, he was elected to office in November. Traveling down to Jefferson City to take his seat in the upper chamber of the legislature for the 25th General Assembly, he surrendered none of his previous work or financial duties or responsibilities, though some were muted. He may have been, however, saddened to learn that George T. Brown had departed his duties, most likely under pressure, in Washington, D.C., and had returned home to Alton. During the time Brown was away, the Wiggins Ferry Company was run by an archenemy of the Eads bridge project, President Bogy, who also faced waterborne competition from upstream. To meet a challenge from the Madison County Ferry Company at Alton, Bogy placed in service two car transfer ferries (steamers, each with a double row of tracks to handle railroad freight cars) and five car transfer barges.

At Jefferson City, Capt. Brown firmly allied himself with those wishing to change the political and franchise direction of Missouri. Six constitutional amendments were prepared for submission to the voters in 1870 (all would pass), including the two dearest to his heart: abolishing the oat of loyalty for voters and abolishing certain disqualifications on account of former acts of disloyalty. In addition, his session voted to ratify the 15th Amendment to the U.S. Constitution and establish the State Agricultural College (later the University of Missouri) at Columbia.

The period of prosperity which followed the Civil War was felt in St. Louis and by 1870 the city was in a wave of expansion with new additions and subdivisions platted and sold and new buildings constructed. During these 12 months, as excavation on the Eads bridge continued, the community of Carondelet and the intervening area between its northern limits and Keokuk Street came within the limits of St. Louis. The city's population was now 310,869 spread out over an area of 17.98 square miles. This growth made St. Louis the nation's fourth largest city.

In February 1870 the founding president of the Atlantic and Mississippi Steamship Company, John J. Roe (1809–1870), a close friend of James Eads as well as a local railroad, insurance, and banking magnet, passed away. He was succeeded by William J. Lewis (1825–1879), merchant, manufacturer, and president of the Memphis and St. Louis Packet Company, where Joseph Brown served as superintendent. In the few short years since its founding, the difficulties of the self-insured Atlantic and Mississippi Steamship Company had increased dramatically. Either through boiler explosions or sinkings caused by snags and other accidents, it lost fifteen of its steamboats. Brown and the respected Lewis were asked to stop the line's fiscal hemorrhage but were not able to do so. The end came with the auction of the remaining eleven vessels. The stockholders suffered greatly from the company's dissolution. "Out of $70,000 I had in stock," Brown later remembered, "I only got $2,600."

In April 1870 the mayor of St. Louis appointed Capt. Brown to a special three-member committee to examine and report on the accounts and books of the city auditor, comptroller, treasurer, board of water commissioners, and board of police commissioners. The work, completed in three weeks, was duly sent off to the city's board of aldermen for its consideration of certain irregularities found in the accounts of a number of departments.

In early summer, Capt. Brown moved to a new home at 948 Chouteau Ave., which address change took him out of the 31st senatorial district. Still, his one term in the legislature had been a productive one. He remained in good standing with both the Democratic Party and thousands of former Confederate soldiers who would soon be able to vote again. Throughout the busy election year, Brown took every opportunity to speak on issues of interest, including the need to pass the constitutional amendments and the economic future of his city.[7]

Brown's economic and political activities, if anything, increased at the beginning of 1871. His service with the Wiggins Ferry Company and the Pacific Railroad brought him into opposition with those backing other railroads as well as the Eads bridge project, which was now falling behind schedule. In addition, the rising power and popularity of the Democratic Party in the wake of the revised Missouri constitution offered the businessman-politician an opening to attain a major public office. The mayoralty of the

City of St. Louis now being open under a revised charter, Capt. Brown campaigned for the office, making numerous speeches and public appearances while also serving as an active superintendent with Wiggins and a director with the Pacific Railroad. Although still personally wealthy, he stressed his support for the newly reenfranchised former supporters and sympathizers of the Confederacy, folks unable to vote for over a decade.

While the campaign progressed, developments in the boardroom maneuvering between his companies and the backers of the Eads bridge intensified in late winter. In a March 27 election, the bridge interests hoped to win sufficient seats on the Pacific Railroad board to guarantee support of its bridge development plans, as well as construction of a central St. Louis rail depot that would serve a number of roads rather than each continuing to operate its own. In this effort they were deeply disappointed, when Capt. Brown was instead elected the railroad president, after, in the words of Hyde and Conard, "endorsing for it to the extent of $500,000." Moving to new offices in St. Louis, Brown kept his financial stake in Wiggins but turned his superintendency over to Samuel C. Clubb, who would later become president of the ferry concern.

When the returns from all the precincts were counted, Joseph Brown had been elected the 25th Mayor of St. Louis on April 4 with a 2,053 majority. Additionally, 10 of the 12 councilmen elected to the board of aldermen were Democrats. The total vote was about 20,000 out of some 28,000 registered. The *St. Louis Daily Missouri Republican* attributed the victory not only to the hard work of the party but also to the absence from the polls of many of the city German-Americans unwilling to reaffirm their previous allegiance to the Republicans. Conflict of interest not being a factor in those days, Brown retained all of his commercial posts and incomes. Six days later he presented his inaugural address before the board of aldermen, labeling himself "the representative of the liberated ballot-box." Brown's first action was to find a way to honor claims against the community for unpaid bills from the Gas-Light Company, without significant cost. In so doing, he also negotiated a rate reduction for all citizens. The mayor's retention of the firm of Sharp & Broadhead to represent the city was, nevertheless, a subject of sharp condemnation by the press due to the $10,000 legal fee.

By the end of March, the underwater caisson work on the Eads bridge was nearing completion and, Brown, as he later indicated at the bridge dedication, supposedly said to himself, *I will not only not oppose the bridge, but I will do everything in my power to hasten its completion.* Although he would now publicly speak openly on behalf of the project, behind the scenes, he would continue to support construction of another crossing downstream at Carondelet and then a boycott. Outwardly in support, the new mayor wanted his administration to both be and appear progressive and productive. To do this, he needed to at least project conciliation in his negotiations with those working against the interests of both Wiggins and the Pacific Railroad as well in the normal to and fro of local politics. As part of this approach, Brown defeated 20-year veteran anti-bridge opponent Bogy in an election for the presidency of the ferry company in a May 9 corporate vote. Interestingly, the defeat does not appear to have become a matter of tension between the two men. Bogy had also just won political office, a seat on the board of aldermen. Within a year, he would become its president and, in essence, acting mayor whenever Brown was out of town.

During the summer following the election, Mayor Brown constructively engaged with bridge supporters and others to find a way to create a new, unified St. Louis rail depot. At least three railroads, under a states statute, were required to certify that such a facility would serve as a public utility. Having, however, found that he did not need to participate in construction of the new facility for his road to continue operations, Brown, acting as CEO of the Pacific Railroad, simply withheld his ascent. This perceived conflict of interest between public need and private enterprise would be held against Brown for years by the local press and political opponents. At the same time, his two principal commercial interests seized almost total control of the railroad car ferry business. Records for the period from July 1872 to July 1873, for example, show that Wiggins transferred 18,755 carloads of freight to St. Louis, with two thirds of the consignments being received by the Pacific Railroad.

A portion of the St. Louis Arsenal grounds, having been ceded to the city for a park by an 1866 Act of Congress, was officially transferred by the U.S. War Department in September. In a letter from the secretary of war to Mayor Brown, the military chief noted that in order for the deal to be permanent St. Louis had to erect a monument to Union patriot Brig. Gen. Nathaniel Lyon within three years.

By September, partially in response to excesses in, or allowed by, previous city administrations, a wave of moral reform had come front and center in the city of St. Louis. A large fight focused on the elimination of open gambling within city limits. Others were smaller. One matter, as historian Stevens reports, caught the eye of the *Missouri Daily Democrat* and resulted in a letter from its editor which began as folows: "We call Mayor Brown's attention to the fact that the skirts of the dresses worn on the streets by many of our fashionable ladies are too long." The solution urged was to have "his honor" ask the chief of police to "notify the ladies that the wearing of such dresses is an indication of bad taste."

Arriving at his office on the morning of October 9, Mayor Brown found a dispatch from Chicago's mayor, Roswell B. Mason, appealing for help, indicating that the Windy City was burning to the ground. The captain immediately drew up a subscription petition, placing his name at the head of it for $10,000. He then made his way to the Union Merchants' Exchange (ME), where he conveyed the news to its president. Business was instantly suspended and Brown gave a short speech detailing the Chicago situation. He then produced his petition and called for subscriptions of no less than $1,000 per signer. In 30 minutes as many men had given him their checks, with 30 more before the hour was finished. By lunchtime, the mayor was able to turn $70,000 in drafts into cash. In addition, several special ME committees were formed that worked throughout the day to collect six boxcars of cooked and uncooked foodstuffs and one of clothing. Cost of the items was covered by the ME, the Pacific Railroad, the St. Louis Gas-Light Company, the Southern Hotel, St. Louis University, the *Daily Republican*, the American Wine Company, and several other concerns, plus James B. Eads personally. Other constituents, many of them religious, in St. Louis also organized relief support, sending help either directly or through organizations. The tragedy inspired the Jewish community to form the United Hebrew Relief Fund specifically to aid their brethren in Chicago, but it remained an important charity for years thereafter. (It would be hard pressed when Jewish refugees from the Illinois city arrived in St. Louis shortly thereafter.)

During the afternoon, the city board of aldermen was called into an unusual session

Mayor Brown and the Chicago Fire. Joseph Brown was elected the 25th Mayor of St. Louis on April 4, 1871. Hardly had the first of his two terms begun than, on October 9, he received word that the city of Chicago, IL, was on fire. Within hours he had organized a massive community-wide relief effort and after giving $10,000 out of his own pocket encouraged other city leaders and concerns to do likewise. By late afternoon he was able to telegraph the Windy City mayor to inform him that $120,000 and seven carloads of provisions would, at 5:30 p.m., depart St. Louis in two special trains, each with delegations comprising leading citizens. No one knew that these trains would be the first of many to arrive in the stricken community from out of town (Currier & Ives, Library of Congress).

at which point Mayor Brown asked that a special motion be made to appropriate relief funds for Chicago from city coffers. By a vote of 16–4, $50,000 was appropriated. Brown immediately telegraphed the Windy City mayor informing him that $120,000 and seven carloads of provisions would, at 5:30 that afternoon, depart St. Louis in two special trains, each with delegations comprising leading citizens. No one knew that these trains would be the first of many to arrive in the stricken community from out of town. The first train to depart carried the uncooked foodstuffs and the clothing. It was followed an hour later by the one transporting the cooked victuals and the fiscal donations. As the latter was preparing to leave it was stopped by a messenger who gave its conductor a large box containing two dozen cooked chickens. These had been personally prepared during the afternoon by Mayor Brown's wife, Virginia K., and his adopted daughter, Virginia ("Jennie") Brown (1857–1883), for delivery to Chicago's mayor. When the train arrived, it was late, so the food, including the Mason fowl, was taken to a nearby church and distributed to a large crowd of destitute people.

7—Joseph Brown, Entrepreneur and Mayor Again: Life After Gunboats

Chicago citizens were not the only ones to benefit from Brown's generosity. As winter approached, he began the annual practice of donating one-half of the mayor's private contingency fund (about $2,500) to two benevolent charitable societies, the St. Vincent de Paul and the Providence Association. The other half was distributed, he recalled in 1897, "to the desperately needy who came to city hall for relief."

In mid–December it was learned that the Russian Grand Duke Alexis, as part of his tour of the United States, would visit St. Louis for four days at the beginning of the new year. Given the large immigrant population of the city, Capt. Joe now found himself in the position of having to effect a compromise between those on the board of aldermen who wanted a lavish reception paid for by the community treasury and those who did not. The mayor worked out an agreement to mount an elaborate event the city would not be asked to pay for. Brown appointed a special committee to oversee arrangements, with $10 donations from the wealthy attending a special ball covering expenses. The Russian prince and his entourage duly arrived at St. Louis and, early on January 7, 1872, was taken on a sleigh tour of the city. His reception was not everywhere eager and at one point he and his party were pelted with snowballs. That evening, the grand duke and his party were taken to a performance by the noted singer Lydia Thompson at the Olympic Theater. Joseph Brown remembered taking two boxes for the party to see the star, "who was then at her best." He continued: "During the performance, the Duke turned to me and said, 'Is that fine-looking young Lady approachable?' I said, 'What do you mean?' 'Oh,' he said, 'anyway, is she free?' I said, 'I don't know.' He said, 'Can't you find out?' I said, 'No sir; but after the play, you can see her, as you are both at the same hotel.' And he did, and the next evening, she had on a pair of bracelets that were said to cost $2,600."

The next day, the Russian and several male members of his group were taken to visit James B. Eads and to inspect work on the great bridge. That evening the grand social ball that paid for the visit was held at the Southern Hotel. January 10 was given over to small intimate receptions and events at the hostelry and next day, the duke's last in town, he went shopping at stores on Fourth Street. Just before noon, he departed after telling Mayor Brown how much he had enjoyed his visit and how he was already making plans for a return stop at some future time. The mayor's thoughts on the prospect are not recorded, although those privileged enough to attend the events would long remember them as the most elaborate functions of their kind ever staged in St. Louis.

A large meeting of railroad officials was held on January 16 at the Southern Hotel. There Joseph Brown was one of a number of rail line presidents who voted to form the Western and Southern Railway Association. Ten days later the board of aldermen passed an ordinance allowing the Pacific Railroad to lay and maintain track on Poplar Street. The move was seen to negatively impact property values and cause "great injury to the southern part of the city."

Sad family duty required Capt. and Mrs. Brown to return to Alton, IL, on February 15. There they met George T. Brown and, with sister Ellen and other members of the Child family, participated in the funeral of Benjamin F. Child, Sr., the next day. The hours following the burial of their brother-in-law at Alton City Cemetery may have occasioned the brothers their first meeting since the Civil War.

To California. Having acquired an interest in the Pacific Railroad of Missouri in 1866 and become a director, Joseph Brown became its president in March 1871 and did not give up the post when he became St. Louis mayor. A year later, he found himself head of a delegation of St. Louis corporate and business leaders, including representatives from several other railroads, embarked on an excursion to California. It was hoped that this delegation could interest civic leaders there and in towns en route of the value in completing another long-haul western railroad in addition to the Central Pacific, this one running along the 35th parallel via Texas, New Mexico, Arizona, and Utah. Brown began an ardent interest in the far West during this trip, later living for a time in California and even becoming president of a New Mexico gold mine (Currier & Ives, Library of Congress).

On March 25, Mayor Brown was unanimously reelected president of the Pacific Railroad and within a few days he found himself head of a delegation of St. Louis corporate and business leaders, including representatives from the Union Merchants' Exchange and several railroads, plus members of their families, 28 total, who had embarked on an excursion to San Francisco. It was hoped that the delegation could interest civic leaders there, and in towns en route, of the value in completing another long-haul western railroad in addition to the Central Pacific, this one running along the 35th parallel via Texas, New Mexico, Arizona, and Utah. Accompanying His Honor was his wife, Virginia K., and their daughter, Jennie. While the party traveled, a specially established Citizens Committee in San Francisco made ready to receive them. The Missourians, traveling in special cars, arrived in San Francisco on April 26. There they were greeted and the California reporters were able to interview many of them. One scribe from the *San Francisco Chronicle* spoke at length with Mayor Brown, whom he described as "a very prominent politician and largely engaged in commercial enterprises besides." The former steamboat man was also noted as being "accounted one of the wealthiest citizens of St. Louis."

After most of a week in discussions with Golden State and San Francisco officials, Brown, who formed a very favorable impression of the city, indicated that it was time for him to return home. The party duly retrained, with one crucial stop left to make. In Salt Lake City Brown visited extensively with Brigham Young, attempting to interest the Mormon leader in joining the undertaking. The party of the Missouri excursionists broke in two at Cheyenne, WY, on the way back, with the Browns and twelve others pushing to return to St. Louis in the fastest time. Chugging in via Omaha, Kansas City, St. Joseph, and Council Bluffs, the notables were back home by May 14.

On May 1, Mayor Brown was appointed a director of the Atlantic and Pacific Railroad, formed in 1866 to open a route from southwestern Missouri to the Pacific Ocean. Also during the month, the *St. Louis Globe*, a Republican newspaper, was founded. Its editor was Joseph B. McCallagh (1842–1896), a noted Civil War journalist and member of the "Bohemian Brigade." McCallagh, it was reported, took an interest in Jennie Brown, but her father was opposed to the two seeing each other, primarily because of the newsman's long hours.

As the year wore on, the mayor was faced with several challenges in local government. For example, in September the Missouri governor stepped in and removed several of the members of the St. Louis board of police commissioners and reorganized that body, which was deemed corrupt and inefficient. Mayor Brown was made an ex-officio member along with several distinguished citizens.

Since at least 1868 the city's board of aldermen had been discussing the need for a new St. Louis city hall. In October, erection was begun on a "temporary" facility, later nicknamed "the barn," bounded by 11th, 12th, Market and Chestnut streets and contracted at $48,750. In his annual message of November 19, the mayor noted that its construction was moving along smoothly and would be finished within a few months. When finished, the facility would be able to group the town's departments "in a manner that will greatly facilitate the transaction of business."

Also in November, in keeping with his pledge to support the bridge project, Brown requested that the board of aldermen authorize a half million dollars in city bonds for the payment of property condemned for the approaches to the Eads structure. He admitted that the bridge was costing more than anticipated due to the difficulty in laying its foundations in the river, but he believed its completion would "stand conspicuous in our history." As part of the endeavor, the Union Depot, located in Chouteau Pond mill tract, as he had negotiated, and the building of a tunnel to connect the two "should create no public dissatisfaction."

Having encountered financial difficulties over the debt incurred in reaching Kansas City, the modest success of the Pacific Railroad so far enjoyed began to dissipate. Progress on the 35h parallel railroad lagged so much that the mayor was forced, on September 6, to publicly deny rumors that the city of St. Louis was not doing anything for the project. He asserted that the reason there had been no action during the summer was because of the intense heat, which had resulted in almost everyone engaged in the effort being out of town.

Joseph Brown resigned as president of the Pacific Railroad on October 9, although he continued to hold his directorship in the A&P. On November 19 the Atlantic and Pacific Railroad took over his line and leased its equipment for 999 years. Much of his investment in the Pacific, however, began to slip away.

Just before the holidays, the police department, under the direction of Mayor Brown, sponsored a ball to raise money for the poor. The affair brought in $1,000 that, while beneficial, was, as the captain remembered in 1897, "not enough."

On December 26 the St. Louis Taxpayer's League was established as an association for the improvement of civic government. Numerous activities and operations would come under its microscope in the next four years, and it would operate a grass-roots campaign leading to the separation of St. Louis from St. Louis County in the years after Mayor Brown left office.[8]

From the time it had been enacted in March 1870, the city's "Social Evil Ordinance," which legalized prostitution in order to regulate it, had been controversial. Ladies of the night were required to register with the police and be inspected, with a special hospital constructed to ensure disease control. St. Louis was the first large U.S. city to undertake such a program, modeled on European plans, thinking that prostitutes could be reformed and their residences and public behavior controlled. The effort was publicly supported by religious, civic, health, and political leaders, including Joseph Brown, but not by numerous reformers, many working medical personnel, or, most important, the prostitutes and their customers. By January 1873 the scheme was shown to not be working as its proponents had hoped; less than half the city's prostitutes had registered as required and fewer still were inspected at the facility known as the Social Evil Hospital. That month Mayor Brown, joined with noted Unitarian minister William Greenleaf Eliot and with Woman Suffrage Movement of Missouri founder Rebecca Hazard, began to bring pressure to repeal the so-called Social Evil Ordinance. It would take fourteen months, but the petition drive they started would bear results the following April when the board of aldermen nullified the local law.

Early in the first quarter Mayor Brown, as has he had the previous year, brought to the attention of the board of aldermen the city's abysmal street situation. Although several experiments had been conducted the previous year concerning possible new types of paving methods and material for use in same, none had been chosen and the streets remained "unsatisfactory." Unlike his street improvement achievement in Alton years earlier, His Honor would have little success in this area in the larger Missouri town.

In March, Lewis Bogy left St. Louis to take a seat as one of Missouri's two U.S. senators. He was succeeded as board of alderman president by Elon G. Smith. A riverboat pilot by trade and also a Democrat, Smith represented the city's Third Ward. Also in March, the U.S. Congress passed a law permitting construction of the St. Clair and Carondelet bridge, which would compete with the Eads bridge. The requirements were so stringent that the project was stalled and work on the Illinois and St. Louis Bridge was able to proceed apace.

Continuing his interest in the railroad business, Mayor Brown was in April named a director and temporary president of the Great Southern Railroad Company. The startup proposed building a line from St. Louis to Belmont, MO, but it was not begun. Simultaneously, he won reelection for a second term as St. Louis mayor. The same month, His Honor was able to put his detailed views on the costs of street paving and materials before a wider audience. In response to an inquiry from the mayor of St. Paul, MN (carried in several regional newspapers north and south of St. Louis), Brown indicated that "the experience with 12 years of wooden pavement in St. Louis has demonstrated the fact that it is not suited to streets with heavy traffic and is expensive under any circumstances. Being something of an expert on wood since his days in the steamboat trade and working with navy ironclads and tinclads, he further indicated that "as to the durability of wood, oak and good white pine give, all things being equal, about the same result."

In mid–May, a large congressional convention, sponsored by the city of St. Louis and the Union Merchants' Exchange, took place at the Southern Hotel. Congressmen and governors from 22 states were in attendance to hear Mayor Brown and others extol the virtues of river improvement and the needs of western commerce. Even as he sought Federal help with those goals and as construction of the Eads bridge continued apace, His Honor found time to celebrate the completion of another structure.

In late May, Capt. Brown took the train to St. Joseph, MO, where, on the last day of the month, the St. Joseph and Elwood Bridge was dedicated in what one historian called "the most brilliant pageant ever witnessed in the city," The St. Louis chief executive was invited to give the keynote address in the ceremony that marked the linking of the Missouri and Kansas cities. Parades, band concerts, and other festivities, topped off by a large banquet for 500 guests, marked the remainder of the day.

In July the St. Louis mayor was faced with an environmental situation he had, frankly, too long ignored. A close friend, Judge John Busby, operated a rendering business onboard a steamer anchored most of the time at the foot of Barton Street. The odious practice of melting animal carcasses for oil enraged local citizens who were forced to continuously smell the process, even though Busby had promised the city since 1871 to run his boat out into the river before boiling his product. Numerous petitions and meetings were held on the matter over a period of almost three years with every city department from the mayor to the health and police departments asked to intervene. None did. In the weeks after Independence Day, mobs threatened to storm the offending vessel and burn it down. Faced with violence, Brown called in Busby and told him he would have to move. To sweeten the ouster of his vessel from its berth, the judge was given a piece of city property on Arsenal Island, in the middle of the Mississippi across from Cahokia, IL.

On July 30, Mayor Brown was able to announce that construction of the city hall building would be completed during the fourth quarter. The decision to add a third story would add another $13,300 to its cost. His Honor and three other officials occupied the new "temporary" city hall on October 22, with other departments following before the end of the year. The three-story block building, which locals came to call "the barn," was the first purpose-built in St. Louis to be employed exclusively as a city hall. It cost $70,000 and would remain in service until 1898. Brown had now overseen the construction of new municipal seats of government in both cities in which he was mayor, Alton, IL, and St. Louis.

In September, as the result of a number of factors—including inflation, the postwar railroad boom, speculative investment, a large trade deficit, the costs of rebuilding

Chicago and Boston after tragic fires, and a change in monetary policy regarding silver—a large banking crisis erupted when several notable firms closed their doors, including those of Jay Cooke & Company and Henry Clewes. Numerous banks from large to small were forced to shut down in the Panic of 1873 in the face of "runs" on their deposits. Even the New York Stock Market closed temporarily for 10 days. Eastern factories laid off workers and depression began to spread west. The downturn would continue for several years after Mayor Brown left office.

As might be expected, the eastern fiscal situation did not go unnoticed in St. Louis. On September 25, Mayor Brown and the leading members of the banking community (the Clearing House Association) met to consider ways to prevent panic striking their city. It was agreed that they would maintain low-key working relationships, cover only small costs, and immediately shut down the banks to prevent failures due to the inability to cover deposits. The result was that no banks failed immediately; however, currency to cover everyday activities became quite scarce and floating bonds was virtually impossible.

When one of the city's largest banks refused to honor the city's drafts for current expenses, Mayor Brown then had an idea, one which would cement his place in St. Louis history. He went to the board of aldermen and recommended that the town "issue warrants as a measure for the relief of existing financial embarrassments." The council met on September 29 and unanimously agreed by ordinance to issue scrip, initially called "shinplasters," in one-, two-, or three-dollar denominations that could be used in place of unavailable greenbacks. A total of $300,000 in scrip was ordered printed on fine paper. The fronts of the bills appeared in four colors and the backs were brown (hence the term "Brown Backs). Embellished on each was a pledge that anyone having one could redeem it at the city treasury and it could be used to pay for anything, including taxes, licenses, and fees. The city and Joseph Brown personally guaranteed the value of the "Brown Backs," and for the duration of the crisis the bills circulated not only in St. Louis but also in the surrounding area. Every dollar they represented was redeemed and neither Brown nor the city lost either money or credit.

While the crisis endured, Mayor Brown knew that some decisive action had to occur to assist the many unemployed laborers and their families affected by the financial crisis and facing starvation in cold weather. He decided to organize a soup kitchen and, almost 25 years later, reluctantly agreed to tell newspaper readers how he personally organized this effort to avoid mass suffering. Out back of the city hall building was a vacant city-owned tobacco warehouse. "I then went to work," he remembered, "entirely alone" except for the "valuable" assistance of a police sergeant from city hall. Using funds from the mayor's contingency fund, he went to retailers and purchased stoves and large soup kettles, etc. He then went to the press and placed ads seeking donations of "bread and meat, crackers, and all sorts of edibles, even though a day old, and also solicited clothing for children, and also adults." There as many as 1,200 destitute people fed every day in cold weather. Years later, he told a reporter from the *St. Louis Post-Dispatch* that the "provisions were all contributed by butchers, bakers, and grocery men and cost the city proper nothing." He did not mention that incidentals in connection with this charity were paid for from his own pocket. The word went out from churches and other locations that the soup kitchen would provide one meal per day and people could take advantage of it for up to 10 days, "after which they would have to give way to others and work their way South." The police would take names and insure both order and fair attendance.

When the kitchen opened at noon on a blustery day, the mayor and his wife were on hand, along with several other city officials and numerous volunteers. He was proud to recollect that "we gave to those in the ware house 700 quart cups of excellent bean soup, with more or less meat that had been donated by the butchers." Additionally, with each quart cup of soup went half a loaf of good bread." When the success of the soup kitchen became known, not everyone approved. Brown remembered being visited by a minister who came to city hall to remonstrate against the whole idea, claiming that the mayor "was only making paupers and at the expense of the city." Capt. Joe told the man, "No, it is not costing the city one dollar except a small amount I have advanced from the mayor's fund, and when the thing's closed up, the outfit will nearly pay the original cost." The unsatisfied minister commented that the people "ought to work and earn their living." He was informed that there were only a few jobs available and more than 1,200 people left over, many of them with little or no warm clothing. "My friend went away unsatisfied," the mayor recalled, "sorrowful to think that someone had eaten a meal that cost only 1½ cents and was furnished by those who never missed it, but gave it cheerfully out of their own abundance."

On November 7, Mayor Brown's position on the Illinois and St. Louis Bridge was officially stated in a letter to James B. Eads, who would later have it published in a U.S. congressional document. The bridge, long in creation and running over estimates, was the subject of much debate and its chief engineer wished all the public support he could rally. His Honor was asked to give his opinion as to whether or not the structure was an obstruction to river navigation. Although he had hoped that its arches might be higher, the famed waterman came down firmly in support of the bridge: "From observation and 20 years experience as a boatman and navigator of the Mississippi River, if I was in charge of one of our largest steamers (numbers of which I have commanded), I would not be afraid to take her through between the piers, even in a storm or any other weather except fog, and it is impracticable to run a steamer anywhere on the river in a fog." Brown went further than just giving his technical opinion but stated the case for the earliest completion of the project: "I consider its completion more vital to the interests of St. Louis than any other public improvement now in progress and to delay or obstruct its completion would be a very great injury, not only to the business of this city, but to the country as a whole, and especially the commercial development of the West.... I consider the time for fault-finding or urging its removal to have more than elapsed.... I consider the structure one of national importance, and in every point of view, past modification or removal."

Though Brown would later chastise Eads regarding his management of the bridge project, for now the mayor stood four-square behind the enterprise as necessary to the growth of St. Louis.[9]

Some 24 months earlier, the state legislature had passed an act permitting the creation of a public park in the western portion of the city. The legislation was nullified by the Missouri Supreme Court, but a new law was passed on March 25, 1874. This time the opposition to the reserve would fail and Forest Park would be officially dedicated a year after Brown left office. On April 22, the secretary of war wrote once more to Mayor Brown asking if the monument to Brig. Gen. Lyon specified in the transfer arrangement of 1871 had been erected. His Honor noted that it would be dedicated soon. In his annual report delivered to the board of aldermen in May, Mayor Brown lauded the accomplishments of his administration in providing public improvements since 1871, including those in many more areas than we are able to detail here. Included in his plus column was work with sewers, parks, the harbor and city wharf, hospitals and schools, and the waterworks. One area of continuing concern was city streets. Unhappily, he sighed, a levy requesting $2.5 million for road improvements had been voted down in the previous election.

Formed as the Public School Library Society of St. Louis in 1865 and chartered by the state legislature, the 12,000-volume collection was transferred to the school board in 1869. During the years Joseph Brown, a supporter of the library, was mayor the collection increased to 36,000 volumes and in May of 1874 home circulation for the previous year was recorded at 96,682. In June, with Brown's backing, the library was opened as a free public library, backed by the school board (a school board public library). Patrons from throughout the community were able to read books on the premises and receive reference information. In 1894, the library became an independent tax-supported institution.

On a personal note for the Brown family, the year's top event was not the political or economic events in the city but the coming out of their 17-year-old daughter, Jennie, who *St. Louis Post-Dispatch* reporter "Antonia" later remembered "was perfectly idolized by her father and mother, as well as by her friends." As an only child, her "life was as cloudless as a dream in girlhood." Over the past several years, Jennie had become rather well known as an amateur actress and musician, performing in numerous plays in the more popular and respectable local theaters. In a society display reminiscent of the visit of Grand Duke Alexis in 1872, Brown and his wife threw an enormous "debut party" for Jennie at the Southern Hotel (in the same ballroom as that used by Alexis), "one unsurpassed in splendor by any before or since [ca. 1889] in St. Louis." It was attended by over 1,400 guests from St. Louis and points as far east as New York. Given that we have the details of one of the proudest moments in the lives of Captain and Mrs. Brown, we offer them here: "The lights and flowers and costumes made a splendid rainbow of beauty. The reception was on the style of a Washington levee, the receiving party standing on one side of the room whilst the guests passed in front. The Mayor first addressing them and presenting them to the receiving party. The beautiful debutante was a queen of loveliness in a Parisian gown of tulle, the gleaming draperies of cream white satin and priceless point face and pearls. She also wore superb pearl ornaments. Mrs. Brown, her mother, was attired in black velvet and point lace." At the end of the following month, the *Alton Telegraph* told its readers that a new steamer, christened the *Jennie Brown* in honor of the mayor's daughter, had been launched for service on the Upper Mississippi.

One of the largest public celebratory occasions in St. Louis history occurred on July 4. After years of political wrangling, economic battles between various interests ranging from railroads and ferry concerns to property owners and out-of-town interests, the Illinois and St. Louis Bridge was ready for dedication. Just two days before, fourteen

7—Joseph Brown, Entrepreneur and Mayor Again: Life After Gunboats   303

Eads Bridge. Underway when Joseph Brown became mayor of St. Louis, the Illinois and St. Louis Bridge over the Mississippi River, built by James B. Eads and usually known by his name, was initially opposed (covertly) and supported (openly) by His Honor, who came to see and support the advantages it offered his city. When the structure was formally opened in great ceremony on July 4, 1874, Mayor Brown waxed eloquent on the political and construction difficulties overcome in completing the bridge, admitting that he had not originally been a supporter of the cross-river enterprise but noting that, as the most important city achievement to occur during his administration, the bridge would prove important to the entire Western half of the nation.

locomotives had been sent across it in a successful final test of its viability and readiness for service. Construction challenges, physically difficult at times, budget overages, and completion finish delays had also been concerns since 1867 but these, too, had not ended Eads' most memorable project. Even though the bridge lacked a few pieces of ornamentation, all was ready for inauguration at the appointed hour of 10 a.m.

Dignitaries from far and wide in two states assembled on a 50-foot-long platform set up at the western end of the structure. Included among these folks were the governors of Missouri and Illinois, U.S. senators and congressmen, the directors and families of the bridge directors, several mayors and their wives, and James B. Eads himself. As these luminaries took their seats, a huge parade began to pass. It traveled some 15 miles through city streets and was seen by upwards of 300,000 people. The *New York Times* reported that it took five hours for it to pass any given point.

Just after the head of the parade passed the reviewing stand the parade halted for the bridge christening ceremony and opening prayer and then continued on its way. At this point, opening remarks were made by the chairman of the arrangements committee. That gentleman was followed by Mayor Brown, who waxed eloquent on the political and construction difficulties overcome in completing the bridge, admitting that he had not originally been a supporter of the cross-river enterprise. Brown's comments, similar in praise to those thoughts printed by Congress earlier, were followed by speeches by several others before Eads himself made a concluding speech acknowledging both the work of various people and the engineering difficulties encountered. Various additional aspects of the ceremony continued far into the afternoon as bands played and chorale groups sang. The evening was capped with fireworks. In a less-impressive September 13 ceremony, an obelisk was dedicated to the memory of Brig. Gen. Lyon and Mayor Brown on behalf of the city, which took official ownership of Lyon Park.

The year in St. Louis society was concluded by the first in a series of lavish events that came to be known as the Charity Ball. The early December evening featured a large social gathering and a musical performance. For some time "a furor of excitement" had built when it was learned that Ms. Brown would have a major role in the night's production of *Faust*. Before a crowd of 1,900, the proud city leader and his wife listened as Jennie sang the role of Marguerite, winning standing applause from the entire audience at the conclusion of the Charles Gounod opera. Local charities received $7,000 in time to cover Christmas.

In early January 1875 a boomlet occurred in Democratic circles when Mayor Brown's name was sponsored as a possible candidate for the U.S. Senate. Brown, along with other possible contenders, traveled to Jefferson City to make themselves available to the Missouri legislature, which made the choice. The move for Brown never got off the ground as former Confederate Brig. Gen. Francis M. Cockrell (1834–1915) was too evidently the choice of the majority of the Missouri state legislature. After his selection, Cockrell would represent his state in Washington for 30 years.

The most widely publicized official action of Mayor Brown in his last several months of office was his sponsorship of a celebratory banquet on March 27 in honor of James B. Eads. Congress had just appropriated funding for the master engineer, who planned to improve river navigation below New Orleans with a series of jetties. The affair was held at the Southern Hotel and speeches of welcome and acceptance were given by his honor and Eads. Joseph Brown completed his two terms as St. Louis mayor on Tuesday, April 13, and, having chosen not to run for another term, was succeeded in office by elected fellow Democrat Arthur Buckner Barrett (1835–1875). It was said by a reporter for a St. Louis newspaper in 1892 that Brown could have had a third term if he had wanted, but he "found that his own business needed attention" and so went out of office.

As was customary, a formal noon inauguration ceremony was laid on for Barrett that day in the chambers of the board of aldermen in city hall. Once the new chief executive was sworn in, the one-time steamboat captain and outgoing mayor began the day's addresses with a valedictory. After a review of the local economic and tax situation, the need for a separation of city and county government, and a lament that the streets could not be improved as much as desired, Brown ticked off a few of the accomplishments of his administration of which he was most proud: the city hospital was increased in size from 200 beds to 450 and under the direction of the board of health the capacity of the special quarantine and smallpox hospitals was doubled; the workhouse was doubled in size with attention paid to its cleanliness; and the social evil hospital had been converted into the St. Louis Female Hospital and functioned as a normal medical center addressing ladies' issues such as pregnancies and adoptions. He did not mention the Panic of 1873 and the role of local government, the Eads bridge, or even the library. Finishing his relatively short remarks (fewer than 20 paragraphs, as reported in the newspaper), Brown applauded his successor, the two shook hands, and Barrett took the podium.

Though now out of office, Brown, aged 52, would remain a player in St. Louis Democratic Party politics for the rest of his life. The battles for city offices would be very rough in those years. In November 1904, one of Missouri's Democratic bosses, former blacksmith Edward ("Boss") Butler (1834–1911), who ran the St. Louis machine after 1876, admitted, in a Chicago newspaper interview, "St. Louis is Republican, too, and if things were on the level here, the Democrats could never have elected any mayor save Joe Brown. Joe was elected twice honestly and he is the only Democrat who did carry St. Louis to the square since the Civil War."[10]

Returning to his Chouteau Ave. residence, Mayor Brown now turned his attention full time to his business affairs as well as his interest in matters pertaining to local civic and political activities and spiritualism. In mid–July there was newspaper speculation that he would become the city's water commissioner, but that did not occur. On October 28 Capt. Joe presided over a lavish testimonial banquet at the Southern Hotel in honor of retiring St. Louis police chief James McDonough, the head of law enforcement in the city during his two administrations. The following month, the former mayor was named a general manager of arrangements for the annual Charity Ball, which was held on December 15.

In February 1876 St. Louis was notified that it had been chosen to host the 12th Democratic National Convention, being the first city west of the Mississippi River to do so. A resident committee was duly assembled, with Brown as treasurer, to make all of the necessary arrangements, including provisions for use of the new Union Merchants' Exchange hall, the largest venue of its kind in America.

Railroad expansion and the associated fiscal problems, along with the success of Democratic politics, were now the issues that gave the former mayor his greatest concerns; however, social ills, as he saw them, occasionally occupied his attention. His response to what was perceived to be one of them would be seen as far less than politically correct a century and a half later. Possessing the same attitudes towards race as many in his locale, party or the railroad business, the captain, like other white Americans of the day, was aghast at the perceived failure of the U.S. Congress to curb the then-rampant immigration of Chinese workers into California. In a spirited letter to the editor in April he lamented the increasing number of new arrivals who were "taking the bread out of our laborers' and artisans' mouths." Though not vitriolic against the Chinese as a people, Brown worried that the flood of what some today call "illegals" (many of whom in Brown's time were originally brought in to work on the western railroads) would impede growth in San Francisco and other Golden State localities that he had visited and appreciated. He closed his column with a call upon the citizens of St. Louis to support California in its grievance with Washington.

The son of a long-time Louisville riverboat captain, perhaps known to Joseph Brown, now entered the picture. Despite an unknown but presumably happy beginning, the story would end sadly. The boy among three children born to Louisville-based steamboat captain Harry Innes Spotts (1824–1864) and Jane Pearce Tunstall (1828–1908), Albert Tunstall Spotts was born in Louisville in December 1849. While he was at home, his father commanded a steamer on the Mississippi, being several times in New Orleans at the same time as Joseph Brown. In 1862 the family, which had quit the river at the beginning of the Civil War, moved to New York City, where Capt. Spotts became proprietor of the St. Nicholas Hotel. There the riverman died on March 5, 1864.

The estate of his father having been placed in trust with his mother (as administrator) and a trust company, Albert attended and graduated from New York University and Columbia Law School, reaching his majority in 1871. At that point, the estate was finally settled out at nearly $400,000. Albert was now a very eligible bachelor, what the newspapers called a "New York beau." At one point during that year Mrs. Spotts and her son visited St. Louis, where testimony on a contested measure related to the estate was taken. One might assume that it was during this time that Albert and Jennie Brown, "a recognized belle," first met.

After getting to know one another, the young people elected to marry and, having won the approval of their parents, vows were publicly announced. Nuptial arrangements were duly made with the Rev. Dr. Edward F. Berkeley at St. Peter's Protestant Episcopal Church on Olive Street (where Mrs. Brown and her daughter worshiped) for a ceremony. Ex-mayor Brown, determined that his only daughter have a grand wedding, duly changed the venue from the small local facility to the city's Episcopal cathedral, Christ Church. There Berkeley would be joined in reciting the marriage service by its rector, the Rev. Dr. Montgomery Schuyler. The groom, Albert T. Spotts, arrived in town with family members on May 31 and took rooms at the Southern Hotel.

Almost two hours before the June 7

Jennie Brown. Her parents having lost two children a decade earlier, seven-year-old Jennie (1857–1883) was the apple of the eye of Capt. Brown and his wife. Jennie accompanied her father everywhere and was often with her mother at social occasions. Additionally, she became a well-known local operatic singer. In 1872 Brown and his wife threw an enormous "debut party" for her at the Southern Hotel that was "one unsurpassed in splendor by any before or since [ca.1889] in St. Louis." It was attended by more than 1,400 guests from St. Louis and points as far east as New York. Her 1876 wedding was just as lavish, though with fewer guests. Jennie and her husband moved to San Francisco, where she died of child birth fever in 1883 (courtesy *St. Louis Post-Dispatch*).

(8:30 p.m.) celebration was due to begin, people in large numbers began to enter the vestibules or congregate on the outside steps of Christ Church, the pavement, and the street. An hour before, the church was filled with people speaking in hushed tones or listening to arrangements from *Faust*, still one of Miss Brown's favorite operas, played on the great organ. Many admired the rare plants and flowers with which Jordan Agriculture had adorned the altar and the grand chancel. It was taken as a compliment to the captain and his "accomplished and beautiful" daughter that so many of their friends and acquaintances had come. In addition to Mr. and Mrs. Brown, several members of the Spotts family were in attendance, including Mrs. Jane Spotts, known as "Mama."

The wedding cortege was slightly late in arriving but made a grand procession to the tones of "The Wedding March." When it reached is place and formed into a V, a calcium light was shown upon the party and the ministers began their recitations, with "old-time grace and dignity." After the final blessing, flower girls spread petals as the bride and groom exited down and out the main aisle to their carriages to strains of triumph gloriously intoned by the enthusiastic organist. Carriages bore the bridal party and selected friends to the home of Capt. Brown, where Spiering's Band played Strauss for dancing and refreshments were consumed until, "at a reasonable hour," everyone went home. During the reception, presents "both numerous and costly" were opened. In addition to a magnificent European-made silver service," the Brown parents' gift was an Eastlake house, which Mr. Brown had ordered constructed for his daughter and the groom on Pacific Avenue in San Francisco, where they would soon take up residence. The *St. Louis Post-Dispatch* employee assigned to report on the event concluded: "From the beginning to the end, in all is appointments, elegance, and dignity, St. Louis never saw such a wedding before." His colleague from the *Globe-Democrat* found that the event "attained an importance much beyond the average weddings in fashionable life."

The next morning the newly wed Spotts, with Mama Spotts, departed for New York, where he needed to wrap up several items from his office. The two would then travel to Philadelphia to take in the Centennial Exposition before departing for their new home in California. As late as 1899 it was said that Jennie Brown's wedding was an affair that even eclipsed the ball given at the Southern Hotel for the Grand Duke Alexis, which had been long considered the gold standard St. Louis social event.

The Brown-Spotts wedding was barely concluded when, on June 27, 28, and 29, the Democratic National Convention was held in St. Louis. Over 5,000 people crowded into the hall of the Union Merchant Exchange, where a platform pledging to end the corruption of the Ulysses S. Grant administration was quickly hammered together. The former mayor, a voting delegate, was a participant when, on the second ballot, Samuel J. Tilden was nominated to be the party standard bearer. On the last night, a grand fireworks was presented from the top of the domed county courthouse, a part of the Jefferson National Expansion Memorial. The convention was considered such a success for the resident committee that it was celebrated by the *Post-Dispatch* in 1887.[11]

Brown continued to publicly demonstrate his devotion to opera and on September 4 authored a letter, signed by many prominent St. Louisians, to French opera star Marie Aimee (1852–1887), who had made her American debut in New York in 1870 and was temporarily in town. Having learned that she would soon be touring to the

St. Louis Democratic Convention. Out of the mayor's office after two terms, Brown, aged 52, remained a player in St. Louis Democratic Party politics for the rest of his life. In February 1876, St. Louis was notified that it had been chosen to host the 12th Democratic National Convention, being the first city west of the Mississippi River to do so. A resident arrangements committee was duly assembled, with Brown as treasurer, to make all of the necessary arrangements, including provisions for use of the new Union Merchants' Exchange hall, the largest venue of its kind in America. Brown was a delegate to the assembly just weeks after his daughter Jennie was married.

west, the men all begged her to perform her specialty, Offenbach, in a St. Louis "complimentary benefit" before she departed. Flattered, she agreed, and a gala event was staged on September 8.

Much of the joy of Brown's business dealings left the ex-mayor only three months after the marriage of his daughter. Having entered receivership in 1875, the Atlantic and Pacific Railroad was sold at a foreclosure auction on September 8, the same day as Aimee's St. Louis performance, for just under half a million dollars. As Capt. Brown's obituary recorded, this railroad investment "proved a disastrous one, however, and some of his real estate was eventually sold to satisfy debts incurred by his connection with it." To help cover his current expenses, the ex-mayor later in the month borrowed $27,000 from the National Bank of the State of Missouri, depositing as collateral $30,000 worth of bonds he held from various railroads. As the bonds had deteriorated in value, the bank demanded that he provide a deed of trust for four St. Louis houses and lots, valued at $10,000 above their first mortgage, agreeing to take over management of the properties.

On September 25 the Democratic Party's county convention nominated a slate to run in the November elections, but within days the selections were, as a newspaper put it, "met with such disapprobation at the hands of the press and party generally" that a "do-over" was required. On October 9, the convention reassembled and nominated a new ticket, with the available Joseph Brown a candidate for the office of sheriff. Brown, a police favorite during his years as St. Louis mayor, lost the ensuing race to a Republican.

The Southern Hotel was not only a fine hotel and social setting but was possessed of an excellent restaurant. After Jennie left for California, Captain and Mrs. Brown took most of their meals there, including many late at night after he returned from his social or political activities. On the evening of April 11, 1877, the structure caught fire and, despite the efforts of many firefighters, burned to the ground by next morning with heavy loss of life. The Browns were among those who were able to escape the conflagration; the former mayor sprained his ankle and Mrs. Brown was forced to walk to a friend's Clinton Ave. home in her stocking feet. This was the second time in their married life that they had escaped a massive fire; the first, readers will recall, was aboard the *Mayflower* back in 1855. Brown returned to the scene next day, with the aid of a cane, to survey the ruins.

As May ended the former steamboat master traveled by train to the city of Omaha to advise anxious residents concerning natural threats occurring in the channel of the Missouri River above the city. Employing his immense knowledge of river conditions dating back to his youth, Brown advised that the difficulty might be remedied with a $100,000 dike such as the one constructed at St. Louis in 1844. It was this kind of expertise that directly led to his next public service opportunity.

At the beginning of October, the Union Merchants' Exchange (ME) appointed a number of delegates, led by ex–Mayor Brown, to attend a multistate River Improvement Convention at St. Paul, MN. It was hoped that this meeting would result in more concrete recommendations for physical waterways improvements on the inland streams than had previously occurred. The convention resolved to petition Congress to provide the means to adequately deepen the main channel of the Mississippi south of St. Paul.

The Southern Hotel. Completed in 1865, the Southern Hotel, the premiere luxury hotel for business travelers and the well-to-do in postwar St. Louis, was located at the corner of Walnut and Fourth streets. It was the scene of many social activities during the mayoralty of Joseph Brown, including a grand ball given in January 1872 to celebrate the visit of the Russian Grand Duke Alexis, a congressional convention on river improvements in May 1873, a huge debutante "coming out" for his daughter Jennie in June, and a great reception in honor of James B. Eads in March 1874. Afterwards, the Browns were frequent visitors to the establishment and were among those able to escape the conflagration which destroyed it on April 11, 1877. The former mayor sprained his ankle and Mrs. Brown was forced to walk to a friend's Clinton Avenue home in her stocking feet. This was the second time in their married life that they had escaped a massive fire (the first was aboard the *Mayflower* back in 1855). Brown returned to the scene next day, with the aid of a cane, to survey the ruins. These two photographs, by Boehl & Koenig, were printed on a stereograph card (Library of Congress).

When the group met on October 11, Brown was elected its president. An executive committee, with Brown as chairman and Sylvester Waterhouse as secretary, was appointed to memorialize Congress. When a document containing the body's objectives was completed, Brown and one of his colleagues were authorized, with confirmation from the ME, to visit Washington, D.C., to lobby senators and Congressmen for needed upgrades. Brown and two companions arrived in the nation's capital on January 10, 1878, and within days were making the rounds of congressional offices. This was the first time we know of that the ex-mayor had returned to the nation's capital since 1865.

Upon his return to St. Louis, Brown reported on his mission to the ME on March 27. The long-time riverman told how he had testified before the House Commerce Committee and the Committee on Levees and the Mississippi River in January and February seeking increased funding, as did officers from the army's Corps of Engineers. Of the $13 million needed, most congressmen, particularly those from eastern states, were inclined to provide less than half. Still, Brown departed feeling that Congress as a whole sympathized with the needs of those living and working on the western waters and might be induced to loosen their purse strings. Hearing this optimistic report, the ME voted to pay the expenses of the two delegates who had been living out of pocket for almost half a year and agreed to have Brown, if he were available, return to Washington again in 1879.

On July 16 Capt. and Mrs. Brown, part of a large party of St. Louis business and political leaders, arrived at Minneapolis, MN, on an excursion. The group spent the next week visiting St. Paul, Lake Superior, and other points of interest. The former steamboat captain was particularly interested in the problems of the Upper Mississippi River.

Ever the politician, Capt. Joe, at the behest of the local Democratic party, agreed to once more run for sheriff of St. Louis County now that that jurisdiction had been separated from the city. It was no more a wise decision this time than it had been two years earlier, as the city and county both ran Republican and the former city mayor lost the race by 5,103 votes. When the vote counting was over that November he was ready to return to the nation's capital on behalf of western waterways.[12]

Ex-Mayor Brown's 1879 stint in the nation's capital went about the same as that in 1877–78, with many discussions on the need for river improvements and several appearances before congressional committees. In early February 1880 Capt. Joe was named chairman of a delegation of St. Louis Democrats who traveled to Washington, D.C., to make a case to the party's national committee as to why their city should host the Democratic convention in early summer. When the Missourians returned home on February 27, all were interviewed by the *Globe-Democrat* and expressed disappointment that their trip was in vain. As Brown indicated, "Cincinnati was a foregone conclusion upwards of a month ago and that fact was apparent as soon as the committee got to Washington."

Not long after coming back from Washington, Brown and several Carrollton, IL, friends and business acquaintances elected to visit places in the West looking for adventure and investment opportunities. The ex-mayor had become interested in the region during his sojourn to San Francisco while in office and by news of gold riches now pouring out of southern New Mexico. An excursion was laid on to Las Vegas, Santa Fe, and El Paso that would return via White Oaks, a major gold-mining boomtown (today a ghost town). On April 29 the *St. Louis Post-Dispatch* announced that the former mayor and others of his party were attacked and killed by Native Americans as they traveled towards White Oaks. Happily for all concerned, the report was wrong.

Sad news arrived from Alton, IL, on June 10. Joseph's brother, the 61-year-old George T., had died the day before after a lingering illness at the home of his sister Ellen. A biographer profiled his post–Washington life, noting that in "his absence from the state, he had lost his prominence in politics and failing resources added to his misfortunes. He was unmarried and led a rather lonely life.... During his later years the journalistic instinct was still strong in him and he was accustomed to frequent the newspaper offices to look over the exchanges and thus keep pace with the world in which he had once borne a prominent part." Capt. Joe, back from the West, immediately boarded a train for Alton, reuniting with Ellen and his nephew George Child the next day. The funeral for George T. was held at the Presbyterian church on June 12. The man who more than any other had helped spark an interest in politics in his younger brother

Death of George T. Brown. When the U.S. Senate elected a new sergeant-at-arms in March 1869, Capt. Brown's older brother retired to his Illinois home. Remembered as "a man of genial manners and generous impulses," he visited the local newspaper office frequently to stay abreast of developments. Brown, aged 61, died on June 9, 1880, without ever having been photographed, a distinction he would share with Joseph. The bachelor, who more than any other had helped spark an interest in politics in his sibling and had helped insure that Joseph received the initial contract needed to build ironclads in 1862, was buried in the Brown family plot at Alton City Cemetery three days later (*Harper's Weekly*, March 28, 1868).

7—Joseph Brown, Entrepreneur and Mayor Again: Life After Gunboats   313

and had helped insure that Joseph received the initial contract needed to build ironclads in 1862 was buried in the Brown family plot at Alton City Cemetery. The bachelor would always be remembered as "a man of genial manners and generous impulses."

Despite his sadness, the ex–St. Louis mayor, a life-long Democrat (unlike his brother), was able to travel to Cincinnati as a Missouri delegate at the June 22–24 National Democratic Convention. There Civil War general Winfield Scott Hancock was nominated for president, but he would lose to another Civil War general, James A. Garfield, in the November election.

The Brown family situation did not improve as the summer advanced. "In consequence of family troubles," as a newspaper later put it, Jennie and her husband separated and began living apart. Believing divorce was possible, the ex-mayor's daughter made out a new will leaving her entire estate and her San Francisco home to her sympathetic father, who agreed to serve as executor.

Back in St. Louis on September 21, the ex-mayor chaired what the newspapers next day called a "rousing" public meeting at the county courthouse. There a report was read from a committee of concerned citizens wishing to petition Congress to open the "unassigned lands" in the Indian Territory west of the Mississippi to settlement. Numerous gentlemen spoke, including Capt. Joe, who, after his excursions in 1872 and the past April, had developed something of an interest in "the Indian question," which had been a "hobby of his for years." Like many of his fellow Americans, Brown was not a champion of minorities and believed the rich lands of areas like New Mexico were occupied by "a few lazy Indians and half-breeds, the Negroes being the better of the two." The federal government's Indian policy was, he claimed, a failure and it was important that the lands to be opened for settlement by homestead and preemption. When the meeting ended, a new committee, with Brown as chair, was created to draw up a petition to Congress, which was duly sent a few weeks later.

During the fall, the health of Mrs. Brown's widowed mother, who had continued to live in Carrolton after her daughter married Capt. Brown, declined significantly. Virginia Brown then returned to Illinois to stay with her mother, offering assistance and comfort. Mrs. Brown's mother passed away on February 7, 1881, and the former mayor, delayed by a Boston blizzard, joined his wife and her family in time for the funeral on February 11. After the service, Capt. Brown returned to Missouri while his wife remained in Carrolton. Not long back in St. Louis, Brown was disappointed to find that the First Spiritual Society of St. Louis, which had met in city hall during his administration, had lost its charter and was forced to suspend its series of weekly spiritualism lectures. Finding that situation intolerable, the city's ex-chief executive agreed to become the group's president and to assist it in obtaining a new state charter. Meetings were resumed in Howard's Hall, at the corner of Thirteenth and Olive streets.

In late September, Mrs. Brown, still in Carrolton, became violently ill with a stomach ailment. When the ailment did not respond to medical attention, the formerly robust first lady of St. Louis, described as "a large, fine-looking lady of, perhaps, 200 pounds weight," began to slim down dramatically. The ex-mayor came to the side of his spouse, but by the middle of October she was unable to eat. On November 1 a message was sent to Mrs. Spotts in San Francisco urging her to return home and, of course, she departed for Illinois immediately. She did not arrive before her mother died on November 7.

Joseph Brown, who had lost his brother just a year earlier, was devastated at the loss of his greatest friend and companion. When news of her passing reached St. Louis, there was genuine sorrow in many quarters, as "her kindly heart and many accomplishments had made her universally admired and loved." Mrs. Brown's funeral was held at the family home on the afternoon of November 15 with her husband, daughter, brother, family members, and local friends, plus many from St. Louis and Alton, present. Flora arrangements were everywhere about the parlor, with the ex-mayor arranging that a large tribute of white flowers, on a black background, be affixed to the wall over the mantel. This devotional from Brown featured lettering which read "Farewell to Earth," reportedly his wife's last words. The Green County Circuit Court was adjourned this day in honor of Virginia K. Brown, who was then interred in her family's vault at the Carrolton cemetery.

The grieving Capt. Brown and Jennie returned to St. Louis in mid–December, taking rooms at the St. James Hotel. On Christmas Eve father and daughter started out for San Francisco. The pair passed Omaha three days later and on New Year's Day arrived at Jennie's Pacific Avenue home, where the ex-mayor could spend time in new surroundings. The visit would get him away from a terrible sense of family loss and, just perhaps, a smoldering love-hate feud he was engaged in with no less a figure than his old river colleague, James B. Eads, for whom he had hosted a banquet in 1875.[13]

Arguably the most famous Mississippi waterman of their day, Eads, having finished the great St. Louis Bridge, had recently developed and installed a series of river jetties at New Orleans designed to improve river navigation at the mouth of the "Father of Waters." Unfortunately, while his engineering feats were universally applauded, many had come with tremendous cost overruns, which Brown now argued did not bode well for those wishing to invest in any of his future enterprises. The disagreement was aired in the *Washington Chronicle* of January 12, 1882, and the *Chicago Daily Tribune* of February 15. Several examples of Eads' financial difficulties, going back over the 30 years the two men had known each other, were recounted by Brown in a short letter. His examples included the Missouri Wrecking Company, a glass company, the St. Louis Bridge, the Columbia Insurance Company, and the jetties, all of which had either failed or suffered significant financial loss. There is no record of an Eads response to Brown's comments but the two men were not really close personally before this flare-up or afterwards, having always supported each other as political or business necessity required.

Finding California to his liking and its beauty an aid during his period of bereavement, Brown extended his stay in the Golden State. By summer, he was traveling up and down the coast enjoying the scenery, being particularly enthralled with the Monterey region. To keep his name before the folks of St. Louis while away he wrote a number of travel accounts and society reports for the *St. Louis Daily Republican*. His breezy air and taste in description, particularly as it applied to ladies and certain public figures, was not always appreciated, winning Brown a stylistic slap from the *Wasp*, San Francisco's satire magazine.

When Brown learned in late fall that Jennie was pregnant, the Missouri senior citizen and visiting tourist elected to stay on for the birth of his first grandchild. What might have been a time of healing and joy instead became one of even deeper sorrow. Fighting between Albert Spotts and Jennie now broke out again and they separated once more over the holidays.

Despite all that could be done, Jennie Brown Spotts died, along with her baby, on May 2, 1883. In a telegram to a St. Louis friend, the ex-mayor stated the cause as "childbirth fever," and concluded "mother and child are now lying side by side." Within a few days, both were laid to rest.

On June 28 a San Francisco attorney, Eugene N. Deuprey (1838–1903), filed suit against Joseph Brown on behalf of St. Louis resident Frank G. Flanagan. It will be recalled that Brown had taken out a note from a St. Louis bank when his railroad investments began to fail in 1876, securing it with $30,000 in railroad bonds and a second mortgage on four city houses and lots he owned worth $10,000 above their first mortgage. In return, the bank promised to manage the properties and pay the interest on the first mortgage, but it did not do so. The first mortgage was then foreclosed and without his consent Brown's collateral bonds were exchanged by the bank for securities that became worthless. For years afterwards, the bank failed to notify Brown of the situation, finally selling the valueless paper to Flanagan for an undisclosed sum and the note itself to J.F. Conroy for $32. Upon the solicitation of Flanagan, Conroy gave the note to him, agreeing that if anything were ever collected upon it would be divided between the two men equally.

When on September 15 the will of Brown's daughter was read there was general disbelief that Jennie had left her entire $20,000 estate (the bulk of which was $14,500 for nearly 4,500 acres in Texas) to her father, along with the house that he had built at the time of her marriage to Spotts. No longer rich, Brown agreed to sell the house to cover a number of debts that had piled up over the past few years. Albert Spotts and his family were aghast and, through his brother-in-law, Thomas J. Blakeman (1842–1915), a long-time St. Louis attorney who had relocated to San Francisco in 1880, filed suit to contest the will and to block the entire probate transaction.

In order that this matter be resolved, Brown offered to set aside the will in order to keep the name of his daughter from being dragged through "the public prints," hoping that the Spotts family would offer a financial settlement. Albert, his mother, and Blakeman were not willing to do so. A probate judge ruled on October 3 that Spotts was entitled to the Texas land, with the remainder and the house going to Brown. Unsatisfied, Brown's "in-laws," as the *San Francisco Chronicle* put it, now endeavored to embarrass the ex-mayor "by pressing for payment on a note which they obtained in a peculiar manner and which was long ago considered worthless."

Flanagan, who knew Blakeman, sent the note and documentation he had obtained from Conroy to California, where the attorney filed suit on his behalf against Jennie's father in San Francisco Circuit Court for $45,000, the principal and interest on the note. It was clearly seen by all that part of the object of this action was to attach the Pacific Avenue house and the remainder of the money from the will in order to apply it as partial payment of the Flanagan note. Depositions were taken by the court commissioner on November 22, but no resolution could be made. Brown offered to reimburse Flanagan $300 for his trouble, but the idea was spurned. When asked about the tenor of the proceedings by a reporter, ex-mayor Brown "was not very reserved about expressing his opinion about his son-in-law or his brother-in-law, Blakeman." While the case limped along over the next year, Brown retained the house and lived in it, making numerous sojourns around the state. When it was learned that J.F. Conroy was the real owner of the note, Brown negotiated a settlement with him and took his deposition as to his dealings with Flanagan and Blakeman.

Capt. Brown came back to St. Louis on November 17, 1884, it being necessary to reengage in his remaining business interests. No sooner had he stepped off the train, however, than many of his old political friends and allies descended upon him seeking his help. An election for St. Louis city mayor would occur the following April and a popular Democrat was needed to wrest the office back from the Republicans, who had held it since 1881. The Democrat party was divided over who should stand and some believed that selection of the ex-mayor would heal any factional wounds and lead to victory. Brown, for his part, advised his supporters to await the will of an upcoming Democratic city convention.

Flanagan v. Brown, meanwhile, continued until December 12. Having received notice to return, the former St. Louis mayor was in the San Francisco courtroom that day when a decision was rendered. Having examined in minute detail the arrangements and deals between Conroy, Flanagan, and Blakeman, the will regarding the house, and Brown's negotiation with Conroy, it was decided that Brown did not owe anyone money and was permitted to retain the house he had constructed for his daughter. The outcome, reported the paper, "relieves ex-mayor Brown from litigation that has been harassing him for nearly two years."

To celebrate his success, Joseph Brown availed himself of a visit to London, England, for Christmas and therein lies another of the many tales he provided the local press. Brown, appreciative of opera ever since his daughter had taken it up, and several companions set off for a performance at the Royal Opera House. Arriving at their stall (box seats), the former St. Louis mayor was halted by the doorkeeper, who refused admittance:

> "Why not?" I asked in surprise, "here are my seat tickets." "Well, you cannot enter," he replied, decisively. "Your coat is a frock, and nothing but dress suits are allowed." I expostulated. I told him my hotel was a long way off and that the ladies would be greatly disappointed. I was an American and I did not know the rule of the theater. Finally, he told me to go into the dressing room where the attendants might be able, perhaps, to fix me out all right. I went, expecting to pay two or three crowns for the loan of a coat. The fellow look at me a second, whipped a pin from his lapel, and pinned my coat-tails back, and I found myself in evening dress. I gave the man half a crown.

Brown returned to St. Louis at the end of December and took up rooms at the Leclede Hotel.[14]

Captain Brown spent much of the first of quarter 1885 involved in his old political passion. The then-current rift between certain factions within the Democratic Party resulted in several members asking Brown not to stand as a candidate for mayor but to consider running for president of the Board of Public Improvement. When the Democrat's city convention was held in an all-night session on March 25, David R. Francis (1850–1927), former president of the Union Merchants' Exchange, was nominated for mayor. In a tough campaign, he would win election as the city's chief executive. Brown, who had accepted nomination to run for president of the Board of Public Improvement, was not so fortunate and lost his bid to Henry Flad (1824–1898), a well-known German émigré engineer and assistant to James B. Eads in the construction of the Illinois–St. Louis Bridge. Having come away from this election cycle without an office, Brown now turned his attention back to business while seeking other political opportunities.

Upon the July 23 death of former president Ulysses S. Grant, Mayor Francis on August 3 appointed a large delegation, including Joseph Brown, to represent the city at the August 8 funeral at Riverside Park in New York City. The group traveled in a special Pullman car that left St. Louis on August 5. Upon his return from New York, Brown traveled to Washington, D.C., in late September to support his own application for the position of St. Louis postmaster. As he wrote a friend, who allowed the letter to be published in the newspapers, Brown believed he could "make it a great lever for the benefit of St. Louis and to the party to which I belong." Wright was introduced to postal and other federal officials by former Confederate brigadier general Marcus J. Wright (1831–1922), agent for the collection of CSA documents for the War Department's Official Records series. Nevertheless, fellow Democrat Grover Cleveland eventually appointed William Hyde, who would serve until 1890.

Now being without a government office, the former mayor made application in 1886 for openings that had come up in St. Louis for both an assessor and a collector of water rates and for a commissioner on the Board of Public Improvement. Mayor Francis chose other candidates. Joining with other, more monied. partners, Brown became president of the Sierra Del Una Gold Mining Company of New Mexico, which was incorporated on September 29 with $1 million capital stock. Its fate is unknown, although it is known that problems with Native Americans slowed bullion extraction for a quarter of a century. In November Capt. Joe became president of the newly reorganized Western Forge and Tool Works. The company, founded in early 1885, had reported the month before that its fiscal situation was improving, especially "in the line of railroad bridge work." The number of orders for machine forgings were also increasing.

On May 2, 1887, Brown, a nonapplicant, was nominated by Mayor Francis before the St. Louis Board of Aldermen to become one of nine district assessors (serving under a president) for the city's Assessment of Revenues Department, or Assessor's Office. The duty of the post would require him to assess the value of real estate and serve as a member of a board of equalization. Much of the work would be "compiling, writing tax books, bills, etc." The city's one-time chief executive was not pleased to learn he had been offered such a minor post (of even less stature than those he had sought the previous year), particularly after the *Globe-Democrat* the next day reported that the announcement of his name "caused some comments on the mutability of political life." Brown declined the honor on June 4 in a letter to Mayor Francis, which was published by the *Post-Dispatch*. Taking the opportunity, he confessed, would cost him more out of pocket than it brought in and so he could not accept it.

Unfortunately, the progress of the Western Force and Tool Works did not continue in the same vein as earlier anticipated, and on October 29 it went over. Remaining to handle the dissolution, Brown made certain that all of the firm's creditors were satisfied,

1888 Democratic National Convention. In February 1888, city leaders learned that St. Louis had once again been chosen to host the year's national Democratic convention, this time in the St. Louis Exposition and Music Hall, completed in 1883. The conclave, in which delegate Joseph Brown played a smaller role than in years before, was still dessert to the dedicated politician. After all, it was a noisy but predictable affair in which anyone could foretell, without a crystal ball, that Grover Cleveland would be renominated for the U.S. presidency (Library of Congress).

but, as with the Atlantic and Mississippi Steamship Company years earlier, the stockholders were left with nothing.[15]

In February 1888, city leaders again learned that St. Louis had been chosen to host the year's national Democratic convention. Once again preparations were made to conduct the conclave, this time in the St. Louis Exposition and Music Hall, completed in 1883. The *Milwaukee Sentinel* stated that the main reason the town was picked over rival Chicago was, first, because it was a Democratic city and, second, "the boys can get as drunk as they please without being arrested or written up."

Just before the Democratic Convention opened on June 5 for its three-day run, the *Post-Dispatch* took time from its normal daily coverage of crime, business, and politics to publish a large article entitled "From the Vasty Deep" devoted to the subject of spiritualism and its practice in St. Louis. All of the most prominent local adherents were profiled. Ex-Mayor Brown, about to participate in the convention, was numbered among the most prominent believers. "He possesses considerable mediumistic power," the article noted, "and is a steady attendant at séances." Brown's conversion to this belief "occurred many years ago and he has ever since remained unshaken in his faith." Brown was not the least bit embarrassed by the newspaper article. For him, the Democratic convention in which he played almost no role was but dessert: a noisy but predictable affair in which anyone could foretell without a crystal ball that Grover Cleveland would be renominated.

Meanwhile, Thomas Dimmock (1830–1909), an old acquaintance of Captain Joe's who was also from Alton, IL, made an appeal that caught Brown's attention. Dimmock, a prewar editor of the *Alton Daily Democrat*, had come to St. Louis in 1865, about the same time as Brown, taking a position as an editorial writer and reviewer with the *St. Louis Daily Republican*. A supporter during the former mayor's two terms, Dimmock now made it his life's goal to erect a monument on the top of the Alton Bluff to Elijah P. Lovejoy.

Earlier, in September 1878, Horace White had established a Lovejoy Monument Association at Alton, IL, to raise funds for the project. A three-person subcommittee was established, with Dimmock charged with taking the message and appeal to St. Louis. In April Dimmock gave a well-regarded lecture on Lovejoy, and the times in which he lived, at the Church of the Unity. During his presentation, he called for the building of a monument to the free-soil martyr. The challenge was accepted by gentlemen in the audience who promised to provide financial and other support. Touched by the appeal made on behalf of his long-ago friend and teacher, Brown promised to join in and fully support the goal. The address was printed and widely distributed and led to the Illinois legislature joining the campaign.

The defeat of the Democratic Party in the November election did little to lessen Capt. Brown's interest in, or hard work on behalf of, his party or the citizens of his town. His name was kept before the larger public not only by the newspapers but also by some of his friends. Early in 1889 he allowed an autobiographical letter to be published in Emerson W. Gould's work *50 Years on the Mississippi*.

On March 23 the former mayor delivered a stirring moral and political address to those assembled, mostly working men, at the Franklin Street Liberty Evangelical Mission. Four days later, Brown was nominated for the office of city auditor, which post he won in the April 3 election. The 1880s, a time of trial and sadness for the 66-year-old one-time steamboat master and ironclad builder, closed as the 1890s promised new challenges and opportunities.[16] Joseph Brown entered into the duties of his new office, one far more important than that of a district assessor, within a few days of his election and turned his full energy into providing effective and honest service to the 400,000-plus residents of St. Louis. During his first term he was involved in numerous high-profile disputes with other officials regarding salaries, perks, and spending

Capt. Joe was not always supported in his activities by local newspapers. Indeed, in March 1891 it was suggested in print that a new city ordinance should, as a cost saving measure, eliminate the office of deputy auditor held by Brown's son. The law was quashed before its enactment, but the reporter apparently was unaware that Brown did not have a living son and that it was his nephew who held the post. In November, the St. Louis press began to run articles previewing the upcoming municipal elections. On the 20th, twelve possible candidates for mayor (six Democrat and six Republican) were profiled by the *Post-Dispatch* based on "whom the politicians are talking about." Auditor Brown was among the Democrats.

About this time, Brown's concern for workers was again demonstrated. In a dispute with other city offices, he supported paying city clerks their December salary a few days earlier than usual. "Buncumbe," shouted several commissioners and department heads who claimed that the men "would squander their money if they got it now." Capt. Joe quietly promised the people working in his office that "they will be paid, at any rate."

Brown was not a candidate for his old job but instead sought return to his current office. In the polling of April 4, 1893, he was the only candidate from his party to win a seat. All other elective offices went to the Republicans, although the former mayor may have been pleased to see that the free library charter amendment also passed. The captain's 1,596-vote margin of victory was contested by the losing GOP standard bearer, who eventually lost a recount months later. Unsatisfied, he sued and lost again. In December after his office was confirmed, Brown traveled to Hardin, IL, to spend the holidays with his aging widowed sister Ellen. In January 1894 the two returned to St. Louis, where she temporarily moved into his home at 3766 Olive Street.

By the early 1890s, the rail traffic passing

Mayor Again? In the decades since leaving the St. Louis mayor's office, the name of Joseph Brown was often mentioned as a candidate for return to the office. On several occasions speculation was more than conjecture as serious boomlets occurred. Brown was elected city auditor in 1889 and seemed to enjoy the post, even though talk of his making a bid for the mayor's office was rampant thereafter. In the polling of April 4, 1893, he stood for auditor once more and was the only candidate from his party to win a seat. All other elective city offices went to the Republicans. As late as 1897 he would be approached regarding the possibility of running for mayor once again (*St. Louis Post Dispatch*, November 20, 1892).

7—Joseph Brown, Entrepreneur and Mayor Again: Life After Gunboats

The Alton Bridge. By the early 1890s, the rail traffic passing over the Mississippi River into downtown St. Louis via the Eads Bridge had become quite congested. Consequently a new structure was built between Alton, IL, and Bellefontaine to speed Illinois-Missouri transport. On May 1, 1894, Capt. Brown was one of those invited to present a speech at the formal opening of the new rail bridge spanning the river between those two communities. His participation was well received and gave him the opportunity to meet a number of old acquaintances (Library of Congress).

over the Mississippi River into downtown St. Louis via the Eads Bridge had become quite congested. Consequently a new structure was built between Alton, IL, and Bellefontaine to speed Illinois-Missouri transport. On May 1 Capt. Brown was one of those invited to present a speech at the formal opening of the new rail bridge spanning the river between those two communities. His participation was well received and gave him the opportunity to meet a number of old acquaintenances. During a lunch at the home of his sister Ellen the day before, the St. Louis official had let it be known that when the time came he wished to be buried in the Alton cemetery "on the knoll overlooking the great river." It was later thought by the editor of his hometown newspaper that this was the time when his mind began "to drift back toward his early religious views."

Brown's second term in the auditor's chair went much as the first. Each year in May he provided an annual report and on other occasions he battled those he perceived as being wrong in their approach to spending city funds. He also found time to speak and write on various aspects of what he called the "Palmy Days of Steamboating" before sundry groups and in regional newspapers and the *Waterways Journal*.

Even though he may secretly have had thoughts regarding the religion of his youth, Brown remained one of the best known spiritualists in St. Louis. As such, he was extensively interviewed by a *Sunday Post-Dispatch* reporter regarding the tenets of his faith on May 31, 1895, for a June 2 article. Never bashful about his faith, the auditor recalled having practiced it for over 35 years, even recently having become convinced of the concept of "materialization," in which a spirit could return to its earthly form. His interest piqued, the correspondent determined to see, and report on, a real-life séance for his readers. The story duly appeared in the June 16 issue under the title "Flashlights and Fair at a Spiritualist's Séance." It is little wonder that Capt. Brown, a true believer who sensed the interest the local public was taking in his faith, used the power of the auditor's office to make certain that those professing to practice the rituals of the faith did not use mediumistic trickery to dupe gullible citizens participating in séances. His

Spiritualism. A follower of the Spiritualist persuasion since the 1850s, Joseph Brown allowed the First Spiritual Society of St. Louis to meet in city hall during his administration and became the group's president in 1881. A friend of leading practitioners, the ex-mayor was often quoted on the subject in the St. Louis newspapers. At the same time, he was almost fanatical about rooting out fake spiritualists and séance leaders, exposing them whenever possible (our illustration shows one being caught in England) and on occasion seeing that they were run out of town. On October 2, 1898, Brown and many others from the St. Louis spiritualism community participated in the dedication of the First Church of Spiritual Unity. The new organization was a direct outgrowth of his presidency of the First Spiritual Society of St. Louis almost two decades earlier. The following year, Brown renounced Spiritualism on his deathbed, returning to Presbyterianism, the religion of his youth (courtesy *St. Louis Post Dispatch*).

best-known targets were the materializing mediums Hugh Moore, his wife, and Mable Abner Jackman, who specialized in the return of dead wives and daughters to their loved ones, and who, in fact, were the subjects of the June 16 *Post-Dispatch* article.

Brown first encountered these three mediums while attending one of their séances at their home on Locust Street in July. Determining, after several visits, that they were frauds and the materialized departed "no more than ordinary buxom girls," the city official wrote the trio a letter threatening exposure and arrest if they did not immediately leave town. The mediums were gone within hours of its receipt.

As he had every August for several years, Joseph Brown traveled to Lily Dale, New York, in August to participate with other believers and general citizens in the spiritualist lectures and séances sponsored by the Cassadaga Lake Free Association, founded in 1886, today called the Lily Dale Assembly. Just off the train, the St. Louisian found Moore and Abner Jackman "installed in great style and holding séances that were drawing like side-shows at a circus." To Brown's great indignation, Brown found them "charging $1 per séance to all comers and reaping in a harvest of gold." After their exposure by the Missourian to the association the two, labeled "cheats," were arrested on August 31, along with four young female assistants. When Brown returned to St. Louis in early September, he was amazed to find that Moore and Abner Jackman had skipped bail in New York and returned to their Locust Street abode, where they were once more holding séances. The auditor immediately alerted the police, who staked out the mediums' house, determined that no more fraud be perpetrated in St. Louis. On September 26 Moore was arrested for beating a lad employed to act as a "spook." When the medium's court case was called two days later, it was found that he had once again skipped bail. On a happier note, the auditor was probably quite pleased on October 14 to offer a requested lecture before the members of the Missouri Historical Society on the subject of his prewar steamboating experiences. The talk was later published in the *Waterways Journal*.

Capt. Joe also continued his support of the Lovejoy Monument Association and others pushing ahead toward the goal of erecting a monument in Alton. The Illinois state government had demanded that as a condition of its own fiscal participation the monument association was required to match the taxpayers' $25,000 contribution with an equal amount, to be in hand by January 1, 1899. On February 6, 1896, the *Alton Telegraph* advised that Capt. Joe would lecture in support of the monument subscription at the city's Temple Theater on February 18, giving his "Early Reminiscences of Alton." In addition to tales of Lovejoy, Daniel Webster, Abraham Lincoln, and steamboating, he would relay "many amusing and memorable anecdotes and incidents." It was expected that many would make a contribution for admittance and that the venue "should be packed to its utmost capacity." The friendly editor, seeking as large a contributing audience as possible, waxed eloquent on Brown's service as mayor of two cities, particularly Alton, "when the first great stride in street improvement was made." A "fluent talker, instructive and humorous," the captain had "a larger store of Alton lore of early days than any other person now living" and, it was promised, his presentation would be "told in an interesting manner that will make the evening pass off most pleasantly."

Brown did not disappoint the many assembled that Tuesday. So popular was the presentation that it was published in a 15-page document by the Lovejoy Monument

Association and widely subscribed to by people unable to attend the talk. The funds collected, like others subscribed before and after, were added to the $25,000 appropriated by the State of Illinois the winter before and, after some political struggle, allowed to pass to the monument association.

In February 1897, as he had several times before, Capt. Brown found himself approached by friends to run for mayor in the upcoming elections. He agreed to submit to the will of his party's convention. When the editor of the *Alton Daily Telegraph* heard of the former townsman's action, he put out a little article entitled "A Lively Old Man." The possible candidate was "about 75 years of age, but his years are no indication of the ex–Mayor's activity and liveliness" the newspaperman proclaimed.

In March, Brown was chosen by the Democrats to stand for the seat of city comptroller against the current occupant, Republican Isaac H. Sturgeon (1821–1908). The two men were close friends and their city hall offices adjoined each other. The captain was soundly defeated, by 20,340 votes. The April 6 election was his last. True to form with his friends, Brown was the first to visit the victor and offer congratulations. "Well, Brown," said Sturgeon, "no one has heard a word from me except in your praise." The auditor responded: "Same here!" Sturgeon would be the only St. Louis political figure to attend Brown's funeral.

Although out of office, the ex-auditor and one-time gunboat builder and mayor was not without opportunities. In late May, he was invited, with fellow Democrat and former governor Norman J. Coleman (1827–1911), to Roodhouse, IL (near Chicago), to offer a keynote speech at the Lower Illinois River Valley Association and Convention. A guest at the new Roodhouse Hotel, Capt. Joe, like his colleague, held sway before a crowd of 7,500, gathered in fine weather on June 5 to participate in consumption of 5,000 pounds of fish that had accompanied the two men on the train from St. Louis. Both speakers discussed the evils of locks and dams on the Illinois River, with Brown, drawing on his mayoral experience, commenting on potential sewage problems of the Chicago Drainage Canal.

The Lovejoy Monument that many had worked so hard to bring to fruition was completed at Alton Cemetery in late fall. Designed by sculptor Robert F. Bringhurst with architect Louis Mulgard, both of St. Louis, it is a 93-foot-high granite column, with two 30-foot-high granite sentinel columns, the former being topped by a 17-foot-high winged statute of Victory and the other two with bronze eagles. The monument was scheduled to be dedicated on November 7, the 60th anniversary of the minister's death. Heavy rain forced the ceremony to be moved inside to the Temple Theater and

Opposite: **The Lovejoy Monument.** One of those who had personally known Elijah Lovejoy, Joseph Brown was keenly interested in efforts to construct a monument to him in Alton, IL. On February 18, 1896, the former two-town mayor lectured in support of the monument subscription at the city's Temple Theater, giving his "Early Reminiscences of Alton." In addition to tales of Lovejoy, Daniel Webster, Abraham Lincoln, and steamboating, he relayed "many amusing and memorable anecdotes and incidents." So popular was the content of the sold-out presentation that it was offered as a booklet, raising even more funds. The Lovejoy Monument that many had worked so hard to bring to fruition was completed at Alton Cemetery and dedicated on November 8, 1897, coinciding with the 60th anniversary of the minister's death (courtesy Catherine E. Bagby, Alton, IL).

held the next day, with Dimmock presenting the principal address. Newspaper coverage of the event does not tell us if Capt. Brown was in attendance.

On December 13 Brown's home was burglarized by Thomas Hood, an African American who stole diamonds and jewelry once belonging to Virginia Brown. An escapee from the Nashville penitentiary, the suspect was arrested on December 23. Three days later the former auditor went to the police station and swore out a warrant. Hood was returned to Tennessee, but there is no information on whether or not Brown's property was returned.[17]

In retirement, Brown found pleasure in writing, preparing a number of articles for the *Waterways Journal*, biographical and historical encyclopedias and histories. All were reminiscences of his time before the Civil War when steamboating was his life. He also continued to support various river improvement projects in the Mississippi Valley and to practice and expound on his faith.

On Sunday night, October 2, 1898, the former mayor and many others from the St. Louis spiritualism community participated in the dedication of the First Church of Spiritual Unity on North Vandeventer Avenue. The use of the word church in the name of the organization on September 6 was necessary, it was explained by the pastor, W. F. Peck, to "give proper expression to the religious aspects of the association." This new organization was a direct outgrowth of Brown's 1880 presidency of the First Spiritual Society of St. Louis.

Brown's last public activity was to serve as one of six representatives of the Union Merchant Exchange of St. Louis at the October 10–11, 1899, Deep Water Convention held at Peoria, IL. There delegates from inland cities discussed the value of a canal running from Lake Michigan to the Gulf of Mexico and a number of other issues, none more controversial than the Chicago Drainage Canal, which the former mayor had decried at Roodhouse, IL, two years earlier.

On one occasion just before Halloween Capt. Brown happened to board a streetcar in front of his Olive Street home. As he sat down, he was spied from the back by two ladies, one of whom, famed Spiritualist medium Maud Lord-Drake (1852–1924), pointed covertly at him and quietly told the other, "I see death very close for that gentleman seated at the front of the car." Both of the women knew him personally, "so well and favorably ... as the old city auditor and at one time Mayor of St. Louis." Calling him back, as one of them was very nearsighted, they engaged him in conversation, during which he indicated he "was feeling quite well, much better than he had felt in some time." He would be dead within two months.

Apparently healthy and still a "pronounced spiritualist and an unusually intelligent man," Brown continued to be active and interested in reliving, for anyone who would listen, the stories of his prewar steamboating business and adventures. Never in any of his reminiscences did he discuss his five-year Civil War stint as a major gunboat contractor. In November he gave permission to the *Waterways Journal* to publish his correspondence with a Memphis friend detailing stories of the *Altona* and the *Mayflower*.

Just after Thanksgiving Capt. Joe became ill from what the *Washington Post* would call a "complication of diseases" and was forced to his bed, where his sister Ellen came to attend him, along with Dr. H. McGee Wilson and his sister, Mrs. E.A. Taylor. His nephew George, Ellen's son and Brown's former auditor's office assistant, came as he could. As Capt. Joe's illness lingered, the colorful man who began his career as a miller went in and out of consciousness, the space between each bout becoming progressively shorter.

At one point late in his sickness several prominent spiritualists arrived and attempted to gain admittance to his room, wishing to convince him to allow them to conduct his funeral. Remaining lucid, he forbade them entrance and sent them away. Brown had decided to die "in the faith of his early life, which was the faith of his fathers." Just before he lost consciousness for the last time late on December 2, Brown told those near his bedside that he knew the end was near. He asked Ellen for a hymnal and a pencil. Slowly he turned the pages and marked three. Handing over the book, he told her he wanted the marked hymns played at his funeral: "Rock of Ages," "Nearer My God to Thee," and "Sweet Hour of Prayer." His strength departing fast, Capt. Joe whispered, mostly inaudibly, to his sister. "Death has no terrors for me," he said, noting almost with pleasure that he would soon meet his wife, Virginia, and daughter Jennie. Just as he fell back into unconsciousness, he whispered to Ellen his final words: "All is well." He died at 11:45 Sunday morning.

A "quiet and unostentatious" funeral service for Joseph Brown was held at his residence on Tuesday morning, December 5. The parlors of his home were filled with flowers and many old friends. "A marked feature of the gathering," recorded the reporter present from the *Post-Dispatch*, "was the number of aged men present." Tears were seen to form in the eyes of some as they stood by the casket of the departed, while others realized that "they, too, belonged to that generation of old St. Louisians rapidly passing away."

The Rev. Dr. John F. Cannon, pastor of the Grand Avenue Presbyterian Church, presided over the solemn readings, and those gathered joined in singing the three hymns Brown had requested. None of the city's ex-mayors were present and "the only representative of the present city administration was Mr. Isaac H. Sturgeon, Comptroller." Later, the Union Merchant Exchange would issue resolutions of respect to the memory of the deceased. After the conclusion of the service, the immediate family and Cannon, Sturgeon, and Thomas Dimmock accompanied the casket to the train station where it departed for Alton at 11:00 a.m.

Per arrangements worked out the night before by Alton mayor A.W. Young, the train was met at the Illinois station by Young and twenty current and former city officials. With the flag on the city building at half-mast, the funeral cortege proceeded to Alton cemetery, where the body would be interred in the family plot while the fire bells all tolled in solemn respect. At the gravesite, the Rev. Cannon spoke again and then, after the casket was lowered, each of the city delegation cast a blossom of their choosing into the grave.[18]

Brown was 76 years old at the time of his death and his long career was both diverse and productive. He was a steamboat, milling, and railroad entrepreneur and a politician—mayor or lesser official from two cities in two states—who earned and lost fortunes but never stepped out of his abode at a loss for either ideas or commentary. Most important to this story, the man employed his prewar skills and connections to obtain construction contracts to build three stopgap river ironclads, coordinating numerous subcontractors to ensure their assembly moved smoothly from the river towns in Indiana and Ohio where they were assembled. Even before the trio was in service, his interpersonal and building abilities won for him the support necessary to remodel more commercial steamers into light-draught Union river gunboats than any other contractor in the Civil War. With a fortune in his pocket from his labors, the enterprising Brown returned to St. Louis in 1865 and launched a successful postwar life.

And yet, 118 years after his death, Capt. Joe's name is one of the great unknowns of the mid–19th century American Midwest. When not condemned for their failures, his wartime vessels, like his political endeavors, are largely forgotten. Prior to my recent biographical compilation, *Civil War Biographies from the Western Waters*, Brown had not received an article-length profile in any encyclopedia or regional history since the 1890s.

In 1896 the one-time student of Elijah P. Lovejoy went home to Alton, IL, and delivered a lecture in support of a subscription monument to his mentor. As his presentation closed, Brown confided his hope to his audience for himself that those who heard of him in the future "will condone my faults and remember me for the good I have done." We hope that this biography will honor his work and memory, and rescue him from obscurity.[19]

Chapter Notes

Introduction

1. *Boston Daily Herald*, March 12, 1862.
2. U.S. Congress, House, *Contracts Made with Bureaus Connected with the Navy Department: Letter from the Secretary of the Navy, July 14, 1862* (House Document; 37th Congress, 2nd sess.; Washington, D.C.: GPO, 1862), 6.
3. Roy P. Basler, ed., *The Collected Works of Abraham Lincoln*, 10 vols. (Springfield, IL: The Abraham Lincoln Association, 1958), vol. 5: 174. Not even a photo of George T. Brown exists, but herein we attempt to convey, however briefly, some sense of his life as well.
4. U.S. Navy Department, *Official Records of the Union and Confederate Navies in the War of the Rebellion*, 31 vols. (Washington, D.C.: GPO, 1894–1922), Series I, Vol. 25, 760.
5. Please see Chapter 3, "The Coming of the Tinclad," in Myron Smith, *Tinclads in the Civil War: Union Light-Draught Gunboat Operations on Western Waters, 1862–1865* (Jefferson, NC: McFarland, 2010), 35–61.
6. Myron J. Smith, *The Fight for the Yazoo, August 1862–July 1864: Swamps, Forts and Fleets on Vicksburg's Northern* Flank (Jefferson, NC: McFarland, 2012).
7. Myron J. Smith, *The CSS* Arkansas: *A Confederate Ironclad on West* Waters (Jefferson, NC: McFarland, 2011).
8. Joseph Brown, *Lecture on Early Reminiscences of Alton* (Alton, IL: Lovejoy Monument Association, 1896), 14.

Chapter 1

1. L.U. Reavis, "Hon Joseph Brown," in *St. Louis: The Commercial Metropolis of the Mississippi Valley* (St Louis: Tribune Publishing, 1874), 228; "Joseph Brown," in Myron J. Smith, Jr., *Civil War Biographies from the Western Waters* (Jefferson, NC: McFarland, 2015), 34–35. Tombstones in the Brown family plot at Alton City Cemetery provide death dates for Thomas, Sr (1771–November 23, 1838); Margaret (1778–March 28, 1866); Thomas, Jr (1866); Joseph the younger and Flora M (July 15, 1855); Leo (January 1, 1880); George T (1880); and Joseph the elder, subject of this book (December 3, 1899); *Portrait and Biographical Album of Pike and Calhoun Counties, Illinois* (Chicago: Biographical, 1891), 501–503. Joseph Brown later gained a reputation as a politician, raconteur and writer but seldom mentioned any of his family members, even his brother George T., born on January 26, 1820, who was, for a while at least, more prominent, although no photo or drawing of this older sibling exists. Julie M. Fenster, *The Case of Abraham Lincoln* (New York: Palgrave-Macmillan, 2007), 35; *Alton Daily Telegraph*, June 9, 1880.
2. E.B. Seitz, "A City With Abiding Faith," *Mississippi Valley Magazine* 3 (June 1919), 10; John Eligon, "Strolling Old Halls and Streets with Ghosts of Civil War," *New York Times* (May 13, 2010); Robert M. Sutton, "Illinois' Year of Decision, 1837," *Journal of the Illinois State Historical Society Journal* 58 (Spring 1965), 44; James T. Hair, *Gazetteer of Madison County* (Alton, IL: Priv. print, 1866), 83–84. Jill Moon, *Godfrey* (Charleston, SC: Arcadia, 2013), 7–8; Judy Hoffman, "'If I Fall, My Grave Shall Be Made in Alton': Elijah Lovejoy, Martyr for Abolition," *Gateway Magazine* 25 (Summer 2005), 1.
3. Following the Lovejoy tragedy, Gilman moved to New York and established an important banking concern (*New York Times*, October 5, 1884). Godfrey, who built Alton's first church, also founded Monticello Female Seminary in 1838, the first woman's school west of the Allegheny Mountains (Moon, *Godfrey*, 8). Krum removed to St. Louis in 1840 and served as that city's 13th mayor in 1848–1849. "John Marshall Krum," *St. Louis Mayors*, http://exhibits.slpl.lib.mo.us/mayors/data/dt43400748.asp (June 10, 2014); Horace White, *The Life of Lyman Trumbull* (Boston and New York: Houghton Mifflin, 1913).
4. Douglas K. Meyer, *Making the Heartland Quilt: A Geographical History of Settlement and Migra-

tion in Early 19th Century Illinois (Carbondale: Southern Illinois University Press, 2000), 88–89; *Portrait and Biographical Album of Pike and Calhoun Counties, Illinois* (Chicago: Biographical, 1891), pp 501–503; Joseph Brown, *Lecture on Early Reminiscences of Alton* (Alton, IL: Lovejoy Monument Association, 1896), 6; September 18, 1835; Sutton, "Illinois' Year of Decision, 1837," 44–45, 48; Hoffman, "'If I Fall,'" 1–2; "Early Days in Alton," *Alton Telegraph*, July 17, 1883.

    5. Brown, *Lecture*, 5–8; Sutton, "Illinois' Year of Decision, 1837," 45–50; Claude Moore Fuess, *Daniel Webster*, 2 vols. (Boston: Little, Brown, 1930), vol. 2: 18, 233; Coleman McCampbell, "H.L. Kinney and Daniel Webster in Illinois in the 1830s," *Journal of the Illinois Historical Society* 47 (Spring 1954), 37–38, 41; *Rochester (NY) Democrat Chronicle*, March 22, 1890; *Alton Daily Telegraph*, August 23, September 27, 1837, December 4, 1899; *Daily National Intelligencer*, June 28, 1837; *Pennsylvania Inquirer and Daily Courier*, July 07, 1837; Edward Beecher, *Narrative of Riots at Alton* (Alton, IL: George Holton, 1838), 86–91; Thomas Dimmock, "Lovejoy: Hero and Martyr," *New England Magazine* 4 (March–August 1891), 373; W.T. Norton, ed., *Centennial History of Madison County, Illinois, and Its People* 2 vols. (Chicago: Lewis, 1912), vol. I: 61–64, 475.

    6. Brown, *Lecture*, 7–8; Howard Louis Conard, "John M. Krum," in *Encyclopedia of the History of Missouri*, 5 vols. (New York; Louisville; St. Louis: Southern History, 1901), vol. I: 561; Dimmock, "Lovejoy: Hero and Martyr," 373–374; *Hayner Public Library District Quarterly Newsletter* 21 (Summer 2012), 1; Sutton, "Illinois' Year of Decision, 1837," 49–51; Paul Simon, *Freedom's Champion: Elijah Lovejoy* (Carbondale: Southern Illinois University Press, 1994), 127–135; Merton L. Dillon, *Elijah P. Lovejoy, Abolitionist Editor* (Urbana: University of Illinois Press, 1961), 122–123, 157–159, 161–169; Louis S. Gerteis, *Civil War St. Louis* (Lawrence: University Press of Kansas, 2001), 16; *Alton Observer*, November 7, 1837; *Alton Daily Telegraph*, November 8, 1837; *Daily Commercial Bulletin and Missouri Literary Register*, November 9–10, 1837; Hoffman, "'If I Fall,'" 10–19; Norton, ed., *Centennial History of Madison County*, i, 65–74, 473; Wounded in the leg and suffering with a limp for the rest of his life, Weller later visited Lovejoy's widow, Celia Ann, in Cincinnati and eventually became her husband (Simon, *Freedom's Champion*, 142). In January 1838 members of both the Gilman warehouse defense and the attacking mob were tried in separate trials and both parties were acquitted. Dimmock, "Lovejoy: Hero and Martyr," 374; Harold Holzer, *Lincoln and the Power of the Press* (New York: Simon and Schuster, 2014), 35–36.

    7. Hoffman, "'If I Fall,'" 19–20; Brown, *Lecture*, 8–9; J. Thomas Scharf, *History of St. Louis City and County*, 2 vols. (Philadelphia: Louis H. Everts, 1883), vol. I: 707–708; "Early Days in Alton," *Alton Telegraph*, July 17, 1883; Bruce Harrison, *The Family Forrest Descendants of Lady Joan Beaufort of Beaufort Castle in England*, 2nd ed (Kamuela, HI: Millisecond, 2011), 4543. Businessman Lamb would be swept into office as town treasurer when Joseph Brown won election as mayor in 1856 and would retain that post until 1860 (Hair, *Gazetteer of Madison County*, 89); James Henry Lea, *A Genealogy of the Ancestors and Descendants of George Augustus and Louisa (Clap) Trumbull* (Worcester, MA: Priv. print., 1886), 32–33; *Semi-Centennial and General Catalogue of the Officers and Students of Shurtleff College* (Upper Alton, IL: Daily Telegraph Steam Print, 1877), 19; *Alton Weekly Courier*, March 13, 1856.

    8. James E. Myers, *The Astonishing Saber Duel of Abraham Lincoln* (Springfield, IL: Lincoln-Herndon Building, 1968), 5–18; David Herbert Donald, *Lincoln* (New York: Simon and Schuster, 1995), 90–93; George W. Smith, *When Lincoln Came to Egypt* (Herrin, IL: Trovillion Private Press, 1940), 100; Brown, *Lecture*, 9–10; *New York Times*, December 3, 1876.

    9. Hair, *Gazetteer of Madison County*, 88–89; U.S. Congress, Senate, Senate Historical Office, "George T. Brown, Sergeant-at-Arms, 1861–1869," *U.S. Senate Homepage*, http://www.senate.gov/artandhistory/history/common/generic/SAA_George_Brown.htm (accessed March 18, 2014); Julie M. Fenster, *Abraham Lincoln: A Story of Adultery, Murder, and the Making of a Great President* (New York: Palgrave Macmillan, 2007), 35, 111, 116–123, 188; Norton, ed., *Centennial History of Madison County*, i, 107, 113–114.

    10. W.R. Brink, *History of Madison County, Illinois* (Edwardsville, IL: W.R. Brink, 1882), 391–392; Joseph Brown, "River Navigation, Steamboat," in William Hyde and Howard I. Conrad, *Encyclopedia of the History of St. Louis*, 5 vols. (New York: Southern History, 1899), vol. 4: 1923; Norton, ed., *Centennial History of Madison County*, i, 92; Brown, *Lecture*, 11–12; "William Shaw Nelson," in Walter Barlow Stevens, *St. Louis: The Fourth City, 1764–1911*, 3 vols. (St. Louis: S.J. Clarke, 1939), vol. 2: 272; Connie Nisiger, "Capt. William P. LaMothe," Find A Grave, http://www.findagrave.com/cgi-bin/fg.cgi?page=gr&GRid=9682637 (accessed June 10, 2014); *Peoria Democratic Union*, June 3, 1858; Roger Matile, "John Frink and Martin Walker: Stagecoach Kings of the Old Northwest," *Journal of the Illinois State Historical Society Journal* 95 (Summer 2002), 124; James Green, *Green's St. Louis Directory* (St Louis: A. Fisher, 1844), 166; Frederick Way, Jr., *Way's Packet Directory, 1848–1994: Passenger Steamboats of the Mississippi River System Since the Advent of Photography in Mid-Continent America*, rev. ed (Athens: Ohio University Press, 1983; Ohio University Press, 1994), 298; Joseph Brown, "Autobiography Statement," in Emerson W. Gould, *50 Years on the Mississippi* (St Louis: Nixon-James, 1889), 674; John M. Palmer, The *Bench and Bar in Illinois*, 2 vols. (Chicago: Lewis, 1899), vol. 2: 719; *Alton Weekly Courier*, April 8, 1853, March 13, 1856; John S. Tomer and Michael J. Brodhead, *A Naturalist in Indian Territory: The Journals of S.W. Woodhouse, 1849–1850* (Norman: University of Oklahoma Press, 1992), 188.

11. *Memphis Daily Appeal*, January 15, 1851; Way, *Way's Packet Directory*, 17; Brown, "Autobiography Statement," in Gould, *50 Years on the Mississippi*, 674. Following his Cincinnati shipbuilding apprenticeship, Maine native Emerson operated, from 1836 to 1841, an important Madison, IN, boatyard on the Ohio River in partnership with James Howard, who gave it his name upon the partner's departure. Over the next decade and a half, Emerson built and repaired boats at a number of Midwestern cities, and with several colleagues was pivotal in the mid-1850s' establishment of the Carondelet Marine Railway and Drydock Company, sometimes known as "Emerson's Ways." When the yard was completed in 1859, it featured Emerson's patented marine railway, which using a 50-horsepower steam engine could pull the largest craft out of the water. Following his work for the Confederacy (1861–1863), he returned home and won a Federal pardon. Emerson was able to resume steamboat work at his Carondelet facilities after the war. In May 1866 part of the uninsured boatyards were destroyed by fire. Emerson estimated the loss at $60,000. Unable to reopen, he became a contract ships carpenter and steamboat constructor (Mary Emerson Branch, "Prime Emerson and Steamboat Building in Memphis," *West Tennessee Historical Society Papers* 38 (1984), 69–71; Branch, "A Story Behind the Story of the *Arkansas* and the *Carondelet*," *Missouri Historical Review* 79 (April 1985), 313–331; "Primus Emerson" in Smith, *Civil War Biographies from the Western Waters*, 71). A native of Kentucky and self-made foundry expert, Gaty (1811–1887) grew his firm by the 1830s to include the construction of nearly every sort of machine part, as well as steamboat, flourmill, and sawmill engines and furnace irons for lead smelters. He was later known as the father of St. Louis's foundry and machine industry (Charles Van Ravenswaay, *St. Louis: An Informal History of the City and Its People, 1764–1865* (St Louis: Missouri Historical Society Press, 1991), 225–226; "Samuel Gaty," FindaGrave http://www.findagrave.com/cgi-bin/fg.cgi?page=gr&GRid=18465 (accessed August 12, 2014)). A native of Pennsylvania early removed to Kentucky, John S. McCune (1809–1874) became a Louisiana miller who in 1841 moved to St. Louis to become a partner of long association in the foundry business of Samuel Gaty. In 1843, believing that a lucrative trade could be established between St. Louis and the intervening river towns to Keokuk, he conceived and organized the Keokuk Packet Company, later the St. Louis and Keokuk Packet Company and later the Northern Line Packet Company. After 1857 he was also president of an iron company (John Edwards, *Edwards's Great West and Her Commercial Metropolis, Embracing a General View of the West, and a Complete History of St. Louis, from the Landing of Ligueste, in 1764, to the Present Time; with Portraits and Biographies of Some of the Old Settlers, and Many of the Most Prominent Buisiness Men* (St Louis: Office of Edwards's Monthly, 1860), 552–555; Connie Nisinger, "John S. McCune," *Find A Grave*, http://www.findagrave.com/cgi-bin/fg.cgi?page=gr&GRid=9349265 [accessed August 12, 2014]).

12. *Memphis Daily Appeal*, January 15, May 29, 1851, March 13, 1852; Branch, "Prime Emerson," 72–73; Way, *Way's Packet Directory*, 17; Brown, "River Navigation, Steamboat," i, 1924; *St. Louis Daily Missouri Republican*, August 28, December 11, 1851; *St. Louis Post-Dispatch*, December 4, 1899; Amy Lehman, *Victorian Women and the Theatre of Trance: Mediums, Spiritualists and Mesmerists in Performance* (Jefferson, NC: McFarland, 2009), 87; Gould, *50 Years on the Mississippi*, 674; Brown, "River Navigation, Steamboat," 1922, 1924; Hair, *Gazetteer of Madison County*, 91; Judy Clark-Wick, "Virginia C. Keach Brown," *Find A Grave*, http://www.findagrave.com/cgi-bin/fg.cgi?page=gr&GRid=52929253 (accessed August 25, 2014); "Hiram Keach," in *History of Greene and Jersey Counties, Illinois* (Springfield, IL: Continental Historical Company, 1885), 841; "John R. Keach," in *History of Greene and Jersey Counties, Illinois* (Springfield, IL: Continental Historical Company, 1885), 841–842; *Alton Daily Telegraph*, May 20 and May 25, 1852; *Alton Telegraph*, July 1, 1918; *St. Louis Globe-Democrat*, November 8, 1881; D.W. Yungmeyer, "An Excursion into the Early History of the Chicago and Alton Railroad," *Journal of the Illinois State Historical Society* 38 (March 1945), 23. Capt. Keach commanded the steamer *Emma* during the 1863 Yazoo Pass expedition and was recompensed by the U.S. government for damages sustained (Myron J. Smith, Jr., *The Fight for the Yazoo, August 1862–July 1864* (Jefferson, NC: McFarland, 2012), 180–191). Interestingly, George T. Brown began publishing the *Alton Daily Morning Courier* on May 29, just 10 days after the *Altona*'s historic run (U.S. Library of Congress, "About *Alton Daily Morning Courier* (Alton, Ill.), 1852–1855," *U.S. Newspaper Directory, 1690-Present*, http://chroniclingamerica.loc.gov/lccn/sn84038318/ (accessed June 14, 2014)). The *Altona* sank twice, being once restored, before her final loss on February 26, 1856. Brown would not be alone among prominent people in accepting spiritualism. Calling it an "ancient philosophy," his fellow riverboat colleague Capt. E.W. Gould wrote about it in an article for the *St. Louis Post-Dispatch* on June 9, 1895.

13. Brown, "River Navigation, Steamboat," 1923; Way, *Way's Packet Directory*, 412; Joseph Brown, *Lecture on Early Reminiscences of Alton*, 13; Scharf, *History of St. Louis City and County*, ii, 1111; "The Plague in the South-West: The Great Yellow Fever Epidemic in 1853," *DeBow's Review* 15 (December 1853), 595–635; John Duffy, *Sword of Pestilence: The New Orleans Yellow Fever Epidemic of 1853* (Baton Rouge: Louisiana State University Press, 1966). The stigma of her original accident together with her poor steaming time made the *St. Louis* an unprofitable boat and she was sold out of service at Memphis in 1856, where she was dismantled and turned into a wharf boat (Way, *Way's Packet Directory*, 412).

14. Brown, "River Navigation, Steamboat," 1923; Hair, *Gazetteer of Madison County*, 88–89; *Alton*

Daily Telegraph, June 9, 1880; U.S. Congress, Senate, Senate Historical Office, "George T. Brown, Sergeant-at-Arms, 1861–1869," U.S. Senate, http://www.senate.gov/artandhistory/history/common/generic/SAA_George_Brown.htm (accessed March 18, 2014); Julie M. Fenster, *Abraham Lincoln: A Story of Adultery, Murder, and the Making of a Great President* (New York: Palgrave Macmillan, 2007), 35, 111, 116–123, 188; Norton, ed., *Centennial History of Madison County*, i, 107, 113–114; Fenster, *The Case of Abraham Lincoln*, 35; Mildred C. Stoler, "Insurgent Democrats of Indiana and Illinois in 1854," *Indiana Magazine of History* 33 (Spring 1937), 1–31; Stoler, "The Democratic Element in the New Republican Party in Illinois, 1856–1860," *Papers in Illinois History and Transactions for the Year 1942* (Springfield: Illinois Historical Society, 1944), 32–70; Ralph J. Roske, *His Own Counsel: The Life and Times of Lyman Trumbull* (Reno: University of Nevada Press, 1979), 56; Mark A. Krug, *Lyman Trumbull: Conservative Radical* (New York: A.S. Barnes, 1965), 170–171; *New York Times*, July 6, 1872; Holzer, *Lincoln and the Power of the Press*, xix; Mark E. Neely, Jr., *The Extra Journal: Rallying the Whigs of Illinois* (Fort Wayne, IN: Louis A. Warren Lincoln Library and Museum, 1982), 3.

15. *Book of Biographies, Containing Biographical Sketches of Leading Citizens of Beaver County, Pennsylvania* (Buffalo, NY: Biographical, 1899), 408; Joseph Brown, "Steamboating in the Old Days on the Mississippi," *American Jewess* 2 (April 1896), 361. On November 17, 1855, Phillips fell off the steamer *Jacob Poe* at Wheeling, VA, and drowned; his body was not recovered.

16. John Stogdell Van Voorhis, *The Old and New Monongahela* (Pittsburgh: Nicholson, Printer, 1893), 179–180; Patricia Lowry, "Who Built the Big Boat?," *Pittsburgh Post-Gazette*, August 3, 2003; Brown, "Steamboating in the Old Days on the Mississippi," 364; Thomas Cushing, *History of Allegeheny County, Pennsylania* (Chicago: A. Warner, 1889), 105 ; *Elizabeth Herald*, June 7, 1900; Way, *Way's Packet Directory*, 317; James V. Swift, "Mayor of Two Cities Also Owned Steamboats," *Waterways Journal* (December 17, 1983), 40; Brown, "River Navigation, Steamboat," 1925; "William Shaw Nelson," in Stevens, *St. Louis: The Fourth City, 1764–1911*, ii, 272; Horatio M. Jones, "*Gaty, et al., Plantiffs in Error, v. Phoenix Insurance Company, Defendant in Error*: March Term, 1860," in vol. 30 of *Reports of Cases Argued and Determined in the Supreme Court of the State of Missouri* (St. Louis: George Knapp, 1861), 56–57.

17. Brown, "Autobiography Statement," in Gould, *50 Years on the Mississippi*, 675; *Memphis Daily Appeal*, September 21, 1855; *Cincinnati Daily Enquirer*, September 21, 1855"; *Gaty, et al, Plantiffs in Error, v. Phoenix Insurance Company*," 58–59; James T. Lloyd, *Lloyd's Steamboat Directory and Disasters on the Western Waters* (Cincinnati: James T. Lloyd, 1856), 321; Swift, "Mayor of Two Cities Also Owned Steamboats," 40; Way, *Way's Packet Directory*, 317; Brown, "Steamboating in the Old Days on the Mississippi," 364; "William Shaw Nelson," in Stevens, *St. Louis: The Fourth City, 1764–1911*, ii, 272; *Memphis Daily Appeal*, December 3, 1855; Brown, *Lecture*, 11. Brown and contemporary authors have given various cost figures for the *Mayflower* ranging downward from $286,000 to $100,000.

18. "James Buchanan Eads," in James Grant Wilson and John Fisk, ed., *Appleton's Cyclopedia of American Biography*, 5 vols. (New York: D. Appleton, 1888), vol. 2: 287; "James Buchanan Eads," *University of Illinois at Urbana-Champagne Riverweb*, http://www.riverweb.uiuc.edu/TECH/TECH20.htm (September 18, 2006); "James Buchanan Eads," in Smith, *Civil War Biographies from the Western Waters*, 67; John D. Milligan, *Gunboats Down the Mississippi* (Annapolis: Naval Institute Press, 1965), 3; Richard Webber and John C. Roberts, "James B. Eads: Master Builder," *The Navy* 8 (March 1965), 23–25; Elmer L. Gaden, "Eads and the Navy of the Mississippi," *American Heritage of Invention and Technology* 9 (Spring 1994), 24–31; "William Shaw Nelson," in Stevens, *St. Louis: The Fourth City, 1764–1911*, ii, 272.

19. Yungmeyer, "An Excursion into the Early History of the Chicago and Alton Railroad," 18, 23; John S. McCune, "St. Louis and Keokuk Packet Company," in Jacob N. Taylor and M.O. Crooks, *Sketch Book of St. Louis* (St. Louis: George Knapp, 1858), 192–195; "John Mitchell of Lancaster County, PA," Ancestry Hints, http://wc.rootsweb.ancestry.com/cgi-bin/igm.cgi?op=GET&db=johnmitchell&id=I0459 (accessed August 10, 2014); Hair, *Gazetteer of Madison County*, 86, 88–89, 92; *Alton Weekly Courier*, April 3–8, 1853; *St. Louis Post-Dispatch*, December 4, 1899; Norton, ed., *Centennial History of Madison County, Illinois and Its People*, 104, 471–472; *Alton Telegraph*, December 4, 1899; L.U. Reavis et al., *St. Louis: The Future City of the World* (St Louis: Gray, Baker, 1875), 649; *Alton Weekly Courier*, September 25–October 9, 1856; *Quincy Daily Whig*, October 4, 1856; *Chicago Daily Journal*, October 4, 1856; *St. Louis Daily Intelligencer*, October 1, 1856; *Daily Cleveland Herald*, October 2, 1856; *Chicago Daily Tribune*, February 15, 1882; "William Shaw Nelson" in Stevens, *St. Louis: The Fourth City, 1764–1911*, ii, 272; George Leighty, "When the State Fair Was Held in Alton in 1856," *Alton Evening Telegraph* (Centennial Edition), January 15, 1936; Viola W. Voss, *Footprints and Echoes from Historical Alton Area* (Alton, IL, 1973), 67; Brown, *Lecture*, 10; Stacy Pratt McDermott, "*Mcready v. City of Alton, Illinois*," *Lincoln Legal Briefs: A Quarterly Newsletter of The Lincoln Legal Papers* 75 (July-September 2005), 3.

20. John Stephen Wright, *Chicago: Past, Present, Future* (Chicago: Horton and Leonard, Printers, 1870), 360; Yungmeyer, "An Excursion into the Early History of the Chicago and Alton Railroad," 23; W.T. Norton, "An Old Time Tragedy at the State Penitentiary at Alton," *Journal of the Illinois State Historical Society* 6 (July 1913), 242–245; Way, *Way's Packet Directory*, 93; McDermott, "*Mcready v. City of Alton,*

Illinois," 3–5; Brown, *Lecture,* 10–11; Nathaniel B. Curran, "Levi Davis, Illinois' Third Auditor," *Journal of the Illinois State Historical Society* 71 (February 1978), 2–12. Carl Sandburg repeated Brown's account in his Lincoln biography, as did Ida Tarbell in hers. Carl Sandburg, *Abraham Lincoln: The Prairie Years* (New York: Harcourt, Brace, 1926), 70; Ida M. Tarbell, *Abraham Lincoln and His Ancestors* (New York: Harper, 1924; rpr. New York: Bison Books, 1997), 299–300; *St. Louis Post-Dispatch,* February 1, 1891. At the time in 1863 when she was converted into the hospital boat *R.C. Wood,* the U.S. Army later noted that the *City of Louisiana* had a seven-foot hold (U.S. Surgeon General's Office, *The Medical and Surgical History of the War of the Rebellion,* 6 vols. (Washington, D.C.: GPO, 1870–1888), vol. 3, part 2, 976.

21. George W. Carpenter, *History of Calhoun County, Illinois* (Jerseyville, IL: Democrat Printing, 1934), 42; Swift, "Mayor of Two Cities Also Owned Steamboats," 40; *Atchison Daily Globe,* December 30, 1893; Allen C. Guelzo, *Lincoln and Douglas: The Debates That Defined America* (New York: Simon and Schuster, 2008), 254–270; Norton, ed., *Centennial History of Madison County,* i, 234–235; Richard Allen Heckman, *Lincoln vs. Douglas: The Great Debates Campaign* (Washington, D.C.: Public Affairs Press, 1967), 125–126; *Alton Weekly Courier,* October 16, 1858; *St. Louis* Daily *Missouri Republican,* October 15, 1858; Charles Dean Harris, "Samuel Pitts, Jr.," Find A Grave, http://www.findagrave.com/cgi-bin/fg.cgi?page=gr&GRid=29618528 (accessed September 30, 2014); Samuel Pitts, Jr., "Samuel Pitts Recalls Lincoln and Douglas Debate, Alton, " *Alton Evening Telegraph,* January 30, 1911; Walter Barlow Stevens, *The Reporter's Lincoln,* ed. Michael Burlingame (Lincoln: University of Nebraska Press, 1998), 57; Brown, *Lecture,* 9.

22. *St. Louis Daily Missouri Republican,* March 13, 1859; Branch, "Prime Emerson," 73; Way, *Way's Packet Directory,* 243; Brown, "Autobiography Statement," in Gould, *50 Years on the Mississippi,* 675–676; The *Jeannie Deans* was also known as the *Jeanie Deans* (named for the heroine of Sir Walter Scott's novel, *The Heart of Midlothian*). She burned at Carondelet on May 12, 1866, in the same fire that destroyed Emerson's docks (Way, *Way's Packet Directory,* 243).

23. *The Encyclopedia of American History,* rev. ed (New York: Harper, 1961), 228–229, with additional details from Kenneth M. Stamp, *And the War Came: The North and the Secession Crisis, 1860–1861* (Baton Rouge: Louisiana State University Press, 1970), 63, 110, 123, 128–140, 215, 217; Stephen D. Engle, *Struggle for the Heartland: The Campaigns from Fort Henry to Corinth* (Lincoln: University of Nebraska Press, 2001), 2; Henry Clyde Hubbart, *The Older Middle West, 1840–1880: Its Social, Economic and Political Life, and Sectional Tendencies Before, During, and After the Civil War* (New York: Russell and Russell, 1936), 74–89, 155–157; E. Merton Coulter, "Effects of Secession Upon the Commerce of the Mississippi Valley," *Mississippi Valley Historical Review* 3 (December 1915), 276–278; David Herbert Donald, *Lincoln* (New York: Simon and Schuster, 1995), 284; Myron J. Smith, Jr., *The Timberclads in the Civil War* (Jefferson, NC: McFarland, 2008), 27–28; *Cincinnati Daily Gazette,* December 11, 24, 1860; *Cincinnati Enquirer,* January 4, 10, 12, 22 and March 8, 1861; "Thomas P. Leathers," in Smith, *Civil War Biographies from the Western Waters,* 138; Brown, "Steamboating in the Old Days on the Mississippi," 362–363.

24. *Cincinnati Enquirer,* January 15, 22, 23 and March 3, 1861; *Cincinnati Daily Commercial,* January 25, 28, 1861; *Evansville Daily Journal,* January 14, 1861; *New Albany Ledger,* January 17, 1861; *Chicago Tribune,* January 22, 1861; *Memphis Evening Argus,* January 17, 1861; S. Chamberlain, "Opening of the Upper Mississippi and the Siege of Vicksburg," *Magazine of Western History* 4 (March 1887), 610; Charles Henry Ambler, *A History of Transportation in the Ohio Valley* (Glendale, CA: Arthur H. Clark, 1932), 242; "First Shots of the War Between the States," *Vicksburg Sunday Post,* January 7, 1996; Gary Matthews, "First Shots of the ACW?," Civil War Navy Messageboard, http://history-sites.com/mb/cw/cwnavy/index.cgi?noframes;read=1005 (August 4, 2006); "John Jones Pettus" and "John Rodgers II," in Smith, *Civil War Biographies from the Western Waters,* 186, 204–205; Henry Lowe, "Reminiscences of Cincinnati in War Time," in *Historical Collections of Ohio,* 3 vols. (Cincinnati: C.J. Krikbiel, 1888), vol. I: 765.

25. Brown, "Steamboating in the Old Days on the Mississippi," 362–363; Brown, "River Navigation, Steamboat," i, 1925; *St. Louis Post-Dispatch,* February 1, 1891; *St. Louis Daily Missouri Democrat,* June 5, 1861; "Joseph Gilbert Totten," in Smith, *Civil War Biographies from the Western Waters,* 239; Louis C. Hunter, *Steamboats on the Western Rivers: An Economic and Technological History* (Cambridge, MA: Harvard University Press, 1949), 548. After Brown left the *City of Louisiana,* she was chartered to the USQM in 1862 for use as a hospital boat (Way, *Way's Packet Directory,* 93). Brown's flag remained aloft throughout the Civil War, hanging at half-mast in April 1865 to mark the passing of President Lincoln. When Brown moved permanently to St. Louis, he gave the flag to his nephew, George Child of Hardin, IL, who it flew at half-mast over his house when Presidents Garfield (1881) and McKinley (1901) were assassinated. During World War I, it hung outside the offices of the *Calhoun News* of Hardin (*Alton Telegraph,* July 1, 1918).

26. Hair, *Gazetteer of Madison County,* 118; "George T. Brown, Sergeant-at-Arms, 1861–1869," U.S. Senate, http://www.senate.gov/artandhistory/history/common/generic/SAA_George_Brown.htm (accessed March 18, 2014); James M. McPherson, *Tried by War: Abraham Lincoln as Commander in Chief* (New York: Penguin, 2008), 23; *New York Times,* July 6, 1872.

Chapter 2

1. Richard Webber and John C. Roberts, "James B. Eads: Master Builder," *The Navy* 8 (March 1965), 23–25; C.B. Boynton, *History of the Navy During the Rebellion*, 2 vols. (New York: D. Appleton, 1867), vol. I: 498; James B. Eads, "Recollections of Foote and the Gunboats," in *Battles and Leaders of the Civil War*, ed. Robert V. Johnson and Clarence C. Buel, 4 vols. (New York: Century, 1884–1887, reprnt. Thomas Yoseloff, 1956), vol. I: 338 (cited hereafter as B&L, followed by a comma, the volume number in Roman numerals, a comma, and the page numbers); "Edward Bates," in Myron J. Smith, Jr., *Civil War Biographies from the Western Waters* (Jefferson, NC: McFarland, 2015), 18; U.S. Navy Department, Naval History Division, *Riverine Warfare* (Washington, D.C.: GPO, 1968), 21; U.S. Navy Department, *Official Records of the Union and Confederate Navies in the War of the Rebellion*, 31 vols. (Washington, D.C.: GPO, 1894–1922), Series I, Vol. 22, 278, 280 (cited hereafter as ORN, followed by a comma, the series number in Roman numerals, a comma, the volume number in Arabic, a colon, and the page in Arabic, e.g., ORN, I, 25: 155). The West and Western Rivers in Civil War literature refers generally to the Western theatre of operations. See Bruce Catton, "Glory Road Began in the West," *Civil War History* 6 (June 1960), 229–237. The location of Brown's residence, which he maintained throughout the Civil War, is confirmed in Richard Edwards, *Edwards' Annual Directory ... the City of St. Louis* (6th ed.; St. Louis: Southern, 1864), 160.

2. Bern Anderson, "The Naval Strategy of the Civil War," *Military Affairs* 26 (Spring 1962), 15; Anderson, *By Sea and By River: The Naval History of the Civil War* (New York: Knopf, 1962), 33–34; John D. Milligan, *Gunboats Down the Mississippi* (Annapolis: Naval Institute Press, 1965), 3–4; "Winfield Scott," in Smith, *Civil War Biographies from the Western Waters*, 212–213; Gideon Welles, *The Diary of Gideon Welles, Secretary of the Navy Under Lincoln and Johnson*, edited by John T. Morse, Jr., 3 vols. (Boston: Houghton, Mifflin, 1911), vol. I: 242; *St. Louis Daily Democrat*, May 10, 1861.

3. Welles to Rodgers, May 16, 1861, ORN, I, 22: 280; Milligan, *Gunboats Down the Mississippi*, 3–4; "George Brinton McClellan" and "Samuel M. Pook" in Smith, *Civil War Biographies from the Western Waters*, 154–155, 191; Robert E. Johnson, *Rear Admiral John Rodgers, 1812–1882* (Annapolis: Naval Institute Press, 1967), 156–157; Jay Slagle, *Ironclad Captain: Seth Ledyard Phelps and the U.S. Navy* (Kent, OH: Kent State University Press, 1996), 33, 115–150; Henry Walke, *Naval Scenes and Reminiscences of the Civil War in the United States on the Southern and Western Waters During the Years 1861, 1862 and 1863 with the History of That Period Compared and Corrected from Authentic Sources* (New York: F.R. Reed, 1877), 17–50. Both Phelps and Walke have left detailed accounts of "timberclad" operations in the fall and winter of 1861–1862.

4. Hair, *Gazetteer of Madison County*, 118; "John Lenthal" " in Smith, *Civil War Biographies from the Western Waters*, 140–141; "George T. Brown, Sergeant-at-Arms, 1861–1869," U.S. Senate Homepage, http://www.senate.gov/artandhistory/history/common/generic/SAA_George_Brown.htm (accessed March 18, 2014); James M. McPherson, *Tried by War: Abraham Lincoln as Commander in Chief* (New York: Penguin, 2008), 23; *New York Times*, July 6, 1872.

5. ORN, I, 22: 295; David W. Miller, *Second Only to Grant: Quartermaster General Montgomery C. Meigs* (Shippensburg, PA: White Mane, 2000), 124–125; Boynton, *History of the Navy During the Rebellion*, i, 503; *St. Louis Daily Missouri Democrat*, July 29, August 1, 1861; "Francis P. Blair, Jr.," and "Montgomery C. Meigs," in Smith, *Civil War Biographies from the Western Waters*, 23, 162; Francis P. Blair, Jr., James S. Rollins, and John W. Noell to Meigs, July 15, 1861, QMG Records; Montgomery Blair to Meigs, July 31, 1861, QMG Records; Johnson, Rear Admiral John Rodgers, 1812–1882, 165; William E. Smith, *The Francis Preston Blair Family in Politics*, 2 vols. (New York: Macmillan, 1933), vol. 2: 52; "Abstract of Bids, August 6, 1861," QMG Records; Temple to Lane, August 14, 1861, QMG Records; Edwin C. Bearss, *Hardluck Ironclad: The Sinking and Salvage of the* Cairo (Baton Rouge: Louisiana State University, 1966), 19–20; Phyllis F. Dorsett, "James B. Eads: Navy Shipbuilder, 1861," *U.S. Naval Institute Proceedings* 101 (August 1975), 77.

6. Mary Emerson Branch, "A Story Behind the Story of the *Arkansas* and the *Carondelet*," *Missouri Historical Review* 79 (April 1985), 314; *St. Louis Daily Missouri Republican*, January 12, 1877; *Memphis Daily Avalanche*, September 10, 1873; Myron J. Smith, Jr., *The CSS* Arkansas: *A Confederate Ironclad on Western Waters* (Jefferson, NC: McFarland, 2011), 26–29; "John T. Shirley," in Smith, *Civil War Biographies from the Western Waters*, 218.

7. U.S. War Department, *The War of the Rebellion: A Compilation of the Official Records of the Union and Confederate Armies*, 128 vols. (Washington, D.C.: GPO, 1880–1901), Series I, Vol. IIII, 390 (cited hereafter as OR, followed by a comma, the series number in Roman numerals, a comma, the volume number in Arabic, a colon, and the page in Arabic, e.g., OR, I, 3: 390; ORN, I, 22: 297; John Niven, *Gideon Welles: Lincoln's Secretary of the Navy* (New York: Oxford University Press, 1973), 378; James M. Hoppin, *The Life of Andrew Hull Foote, Rear Admiral, United States Navy* (New York: Harper and Brothers, 1874), 152–153; Spencer C. Tucker, *Andrew Foote: Civil War Admiral on Western Waters* (Annapolis: Naval Institute Press, 2000), 114–115; "Andrew Hull Foote," " in Smith, *Civil War Biographies from the Western Waters*, 79–80; Roland L. Meyer, Jr., "Inland Shipyard Saga," *Marine Engineering and Shipping Review* 51

(February 1946), 127–129; James M. Merrill, "Union Shipbuilding on Western Waters During the Civil War," *Smithsonian Journal of History* 3 (Winter 1968–1969), 17–44; The building and outfitting of the City Series ironclads of the Western Flotilla is told not only by Eads in his B&L article, but also, most completely, by the National Park Service historian in charge of salvaging one of them in the 1960s, Edwin C. Bearss. See his *Hardluck Ironclad: The Sinking and Salvage of the* Cairo, 10–27. I made a review of another in *The USS* Carondelet: *A Civil War Ironclad on Western Waters* (Jefferson, NC: McFarland, 2010, 5–38), where I also noted subcontractors, 23.

    8. Alfred T. Mahan, *The Gulf and Inland Waters* (Vol. 3 of *The Navy in the Civil War* (New York: Scribner's, 1883, 19–21); Charles Dana Gibson, with E. Kay Gibson, *Assault and Logistics*, vol. 2: *Union Army Coastal and River Operations, 1861–1866* (Camden, ME: Ensign, 1995), 65–66; Tucker, *Andrew Foote: Civil War Admiral on Western Waters*, 129–130. Documents for the Belmont campaign are provided in ORN, I, 22:398–427 and OR, I, III: 267–310, while the whole is most recently reviewed by Nathaniel Cheairs Hughes in *The Battle of Belmont: Grant Strikes South* (Chapel Hill: University of North Carolina Press, 1991). The Kentucky political and military developments are covered in Lowell H. Harrison, *The Civil War in Kentucky* (Lexington: University Press of Kentucky, 1975), 14–32, and OR, I, 4: 179–181. The *St. Louis Daily Democrat*, January 24, 1862, reported on expected sailor life, but the cheerful reporter was wrong about the grog—there was no booze in any squadron commanded by Andrew H. Foote.

    9. Allan Nevins, *The War for the Union: War Becomes Revolution* (New York: Charles Scribner's Sons, 1960), 14–15; Stephen E. Ambrose, "The Union Command System and the Donelson Campaign," *Military Affairs* 24 (Summer 1960), 78–86; Benjamin F. Cooling, *Forts Henry and Donelson: The Key to the Confederate Heartland* (Knoxville: University of Tennessee Press, 1987), xiv; "Henry Halleck," in Smith, *Civil War Biographies from the Western Waters*, 103–104; Tucker, *Andrew Foote: Civil War Admiral on Western Waters*, 125–126. Rowena Reed reviews Yankee strategy for Tennessee in her *Combined Operations in the Civil War* (Annapolis: Naval Institute Press, 1978), 64–84.

    10. ORN, I, 22: 540–615; OR, I, 4: 620–639, 861–862; Gibson, *Assault and Logistics*, Vol. 2: *Union Army Coastal and River Operations, 1861–1866*, 67–73; Byrd Douglas, *Steamboatin' on the Cumberland* (Nashville: Tennessee Book, 1961), 118–121; *Cincinnati Daily Gazette*, February 18, 1862; Cooling, *Forts Henry and Donelson: The Key to the Confederate Heartland*, 57, 128–227; Tucker, *Andrew Foote: Civil War Admiral on Western Waters*, 146–162; Edwin C. Bearss, *The Fall of Fort Henry* (Dover, TN: Eastern National Park and Monument Association, 1989), 26; Bearss, *Unconditional Surrender: The Fall of Fort Donelson* (Dover, TN: Eastern National Park and Monument Association, 1991), 35–45; Mahan, *The Gulf and Inland Waters*, 26–28; David Dixon Porter, *Naval History of the Civil War* (New York: Sherman, 1886), 144–150; "Ulysses Simpson Grant," in Smith, *Civil War Biographies from the Western Waters*, 94–95.

    11. Anderson, *By Sea and By River*, 99; "Pierre G.T. Beauregard" and "Albert Sidney Johnston," in Smith, *Civil War Biographies from the Western Waters*, 20, 127–128; Byrd Douglas, *Steamboatin' on the Cumberland*, 124–125; Gibson, *Assault and Logistics*, Vol. 2: *Union Army Coastal and River Operations, 1861–1866*, 74–75; M.F. Force, *From Fort Henry to Corinth: Campaigns of the Civil War* (New York: Scribner's, 1882; reprnt. Broadfoot, 1989), 64–65; Stanley F. Horn, *The Army of Tennessee* (Indianapolis: Bobbs-Merrill, 1941), 99–105. Beauregard's Feb. 7 plans and resultant defensive line summary is cited in OR, I, 4:861–862, 911, 915.

Chapter 3

    1. *New York Times*, February 15, 1862; *New York Tribune*, February 21, 28, 1862; *Boston Herald*, March 12, 1862; *Chicago Daily Tribune*, March 28, 1862; Edward William Sloan III, *Benjamin Franklin Isherwood, Naval Engineer: The Years as Engineer-in-Chief, 1861–1869* (Annapolis: Naval Institute Press, 1965), 57; "Gustavus Vasa Fox," "Edward Hartt," "William David ('Dirty Bill') Porter," and "Edwin Stanton" in Myron J. Smith, Jr., *Civil War Biographies from the Western Waters* (Jefferson, NC: McFarland, 2015), 82–83, 107, 193–194, 225; David A. Mindell, *Iron Coffin: War, Technology, and Experience Aboard the USS* Monitor (Baltimore: Johns Hopkins University Press, 2012), 160; U.S. Navy Department, Official Records of the Union and Confederate Navies in the War of the Rebellion, 31 vols. (Washington, D.C.: GPO, 1894–1922), Series I, Vol. 22, 659, 688 (cited hereafter as ORN, followed by a comma, the series number in Roman numerals, a comma, the volume number in Arabic, a colon, and the page in Arabic, e.g., ORN, I, 22: 659, 688); ORN, I, 23: 83; U.S. Surgeon General's Office, *The Medical and Surgical History of the War of the Rebellion*, 6 vols. (Washington, D.C.: GPO, 1870–1888), Vol. III, Part 2, 976; Louis S. Gerteis, *Civil War St. Louis* (Lawrence: University Press of Kansas, 2001), 252; John D. Milligan, "From Theory to Application: The Emergence of the American Ironclad War Vessel," *Military Affairs* 48 (July 1984), 130; Eads, "Recollections of Foote and the Gunboats," 345; William H. Roberts, *Civil War Ironclads: The U.S. Navy and Industrial Mobilization* (Baltimore: Johns Hopkins University Press, 2002), 48,115; Jacob N. Taylor and M.O. Crooks, "Franklin Foundry," in *Sketch Book of St. Louis* (St Louis: George Knapp, 1858), 225–226; Charles C. Nott and Archibald Hopkins, *Cases Decided in the Court of Claims*

at the December Term, 1873, and the Decisions of the Supreme Court in the Appealed Cases from October 1873–May 1874 (Washington, D.C.: GPO, 1874), 155–170; Lewis and Richard H. Collins, *History of Kentucky*, 3 vols. (Chicago: S.J. Clarke, 1928), vol. I: 206; Jan Onofrio, "James Harrison," in *Missouri Biographical Dictionary*, 3rd ed.; 3 vols. (St. Clair Shores, MI: Somerset, 2001), vol. I: 140; Albert N. Marquis, "James Harrison," in *Book of St. Louisians*, 2nd ed (Chicago: A.N. Marquis, 1912), 265; James Neal Primm, *Lion of the Valley: St. Louis, Missouri, 1764–1980*, 3rd ed (St Louis: Missouri Historical Society Press, 1998), 200.

2. ORN, I, 22, 672; *New York Tribune*, March 24, 1862; *New York Times*, March 25, 1862; *Daily Cleveland Herald*, March 24, 1862; *Cincinnati Daily Commercial*, March 29, 1862. The ironclads under discussion at the War Department were actually those being built at New Orleans, and not the CSS *Arkansas*, then being constructed with great difficulty at Memphis by Primus Emerson. Myron J. Smith, Jr., *CSS* Arkansas: *A Confederate Ironclad on Western Waters* (Jefferson, NC: McFarland, 2011), 38–56.

3. Roy P. Basler, ed., *The Collected Works of Abraham Lincoln*, 10 vols. (Springfield, IL: Abraham Lincoln Association, 1958), vol. 5: 174; Sloan, *Benjamin Franklin Isherwood, Naval Engineer: The Years as Engineer-in-Chief, 1861–1869*, 57. In Brown's obituary in his hometown newspaper it was bluntly stated that the captain "continued steamboating until the opening of the war, when he went to Washington and, through the aid of his brother, who was sergeant-at-arms of the Senate, was awarded a contract to build gun-boats for the Federal government" (*Alton Daily Telegraph*, December 4, 1899).

4. Donald L. Canney, *The Old Steam Navy*, 2 vols. (Annapolis: Naval Institute Press, 1993), vol. 2: 95–96; Paul H. Silverstone, *Civil War Navies, 1855–1883* (New York: Taylor and Francis, 2006), 109–112; *Boston Daily Advertiser*, April 2, 1862; Sloan, *Benjamin Franklin Isherwood, Naval Engineer: The Years as Engineer-in-Chief, 1861–1869*, 57; ORN, I, 12: 813–814; *Cleveland Morning Daily Herald*, April 15, 1862; Roberts, *Civil War Ironclads*, 52–53; James M. Merrill, "Union Shipbuilding on Western Waters During the Civil War," *Smithsonian Journal of History* 3 (Winter 1868–1969), 33; Nicholas F. Budd, "The Adaptation of the Vessels of the Western Gunboat Flotilla to the Circumstances of Riverine Warfare During the American Civil War" (Master's thesis, U.S. Army Command and General Staff College, 1997), 62; *St. Louis Daily Republican*, August 4, 1862; *New York Times*, August 10, 1862; *San Francisco Daily Evening Bulletin*, April 1, 1863; U.S. Congress, House of Representatives, "Contracts Made With Bureaus Connected with the Navy Department: Letter from the Secretary of the Navy, July 14, 1862," in *House Executive Documents* (37th Cong., 2nd sess.; Washington, D.C.: GPO, 1862), 6. Interestingly enough, in the same May 6 report in which he castigated center wheel propulsion systems, Com. William D. Porter wrote even less kindly about propellers. In addition to the problems of driftwood shared with center wheels, propellers had to be quite small in order to accommodate themselves to the shoal depths of water. Small diameter propellers on large steamers would be "useless to obtain speed." He does not offer any opinion regarding their possible use in combination with side wheels (ORN, I, 23: 83). The *Marietta* and *Sandusky* did not see Civil War service. All of the ironclads built in Western yards hereafter would be monitors, though many were not commissioned.

5. Louis C. Hunter, *Steamboats on the Western Rivers: An Economic and Technological History* (Cambridge, MA: Harvard University Press, 1949), 548–549; Lawrence M. Pockras, "October 1959: That Damned Black Hulk—The U.S.S. *Chickasaw*," *Cincinnati Civil War Roundtable Talks*, http://www.cincinnaticwrt.org/data/ccwrt_history/talks_text/pockras_chickasaw.html (November 12, 2014); Smith, *CSS* Arkansas, 41–46; Mindell, *Iron Coffin*, 43–48; U.S. Congress, House of Representatives, "Contracts Made with Bureaus Connected with the Navy Department: Letter from the Secretary of the Navy, July 14, 1862," 6; Roberts, *Civil War Ironclads*, 26–28, 56, 70. U.S. Navy RAdm. David Dixon Porter required a number of structural changes in the three Brown vessels (discussed below) that raised their completion cost. When Brown was paid, he received a total of $503,292.29 for the group: $92,960 for the *Chillicothe*, $182,662.56 for the *Indianola*, and $227.669.72 for the *Tuscumbia* (ORN, II, 1: 56, 107, 227).

6. Victor M. Bogle, "New Albany's Attachment to the Ohio River," *Indiana Magazine of History* 49 (September 1953), 257; Myron J. Smith, Jr., *The Timberclads in the Civil War* (Jefferson, NC: McFarland, 2008), 21, 25, 59–62; "William J. Kountz," in Smith, *Civil War Biographies from the Western Waters*, 135; Theodore R. Parker, "William J. Kountz, Superintendent of River Transportation Under McClellan, 1861–62," *Western Pennsylvania Historical Magazine* 21 (December 1938), 239; Hunter, *Steamboats on the Western Rivers*, 109, 219–222, 225, 231, 233–236; OR, I, 52, 1: 158, 164; ORN, I, 23: 360; Roberts, *Civil War Ironclads*, 49; Theodore R. Parker, "Western Pennsylvania and the Naval War on the Inland Waters, 1861–1863," *Pennsylvania History* 16 (July 1949), 223–224; *Louisville Daily Journal*, May 21, 1862; *Pittsburg Gazette*, October 25, 1862.

7. Charles Cist, *Sketches and Statistics of Cincinnati in 1858* (Cincinnati: Priv. print, 1859), 552; Hunter, *Steamboats on the Western Rivers*, 549; Roberts, *Civil War Ironclads*, 51; Smith, *Timberclads in the Civil War*, 60 ; "Daniel H. Morton," in Smith, *Civil War Biographies from the Western Waters* (Jefferson, NC: McFarland, 2015), 171; John H. White, Jr., "Captain Hercules Carrel and the Cincinnati Marine Railway," *S & D Reflector* 45 (Summer 2008), 11, 14 ; White, "The Cincinnati Marine Railway," *Queen City Heritage* 57 (Summer-Fall 1999), 69–70, 82; Federal Writers' Project, *Cincinnati: A Guide to the Queen City and Its Neighbors* (Columbus: Ohio State Archaeological and Historical Society, 1943), 242; Mark

Tellon, "In the Heyday of Steamboating in New Albany," *New Albany Weekly Ledger,* May 24, 1924; David Dixon Porter, "Report Relative to the *Tuscumbia,*" in U.S. Navy Department, *Report of the Secretary of the Navy in Relation to Armored Vessels* (Washington, D.C.: GPO, 1864), 522. A native of Rochelle, France, Peter Tellon arrived at New Albany via Baltimore in 1817. The shipbuilder was "a highly respected citizen"; he died on December 8, 1862 (*Zif Lodge No. 8 Register and Minutes Ledger, 1819–1827,* http://ww-bbs.com/39/roll.htm (accessed November 15, 2014)).

   8. White, "The Cincinnati Marine Railway," 76; Don Prout, "Cincinnati Marine Railway," *Cincinnati Views,* http://www.cincinnativiews.net/ohio%20river.htm (accessed December 1, 2014); *Cleveland Daily Herald,* May 27, 1862. The *Daily Herald* briefing was reprinted in other local Ohio newspapers—but not until summer (*Western Reserve Chronicle* (Warren, OH), July 30, 1862, and the *Jeffersonian Democrat* (Chardon, OH), August 15, 1862). Lorenzo P. Sanger (1809–1875) was a U.S. Army colonel in Kentucky in 1862, the same year William Alexander Steel (1836–1880) married Sanger's daughter in St. Louis, where the one-time Pennsylvanian performed legal work for the firm Sanger, Wallace and Mix, an army mule supplier. The previous year, Steel, a pro-war Democrat, had cofounded with Sanger and Charles W. McCord the National Iron Works and served as major in its local defense force, the National Iron Works Battalion. It was, in fact, Steel who worked closely with McCord and Brown on Brown's ironclads; however, Steel would also partner with McCord on his monitor projects and oversee supply armor plate to James B. Eads for his. We were alerted to the Sanger-Steel relationship by a Steel relative, University of Mississippi music professor Warren Steel, in a May 29, 2014, e-mail. Those interested should also see *The History of Will County, Illinois* (Chicago: William Le Baron, Jr., 1878), 711–714; Huntington Library, "Letterbooks of William A. Steel, August 28, 1862–October 22, 1877," Archivegrid, http://184.168.105/185/archivegrid/collection/data/753739653 (accessed May 30, 2014); Newton Bateman, Paul Selby, and Charles A. Martin, vol. I of *Historical Encyclopedia of Illinois* (Chicago: Munsell, 1915), 465–466.

   9. Mark Tellon, "In the Heyday of Steamboating in New Albany," *New Albany Weekly Ledger,* May 24, 1924; *New Albany Daily Ledger,* January 28, 1863. Peter Tellon died on December 6, 1862, and completion of the *Tuscumbia,* as Brown's largest gunboat was named, was finished by his sons (*New Albany Daily Ledger,* December 8, 1862).

   10. Lewis R. Hamersly, comp., *Records of the Living Officers of the United States Navy and Marine Corps,* 3rd ed (Philadelphia: J.B. Lippincott, 1878), 76; Spencer C. Tucker, "Joseph Bartine Hull," in Tucker, ed., *The Civil War Naval Encyclopedia,* 2 vols. (Santa Barbara, CA: ABC-Clio, 2011), vol. I: 305–306; *Philadelphia Inquirer,* January 18, 1890; Edward W. Callahan, *List of Officers of the Navy of the United States and of the Marine Corps, from 1775 to 1900, Comprising a Complete Register of All Present and Former Commissioned, Warranted, and Appointed Officers of the United States Navy, and of the Marine Corps, Regular and Volunteer; Compiled from the Official Records of the Navy Department* (New York: L.R. Hamersly, 1901; Reprnt., New York: Haskell House, 1969), 251; U.S. Navy Department, *Report of the Secretary of the Navy for 1883–1884* (Washington, D.C.: GPO, 1884), 188; B. K. Genie, "Edward Hartt," Find A Grave, http://www.findagrave.com/cgi-bin/fg.cgi?page=gr&GRid=57881901 (accessed November 13, 2011); ORN, I, 12: 814; ORN, I, 23: 98–113; ORN, I, 24: 446–447. Hartt actually arrived in St. Louis at the end of May and, although he had assumed his duties, was unable to directly report to Hull until the latter's arrival on June 30 (*Milwaukee Morning Sentinel,* July 1, 1862). Hartt's role in the design of Brown's ironclads is found in Paul H. Silverstone, *Civil War Navies, 1855–1883* (New York: Routledge, 2006), 113, and Angus Konstam, *Union River Ironclads, 1861–1865* (Oxford, UK: Osprey, 2002), 12–13; *St. Louis Daily Republican,* August 4, 1862; Canney, *The Old Steam Navy,* ii, 95, 98; John A. Kouwenhoven, "The Designing of the Eads Bridge," *Technology and Culture* 23 (October 1982), 545–546; "Joseph Bartine Hull," in Smith, *Civil War Biographies from the Western Waters,* 127; Gustavus Vasa Fox, *Confidential Correspondence of Gustavus Vasa Fox, Assistant Secretary of the Navy, 1861–1865,* ed. Robert Means Thompson and Richard Wainwright, 2 vols. (New York: De Vinne, 1920), vol. 2: 458.

   11. ORN, I, 24: 446; Edward D. Parent, "Modeling the Ironclad USS *Indianola* (1862–1863)," *Ships in Scale* 19 (May-June 2007), 44–45; *St. Louis Daily Republican,* March 14, 1863; James M. Merrill, "Union Shipbuilding on Western Waters During the Civil War," *Smithsonian Journal of History* 3 (Winter 1968–1969), 34; Canney, *The Old Steam Navy,* ii, 95–96, 98, 100; Budd, "The Adaptation of the Vessels of the Western Gunboat Flotilla," 63–65; *St. Louis Daily Republican,* August 4, 1862; ORN, II, 1: 56; Henry H. Saylor, *Dictionary of Architecture* (New York: John Wiley, 1953), 66; *Louisville Journal,* August 13, 1862; *San Francisco Daily Evening Bulletin,* April 1, 1863; "John Hunt Morgan" and "Edmund Kirby Smith" in Smith, *Civil War Biographies from the Western Waters,* 170, 221–222; Steven E. Woodworth, *Jefferson Davis and His Generals: The Failure of Confederate Command in the West* (Lawrence: University Press of Kansas, 1990), 135; Kenneth W. Noe, *Perryville: This Grand Havoc of Battle* (Frankfurt: University Press of Kentucky, 2001), 29–31; *Milwaukee Daily Sentinel,* October 4, 1862.

   12. *St. Louis Daily Republican,* August 4, 1862; ORN, I, 23: 291, 449; ORN, I, 24: 446; *Louisville Daily Journal,* September 10, 1862; Merrill, "Union Shipbuilding," 35. As was common newspaper practice during the war, articles from different journals were widely reprinted. The *Daily Republican* report also appeared in the *New York Times* (August 10, 1862); the *Louisville Daily Democrat* (August 12, 1862); *Scientific American* (August 23, 1862), and, as far away as Auckland, New Zealand, in the November 4

number of the *Daily Southern Cross*. Shaw was the first volunteer officer chosen by Cmdr. John Rodgers II the previous year and within three months would become the first captain of the light-draught gunboat *Juliet* (Tinclad No. 4). Poor health would force his resignation in mid-1863 ("Edward Shaw," in Smith, *Civil War Biographies from the Western Waters*, 215).

13. Noe, *Perryville*, 25–35; Woodworth, *Jefferson Davis and His Generals*, 135–140; Shelby Foote, *The Civil War, A Narrative: Second Manassas to Pocotaligo* (Random House, 1958), 25; Gary Donaldson, "'Into Africa': Kirby Smith and Braxton Bragg's Invasion of Kentucky," *Filson Club Historical Quarterly* 61 (October 1987), 450; Roger C. Adams, "Panic on the Ohio: The Defense of Cincinnati, Covington, and Newport, September 1862," *Journal of Kentucky Studies* 9 (September 1992), 81; ORN, I, 23: 288, 291; "Edward Shaw," in Smith, *Civil War Biographies from the Western Waters*, 215.

14. Adams, "Panic on the Ohio," 81–86; U.S. War Department, *The War of the Rebellion: A Compilation of the Official Records of the Union and Confederate Armies*, 128 vols. (Washington, D.C.: GPO, 1880–1901), Series I, Vol. XVI, Part II, 479 (cited hereafter as OR, followed by a comma, the series number in Roman numerals, a comma, the volume number in Arabic, a colon, and the page in Arabic, e.g., OR, I, 2: 479); *St. Louis Daily Republican*, March 14, 1863; *Cincinnati Daily Enquirer*, September 2, 1862; *Cincinnati Daily Commercial*, September 2, 1862; ORN, I, 23: 335–338, 369, 418–419; James Morrison, ed., *The Memoirs of Henry Heath* (Westport, CT: Greenwood, 1974), 165–166. Anschutz and Yates remained with the *Indianola* and were captured with most of the rest of her crew below Vicksburg in February 1863 ("William J ("W. J.") Anschutz," "Oscar Badger," "John A. Duble," "Thomas Doughty," "Henry ('Harry') Heath," "Oliver P. Morton," "Alexander M. Pennock," "Lew Wallace," "Horatio Gouverneur Wright," and "John A. Yates," in Smith, *Civil War Biographies from the Western Waters*, 12, 15, 64–65, 110, 172, 184, 250–251, 267–268).

15. ORN, I, 23: 340–341, 345, 348; *Louisville Daily Journal*, September 10, 1862; Adams, *Panic on the Ohio*, 87. Also on September 10, the leadership of the Western Flotilla was informed that effective October 1 the unit would be transferred from the War Department to the Navy Department and be known as the Mississippi Squadron (ORN, I, 23: 348–349).

16. ORN, I, 23: 347, 352–353; 355–356, 364–365, 367–368, 383, 418–419; Merrill, "Union Shipbuilding," 35; Canney, *The Old Steam Navy*, ii, 97; Adams, *Panic on the Ohio*, 87–90; "Charles Henry Davis," in Smith, *Civil War Biographies from the Western Waters*, 58–59; David M. Smith, "January 1998, The Defense of Cincinnati: The Battle That Never Was," Cincinnati Civil War Roundtable Talks, http://www.cincinnaticwrt.org/data/ccwrt_history/smith_defense_cin.html (accessed November 12, 2014); Stephen I. Rockenbach, "A Border City at War: Louisville and the 1862 Invasion of Kentucky," *Ohio Valley History* 3 (Winter 2003), 38–41, 45; OR, I, XVI, 2: 516, 527, 532, 540; *Louisville Daily Journal*, September 18, 24–25, 1862; Robert S. Cameron, *Staff Ride Handbook for the Battle of Perryville, 8 October 1862* (Fort Leavenworth, KA: Combat Studies Institute Press, 2005), 88–99. Wounded in the ankle by shrapnel during the March 1863 Battle of Fort Pemberton, Kentuckian Underwood would remain aboard the *Chillicothe* until his honorable discharge on April 14, 1864. He died in Lawrence County, IN, on April 19, 1877 (Michael and Betsy Johnson, "Theodore E. Underwood, 1836–1877," RootsWeb, http://archiver.rootsweb.ancestry.com/th/read/UNDERWOOD/2013-07/1373742216 (accessed March 23, 2015).

17. ORN, I, 23: 388; ORN, I, 24: 377, 446–447; Chester G. Hearn, *Admiral David Dixon Porter: The Civil War Years* (Annapolis: Naval Institute Press, 1996), 119–145; Gideon, Welles, *The Diary of Gideon Welles*, ed. Edgar T. Welles, 3 vol (New York: Houghton Mifflin, 1911), vol. I: 157; "David Dixon Porter," "Watson Smith" in Smith, *Civil War Biographies from the Western Waters*, 192–193, 224; Fox, *Confidential Correspondence* 2, 458; David Dixon Porter, "Report Relative to the *Tuscumbia*," 522; Smith, *The Timberclads in the Civil War*, 363; Smith, *Tinclads in the Civil War* (Jefferson, NC: McFarland, 2010), 49–50. Mexican War veteran Watson Smith served in Cmdr. Porter's mortar flotilla during the Battle of New Orleans and the first Vicksburg campaign (April–July 1862), after which he was promoted to his current rank. Transferred to the Mississippi Squadron in early fall, he supervised naval activities in Cincinnati, helped to scout out civilian steamers for conversion by Brown into tinclads, and oversaw their building, as well as their delivery downstream to Cairo for completion of naval outfitting. At the beginning of 1863 he would be transferred to the Yazoo River area where he would shortly thereafter command a force that included not only several of his tinclads but the *Chillicothe* as well ("Watson Smith," in Smith, *Civil War Biographies*, 224).

18. ORN, I, 23: 418–419, 441; "George Brown," "John Grimes Walker" and "John Y. Yates" in Smith, *Civil War Biographies from the Western Waters*, 32. 249–250, 268; *St. Louis Daily Republican*, March 14, 1863. The Yates retention did not end well, as the old timer, according to his captain, was exceptionally ineffective. Later in the war he resigned, thereafter entering the mercantile business in Richmond, IN. There are a number of Farragut biographies; we used Chester G. Hearn's *Admiral David Glasgow Farragut: The Civil War Years* (Annapolis: Naval Institute Press, 1998).

19. ORN, I, 23: 448–449; Canney, *The Old Steam Navy*, ii, 97; Merrill, "Union Shipbuilding," 35; "Glossary of Steamboat Terms," Steamboats.org, http://www.steamboats.org/history-education/glossary/hog_chains.html (accessed January 4, 2011).

20. ORN, I, 22: 550; ORN, I, 23: 442, 449, 453; ORN, I, 24: 446; Canney, *The Old Steam Navy*, ii,

98, 100; Merrill, "Union Shipbuilding," 35; *St. Louis Daily Republican,* October 31, 1862; *Boston Daily Advertiser,* November 1, 1862; *Milwaukee Daily Sentinel,* November 5, 1862; *North American and United States Gazette,* November 8, 1862; David Dixon Porter, "Report Relative to the *Tuscumbia,*" in U.S. Navy Department, *Report of the Secretary of the Navy in Relation to Armored Vessels* (Washington, D.C.: GPO, 1864), 522. It was at this time that RAdm. Porter ordered the use of African-American contrabands as firemen and coalheavers throughout the Mississippi Squadron, thereby freeing up recruits to serve in combat billets (ORN, I, 23: 449). Formerly third master of the timberclad *Conestoga,* Sebastian, whose life vitals are unknown, was heavily involved in Mississippi Squadron recruiting during the remainder of the war and also worked closely with Joseph Brown in the preparation and delivery of light-draught gunboats ("Benjamin Sebastian" in Smith, *Civil War Biographies from the Western Waters,* 213).

21. ORN, I, 23: 471; *St. Louis Daily Republican,* November 8, 1862; *Louisville Daily Journal,* November 10, 1862; *Milwaukee Daily Sentinel,* November 10, 1862; *Philadelphia Inquirer,* November 11, 1862.

22. ORN, I, 23: 474, 483, 498–499, 504, 507, 531, 542, 634. 641; ORN, I, 24: 152; Steven E. Woodworth, *Nothing but Victory: The Army of the Tennessee, 1861–1865* (New York: Alfred A. Knopf, 2005), 264–265; *New York Tribune,* November 11, 1862; *New York Herald,* February 27, 1863; *Louisville Daily Journal,* October 22, 1862; "James P. Foster," "William Strong Pease," and "William Tecumseh Sherman" in Smith, *Civil War Biographies from the Western Waters,* 81, 183–184, 216–217; *Detroit Free Press,* December 28, 1862; "James P. Foster," in James Grant Wilson and John Fiske, eds., *Appletons' Cyclopaedia of American Biography,* 6 vols. (New York: D. Appleton, 1888), vol. 2: 511. Initially assigned command of the new Eads monitor *Neosho,* Foster was instead transferred to the Brown-built ironclad, arriving at Jeffersonville on November 14. Acting Master Shaw assisted his nephew in obtaining his October 1862 appointment as an acting master's mate (later acting ensign). Immediately upon joining, William was cautioned by his mother to say his prayers and be sure to wear his overcoat while on watches during wet weather because "you have been delicately brought up and cannot stand everything." Captured with the *Indianola* and also later while on a mission ashore from the *Choctaw,* Ward's health failed and he resigned from the service in January 1864. Graduating from Princeton University, he then entered the mining business ("William Shaw Ward," in Smith, *Civil War Biographies from the Western Waters,* 251–252; Geoffrey C. Ward, *A Disposition to Be Rich* (New York: A. Knopf, 2012), 93.

23. ORN, I, 23: 664–665; ORN, I, 24: 133; *New York Times,* November 29, 1862; Canney, *The Old Steam Navy,* ii, 97; Jennifer L. Weber, *Copperheads: The Rise and Fall of Lincoln's Opponents in the North* (New York: Oxford University Press, 2006), 79–80; Frank L.Klement, *Dark Lanterns: Secret Political Societies, Conspiracies, and Treason Trials in the Civil War* (Baton Rouge: Louisiana State University Press, 1984), 21–27.

24. ORN, I, 24: 95, 139, 152, 172; *New York Herald,* March 20, 1863; *Chicago Daily Tribune,* March 27, 1863; "Henry Walke" in Smith, *Civil War Biographies from the Western Waters,* 247–248; "The Civil War Diary of John G. Morrison, 1861–1865," New York State Military Museum and Veterans Research Center, http://dmna.ny.gov/historic/reghist/civil/infantry/30thInf/30thInf_Diary_Morrison.htm (accessed March 31, 2015); "Terry P. Robinson Journal, January 10, 1863," Journal Kept on Board the U.S. Steam Gunboat Carondelet and Lafayette, January 8–20, 1863, Manuscript Division, Library of Congress. The Robinson title has long been attributed to Thomas Lyons; however, the author's true identify was clarified by Mark Jenkins in 2013. James Hathaway, a native of New Bedford, MA, is the only "plank-owning" *Chillicothe* officer for whom we have a biography other than Foster and Underwood. The gunboat's purser served aboard throughout her deployment through the end of July 1864, after which he was transferred to the Mound City naval station. Following the war he was repeatedly elected treasurer of his home town ("James H. Hathaway," in Smith, *Civil War Biographies from the Western Waters,* 109).

25. *New York Times,* January 29, 1863; *St. Louis Daily Republican,* March 14, 1863; ORN, I, 24: 122, 192, 199, 207, 322; "Seth Ledyard Phelps" and "James Whitehall Shirk," in Smith, *Civil War Biographies from the Western Waters,* 186–187, 217–218; Gary D. Joiner, "James W. Shirk," in Tucker, ed., *The Civil War Naval Encyclopedia,* ii, 634–635.

26. ORN, I, 24: 446–447; ORN, II, 1: 56, 107, 227; ORN, I, 25: 760; *New Albany Daily Ledger,* January 28, 1863; *Scientific American* 8 (February 21, 1863), 115; Mark Tellon, "In the Heyday of Steamboating in New Albany," *New Albany Weekly Ledger,* May 24, 1924; David Dixon Porter, "Report Relative to the *Tuscumbia,*" in U.S. Navy Department, *Report of the Secretary of the Navy in Relation to Armored Vessels* (Washington, D.C.: GPO, 1864), 522; Smith, *Tinclads in the Civil War,* 52.

Chapter 4

1. U.S. Navy Department, *Official Records of the Union and Confederate Navies in the War of the Rebellion,* 31 vols., Washington, D.C.: GPO, 1894–1922), Series I, Vol. 24, 122–123, 208, 211, 244, 321, 324–325, 351, 431 (cited hereafter as ORN, followed by a comma, the series number in Roman numerals, a comma, the volume number in Arabic, a colon, and the page in Arabic, e.g, ORN, I, 24: 122–123, 208,

211, 244, 321, 324–325, 351, 431); *New York Herald*, January 31, 1863; *Chicago Daily Tribune*, February 2, 1863; *Erie (PA) Observer*, April 8, 1863; Thomas Bangs Thorpe, *The Mysteries of the Backwoods; or, Sketches of the Southeast, Including Character, Scenery, and Rural Sports* (Philadelphia: Carey & Hart, 1846), 173–174; Alfred T. Mahan, *The Gulf and Inland Waters*, vol. 3 of *The Navy in the Civil War* (New York: Scribner's, 1883), 141, 144–147; U.S. War Department, *The War of the Rebellion: A Compilation of the Official Records of the Union and Confederate Armies*, 128 vols. (Washington, D.C.: GPO, 1880–1901), Series I, Vol. 24, Pt. 1: 37 (cited hereafter as OR, followed by a comma, the series number in Roman numerals, a comma, the volume number in Arabic, any part number in Arabic, a colon, and the page in Arabic, e.g., OR, I, 24, 1: 37); John D. Milligan, *Gunboats Down the Mississippi* (Annapolis: Naval Institute Press, 1965), 132–135. Pennsylvanian and college dropout Keim went to work for the *Herald* in April 1861, being sent west the next spring. His uncle, Brig. Gen. William High Keim, introduced the reporter to Ulysses S. Grant, with whom he would form a lifelong friendship. Keim was imbedded with Union troops in the western theater during the Civil War and on the frontier afterwards ("DeBenneville Raldoph Keim," in Bertolet Family Association, *A Genealogical History of the Bertolet Family: The Descendants of Jean Bertolet* (Harrisburg, PA: Press of United Evangelical Publishing House, 1914), 166.

 2. Jean Edward Smith, *Grant* (New York: Simon and Schuster, 2001), 226–229; Timothy B. Smith, "Victory at Any Cost: The Yazoo Pass Expedition," *Journal of Mississippi History* 67 (Summer 2007), 147–148; William L. Shea and Terrence J. Winschel, *Vicksburg Is the Key: The Struggle for the Mississippi River* (Lincoln: University of Nebraska Press, 2003), 69; Ulysses S. Grant, *Personal Memoir of U.S. Grant*, 2 vols. (New York: Charles L. Webster, 1885), vol. I: 440–443, 448; David Dixon Porter, *Naval History of the Civil War* (New York: Sherman, 1886; Reprnt., Secaucus, NJ: Castle, 1984), 300; Richard S. West, Jr., "Gunboats in the Swamps: The Yazoo Pass Expedition," *Civil War History* 9 (June 1963), 157; Francis Vinton Greene, *The Mississippi: Campaigns of the Civil War*, vol. 8 (New York: Charles Scribner's Sons, 1885; Reprnt., The Blue & The Gray Press, n.d.), 91, 94; Rowena Reed, *Combined Operations in the Civil War* (Annapolis: U.S. Naval Institute Press, 1978), 240; Myron J. Smith, Jr., *The Fight for the Yazoo, August 1862–July 1864: Swamps, Forts, and Fleets on Vicksburg's Northern Flank* (Jefferson, NC: McFarland, 2012), 131–134. A recent student of the logistical side of the war, Charles Dana Gibson, believes this view of what might appear to be a haphazard initiative into Yazoo Pass "a common misconception." The purpose of the incursion was "pure and simple": to "cut off supply communications to Vicksburg which emanated from the Coldwater-Sunflower-Yazoo basin." The push into Steele's Bayou was a diversion to that initial incursion designed to help take pressure from it as it faltered (Charles Dana Gibson, with E. Kay Gibson, *Assault and Logistics*, Vol. 2: *Union Army Coastal and River Operations, 1861–1866* (Camden, ME: Ensign Press, 1995), 266).

 3. OR, I, 24: 207; 211; Smith, *Fight for the Yazoo*, 133; "James Harrison Wilson," in Smith, *Civil War Biographies from the Western Waters* (Jefferson, NC: McFarland, 2015), 262.

 4. ORN, I, 23: 406; ORN, I, 24: 228, 249, 253, 345; OR, I, 24, 1: 371–374, 386–387; OR, I, 24, 3: 38–39; Timothy Smith, "Victory at Any Cost," 149–150; Edward G. Longacre, *Grant's Cavalryman: The Life and Wars of General James H. Wilson* (Mechanicsburg, PA: Stackpole, 1996), 68–69; Smith, *Fight for the Yazoo*, 150–151; West, "Gunboats in the Swamps," 158; Ulysses S. Grant, *The Papers of Ulysses S. Grant:* vol. 7: *December 9, 1862–March 31–1863*, ed. John Y. Simon, 31 vols. (Edwardsville: Southern Illinois University Press, 1967–2009), 256, 299–300; Greene, *The Mississippi*, 97; Robert W. Harrison, "Levee Building in Mississippi Before the Civil War," *Journal of Mississippi History* 12 (April 1950), 69; Michael B. Ballard, *The Civil War in Mississippi: Major Campaigns and Battles* (Jackson: University Press of Mississippi, 2011), 132. For a brief and insightful examination of the problems of recruiting for the Mississippi Squadron, see Michael J. Bennett, *Union Jacks: Yankee Sailors in the Civil War* (Chapel Hill: University of North Carolina Press, 2004), 79–81.

 5. ORN, I, 23: 406; ORN, I, 24: 244–245, 249–250, 252, 261; OR, I, 24, 1: 17; OR, I, 24, 3: 36, 39; *Chicago Daily Times*, February 26, 1863; *Brooklyn Daily Eagle*, March 2, 1863; *New York Herald*, March 25, 1863; West, "Gunboats in the Swamps," 158–159; Longacre, *Grant's Cavalryman*, 70; Timothy Smith, "Victory at Any Cost," 150; Smith, *Fight for the Yazoo*, 151–153. Regarding the neck of land near where the Rebels would build Fort Pemberton, the modern visitor will find that some of the Tallahatchie now flows through a crossover channel near the site of the improvised Southern defense. This crossover was not present in 1863 and now makes the previous neck of land into an island. In addition, early in August 2010 my friend the historian David Meagher visited Fort Pemberton and sent back his impressions: "Today a double highway cuts through Pemberton from east to west, there is a spillway canal going north to south through it and all that is left is a tiny park about the size of a baseball diamond, with a few rounded trenches and a granite marker" (David Meagher to author, August 15, 2010).

 6. ORN, I, 24: 251, 254, 311; OR, I, 24, 1: 324–325, 342–346, 374–375, 387,404; OR, I, 24, 3: 38–39, 42, 622–623; *Chicago Daily Times*, March 2, 10, 1863; *Milwaukee Daily Sentinel*, March 14, 1863; *Yazoo Daily Banner*, February 8, 1863; *St. Louis Daily Missouri Democrat*, February 19, 1863; *Brooklyn Daily Eagle*, February 27, 1863; *Chicago Daily Times*, March 2, March 10, 1863; *Dubuque Daily Times*, March 5, 1863; West, "Gunboats in the Swamps," 158–159; George W. Brown, "Service in the Mississippi Squadron," 308; Smith, *Fight for the Yazoo*, 153–154; Longacre, *Grant's Cavalryman*, 70; Grant, *The Papers*

of Ulysses S. Grant: vol. 7, 299; Timothy Smith, "Victory at Any Cost," 150; Edwin C. Bearss, *Decision in Mississippi* (Little Rock: Pioneer, 1962), 149.

7. OR, I, 24, 1: 375, 387; OR, I, 24, 3: 620, 622–623; ORN, I, 24: 252–254, 259, 265; *Chicago Daily Times,* March 10, 1863; *Milwaukee Daily Sentinel,* March 14, 1863; Grant, *The Papers of Ulysses S. Grant:* Vol. 7, 334–335; Bettye E. Burkhalter, *Raised Country Style from South Carolina to Mississippi: Civil War Transforms America* (Bloomington, IN: AuthorHouse, 2010), 119; Smith, *Fight for the Yazoo,* 154–162; West, "Gunboats in the Swamps," 159; Timothy Smith, "Victory at Any Cost," 150; "John L. Morton," in Walter Williams, ed., *A History of Northwest Missouri,* 3 vols. (Chicago: Lewis, 1915), vol. 2: 643; "William Wing ('Old Blizzards') Loring," in Smith, *Civil War Biographies from the Western Waters,* 145–146.

8. ORN, I, 24: 254–255, 265; OR, I, 24: 1, 376, 381, 401–402; OR, I, 24, 3: 54, 57–58, 626, 629–630; Smith, *Fight for the Yazoo,* 163–168; *New York Times,* February 19, 1863; *New York Herald,* March 17, 1863; *Chicago Daily Tribune,* March 19, 1863; *Erie (PA) Observer,* April 8, 1863; "Benjamin Mayberry Prentiss" and "Leonard Fulton ("Judge") Ross," in Smith, *Civil War Biographies from the Western Waters,* 195–196, 207.

9. OR, I, 23, 2: 641; OR, I, 24, 1: 415, 360–361, 376; OR, I, 24, 3: 629–630, 632–634, 636–638, 641, 644; OR, I, 52, 2: 423–425; ORN, I, 24: 255–258; *Chicago Daily Tribune,* February 21, 1863; Smith, *Fight for the Yazoo,* 169–176; William A. Gillespie, "Fort Pemberton," Civil War Album, http://www.civilwaralbum.com/vicksburg/fort_pemberton_1904.htm (accessed February 1, 2011); William H. Tunnard, *A Southern Record: The History of the Third Regiment Louisiana Infantry* (Baton Rouge: Printed for the Author, 1866), 219; Frederic E. Davis to parents, February 17, 1863, Frederic E. Davis Papers, 1860–1863, Manuscript, Archives, and Rare Book Library, Emory University, Atlanta, GA; West, "Gunboats in the Swamps," 160; Harry P. Owens, *Steamboats and the Cotton Economy: River Trade in the Yazoo-Mississippi Delta* (Jackson: University of Mississippi Press, 1990), 57; Charles M. Getchell, Jr., "Defender of Inland Waters: The Military Career of Isaac Newton Brown, Commander, Confederate States Navy, 1861–1865," Master's thesis, University of Mississippi, 1978), 94–96; "John Clifford Pemberton," in Smith, *Civil War Biographies from the Western Waters,* 184.

10. OR, I, 24, 1: 376, 399; OR, I, 24, 3: 74, 163, 637–640, 644; ORN, I, 24: 245, 258–260; *Chicago Daily Times,* March 2, 1863; *New York Times,* March 6, 1863; John Bakeless, *Spies of the Confederacy* (Philadelphia: J.B. Lippincott, 1970), 213; James W. Raab, *W.W. Loring: Florida's Forgotten General* (Manhattan, KA: Sunflower University Press, 1996), 93; William A. Gillespie, "Fort Pemberton," Civil War Album, http://www.civilwaralbum.com/vicksburg/fort_pemberton_1904.htm (accessed February 1, 2011); Owens, *Steamboats and the Cotton Economy,* 55–56; Smith, *Fight for the Yazoo,* 176–178; Timothy Smith, "Victory at Any Cost, 151, 156; Frank E. Smith, *The Yazoo River* (New York: Rinehart, 1944; Reprnt., Jackson: University Press of Mississippi, 1988), 113; "Thomas Neville Waul," in Smith, *Civil War Biographies from the Western Waters,* 255.

11. OR, I, 24, 1: 376–377, 380, 394, 397–399; OR, I, 24, 3: 22, 640–641, 643–646, 648–650; ORN, I, 24: 244, 246, 259–261; *Richmond Daily Dispatch,* February 28, 1863; *Dubuque Daily Times,* March 5, 1863; *Chicago Daily Times,* March 10, 1863; *Milwaukee Daily Sentinel,* March 14, 1863; *New York Herald,* March 17, 1863; *Chicago Daily Tribune,* March 19, 1863; Grant, *The Papers of Ulysses S. Grant:* Vol. 7, 409; Allen Woods Miller, Diary, February 25, 1863, Manuscript Division, Library of Congress, Washington, D.C.; Milton W. Shaw to Alf Giague, March 10, 1863, Milton Shaw Letters, McCain Library and Archives, University of Southern Mississippi; *Charles O. Musser, Soldier Boy: The Civil War Letters of Charles O. Musser, 29th Iowa,* ed. Barry Popchock (Iowa City: University of Iowa Press, 1995), 30–34; William A. Gillespie, "Fort Pemberton," Civil War Album, http://www.civilwaralbum.com/vicksburg/fort_pemberton_1904.htm (accessed February 1, 2011); John S. Morgan, "Diary of John S. Morgan, Company G, Thirty-Third Iowa Infantry," *Annals of Iowa* 13 (January 1923), 484, 501; Smith, "Victory at Any Cost, 151–152; George M. Blackburn, ed., *"Dear Carrie": The Civil War Letters of Thomas M. Stevens* (Mount Pleasant: Central Michigan University Press, 1984), 61; Alonzo Leighton Brown, *History of the Fourth Regiment of Minnesota Volunteers During the Great Rebellion, 1861–1865* (St. Paul, MN: Pioneer, 1892), 168–169; Burkhalter, *Raised Country Style from South Carolina to Mississippi,* 119–120; West, "Gunboats in the Swamps," 159–160; John M. Carson, "The Capture of the *Indianola,*" *Confederate Veteran* 32 (1924), 380–381; W.F. Brand, "The Capture of the *Indianola,*" *Maryland Historical Magazine* 4 (December 1909), 353–361; Ralph R. Rea, ed., "Diary of Private John P. Wright, 29th Iowa, U.S.A., 1863–1865," *Arkansas Historical Quarterly* 16 (Autumn 1957), 307; Chester G. Hearn, *Ellet's Brigade: The Strangest Outfit of All* (Baton Rouge: Louisiana State University Press, 2000), 125–126; Hearn, *Admiral David Dixon Porter: The Civil War Years* (Annapolis: U.S Naval Institute Press, 1996), 178–182; Smith, *Fight for the Yazoo,* 176–189.

12. OR, I, 24, 1: 393, 406; OR, I, 24, 3: 86–87, 105, 649–650; OR, I, 52, 2: 429; ORN, I, 24: 261–264; Grant, *The Papers of Ulysses S. Grant:* Vol. 7, 369, 415; *New York Tribune,* February 27 and March 12, 1863; *Chicago Daily Times,* March 10, 1863; *Chicago Daily Tribune,* March 12, 24,1863; *Detroit Free Press,* March 12, 1863; *Milwaukee Daily Sentinel,* March 14, 1863; *New York Times,* March 15–16, 1863; *Brooklyn Daily Eagle,* March 16, 1863; *New York Herald,* March 17, 25, 1863; *Chicago Daily Tribune,* March 7, 19, 1863; Frederic E. Davis to his parents, March 2, 1863, *Frederic E. Davis Papers;* Steven E. Woodworth,

Nothing but Victory: The Army of the Tennessee, 1861–1865 (New York: Alfred A. Knopf, 2005), 306; Gibson. *Assault and Logistics*, Vol. 2: *Union Army Coastal and River Operations, 1861–1866*, 269; Frank E. Smith, *The Yazoo River* (New York: Rinehart, 1944; Reprnt., Jackson: University Press of Mississippi, 1988), 114; Owens, *Steamboats and the Cotton Economy*, 56–57; Musser, *Soldier Boy*, 34–35; Smith, *Fight for the Yazoo*, 189–193; "Isaac Newton Brown," in Smith, *Civil War Biographies from the Western Waters*, 33–34; "James Birdseye McPherson," in Smith, *Civil War Biographies from the Western Waters*, 160; "Isaac Ferdinand Quinby," in Smith, *Civil War Biographies from the Western Waters*, 197.

13. ORN, I, 24: 109, 246, 263–269, 271–273, 296, 299, 421, 541, 693–694; OR, I, 24, 1: 19–20, 295, 379–380, 388, 393–395, 399, 406, 412, 414–417, 421; OR, I, 24, 3: 90–91, 93–94, 96, 98–99, 105, 110, 649, 654, 656–660, 662–663, 668; *Chicago Daily Tribune*, March 12, 1863; *Jackson Daily Mississippian*, March 13, 1863; *Chicago Daily Times*, March 17, 23, 1863; *Brooklyn Daily Eagle*, March 19, 25, 1863; *Philadelphia Press*, March 20, 1863; *New York Times*, March 20, 1863;*Cincinnati Daily Commercial*, March 23, 1863; *Bangor (ME) Daily Whig and Courier*, March 23, 1863; *Chicago Daily Tribune*, March 24, 1863; *New York Herald*, March 25, 1863; Milton W. Shaw to Alf Giague, March 10, 1863, Milton Shaw Letters, McCain Library and Archives, University of Southern Mississippi; Woodworth, *Nothing but Victory: The Army of the Tennessee, 1861–1865*, 307; John C. Stiles, "A Remarkable Shot," *Confederate Veteran* 28 (1920), 358; Owens, *Steamboats and the Cotton Economy*, 56–57; Donald L. Canney, *The Old Steam Navy*, 2 vols. (Annapolis: Naval Institute Press, 1993), vol. 2: 97; Timothy Smith, "Victory at Any Cost," 153–155, 157–158; West, "Gunboats in the Swamps," 162–163; Rae, ed., *Diary of Private John P. Wright*, 308; Musser, *Soldier Boy*, 35–37; "Letters of Thomas N. Stevens, n.d."; "Letters of Lauren Barker, n.d."; "Letters of George Sawyer, n.d.," 28th Wisconsin Volunteer Infantry, http://www.28thwisconsin.com/letters/enos_12mar1863.html (accessed February 12, 2011); Newton Robert Scott to Hannah Cone, March 9, 1863, *Letters from an Iowa Soldier in the Civil War*, http://www.civilwarletters.com/scott_3_9_1863.html (accessed March 3, 2011); Raab, *W.W. Loring*, 94; Ron Field and Adam Hook, *American Civil War Fortifications (3): The Mississippi and River Forts* (Fortress, no. 68; Oxford, UK: Osprey, 2007), 25; Smith, *Fight for the Yazoo*, 193–207; James A. Newman, *The Autobiography of an Old Fashioned Boy* (Oklahoma City, Okla.?: s.n., 1923), 18; Warren E. Grabau, *Ninety-Eight Days: A Geographer's View of the Vicksburg Campaign* (Knoxville: University of Tennessee Press, 2000), 42; Getchell, "Defender of Inland Waters," 96–98; Edwin Olmstead, Wayne E. Stark, and; Spencer C. Tucker, *The Big Guns: Civil War Siege, Seacoast, and Naval Cannon* (Bloomfield, Ontario, and Alexandria Bay, NY: Museum Restoration Service, 1997), 125–126; "Brooke Rifles and Smoothbore Guns," in *The Encyclopedia of Civil War Artillery*, http://www.cwartillery.org/ve/brooke.html (accessed October 13, 2009); Paul Branch, "Armament of Fort Macon," in *The Fort Macon Ramparts, Spring 1996*, http://www.clis.com/friends/armament.htm (accessed October 13, 2009); Leonard Fullenkamp, Stephen Bosman, and Jay Luvaas, *Guide to the Vicksburg Campaign* (Lawrence: University of Kansas Press, 1998), 376; Hearn, *Admiral David Dixon Porter*, 183.

14. ORN, I, 24: 273–276, 379, 555, 694; OR, I, 24, 1: 404–405, 416–417; OR, I, 24, 3: 105–107, 663, 665–667, 672; OR, I, 52, 2: 433–434; *New York Tribune*, March 12, 1863; *Cincinnati Daily Gazette*, March 16, 1863; *Brooklyn Daily Eagle*, March 16, 1863; *New York Times*, March 17, 19, 1863; *Chicago Daily Tribune*, March 25, 1863; *New York Herald*, March 25, 1863; *Yazoo City Banner*, n.d., quoted in *Richmond Daily Dispatch*, April 3, 1863; Smith, *Fight for the Yazoo*, 207–213; Frederic E. Davis to his parents, March 12, 1863, Frederic E. Davis Papers, 1860–1863, Manuscript, Archives, and Rare Book Library, Emory University, Atlanta, GA; Edwin E. Rice, "Diary, March 12–13, 1863," in *Diary of Edwin E. Rice, April 15, 1862–April 5, 1863*, trans. David S. Pettus, Galveston and Texas History Center, Rosenberg Library, Galveston; Edwin C. Bearss, *Decision in Mississippi* (Little Rock: Pioneer, 1962), 209; Claude E. Fike, ed., "Diary of James Oliver Hazard Perry Sessions of Rokeby Plantation on the Yazoo River, January 1862 to June 1872," *Journal of Mississippi History* 39 (August 1977), 248; Timothy Smith, "Victory at Any Cost," 159; Burkhalter, *Raised Country Style from South Carolina to Mississippi*, 120; Owens, *Steamboats and the Cotton Economy*, 58; Raab, *W.W. Loring*, 96; Hearn, *Admiral David Dixon Porter*, 183–184.

15. OR, I, 24, 1: 20–21, 379–386, 391–392, 396, 406, 413–414; OR, I, 24, 3: 110–112, 118–119 668–670, 672, 677–678; ORN, I, 24: 276–286, 293, 301–302, 484–485, 515, 694; OR, I, 52, 1: 439; OR, I, 52, 2: 435; *New Albany Daily Ledger*, January 28, 1863; *Memphis Daily Appeal*, March 14, 19, 1863; *Richmond Daily Dispatch*, March 14, 18, 1863; *Mobile Advertiser and Register*, March 14, 18, 1863; *Chicago Daily Times*, March 26, 1863; *Brooklyn Daily Eagle*, March 14, 28, 1863; *New York Times*, March 16, 1863; *New York Herald*, March 20, 1863; *Philadelphia Press*, April 28, 1863; Grant, *The Papers of Ulysses S. Grant*: Vol. 7, 420–422, 427–429, 439; Edwin E. Rice, "Diary, March 14–19, 1863," in *Diary of Edwin E. Rice, April 15, 1862–April 5, 1863*, trans. David S. Pettus, Galveston and Texas History Center, Rosenberg Library, Galveston; Fike, ed., *Diary of James Oliver Hazard Perry Sessions*, 248; "Letters of Lauren Barker, n.d.," 28th Wisconsin Volunteer Infantry, http://www.28thwisconsin.com/letters/enos_12mar1863.html> (accessed February 12, 2011); Nicholas F. Budd, "The Adaptation of the Vessels of the Western Gunboat Flotilla to the Circumstances of Riverine Warfare During the American Civil War" (Master's thesis, U.S. Army Command and General Staff College, 1997), 66–67; Longacre, *Grant's Cavalryman*, 73; James H. Wilson, *Under the Old Flag*, 2 vols. (New York: D. Appleton, 1912), vol. I: 153; Gibson, *Assault and Logistics*, 269; David Dixon Porter, *Naval History of the Civil War* (New York: Sherman, 1886; Reprnt., Se-

caucus, NJ: Castle, 1984), 301; Porter, *Incidents and Anecdotes of the Civil War* (New York: D. Appleton, 1885; Reprnt., Harrisburg, PA: Archive Society, 1997), 240; Musser, *Soldier Boy*, 38–39; Winston Groom, *Vicksburg, 1863* (New York: Alfred A. Knopf, 2009), 253; Glenna R. Schroeder-Lein, *The Encyclopedia of Civil War Medicine* (Armonk, NY: M.E. Sharpe, 2008), 86–87; Rae, ed., "Diary of Private John P. Wright," 308–309; George S. Burkhardt, ed., *Double Duty in the Civil War: The Letters of Soldier and Sailor Edward W. Bacon* (Carbonedale: Southern Illinois University Press, 2009), 226; Smith, "Victory at Any Cost," 160–161; West, "Gunboats in the Swamps," 161–162, 164–165; Smith, *Fight for the Yazoo*, 213–224.

16. ORN, I, 24: 70, 269, 283–291, 302–304, 392–393, 489–490, 514–515, 541–544, 547, 693–694; OR, I, 24, 1: 66, 407–409, 416–420; OR, I, 24, 3: 127, 132–135, 148–149, 151, 696, 679–680, 682, 687, 719, 722, 795–796; OR, I, 52, 1: 445, 447–448, 451–453; *Chicago Daily Times*, March 26, 1863; *Brooklyn Daily Eagle*, March 28, 1863; *Chicago Daily Tribune*, April 4, 1863; *Evansville Daily Journal*, April 10, 15, 29, May 7, 1863; *Erie Observer*, April 18, 1863; Edwin E. Rice, "Diary, March 19–March 25, March 29, April 1–2, 5, 1863," *Diary of Edwin E. Rice, April 15, 1862–April 5, 1863*; Timothy Smith, "Victory at Any Cost," 163–166; Raab, *W.W. Loring*, 235; Smith, *Fight for the Yazoo*, 224–237; Porter, *Incidents and Anecdotes of the Civil War*, 144; Donald C. Elder III, ed., *Love and the Turmoil: The Civil War Letters of William and Mary Vermilion* (Iowa City: University of Iowa Press, 2003), 74; Joseph Stockton, *War Diary of Brevet Brigadier General Joseph Stockton* (Chicago: John T. Stockton, 1910), 11. Lt. Gen. Pemberton was advised by Col. Waul to maintain Fort Pemberton as an active post until about mid–May, when the falling rivers would make a fresh Union advance unlikely. During that time, his troops, plus about 150 African American slaves, would make necessary improvements (OR, I, 24, 3: 796).

17. ORN, I, 24: 637, 679, 694; ORN, I, 25: 153, 333; *Philadelphia Press*, May 2, 1863; "Mound City Illinois Shipyards, Hospital," Southernmost Illinois History, http://www.southernmostillinoishistory.net/mound-city-il-shipyards-hospital.html (accessed April 21, 2015).

18. ORN, I, 25: 153, 179, 219, 333, 378, 412, 426–427, 452, 459, 482–483, 519, 562; Smith, *Tinclads in the Civil War* (Jefferson, NC: McFarland, 2010), 126–127; "Joseph Pitty Couthouy," "Henry St. Clair Eytinge," "Francis Munroe ('Frank') Ramsay," in Smith, *Civil War Biographies from the Western Waters*, 55, 72–73, 197–198; Gary D. Joiner and Jimmy H. Sandefur, ed., "Joseph Pitty Couthouy: The Death of a Sailor-Scientist," in Gary D. Joiner, ed., *Little to Eat and Thin Mud to Drink: Letters, Diaries, and Memoirs from the Red River Campaigns, 1863–1864* (Knoxville: Univ. of Tennessee Press, 2007), 317–329; W.H. Dall, "Some American Conchologists," *Proceedings of the Biological Society of Washington* 4 (1888), 95–134. Eytinge, having grounded two vessels, was dismissed from the service and his appointment was revoked on December 1, 1863. David J. Gerelman, "Acting Masters of Disaster," *Lincoln Editor: The Quarterly Newsletter of the Papers of Abraham Lincoln* 11 (July-September 2011), 4–8.

19. OR, I, 26, 1: 384, 559, 653, 673; ORN, I, 25: 734–736, 770–773; ORN, I, 26: 286; U.S., Congress, Joint Committee on the Conduct of the War, *Report: Red River* (38th Cong., 2nd sess.; Washington, D.C.: GPO, 1864; reprnt., Greenwood, 1971), 5 (cited hereafter as *Joint Committee*, with page number in Arabic); Selfridge, *op. cit.*, 87–88; William Riley Brooksher, *War Along the Bayous: The 1864 Red River Campaign in Louisiana* (Washington, D.C.: Brassey's, 1998), xi–xii, 1–24; *A Brief and Condensed History of Parsons' Texas Cavalry Brigade* (Waxhachie, TX: J.M. Flemister, 1893), 268; Elias P. Pellet, *History of the 114th Regiment, New York State Volunteers* (Norwich, NY: Telegraph & Chronicle, 1866), 166–167.

20. OR, I, 34, 1: 168, 304, 476; OR, I, 34, 2: 448–449, 494–496, 554, 616; ORN, I, 26: 23–26, 776, 789; *New York Daily Tribune*, March 28, 1864; *St. Louis Daily Missouri Republican*, March 28, 1864; *Philadelphia Inquirer*, March 30, 1864; *Joint Committee, op. cit.*, 21; Porter, *Naval History*, 494–496; Porter, *Incidents and Anecdotes of the Civil War*, 213"; Andrew Jackson ('Whiskey') Smith," "Richard ('Dick') Taylor," in Smith, *Civil War Biographies from the Western Waters*, 220, 233–234; Richard Taylor, *Destruction and Reconstruction: Personal Experiences of the Late War* (New York: D. Appleton, 1879), 180–181; Richard B. Irwin, "The Red River Campaign," in *Battles and Leaders of the Civil War*, ed. Robert V. Johnson and Clarence C. Buel, 4 vols. (New York: Century, 1884–1887, reprinted Thomas Yoseloff, 1956), IV, 349–351; Thomas O. Selfridge, Jr., "The Navy in the Red River," B & L, IV, 362; David Dixon Porter, "The Mississippi Flotilla in the Red River Expedition," B & L, IV, 367; Walter G. Smith, ed., *Life and Letters of Thomas Kilby Smith* (New York: G.P. Putnam, 1898), 356; Gary D. Joiner, *Through the Howling Wilderness: The 1864 Red River Campaign and Union Failure in the West* (Knoxville: University of Tennessee Press, 2006), 54–57; Joiner and Charles E. Vetter, "The Union Naval Expedition on the Red River, March 12–May 22, 1864," *Civil War Regiments: A Journal of the American Civil War* 4 (1994), 26–41; Curtis Milbourn and Gary D. Joiner, "The Battle of Blair's Landing," *North and South* 9 (February 2007), 12; Hearn, *Admiral David Dixon Porter: The Civil War Years*, 245–246.

21. OR, 34, 1: 305, 313, 338–339, 500, 506, 561; OR, I, 34, 2: 494, 610–611; ORN, I, 26: 29–31, 35, 41, 50, 776–777, 781, 784–785, 789; Mahan, *op. cit.*, 190–191; *New York Daily Tribune*, April 4, 1864; *St. Louis Daily Missouri Republican*, March 26, 1864; *Columbus (WI) Democrat*, May 29, 1895; Porter, *Naval History*, 499–500; Taylor, *Destruction and Reconstruction*, 156, 181–183; Joiner and Vetter, "The Union Naval Expedition on the Red River," 41–49; Selfridge, "The Navy in the Red River," B & L, IV, 362; John D. Winters, *The Civil War in Louisiana* (Baton Rouge: Louisiana State University Press, 1963), 330–331;

Ludwell H. Johnson, *Red River Campaign: Politics and Cotton in the Civil War* (Kent, OH: Kent State University Press, 1993), 99–105; Ivan Musicant, *Divided Waters: The Naval History of the Civil War* (New York: HarperCollins, 1995), 295–296; Irwin, "The Red River Campaign," *B & L*, IV, 349–350; Robert L. Kerby, *Kirby Smith's Confederacy: The Trans-Mississippi South, 1863–1865* (New York: Columbia University Press, 1972), 297; Hearn, *Admiral David Dixon Porter*, 246–248.

22. OR, I, 34, 1: 179–180; 282, 308–309, 322, 324, 331, 341, 379–381, 384, 388–393, 407, 428, 445, 452, 468, 471–472, 633–634; OR, I, 34, 2: 610–611; OR, I, 34, 3: 98–99; *New York World*, April 16, 1864; *Columbus (WI) Democrat*, May 29, 1895; Joint Committee, *op. cit.*, 35, 210, 275–276, 282, 286–287, 323; ORN, I, 26: 38–39, 42–43, 46, 50–51, 54, 60–61, 776–778, 781, 785, 789; Joiner and Sandefur, ed., "Joseph Pitty Couthouy: The Death of a Sailor-Scientist," in Joiner, ed., *Little to Eat and Thin Mud to Drink*, 326–327; "Joseph Pitty Couthouy," "Thomas Kilby Smith," in Smith, *Civil War Biographies from the Western Waters*, 55, 224; Thomas O. Selfridge, Jr., "The Navy in the Red River," *B & L*, IV, 363; Selfridge, *Memoirs*, *op. cit.*, 99–101; Brooksher, *War Along the Bayous*, 69–78; Irwin, "The Red River Campaign," *B & L*, IV, 351–356; Porter, *Naval History*, 502, 511–512; Joiner, *Through the Howling Wilderness*, op. cit., 32, 131–136; Joiner and Vetter, "The Union Naval Expedition on the Red River," 49–51; Hearn, *Admiral David Dixon Porter*, 248–250; Steven D. Smith and George J. Castille III, "Bailey's Dam," *Louisiana Department of Culture, Recreation and Tourism Anthropological Study*, no. 8, March 1986, http://www.crt.state.la.us/archaeology/BAILEYS/baileys.htm (August 7, 2006).

23. OR, I, 34, 1: 310, 382–383; ORN, I, 26: 66, 69, 72–78; 773–774, 777–780, 790; *Philadelphia Press*, April 29, 1864; *St. Louis Daily Missouri Democrat*, May 10, 1864; *Columbus (WI) Democrat*, May 29, 1895; "Thomas Green," in Smith, *Civil War Biographies from the Western Waters*, 95–96; Selfridge, *Memoirs*, 99–101; Brooksher, *War Along the Bayous*, 158–159; Joiner and Vetter, "The Union Naval Expedition on the Red River," 58–59; Selfridge, Jr., "The Navy in the Red River," *B & L*, IV, 364; Hearn, *Admiral David Dixon Porter*, 253–254; Porter, *Naval History*, 515–519; Porter, *Incidents and Anecdotes*, 235–239; Pellet, *History of the 114th Regiment, New York State Volunteers*, 222.

24. ORN, I, 26: 73–76, 79–81, 83, 166–169, 176, 779, 787–787, 790–791; OR, I, 34,1, 583–584, 632, 634. 782, 790–791; *Columbus (WI) Democrat*, May 29, 1895; Taylor, *Destruction and Reconstruction*, 183–185; Hearn, *Admiral David Dixon Porter*, 255–257; Joiner, *Through the Howling Wilderness*, 138–140; Joiner and Vetter, "The Union Naval Expedition on the Red River," 60–62; Selfridge, Jr., "The Navy in the Red River," *B & L*, IV, 364–365; Brooksher, *War Along the Bayous*, 190–193; Porter, *Naval History*, 520–524; Porter, *Incidents and Anecdotes*, 239–243; Musicant, *Divided Waters*, 301–302.

25. ORN, I, 26: 92–96, 112, 124, 129–132, 137–138, 142–145, 150–154, 317. 775–776, 779, 793; OR, I, 34, 1: 209, 310, 402–406, 491, 585–586; OR, I, 34, 3: 65–66; *New Orleans Era*, May 17, 1864; *New Orleans Times*, May 18, 1864; *Columbus (WI) Democrat*, May 29, 1895; "Joseph Bailey," in Smith, *Civil War Biographies from the Western Waters*, 15–16; Albert B. Paine, "The Red River Dam," *Morning Oregonian*, March 19, 1895; Steven D. Smith and George J. Castille III, "Bailey's Dam," *Louisiana Department of Culture, Recreation and Tourism Anthropological Study*, no. 8, March 1986, http://www.crt.state.la.us/archaeology/BAILEYS/baileys.htm (August 7, 2006); Porter, *Incidents and Anecdotes*, 248–249; Porter, *Naval History*, 525–534; Johnson, *Red River Campaign*, 256–262; Musicant, *Divided Waters*, 303–304; Taylor, *Destruction and Reconstruction*, 186–189; Irwin, "The Red River Campaign," *B & L*, IV, 358–362; Hearn, *Admiral David Dixon Porter*, 258–265; Joiner and Vetter, "The Union Naval Expedition on the Red River," 60–62; 64–67; Selfridge, Jr., "The Navy in the Red River," *B & L*, IV, 365–366; Brooksher, *War Along the Bayous*, 209–215.

26. ORN, I, 26: 445; Samuel S. Armstrong, "Trenton in the Mexican, Civil, and Spanish-American Wars," in *A History of Trenton, 1679–1929*," Trenton Historical Society, http://trentonhistory.org/His/Wars.html (accessed January 11, 2012).

27. ORN, I, 24: 369–373, 779–780; OR, I, 34: 1: 987; ORN, II, 1: 56; Arthur W. Bergeron, Jr., *Guide to Louisiana Confederate Military Units, 1861–1865* (Baton Rouge: Louisiana State University Press, 1996), 20–21, 28–29; David M. Rubenstein, "Guide to the Eltinge-Lord Family Papers, 1856–1871," *Duke University Libraries*, http://library.duke.edu/digitalcollections/rbmscl/eltinge/inv/ (accessed November 18, 2011); "George P. Lord," in Smith, *Civil War Biographies from the Western Waters*, 145; Canney, *The Old Steam Navy* II, 97; Frederick Way, Jr., *Way's Packet Directory, 1848–1994: Passenger Steamboats of the Mississippi River System Since the Advent of Photography in Mid-Continent America* (Athens:Ohio University Press, 1983, rev. ed. (Athens OH: Ohio University, 1994), 86. Without cannon, Lt. Bennett and his surviving men returned to Alexandria, where they were stationed for the remainder of the war.

Chapter 5

1. U.S. Navy Department, *Official Records of the Union and Confederate Navies in the War of the Rebellion*, 31 vols. (Washington, D.C.: GPO, 1894–1922), Series I, Vol. 24, 217–225, 370–374 (cited hereafter as ORN, followed by a comma, the series number in Roman numerals, a comma, the volume number in Arabic, a colon, and the page in Arabic, e.g., ORN, I, 24: 217–225, 370–374); Alfred T. Mahan, *The

Gulf and Inland Waters, vol. 3 of *The Navy in the Civil War* (New York: Scribner's, 1883), 124–126; *Chicago Daily Tribune*, February 2, 1863; *New York Herald*, February 27, 1863; *Daily National Intelligencer*, March 4, 1863; Marshall Scott Legan, "The Confederate Career of a Union Ram," *Louisiana History* 33 (Summer 2000), 283–285; William Shaw Ward, "How We Ran the Vicksburg Batteries," *Magazine of American History and Notes and Queries* 14 (July-December 1885), 600; "Charles Rivers Ellet," in Myron J. Smith, Jr., *Civil War Biographies from the Western Waters* (Jefferson, NC: McFarland, 2015), 70. A medical student at the outbreak of the war, CRE joined the unorthodox ram squadron his father, Charles Ellet, Jr., had established the previous spring. Following this adventure below Vicksburg, he would, beginning in May, command the infantry of the Mississippi Marine Brigade until his health failed.

2. ORN, I, 24: 370–371, 374, 376–377, 383–384, 391; Ward, "How We Ran the Vicksburg Batteries," 601–602; *Brooklyn Daily Eagle*, February 16, 1863; *New York Tribune*, February 15, 1863; *Chicago Daily Tribune*, March 1, 1864; *Memphis Daily Appeal*, March 2, 1863; *New York Herald*, March 8, 1863; Chester G. Hearn, *Ellet's Brigade: The Strangest Outfit of All* (Baton Rouge: Louisiana State University Press, 2000), 95–102; Mahan, *The Gulf and Inland Waters*, 126–127, 130; Steven M. Mayeux, *Earthen Walls and Iron Men: Fort DeRussy, Louisiana, and the Defense of the Red River* (Knoxville: University of Tennessee Press, 2007), 14–18, 34–35; Frederick Way, Jr., *Way's Packet Directory, 1848–1994: Passenger Steamboats of the Mississippi River System Since the Advent of Photography in Mid-Continent America* (Athens: Ohio University Press, 1983, rev. ed. 1994), 488; ORN, II, 1: 107, 271; Legan, "Confederate Career," 284–285; Donald L. Canney, *The Confederate Steam Navy, 1861–1865* (Atglen, PA: Schiffer, 2016), 145–146.

3. ORN, I, 24: 376–378; *Brooklyn Daily Eagle*, March 6, 1863; Ward, "How We Ran the Vicksburg Batteries," 601–604; *Chicago Daily Tribune*, February 20, 1863; *New York Herald*, February 27, 1863; Hearn, *Ellet's Brigade*, 109–110; Mahan, *The Gulf and Inland Waters*, 126; Legan, "Confederate Career," 286–287.

4. ORN, I, 24: 374, 384–385, 400; *New York Tribune*, February 15, 1863; *Richmond Examiner*, February 21, 1863; *New York Times*, February 25, 1863; *Chicago Daily Tribune*, March 1, 1863; *Cincinnati Daily Commercial*, March 4, 1863; *St. Joseph Gazette*, quoted in *Natchez Courier*, March 11, 1863; Hearn, *Ellet's Brigade*, 102–103; Mahan, *The Gulf and Inland Waters*, 127–128; Mayeux, *Earthen Walls and Iron Men*, 18–32.

5. ORN, I, 24: 376–380, 385–386, 393, 398–399; U.S. War Department, *The War of the Rebellion: A Compilation of the Official Records of the Union and Confederate Armies* (128 vols., Washington, D.C.: GPO, 1880–1901), Series I, Vol.24, Part1, 346 (cited hereafter as OR, followed by a comma, the series number in Roman numerals, a comma, the volume number in Arabic, a colon, and the page in Arabic, e.g., OR, I, 24: 1: 346; *Natchez Weekly Courier*, February 27, 1863; *Chicago Daily Tribune*, March 1, 1864; *Cincinnati Daily Commercial*, March 4, 1863; *New York Herald*, March 8, 1863; Legan, "Confederate Career," 286–288; Hearn, *Ellet's Brigade*, 102–103, 109–114; Mahan, *The Gulf and Inland Waters*, 128–129; Mayeux, *Earthen Walls and Iron Men*, 33–36, 40–44, 48–49, 55; "Career of Gen. Joseph Lancaster Brent," *Confederate Veteran* 17 (1909), 345–347; H.D. Barrows, "J. Lancaster Brent," *Quarterly of the Historical Society of Southern California*, VI (1905), 238–241; "Joseph Lancaster Brent" and "William Farley Storrow Lovell," in Myron J. Smith, Jr., *Civil War Biographies*, 30, 146; Jonathan Malcolm Lambley, "Joseph Alexander Smith Acklen," Find A Grave, http://www.findagrave.com/cgi-bin/fg.cgi?page=gr&GRid=21012245 (cited June 10, 2015); Way, *Way's Packet Directory*, 196. Special Order 49 is quoted on p. 13 of Brent's memoir, *The Lugo Case: Capture of the Ironclad Indianola* (New Orleans: Searcy & Pfaff, 1926), while his efforts to ready his flotilla are described on pp. 14–30.

6. ORN, I, 24: 372, 380. 382–383, 393–394, 401; *St. Louis Daily Missouri Republican*, March 6, 1863; *Chicago Daily Tribune*, March 3, 1863; *New York Herald*, March 8, 1863; *New York Times*, March 19, 1863; Mahan, *The Gulf and Inland Waters*, 129–130; Mayeux, *Earthen Walls and Iron Men*, 50–63; Way, *Way's Packet Directory*, 130; Brent, *The Lugo Case*, 31–59; Legan, "Confederate Career," 289–290; Arthur W. Bergeron, Jr., *Guide to Louisiana Confederate Military Units, 1861–1865* (Baton Rouge: Louisiana State University Press, 1989), 144–145; Hearn, *Ellet's Brigade*, 115; "Charles H. Frith," Ancient Faces, http://www.ancientfaces.com/person/charles-h-frith/117731647 (accessed October 28, 2015).

7. ORN, I, 24: 376, 380–381, 388–390, 392, 394–396, 403–404, 408; OR, I, 24, 1: 363–368; *Memphis Daily Appeal*, March 11, 1863; Mahan, *The Gulf and Inland Waters*, 130–133; Mayeux, *Earthen Walls and Iron Men*, 63–68; Brent, *The Lugo Case*, 59–66; Legan, "Confederate Career," 291–292; Hearn, *Ellet's Brigade*, 115–117; *Shreveport Weekly News*, March 23, 1863; "Henry M. Mixer," in Smith, *Civil War Biographies*, 166–167. In addition to Isaac and his companions, the *New York Times* later reported, "eight or nine of the crew escaped by jumping from the bow and running to the woods" (*New York Times*, March 19, 1863).

8. ORN, I, 24: 390, 397, 401–402, 411; OR, I, 24, 1: 363–368; *Natchez Weekly Courier*, March 4, 1863; *Memphis Daily Appeal*, March 2, 1863; *Chicago Daily Tribune*, March 5, 7, 1863; *New York Times*, March 12, 1863; *New York Herald*, March 12, 1863; Mahan, *The Gulf and Inland Waters*, 132; Mayeux, *Earthen Walls and Iron Men*, 69–72; Brent, *The Lugo Case*, 66–73; Legan, "Confederate Career," 290–292, 294; Robert Collins Suhr, "The Union's Hard-Luck Ironclad," *American Civil War* 6 (1993), 34–40;

Hearn, *Ellet's Brigade*, 116; "William Wirt Adams," in Smith, *Civil War Biographies*, 10; John J. McAfee, "Charles H. Hays," in *Kentucky Politicians* (Louisville: Press of the Courier-Journal, 1886), 78. The POWs arrived at Jackson, MS, on March 10 (*Vicksburg Whig*, March 11, 1863).

9. ORN, I, 24: 388–392, 395–397, 408–412, 686, 714; Mahan, *The Gulf and Inland Waters*, 132–133; Mayeux, *Earthen Walls and Iron Men*, 72–80; Legan, "Confederate Career," 294–296; Suhr, "The Union's Hard-Luck Ironclad," 34–40; Hearn, *Ellet's Brigade*, 117–118; David Dixon Porter, *Incidents and Anecdotes of the Civil War* (New York: D. Appleton, 1886), 134; *Chicago Daily Tribune*, February 12, 24, 27, March 5, 1863; *Jackson Mississippian*, March 5, 1863; *Vicksburg Whig*, February 27, March 5, 1863; *St. Louis Daily Missouri Democrat*, March 6, 1863; *Weekly Mississippian*, March 11,1863; *Memphis Daily Appeal*, March 11, 1863; *New York Herald*, March 12, 1863; *Richmond Examiner*, March 12, 1863; *Brooklyn Daily Eagle*, March 16, 1863; *New York Times*, March 12, 19, 25, 29, 1863; *Harper's Weekly*, March 28, 1863; E. Cort Williams, "The Cruise of 'The Black Terror,'" in Robert Hunter, ed., *Sketches of War History: Papers Prepared for the Ohio Commandery of the Loyal Legion of the United States* (3 vols. (Cincinnati: Robert Clarke, 1890), vol. 3, 151; *Harper's Weekly*, April 11, 1863. Lt. Hassler had enlisted in his regiment near Cleveland, OH, in 1861 for three years. Previously 2nd lieutenant of Co. K, he would be killed in action near Vicksburg on May 10. "Sebaldus Hassler" in volume 4 of *Official Roster of the Soldiers of the State of Ohio in the War of the Rebellion, 1861–1865* (Akron: Werner, 1887), 16; "William F.G. Shanks," in volume 3 of *The National Cyclopedia of American Biography* (New York: James T. White, 1893), 459–460; Albert H. Bodman, "'In Sight of Vicksburg': Private Diary of a Northern War Correspondent," ed. Leo M. Kaiser, *Chicago Historical Society Bulletin* 34 (May 1956), 209. Exceptions to Mahan and Williams are few. The inaccurate reporting on Porter's dummy gunboat has appeared in every book and article for over a hundred years except for Mayeux's retelling of the *Indianola* story. The list is too long to footnote here. Lt. Col. Woods, a prominent Buckeye lawyer and speaker of the state house, was appointed a federal circuit court judge before serving (1880–1887) as an associate U.S. Supreme Court justice (Timothy L. Hull, *Supreme Court Justices: A Biographical Dictionary* (New York: Facts on File, 2001), 179).

10. ORN, I, 19: 644; ORN, I, 20: 28, 31; ORN, I, 24: 533, 541, 765; *Chicago Daily Times*, March 4, 1863; *Chicago Daily Tribune*, March 28, 1863; *Brooklyn Daily Eagle*, March 6, 16, 27, April 4, 1863; *St. Louis Daily Missouri Republican*, March 14, 1863; *New York Times*, March 16, 1863; *Jackson Mississippian*, March 11, 1863; "Gustavus Vasa Fox," in Smith, *Civil War Biographies from the Western Waters*, 82–83; Robert Mean Thompson and Richard Wainwright, ed., *Confidential Correspondence of Gustavus Vasa Fox, Assistant Secretary of the Navy, 1861–1865*, 2 vols. (New York: De Vinne, 1918), vol. I: 327–328, and II, 158, 160, 165–166; Legan, "Confederate Career," 297; Loyal Farragut, "Farragut at Port Hudson," *Putnam's Magazine* 5 (October 1908), 44.

11. ORN, I, 24: 543, 552, 567–568, 572, 701, 705, 707; OR, I, 24, 3: 200–201; "William Rion Hoel," "John Alexander McClernand," "Elias Kenneth Owen," and "Byron Wilson," in Smith, *Civil War Biographies from the Western Waters*, 114–115, 155, 179, 261; "The Civil War Diary of Confederate Soldier George D. Wise," *The North Jersey History and Genealogical Collections*, http://cdm15387.contentdm.oclc.org/cdm/landingpage/collection/p16100coll2 (accessed November 12, 2015). The date on Hoel's report regarding his examination of the *Indianola*'s wreck site is incorrect and hence is out of order in ORN (ORN, I, 24: 543, 552, 705).

12. ORN, I, 25: 28–29, 54–55, 59, 141, 147–148, 172; "Charles Anderson Dana," "John McLeod Murphy," "Oliver Donaldson," "John George Walker" in Smith, *Civil War Biographies from the Western Waters*, 58, 63, 173–174, 248–249; Richard Taylor, *Destruction and Reconstruction: Personal Experiences of the Late War* (New York: D. Appleton, 1879), 137–139; Joseph P. Blessington, *The Campaigns of Walker's Texas Division* (Austin: Pemberton, 1968), 79–93; Hearn, *Admiral David Dixon Porter*, 228; John D. Winters, *The Civil War in Louisiana* (Baton Rouge: Louisiana State University Press, 1963), 198–203; Joseph H. Parks, *General Edmund Kirby Smith, C.S.A* (Baton Rouge: Louisiana State University Press, 1954), 277–278; Robert L. Kerby, *Kirby Smith's Confederacy: The Trans-Mississippi South, 1863–1865* (New York: Columbia University Press, 1972), 112–114; N.H. Winchell, "A Sketch of Richard Owen," *American Geologist* 6 (September 1890), 135–145. In August 1872, Owen became the first president of Purdue University.

13. ORN, I, 25: 172, 182–183, 218; Scott D. Jordan to his wife, June 30, July 5, 1863, in *Civil War Letters of Scott D. Jordan, Produced for Eleanor Jordan West* (CD-ROM; Glendale, AZ: Doug@Bellnotes.com, 2007), cited hereafter as Jordan Letters, with date. Nelson was correct; it would be well over a year before the *Indianola* was raised. Fortunately, the USN had by then a skilled expert of its own on hand to prevent her subsequent loss.

14. ORN, I, 25: 301–302; Jordan Letters, August 8, 12, 1863.

15. ORN, I, 25: 378, 383, 401, 507, 583, 609, 624–625, 638, 678, 692, 726; Jordan Letters, August 8, October 24, 27, December 6, 1863, January 6, February 6, 1864; William H. Elder, "September 1, 1863," in *Civil War Diary (1862–1863) of Bishop William Henry Elder, Bishop of Nashville* (Jackson, MS: R.O. Gerow, Bishop of Natchez-Jackson, 1960), 125. Though hope for his return was retained by Carondelet crewmen, the popular Murphy was unable to return; indeed, he eventually resigned his commission, on July 30, 1864. Having been appointed an acting ensign the previous October, James C. Gipson would be

promoted to acting master on October 24. When Lt. Cmdr. Mitchell assumed command of the *Carondelet* in November, Gipson was given the new tinclad *Exchange*. Near Greenville, MS, on June 5, 1864, his light draught was attacked by Confederate masked batteries. She was heroically fought and took severe damage. For his gallantry, Gipson was appointed an acting volunteer lieutenant on July 9. He would be honorably discharged on November 14, 1865 (Edward W. Callahan, *List of Officers of the Navy of the United States and of the Marine Corps, from 1775 to 1900, Comprising a Complete Register of All Present and Former Commissioned, Warranted, and Appointed Officers of the United States Navy, and of the Marine Corps, Regular and Volunteer. Compiled from the Official Records of the Navy Department* (New York: L.R. Hamersly, 1901; reprnt., New York: Haskell House, 1969), 220; ORN, I, 26: 354–355, 385).

16. ORN, I, 25: 715, 738; ORN, I, 26: 5–6; "James Augustin Greer," "Amos R. Langthorne," and "James Lanning," in Smith, *Civil War Biographies from the Western Waters*, 97, 136–137.

17. ORN, I, 26: 178, 283, 322 330–331, 357,576–577 704; ORN, I, 27: 53; *St. Louis Daily Missouri Republican*, March 9, 1864; "Samuel Phillips Lee," in Smith, *Civil War Biographies from the Western Waters*, 139.

18. ORN, I, 26: 722–723; ORN, I, 27: 24, 34, 53; "James Lanning," in Smith, *Civil War Biographies from the Western Waters*, 137.

19. The newspapers also advertised the auction of 5,000 tons of the ex-fleet's coal and a number of coal barges for November 28.

20. *St. Louis Daily Missouri Democrat*, November 21, 30, 1865; *Cincinnati Daily Commercial*, December 19, 1865.

21. ORN, II, 1: 107; Frederick Way, Jr., *Way's Packet Directory, 1848–1994: Passenger Steamboats of the Mississippi River System Since the Advent of Photography in Mid-Continent America* (Athens: Ohio University Press, 1983; rev. ed., 1994), 224.

Chapter 6

1. U.S. Navy Department, *Official Records of the Union and Confederate Navies in the War of the Rebellion*, 31 vols. (Washington, D.C.: GPO, 1894–1922), Series I, Vol. XXIV, 50–56, 58–60, 318, 453–454, 463–464, 469–470, 472, 564, 659–660 (cited hereafter as ORN, followed by a comma, the series number in Roman numerals, a comma, the volume number in Arabic, a colon, and the page in Arabic); ORN, I, 27: 127; U.S. War Department, *The War of the Rebellion: A Compilation of the Official Records of the Union and Confederate Armies*, 128 vols. (Washington, D.C.: GPO, 1880–1901), Series I, Vol. 23, Pt. 2: 136 (cited hereafter as OR, followed by a comma, the series number in Roman numerals, a comma, the volume number in Arabic, a colon, and the page in Arabic); Benjamin Franklin Cooling, *Fort Donelson's Legacy: War and Society in Kentucky and Tennessee, 1862–1863* (Knoxville: University of Tennessee Press, 1997), 216–217; Lurton Dunham Ingersoll, *Iowa and the Rebellion* (Philadelphia, PA: J.B. Lippincott, 1866), 441–456; John A. Eisterhold, Fort Heiman, Forgotten Fortress," *West Tennessee Historical Society Papers* 38 (1974), 47–50; "Thomas M. Farrell," "John W. Hartupee," "Stephen Augustus Hurlburt" and "George Augustus Lyon," in Myron J. Smith, Jr., *Civil War Biographies from the Western Waters* (Jefferson, NC: McFarland, 2015), 73, 107, 122–123, 147; "Alexander Asboth," in Ezra J. Warner, *Generals in Blue: Lives of the Union Commanders* (Baton Rouge: Louisiana State University Press, 1964), 11–12; "Frederick E. Potter, MD," *New Hampshire Medical Society Transactions* (Concord, N.H.: Ira C. Evans, 1903), 240.

2. ORN, I, 24:207, 517–518. 520, 523, 552, 703, ORN, I, 25: 29; OR, I, 24, 1: 25; OR, I, 24, 3:151–152; *New York Times*, April 4, 16, 1863; *Chicago Daily Tribune*, April 4,1863; William L. Shea and Terrence J. Winschel, *Vicksburg Is the Key: The Struggle for the Mississippi Valley* (Great Campaigns of the Civil War Series; Lincoln: University of Nebraska Press, 2003), 74–75, 90–91; Michael B. Ballard, *Vicksburg: The Campaign That Opened the Mississippi* (Chapel Hill: University of North Carolina Press, 2004), 186–187; Chester G. Hearn, *Admiral David Dixon Porter: The Civil War Years* (Annapolis: Naval Institute Press, 1996),190–192, 207–208; Samuel Carter III, *The Final Fortress: The Campaign for Vicksburg, 1862–1863* (New York: St. Martin's, 1980), 147–149; Jack D. Coombe, *Thunder Along the Mississippi: The River Battles That Split the Confederacy* (New York: Bantam, 1996), 210–211; David Dixon Porter, *Incidents and Anecdotes of the Civil War* (New York: Sherman, 1885), 163–165; William T. Sherman, *Memoirs of General W.T. Sherman, Written by Himself*, 2 vols. (New York: Appleton, 1875; reprnt., New York: Penguin, 2000), vol. I: 309–310; William H.C. Michael, "How the Mississippi Was Opened," *Civil War Sketches and Incidents; Papers Read Before the Nebraska Commandery, Military Order of the Loyal Legion of the United States* (Omaha: The Commandery, 1902), 48; Francis V. Green, *The Mississippi*, vol. 8 of *Campaigns of the Civil War* (New York: Scribners, 1883), 178; James R. Soley, *Admiral Porter* (New York: D. Appleton, 1903), 311; Edwin C. Bearss and Warren E. Grabau, "How Porter's Flotilla Ran the Gauntlet Past Vicksburg," *Civil War Times Illustrated* 1 (December 1962), 38; James R. Arnold, "Rough Work on the Mississippi," *Naval History* 13, no. 5 (1999), 38; Gustavus Vasa Fox, *Confidential Correspondence of Gustavas Vasa Fox, Assistant Secretary of the Navy, 1861–1865*, ed. Robert M. Thompson and Richard Wainwright, 2 vols. (New York: Naval History Society, 1919; reprnt., Freeport, NY: Books for Libraries,

1972), vol. 2: 172). Porter nearly lost his fleet, including the *Tuscumbia*'s sister ship *Chillicothe*, a year later in the Red River Campaign.

    3. OR, I, 24, 1: 67–68, 70, 74; OR, I, 24, 3: 151–152, 167–168,; ORN, I, 24: 520–521, 659, 671, 689, 703; *New York Times*, April 10, 1863; *Harrisburg Daily Patriot and Union*, April 23, 1863; *Memphis Daily Appeal*, April 9, 11, 1863; *Mobile Daily Advertiser and Register*, April 12, 1863; Ulysses S. Grant, *Memoirs and Selected Letters: Personal Memoirs of U.S. Grant, Selected Letters, 1839–1865*, ed. Mary D. and William S. McFeely; New York: Library of America, 1990), 295–296, 305; "Fred Grant as a Boy with the Army," *Confederate Veteran* 16 (January 1908), 10; Richard L. Kiper, *Major General John A. McClernand: Politician in Uniform* (Kent, OH: Kent State University, 1999), 204; Ballard, *The Civil War in Mississippi*, 139–140 "Richard James ('Uncle Dick') Oglesby" and "William Henry Tunnard," in Smith, *Civil War Biographies from the Western Waters*, 155, 178, 241–242; Mark A. Plummer, *Lincoln's Rail Splitter: Governor Richard J. Oglesby* (Urbana: University of Illinois Press, 2001); William H. Tunnard, *A Southern Record: The History of the Third Regiment Louisiana Infantry* (Baton Rouge: Printed for the Author, 1866), 223–224; Edwin C. Bearss, *The Vicksburg Campaign*, 3 vols. (Dayton, OH: Morningside, 1985–1986), vol. 2: 27); Harry P. Owens, *Steamboats and the Cotton Economy: River Trade in the Yazoo-Mississippi Delta* (Jackson: University of Mississippi Press, 1990), 60–61. The Duckport Canal, like the Williams and Lake Providence efforts, would be unsuccessful (Michael B. Ballard, *The Civil War in Mississippi: Major Campaigns and Battles* (Jackson: University Press of Mississippi, 2011), 138; Bearss, *The Vicksburg Campaign*, II, 43–51).

    4. ORN, I, 24: 521, 537, 544–545, 553–555, 659–660, 690; OR, I, 24, 1: 489–493; OR, I, 24, 2: 336–337; OR, I, 24, 3: 207–208, 688; *New York Times*, April 10, 29, 1863; *Chicago Daily Tribune*, April 28, 1863; Hearn, *Admiral David Dixon Porter*, 208–209; Arnold, "Rough Work on the Mississippi," 39–41); Edwin C. Bearss, *The Campaign for Vicksburg*, 3 vols. (Dayton, OH: Morningside, 1986), vol. 2: 64; Ballard, *The Civil War in Mississippi*, 197–198; Coombe, *Thunder Along the Mississippi*, 211–213; Bearss and Grabau, "How Porter's Flotilla Ran the Gauntlet Past Vicksburg," 39–41; "Daniel Beltzhoover," "Edward Higgins," "Andrew Jackson, 3rd," and "Frederick Nash Ogden," in Smith, *Civil War Biographies from the Western Waters*, 21, 112–113, 124, 177; Robert Dabney Calhoun, "The John Perkins Family of Northeast Louisiana," *Louisiana Historical Quarterly* 19 (1936), 70–88; Warren E. Grabau, *98 Days: A Geographer's View of the Vicksburg Campaign* (Knoxville: University of Tennessee Press, 2000), 39–50; Frederick Way, Jr., *Way's Packet Directory, 1848–1994: Passenger Steamboats of the Mississippi River System Since the Advent of Photography in Mid-Continent America* (Athens: Ohio University Press, 1983; rev. ed., 1994), 169, 211,427–428; "Fred Grant as a Boy with the Army," 10; The *Forest Queen*'s September escape is detailed in Smith, *Tinclads in the Civil War* (Jefferson, NC: McFarland, 2010), 67; Michael Wayne, *The Reshaping of Plantation Society: The Natchez District, 1860–1880* (Baton Rouge: Louisiana State University Press, 1983), 31–32; Oran Perry, "Regimental History," in Carolyn S. Bridge, comp., *These Men Were Heroes Once: The 69th Indiana Volunteer Infantry* (West Lafayette, IN: Twin, 2005), 13–14 (1–32); Perry, "The Entering Wedge," in vol. I of *Indiana MOLLUS War Papers* (New York: Military Order of the Loyal Legion of the United States, 1898; reprnt. as vol. 24, Wilmington, DE: Broadfoot, 1992), 365–370 (362–365); "Oran D. Perry," USGenWeb, http://ucgenweb.org/Union%20County%20Personalities/oran_d%20Perry.htm (accessed December 1, 2015).

    5. ORN, I, 24: 563, 565, 701, 704; *Chicago Daily Tribune*, April 28, 1863; Mary Bobbitt Townsend, *Yankee Warhorse: A Biography of Major General Peter Osterhaus* (Columbia: University of Missouri Press, 2010), 82–84; "Grant to McClernand, April 14, 16, 1863" and "Porter to Grant, April 15, 1863," in vol. 8, Ulysses S. Grant, *The Papers of Ulysses S. Grant*, ed. John Y. Simon, 32 vols. (Edwardsville: Southern Illinois University Press, 1967–2012), 81; Charles E. Affeld, "Charles Affeld Diary Transcription from April 15 through July 4th, 1863," The Taylor—Taylor's Battery, http://www.taylorsbattery.org/Affeld%20Diary%20transcription.htm (accessed December 1, 2015); "Company D, 29th Illinois Regiment," Illinois Civil War Rosters, http://civilwar.illinoisgenweb.org/r050/029-d-in.html (accessed November 29, 2015); Shea and Winschel, *Vicksburg Is the Key*, 98; Perry, "The Entering Wedge," 372–373; Charles Heckman ("Heck") Gulick: Letters from 'Heck,'" ed. Stan Hamper, *Civil War Times Illustrated* 21 (June 1982), 24. Born in Kentucky and the brother of a steamboat pilot, Gulick also took to the river. He reportedly died in Kentucky three years after the war ("Charles Heckman Gulick, Circa 1836-Circa 1868," MyHeritage, http://www.myheritage.com/names/charles_gulick (accessed November 29, 2015); Bearss and Grabau, "How Porter's Flotilla Ran the Gauntlet Past Vicksburg," 41; Franc Bang Wilkie, *Pen and Powder* (Boston: Ticknor, 1888), 313.

    6. ORN, I, 24: 521, 553–555, 561–567, 682, 690, 717; *Vicksburg Whig*, April 17, 20, 1863; *Jackson Daily Mississippian*, April 18, 1863; *Memphis Daily Appeal*, April 18, 1863; *Chicago Evening Journal*, April 21, 1863; *New York Times*, April 23, 1863; *Daily Cleveland Herald*, April 27, 1863; *Chicago Daily Tribune*, April 28, 1863; *National Tribune*, January 20, 1887; Henry Walke, *Naval Scenes and Reminiscences of the Civil War in the United States on the Southern and Western Waters During the Years 1861, 1862 and 1863, with the History of That Period Compared and Corrected from Authentic Sources* (New York: F.R. Reed, 1877), 354–355, 363; Wilkie, *Pen and Powder*, 313–317; "Fred Grant as a Boy with the Army," 10; Charles A. Dana, *Recollections of the Civil War* (New York: D. Appleton, 1898), 37–38; Affeld, "Charles Affeld Diary Transcription from April 15 through July 4th, 1863," The Taylor—Taylor's Battery, http://www.tay

lorsbattery.org/Affeld%20Diary%20transcription.htm (accessed December 1, 2015); David D. Porter, *Incidents and Anecdotes of the Civil War* (New York: D. Appleton, 1885; reprnt., Harrisburg, PA: The Archive Society, 1997), 175–178; Perry, "The Entering Wedge," 373–375; James T. Hogane, "Reminiscences of the Siege of Vicksburg," *Southern Historical Society Papers* 11 (April-May 1883), 4854–4886; Hearn, *Admiral David Dixon Porter*, 209–219; Ulysses S. Grant, *Memoirs and Selected Letters: Personal Memoirs of U.S. Grant, Selected Letters, 1839–1865*, ed. Mary D. and William S. McFeely; New York: Library of America, 1990), 315; Gulick, "Letters from 'Heck,'" 26 (24–31); Shea and Winschel, *Vicksburg Is the Key,* 98–100; Arnold, "Rough Work on the Mississippi," 41–42; Bearss, *The Campaign for Vicksburg*, II, 64–74; Coombe, *Thunder on the Mississippi*, 213–214; Bearss and Grabau, "How Porter's Flotilla Ran the Gauntlet Past Vicksburg," 43–46; Ballard, *The Civil War in Mississippi*, 199–202; Peter F. Walker, *Vicksburg: A People at War, 1860–1865* (Chapel Hill: University of North Carolina Press, 1960), 151–152; Fox, *Confidential Correspondence*, II, 458; "Frank Arnold," Vicksburg Tombstone Database, http://www.vicksburg.org/index.php/component/easytablepro/tombstone-database/405/arnold-frank (accessed December 15, 2015); James R. Soley, "Naval Operations in the Vicksburg Campaign," in *Battles and Leaders of the Civil War*, ed. Robert V. Johnson and Clarence C. Buel, 4 vols. (New York: Century, 1884–1887, reprnt. Thomas Yoseloff, 1956), vol. 3: 566; Townsend, *Yankee Racehorse*, 84.

    7. OR, I, 24, 3: 200–201; ORN, I, 24: 704; *St. Louis Daily Missouri Republican*, April 21, 1863; *St. Louis Daily Missouri Democrat*, April 21, 1863; *Chicago Daily Tribune*, April 21, 1863; *New York Times*, April 22, 1863; *Daily Cleveland Herald*, April 22, 1863; *Cincinnati Daily Commercial*, April 22, 1863; *New York Herald*, April 22, 1863; *Boston Daily Advertiser*, April 22, 1863; *North American and United States Gazette*, April 22, 1863; Henry Clay Warmoth, *War, Politics and Reconstruction* (Columbia: University of South Carolina Press, 2006); Paul H. Hass, ed., "The Vicksburg Diary of Henry Clay Warmoth," *Journal of Mississippi History* 71 (November 1969–February 1970), 341–342; Townsend, *Yankee Racehorse*, 84; Porter, *Incidents and Anecdotes*, 179–180; Edwin C. Bearss, "Grand Gulf's Role in the Civil War," *Civil War History* 5 (March 1959), 19–22; John David Winters, *The Civil War in Louisiana* (Baton Rouge: Louisiana State University Press, 1963), 192; Hearn, *Admiral David Dixon Porter*, 219. Pilot John Taylor of the *Henry Clay* reached Memphis aboard the transport *Crescent City* on April 20 and he offered his observations to a reporter from the *Chicago Daily Tribune* (April 21,1863).

    8. ORN, I, 24: 600–606, 626–628, 704–705; OR, I, 24, 1: 79–80, 663–664; OR, I, 24, 3: 225–228; *New York Herald*, April 28, 1863; *New York Times*, May 12, 1863; Hearn, *Admiral David Dixon Porter*, 219–221; "John Stevens Bowen," in Smith, *Civil War Biographies from the Western Waters*, 26–27; Bearss, "Grand Gulf's Role in the Civil War," 21–22.

    9. ORN, I, 24: 606–609, 612, 626–628, 660, 682–683, 705; OR, I, 24, 1: 27–28, 79–82, 142, 663–664; OR, I, 24, 3: 204–205, 207–208, 211, 221, 225–226, 228, 231, 237–238; *New York Times*, May 11, 1863; Walke, *Naval Scenes*, 366, 372–373; Shea and Winschel, *Vicksburg Is the Key*, 100–103; Dana, *Recollections of the Civil War*, 41–42; Soley, "Navy in the Vicksburg Campaign," III, 567; 3 Grant, *Memoirs and Selected Letters: Personal Memoirs of U.S. Grant, Selected Letters, 1839–1865,* 95; Alfred T. Mahan, *The Gulf and Inland Waters*, vol. 3 of *The Navy in the Civil War* (New York: Scribner's, 1883),158–159; Arnold, "Rough Work on the Mississippi," 43; Fox, *Confidential Correspondence*, II, 458; Ballard, *Vicksburg*, 214–217; Coombe, *Thunder on the Mississippi*, 215; Hearn, *Admiral David Dixon Porter*, 220–223; Bearss, *The Campaign for Vicksburg*, II, 271–274, 277; Bearss, "Grand Gulf's Role in the Civil War," 20–22. To help prevent the reinforcement of Grand Gulf, Maj. Gen. Sherman, with support from the squadron's upper division, conducted a two-day feint up the Yazoo. Col. Benjamin Grierson also led a cavalry raid through Mississippi into Louisiana (Shea and Winschel, *Vicksburg Is the Key*, 102–103; Myron J. Smith, Jr., *The Fight for the Yazoo, August 1862–July 1864* (Jefferson, NC: McFarland, 2012), 307–318; Winters, *The Civil War in Louisiana*, 95).

    10. ORN, I, 24: 610–628, 684, 690, 699, 702, 705–706; OR, I, 24, 1, 142, 574–576; OR, I, 24, 3: 792–793, 797, 800; *New York Times*, May 11, 1863; *New York Herald*, May 11, 1863; *Chicago Daily Times*, May 11, 1863; *Jackson Daily Mississippian*, April 30, 1863; *Brooklyn Daily Eagle*, May 21, 1863; Walke, *Naval Scenes and Reminiscences*, 374–376, 387–389; Fox, *Confidential Correspondence*, II, 458; Coombe, *Thunder on the Mississippi*, 215–216; Ballard, *Vicksburg,* 218–219; Joseph O. Jackson, ed., *Some of the Boys: The Civil War Letters of Isaac Jackson, 1862–1865* (Carbondale: Southern Illinois University Press, 1960), 86–87; Shea and Winschel, *Vicksburg Is the Key,* 102–105; Mahan, *The Gulf and Inland Waters*, 160–162; Warren E. Grabau, *98 Days: A Geographer's View of the Vicksburg Campaign* (Knoxville: University of Tennessee Press, 2000), 135–138; Dana, *Recollections of the Civil War*, 43; Hearn, *Admiral David Dixon Porter*, 223–225; Bearss, *The Campaign for Vicksburg*, II, 285–289; Bearss, "Grand Gulf's Role," 23–27; *The Pine Bluff (MS) Commercial*, December 17, 1904; Adam Kane, *The Western River Steamboat* (College Station: Texas A & M University Press, 2004), 118; Donald L. Canney, *The Old Steam Navy*, 2 vols. (Annapolis: Naval Institute Press, 1993), vol. 2: 98–99.

    11. ORN, I, 24:664–665, 706–707; ORN, I, 25: 15–20, 26; OR, I, 24, 3: 285, 326–327; Hearn, *Admiral David Dixon Porter*, 225–226, 228; William T. Sherman, *Memoirs of W.T. Sherman* (New York: Library of America, 1990), 351; F.G. Carnes, comp., "'We Can Hold Our Ground': Calvin Smith's Diary," *Civil War Times Illustrated* 24 (April 1985), 29.

12. ORN, I, 25: 21–33, 81, 90, 99; OR, I, 24, 2: 331–332, 337, 342–343, 345; Mahan, *The Gulf and Inland Waters*, 169; David Martin, *The Vicksburg Campaign* (Conshohocken, PA: Combined, 1994), 128; Hearn, *Admiral David Dixon Porter*, 230–231; Carnes, comp., "'We Can Hold Our Ground,'" 30; Edwin C. Bearss, "The Vicksburg River Defenses and the Enigma of 'Whistling Dick,'" *Journal of Mississippi History* 29 (January 1957), 21–24; Gulick, "Letters from 'Heck,'" 29–31. A member of the 1st Louisiana Heavy Artillery directly involved in the actions of May 19–22, Lt. A.L. Slack later indicated that from conversations he held with Union officers after Vicksburg's surrender all Federal officers confused "Whistling Dick" and the "Widow Blakely" (*Vicksburg Daily Herald*, May 23, 1900).

13. ORN, I, 25: 517; ORN, I, 26: 21, 318, 320, 459, 717, 750, ORN, I, 27: 56. Also, in May 1864, the bulk of the ironclad's ammunition, left behind when she departed Memphis the previous fall, was removed from the navy yard to the magazine at Fort Pickering (ORN, I, 26: 280).

14. ORN, I, 27: 278–279, 344; ORN, II, 1:227; David Stephen Heidler, *Encyclopedia of the War of 1812* (Annapolis: Naval Institute Press, 2004), 591; "John William Livingston," in Smith, *Civil War Biographies from the Western Waters*, 144; *St. Louis Daily Missouri Democrat*, November 21, 30, 1865; *Cincinnati Daily Commercial*, December 19, 1865; Way, *Way's Packet Directory*, 460.

Chapter 7

1. U.S. Navy Department, *Official Records of the Union and Confederate Navies in the War of the Rebellion*, 31 vols. (Washington, D.C.: GPO, 1894–1922), Series I, Vol. XXIII, 373, 379–380, 388–390, 394–395, 444, 449 451–452, 472, 477, 487, 494, 630 (cited hereafter as ORN, followed by a comma, the series number in Roman numerals, a comma, the volume number in Arabic, a colon, and the page in Arabic); ORN, I, 24: 164–165, 417, 440–441, 466, 468, 470–471, 505, 540, 571, 634, 670, 677; ORN, I, 25: 596–596, 681, 698–700, 733, 741; ORN, I, 26: 476, 488, 566, 573, 577, 724, 738–741; ORN, II, 1: 221; *Chicago Daily Tribune*, December 1, 1863; Chester G. Hearn, *Admiral David Dixon Porter: The Civil War Years* (Annapolis: Naval Institute Press, 1996), 145, 151–152; William H. Roberts, *Civil War Ironclads: The U.S. Navy and Industrial Mobilization* (Baltimore: Johns Hopkins University Press, 2002), 52; Donald L. Caney, *The Old Steam Navy:* vol. 2, *The Ironclads, 1842–1885* (Annapolis: Naval Institute Press, 1993), 95; Gustavus Vasa Fox, *Confidential Correspondence of Gustavus Vasa Fox, Assistant Secretary of the Navy, 1861–1865*, ed. Robert Means Thompson and Richard Wainwright, 2 vols. (New York: De Vinne, 1918–1919; eeprnt., Freeport, NY: Books for Libraries, 1971), vol. 2: 137–138); James R. Soley, *Admiral Porter* (New York: D. Appleton, 1903), 239; "Virginia Brown," *Tunstall Descendants*, http://wc.rootsweb.ancestry.com/cgi-bin/igm.cgi?op=GET&db=tunstall&id=I02811 (accessed December 1, 2015); Frederick Way, Jr., *Way's Packet Directory, 1848–1994: Passenger Steamboats of the Mississippi River System Since the Advent of Photography in Mid-Continent America* (Athens: Ohio University Press, 1983; re. ed. Athens: Ohio University Press, 1994), 448; "Tempest," in *Dictionary of American Naval Fighting Ships*, U.S. Navy Department, Naval Historical Center, http://www.history.navy.mil/danfs/t3/tempest.htm (accessed February 9, 2008). For a detailed review of the tinclad acquisition program, please see Chapter 3, "The Coming of the Tinclad," in *Tinclads in the Civil War: Union Light-Draught Gunboat Operations on Western Waters, 1862–1865* (Jefferson, NC: McFarland, 2010), 35–61.

2. ORN, II, 1: 27–246; Paul H. Silverstone, *Warships of the Civil War Navies* (Annapolis: Naval Institute Press, 1989), 164–180.

3. "Lewis Vital Bogy," *Biographical Directory of the United States Congress*, http://bioguide.congress.gov/scripts/biodisplay.pl?index=B000595 (accessed December 27, 2015); *Memorial Addresses on the Life and Character of Lewis V, Bogy, a Senator from Missouri* (44th Congress, 2nd sess.; Washington, D.C.: GPO, 1878); Agnes Wallace, "The Wiggins Ferry Monopoly," *Missouri Historical Review* 42 (October 1947), 8; John W. Leonard, *The Industries of St. Louis* (St. Louis: John W. Leonard, 1887), 76; ORN, II, 1: 67, 187; Smith, *Tinclads in the Civil War*, 52–54, 56; Richard Edwads, *Edwards' Annual Directory ... the City of St. Louis* (8th ed.; St Louis: Richard Edwards, 1866), 257; *St. Louis Post-Dispatch*, December 4, 1899; Walter Barlow Stevens, *St. Louis: The Fourth City, 1764–1911*, 3 vols. (St Louis: S.J. Clarke, 1939), vol. I: 108. Newspaper articles at the time of his death suggest various figures paid to Brown for his wartime work. The *San Francisco Chronicle* of December 4, 1899 flatly states that he "made nearly a million dollars in four years."

4. *St. Louis Post-Dispatch*, December 4, 1899; *Buffalo Evening Courier*, September 8, 1866; *New York Times*, September 9, 1866; *Warsaw Northern Indianan*, April 5, 1866; *St. Louis Post Dispatch*, December 4, 1899; Norbury Wayman, "The Physical Growth of the City of St. Louis, 1969," St. Louis City Planning Commission, https://www.stlouis-mo.gov/archive/history-physical-growth-stlouis/#golden (accessed December 31, 2015); William Hyde and Howard I. Conard, *Encyclopedia of the History of St. Louis*, 5 vols. (New York: Southern History, 1899), vol. 4: 2123; James Lowell Moore, *Introduction to the Writings of Andrew Jackson Davis* (Boston: Christopher, 1930); Louis C. Hunter, *Steamboats on the Western Rivers: An Economic and Technological History* (Cambridge, MA: Harvard University Press, 1949), 561–566, 632; Joseph Brown, "Autobiography Statement," in Emerson W. Gould, *50 Years on the Mississippi* (St

Louis: Nixon-James, 1889), 675; Gould, "The Atlantic and Mississippi Steamship Company," in Gould, *50 Years on the Mississippi*, 386–388; Missouri Pacific Historical Society, "MoPac's First 125 Years," Missouri Pacific Historical Society, http://www.mopac.org/corporate-history/73-missouri-pacific-railroad (accessed December 31, 2015); William E. Parish, Charles T. Jones, Jr., and Lawrence O. Christensen, *Missouri: The Heart of the Nation* (2nd ed.; Arlington Heights, IL: Harlan Davidson, 1992), 183–184,189–193; Richard J. Hardy, Richard R. Dohm, and David A. Leuthold, ed., *Missouri Government and Politics*, rev. and enl. ed. (Columbia: University of Missouri Press, 1995), 58; Walter A. Stevens, "The Missouri Tavern," *Missouri Historical Review* 15 (January 1921), 256; Joseph Brown, *Lecture on Early Reminiscences of Alton* (Alton, IL: Lovejoy Monument Association, 1896), 14; Philip Rose, *Andrew Johnson's Circle Trip* (Bloomington: Trafford, 2011), 129–135. C.C. Duble, son of Capt. John A. Duble, who had led a pick-up squadron of army gunboats at Cincinnati in 1862, wrote years later in a letter to the *Literary Digest* that his father was in command of the *Ruth* at this time (*Literary Digest* 38 (June 12, 1909), 1038.

    5. *St. Louis Daily Democrat*, July 21, 1867; Robert W. Jackson, *Rails Across the Mississippi: A History of the St. Louis Bridge* (Urbana: University of Illinois Press, 2001), 22–41; Union Merchants' Exchange of St. Louis, *Proceedings of the Mississippi River Improvement Convention Held in St. Louis, February 12–13, 1867* (St Louis: George Knapp, 1867), 55–60.

    6. *St. Louis Post-Dispatch*, December 4, 1899; James Cox, *St. Louis Through a Camera* (St Louis: Woodward and Tiernan, 1896), 57; Ernst D. Kargau et al., *The German Element in St. Louis* (Baltimore: Genealogical, 2000), 59; *The Statesman*, I (October 17, 1868), 10; *London Morning Republican*, December 4, 1868; *American Agriculturalist* 27 (December 1868), 430; *North American and United States Gazette*, March 8, 1869; Hunter, *Steamboats on the Western Rivers*, 632; *Harper's Weekly*, March 28, 1868; *New York Times*, July 6, 22, 1872; "George T. Brown," U.S. Senate, http://www.senate.gov/artandhistory/history/common/generic/SAA_George_Brown.htm (accessed March 18, 2014); Wilker T. Norton, ed. and comp., *Centennial History of Madison County, Illinois, and Its People, 1812–1912*, 2 vols., Chicago: Lewis, 1912), vol. I: 113–114; W.A. Newell and George H. Williams, "George T. Brown (1820–1880) *WoodBeeCarver*, http://woodbeecarver.com/lincoln/?p=21 (accessed March 19, 2014).

    7. *St. Louis Daily Republican*, July 15, 1879; *St. Louis Post-Dispatch*, December 4, 1899; Missouri (Secretary of State), "Joseph Brown," in *Missouri State Legislators, 1820–2000*, http://s1.sos.mo.gov/archives/history/historicallistings/molegb (accessed December 31, 2015); Jackson, *Rails Across the Mississippi*, 138, 209; William Franklin Switzler et al., *Switzler's Illustrated History of Missouri from 1541–1877* (St Louis: C.R. Barnes, 1879), 465–470; L.U. Reavis, "William J. Lewis," and "Hon Joseph Brown," in *St. Louis: The Commercial Metropolis of the Mississippi Valley* (St Louis: Tribune, 1874), 148–149, 229; Norton, *Centennial History of Madison County, Illinois, and Its People, 1812–1912*, I, 113–114; W.A. Newell and George H. Williams, "George T. Brown (1820–1880)" *WoodBeeCarver*, http://woodbeecarver.com/lincoln/?p=21 (accessed March 19, 2014); "George T. Brown," U.S. Senate, http://www.senate.gov/artandhistory/history/common/generic/SAA_George_Brown.htm (accessed March 18, 2014); Norbury Wayman, "The Physical Growth of the City of St. Louis, 1969," St. Louis City Planning Commission, https://www.stlouis-mo.gov/archive/history-physical-growth-stlouis/#golden (accessed December 31, 2015); "John James Roe," in Hyde and Conard, III, 1879; Conard, *Encyclopedia of the History of Missouri*, 5 vols. (New York: Southern History, 1901), vol. I: 214 Walter Barlow Stevens, *Missouri, the Center State, 1821–1915*, 4 vols. (Chicago, S.J. Lewis, 1915), vol. 4: 113; Joseph Brown, "Autobiography Statement," in Gould, *50 Years on the Mississippi*, 674; Gould, "The Atlantic and Pacific Steamship Company," in Gould, *50 Years on the Mississippi*, 386–387; St. Louis, Board of Aldermen, *Journal of the City Council of the City of St. Louis, April 1870–April 1871* (St Louis: George Knapp, 1871), 29,95. The operational story of the cross-river transfer concerns after 1869 are beyond the space available for its presentation here. For a full but brief accounting, the reader is directed to "The History of St. Louis Terminals," by Wiggins Ferry Company general freight agent J.J. Baulch in Hyde and Conrad, *Encyclopedia of the History of St. Louis*, III, 1863–1872.

    8. *Newark Advocate*, April 7, 1871; *Milwaukee Sentinel*, April 8, 1871; *Alton Daily Telegraph*, February 16, 1872; Lee A. Farrow, *Alexis in America: A Russian Grand Duke's Tour, 1871–1872* (Baton Rouge: Louisiana State University Press, 2014), 136–143; *St. Louis Daily Missouri Democrat*, January 7–12, 1872; *St. Louis Post-Dispatch*, June 2, 1896, January 31, 1897; Brown, *Lecture on Early Reminiscences of Alton*, 14; Hyde and Conard, *Encyclopedia of the History of St. Louis*, I, 352; *Railroad Gazette* 4 (January 27, April 6, June 8, December 14, 1872), 38, 155, 246, 535; Charles C. Clayton, *Joseph B. McCallagh of the St. Louis Globe Democrat* (Carbondale: Southern Illinois University Press, 1969), 225; *St. Louis Daily Missouri Democrat*, May 15, 1872; *St. Louis Daily Missouri Republican*, April 7, 1871, October 9, 1872; *East St. Louis Gazette*, October 18, 1873; *St. Louis Post-Dispatch*, April 6, 1885, January 31, 1897; December 4, 1899; Jackson, *Rails Across the Mississippi*, 115, 121–124, 203; Walter Barlow Stevens, *St. Louis: The Fourth City*, 108, 145; J. Thomas Scharf, *History of St. Louis City and County*, 2 vols. (Philadelphia: Louis H. Everts, 1883), vol. I: 704–706, 727, 757; Scharf, *History of St. Louis City and County, II, 1073; Railroad Gazette* 3 (May 20, 1871), 89; *Railroad Gazette* 5 (January 12, 1873), 29; *San Francisco Chronicle*, April 27, May 23, 1872; *San Francisco Daily Evening Bulletin*, April 23, September 7, 1872; R.E. Riegel, "The Missouri-Pacific Railroad to 1879," *Missouri Historical Review* 18 (October 1923), 15; *Memorial Addresses*

on the Life and Character of Lewis V, Bogy, a Senator from Missouri, 11; Mike Schaefer, *Classic American Railroads*, 3 vols. (St. Paul, MN: MBI, 2003), vol. 3: 121; Alfred Theodore Andreas, *History of Chicago from 1857 to the Fire of 1871* , 3 vols. (Chicago: A.T. Andreas, 1885), vol. 2: 770–771; George S. Pabis, *Daily Life Along the Mississippi* (Westport, CT: Greenwood, 2007), 155.

9. *St. Louis Post Dispatch*, September 26, 1893, January 31, 1897; December 4, 1899; Jackson, *Rails Across the Mississippi*, 147,188; *Railroad Gazette* 5 (April 19, 1873), 162; Andrew Hurley, "Busby's Stink Boat and the Regulation of Nuisance Trades, 1865–1918," in Andrew Hurley, ed., *Common Fields: An Environmental History of St. Louis* (St Louis: Missouri Historical Society Press, 1997), 145–148; Scharf, *History of St. Louis City and County*, I, 706, 728; Scharf, *History of St. Louis City and County*, II, 1382–1383; Katherine T. Corbett, *In Her Place: A Guide to St. Louis Women's History* (St Louis: Missouri Historical Society Press, 1999), 126–129; John C. Burnham, "The Social Evil Ordinance: A Social Experiment in Nineteenth Century St. Louis," *Bulletin of the Missouri Historical Society* 27 (April 1971), 203–217; James Wunsuch, "The Social Evil Ordinance," *American Heritage* 33 (February 1982), 50–55; Alan Lucibello, "Panic of 1873," in Daniel Leab, ed., *Encyclopedia of American Recessions and Depressions* (Santa Barbara, CA: ABC-CLIO, 2014), 227–276; *Little Rock Daily Republican*, April 22, 1873; Hyde and Conard, *Encyclopedia of the History of St. Louis*, I, 353; United States, War Department, *Executive Document 194: Letter from the Secretary of War Transmitting Reports of the Construction of the St. Louis and Illinois Bridge Across the Mississippi River* (43rd Cong., 1st sess.; Washington, D.C.: GPO, 1874), 36–37; *Proceedings of the Congressional Convention Held in the City of St. Louis on the 13th, 14th, and 15th Days of May 1873* (St Louis: Woodward, Tiernan and Hale, 1873); Patrick Leopoldo Gray, *Gray's Doniphan County History* (Bendenta, KA: Roycroft, 1905), 53.

10. *St. Louis Daily Republican*, July 5, 1874; *Chicago Daily Tribune*, July 5, 1874, November 20, 1904; *Chicago Times*, July 5, 1874; *New York Times*, July 3, 5, 1874; *St. Louis Post Dispatch*, November 23, 1879, November 17, 1889, November 20, 1892; *Alton Telegraph*, July 30, 1874; *Chicago Daily Inter-Ocean*, January 6, 1875; *St. Louis Post-Dispatch*, April 13, 1875; John Kouwenhoven, "Eads Bridge: The Celebration," *Bulletin of the Missouri Historical Association* 30 (April 1974), 159–180; Jackson, *Rails Across the Mississippi*, 194–206; Scharf, *History of St. Louis City and County*, I, 707–708, 750–751, 757, 761–762; William T. Harris, "Schools, Public," in Hyde and Conrad, *Encyclopedia of the History of St. Louis*, IV, 2016; St. Louis Public Library, "History and Mission," *St. Louis Public Library About Us*, http://www.slpl.org/slpl/library/article240165754.asp (accessed December 2, 2015); Edward C. Rafferty, "The Boss Who Never Was: Col. Ed Butler and the Limit of Practical Politics in St. Louis, 1875–1904," *Gateway Heritage* 12 (Winter 1992), 54–73; Estill McHenry, ed., *Addresses and Papers of James B. Eads, Together with a Biographical Sketch* (St Louis: Slawson, 1884), 46–48.

11. *St. Louis Post-Dispatch,* October 29, 1875, April 8, May 31, June 8, 1876, October 27, 1887; December 4, 1899; *St. Louis Globe-Democrat*, July 14, December 7, 1875, March 8, June 8, 1876; *St. Louis Dispatch,* June 29,1876; *Little Rock Daily Arkansas Gazette,* March 11, 1876; Charles Henry Browning, *Americans of Royal Descent* (Baltimore: Genealogical, 1998), 457; "Harry Innes Spotts," "Jane Pearce Tunstall," and "Albert Tunstall Spotts," *Tunstall Descendants*, http://wc.rootsweb.ancestry.com/cgi-bin/igm.cgi?op=PED&db=tunstall&id=I0281 (accessed January 12, 2016); *New York Times*, March 7, 1864; New York Superior Court, *General Term, 1876* (New York: Evening Post Steam Presses, 1876), 1–72; *San Francisco Call*, July 26, 1894; St. Louis Public Library, "C" and "S," *Two Hundred Years of St. Louis Places of Worship, 1770–1970*, http://previous.slpl.org/libsrc/s-stlworship.htm (accessed January 12, 2016); *Omaha Herald*, June 1, 1877; *Washington Evening Star,* December 13, 1915.

12. *St. Louis Post-Dispatch*, April 11, October 8, 1877, March 27, October 26, 1878; *Milwaukee Daily Sentinel,* October 10, 1876; *Omaha Herald,* June 1, 1877; *St. Louis Globe-Democrat,* September 7, 1876; April 12, June 2, October 12, 1877, January 10, 1878; *Alton Daily Telegraph,* April 12, 1877; December 4, 1899; *Chicago Daily Inter-Ocean*, July 16, 1878; *Commercial and Financial Chronicle* 42 (February 1886), 81; "Marie Aimee," in Charles Ralph, *Opera in Old Colorado*, http://www.operaoldcolo.info/personages/company10.html (accessed February 12, 2016); Schaefer, *Classic American Railroads*, III, 121; *San Francisco Chronicle,* December 4, 1879; Riegel, "The Missouri-Pacific Railroad to 1879," 16–18; Sylvester Waterhouse, *A Memorial to Congress to Secure an Adequate Appropriation for a Prompt and Thorough Improvement of the Mississippi River* (St Louis: John Daly, 1877), 1–9.

13. *St. Louis Post-Dispatch,* April 26, 1880; *Alton Telegraph,* June 9, 11, 12, 1880; *St. Louis Globe-Democrat,* February 27, June 6, 11, September 22, 1880; February 10, November 8,16. December 11, 1881; *San Francisco Daily Evening Bulletin*, October 3, 1883; *Alton Daily Telegraph*, November 17, December 24, 1881; Hyde and Conrad, *Encyclopedia of the History of St. Louis*, IV, 2123; "George T. Brown," U.S. Senate, http://www.senate.gov/artandhistory/history/common/generic/SAA_George_Brown.htm (accessed March 18, 2014); *San Francisco Daily Evening Bulletin*, December 29, 1881; Herbert J. Clancy, *The Presidential Election of 1880* (Chicago: Loyola University Press, 1958). A "land rush" into central Oklahoma was permitted in April 1889 (*New York Times*, April 22, 1889; William W. Howard," The Rush to Oklahoma," *Harper's Weekly* 33 (May 18, 1889), 391–394.

14. *St. Louis Post-Dispatch,* May 25, 1876, July 9, 1877, September 23, 1882, December 3, 1884, February 24, 1885; *Washington Chronicle,* January 12, 1882; *Chicago Daily Tribune*, February 15, 1882; St.

Louis Daily Republican, August 13, 1882; *St. Louis Globe-Democrat*, May 4, 1883; *The Wasp*, August 21, 1882; *New Orleans Times-Picayune*, September 10, 2011; *San Francisco Daily Evening Bulletin*, June 30, October 3, 1883, November 7, 1891; *San Francisco Chronicle*, November 18, 1883, December 16, 1884; *San Francisco Call*, October 5, 1903; U.S. Army, Corps of Engineers, *Eads' South Pass Jetties* (New Orleans: U.S. Army, Corps of Engineers, New Orleans District, n.d ; Gaye Hill, "Albert Tunstall Spotts," Find A Grave, http://www.findagrave.com/cgi-bin/fg.cgi?page=gr&GRid=53822361 (accessed January 12, 2016); John P. Young, "Theodore Z. Blakeman," in *Journalism in California* (San Francisco: Chronicle, 1915), 239; *St. Louis Chronicle*, November 1, 1891; The remains of Jennie B. Spotts and several other family members were removed and shipped to Cave Hill Cemetery, Louisville, KY, on August 19, 1921, by arrangement of Leontine Spotts Blakeman McMillan ("Virginia Brown," Tunstall Descendants, http://wc.rootsweb.ancestry.com/cgi-bin/igm.cgi?op=GET&db=tunstall&id=I02811 (accessed January 12, 2016). There was no contact between Brown and his son-in-law after settlement of the bond case. Spotts served as San Francisco county recorder (1886–1889) and later as coiner of the U.S. Mint.

15. *St. Louis Post-Dispatch*, February 24, August 3, September 29, 1885, March 26, June 4, October 29, 1887; *St. Louis Globe-Democrat*, September 25, 1885, September 30, 1886, May 4, 1887; *Galveston Daily News*, March 27, 1885; Harper Barnes, *Standing on a Volcano: The Life and Times of David Rowland Francis* (Carbondale: Southern Illinois University Press, 2001); *New York Times*, June 21, 1898; *The Railway Purchasing Agent* 8 (October 1885), 152; "Marcus J. Wright," in Ezra J. Warner, *Generals in Gray: Lives of the Confederate Commanders* (Baton Rouge: Louisiana State University Press, 1959), 346: *Christian Science Monitor*, November 1, 1909. The office of district assessor which Brown turned down was described in the *St. Louis Post-Dispatch*, January 27, 1885.

16. *St. Louis Globe-Democrat*, September 20, 1878; *Milwaukee Sentinel*, February 27, 1888; *St. Louis Post-Dispatch*, June 5, 17, 1888, March 23, April 3, 1889; *Charles W. Calhoun, Minority Victory: Gilded Age Politics and the Front Porch Campaign of 1888* (Lawrence: University Press of Kansas, 2008); *Chicago Daily Inter-Ocean, March 28, 1889*; Stevens, *St. Louis: The Fourth City, 1764–1911*, I, 172; "Thomas Dimmock," Find A Grave, http://www.findagrave.com/cgi-bin/fg.cgi?page=gr&GRid=11148 (accessed January 12, 2016); Brown, "Autobiography Statement," in Gould, *50 Years on the Mississippi*, 675.

17. *St. Louis Post-Dispatch*, April 9, 16, 1890, March 22, December 23, 1891, November 16, 20, 1892, January 23, March 4, April 5, April 23, October 26, November 11, December 10, 26, 1893; May 1, 1894; June 2, 16, September 1, 15, October 5, 1895; March 30, April 7, June 6, December 27, 1897; December 4, 1899; August 23, 1908; *Poughkeepsie Daily Eagle*, February 23, 1894; *Chicago Daily Inter-Ocean*, July 26, 1895; Hyde and Conrad, *Encyclopedia of the History of St. Louis*, IV, 2170; Joe Nickell, *The Mystery Chronicles: More Real Life X-Files* (Lexington: University Press of Kentucky, 2004), 32, 320–321; *The Waterways Journal* (November 23–30, 1895), 4–5; *Alton Telegraph*, February 6, 19, 1896, February 25, November 5, 11, 1897, December 4, 1899; *Rocky Mountain News*, November 9, 1897; Norman Dwight Harris, *The History of Negro Servitude in Illinois* (Chicago: A.C. McClurg, 1904), 254; *Monumental News* 9 (October 1897), 579; John L. Wright, "A Forerunner to Freedom," *Goody's Magazine* 136 (June 1898), 655; Arnold P. Powers, *Devour Us Not: Short Stories of African American History* (Bloomington: XLibris.com, 2013), 102; "Norman Jay Coleman," in vol. 6 of Albert N. Marquis, comp., *Who's Who in America* (Chicago: Marquis, 1911), 399.

18. *Chicago Daily Tribune*, October 11, 1899; *St. Louis Post-Dispatch*, October 3, 1898; October 27, December 4–5, 1899; *Modern Miller* 25 (July 1, 1899), 24; *Railroad Gazette* 31 (October 20, 1899), 733; Maud Lord-Drake, *Psychic-Light: The Continuity of Law and Life* (Kansas City: Frank T. Riley, 1904), 364; "Maud Lord-Drake," in Victoria Barnes, ed., *Centennial Book of Modern Spiritualism in America* (Chicago: National Spiritualist Association, 1948), 226; *Waterways Journal* (December 2, 9, 1899), 5, 4; *Washington Post*, December 4, 1899; *Alton Telegraph*, December 4–5 1899; *St Louis Globe-Democrat*, December 4, 1899; *Weekly Northwestern Miller* 48 (December 6, 1899), 1099.

19. Brown, *Lecture on Early Reminiscences of Alton*, 14.

Bibliography

Primary Sources

Beecher, Edward. *Narrative of Riots at Alton.* Alton, IL: George Holton, 1838.
Brown, Joseph. "Autobiography Statement." In Emerson W. Gould. *50 Years on the Mississippi* (St. Louis: Nixon-James, 1889), p. 674.
_____. *Lecture on Early Reminiscences of Alton.* Alton, IL: Lovejoy Monument Association, 1896.
Civil War Collection. Missouri Historical Society, St. Louis, MO.
Civil War, Confederate and Federal Collection. Tennessee State Library and Archives, Nashville.
Civil War Times Illustrated. Collection. U.S. Army Military History Institute, Carlisle Barracks, PA.
Davis, Frederic E. *Frederic E. Davis Papers.* 1860–1863. Manuscript, Archives, and Rare Book Library, Emory University, Atlanta, GA;
Eads, James B. *Addresses and Papers of James B. Eads, Together with a Biographical Sketch.* Edited by Estill McHenry. St. Louis: Slawson, 1884.
_____. Papers, Missouri Historical Society, St. Louis.
Green, James. *Green's St. Louis Directory.* St. Louis: A. Fisher, 1844.
Hair, James T. *Gazetteer of Madison County.* Alton, IL: Priv. print, 1866.
Jones, Horatio M. "*Gaty, et al, Plantiffs in Error, v. Phoenix Insurance Company, Defendant in Error*: March Term, 1860." In vol. 30, *Reports of Cases Argued and Determined in the Supreme Court of the State of Missouri.* St. Louis: George Knapp, 1861.
Jordan, Scott D. *Civil War Letters of Scott D. Jordan, Produced for Eleanor Jordan West.* CD-ROM. Glendale, AZ: doug@bellnotes.com, 2007).
Meigs, Montgomery C. Papers. Manuscript Division, Library of Congress, Washington, D.C.
Miller, Allen Woods. Diary. Manuscript Division, Library of Congress, Washington, D.C.
Nott, Charles C., and Archibald Hopkins. *Cases Decided in the Court of Claims at the December Term, 1873, and the Decisions of the Supreme Court in the Appealed Cases from October 1873-May 1874.* Washington, D.C.: GPO, 1874.
Porter, David Dixon. Papers. Manuscript Division, Library of Congress, Washington, D.C.
_____. Papers. Missouri Historical Society, St. Louis.
Rice, Edwin E. *Diary of Edwin E. Rice, April 15, 1862-April 5, 1863.* Transcribed by David S. Pettus. Galveston: Galveston and Texas History Center, Rosenberg Library.
Robinson, Terry P. Journal Kept on Board the U.S. Steam Gunboat *Carondelet* and *Lafayette*, January 8–20, 1863. Manuscript Division, Library of Congress, Washington, D.C.
Sawyer, William D. "The Western River Engine." *Steamboat Bill* 24 (1978), 71–80.
Sessions, James O.H. "Diary of James Oliver Hazard Perry Sessions of Rileby Plantation, on the Yazoo, January 1, 1862-June 1872." *Journal of Mississippi History* 39 (August 1977), 239–254.
Shaw, Milton. Milton Shaw Letters. McCain Library and Archives, University of Southern Mississippi, Hattiesburg.
United States. Congress. House of Representatives. "Contracts Made With Bureaus Connected With the Navy Department: Letter from the Secretary of the Navy, July 14, 1862." In *House Executive Documents.* 37th Cong., 2nd sess. Washington, D.C.: GPO, 1862.
_____. _____. _____. Joint Committee on the Conduct of the War. *Report: Red River.* 38th Cong., 2nd sess.; Washington, D.C.: GPO, 1864; reprnt., Greenwood, 1971.
_____. Navy Department. *Official Records of the Union and Confederate Navies in the War of the Rebellion.* 31 vols. Washington, D.C.: GPO, 1894–1922.
_____. _____. Records of the Bureau of Naval Personnel: Record Group 24. National Archives, Washington, D.C.
_____. _____. Records of the Office of Naval Records and Library. Naval Records Collection: Record.
_____. _____. *Report of the Secretary of the Navy.* Washington, D.C.: GPO, 1860–1884.

_____. _____. *Report of the Secretary of the Navy in Relation to Armored Vessels.* Washington, D.C.: GPO, 1864. Group 45. National Archives, Washington, D.C.

_____. War Department. *Atlas to Accompany the Official Records of the War of the Rebellion.* Compiled by Calvin D. Cowles. 3 vols. Washington, D.C.: GPO, 1891–1895.

_____. _____. Quartermaster General. Records of the Office of the Quartermaster General. Record Group 92. National Archives, Washington, D.C.

_____. _____. *The War of the Rebellion: A Compilation of the Official Records of the Union and Confederate Armies* [OR]. 128 vols. Washington, D.C.: GPO, 1880–1901.

Newspapers

Alton Daily Telegraph
Alton Observer
Alton Telegraph
Alton Weekly Courier
Atchison Daily Globe
Bangor Daily Whig & Courier
Boston Daily Advertiser
Boston Morning Journal
Brooklyn Daily Eagle
Buffalo Evening Courier
Cairo (IL) City Weekly Gazette
Cairo (IL) Daily Journal
Charleston Daily Courier
Charleston Mercury
Chattanooga Daily Gazette
Chicago Daily Inter-Ocean
Chicago Daily Journal
Chicago Daily Post
Chicago Daily Times
Chicago Daily Tribune
Chicago Evening Journal
Christian Science Monitor
Cincinnati Daily Commercial
Cincinnati Daily Enquirer
Cincinnati Daily Gazette
Cincinnati Daily Times
Columbus Crisis
Columbus Democrat
Commercial and Financial Chronicle
Daily Cleveland Herald
Daily Commercial Bulletin and Missouri Literary Register
Daily National Intelligencer
Daily Southern Cross
Detroit Free Press
Dubuque Daily Times
Dubuque Telegraph-Herald
East St. Louis Gazette
Elizabeth Herald
Erie Observer
Evansville Daily Journal
Frank Leslie's Illustrated Newspaper
Harper's Weekly
Illinois Weekly State Journal
Indiana Herald
Indianapolis Daily Journal
Indianapolis News
Jackson Daily Appeal
Jackson Daily Mississippian
Jeffersonian Democrat
Little Rock Daily Arkansas Gazette
Little Rock Daily Republican
Little Rock True Democrat
London Morning Republican
Louisville Courier
Louisville Daily Journal
Memphis Daily Appeal
Memphis Daily Avalanche
Milwaukee Daily Sentinel
Missouri Daily Evening Herald
Mobile Daily Advertiser and Register
Mobile Daily Tribune
Mobile Evening News
Morning Oregonian
Nashville Banner
Nashville Daily Patriot
Nashville Daily Union
Nashville Dispatch
Nashville Times
Nashville Union and American
Natchez Courier
Natchez Weekly Courier
National Intelligencer
National Tribune
New Albany Daily Ledger
New Albany Weekly Ledger
New Orleans Daily Crescent
New Orleans Daily Delta
New Orleans Daily Picayune
New Orleans Era
New Orleans Times
New York Herald
New York Times
New York Tribune
New York World
Newark Advocate
North American and United States Gazette
Omaha Herald
Pennsylvania Inquirer and Daily Courier
Peoria Democratic Union
Philadelphia Inquirer
Philadelphia Press
Pine Bluff Commercial
Pittsburgh Gazette-Times
Pittsburgh Post-Gazette
Poughkeepsie Daily Eagle
Quincy Daily Whig
Richmond Daily Dispatch
Richmond Daily Examiner
Rochester Democrat Chronicle
Rocky Mountain News
St. Louis Chronicle
St. Louis Daily Intelligencer
St. Louis Daily Missouri Democrat
St. Louis Daily Missouri Republican
St. Louis Globe-Democrat
St. Louis Post-Dispatch
San Francisco Call
San Francisco Chronicle
San Francisco Daily Evening Bulletin
Shreveport Weekly News
Vicksburg Daily Herald
Vicksburg Sunday Post
Vicksburg Whig
Warsaw Northern Indianian
Washington Evening Star
Washington Post
Waterways Journal
Weekly Northwestern Miller
Western Reserve Chronicle
Yazoo Daily Banner

Internet Sources

Affeld, Charles E. "Charles Affeld Diary Transcription from April 15 through July 4th, 1863." *The Taylor—Taylor's Battery.* http://www.taylorsbattery.org/Affeld%20Diary%20transcription.htm (accessed December 1, 2015).

"Another Misidentified *Indianola*." Civil War Talk. http://civilwartalk.com/threads/another-misidentified-indianola.88583 (accessed March 13, 2016).
Armstrong, Samuel S. "Trenton in the Mexican, Civil, and Spanish-American Wars." In *A History of Trenton, 1679–1929*." Trenton Historical Society. http://trentonhistory.org/His/Wars.html (accessed January 11, 2012).
Biographical Directory of the United States Congress, 1774-Present. http://bioguide.congress.gov/scripts/biodisplay.pl?index=B000231 (October 1, 2006).
Branch, Paul. "Armament of Fort Macon." *The Fort Macon Ramparts* (Spring 1996). http://www.clis.com/friends/armament.htm (accessed October 13, 2009).
"Charles H. Frith." *Ancient Faces*. http://www.ancientfaces.com/person/charles-h-frith/117731647 (accessed October 28, 2015).
"Charles Heckman Gulick, Circa 1836–Circa 1868." MyHeritage. http://www.myheritage.com/names/charles_gulick (accessed November 29, 2015).
Clark-Wick, Judy. "Virginia C. Keach Brown." Find A Grave. http://www.findagrave.com/cgi-bin/fg.cgi?page=gr&GRid=52929253 (accessed August 25, 2014).
"Company D, 29th Illinois Regiment." *Illinois Civil War Rosters*. http://civilwar.illinoisgenweb.org/r050/029-d-in.html (accessed November 29, 2015);
"Dahlgren Guns and Rifles." *The Encyclopedia of Civil War Artillery*. http://www.cwartillery.org/ve/dahlgrens.html (accessed October 13, 2009).
"Dahlgrens, Brookes, and Parrotts." *Ironclads and Blockade Runners of the Civil War*. http://www.wideopenwest.com/~jenkins/ironclads/ironguns.htm. (accessed October 13, 2009).
"Frank Arnold." Vicksburg Tombstone Database. http://www.vicksburg.org/index.php/component/easytablepro/tombstone-database/405/arnold-frank (accessed December 15, 2015).
"Gen. Joseph Lancaster Brent." Find A Grave. http://www.findagrave.com/cgi-bin/fg.cgi?page=gr&GRid=6778835> (accessed July 15, 2012).
Genie, B.K. "Edward Hartt." Find A Grave. http://www.findagrave.com/cgi-bin/fg.cgi?page=gr&GRid=57881901 (accessed November 13, 2011).
Gillespie, William A. "Fort Pemberton." *Civil War Album*. http://www.civilwaralbum.com/vicksburg/fort_pemberton_1904.htm (accessed February 1, 2011).
"Glossary of Steamboat Terms." Steamboats.org. http://www.steamboats.org/history-education/glossary/hog_chains.html (accessed January 4, 2011).
Harris, Charles Dean. "Samuel Pitts, Jr." Find A Grave. http://www.findagrave.com/cgi-bin/fg.cgi?page=gr&GRid=29618528 (accessed September 30, 2014).
Huntington Library. "Letter of William A. Steel, August 28, 1862-October 22, 1877." Archivegrid. http://184.168.105/185/archivegrid/collection/data/753739653 (accessed May 30, 2014).
"James Buchanan Eads." University of Illinois at Urbana-Champagne Riverweb. http://www.riverweb.uiuc.edu/TECH/TECH20.htm (accessed September 18, 2006).
"John Marshall Krum," *St. Louis Mayors* . http://exhibits.slpl.lib.mo.us/mayors/data/dt43400748.asp> (accessed June 10, 2014).
"John Mitchell of Lancaster County, PA." Ancestry Hints. http://wc.rootsweb.ancestry.com/cgi-bin/igm.cgi?op=GET&db=johnmitchell&id=I0459 (accessed August 10, 2014).
Johnson, Michael, and Betsy. "Theodore E. Underwood, 1836–1877." *RootsWeb*. http://archiver.rootsweb.ancestry.com/th/read/UNDERWOOD/2013–07/1373742216 (accessed March 23, 2015).
Lambley, Jonathan Malcolm. "Joseph Alexander Smith Acklen." Find A Grave. http://www.findagrave.com/cgi-bin/fg.cgi?page=gr&GRid=21012245 (cited June 10, 2015).
"Marie Aimee." In Charles Ralph, *Opera in Old Colorado*. http://www.operaoldcolo.info/personages/company10.html (accessed February 12, 2016).
Matthews, Gary. "First Shots of the ACW?" *Civil War Navy Messageboard*. http://history-sites.com/mb/cw/cwnavy/index.cgi?noframes;read=1005 (accessed August 4, 2006).
Missouri Pacific Historical Society. "MoPac's First 125 Years." Missouri Pacific Historical Society. http://www.mopac.org/corporate-history/73-missouri-pacific-railroad (accessed December 31, 2015).
Missouri. Secretary of State. "Joseph Brown." In *Missouri State Legislators, 1820–2000*. http://s1.sos.mo.gov/archives/history/historicallistings/molegb (accessed December 31, 2015).
Morrison, John G. "The Civil War Diary of John G. Morrison, 1861–1865." New York State Military Museum and Veterans Research Center. http://dmna.ny.gov/historic/reghist/civil/infantry/30thInf/30thInf_Diary_Morrison.htm (accessed March 31, 2015).
"Mound City Illinois Shipyards, Hospital." *Southernmost Illinois History*. http://www.southernmostillinoishistory.net/mound-city-il-shipyards-hospital.html (accessed April 21, 2015).
Nautical Terms and Phrases: Their Meaning and Origin. http://www.history.navy.mil/trivia/trivia03.htm (accessed January 12, 2010).
Newell, W.A., and George H. Williams. "George T. Brown (1820–1880)." *WoodBeeCarver*. http://woodbeecarver.com/lincoln/?p=21 (accessed March 19, 2014).

Nisiger, Connie. "Capt. William P. LaMothe." Find A Grave. http://www.findagrave.com/cgi-bin/fg.cgi?page=gr&GRid=9682637 (accessed June 10, 2014).

———. "John S. McCune." Find A Grave. http://www.findagrave.com/cgi-bin/fg.cgi?page=gr&GRid=9349265 (accessed August 12, 2014).

"Oran D. Perry." USGenWeb. http://ucgenweb.org/Union%20County%20Personalities/oran_d%20Perry.htm (accessed December 1, 2015).

Pockras, Lawrence M. "October 1959: That Damned Black Hulk—The U.S.S. *Chickasaw*." *Cincinnati Civil War Roundtable Talks.* http://www.cincinnaticwrt.org/data/ccwrt_history/talks_text/pockras_chickasaw.html (November 12, 2014).

Prout, Don. "Cincinnati Marine Railway." *Cincinnati Views.* http://www.cincinnativiews.net/ohio%20river.htm (Accessed December 1, 2014).

Rubenstein, David M. "Guide to the Eltinge-Lord Family Papers, 1856–1871." Duke University Libraries. http://library.duke.edu/digitalcollections/rbmscl/eltinge/inv/ (accessed November 18, 2011).

St. Louis Public Library. "History and Mission." St. Louis Public Library. "About Us." http://www.slpl.org/slpl/library/article240165754.asp (accessed December 2, 2015).

———. *Two Hundred Years of St. Louis Places of Worship, 1770–1970.* http://previous.slpl.org/libsrc/s-stlworship.htm (accessed January 12, 2016).

"Samuel Gaty." Find A Grave. http://www.findagrave.com/cgi-bin/fg.cgi?page=gr&GRid=18465 (accessed August 12, 2014).

Sawyer, George. "Letters of George Sawyer." *28th Wisconsin Volunteer Infantry.* http://www.28thwisconsin.com/letters/enos_12mar1863.html (accessed February 12, 2011).

Scott, Newton Robert. *Letters from an Iowa Soldier in the Civil War.* http://www.civilwarletters.com/scott_3_9_1863.html (accessed March 3, 2011).

Smith, David M. "January 1998: The Defense of Cincinnati: The Battle That Never Was." *Cincinnati Civil War Roundtable Talks.* http://www.cincinnaticwrt.org/data/ccwrt_history/smith_defense_cin.html (accessed November 12, 2014).

Smith, Steven D., and George J. Castille III. "Bailey's Dam." *Louisiana, Department of Culture, Recreation and Tourism Anthropological Study No. 8*, March 1986. http://www.crt.state.la.us/archaeology/BAILEYS/baileys.htm (August 7, 2006).

Tarbell, Rose, comp. *Joseph L. Brent Papers: Inventory.* Louisiana State University Libraries. http://www.lib.lsu.edu/sites/default/files/sc/findaid/1477.pdf (accessed October 1, 2014).

"Thomas Dimmock." Find A Grave. http://www.findagrave.com/cgi-bin/fg.cgi?page=gr&GRid=11148 (accessed January 12, 2016).

United States Congress. Senate. Senate Historical Office. "George T. Brown, Sergeant-at-Arms, 1861–1869," U.S. Senate. http://www.senate.gov/artandhistory/history/common/generic/SAA_George_Brown.htm (accessed March 18, 2014).

———. Library of Congress. "About Alton *Daily Morning Courier* (Alton, Ill.), 1852–1855." *U.S. Newspaper Directory, 1690-Present.* http://chroniclingamerica.loc.gov/lccn/sn84038318/ (accessed June 14, 2014).

"Virginia Brown." *Tunstall Descendants.* http://wc.rootsweb.ancestry.com/cgi-bin/igm.cgi?op=GET&db=tunstall&id=I02811 (accessed December 1, 2015).

Wayman, Norbury. "The Physical Growth of the City of St. Louis, 1969." St. Louis City Planning Commission. https://www.stlouis-mo.gov/archive/history-physical-growth-stlouis/#golden (accessed December 31, 2015).

Williams, Scott K. "St Louis' Ships of Iron: The Ironclads and Monitors of Carondelet (St. Louis), Missouri." Missouri Civil War Museum Home. http://www.missouricivilwarmuseum.org/1ironclads.htm (July 12, 2005).

Wise, George D. "The Civil War Diary of Confederate Soldier George D. Wise." North Jersey History and Genealogical Collections. http://cdm15387.contentdm.oclc.org/cdm/landingpage/collection/p16100coll2 (accessed November 12, 2015).

Zif Lodge No. 8 Register and Minutes Ledger, 1819–1827. http://ww-bbs.com/39/roll.htm (accessed November 15, 2014).

Books

Abbott, John S.C. *The History of the Civil War in America.* 2 vols. New York: H. Bill, 1863.

Allen, John W. *Legends and Lore of Southern Illinois.* Carbondale: University Graphics, 1978.

Ambler, Charles Henry. *A History of Transportation in the Ohio Valley.* Glendale, CA: Arthur H. Clark 1932.

Ambrose, Stephen E. *Halleck: Lincoln's Chief of Staff.* Baton Rouge: Louisiana State University Press, 1962.

Anders, Curt. *Disaster in Damp Sand: The Red River Expedition.* Carmel: Guild Press of Indiana, 1997.

_____. *Henry Halleck's War: A Fresh Look at Lincoln's Controversial General-in-Chief*. Indianapolis: Guild Press of Indiana, 1999.
Anderson, Bern. *By Sea and By River: The Naval History of the Civil War*. New York: Knopf, 1962.
Andreas, Alfred Theodore. *History of Chicago from 1857 to the Fire of 1871*. 3 vols. Chicago: A.T. Andreas, 1885.
Andrews, J. Cutler. *The North Reports the Civil War*. Pittsburgh: University of Pittsburgh Press, 1985.
_____. *The South Reports the Civil War*. Pittsburgh: University of Pittsburgh Press, 1985.
Angle, Paul M., ed. *Illinois Guide and Gazetter: Prepared Under the Supervision of the Illinois Sesquicentennial Commission*. Chicago: Rand McNally, 1969.
Bakeless, John. *Spies of the Confederacy*. Philadelphia: J.B. Lippincott, 1970.
Ballard, Michael B. *The Civil War in Mississippi: Major Campaigns and Battles*. Jackson: University Press of Mississippi, 2011.
_____. *Civil War Mississippi: A Guide*. Jackson: University Press of Mississippi, 2000.
_____. *Vicksburg: The Campaign that Opened the Mississippi*. Chapel Hill: University of North Carolina Press, 2004.
Banta, Richard E. *The Ohio*. Rivers of America. New York: Rinehard, 1949.
Barnes, Harper. *Standing on a Volcano: The Life and Times of David Rowland Francis*. Carbondale: Southern Illinois University Press, 2001.
Barrett, Edward. *Gunnery Instruction Simplified for the Volunteer Officers of the U.S. Navy, with Hints for Executive and Other Officers*. New York: D. Van Nostrand, 1863.
Bartols, Barnabas H. *A Treatise on the Marine Boilers of the United States*. Philadelphia: R.W. Barnard, 1851.
Basler, Roy P., ed. *The Collected Works of Abraham Lincoln*. 10 vols. Springfield, IL: The Abraham Lincoln Association, 1958.
Bastian, David F. *Grant's Canal: The Union's Attempt to Bypass Vicksburg*. Shippensburg, PA: Burd Street, 1995; reprnt., Shippensburg, PA: White Mane, 1998.
Baxter, James P., III. *Introduction of the Ironclad Warship*. Cambridge, MA: Harvard University Press, 1933; reprnt., Annapolis: U.S. Naval Institute, 2000.
Bearss, Edwin C. *Decision in Mississippi*. Little Rock: Pioneer, 1962
_____. *The Fall of Fort Henry*. Dover, TN: Eastern National Park and Monument Association, 1989.
_____. *Hardluck Ironclad: The Sinking and Salvage of the Cairo*. Baton Rouge: Louisiana State University, 1966.
_____. *Unconditional Surrender: The Fall of Fort Donelson*. Dover, TN: Eastern National Park and Monument Association, 1991.
_____. *The Vicksburg Campaign*. 3 vols. Dayton, OH: Morningside, 1985–1986.
Bennett, Frank M. *The Monitor and the Navy Under Steam*. Boston: Houghton, Mifflin, 1900.
_____. *Steam Navy of the United States: A History of the Growth of the Steam Vessel of War in the U.S. Navy, and of the Naval Engineer Corps*. Pittsburgh: Warren, 1896; Reprnt., New York: Greenwood, 1970.
Bennett, Michael J. *Union Jacks: Yankee Sailors in the Civil War*. Chapel Hill: University of North Carolina Press, 2004.
Bergeron, Arthur W., Jr. *Guide to Confederate Military Units, 1861–1865*. Baton Rouge: Louisiana State University Press, 1989.
Bertolet Family Association. *A Genealogical History of the Bertolet Family: The Descendants of Jean Bertolet*. Harrisburg, PA: United Evangelical, 1914.
Blackburn, George M., ed. *"Dear Carrie": The Civil War Letters of Thomas M. Stevens*. Mount Pleasant: Central Michigan University Press, 1984.
Blessington, Joseph P. *The Campaigns of Walker's Texas Division*. Austin: Pemberton, 1968.
Boatner, Mark M., III. *The Civil War Dictionary*. New York: David McKay, 1959.
Book of Biographies, Containing Biographical Sketches of Leading Citizens of Beaver County, Pennsylvania. Buffalo, NY: Biographical, 1899.
Boynton, Charles B. *History of the Navy During the Rebellion*. 2 vols. New York: D. Appleton, 1867.
Bradford, Gershom. *The Mariner's Dictionary*. New York: Weathervane, 1970.
Bragg, Marion. *Historic Names and Places on the Lower Mississippi River*. Vicksburg: Mississippi River Commission, 1977.
Brandt, J. D. *Gunnery Catechism, as Applied to the Service of Naval Ordnance*. New York: D. Van Nostrand, 1864.
Brent, Joseph L. *The Lugo Case: Capture of the Ironclad Indianola*. New Orleans: Searcy & Pfaff, 1926.
A Brief and Condensed History of Parsons' Texas Cavalry Brigade. Waxhachie, TX: J.M. Flemister, 1893.
Brooksher, William Riley. *War Along the Bayous: The 1864 Red River Campaign in Louisiana*. Washington, D.C.: Brassey's, 1998.
Brown, Alonzo Leighton. *History of the Fourth Regiment of Minnesota Volunteers During the Great Rebellion, 1861–1865*. St. Paul, MN: Pioneer, 1892.

Browne, Henry R., and Symmes E. *From the Fresh Water Navy, 1861–1864: Letters of Acting Master's Mate Henry R. Browne and Acting Ensign Symmes E. Browne.* Edited by John D. Milligan. Naval Letters Series. Volume 3. Annapolis: Naval Institute Press, 1970.

Browning, Charles Henry. *Americans of Royal Descent.* Baltimore: Genealogical, 1998.

Burkhalter, Bettye E. *Raised Country Style from South Carolina to Mississippi: Civil War Transforms America.* Bloomington, IN: AuthorHouse, 2010.

Burkhardt, George S., ed. *Double Duty in the Civil War: The Letters of Soldier and Sailor Edward W. Bacon.* Carbonedale: Southern Illinois University Press, 2009.

Calhoun, Charles W. *Minority Victory: Gilded Age Politics and the Front Porch Campaign of 1888.* Lawrence: University Press of Kansas, 2008.

Callahan, Edward W. *List of Officers of the Navy of the United States and of the Marine Corps, from 1775 to 1900, Comprising a Complete Register of All Present and Former Commissioned, Warranted, and Appointed Officers of the United States Navy, and of the Marine Corps, Regular and Volunteer; Compiled from the Official Records of the Navy Department.* New York: L.R. Hamersly, 1901; Reprnt., New York: Haskell House, 1969.

Calore, Paul. *Naval Campaigns of the Civil War.* Jefferson, NC: McFarland, 2002.

Cameron, Robert S. *Staff Ride Handbook for the Battle of Perrysville, 8 October 1862.* Fort Leavenworth, KA: Combat Studies Institute, 2005.

Campbell, R. Thomas. *Confederate Naval Forces on Western Waters: The Defense of the Mississippi River and Its Tributaries.* Jefferson, NC: McFarland, 2005.

_____. *Gray Thunder.* Exploits of the Confederate Navy. New Orleans: Burd Street, 1996.

_____. *Southern Thunder.* Exploits of the Confederate Navy. New Orleans: Burd Street, 1996.

Canfield, Eugene B. *Civil War Naval Ordnance.* Washington, D.C.: Naval History Division, U.S. Navy Department, 1969.

Canney, Donald L. *The Confederate Steam Navy, 1861–1865.* Atglen, PA: Schiffer, 2016.

_____. *Lincoln's Navy: The Ships, Men and Organization, 1861–65.* London and New York: Conway Maritime, 1998.

_____. *The Old Steam Navy.* Vol. 2: *The Ironclads, 1842–1885.* Annapolis: Naval Institute Press, 1993.

Capers, Gerald M. *The Biography of a River Town: Memphis—Its Heroic Age.* Chapel Hill: University of North Carolina Press, 1939.

Carpenter, George W. *History of Calhoun County, Illinois.* Jerseyville, IL: Democrat, 1934.

Carter, Samuel, III. *The Final Fortress: The Campaign for Vicksburg, 1862–1863.* New York: St. Martin's, 1980.

Catton, Bruce. *The American Heritage Picture History of the Civil War.* New York: American Heritage, 1960.

_____. *The Centennial History of the Civil War.* 3 vols. Garden City, NY: Doubleday, 1961–1965.

_____. *Grant Moves South.* Boston: Little, Brown, 1960.

Chamberlain, William H., ed. *Sketches of War History, 1861–1865: Papers Prepared for the Ohio Commandry of the Military Order of the Loyal Legion of the United States.* 6 vols. Cincinnati: R Clarke, 1890–1908.

Cist, Charles. *Sketches and Statistics of Cincinnati in 1858.* Cincinnati: Priv. print, 1859.

Clancy, Herbert J. *The Presidential Election of 1880.* Chicago, Illinois: Loyola University Press, 1958.

Clayton, Charles C. *Joseph B. McCallagh of the St. Louis Globe Democrat.* Carbondale: Southern Illinois University Press, 1969.

Cogar, William B. *Dictionary of Admirals of the U.S. Navy.* 2 vols. Annapolis: Naval Institute Press, 1989.

Collins, Lewis, and Richard H. *History of Kentucky.* 3 vols. Chicago: S.J. Clarke, 1928.

Conard, Howard Louis. *Encyclopedia of the History of Missouri.* 5 vols. New York; Louisville; St. Louis: Southern History, 1901.

Cooling, Benjamin F. *Fort Donelson's Legacy: War and Society in Kentucky and Tennessee, 1862–1863.* Knoxville: University of Tennessee Press, 1997.

_____. *Forts Henry and Donelson: The Key to the Confederate Heartland.* Knoxville: University of Tennessee Press, 1987.

Coombe, Jack D. *Thunder Along the Mississippi: The River Battles That Split the Confederacy.* New York: Sarpedon, 1996.

Corbett, Katherine T. *In Her Place: A Guide to St. Louis Women's History.* St. Louis: Missouri Historical Society Press, 1999.

Cornwell, Charles H. *St. Louis Mayors: Brief Biographies.* St. Louis: St. Louis Public Library, 1965.

Cotton, Gordon A., and Jeff T. Giambrone. *Vicksburg and the War.* Gretna, LA: Pelican, 2004.

Cox, James. *St. Louis Through a Camera.* St. Louis: Woodward and Tiernan, 1896.

Crandall, Warren D., and Isaac D. Newell. *History of the Ram Fleet and Mississippi Marine Brigade.* St. Louis: Buschart Brothers, 1907.

Cunningham, Edward. *The Port Hudson Campaign, 1862–1863.* Baton Rouge: Louisiana State University Press, 1963.

Cushing, Thomas. *History of Allegehny County, Pennsylvania*. Chicago: A. Warner, 1889.
Dana, Charles A. *Recollections of the Civil War*. New York: D. Appleton, 1898; Reprnt., New York: Collier, 1963.
Dickey, Thomas S., and Peter C. George. *Field Artillery Projectiles of the American Civil War*. Revised and Supplemented 1993 Edition™. Mechanicsville, VA: Arsenal II, 1993.
Dictionary of American Naval Fighting Ships. 8 vols. Washington, D.C.: GPO, 1916–1981.
Dillon, Merton L. *Elijah P. Lovejoy, Abolitionist Editor*. Urbana: University of Illinois Press, 1961.
Donald, David Herbert. *Lincoln*. New York: Simon & Schuster, 1995.
Dorsey, Florence. *Road to the Sea: The Story of James B. Eads and the Mississippi River*. New York: Rinehart, 1947.
Dossman, Steven Nathaniel. *Vicksburg, 1863: The Deepest Wound*. Santa Barbara, CA: ABC-Clio, 2014.
Douglas, Byrd. *Steamboatin' on the Cumberland*. Nashville: Tennessee Book, 1961.
Drury, Ian, and Tony Gibbons. *The Civil War Military Machine: Weapons and Tactics of the Union and Confederate Armed Forces*. New York: Smithmark, 1993.
Duffy, John. *Sword of Pestilence: The New Orleans Yellow Fever Epidemic of 1853*. Baton Rouge: Louisiana State University Press, 1966.
Dunphy, John J. *Abolitionism and the Civil War in Southwestern Illinois*. Charleston, SC: History, 2011.
Dyer, Frederick H. *A Compendium of the War of the Rebellion*. 3 vols. Des Moines: Dyer, 1908. Reprnt., New York: Thomas Yoseloff, 1959.
Edwards, John. *Edwards's Great West and Her Commercial Metropolis, Embracing a General View of the West, and a Complete History of St. Louis, from the Landing of Liguest, in 1764, to the Present Time; with Portraits and Biographies of Some of the Old Settlers, and Many of the Most Prominent Buisiness Men*. St. Louis: Office of Edwards's Monthly, 1860.
Edwards, Richard. *Edwards' Annual Directory ... the City of St. Louis*. 6th ed. St. Louis: Southern, 1864; 8th ed.. St. Louis: Richard Edwards, 1866.
Eicher, David J. *The Longest Night: A Military History of the Civil War*. New York: Simon & Schuster, 2001.
Elder, Donald C., III, ed. *Love and the Turmoil: The Civil War Letters of William and Mary Vermilion*. Iowa City: University of Iowa Press, 2003.
Elder, William H. *Civil War Diary (1862–1863) of Bishop William Henry Elder, Bishop of Nashville*. Jackson, MS: R.O. Gerow, Bishop of Natchez-Jackson, 1960.
The Encyclopedia of American History. Rev. ed. New York: Harper, 1961.
Engle, Stephen D. *Struggle for the Heartland: The Campaigns from Fort Henry to Corinth*. Lincoln: University of Nebraska Press, 2001.
Fairbanks, Merwin G. *A History of Newspaper Journalism in Alton, Illinois, from 1836 to 1962, as Represented by the Alton Evening Telegraph and Its Predecessors*. Carbondale: Southern Illinois University Press, 1973.
Farrow, Lee A. *Alexis in America: A Russian Grand Duke's Tour, 1871–1872*. Baton, Rouge: Louisiana State University Press, 2014.
Federal Writers' Project. *Cincinnati: A Guide to the Queen City and Its Neighbors*. Columbus: Ohio State Archaeological and Historical Society, 1943.
Feis, William B. *Grant's Secret Service: The Intelligence War from Belmont to Appomattox*. Lincoln: University of Nebraska Press, 2002.
Fenster, Julie M. *Abraham Lincoln: A Story of Adultery, Murder, and the Making of a Great President*. New York: PalGrave. Macmillan, 2007.
_____. *The Case of Abraham Lincoln*. New York: Palgrave-Macmillan, 2007.
Field, Ron, and Adam Hook, *American Civil War Fortifications (3): The Mississippi and River Forts*. Fortress, no. 68. Oxford,UK: Osprey, 2007.
Fiske, John. *The Mississippi Valley in the Civil War*. Boston: Houghton, Mifflin, 1900.
Foote, Shelby. *The Civil War: A Narrative*. 3 vols. New York: Random House, 1958–1974; reprnt., New York: Vintage, 1986.
Force, Manning F. *From Fort Henry to Corinth*. Campaigns of the Civil War. No. 2. New York: Scribner's, 1882, reprnt., T.Y. Yoseloff, 1963.
Fox, Gustavus Vasa. *Confidential Correspondence of Gustavus Vasa Fox, Assistant Secretary of the Navy, 1861–1865*. Edited by Robert Means Thompson and Richard Wainwright. 2 vols. New York: De Vinne, 1920.
Fuess, Claude Moore. *Daniel Webster*. 2 vols. Boston: Little, Brown, 1930.
Fullenkamp, Leonard, Stephen Bosman, and Jay Luvaas. *Guide to the Vicksburg Campaign*. Lawrence: University of Kansas Press, 1998.
Fuller, Howard J. *Clad in Iron: The American Civil War and the Challenge of British Naval Power*. Westport, CT: Praeger, 2008.
Gabel, Christopher R.. and the Staff Ride Team. *Staff Ride Handbook for the Vicksburg Campaign, December 1862–July 1863*. Fort Leavenworth, KS: Combat Studies Institute, U.S. Army Command and General Staff College, 2001.

Gerteis, Louis S. *Civil War St. Louis*. Lawrence: University Press of Kansas, 2001.
Gibbons, Tony. *Warships and Naval Battles of the Civil War*. New York: Gallery, 1989.
Gibson, Charles Dana, with E. Kay Gibson. *Assault and Logistics, Vol. 1: Dictionary of Transports and Combat Vessels Steam and Sail Employed by the Union Army, 1861–1868*. Camden, ME: Ensign, 1995.
_____. *Assault and Logistics*. Vol. 2: *Union Army Coastal and River Operations, 1861–1866*. Camden, ME: Ensign, 1995.
Gosnell, H. Allen. *Guns on the Western Waters: The Story of the River Gunboats in the Civil War*. Baton Rouge: Louisiana State University Press, 1949; Reprnt., 1993.
Gould, Emerson W. *50 Years on the Mississippi*. St. Louis: Nixon-James, 1889.
Grabau, Warren. *98 Days: A Geographer's View of the Vicksburg Campaign*. Knoxville: University of Tennessee Press, 2000,
Grant, Ulysses S. *Memoirs and Selected Letters: Personal Memoirs of U.S. Grant, Selected Letters, 1839–186*. Edited by Mary D. McFeely and William S. McFeely. 2 vols. in 1. New York: Library of America, 1990.
_____. *The Papers of Ulysses S. Grant*. Edited by John Y. Simon. 31 vols. Edwardsville: Southern Illinois University Press, 1967–2009.
_____. *Personal Memoirs of U.S. Grant*. 2 vols. New York: C. L. Webster & Co., 1885–1886. Reprnt. 2 vols. in 1. New York: Penguin, 1999.
_____. *Personal Memoirs of U.S. Grant: A Modern Abridgment*. New York: Premier, 1962.
Gray, Patrick Leopoldo. *Gray's Doniphan County History*. Bendenta, KA: The Roycroft Press, 1905.
Green, Francis Vinton. *The Mississippi*. Campaigns of the Civil War. vol. 8. New York: Charles Scribner's Sons, 1885. Reprnt., Blue & Gray, n.d.
Groom, Winston. *Vicksburg 1863*. New York: Alfred A. Knopf, 2009.
Guelzo, Allen C. *Lincoln and Douglas: The Debates That Defined America*. New York: Simon & Schuster, 2008.
Hackemer, Kurt. *The U.S. Navy and the Origins of the Military-Industrial Complex, 1847–1883*. Annapolis: Naval Institute Press, 2001.
Haites, Erik F., James Mak, and Gary M. Walton. *Western River Transportation: The Era of Early Internal Developments, 1810–1860*. Baltimore: Johns Hopkins University Press, 1975.
Hall, Henry. *Report on the Ship-Building Industry of the United States*. Washington, D.C.: GPO, 1884; Reprnt., New York: Library Editions, 1970.
Hamersly, Lewis R., comp. *Records of the Living Officers of the United States Navy and Marine Corps*. 3rd ed. Philadelphia: J.B. Lippincott, 1878.
Hanson, Joseph Miles. *Conquest of the Missouri: The Story of the Life and Exploits of Capt. Grant Marsh*. Harrisburg, PA: Stackpole, 2003.
Hardy, Richard J., Richard R Dohm, and David A. Leuthold, ed. *Missouri Government and Politics*. Rev. and enl. ed. Columbia: University of Missouri Press, 1995.
Harris, NiNi. *History of Carondelet*. St. Louis: Southern Commercial Bank, 1991.
Harris, Norman Dwight. *The History of Negro Servitude in Illinois*. Chicago: A.C. McClurg, 1904.
Harrison, Bruce. *The Family Forrest Descendants of Lady Joan Beaufort of Beaufort Castle in England*. 2nd ed. Kamuela, HI: Millisecond, 2011.
Harrison, Lowell H. *The Civil War in Kentucky*. Lexington: University Press of Kentucky, 1975.
Hearn, Chester G. *Admiral David Dixon Porter: The Civil War Years*. Annapolis: Naval Institute Press, 1996.
_____. *Admiral David Glasgow Farragut: The Civil War Years*. Annapolis: Naval Institute Press, 1998.
_____. *Ellet's Brigade: The Strangest Outfit of All*. Baton Rouge: Louisiana State University Press, 2000.
Heath, Henry. *The Memoirs of Henry Heath*. Edited by James Morrison. Westport, CT: Greenwood, 1974.
Heckman, Richard Allen. *Lincoln vs. Douglas: The Great Debates Campaign*. Washington, D.C.: Public Affairs, 1967.
Heidler, David Stephen. *Encyclopedia of the War of 1812*. Annapolis: Naval Institute Press, 2004.
Hewitt, Lawrence Lee. *Port Hudson: Confederate Bastion on the Mississippi*. Baton Rouge: Louisiana State University Press, 1987.
Hill, Richard, and John Keegan. *War at Sea in the Ironclad Age*. Smithsonian History of Warfare. New York: Harper, 2006.
Historical Collections of Ohio. 3 vols. Cincinnati: C.J. Krikbiel, 1888.
History of Greene and Jersey Counties, Illinois. Springfield, IL: Continental Historical, 1885.
The History of Will County, Illinois. Chicago: William Le Baron, Jr., 1878.
Hoeling, Adolph A. *Vicksburg: 47 Days of Siege*. Mechanicsburg, PA: Stackpole, 1996.
Holzer, Harold. *Lincoln and the Power of the Press*. New York: Simon & Schuster, 2014.
Hoppin, James M. *The Life of Andrew Hull Foote, Rear Admiral, United States Navy*. New York: Harper, 1874.
Horn, Stanley F. *The Army of Tennessee: A Military History*. Indianapolis: Bobbs-Merrill, 1941.

Howard, Robert P. *Illinois: A History of the Prairie State*. Grand Rapids: William B. Eerdmans, 1973.
Hubbart, Henry Clyde. *The Older Middle West, 1840–1880: Its Social, Economic and Political Life, and Sectional Tendencies Before, During, and After the Civil War*. New York: Russell and Russell, 1936.
Hubbell, John T., and James W. Geary, ed. *Biographical Dictionary of the Union: Northern Leaders of the Civil War*. Westport, CT: Greenwood, 1995.
Hughes. Nathaniel Cheairs. *The Battle of Belmont: Grant Strikes South*. Chapel Hill: University of North Carolina Press, 1991.
Hull, Timothy L. *Supreme Court Justices: A Biographical Dictionary*. New York: Facts on File, 2001.
Hunter, Louis C. *Steamboats on the Western Rivers: An Economic and Technological History*. Cambridge, MA: Harvard University Press, 1949.
Hyde, William, and Howard I. Conard. *Encyclopedia of the History of St. Louis*. 5 vols. New York: Southern History, 1899.
Ingersoll, Lurton Dunham. *Iowa and the Rebellion*. Philadelphia: J.B. Lippincott, 1866.
Jackson, Joseph O., ed. *Some of the Boys: The Civil War Letters of Isaac Jackson 1862–1865*. Carbondale: Southern Illinois University Press, 1960.
Jackson, Rex T. *James B. Eads: The Civil War Ironclads and His Mississippi*. Westminster, MD: Heritage, 2004.
Jackson, Robert W. *Rails Across the Mississippi: A History of the St. Louis Bridge*. Urbana: University of Illinois Press, 2001.
James, Uriah Pierson. *James' River Guide*. Cincinnati: U.P. James, 1866.
Jett, Cheryl E. *Alton*. Images of America Series. Charleston, SC: Arcadia, 2009.
Johnson, Ludwell H. *Red River Campaign: Politics and Cotton in the Civil War*. Kent, OH: Kent State University Press, 1993.
Johnson, Robert E. *Rear Admiral John Rodgers, 1812–1882*. Annapolis: Naval Institute Press, 1967.
Johnson, Robert V., and Clarence C. Buel. *Battles and Leaders of the Civil War*. 4 vols. New York: Century, 1884–1887; reprnt., Thomas Yoseloff, 1956.
Joiner, Gary. *Mr. Lincoln's Brown Water Navy: The Mississippi Squadron*. Lanham, MD: Rowman and Littlefield, 2007.
_____. _____. *One Damn Blunder from Beginning to End: The Red River Campaign of 1864*. Lanham, MD: Rowman and Littlefield, 2003.
_____. *Through the Howling Wilderness: The 1864 Red River Campaign and Union Failure in the West*. Knoxville: University of Tennessee Press, 2006.
_____, ed. *Little to Eat and Thin Mud to Drink: Letters, Diaries, and Memoirs from the Red River Campaigns, 1863–1864*. Knoxville: University of Tennessee Press, 2007.
Kane, Adam. *The Western River Steamboat*. College Station: Texas A & M University Press, 2004.
Kargau, Ernst D., et al. *The German Element in St. Louis*. Baltimore: Genealogical, 2000.
Kerby, Robert L. *Kirby Smith's Confederacy: The Trans-Mississippi South, 1863–1865*. New York: Columbia University Press, 1972.
King, William H. *Lessons and Practical Notes on Steam*. Revised by James W. King. New York: D. Van Nostrand, 1864.
Kiper, Richard L. *Major General John Alexander McClernand: Politician in Uniform*. Kent, OH: Kent State University Press, 1999.
Klement, Frank L. *Dark Lanterns: Secret Political Societies, Conspiracies, and Treason Trials in the Civil War*. Baton Rouge: Louisiana State University Press, 1984.
Knight, Edward Henry. *Knight's American Mechanical Dictionary*. 3 vols. Boston: Hurd and Houghton, 1876.
Konstam, Angus. *Union River Ironclad, 1861–1865*. New Vanguard Series 56. London: Osprey, 2002.
Lane, Carl D, *American Paddle Steamboats*. New York: Coward-McCann, 1943.
Lea, James Henry. *A Genealogy of the Ancestors and Descendants of George Augustus and Louisa (Clap) Trumbull*. Worcester, MA: Priv. print., 1886.
Lehman, Amy. *Victorian Women and the Theatre of Trance: Mediums, Spiritualists and Mesmerists in Performance*. Jefferson, NC: McFarland, 2009.
Leonard, John W. *The Industries of St. Louis*. St. Louis: John W. Leonard, 1887.
Lewis, Lloyd. *Sherman: Fighting Prophet*. New York: Harcourt, Brace and World, 1960.
Lloyd, James T. *Lloyd's Steamboat Directory and Disasters on the Western Waters*. Cincinnati: James T. Lloyd, 1856.
Longacre, Edward G. *Grant's Cavalryman: The Life and Wars of General James H. Wilson*. Mechanicsburg, PA: Stackpole, 1996.
Lord-Drake, Maud. *Psychic-Light: The Continuity of Law and Life*. Kansas City, MO: Frank T. Riley, 1904.
Luraghi, Raimondo. *A History of the Confederate Navy*. Translated by Paolo E. Coletta. Annapolis: Naval Institute Press, 1996.
Lytle, William C., comp. *Merchant Steam Vessels of the United States, 1807–1868 "The Lytle List."* Publication No. 6. Mystic, CT: Steamship Historical Society of America, 1952.

Mahan, Alfred T. *The Gulf and Inland Waters.* Vol. 3 of *The Navy in the Civil War.* New York: Scribner's, 1883.
Mahoney, Timothy R. *River Towns in the Great West: The Structure of Provincial Urbanization in the American West, 1820–1870.* Cambridge, MA: Cambridge University Press, 1990.
Marquis, Albert N. *Book of St. Louisians.* 2nd ed. Chicago: A.N. Marquis, 1912.
Marszalek, John F. *Sherman: A Soldier's Passion for Order.* Carbondale: Southern Illinois University Press, 2007.
Martin, David. *The Vicksburg Campaign.* Conshohocken, PA: Combined, 1994.
Mayeux, Steven M. *Earthen Walls and Iron Men: Fort DeRussy, Louisiana, and the Defense of the Red River.* Knoxville: University of Tennessee Press, 2007.
McAfee, John J. *Kentucky Politicians.* Louisville: Press of the Courier-Journal, 1886.
McCune, Gill. *Mayors of St. Louis.* St. Louis: Title Insurance Company, 1949.
McPherson, James M. *Tried by War: Abraham Lincoln as Commander in Chief.* New York: Penguin, 2008.
_____. *War on the Waters: The Union and Confederate Navies, 1861–1865.* Charlotte: University of North Carolina Press, 2012.
Memorial Addresses on the Life and Character of Lewis V. Bogy, a Senator from Missouri. 44th Congress, 2nd sess. Washington, D.C.: GPO, 1878.
Merrill, James M. *Battle Flags South: The Story of the Civil War Navies on Western Waters.* Rutherford, NJ: Fairleigh Dickinson University Press, 1970.
_____. *The Rebel Shore: The Story of Union Sea Power in the Civil War.* Boston: Little, Brown, 1957.
Meyer, Douglas K. *Making the Heartland Quilt: A Geographical History of Settlement and Migration in Early 19th Century Illinois.* Carbondale: Southern Illinois University Press, 2000.
Miles, Jim. *A River Unvexed: A History and Tour Guide of the Campaign for the Mississippi River.* Nashville: Rutledge Hill, 1994.
Miller, David W. *Second Only to Grant: Quartermaster General Montgomery C. Meigs.* Shippensburg, PA: White Mane, 2000.
Miller, Francis Trevelyan, ed. *The Photographic History of the Civil War.* Vol. 6: *The Navies.* New York: Castle, 1911; Reprnt., New York: Thomas Yoseloff, 1957.
Milligan, John D. *Gunboats Down the Mississippi.* Annapolis: Naval Institute Press, 1965.
Mindell, David A. *Iron Coffin: War, Technology, and Experience Aboard the USS Monitor.* Baltimore: Johns Hopkins University Press, 2012.
Miner, H. Craig. *The St. Louis-San Francisco Transcontinental Railroad: The Thirty-fifth Parallel Project, 1853–1890.* Lawrence: University Press of Kansas, 1972.
Missouri Biographical Dictionary. 3 vols. 3rd ed. St. Clair Shores, MI: Somerset, 2001.
Moon, Jill. *Godfrey.* Charleston, SC: Arcadia, 2013.
Moore, Frank, ed. *The Rebellion Record: A Diary of American Events.* 12 vols. New York: G.P. Putnam, 1861–1863; D. Van Nostrand, 1864–1868; Reprnt., Arno, 1977.
Moore, James Lowell. *Introduction to the Writings of Andrew Jackson Davis.* Boston: Christopher, 1930.
Musicant, Ivan. *Divided Waters: The Naval History of the Civil War.* New York: HarperCollins, 1995.
Musser, Charles O. *Soldier Boy: The Civil War Letters of Charles O. Musser, 29th Iowa.* Edited by Barry Popchock. Iowa City: University of Iowa Press, 1995.
Myers, James E. *The Astonishing Saber Duel of Abraham Lincoln.* Springfield, IL: Lincoln-Herndon Building, 1968,
The National Cyclopedia of American Biography. New York: James T. White, 1893.
Neely, Mark E., Jr. *The Extra Journal: Rallying the Whigs of Illinois.* Fort Wayne: Louis A. Warren Lincoln Library and Museum, 1982.
Nevins, Allan. *The War for the Union: War Becomes Revolution.* New York: Charles Scribner's Sons, 1960.
Newman, James A. *The Autobiography of an Old Fashioned Boy.* Oklahoma City, OK?: s.n., 1923.
Nickell, Joe. *The Mystery Chronicles: More Real Life X-Files.* Lexington: University Press of Kentucky, 2004.
Niven, John. *Gideon Welles: Lincoln's Secretary of the Navy.* New York: Oxford University Press, 1973.
Noe, Kenneth W. *Perryville: This Grand Havoc of Battle.* Frankfurt: University Press of Kentucky, 2001.
Norton, Wilker T., ed. and comp., *Centennial History of Madison County, Illinois and Its People.* 2 vols. Chicago: Lewis, 1912.
Olmstead, Edwin, Wayne E. Stark, and Spencer C. Tucker. *The Big Guns: Civil War Siege, Seacoast and Naval Cannon.* Ontario, Bloomfield, NY: Alexandria Bay: Museum Restoration Service, 1997.
Owens, Harry P. *Steamboats and the Cotton Economy: River Trade in the Yazoo-Mississippi Delta.* Jackson: University of Mississippi Press, 1990.
Pabis, George S. *Daily Life Along the Mississippi.* Westport, CT: Greenwood, 2007.
Palmer, John M. The *Bench and Bar in Illinois.* 2 vols. Chicago: Lewis, 1899.
Parish, William E., Charles T. Jones, Jr., and Lawrence O. Christensen. *Missouri: The Heart of the Nation.* 2nd ed. Arlington Heights, IL: Harlan Davidson, 1992.
Parks, Joseph H. *General Edmund Kirby Smith, C.S.A.* Baton Rouge: Louisiana State University Press, 1954.

Parrish, T. Michael. *Richard Taylor: Soldier Prince of Dixie*. Chapel Hill: University of North Carolina Press, 1992.
Pellet, Elias P. *History of the 114th Regiment, New York State Volunteers*. Norwich, NY: Telegraph & Chronicle, 1866.
Perry, James M. *A Bohemian Brigade: The Civil War Correspondents, Mostly Rough, Sometimes Ready*. New York: John Wiley, 2000.
Petersen, William J. *Steamboating on the Upper Mississippi*. Iowa City: State Historical Society of Iowa, 1968; rpr. New York: Dover, 1995.
Plummer, Mark A. *Lincoln's Rail Splitter: Governor Richard J. Oglesby*. Urbana: University of Illinois Press, 2001.
Porter, David D. *Incidents and Anecdotes of the Civil War*. New York: D. Appleton, 1885; Reprnt., Harrisburg, PA: Archive Society, 1997.
_____. *Naval History of the Civil War*. New York: Sherman, 1886; Reprnt., Secaucus, NJ: Castle, 1984.
Portrait and Biographical Album of Pike and Calhoun Counties, Illinois. Chicago: Biographical, 1891.
Powers, Arnold P. *Devour Us Not: Short Stories of African American History*. Bloomington, IN: XLibris.com, 2013.
Powers, Ron. *Mark Twain: A Life*. New York: Free Press, 2005.
Pratt, Fletcher. *The Civil War on Western Waters*. New York: Holt, 1958.
Primm, James Neal. *Lion of the Valley: St. Louis, Missouri, 1764–1980*. 3rd ed. St. Louis: Missouri Historical Society Press, 1998.
Proceedings of the Congressional Convention Held in the City of St. Louis on the 13th, 14th, and 15th Days of May 1873. St. Louis: Woodward, Tiernan and Hale, 1873.
Raab, James W. W.. *Loring: Florida's Forgotten General*. Manhattan, KA: Sunflower University Press, 1996.
Reavis, L.U. *St. Louis: The Commercial Metropolis of the Mississippi Valley*. St. Louis: Tribune, 1874.
Reavis, L.U., et al. *St. Louis: The Future City of the World*. St. Louis: Gray, Baker, 1875.
Reed, Rowena. *Combined Operations in the Civil War*. Annapolis: Naval Institute Press, 1978.
Richard, Allen C., Jr., and Mary Margaret Higgeinbotham Richard. *The Defense of Vicksburg: A Louisiana Chronicle*. Williams-Ford Texas A&M University Military History Series. College Station: Texas A & M University Press, 2003.
Ringle, Dennis J. *Life in Mr. Lincoln's Navy*. Annapolis: Naval Institute Press, 1998.
Roberts, William H. *Civil War Ironclads: The U.S. Navy and Industrial Mobilization*. Baltimore: Johns Hopkins University Press, 2002.
Roe, Francis Asbury. *Naval Duties and Discipline, with the Policy and Principles of Naval Organization*. New York: D. Van Nostrand, 1865.
Rombauer, Robert J. *The Union Cause in St. Louis in 1862*. St. Louis: Press of Nixon-Jones, 1909.
Rose, Philip. *Andrew Johnson's Circle Trip*. Bloomington, IN: Trafford, 2011.
Roske, Ralph J. *His Own Counsel: The Life and Times of Lyman Trumbull*. Reno: University of Nevada Press, 1979.
St. Louis Board of Aldermen. *Journal of the City Council of the City of St. Louis, April 1870-April 1871*. St. Louis: George Knapp, 1871.
Sandburg, Carl. *Abraham Lincoln: The Prairie Years*. New York: Harcourt, Brace, 1926.
Saylor, Henry H. *Dictionary of Architecture*. New York: John Wiley, 1953.
Schaefer, Mike. *Classic American Railroads*. 3 vols. St. Paul, MN: MBI, 2003.
Scharf, J. Thomas. *History of the Confederate Navy from Its Organization to the Surrender of Its Last Vessel*. New York: Rodgers and Sherwood, 1887, Reprnt., New York: Fairfax, 1977.
_____. *History of St. Louis City and County*. 2 vols. Philadelphia: Louis H. Everts, 1883.
Schroeder-Lein, Glenna R. *The Encyclopedia of Civil War Medicine*. Armonk NY: M.E. Sharpe, 2008.
Scott, H.L. *Military Dictionary, Comprising Technical Definitions*. New York: D. Van Nostrand, 1864.
Selfridge, Thomas O., Jr. *Memoirs of Thomas O. Selfridge, Jr., Rear Admiral, U.S.N.* New York: Knickerbocker, 1924; reprnt., Columbia, University of South Carolina Press, 1987.
Semi-Centennial and General Catalogue of the Officers and Students of Shurtleff College. Upper Alton IL: Daily Telegraph, 1877.
Shea, William L., and Terrence J. Winschel. *Vicksburg Is the Key: The Struggle for the Mississippi Valley*. Great Campaigns of the Civil War Series. Lincoln: University of Nebraska Press, 2003.
Sherman, William Tecumseh. *Memoirs*. 2 vols. New York: Appleton, 1875; reprnt., Penguin Classics. New York: Penguin, 2000.
_____. *Sherman's Civil War: Selected Correspondence of William T. Sherman, 1860–1865*. Edited by Brooks D. Simpson and Jean V. Berlin. Chapel Hill: University of North Carolina Press, 1999.
Shomette, Donald G. *Shipwrecks of the Civil War: The Encyclopedia of Union and Confederate Naval Losses*. Washington, D.C.: Donic Ltd., 1973.
Silverstone, Paul. *Civil War Navies, 1855–1883*. New York: Routledge, 2006.
_____. *Warships of the Civil War Navies*. Annapolis: Naval Institute Press, 1989.
Simon, Paul. *Freedom's Champion: Elijah Lovejoy*. Carbondale: Southern Illinois University Press, 1994.

Simpson, Brooks D. *Ulysses S. Grant: Triumph Over Adversity, 1822–1865.* New York: Houghton Mifflin Harcourt, 2000.
Simpson, Edward. *A Treatise on Ordnance and Naval Gunnery, Compiled and Arranged as a Text-Book for the U.S. Naval Academy.* 2nd ed. New York: D. Van Nostrand, 1862.
Simson, Jay W. *Naval Strategies of the Civil War: Confederate Innovations and Federal Opportunism.* Nashville: Cumberland House, 2001.
Sketch Book of St. Louis. St. Louis: George Knapp, 1858.
Slagle, Jay. *Ironclad Captain: Seth Ledyard Phelps and the U.S. Navy.* Kent, OH: Kent State University Press, 1996.
Sloan, Edward William, III. *Benjamin Franklin Isherwood, Naval Engineer: The Years as Engineer-in-Chief, 1861–1869.* Annapolis: Naval Institute Press, 1965.
Smith, Frank E. *The Yazoo River.* Rivers of America. New York: Rinehart, 1954; Reprnt., Jackson: University Press of Mississippi, 1988.
Smith, George W. *When Lincoln Came to Egypt.* Herrin, IL: Trovillion, 1940.
Smith, Jean Edward. *Grant.* New York: Simon & Schuster, 2001.
Smith, Myron J., Jr. *Civil War Biographies from the Western Waters.* Jefferson, NC: McFarland, 2015.
_____. *The CSS Arkansas: A Confederate Ironclad on Western Waters.* Jefferson, NC: McFarland, 2011.
_____. *The Fight for the Yazoo, August 1862–July 1864: Swamps, Forts, and Fleets on Vicksburg's Northern Flank.* Jefferson, NC: McFarland, 2012.
_____. *The Timberclads in the Civil War.* Jefferson, NC: McFarland, 2008.
_____. *The Tinclads in the Civil War: Union Light-Draught Gunboat Operations on Western Waters, 1862–1865.* Jefferson, NC: McFarland, 2010.
_____. *The USS Carondelet: A Civil War Ironclad on Western Waters.* Jefferson, NC: McFarland, 2010.
Smith, Walter George. *The Life and Letters of Thomas Kilby Smith, Brevet Major General United States Volunteers, 1820–1887.* New York: G.P. Putnam's, 1898.
Smith, William E. *The Francis Preston Blair Family in Politics.* 2 vols. New York: Macmillan, 1933.
Soley, James R, *Admiral Porter.* New York: D. Appleton, 1903.
Speer, Lonnie R. *Portals to Hell: Military Prisons of the Civil War.* Mechanicsburg, PA: Stackpole, 1997.
Stamp, Kenneth M. *And the War Came: The North and the Secession Crisis, 1860–1861.* Baton Rouge: Louisiana State University Press, 1970.
Stevens, Walter Barlow. *Missouri, the Center State, 1821–1915.* 4 vols. Chicago, S.J. Lewis, 1915.
_____. *The Reporter's Lincoln.* Edited by Michael Burlingame. Lincoln: University of Nebraska Press, 1998.
_____. *St. Louis, the Fourth City, 1764–1911.* 3 vols. St. Louis: S.J. Clarke, 1939.
Stockton, Joseph. *War Diary of Brevet Brigadier General Joseph Stockton.* Chicago: John T. Stockton, 1910.
Switzler, William Franklin, et al. *Switzler's Illustrated History of Missouri from 1541–1877.* St. Louis: C. R. Barnes, Publisher, 1879.
Symonds, Craig L. *The Civil War at Sea.* Santa Barbara, CA: ABC/CLIO, 2009.
_____. *Lincoln and His Admirals: Abraham Lincoln, the U.S. Navy, and the Civil War.* New York: Oxford University Press, 2008.
Tarbell, Ida M. *Abraham Lincoln and His Ancestors.* New York: Harper, 1924; reprnt. New York: Bison, 1997.
Taylor, Richard. *Destruction and Reconstruction: Personal Experiences of the Late War.* New York: D. Appleton, 1879.
Thorpe, Thomas Bangs. *The Mysteries of the Backwoods; or, Sketches of the Southeast, Including Character, Scenery, and Rural Sports.* Philadelphia: Carey & Hart, 1846.
Tomer, John S., and Michael J. Brodhead. *A Naturalist in Indian Territory: The Journals of S.W. Woodhouse, 1849–1850.* Norman: University of Oklahoma Press, 1992.
Townsend, Mary Bobbitt. *Yankee Warhorse: A Biography of Major General Peter Osterhaus.* Columbia: University of Missouri Press, 2010.
Tucker, Louis L. *Cincinnati During the Civil War.* Publications Ohio Civil War Centennial Commission, no. 9. Columbus: Ohio State University Press, 1962.
Tucker, Spencer C. *Andrew Foote: Civil War Admiral on Western Waters.* Annapolis: Naval Institute Press, 2000.
_____. *Arming the Fleet: U.S. Navy Ordnance in the Muzzle-Loading Era.* Annapolis: Naval Institute Press, 1988
_____. *Blue & Gray Navies: The Civil War Afloat.* Annapolis: U.S. Naval Institute, 2006.
_____, ed. *The Civil War Naval Encyclopedia.* 2 vols. Santa Barbara, CA: ABC-Clio, 2011.
Tunnard, William H. *A Southern Record: The History of the Third Regiment Louisiana Infantry.* Baton Rouge: Printed for the Author, 1866.
Twain, Mark. *Life on the Mississippi.* New York: Harper, 1950.
Union Merchants' Exchange of St. Louis. *Proceedings of the Mississippi River Improvement Convention Held in St. Louis, February 12–13, 1867.* St. Louis: George Knapp, 1867.

United States. Navy Department. *Laws of the United States Relating to the Navy.* Washington, D.C.: GPO, 1866.
____. ____. Mississippi Squadron. *General Orders, Rear Adm. D.D. Porter, Commanding, from Oct. 16th 1862 to Oct. 26th, 1864.* St. Louis: R.P. Studley, 1864.
____. ____. Naval History Division. *Civil War Naval Chronology, 1861–1865.* 6 vols. in 1. Rev. ed. Washington, D.C.: GPO, 1966.
____. ____. *Regulations for the Government of the United States Navy.* Washington, D.C.: GPO, 1865.
____. ____. ____. *Riverine Warfare.* Washington, D.C.: GPO, 1968.
____. ____. Office of the Secretary of the Navy. *Report of the Secretary of the Navy.* 6 vols. Washington, D.C.: GPO, 1861–1866.
____. Surgeon General's Office. *The Medical and Surgical History of the War of the Rebellion.* 6 vols. Washington, D.C.: GPO, 1870–1888.
United States. War Department. *Executive Document 194: Letter from the Secretary of War Transmitting Reports of the Construction of the St. Louis and Illinois Bridge Across the Mississippi River.* 43rd Cong., 1st sess.Washington, D.C.: GPO, 1874.
Van Ravenswaay, Charles. *St. Louis: An Informal History of the City and Its People, 1764–1865.* St. Louis: Missouri Historical Society Press, 1991.
Van Voorhis, John Stogdell. *The Old and New Monongahela.* Pittsburgh: Nicholson, 1893.
Voss, Viola W. *Footprints and Echoes from Historical Alton Area.* Alton, IL: Priv. print, 1973.
Wakelyn, John L. *Biographical Dictionary of the Confederacy.* Westport, CT: Greenwood, 1977.
Walke, Henry. *Naval Scenes and Reminiscences of the Civil War in the United States on the Southern and Western Waters During the Years 1861, 1862 and 1863 with the History of That Period Compared and Corrected from Authentic Sources.* New York: F.R. Reed, 1877.
Walker, Peter F. *Vicksburg: A People at War, 1860–1865.* Chapel Hill: University of North Carolina Press, 1960.
Wallace, Lew. *An Autobiography.* 2 vols. New York: Harper, 1906.
____. *Smoke, Sound and Fury: The Civil War Memoirs of Major General Lew Wallace, U.S. Volunteers.* Edited by Jim Leeke. Portland, OR: Strawberry Hill, 1998.
Ward, Geoffrey C. *A Disposition to Be Rich.* New York: A.A. Knopf, 2012.
Warmoth, Henry Clay. *War, Politics and Reconstruction.* Columbia: University of South Carolina Press, 2006.
Warner, Ezra. *Generals in Blue: Lives of Union Commanders.* Baton Rouge: Louisiana State University Press, 1964.
____. *Generals in Gray. Lives of Confederate Commanders.* Baton Rouge: Louisiana State University Press, 1959.
Waterhouse, Sylvester. *A Memorial to Congress to Secure an Adequate Appropriation for a Prompt and Thorough Improvement of the Mississippi River.* St. Louis: John Daly, 1877.
Way, Frederick, Jr. *Way's Packet Directory, 1848–1994: Passenger Steamboats of the Mississippi River System Since the Advent of Photography in Mid-Continent America.* Athens: Ohio University Press, 1983; rev. ed., 1994.
Wayne, Michael. *The Reshaping of Plantation Society: The Natchez District, 1860–1880.* Baton Rouge: Louisiana State University Press, 1983.
Weber, Jennifer L. *Copperheads: The Rise and Fall of Lincoln's Opponents in the North.* New York: Oxford University Press, 2006.
Webster's Geographical Dictionary. Rev. ed. Springfield, MA: G. & C. Merriam, 1966.
Weigley, Russell F. *Quartermaster General of the Union Army: A Biography of M.C. Meigs.* New York: Columbia University Press, 1959.
Welcher, Frank J. *The Union Army, 1861–1865.* Vol. 3: *Organization and Operations—The Western Theater.* Bloomington: Indiana University Press, 1993.
Welles, Gideon. *The Diary of Gideon Welles, Secretary of the Navy Under Lincoln and Johnson.* Edited by John T. Morse, Jr. 3 vols. Boston: Houghton, Mifflin, 1911; Reprnt., New York: W.W. Norton, 1960.
West, Richard S. *Gideon Welles: Lincoln's Navy Department.* Indianapolis: Bobbs-Merrill, 1943.
____. *Mr. Lincoln's Navy.* New York: Longman's, Green, 1957.
____. *The Second Admiral: A Life of David Dixon Porter, 1813–1891.* New York: Coward-McCann, 1937.
White, Horace. *The Life of Lyman Trumbull.* Boston and New York: Houghton Mifflin, 1913.
Wilkie, Franc B. *Pen and Powder.* Boston: Ticknor, 1888.
Williams, Walter, ed. *A History of Northwest Missouri.* 3 vols. Chicago: Lewis, 1915.
Wilson, James Grant, and John Fisk, ed. *Appleton's Cyclopedia of American Biography.* 5 vols. New York: D. Appleton, 1888.
Wilson, James H. *Under the Old Flag.* 2 vols. New York: D. Appleton, 1912.
Winschel, Terrence J. *Triumph and Defeat: The Vicksburg Campaign.* 2 vols. New York: Savas Beatie, 2006.
Winters, John D. *The Civil War in Louisiana.* Baton Rouge: Louisiana State University Press, 1963.

Woodworth, Steven E. *Jefferson Davis and His Generals: The Failure of Confederate Command in the West.* Lawrence: University Press of Kansas, 1990.
_____. *Nothing but Victory: The Army of the Tennessee, 1861–1865.* New York: Alfred A. Knopf, 2005.
_____. *Sherman.* Great Generals Series. New York: Palgrave Macmillan, 2009.
_____., ed. *Grant's Lieutenants: From Cairo to Vicksburg.* Lawrence: University Press of Kansas, 2001.
W.R. Brink & Co. *History of Madison County, Illinois.* Edwardsville, IL: W.R. Brink, 1882.
Wright, Howard C. *Port Hudson: Its History from an Interior Point of View as Sketched from the Diary of an Officer.* St. Francisville, LA: St. Francisville Democrat, 1937.
Wright, John Stephen. *Chicago: Past, Present, Future.* Chicago: Horton and Leonard, 1870.
Young, John P. *Journalism in California.* San Francisco: Chronicle, 1915.

Articles, Essays and Journals

Adams, Roger C. "Panic on the Ohio: The Defense of Cincinnati, Covington, and Newport, September 1862." *Journal of Kentucky Studies* 9 (September 1992), 81–98.
Ambrose, Stephen E. "The Union Command System and the Donelson Campaign." *Military Affairs* 24 (Summer 1960), 78–86.
Anderson, Bern. "The Naval Strategy of the Civil War." *Military Affairs* 26 (Spring 1962), 11–21.
Aptheker, Herbert. "The Negro in the Union Navy." *Journal of Negro History* 32 (April 1947), 169–200.
Arnold, James R. "Rough Work on the Mississippi." *Naval History* 13, no. 5 (1999), 38–43.
Barrows, H.D. "J. Lancaster Brent." *Quarterly of the Historical Society of Southern California* 6 (1905), 238–241.
Bearss, Edwin C. "Grand Gulf's Role in the Civil War." *Civil War History* 5 (March 1959), 5–29.
_____. "The Vicksburg River Defenses and the Enigma of 'Whistling Dick.'" *Journal of Mississippi History* 29 (January 1957), 21–30.
Bearss, Edwin C., and Warren E. Grabau. "How Porter's Flotilla Ran the Gauntlet Past Vicksburg." *Civil War Times Illustrated* 1 (December 1962), 38–47.
Bodman, Albert H. "'In Sight of Vicksburg': Private Diary of a Northern War Correspondent." Edited by Leo M. Kaiser. *Chicago Historical Society Bulletin* 34 (May 1956), 202–221.
Bogle, Victor M. "New Albany's Attachment to the Ohio River." *Indiana Magazine of History* 49 (September 1953), 249–266.
Bonham, Milledge L., Jr. "Man and Nature at Port Hudson, 1863." *Military Historian & Economist* 2, 3 (October 1917-January 1918), 20–38.
Branch, Mary Emerson. "Prime Emerson and Steamboat Building in Memphis." *West Tennessee Historical Society Papers* 38 (1984), 69–83.
_____. "A Story Behind the Story of the *Arkansas* and the *Carondelet*." *Missouri Historical Review* 79 (April 1985), 313–331.
Brand, W.F. "The Capture of the *Indianola*." *Maryland Historical Magazine* 4 (December 1909), 353–361.
Brewer, Charles C. "African-American Sailors and the Unvexing of the Mississippi River." *Prologue* 30 (Winter 1996), 279–286.
Brown, George W. "Service in the Mississippi Squadron and Its Connection with the Siege and Capture of Vicksburg." In: vol. 1 of James Grant Wilson and Titus Munson Con, eds., *Personal Recollections of the War of the Rebellion: Addresses Delivered Before the New York Commandery of the Loyal Legion of the United States, 1883–1891.* New York: Commandery, 1891.
Brown, Joseph. "River Navigation, Steamboat." In William Hyde and Howard I. Conrad, *Encyclopedia of the History of St. Louis.* 5 vols. New York: Southern History, 1899, IV, 1923.
_____. "Steamboating in the Old Days on the Mississippi." *American Jewess* 2 (April 1896), 360–364.
Burnham, John C. "The Social Evil Ordinance: A Social Experiment in Nineteenth Century St. Louis." *Bulletin of the Missouri Historical Society* 27 (April 1971), 203–217.
Calhoun, Robert Dabney. "The John Perkins Family of Northeast Louisiana." *Louisiana Historical Quarterly* 19 (1936), 70–88.
"Career of Gen. Joseph Lancaster Brent." *Confederate Veteran* 17 (1909), 345–347.
Carnes, F.G., comp. "'We Can Hold Our Ground': Calvin Smith's Diary." *Civil War Times Illustrated* 24 (April 1985), 24–31.
Carson, John M. "The Capture of the *Indianola*." *Confederate Veteran* 32 (1924), 380–381.
Catton, Bruce. "Glory Road Began in the West." *Civil War History* 6 (June 1960), 229–237.
Chamberlain, S. "Opening of the Upper Mississippi and the Siege of Vicksburg." *Magazine of Western History* 4 (March 1887), 609–624.
Coggins, Jack. "Civil War Naval Ordnance: Weapons and Equipment." *Civil War Times Illustrated* 4 (November 1964), 16–20.
Coulter, E. Merton. "Effects of Secession Upon the Commerce of the Mississippi Valley." *Mississippi Valley Historical Review* 3 (December 1915), 275–300.

Curran, Nathaniel B. "Levi Davis, Illinois' Third Auditor." *Journal of the Illinois State Historical Society* 71 (February 1978), 2–12.
Dall, W.H. "Some American Conchologists." *Proceedings of the Biological Society of Washington* 4 (1888), 95–134.
Dimmock, Thomas. "Lovejoy: Hero and Martyr." *New England* 4 (March-August 1891), 364–378.
Donaldson, Gary. "'Into Africa': Kirby Smith and Braxton Bragg's Invasion of Kentucky." *Filson Club Historical Quarterly* 61 (October 1987), 444–465.
Dorsett, Phyllis F. "James B. Eads: Navy Shipbuilder, 1861." *U.S. Naval Institute Proceedings* 101 (August 1975), 76–79.
East, Sherrod E. "Montgomery C. Meigs and the Quartermaster Department." *Military Affairs* 25 (Winter 1961–1962), 183–196.
Eisterhold, John A. "Fort Heiman: Forgotten Fortress." *West Tennessee Historical Society Papers* 28 (1974), 43–54.
Farragut, Loyal. "Farragut at Port Hudson." *Putnam's* 5 (October 1908), 44–53.
"Fred Grant as a Boy with the Army." *Confederate Veteran* 16 (January 1908), 10–14.
"Frederick E. Potter, MD." *New Hampshire Medical Society Transactions* (Concord, NH: Ira C. Evans, 1903), 240.
Gaden, Elmer L. "Eads and the Navy of the Mississippi." *American Heritage of Invention and Technology* 9 (Spring 1994), 24–31.
Gerelman, David J. "Acting Masters of Disaster." *Lincoln Editor: The Quarterly Newsletter of the Papers of Abraham Lincoln* 11 (July-September 2011), 4–8.
Gould, Emerson W. "The Atlantic and Mississippi Steamship Company." In Emerson W. Gould, *50 Years on the Mississippi*. St. Louis: Nixon-James, 1889.
Gulick, Charles Heckman "Heck". "Letters from 'Heck.'" Edited by Stan Hamper. *Civil War Times Illustrated* 21 (June 1982), 24–31.
Haites, Erick F., and James Mak. "The Decline of Steamboating on the Antebellum Western Rivers: Some New Evidence and an Alternative Hypothesis." *Explorations in Economic History* 11 (Fall 1973), 25–36.
Harrison, Robert W. "Levee Building in Mississippi Before the Civil War." *Journal of Mississippi History* 12 (April 1950), 63–97.
Hass, Paul H., ed. "The Vicksburg Diary of Henry Clay Warmoth." *Journal of Mississippi History* 71 (November 1969-February 1970), 334–347, 69–74.
Hoffman, Judy. "'If I Fall, My Grave. Shall Be Made in Alton': Elijah Lovejoy, Martyr for Abolition." *Gateway* 25 (Summer 2005), 1+.
Hogane, James T. "Reminiscences of the Siege of Vicksburg." *Southern Historical Society Papers* 11 (April-May 1883), 4854–4886.
Hurley, Andrew. "Busby's Stink Boat and the Regulation of Nuisance Trades, 1865–1918." In Andrew Hurley, ed. *Common Fields: An Environmental History of St. Louis. St. Louis:* Missouri Historical Society Press, 1997.
Joiner, Gary D. "The Congressional Investigation Following the Red River Campaign." *North Louisiana History* 35 (Fall 2004), 147–167.
_____. "The Red River Campaign." *Louisiana Cultural Vistas* (Fall 2006), 58–69.
_____. "Up the Red River and Down to Defeat." *America's Civil War* (March 2004), 22–29.
Joiner, Gary D., and Charles E. Vetter. "The Union Naval Expedition on the Red River, March 12-May 22, 1864." *Civil War Regiments: A Journal of the American Civil War* 4, no. 2 (1994), 26–67.
Kouwenhoven, John A. "The Designing of the Eads Bridge." *Technology and Culture* 23 (October 1982), 535–568.
_____. "Downtown St. Louis as James B Eads Knew It When the Bridge was Opened a Century Ago." *Bulletin of the Missouri Historical Association* 30 (April 1974), 181–195.
_____. "Eads Bridge: The Celebration." *Bulletin of the Missouri Historical Association* 30 (April 1974), 159–180.
Landers, H.L. "Wet Sand and Cotton: Banks' Red River Campaign." *Louisiana Historical Quarterly* 19 (January 1936), 150–195.
Legan, Marshall S. "The Confederate Career of a Union Ram [*Queen of the West*]." *Louisiana History* 33 (Summer 2000), 277–300.
Lucibello, Alan. "Panic of 1873." In Daniel Leab, ed. *Encyclopedia of American Recessions and Depressions.* Santa Barbara, CA: ABC-CLIO, 2014.
Mak, James, and Gary M. Walton. "Steamboats and the Great Productivity Surge in River Transportation." *Journal of Economic History* 3 (September 1972), 619–640.
Matile, Roger. "John Frink and Martin Walker: Stagecoach Kings of the Old Northwest." *Journal of the Illinois State Historical Society Journal* 95 (Summer 2002), 119–130.
"Maud Lord-Drake." in Victoria Barnes, ed. *Centennial Book of Modern Spiritualism in America.* Chicago: National Spiritualist Association, 1948.

Mayeux, Steven W. "Joseph L. Brent: Lawyer, Warrior, and Prophet of Tank Warfare." In Lawrence Lee Hewitt and Thomas E. Schott, eds. *Confederate Generals in the Trans-Mississippi.* Vol. 2: *Essays on America's Civil War.* Knoxville: University of Tennessee Press, 2015.
McCammack, Brian. "Competence, Power, and the Nostaligic Romance of Piloting in Mark Twain's *Life on the Mississippi*." *Southern Literary Journal* 39 (March 2006), 1–18.
McCampbell, Coleman. " H.L. Kinney and Daniel Webster in Illinois in the 1830s." *Journal of the Illinois Historical Society* 47 (Spring 1954), 36–42.
McCune, John S. "St. Louis and Keokuk Packet Company." In Jacob N. Taylor and M.O. Crooks. *Sketch Book of St. Louis.* St. Louis: George Knapp, 1858.
McDermott, Stacy Pratt. "*Mcready v. City of Alton, Illinois*." *Lincoln Legal Briefs: A Quarterly Newsletter of the Lincoln Legal Papers,* no. 75 (July-September 2005), 3–5.
Merrill, James M. "Cairo, Illinois: Strategic Civil War River Port." *Journal of the Illinois State Historical Society* 76 (Winter 1983), 242–257.
_____. "Union Shipbuilding on Western Waters During the Civil War." *Smithsonian Journal of History* 3 (Winter 1968–1969), 17–44.
Meyer, Roland L., Jr., "Inland Shipyard Saga." *Marine Engineering and Shipping Review* 51 (February 1946), 127–129.
Michael, William H.C. "How the Mississippi Was Opened." In *Civil War Sketches and Incidents; Papers Read Before the Nebraska Commandery, Military Order of the Loyal Legion of the United States.* Omaha: Commandery, 1902.
Miller, Milford M. "Evansville Steamboats During the Civil War," *Indiana Magazine of History* 37 (December 1941), 359–381.
Milligan, John D. "Expedition into the Bayous." *Civil War Times Illustrated* 15 (January 1977), 12–21.
_____. "The First American Ironclads: The Evolution of a Design," *Missouri Historical Society Bulletin* 22 (October 1965), 3–13
_____. "From Theory to Application: The Emergence of the American Ironclad War Vessel." *Military Affairs* 48 (July 1984), 126–132.
_____. "Navy Life on the Mississippi River." *Civil War Times Illustrated* 33 (May-June 1994), 16, 66–73.
Milligan, John D., ed. "The Dark and the Light Side of the River War." *Civil War Times Illustrated* 9 (December 1970), 12–19.
Morgan, John S. "Diary of John S. Morgan, Company G, Thirty-Third Iowa Infantry." *Annals of Iowa* 13 (January 1923), 483–508.
Norton, W.T. "An Old Time Tragedy at the State Penitentiary at Alton." *Journal of the Illinois State Historical Society* 6 (July 1913), 242–245.
Parent, Edward D. "Modeling the Ironclad USS *Indianola* (1862–1863)." *Ships in Scale,* 19 (May-June 2007), 44–53.
Parker, Theodore R. "Western Pennsylvania and the Naval War on the Inland Waters, 1861–1863." *Pennsylvania History* 16 (July 1949), 221–229.
_____. "William J. Kountz, Superintendent of River Transportation Under McClellan, 1861–62." *Western Pennsylvania Historical Magazine* 21 (December 1938), 237–254.
Perry, Oran. "The Entering Wedge." In *Indiana MOLLUS War Papers.* Vol. 1. New York: Military Order of the Loyal Legion of the United States, 1898; reprnt., vol. 24, Wilmington, DE: Broadfoot, 1992.
_____. "Regimental History." In Carolyn S. Bridge, comp. *These Men Were Heroes Once: The 69th Indiana Volunteer Infantry.* West Lafayette, IN: Twin, 2005.
"The Plague in the South-West: The Great Yellow Fever Epidemic in 1853." *DeBow's Review* 15 (December 1853), 595–635.
Rafferty, Edward C. "The Boss Who Never Was: Col. Ed Butler and the Limit of Practical Politics in St. Louis, 1875–1904." *Gateway Heritage* 12 (Winter 1992), 54–73.
Rea, Ralph R., ed. "Diary of Private John P. Wright, 29th Iowa, U.S.A., 1863–1865." *Arkansas Historical Quarterly* 16 (Autumn 1957), 304–318.
Riegel, R.E. "The Missouri-Pacific Railroad to 1879." *Missouri Historical Review* 18 (October 1923), 3–26.
Rockenbach, Stephen I. "A Border City at War: Louisville and the 1862 Invasion of Kentucky." *Ohio Valley History* 3 (Winter 2003), 35–52.
Seitz, E.B. "A City With Abiding Faith." *Mississippi Valley Magazine* 3 (June 1919), 10.
Smith, Timothy B. "Victory at Any Cost: The Yazoo Pass Expedition." *Journal of Mississippi History* 67 (Summer 2007), 147–166.
Stevens, Walter A. "The Missouri Tavern." *Missouri Historical Review* 15 (January 1921), 241–276.
Stiles, John C. "A Remarkable Shot." *Confederate Veteran* 28 (1920), 358.
Still, William N., Jr. "The Common Sailor—The Civil War's Uncommon Man: Part I, Yankee Blue Jackets." *Civil War Times Illustrated* 23 (February 1985), 25–39.
Stoler, Mildred C. "The Democratic Element in the New Republican Party in Illinois, 1856–1860." *Papers in Illinois History and Transactions for the Year 1942.* Springfield: Illinois Historical Society, 1944.

____. "Insurgent Democrats of Indiana and Illinois in 1854." *Indiana Magazine of History* 33 (Spring 1937), 1–31.
Suhr, Robert Collins. "The Union's Hard-Luck Ironclad." *American Civil War* 6 (1993), 34–40
Sutton, Robert M. "Illinois' Year of Decision, 1837." *Journal of the Illinois State Historical Society Journal* 58 (Spring 1965), 34–53.
Tucker, Spencer C. "Capturing the Confederacy's Western Waters." *Naval History* 20 (June 2006), 16–23.
Vitz, Carl. "Cincinnati: Civil War Port." *Museum Echoes* 34 (July 1961), 51–54.
Wallace, Agnes. "The Wiggins Ferry Monopoly." *Missouri Historical Review* 42 (October 1947), 1–19.
Ward, William Shaw. "How We Ran the Vicksburg Batteries." *Magazine of American History and Notes and Queries* 14 (July-December 1885), 600–605.
Webber, Richard, and John C. Roberts. "James B. Eads: Master Builder." *The Navy* 8 (March 1965), 23–25.
Wegner, Dana S. "Commodore William D. 'Dirty Bill' Porter." *U.S. Naval Institute Proceedings* 103 (February 1977), 40–49.
Weigley, Russel F. "Montgomery C. Meigs: A Personality Profile." *Civil War Times Illustrated* 3 (November 1964), 42–48.
West, Richard S., Jr. "Gunboats in the Swamps: The Yazoo Pass Expedition." *Civil War History* 9 (June 1963), 157–166.
____. "Lincoln's Hand in Naval Matters," *Civil War History* 4 (June 1958), 175–181.
White, John H., Jr. "Captain Hercules Carrel and the Cincinnati Marine Railway." *S & D Reflector* 45 (Summer 2008), 10–19.
____. "The Cincinnati Marine Railway." *Queen City Heritage* 57 (Summer-Fall 1999), 69–83.
Williams, E. Cort "The Cruise of 'The Black Terror.'" In Robert Hunter, ed., *Sketches of War History: Papers Prepared for the Ohio Commandery of the Loyal Legion of the United States.* 3 vols. Cincinnati: Robert Clarke, 1890.
Winchell, N.H. "A Sketch of Richard Owen." *American Geologist* 6 (September 1890), 135–145.
Wright, John L. "A Forerunner to Freedom." *Goody's* 136 (June 1898), 653–657.
Wunsuch, James. "The Social Evil Ordinance." *American Heritage* 33 (February 1982), 50–55.
Yungmeyer, D.W. "An Excursion into the Early History of the Chicago and Alton Railroad." *Journal of the Illinois State Historical Society* 38 (March 1945), 7–37.

Dissertations and Masters' Theses

Bogle, Victor M. "A 19th Century River Town: A Social-Economic Study of New Albany, Indiana." PhD Diss., Boston University, 1951.
Budd, Nicholas F. "The Adaptation of the Vessels of the Western Gunboat Flotilla to the Circumstances of Riverine Warfare During the American Civil War." Master's thesis, U.S. Army Command and General Staff College, 1997.
Chapman, Jesse L. "The Ellet Family and Riverine Warfare in the West, 1861–1865." Master's thesis, Old Dominion University, 1985.
Getchll, Charles M., Jr. "Defender of Inland Waters: The Military Career of Isaac Newton Brown, Commander, Confederate States Navy, 1861–1865." Master's thesis, University of Mississippi, 1978.
Goodman, Michael Harris. "The Black Tar: Negro Seamen in the Union Navy." PhD Diss., University of Nottingham, 1975.
Parker, Theodore R. "The Federal Gunboat Flotilla on the Western Waters During Its Administration by the War Department to October 1, 1862." PhD Diss., University of Pittsburgh, 1939.
Polser, Aubrey Henry. "The Administration of the United States Navy, 1861–1865." PhD Diss., University of Nebraska, 1975.

Correspondence and Interviews

Meagher, David, to Myron J. Smith, Jr., August 15, 2010 (e-mail).
Prout, Don, to Myron J. Smith, Jr., February 11, 2014 (e-mail).
Steel, Warren, to Myron J. Smith, Jr., May 29, 2014 (e-mail).
Wright, George, to Myron J Smith, Jr., April 23, 2014 (e-mail).

Index

Numbers in ***bold italics*** indicate pages with photographs.

Able, Capt. Bart 287; *see also* Johnson, Andrew; *Ruth* (steamboat)
Acklen, Joseph A.S. (Confederate colonel) 191; *see also* Palmyra Island, battle off (February 24, 1863)
Adams, William Wirt (Confederate colonel) 203–204
Adams, W.K. (ship broker) 277
Aimee, Marie (French opera star): St. Louis visit (1876) 307–308
Alexis, Russian Grand Duke: St. Louis visit (1872) 295, 307
Alton, IL 1–41
Alton-Bellefontaine Bridge (1894) ***321***
Alton Daily Morning Courier 15, 23, 41; *see also* Brown, George T.
Alton Gas Co. 28; *see also* Illinois Agricultural Fair, Alton, IL (1856)
Alton House Hotel 11, 32; *see also* Lincoln-Douglas Debate, October 1858; Webster, Daniel
Alton Manufacturing Company 17; *see also* S & P Wise; Wise, Peter; Wise, Sebastian
Alton Penitentiary Inquest (1857) 31
Alton-St. Louis Packet Co. 26, 28–29, 31
Altona (steamboat) 18–22, 32; *see also* Brown, Helen ("Ellen"); Chicago and Sangamon Railroad; Emerson, Primus; Gaty, McCune & Co.; LaMothe, Capt. William Pierre; Wise, Peter

American Foundry *see* Peter Tellon & Son
American Wine Company 293
Anaconda Plan 42–***44***; *see also* Eads, Capt. James Buchanan; Scott, Winfield (U.S. general)
Andy Johnson (steamboat) 287; *see also* Johnson, Andrew
Anschutz, William J. (chief pilot, *Indianola*) 86, 99
A.O. Tyler (steamboat) 36; *see also* Tyler (U.S. timberclad); "Wideawakes"
Arkansas (Confederate ironclad) 21, 47, 65, 82–83, 143, 198–199, 214; *see also* Emerson, Primus; Fort Pemberton, MS
Arkansas Post, Battle of (1863) 107, 136
Asboth, Alexander (U.S. brigadier general) 231–232; *see also* Fort Heiman, TN, U.S. occupation of (1863)
Ashten, Isaac N. (pilot, *Tuscumbia*) 229, 255
Atchafalaya River expedition (1864) 174–175; *see also* Red River campaign (March–May 1864)
Atlantic and Mississippi Steamship Company 286, 291, 318
Atlantic and Pacific Railroad 297–298, 309

Badger, Lt. Cmdr. Oscar C. (assistant ordnance inspector; acting captain, *Indianola*) 85–88, 90–91, 93, 97, 101
Bagley, Samuel (U.S. lieutenant) 247, 265, 268; *see also* Grand Gulf, MS, Battle of (April 29, 1863); Vicksburg batteries, passage of by *Tuscumbia* (April 16, 1863)
Bailey, Joseph (U.S. lieutenant colonel) 169–171; *see also* Red River campaign (March–May 1864)
Baker, Henry (master's mate, *Chillicothe*) 103
Banks, Nathaniel (U.S. major general) 155–160, 162, 164–165, 168–169, 171, 172, 220; *see also* Red River campaign (March–May, 1864)
Baron de Kalb (U.S. ironclad) 111, 122, 124, 126–127, 131–132, 135–151, 233; *see also* Fort Pemberton, MS; Yazoo Pass Expedition (March–April 1863)
Barrett, Arthur Buckner (St. Louis mayor) 304–305
Bates, Edward (U.S. attorney general) 42; *see also* Eads, Capt. James Buchanan
Beltzhoover, Daniel (Confederate lieutenant colonel) 241; *see also* Vicksburg campaign (1862–1863)
Benefit (steamboat) 162, 165; *see also* Red River campaign (March–May 1864)
Bennett, Maunsel (Confederate lieutenant) 174; *see also* Atchafalaya River expedition (1864); Red River campaign (March–May 1864)
Benton (U.S. ironclad) 48, 57, 216–217, 222, 224, 242, 244, 248–250, 255, 257–258, 260–263, 266, 270–273; *see also* Grand Gulf, MS, Battle of (April 29, 1863); Vicksburg

batteries, passage of by *Tuscumbia* (April 16, 1863)
Berkeley, Rev. Dr. Edward F. 306; *see also* Brown, Virginia ("Jennie"); Christ Church Episcopal Cathedral, St. Louis, MO; St. Peter's Protestant Episcopal Church, St. Louis, MO
Berrien, Cmdr. John M. (assistant ordnance inspector) 85
Bethel Mission *see* St. Louis Bethel Association
Billings, Henry W. (attorney) 31; *see also* Lincoln, Abraham; Mcready, Mary
Bishop, Lyman 12; *see also* Lovejoy, Elijah Parish
Black Hawk (Mississippi Squadron flagboat) 103, 115, 158, 162, 178, 221, 233, 238–239, 242, 270, 282
Black Hawk (steamboat) 165, 167; *see also* Red River campaign (March–May 1864)
Black Terror see Porter's Hoax (February 1863)
Blair, Francis P. (politician) 46
Blair, Montgomery (U.S. postmaster general) 46
Blair's Landing, Battle of (1864) 165–166; *see also* Red River campaign (March–May 1864)
Blake, Josephus (third assistant engineer, *Indianola*) 99
Blakeman, Thomas J. (San Francisco attorney) 315–316; *see also Flanagan v. Brown*
Blenker, William (clerk, *Forest Queen*) 244
Bloomington (IL) Republican Convention 23; *see also* Brown, George T.
Bogy, Lewis Vital (U.S. senator) 284–285, 292, 298; *see also* Wiggins Ferry Company
Boice, George A (third assistant engineer, *Indianola*) 99
Boone, Richard M. (Confederate captain) 174; *see also* Atchafalaya River expedition (1864)
Bowen, John S. (Confederate colonel) 260–261; *see also* Grand Gulf, MS, Battle of (April 29, 1863)
Bragg, Braxton (Confederate general) 83–84, 89, 91; *see also* Kentucky, Confederate campaign (1862)

Brand, Frederick B. (Confederate lieutenant colonel; captain, *Dr. Beatty*) 195–196, 202–204, 212; *see also* Palmyra Island, battle off (February 24, 1863)
Brent, Joseph L. (Confederate major) 192–193, 195–199, 201–204, 214; *see also* Palmyra Island, battle off (February 24, 1863)
Briggs, John J. (third assistant engineer, *Chillicothe*) 103
Bringhurst, Robert F. (sculptor) 324; *see also* Lovejoy Monument
Brown, Flora M. 5
Brown, Lt. Cmdr. George (captain of *Indianola*) 93–95, 97–99,101–102, *181*, 182, 184–186, 189–203, 206, 214, 219–220; *see also* Palmyra Island, battle off (February 24,1863); Vicksburg batteries, passage of by *Indianola* (February 13, 1863)
Brown, George T. (newsman, politician, U.S. Senate sergeant at arms) 5,8, 10–15, 17, 23, 32–33, 41, 45, 60–62, 289, 295, 311–*313*; *see also* Johnson, Andrew; Lincoln, Abraham; Lovejoy, Elijah Parish; Trumbull, S Lyman
Brown, Helen ("Ellen") 5, 32, 295, 311, 320–321, 326–327; *see also Altona* (steamboat); Child, Benjamin F.; Child, George
Brown, Cmdr. Isaac Newton (Confederate naval officer) 129; *see also Arkansas* (Confederate ironclad); Yazoo Pass Expedition (March–April 1863)
Brown, Jennie *see* Brown, Virginia ("Jennie")
Brown, Capt. Joseph (miller, riverman, steam and gunboat builder, politician): Alton mayor 26–32; Atlantic and Mississippi Steamship Company official/president 286, 291–292; Atlantic and Pacific Railroad director 297–298, 309; commodore of Johnson visit flotilla (1866) 286–288; designs, builds, or converts ironclads/tinclads (1862–186), 57–105, 145–146, 279–284; escape from New Orleans, LA (1861) 37–40; funeral

327; Lincoln acquaintance 14–15, 30–33, 61–62; Lovejoy protégé 10–13; miller 14–17; Missouri state senator (1869–1870) 290–291; Pacific Railroad of Missouri official/president 285, 291–292, 295, 297; riverman/steamboat captain 16–41; St. Louis auditor 318, 320–324; St. Louis mayor (1871–1875) 291–304; Sierra Del Una Gold Mining Company president 317; spiritualism practice 20, 285, 313, 318, 322–323; Western Forge and Tool Works president 317–318; Wiggins Ferry Company superintendent/president 284, 291–292
Brown, Leo 5
Brown, Margaret 5, 286
Brown, Thomas, Jr. 5
Brown, Thomas, Sr. (merchant) 5, 8–10, 14
Brown, Virginia ("Jennie") 294, 296–297, 302, 304, *306*–307, 313–315; *see also* McCallagh, Joseph B.; St. Louis Charity Ball; Spots, Albert Tunstall
Brown, Virginia K. 19, 26, 68, 285, 294–296, 302, 309, 311, 313–314,326; *see also Altona* (steamboat); *City of Louisiana* (steamboat); *Mayflower* (steamboat); Shurtleff College
Brown Backs *see* Panic of 1873
Buchanan, James (U.S. president) 30
Buchanan, William C. 221; *see also* Salvage of *Indianola* (1863–1865)
Buckeye State (steamboat) 24; *see also Mayflower* (steamboat)
Burnet House, Cincinnati, OH *69*, 214, 285
Buell, Don Carlos (U.S. major general) 49, 91
Busby, Judge John (meatpacker) 299
Butler, Edward (blacksmith/Democratic political boss) 305

Cairo (U.S. ironclad) 48, 262
Callender, Franklin D. (brevet brigadier general) 87
Calvert, Acting Ensign C.A. (officer, *Chillicothe*) 159

Campti, LA, Battle of (1864) 161–162
Carondelet (U.S. ironclad) 47–48, 51, **57**, 103, 111, 126, 160, 168, 171, 218–222, 242–243, 247, 267, 270, 273–274; *see also* Grand Gulf, MS, battle of (April 29, 1863); Perkin's Landing, MS, battle of (May 31, 1863); Salvage of *Indianola* (1863–1865); Vicksburg batteries, bombardment by *Tuscumbia* (May 19–22, 1863); Vicksburg batteries, passage of by *Tuscumbia* (April 16, 1863)
Carondelet Marine Railway and Dock Co. 33, 47; *see also* Eads, Capt. James Buchanan; Emerson, Primus; McAlister, Roger C.; Union Iron Works
Carrel, Hercules (CEO) 69, 71–72, 85, 279; *see also* Cincinnati Marine Railway
Carstairl, Thomas (acting assistant paymaster, *Indianola*) 99
Cassadaga Lake Free Association 323; *see also* spiritualism
Champion (steamboat) 8
Chicago (IL) fire (1871) 293–**294**
Chicago and Mississippi Railroad 26, 28, 31; *see also* Alton-St. Louis Packet Co.; St. Louis, Alton and Chicago Railroad
Chicago and Sangamon Railroad 20; *see also* Altona (steamboat); Chicago and Mississippi Railroad
Child, Benjamin F. 32, 295; *see also* Brown, Helen ("Ellen"); Child, George
Child, George 32, 295, 311, 320, 327; *see also* Brown, Helen ("Ellen"); Child, Benjamin F.
Chillicothe (U.S. ironclad) *see* Atchafalaya River expedition (1864); Brown, Joseph; Cutting & Ellis; Fort Pemberton, MS; Foster, James P.; Red River campaign (March–May, 1864); Yazoo Pass Expedition (March–April 1863)
Choctaw (U.S. ironclad) 154, 175, 224, 242, 279; *see also* Laning, James; Ramsay, Frank; Vicksburg campaign (1862–1863)
Chouteau, Harrison & Valle 60, 77–78; *see also* Harrison, James
Christ Church Episcopal Cathedral, St. Louis, MO 306; *see also* Berkeley, Rev. Dr. Edward F.; Brown, Virginia ("Jennie"); Schuyler, Rev. Dr. Montgomery
Cincinnati (U.S. ironclad) 48, 51, 111
Cincinnati, OH, defense of (1862) 82–91
Cincinnati Marine Railway 67–**68**, 69–**70**, 71–72, 79, **80**–**81**, 99–100, 279, 285; *see also* Morton, Capt. Daniel H.
City of Louisiana (steamboat) 31–32, 34–40, 60, 62; *see also* *A. O. Tyler* (steamboat); Lincoln-Douglas Debate, October 1858
City of Vicksburg (steamboat) 178–180, **181**; *see also* Queen of the West (U.S./Confederate ram)
Clara Bell (steamboat) 162; *see also* Red River campaign (March–May 1864)
Clubb, Samuel C. 292; *see also* Wiggins Ferry Company
Coleman, Norman J. (Illinois governor) 324
Collier, Capt. John 36; *see also* *A. O. Tyler* (steamboat)
Conestoga (U.S. timberclad) 43, 67, 111; *see also* Cincinnati Marine Railway; Morton, Capt. Daniel H.
Congress (U.S. frigate) 56; *see also* Virginia (Confederate ironclad)
Conroy, J.F. *see Flanagan v Brown*
Conway, C. Dan (captain, *Forest Queen*) 244, 247, 254–256, 259; *see also* Vicksburg batteries, passage of by *Tuscumbia* (April 16, 1863)
Copperheads 101–**102**
Couthouy, Acting Volunteer Lt. Joseph Pitty (captain, *Osage/Chillicothe*) 154, 158–159, 161–162; *see also* Red River campaign (March–May 1864)
Covington (Tinclad No. 25) 174, 176, 285; *see also* Red River campaign (March–May 1864)
Cricket (Tinclad No. 6) 162, 165–166, 223; *see also* Red River campaign (March–May 1864)
Crittenden, John J. (U.S. senator) and Crittenden Compromise 35
Crittenden, Thomas L. (U.S. major general) 91
Cronin, John (carpenter, *Tuscumbia*) 262, 266, 268
Cumberland (U.S. frigate) 56; *see also* Virginia (Confederate ironclad)
Cutting & Ellis 176

Dahlia (U.S. tug) 159, 162, 165; *see also* Red River campaign (March–May 1864)
Dan Morton & Co. *see* Morton, Capt. Daniel H.
Dana, Charles A. (U.S. assistant war secretary) 150, 220, 230, 240, 247, 250, 256, 263; *see also* Stanton, Edwin; Vicksburg campaign (1862–1863)
Davis, Andrew Jackson 285; *see also* First Spiritual Society of St. Louis
Davis, RAdm. Charles H. 90–93, 279
Davis, Frederic E. (seaman, *Baron de Kalb*) 122, 140, 149; *see also* Fort Pemberton, MS; Yazoo Pass Expedition (March–April 1863)
Davis, Levi (attorney) 31; *see also* Lincoln, Abraham; Mcready, Mary
Dean, John (pilot, *Chillicothe*) 172
Deep Water Convention (1899) 326
Democratic National Convention (1876) 305, 307–**308**
Democratic National Convention (1880) 312–313
Democratic National Convention (1888) 318–*319*
De Soto (steamboat) 183, 187, 189; *see also* Queen of the West (U.S./Confederate ram)
Deuprey, Eugene N. (San Francisco attorney) 315
Dignan, Arthur (assistant barkeeper) 26; *see also* *Mayflower* (steamboat)
Dimmock, Thomas 12, 318, 326–327; *see also* Lovejoy, Elijah Parish
Dr. Beatty (Confederate gunboat) 195–198, 200, 202–

203; *see also* Brand, Frederick B.; Palmyra Island, battle off (February 24, 1863)
Donaldson, Acting Ensign Oliver (executive officer, Carondelet) 219, 222; *see also* Salvage of *Indianola* (1863–1865)
Doughty, Thomas (chief engineer, *Indianola, Ozark*) 86, 99
Douglas, Stephen (U.S. senator) 22, **30**, 32–33; *see also* Lincoln, Abraham; Lincoln-Douglas Debate, October 1858
Doyden, David M. (pilot, *Chillicothe*) 103
Duble, John A. (first master, *Conestoga*) 85, 89–91; *see also* Cincinnati, OH, Defense of (1862); Kentucky, Confederate campaign (1862)
Du Pont, RAdm. Samuel Francis 63

Eads, Capt. James Buchanan (engineer, gunboat builder) 29–30, 40, 42, 46–48, 58, 63–65, 74–75, 92, 106, 154, 286–288, 290–291, 293, 295, 301, 303–304, 314; *see also* Bates, Edward (U.S. attorney general); Illinois Agricultural Fair, Alton, IL (1856); Illinois and St. Louis Bridge; Johnson, Andrew; Nelson, Capt. William Shaw
Eads Bridge *see* Illinois and St. Louis Bridge
Easton, Rufus 5
Eastport (U.S. ironclad) 159, 168, 238; *see also* Red River campaign (March–May 1864)
Edson, Acting Ensign A.H. (officer, *Tuscumbia*) 231
Edward J. Gay (steamboat) 123, 150; *see also* Fort Pemberton, MS; Yazoo Pass Expedition (March–April 1863)
Elder, Rev. William Henry (archbishop of Natchez) 222; *see also* Murphy, John McLeod
Eliot, William Greenleaf 298; *see also* St. Louis Social Evil Hospital
Ellet, Charles Rivers (U.S. lieutenant colonel) 179–180, 183, 186–193, 196; *see also* *Era No. 5* (steamboat); *Queen of the West* (U.S./Confederate ram)
Elliot, Benjamin (seaman, *Indianola*) 206; *see also* Palmyra Island, battle off (February 24, 1863); Porter's Hoax (February 1863)
Eltinge, Peter *see* Lord, Acting Volunteer Lt. George P.
Emerson, Primus (boatbuilder) 18–19, 21, 47, 65; *see also* *Altona* (steamboat); *Arkansas* (Confederate ironclad)
Era No. 5 (steamboat), 187–191; *see also* Ellet, Charles Rivers; *Queen of the West* (U.S./Confederate ram);
Ericsson, John (engineer) 65; *see also* *Monitor* (U.S. ironclad)
Essex (U.S. ironclad) 48, 51
Etlah (U.S. ironclad) 58; *see also* McCord, Charles W.
Eytinge, Acting Volunteer Lt. Henry St. Clair (captain, *Chillicothe*) 154

Farragut, RAdm. David Glasgow 94, 189, 214–**215**, 243, 286–287
Farrell, Acting Ensign Thomas M.(officer, *Tuscumbia*) 231, 256, 273–274
Faust 304, 307; *see also* Brown, Virginia ("Jennie")
Filbrun, Henry (clerk) 25; *see also* *Mayflower* (steamboat)
First Church of Spiritual Unity, St. Louis, MO 326
First Spiritual Society of St. Louis 285, 313, 322, 326
Fitch, Gardner (acting master's mate, *Indianola*) 99
Fitch, Lt. Cmdr. Le Roy 153, 195
Flanagan, Frank G. (St. Louis resident) *see* Flanagan v Brown
Flanagan v Brown 315–316
Fleming, Watson B. (third assistant engineer, *Chillicothe*) 103
Foote, RAdm. Andrew Hull 48, **50**, 56–58, 61–62, 92
Forest Park, St. Louis, MO 301
Forest Queen (steamboat) 220–221, 244, 246–247, 252–257, 259, 261; *see also* Perkin's Landing, MS, battle of (May 31, 1863); Vicksburg batteries, passage of by *Tuscumbia* (April 16, 1863)
Forest Rose (Tinclad No. 9) 119, 172, 222, 280; *see also* Yazoo Pass Expedition (March–April 1863)
Fort Cobun, MS *see* Grand Gulf, MS, Battle of (April 19, 1863)
Fort De Russy, LA 157–158, 174; *see also* Red River campaign (March–May 1864)
Fort Donelson, TN, battle of 51–**52**
Fort Heiman, TN, U.S. occupation of (1863) 229, **230**–232
Fort Henry, TN, battle of 50–**52**
Fort Hindman, AR *see* Arkansas Post, battle of (1863)
Fort Hindman (Tinclad No. 13), 160–162, 166, 170, 174–175; *see also* Atchafalaya River expedition (1864); Red River campaign (March–May 1864)
Fort Pemberton, MS 123–124, **133**–151; *see also* Yazoo Pass Expedition (March–April 1863)
Fort Wade, MS *see* Grand Gulf, MS, battle of (April 19, 1863)
Foster, Lt. Cmdr. James P. (captain, *Chillicothe/Lafayette*) 98, 100–101, 103, 107, 110–**111**, 116, 134, 137, 140–141, 143, 145–153; *see also* Fort Pemberton, MS; Yazoo Pass Expedition (March–April 1863)
Foster, Dr. William C., Jr. (acting assistant surgeon, *Chillicothe*) 103
Fox, Gustavus Vasa (U.S. assistant navy secretary) 55–56, 74, 92, 214–215, 236, 255, 263, 266
Fox, Kate (spiritualist) 20
Fox, Margaret (spiritualist) 20
Francis, David R. (St. Louis mayor) 316–317
Franklin Foundry 58, 64, 105; *see also* McCord & Co.
Franklin House Hotel, Alton, IL 30, 32; *see also* Lincoln-Douglas Debate, October 1858
Fremont, John C. (Republican presidential candidate 1856) 30
Frink, John 16–17; *see also*

Frink & Walker Stagecoach Line; Walker, Martin; *General Briggs* (steamboat)
Frink & Walker Stagecoach Line 16–18
Frith, Charles H. (Confederate lieutenant) 195, 203, 206, 212–213; *see also Dr. Beatty*; Palmyra Island, battle off (February 24, 1863); Porter's Hoax (February 1863)
Frolic (steamboat) 205; *see also* Hayes, Thomas H.; Vicksburg campaign (1862–1863)

Gaty, Samuel (engineer) 19, 23, 25, 58; *see also* Alton-St. Louis Packet Co.; *Altona* (steamboat); *City of Louisiana* (steamboat); Gaty, McCune & Co.; *Mayflower* (steamboat); Phoenix Insurance Co.
Gaty, McCune & Co. 19, 26, 33; *see also* Alton-St. Louis Packet Co.; *Altona* (steamboat); *Jeannie Deans* (steamboat); *Mayflower* (steamboat); Phoenix Insurance Co.
Gaylord, Son & Company (ironworks) 48
General Briggs (steamboat) 16–17; *see also* Starr, Capt. James E.
General Price (U.S. gunboat) *see General Sterling Price*
General Sterling Price (U.S. gunboat) 229, 238–239, 242, 259, 261, 263, 270, 274; *see also* Grand Gulf, MS, battle of (April 29, 1863); Vicksburg batteries, passage of by *Tuscumbia* (April 16, 1863)
George Collier (steamboat) 26; *see also Mayflower* (steamboat)
Gettysburg, PA, battle of (1863) 222
Gilman, Winthrop Sargeant 6, 10, 12–13
Gipson, Acting Ensign James C. (captain, *Carondelet*) 222–223; *see also* Salvage of *Indianola* (1863–1865)
Godfrey, Benjamin 6, 13–14
Godfrey, Gilman & Co. 8, 12–13, 17; *see also* Lovejoy, Elijah Parish
Gough, Oliver (third assistant engineer, *Tuscumbia*) 231

Grand Duke (Confederate gunboat) 189
Grand Era (Confederate gunboat) 193, 196–197, 202–203, 212; *see also* Palmyra Island, battle of (February 24, 1863)
Grand Gulf, MS, battle of (April 29, 1863), 259–268
Granger, Gordon (U.S. brigadier general) 88
Grant, Fred 247, 250–251; *see also* Grant, Ulysses Simpson; Vicksburg batteries, passage of by *Tuscumbia* (April 16, 1863)
Grant, Julia 247; *see also* Grant, Ulysses Simpson; Vicksburg batteries, passage of by *Tuscumbia* (April 16, 1863)
Grant, Ulysses Simpson (U.S. major general) 50–**51**, 52, 97–98, 111, 113, 116, 121, 124, 131, 142, 149–150, 155, 205, 216, 220, 234, 236–**237**, 238–242, 244-247, 250, 256, 259–261, 263, 267–270, 272, 274, 286–287, 307, 317; *see also* Fort Donelson, TN; Fort Henry, TN; Vicksburg campaign (1862–1863); Yazoo Pass Expedition (March–April 1863)
Great Southern Railroad Company 298
Green, Thomas (Confederate brigadier general) 166; *see also* Blair's Landing, battle of (1864); Red River campaign (March–May 1864)
Greenslade, Thomas (quarter gunner, *Chillicothe*) 149; *see also* Fort Pemberton, MS
Greer, Lt. Cmdr. James A. (captain, *Benton*) 224–225, 250, 257, 270–271; *see also* Vicksburg batteries, passage by the *Tuscumbia* (April 16, 1863)
Gulick, Acting Master's Mate Charles Heckman (captain, *Ivy*) 248, 253, 256, 273–274; *see also* Vicksburg batteries, passage of by *Tuscumbia* (April 16, 1863)

Halleck, Henry (U.S. major general) 49, *51*, 155
Hambleton, Samuel T. 64–65; *see also* Hambleton, Collier & Company

Hambleton, William 64–65; *see also* Hambleton, Collier & Company
Hambleton, Collier & Company 64–65, 152–153; *see also* Hambleton, Samuel T.; Hambleton, William
Hamond, Horace J. (master's mate, *Chillicothe*) 103
Handy, Thomas (Confederate lieutenant) 203, 213; *see also William H. Webb* (Confederate ram)
Hanson, Acting Ensign H. A. (officer, *Chillicothe*) 158, 165
Hardy, H.W. (chief engineer, *Chillicothe*) 103
Harrison, James (engineer) 60, 71–72, 77–78; *see also* Chouteau, Harrison & Valle
Hartt, Edward (U.S. assistant naval constructor) 55, 72–74, 83, 88, 90, 92, 105, 279; *see also* Hull, Com. Joseph B.; Ironclad Board (1862)
Hartupee, John W. (chief engineer, *Tuscumbia*) 231, 262, 265, 267
Hartupee and Company (engine builders) 48
Hassler, Sebaldus (U.S. lieutenant) 206; *see also* Porter's Hoax (February 1863)
Hawksworth, David (second assistant engineer, *Indianola*) 99
Hawley, Capt. George E. 17–18; *see also Luella* (steamboat)
Hayes, Thomas H. (Confederate major) 205; *see also Frolic* (steamboat)
Hazard, Rebecca 298; *see also* St. Louis Social Evil Hospital
Heartland Offensive, Confederate *see* Kentucky, Confederate campaign (1862)
Heath, Henry ("Harry") 85, 88–89; *see also* Cincinnati, OH, Defense of (1862); Kentucky, Confederate campaign (1862)
Henry Clay (steamboat) 244, 246–247, 252–257; *see also* Vicksburg batteries, passage of by *Tuscumbia* (April 16, 1863)
Henry von Phul (steamboat) 247–249, 251, 256; *see also* Grant, Ulysses Simpson; Vicksburg batteries, passage

of by *Tuscumbia* (April 16, 1863)
Higgins, Edward (Confederate colonel) 241, 249; *see also* Vicksburg campaign (1862–1863)
Hilliard, Joseph (first assistant engineer, *Tuscumbia*) 231
Hipps, P.H. (acting master's mate, *Indianola*) 99
H.L. Kinney (steamboat) 10; *see also* Webster, Daniel
Hoel, Acting Volunteer Lt. William R. (captain, *Pittsburg*) 216–**218**, 243, 257, 263; *see also* Grand Gulf, MS, Battle of (April 29, 1863); salvage of *Indianola* (1863–1865)
Hood, Thomas (thief) 326
Hope (steamboat) 123; *see also* Yazoo Pass Expedition (March–April 1863)
Hovey, Wallace B. (first assistant engineer, *Indianola*) 99
Hull, Com. Joseph B. (gunboat construction superintendent) 72, 74, 81, 83, 87–88, 90–92, 96–97, 99, 101, 105, 141, 218–219, 221, 229, 231, 279; *see also* Salvage of *Indianola* (1863–1865)
Hunter, Charles 11; *see also* Webster, Daniel
Hurlbut, Stephen A. (U.S. major general) 231; *see also* Fort Heiman, TN, U.S. occupation of (1863)
Hutton, Thomas H. (Confederate captain) 174; *see also* Atchafalaya River expedition (1864); Red River campaign (March–May 1864)
Hyacinth (U.S. tug) 224; *see also* Salvage of *Indianola* (1863–1865)
Hyde, William (St. Louis postmaster) 317

Illinois Agricultural Fair, Alton, IL (1856) 28–30
Illinois and St. Louis Bridge (Eads Bridge) 290, 292, 297–298, 301, **303**–305, 314
Illinois State Bank 8
Indianola (U.S. ironclad) *see* Palmyra Island, battle off (February 24, 1863); Porter's Hoax (March 1863); salvage of *Indianola* (1863–1865); Vicksburg batteries, passage of by *Indianola* (February 13, 1863)

Ironclad Board: 1861 55; 1862 55, 61–63; *see also* Smith, Com. Joseph
Isaac (fireman, *Indianola*) 201, 213; *see also* Palmyra Island, battle off (February 24, 1863)
Isherwood, Benjamin (naval engineer) 55; *see also* Ironclad Board (1862)
Island No. 10, battle of 58–**59**, 60, 243
Ivy (U.S. tug) 242, 248, 253, 256–257, 260–261, 263, 267, 273–274; *see also* Grand Gulf, MS, battle of (April 19, 1863); Vicksburg batteries, passage of by *Tuscumbia* (April 16, 1863)

Jackman, Mable Abner (spiritualist) 323
Jackson, Andrew 3rd (Confederate colonel) 241, 252; *see also* Vicksburg campaign (1862–1863)
James, Joshua (owner, *Ion* plantation) 245, 247, 251, 257; *see also* Vicksburg batteries, passage of by *Tuscumbia* (April 16, 1863)
Jeannie Deans (steamboat) 33–34; *see also* St. Louis and Keokuk Line
Jennie Brown (steamboat) 302
John Simmonds (steamboat) 24
John Walsh (steamboat) 137; *see also* Fort Pemberton, MS
John Warner (steamboat) 167, 176; *see also* Red River campaign (March–May 1864)
Johnson, Andrew (U.S. president) 286, **287**–288, 290
Johnson, George L. (acting master, U.S. gunboat *General Bragg*) 90
Johnston, Albert S. (Confederate general) 53
Jordan, Acting Ensign Scott D. (officer, *Carondelet*) 222–223; *see also* salvage of *Indianola* (1863–1865)
Juliet (Tinclad No. 4) 93, 280; *see also* Shaw, Acting Master Edward

Keach, Hiram 19
Keach, Capt. John R. 19
Keach, Virginia K. *see* Brown, Virginia K.
Kendall, Charles F. (U.S. naval constructor) 276, 281

Kenny, Lewis (acting master's mate, *Indianola*/Acting Ensign, *Tuscumbia*) 99, 231
Kentucky, Confederate campaign in (1862) 77, 82–91; *see also* Cincinnati, OH, defense of (1862)
Key West No. 2 (steamboat) 125; *see also* Yazoo Pass Expedition (March–April 1863)
Keys, Joseph F. (acting gunner, *Indianola*) 99
Knights of the Golden Circle *see* Copperheads
Koontz, George W. (Confederate government agent) 188
Kouns, John H. and George L. *see* Grand Era (Confederate gunboat)
Kountz, Capt. William J. 66
Krum, John Marshall 8, 12; *see also* Lovejoy, Elijah Parish

Lafayette (U.S. ironclad) 153, 224, 242, 250, 252, 267, 279; *see also* Foster, Lt. Cmdr. James P.; Grand Gulf, MS, battle of (April 29, 1863); Laning, James; Vicksburg batteries, passage of by *Tuscumbia* (April 16, 1863); Walke, Capt. Henry
Lamb, Joshua G. (miller) 14, 17; *see also* Madison Mills
LaMothe, Capt. William Pierre 16–17; *see also* Alton-St. Louis Packet Co.; *Altona* (steamboat); *Little Eagle* (steamboat); *Luella* (steamboat)
Lancaster (U.S. ram) 129; *see also* Yazoo Pass Expedition (March–April 1863)
Lane, Henry S. (U.S. senator) 46
Langthorne, Acting Volunteer Lt. Amos R. (captain, *Mound City*) 223–224; *see also* Salvage of *Indianola* (1863–1865)
Laning, Acting Volunteer Lt. James (captain, *Rattler*) 224–226; *see also* salvage of *Indianola* (1863–1865)
Lantz, Daniel (third assistant engineer, *Chillicothe*) 103
Lavinia Logan (steamboat) 128; *see also* Yazoo Pass Expedition (March–April 1863)
Lea, Henry (miller) 14, 17; *see also* Madison Mills

Leathers, Capt. Thomas P. 37–38; *see also* Natchez No. 5 (steamboat)

Leclede Hotel, St. Louis, MO 316

Lee, Acting RAdm. Samuel Phillips 225–226, 276; *see also* salvage of *Indianola* (1863–1865)

Lenthall, John (Bureau of Construction chief) 44–45, 55–**56**, 63, 218, 231; *see also* Ironclad Board (1862)

Lewis, William J. 291; *see also* Atlantic and Mississippi Steamship Company; Memphis and St. Louis Packet Company

Lexington (U.S. timberclad) 43, 67, 104, 111, 160–162, 166–167, 200, 217; *see also* Cincinnati Marine Railway; Red River campaign (March–May 1864)

Lily Dale Association *see* Cassadaga Lake Free Association

Lincoln, Abraham (U.S. president) 14–**15**, **30**, 31–33, 35, 42, 61–**62**, 91, 289–290; *see also* Brown, George T.; Douglas, Stephen; Eads, Capt. James Buchanan; Lincoln-Douglas Debate, October 1858; Lincoln-Shields "duel" (1842); Mcready, Mary; Red River campaign (March–May, 1864); Shields, James; Trumbull, Lyman; Vicksburg campaign (1862–1863); Welles, Gideon

Lincoln, Mary Todd 14; *see also* Lincoln, Abraham; Shields, James

Lincoln-Douglas Debate, October 1858 32–**33**; *see also* City of Louisiana (steamboat); Douglas, Stephen; Lincoln, Abraham; McKenna, Jerry

Lincoln-Shields "duel" (1842) 14–15

Linden (Tinclad No. 10) 237–239

Lioness (U.S. ram) 137; *see also* Yazoo Pass Expedition (March–April 1863)

Little Eagle (steamboat) 16; *see also* LaMothe, William Pierre

Livingston, Com. John W. 276

Lord, Acting Volunteer Lt. George P. (captain, *Chillicothe*) 175–176, 276

Lord-Drake, Maud (spiritualist) 326

Loring, William Wing (Confederate major general) 119, 122–124, 132–137, 139–144, 148–149, 151; *see also* Fort Pemberton,MS; Yazoo Pass Expedition (March–April 1863)

Louis d'Or (Confederate gunboat) 189; *see also* Palmyra Island, battle of (February 24, 1863)

Louisville (U.S. ironclad) 48, 51, 103, 111, 168, 171, 223, 255, 263, 267, 269; *see also* Grand Gulf, MS, Battle of (April 29, 1863); Vicksburg batteries, passage of by *Tuscumbia* (April 16, 1863)

Lovejoy, Elijah Parish (minister/newspaperman) 10–13

Lovejoy Monument, Alton, IL 318, 323–325, 328

Lovell, Mansfield (Confederate major general) *see* Lovell, William S. (Confederate lieutenant)

Lovell, William S. (Confederate lieutenant colonel, captain *Queen of the West*) 189–192; *see also* Queen of the West (U.S./Confederate ram)

Lower Illinois River Valley Association and Convention (1897) 324

Luella (steamboat) 16–18; *see also* LaMothe, Capt. William Pierre; Tempest (steamboat)

Lyon, George A.(acting assistant paymaster, *Tuscumbia/Lexington*) 231

Madison Marine Railway Company 46; *see also* Temple, Capt. A.F. (boatbuilder)

Madison Mills 17; *see also* Lamb, Joshua G.; Lea, Henry

Marietta (U.S. ironclad) 64

Marmora (Tinclad No. 2) 125; *see also* Yazoo Pass Expedition (March–April 1863)

Marshall, Acting Ensign James (officer and acting captain, *Tuscumbia*) 231, 273, 275–276

Martin, Daniel (naval engineer) 55; *see also* Ironclad Board (1862)

Mary Hunt (wharfboat) 26; *see also* Mayflower (steamboat)

Mason, Roswell B. (Chicago mayor) 293–294; *see also* Chicago Fire (1871)

Mayflower (steamboat) 24, **25**–27, 33, 61, 66, 309; *see also* Phoenix Insurance Co.

McAlister, Roger C. (CEO) 33, 47; *see also* Carondelet Marine Railway and Dock Co.

McCallagh, Joseph B. 297; *see also* Brown, Virginia ("Jennie"); *St. Louis Globe*

McCammant, Joseph (pilot, *Tuscumbia*) 229, 255, 263

McClellan, George B. (U.S. major general) 43; *see also* Rodgers, Capt. John

McClernand, John A. (U.S. major general) 113, 216, 240, 246–247, 251, 257, 261, 273; *see also* Vicksburg campaign (1862–1863)

McCloskey, James (Confederate captain, captain *William H. Webb*) 193, 198–199, 203, 212; *see also* Palmyra Island, battle off (February 24, 1863)

McCord, Charles W. (engineer) 58, 60, 63, 77, 87, 105; *see also* Franklin Foundry; McCord & Co.

McCord & Co. 58, 71–72, 77, 105; *see also* Franklin Foundry; McCord, Charles W.

McCune, John S. 19, 23, 31; *see also* Alton-St. Louis Packet Co.; *Altona* (steamboat); *City of Louisiana* (steamboat); Gaty, Samuel; Gaty, McCune & Co.; *Mayflower* (steamboat)

Mcdonough, James (St. Louis police chief) 305

McElwill, Acting Ensign Thomas (officer, *Indianola*) 99, 184

McKenna, Jerry (sculptor) 33; *see also* Lincoln-Douglas Debate, October 1858

McMillen, John S. (captain, *Silver Wave*) 244

McPherson, James B. (U.S. major general) 131, 149, 262; *see also* Yazoo Pass Expedition (March–April 1863)

Mcready, Mary (actress) 30–32; *see also* Lincoln, Abraham (U.S. president)

Meeker, John H. (pilot, *Forest Queen*) 244, 255
Meigs, Montgomery C. (U.S. QM general) 45–*47*, 55, 61
Memphis and St. Louis Packet Company 291; *see also* Atlantic and Mississippi Steamship Company; Lewis, William J.
Miller, J.A. (Illinois Agricultural Fair superintendent) 28; *see also* Illinois Agricultural Fair, Alton, IL (1856)
Miller, John James (miller) 26; *see also* Alton–St. Louis Packet Co.
Milligan, William J. (second assistant engineer, *Tuscumbia*) 231
Mississippi River Improvement Convention: 1867 288; 1877 309–311
Missouri Wrecking Company *see* Eads, Capt. James Buchanan; Nelson, Capt. William Shaw
Mixer, Dr. Henry (acting assistant surgeon, *Chillicothe, Indianola*) 99, 200–201; *see also* Palmyra Island, battle off (February 24,1863)
Monitor (U.S. ironclad) 55, 62, 76, 177; *see also* Ericcson, John; Ironclad Board (1861); *Virginia* (Confederate ironclad)
Monticello Female Seminary *see* Shurtleff College
Moore, Hugh (spiritualist) 323
Morgan, John Hunt (Confederate brigadier general) 77, 82
Morrison, John G. 103; *see also Carondelet* (U.S. ironclad)
Morton, John L. (U.S. special pilot) 120, 137; *see also* Yazoo Pass Expedition (March–April 1863)
Morton, Oliver P. (Indiana governor) 84; *see also* Kentucky, Confederate campaign (1862)
Mound City (U.S. ironclad) 48, 168, 171, 223–225, 242, 263, 267, 270, 273; *see also* Grand Gulf, MS, battle of (April 29, 1863) ; salvage of *Indianola* (1863–1865); Vicksburg batteries, passage of by *Tuscumbia* (April 16, 1863)
Mozelle (steamboat) 12

Muir, Acting Ensign Walter (executive officer/acting captain, *Chillicothe*) 103, 152, 154, 165
Mulgard, Louis (architect) 324; *see also* Lovejoy Monument
Murphy, Acting Volunteer Lt. John McLeod (captain, *Carondelet*) **218**–222; *see also* salvage of *Indianola* (1863–1865)
Myrick, John D. (Confederate captain) 134; *see also* Fort Pemberton, MS; Yazoo Pass Expedition (March–April 1863)

Natchez (steamboat) 24; *see also Mayflower* (steamboat)
Natchez No. 5 (steamboat) 37–38; *see also* Leathers, Capt. Thomas P.
Nelson, William (U.S. major general) 89; *see also* Kentucky, Confederate campaign (1862)
Nelson, Capt. William Shaw 29, 40, 47, 219, 221; *see also* Eads, Capt. James Buchanan; Missouri Wrecking Company; salvage of *Indianola* (1863–1865)
Neosho (U.S. ironclad) 160, 170, 174–175; *see also* Atchafalaya River expedition (1864); Red River campaign (March–May 1864)
New Era (Tinclad No. 7) 280
New Falls City (steamboat) 163–164; *see also* Red River campaign (March–May 1864)
New Orleans yellow fever epidemic (1853) 22; *see also St. Louis* (steamboat)
North Alabama (steamboat) 16

Ogden, Frederick (Confederate major) 241, 250; *see also* Vicksburg campaign (1862–1863)
Oglesby, Richard (U.S. major general) 238
Olive Branch (steamboat) 287; *see also* Johnson, Andrew
Osage (U.S. ironclad) 99, 154, 158, 160, 162, 164, 166, 170; *see also* Red River campaign (March–May 1864)
Osterhaus, Peter (U.S. brigadier general) 246–247,

251, 257–258, 261; *see also* Vicksburg batteries, passage of by *Tuscumbia* (April 16, 1863)
Owen, Lt. Cmdr. Elias K. (captain, *Louisville*) 219, 223, 269; *see also* salvage of *Indianola* (1863–1865)
Owen, Richard (U.S. colonel) 220–221; *see also* Perkin's Landing, MS, battle of (May 31, 1863)
Ozark (U.S. ironclad) 63, 168, 171–172; *see also* Red River campaign (March–May 1864)

Pacific Railroad of Missouri 285, 291–293, 295, 297
Palmyra Island, battle off (February 24, 1863), 128, 189–203
Panic of 1873 300–301, 305
Paschall, Nathaniel (*St. Louis Daily Republican* CEO) 79
Paschall House, St. Louis, MO 285, 289
Paul Jones (steamboat) 8
Pease, Acting Ensign William S. (officer, *Indianola*) 99, 184
Pemberton, John C. (Confederate lieutenant general) 122, 129, 133, 136, 139, 143, 148, 151, 189, 204, 212, 214, 217, 220, 240, 256; *see also* Vicksburg campaign (1862–1863); Yazoo Pass Expedition (March–April 1863)
Pennock, Capt. Alexander M. (U.S. fleet captain) 85, 87, 90, 99–102, 104, 152–153, 225, 229–231
Perkins, John, Jr. (owner, *Perkins/Somerset* plantations) 245, 257–258; *see also* Perkin's Landing, MS, battle of (May 31, 1863); Vicksburg batteries, passage of by *Tuscumbia* (April 16, 1863)
Perkin's Landing, MS, battle of (May 31, 1863) 220–221; *see also Carondelet* (U.S. ironclad)
Perrysville, KY, battle of (1862) 91
Peter Tellon & Son 67–68, 72, 83–84, 97, 105; *see also* American Foundry; Tellon, Capt. Peter
Pettis, John J. (Mississippi governor) 36; *see also Silver*

Lake (steamboat); "Wide-awakes"
Phelps, Lt. Cmdr. Seth Ledyard 104, 159, 195, 200; *see also Eastport* (U.S. ironclad); Red River campaign (March–May, 1864)
Philadelphia Centenial Exposition (1876) 307
Phillips, Stephen (boatbuilder) 23–24
Phoenix Insurance Co. 24–26, 33; *see also Mayflower* (steamboat)
Pierce, Charles J. (Confederate captain; captain, Queen of the West) 193, 199, 201
Pittsburg (U.S. ironclad) 48, 51, 168, 216, 242, 252, 257, 263, 267; *see also* Grand Gulf, MS, Battle of (April 29, 1863); Vicksburg batteries, passage of by *Tuscumbia* (April 16, 1863)
Pook, Samuel M. (U.S. naval constructor) 43–45, 67
Pope, Archy (slave superintendent) 187
Porter, RAdm. David Dixon 68, 73–74, 92, 94–99, 102–108, 111, 113–116, 121, 125–126, 129, 139, 142, 146–148, 150, 152, 156–160, 162–166, 168–172, 177–178, 180–183, 186, 192–197, 201, ***204***, 205–225, 229, 232–233, 236–***243***, 244, 246–250, 255, 258–263, 266–276, 279–281; *see also* Grand Gulf, MS, battle of (April 29, 1863); Porter's Hoax (February–March 1863); Red River campaign (March–May, 1864); Vicksburg campaign (1862–1863)
Porter, Com. William D. 58; *see also Essex* (U.S. ironclad)
Porter's Hoax (February–March 1863) 205–207, ***208***, 209, ***210***–213
Potter, Dr. Frederick E. (acting assistant surgeon, *Tuscumbia*) 231, 267–268
Powers, Acting Ensign William T. (officer, *Chillicothe*) 103
Prentiss, Benjamin M. (U.S. brigadier general) 120, 124–125, 132, 142, 151–152; *see also* Yazoo Pass Expedition (March–April 1863)
Providence Association, St. Louis, MO 295

Public School Library Society of St. Louis 302

Queen City (Tinclad No. 26) 281–282, 285
Queen of the West (U.S./Confederate ram) 128, 178–180, ***181–182***, 183–184, 187, ***189***, 190–193, 195–205, 207, 212–213, 216, 246; *see also* Ellet, Charles Rivers; Palmyra Island, battle of (February 24, 1863); Pierce, Charles J.
Quinby, Isaac F. (U.S. brigadier general) 131, 148–151; *see also* Yazoo Pass Expedition (March–April 1863)
Quincy (steamboat) ***9***

Ramsay, Lt. Cmdr. Frank (captain, *Choctaw/Chillicothe*) 153–154, 156, ***173***, 174–175; *see also* Atchafalaya River expedition (1864)
Rattler (Tinclad No.1) 115, 120, 122–125, 127, 131–133, 137, 139, 146, 225, 280; *see also see also* Laning, James; salvage of *Indianola* (1863–1865); Smith, Lt. Cmdr. Watson; Yazoo Pass Expedition (March–April 1863)
Red River campaign (March–May 1864) 155–173; *see also* Porter, RAdm. David Dixon
Red River dams 169–171; *see also* Red River campaign (March–May 1864)
Reindeer (steamboat) 26; *see also* Alton-St. Louis Packet Co.
Reno, Francis (seaman, *Tuscumbia*) 274
Reynolds, Charles W. (second assistant engineer, *Chillicothe*) 103
Rice, J.D. (first assistant engineer, *Chillicothe*) 103
Richmond, KY, battle of (1862) 84
Riley, John (ship broker) 226–228; *see also* salvage of *Indianola* (1863–1865)
Rob Roy (steamboat) 162; *see also* Red River campaign (March–May 1864)
Rodgers, Capt. John 36, 43–***45***, 46, 48, 65–67, 92, 104; *see also Tyler* (U.S. timberclad)
Roe, John J. 291; *see also* At-

lantic and Mississippi Steamship Company
Romeo (Tinclad No. 3) 280
Roodhouse Hotel, Roodhouse, Il 324
Ross, Leonard F. (U.S. brigadier general) ***121***, 124–125, 128, 130–132, 134–136, 144, 146–149; *see also* Fort Pemberton, MS; Yazoo Pass Expedition (March–April 1863)
Ruth (steamboat) 287; *see also* Able, Capt. Bart; Johnson, Andrew
Ryan, Alfred (captain's clerk, *Chillicothe*) 103

S & P Wise 17; *see also* Alton Manufacturing Company; Wise, Peter; Wise, Sebastian
Sabine Cross-Roads, battle of (1864) 164; *see also* Red River campaign (March–May 1864)
St. James Hotel, St. Louis, MO 314
St. Joseph and Elwood Bridge 299
St. Louis (steamboat) 20–22; *see also* New Orleans yellow fever epidemic (1853); Taylor, Capt. George
St. Louis, Alton and Chicago Railroad 31
St. Louis and Keokuk Line 29–31; *see also City of Louisiana* (steamboat); Illinois Agricultural Fair, Alton, IL (1856); *Jeannie Deans* (steamboat)
St. Louis Bethel Association 290
St. Louis Charity Ball 304
St. Louis city hall 297, 299
St. Louis Clearing House Association 300; *see also* Panic of 1873
St. Louis Female Hospital 305
St. Louis Gas-Light Company 292–293
St. Louis Globe 297; *see also* McCallagh, Joseph B.
St. Louis Public Library 302
St. Louis Social Evil Hospital 298; *see also* St. Louis Female Hospital
St. Louis Taxpayer's League 298
St. Louis University 293
St. Peter's Protestant Episcopal Church, St. Louis, MO 306

St. Vincent de Paul Society, St. Louis, MO 294
salvage of *Indianola* (1863–1865) 216–228, 246
Sandusky (U.S. ironclad) 64
Sanford, Lt. Cmdr. Joseph P. (acting captain, *Chillicothe*) 87–88, 90, 94–95, 281
Scholes, Thomas E. (third assistant engineer, *Indianola*) 99
Schuyler, Rev. Dr. Montgomery 306; *see also* Brown, Virginia ("Jennie"); Christ Church Episcopal Cathedral, St. Louis, MO
Scott, Sir Walter 5
Scott, Winfield (U.S. general) 42; *see also* Anaconda Plan
Sedgwick, Charles Baldwin (U.S. congressman) 55
Seward, William H. (U.S. secretary of state) 286
Shaw, Acting Master Edward (first master, *Tyler* and acting captain, *Indianola*) 82, 90–91, 93; *see also Juliet* (Tinclad No. 4)
Sherman, William T. (U.S. major general) 97, 99, 108, 114, 155–156, 164, 236, 238, **255**–256, 259–260, 271, 274, 286–287; *see also* Red River campaign (March–May, 1864); Vicksburg campaign (1862–1863)
Shields, James (Illinois state auditor) 14–**15**; *see also* Lincoln, Abraham; Lincoln, Mary Todd; Lincoln-Shields "duel" (1842)
Shiloh (U.S. ironclad) 58; *see also* McCord, Charles W.
Shirk, Lt. Cmdr. James W. (captain, *Tuscumbia*) 104, 229, 231–**232**, 233, 242, 246–247, 252–256, 258–259, 262, 265–268, 270–276; *see also* Fort Heiman, TN, U.S. occupation of (1863); Vicksburg batteries, bombardment by *Tuscumbia* (May 19–22, 1863); Vicksburg batteries, passage of by *Tuscumbia* (April 16, 1863)
Shirley, John T. (boatbuilder) 47; *see also* Arkansas (Confederate ironclad)
Shurtleff College 13–14, 19; *see also* Brown, Virginia K.; Godfrey, Benjamin; Keach, Capt. John R.

Sierra Del Una Gold Mining Company, New Mexico 317
Signal (Tinclad No. 8) 92
Silver Lake (steamboat) 36; *see also* "Wideawakes"
Silver Lake (Tinclad No. 23) 280
Silver Wave (steamboat) 244, 252–253, 259; *see also* Vicksburg batteries, passage of by *Tuscumbia* (April 16, 1863)
Sioux City (steamboat) 166–167; *see also* Red River campaign (March–May 1864)
Smith, A.J. (U.S. major general) 156–161, 164, 167, 172; *see also* Red River campaign (March–May 1864)
Smith, Edmund Kirby (Confederate lieutenant general) 82–83, 85,89, 155, 220; *see also* Kentucky, Confederate campaign in (1862); Red River campaign (March–May, 1864)
Smith, Elon G. (pilot, St. Louis alderman) 298
Smith, Jake (constable) 14; *see also* Lincoln-Shields "duel" (1842)
Smith, Com. Joseph 55, 61–63; *see also* Ironclad Board (1862)
Smith, Perry (first assistant engineer, *Tuscumbia*) 265
Smith, Thomas Kilby (U.S. brigadier general) 161, 164–165, 167; *see also* Red River campaign (March–May 1864)
Smith, Lt. Cmdr. Watson (task force commander later captain, *Chillicothe*) 93, 115–116, 119–120, 122–126, 128, 130–142, 144, 146, 162–163, 166–168, 170–173, 280–281; *see also* Red River campaign (March–May 1864); Yazoo Pass Expedition (March–April 1863)
Social Evil Hospital *see* St. Louis Social Evil Hospital
Soup Kitchen *see* Panic of 1873
South, Perry (first assistant engineer, *Tuscumbia*) 231
South Fort *see* Vicksburg batteries, bombardment by *Tuscumbia* (May 19–22, 1863)
Southern Hotel, St. Louis, MO

293, 295, 299, 302, 304–305, 309–**310**
Southwestern (steamboat) 166; *see also* Red River campaign (March–May 1864)
spiritualism 20, 285, 313, 318, 322–323
Spots, Albert Tunstall 306–307, 315; *see also* Brown, Virginia ("Jennie"); *Flanagan v Brown*
Spots, Harry Innes (steamboat captain) 306; *see also* Spots, Albert Tunstall
Spots, Jane ("Mama") 307, 315; *see also* Spots, Albert Tunstall
Stanton, Edwin (U.S. war secretary) 55–56, 60–61, 63, 92, 150, 230
Starnes & Springer (grocers) 16; *see also* LaMothe, Capt. William Pierre
Starr, Capt. James E. 16; *see also General Briggs* (steamboat); *S & P Wise*; *Tempest* (steamboat)
State Agricultural College of Missouri 291
Steele, Frederic (U.S. major general) 156; *see also* Red River campaign (March–May 1864)
Stephen Bayard (steamboat) 119, 124, 132; *see also* Yazoo Pass Expedition (March–April 1863)
Stevenson, Carter L. (Confederate major general) 204, 213–214; *see also* Vicksburg campaign (1862–1863)
Stewart, Daniel V. (pilot, *Indianola*) 99
Sturgeon, Isaac H. (St. Louis city comptroller) 324, 327
Submarine No. 7 (snagboat) *see* Benton (U.S. ironclad)
Sweeney, Thomas C. and Andrew J. *see* Signal (Tinclad No. 8)

Taylor, Capt. George 22; *see also St. Louis* (steamboat)
Taylor, John (pilot, *Henry Clay*) 244, 253–254; *see also* Vicksburg batteries, passage of by *Tuscumbia* (April 16, 1863)
Taylor, Richard (Confederate major general) 156, 158, 165, 189, 192, 196, 220; *see also* Red River campaign (March–May 1864)

Tayon, Acting Master Augustus S. (executive officer, *Tuscumbia*) 231, 275
Tellon, Capt. Peter (boatbuilder) 67–68, 72, 105; *see also* American Foundry; Peter Tellon & Son
Tellon, Martin *see* Peter Tellon & Son
Tellon, William *see* Peter Tellon & Son
Tempest (steamboat) 17–18; *see also Luella* (steamboat); S & P Wise; Starr, Capt. James E.
Tempest (Tinclad No. 1) 282
Temple, Capt. A. F. (boatbuilder) 46; *see also* Madison Marine Railway Company
Tharp, Oliver P. (superintendent) 69, 72, 279; *see also* Cincinnati Marine Railway
35th Parallel (steamboat) 133; *see also* Yazoo Pass Expedition (March–April 1863)
Thistle (U.S. tug) 246; *see also* Vicksburg batteries, passage of by *Tuscumbia* (April 16, 1863)
Thompson, James D. (first master, *Queen of the West*) 183, 187
Tilden, Samuel J. (Democratic presidential candidate 1876) 307
Timmons, Barnard (Confederate lieutenant colonel) 148; *see also* Fort Pemberton, MS
Tiskilwa (steamboat) 8, 18
Tomlinson and Hartupee 64
Totten, Joseph (U.S. brigadier general) 41, 44, 66
Treat, Samuel (judge) 31–32; *see also* Lincoln, Abraham; Mcready, Mary
Trotten, Charles (first assistant engineer, *Chillicothe*) 103
Trumbull, Lyman (U.S. senator) 8–**9**, 23, 32, 44–45, 290; *see also* Brown, George T.; Lincoln, Abraham
Tunnard, William H. (Confederate sergeant) 237–238
Tunstall, Jane Pearce 306; *see also* Spots, Albert Tunstall
Tuscumbia (U.S. ironclad) *see* Fort Heiman, TN, U.S. occupation of (1863); Grand Gulf, MS, battle of (April 29, 1863); Vicksburg batteries, bombardment by *Tuscumbia* (May 19–22, 1863);

Vicksburg batteries, passage of by *Tuscumbia* (April 16, 1863); Warrenton, MS, bombardment by *Tuscumbia* (May 15, 1863)
Tyler (U.S. timberclad) 36, 43, 67; *see also A. O. Tyler* (steamboat); Cincinnati Marine Railway; Shaw, Acting Master Edward

Underwood, Theodore E. (chief pilot, *Chillicothe*) 90, 99, 103
Union Iron Works 47; *see also* Carondelet Marine Railway and Dock Co., Eads, Capt. James Buchanan; Nelson, Capt. William Shaw
United Hebrew Relief Fund, St. Louis, MO 293

Vicksburg batteries: bombardment by *Tuscumbia* (May 19–22, 1863) 270, 272–**275**; passage of by *Indianola* (February 13, 1863) 184–**186**; passage of by *Tuscumbia* (April 16, 1863), 216, 236–257
Vicksburg campaign (1862–1863) 98, 107–278
Vindicator (U.S. ram) 225–226; *see also* salvage of *Indianola* (1863–1865)
Virginia (Confederate ironclad) 56, 62; *see also Congress* (U.S. frigate); *Cumberland* (U.S. frigate); *Monitor* (U.S. ironclad)
Volunteer (steamboat) 125, 127, 132, 142; *see also* Yazoo Pass Expedition (March–April 1863)

Wade, William B. (Confederate colonel) 260; *see also* Grand Gulf, MS, battle of (April 29, 1863)
Walke, Capt. Henry (captain, *Carondelet/Lafayette*) 103–104, 111, 242–243, 250, 260, 263, 265; *see also* Vicksburg campaign (1862–1863)
Walker, John George (Confederate major general) 220
Walker, Lt. Cmdr. John G. (captain, *Chillicothe*) 93–98, 135–136, 148; *see also Baron de Kalb* (U.S. ironclad); Fort Pemberton, MS; Yazoo Pass Expedition (March–April 1863)

Walker, Martin 16–17; *see also* Frink, John; Frink & Walker Stagecoach Line; *General Briggs* (steamboat)
Walker, Samuel (boatbuilder) 24; *see also Mayflower* (steamboat)
Wallace, Lew (U.S. major general) **84**–85, 87, 89–90; *see also* Kentucky, Confederate campaign (1862)
Ward, William Shaw (acting master's mate, *Indianola*) 99, 177, 182, 184–186
Wardell, George (third assistant engineer, *Indianola*) 99
Warrenton, MS, bombardment by *Tuscumbia* (May 15, 1863) 270
Waters, Terry P. 103; *see also Carondelet* (U.S. ironclad)
Waul, Thomas N. (Confederate colonel) 123, 134–135, 148; *see also* Fort Pemberton, MS; Yazoo Pass Expedition (March–April 1863)
Webb see William H. Webb (Confederate ram)
Webster, Daniel (U.S. senator) 10–**11**
Weller, Royal (merchant) 8, 12–13; *see also* Lovejoy, Elijah Parish
Welles, Gideon (U.S. navy secretary) 42, 55–**56**, 63, 85, 87–88, 90–91, 99, 104, 159, 168, 173, 180, 207, 214, 217, 226, 229, 236, 238, 244, 279–280, 286
Western Forge and Tool Works, St. Louis, MO 317–318
Western Seaman's Friends Association, St. Louis, MO 290
White Cloud (steamboat) 168; *see also* Red River campaign (March–May 1864)
Wickliffe, Charles A. (U.S. congressman) 55
"Wideawakes" 36; *see also Silver Lake* (steamboat)
Wiggins, William C. 284; *see also* Wiggins Ferry Company
Wiggins Ferry Company 281, 284–286, 291–292
William H. Brown (steamboat) 162, 167; *see also* Red River campaign (March–May 1864)
William H. Webb (Confederate

ram) 183, 189–191, 196–199, 201–203, 207, 212–213; *see also* McCloskey, James; Palmyra Island, battle off (February 24, 1863)
Wilson, Byron (captain, *Mound City*) 217, 223, 270; *see also* salvage of *Indianola* (1863–1865);
Wilson, James H. (U.S. lieutenant colonel) 113–114, 116–**117**, 120–121, 123–124, 128, 134–135, 142, 144, 147–151; *see also* Yazoo Pass Expedition (March–April 1863)
Winchester (steamboat) 26, 29–30; *see also* Alton-St. Louis Packet Co.; Eads, James Buchanan; Illinois Agricultural Fair, Alton, IL (1856)
Wise, George D. (Confederate captain) 217; *see also* Salvage of *Indianola* (1863–1865)
Wise, Peter 17–19; *see also* *Altona* (steamboat); S & P Wise; Wise, Sebastian
Wise, Sebastian 17; *see also* S & P Wise; Wise, Peter
Woodhouse, S.W. (naturalist) 17; *see also* *Luella* (steamboat)
Worthington, James (hospital steward, *Henry Clay*) 254; *see also* Vicksburg batteries, passage of by *Tuscumbia* (April 16, 1863)
Wright, Horatio (U.S. major general) 84, 89; *see also* Kentucky, Confederate campaign (1862)
Wright, Marcus J. 317

Yates, Acting Master John A. (executive officer, *Indianola*) 86, 90, 95
Yazoo Pass Expedition (March–April 1863) 113–152, 193, 233, 266
Young, A W. (Alton, IL, mayor) 327
Young, Brigham 297

www.ingramcontent.com/pod-product-compliance
Lightning Source LLC
Chambersburg PA
CBHW081534300426
44116CB00015B/2621